Advanced Excel Formulas

Unleashing Brilliance with Excel Formulas

Alan Murray

Apress®

Advanced Excel Formulas: Unleashing Brilliance with Excel Formulas

Alan Murray
IPSWICH, UK

ISBN-13 (pbk): 978-1-4842-7124-7   ISBN-13 (electronic): 978-1-4842-7125-4
https://doi.org/10.1007/978-1-4842-7125-4

Managing Director, Apress Media LLC: Welmoed Spahr
Acquisitions Editor: Smriti Srivastava
Development Editor: Laura Berendson
Coordinating Editor: Shrikant Vishwakarma

Cover designed by eStudioCalamar

Cover image designed by Pexels

Distributed to the book trade worldwide by Springer Science+Business Media LLC, 1 New York Plaza, Suite 4600, New York, NY 10004. Phone 1-800-SPRINGER, fax (201) 348-4505, email orders-ny@springer-sbm.com, or visit www.springeronline.com. Apress Media, LLC is a California LLC and the sole member (owner) is Springer Science + Business Media Finance Inc (SSBM Finance Inc). SSBM Finance Inc is a **Delaware** corporation.

For information on translations, please e-mail booktranslations@springernature.com; for reprint, paperback, or audio rights, please e-mail bookpermissions@springernature.com, or visit http://www.apress.com/rights-permissions.

Apress titles may be purchased in bulk for academic, corporate, or promotional use. eBook versions and licenses are also available for most titles. For more information, reference our Print and eBook Bulk Sales web page at http://www.apress.com/bulk-sales.

Any source code or other supplementary material referenced by the author in this book is available to readers on GitHub via the book's product page, located at https://link.springer.com/book/10.1007/978-1-4842-7124-7.

Printed on acid-free paper

To my children, George and Lily.
And to all the Excel functions. I love you all. And without you,
there would be no book.

Table of Contents

About the Author

Alan Murray is a Microsoft MVP and Excel trainer. He has been helping people in Excel for over 20 years. He loves training and the joy he gets from knowing he is making people's working lives easier.

Alan runs his own blog – Computergaga (https://computergaga.com) – and writes for multiple other websites. His YouTube channel has over 550 videos and over 30 million views.

He organizes a free monthly Excel meetup in London where anyone can come learn Excel, chat, and enjoy each other's company (www.meetup.com/London-Excel-Meetup-Group/).

About the Technical Reviewer

Mark Proctor is a senior finance professional, qualified accountant, and blogger who has been applying spreadsheet-based solutions to solve real-world problems for the last 20 years. He has built a variety of Excel-based reporting, predictive, decision-making, and automation tools for achieving process efficiency in multinational companies in the media, food, retail, and manufacturing sectors.He is also the owner of Excel Off The Grid (https://exceloffthegrid.com), one of the most popular Excel blogs on the Internet, which focuses on teaching intermediate and advanced Excel techniques.

Acknowledgments

The MAX thank you goes to the Excel community. Together, we help and inspire each other to get the best from the behemoth that is Excel. A beautiful collection of millions of cells that invite us to calculate, analyze, track, and model our data however we choose. We often encounter cute and not-so-cute problems in the pursuit of our Excel dreams. The help of others to find the solution to these problems is vital, and the Excel community is very generous with their support.

A UNIQUE thanks to Mark Proctor, Tea Kuseva, Celia Alves, Abiola David, Danielle Stein Fairhurst, Faraz Shaikh, David Benaim, and many others who I hope not to disappoint by not naming them specifically.

My gratitude to the Excel MVPs who somehow find 30 hours in a 24-hour day. They seem to answer messages at any hour of the day. And to all members of the London Excel Meetup group, the subscribers of my YouTube channel (Computergaga), and followers on other channels. You challenge and motivate me to do better.

A LARGE thank you to team Excel at Microsoft. They listen to our feedback (for the most part anyhow) and push Excel to be a better product every day. During the writing of this book, functions were being developed and changed. This makes the task of teaching and producing learning content very difficult, but also exciting, and I wouldn't have it any other way.

Finally, as always, thank you to my children, George and Lily. I'm very lucky.

Introduction

Formulas are what made me fall in love with Excel. How is that for an opening line?

They are the muscles and the connective tissue of your workbooks. Making decisions, performing calculations, linking cells, converting data types, and so much more. And boy, they are fun.

Advanced Excel Formulas is a comprehensive book containing more than 500 Excel formula examples. It is also fully updated to include the new functions released in recent years including more than ten functions released in 2022.

This book will benefit anyone who works with Excel regularly. The focus is on users who understand formulas but want to push their skills to the next level and fill any gaps in their knowledge.

When your company sends you for Excel training (if they do), you are normally taught functions such as VLOOKUP, IF, and SUMIFS. And this book covers those functions too because they are fantastic. But it also goes far beyond, venturing down the less trekked path to the functions such as AGGREGATE, SEQUENCE, VSTACK, SWITCH, and many more. In fact, more than 150 Excel functions are demonstrated in this book.

And do not be mistaken. This is not just a cursory look at the different functions. You will see multiple "real-world" examples of the different functions, fully explained, with "pro" tips to get the maximum out of them.

Advanced Excel Formulas is divided into 15 chapters:

- **Chapter 1:** The first chapter is a primer on Excel formulas. It explains the anatomy of formulas and functions and the role of the different characters in Excel formulas. This is an advanced formulas book, but this chapter is included to lay a strong base and reference point for the coming chapters.

- **Chapter 2:** This chapter explores the logical functions of Excel. This includes IF, IFS, SWITCH, AND, OR, XOR, IFERROR, and IFNA. These are key decision-making functions to automate our Excel models and reports.

- **Chapter 3:** In this chapter, we explain defined names in depth. This little-known feature has huge benefits in how we use and deploy ranges and formulas in Excel. The importance of this feature has grown further with the recent changes to the calculation engine of Excel.

- **Chapter 4:** This chapter is about using tables in Excel. It covers the many benefits of using tables instead of ranges and explains how to use them effectively.

- **Chapter 5:** This chapter is all about the text functions of Excel. Use these functions to extract, combine, replace, and format text.

- **Chapter 6:** In this chapter, we work with the many date and time functions of Excel. Almost every user has a need to perform calculations or analysis based on date or time values. Fortunately, Excel has the functions to achieve these tasks.

- **Chapter 7:** In this chapter, we learn the VLOOKUP function. Incredibly popular among Excel users and very useful. We will cover this function inside-out and explain it like you have never heard before. We will also cover insider tricks to avoid common VLOOKUP limitations and mistakes.

- **Chapter 8:** This chapter focuses on two of the most useful functions of Excel – SUMIFS and COUNTIFS. A variety of examples are shown to fully appreciate these gems. The chapter will also cover the AVERAGEIFS, MAXIFS, and MINIFS functions.

- **Chapter 9:** This chapter is all about the SUMPRODUCT and AGGREGATE functions of Excel. These are next-level aggregation functions. They are very powerful, and SUMPRODUCT is especially useful for users not on Excel 365.

- **Chapter 10:** In this chapter, you will learn how to efficiently use the dynamic array formulas of Excel. It is important to know how to best use these formulas and how they change the way spreadsheets calculate in modern Excel.

- **Chapter 11:** This chapter dives further into the world of lookup formulas in Excel. INDEX, INDIRECT, OFFSET, CHOOSE, VSTACK, and more are covered to extend your lookup formula arsenal.

- **Chapter 12:** This chapter covers the new XLOOKUP function. This is a complete lookup formula with many options. Numerous examples are shown in this chapter to showcase its power.

- **Chapter 13:** In this chapter, we cover the FILTER function. This function is a real game changer. A lookup formula that can handle complex lookup criteria and return multiple results.

- **Chapter 14:** In this chapter, we will learn the rich data types in Excel and how to access and analyze their data using formulas. A recently added feature enabling multiple columns to be stored in a single cell. Data types are incredible. The new STOCKHISTORY and FIELDVALUE functions are covered in this chapter too.

- **Chapter 15:** This chapter covers the new LET and LAMBDA functions. They provide the ability to break down complex formulas and even create your own custom functions. Very cool and incredibly powerful.

Notation

You can expect the following notation in this book:

- The name of a button, keystrokes, or tab of the Ribbon or a window that we click will be in **bold** text. For example, click the **Formulas** tab of the Ribbon.

- Titles and other text that you see on screen and are referenced in the book will be shown in *italics*. For example, in the *Name Manager* window.

- Names of files, sheet tabs, tables, or columns will be shown with square brackets. For example, on the [Report] sheet.

- Written text will be enclosed in double quotations. For example, type "chart_labels" in the box.

Excel Versions

Excel is constantly evolving and improving. Because of this, we should be aware of the version of Excel that we are using and bear in mind the versions that others we collaborate with use when sharing files.

Regarding Excel versions, please note the following:

- All screenshots and step-by-step processes shown in the book are performed using Excel for Microsoft 365.

- Whenever a new function is introduced, a listing of the Excel versions that it is available is shown.

- When the availability of a function is labeled as "all versions," the cut-off point is Excel 2010 and Excel for Mac 2011. So, for clarity, if a function was released in a version prior to these, it is stated as being available in "all versions."

Download the Example Files

You are encouraged to download the example files used by me throughout the book to practice on. The best way of learning is by doing. Follow along, and this will benefit your learning greatly.

You can download the example files from the Apress GitHub page (`https://github.com/Apress/advanced-excel-formulas`).

The files are organized into folders that match the chapters of this book.

CHAPTER 1

Excel Formulas: A Quick Primer

This is a short chapter to lay a solid foundation on using formulas in Excel before we get to the really exciting stuff.

Although this is an advanced Excel formulas book, I felt this chapter would be useful to plug any gaps that may exist in your knowledge. Also, it can serve as a reference point that you can revisit to help understand some of the formulas later.

This chapter will begin by explaining the anatomy of formulas and the use of the different characters, for example, !, $, >. We then explain the use of workbook and worksheet references and absolute addresses. It then concludes with the different types of errors and other alerts you experience when using Excel formulas.

Anatomy of an Excel Formula

Now, let's begin with a question that you may be surprised to read in this book: What exactly is an Excel formula?

An Excel formula is an expression that returns a result. In Excel, this result can be a value (number, string, or Boolean), multiple values, or a range. Excel formulas always begin with =.

Formulas cannot delete, unhide, or format. They return something. However, they can be used with other Excel features to perform actions such as format or chart.

Breakdown of a Function

The terms formula and function are often used interchangeably. However, they are different. A function is a prewritten expression. It has a name and a purpose. A function can be included as part of a formula.

1

© Alan Murray 2022
A. Murray, *Advanced Excel Formulas*, https://doi.org/10.1007/978-1-4842-7125-4_1

There are many functions in Excel. They each have their own unique characteristics. The good news – they all follow the same syntax.

The syntax of an Excel function is

```
=FunctionName(argument1, argument2, ...)
```

A function always has brackets after its name. This is true even when it has no arguments. The best example of this is probably the TODAY function:

```
=TODAY()
```

Its job is to return today's date. It does this by using the system date and therefore requires no information from the user. However, you must still enter brackets after its name.

Most functions will prompt for arguments. An argument is information that the function needs to fulfill its purpose. Figure 1-1 shows the arguments of the SUM function.

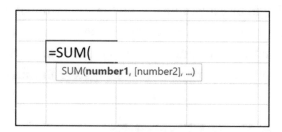

Figure 1-1. *The arguments of the SUM function*

The SUM function prompts for one or multiple values. It needs values to fulfill its purpose, which is to sum.

The second argument is enclosed in square brackets: [number2]. This indicates that it is an optional argument.

Figure 1-2 shows the VLOOKUP function and its arguments. You can see that the first three arguments are mandatory, and the last argument is optional.

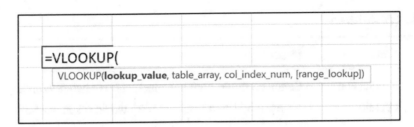

Figure 1-2. *The arguments of the VLOOKUP function*

Arguments are separated by a comma, and your position in the syntax is highlighted in bold.

Note   In regions where a comma is used as a decimal separator, a semicolon ";" is used as the function argument separator.

Table of Formula Characters

Table 1-1 is a list of the different characters used in Excel formulas. This book includes examples that demonstrate the use of all these characters.

Table 1-1. *Table of formula characters*

Characters	Name	Description
=	Equals	All formulas start with =.
		The equal is also the logical operator for equal to.
( )	Brackets or parentheses	Used to enclose the arguments of a function.
		Also, used to specify the order of calculation in a formula.
,	Separator or union operator	Primarily used to separate the arguments of a function.
		Also, creates a range from multiple references. For example, =SUM(A2:A5,C2:C5).
:	Range operator	Creates a range of all cells between two references. For example, =SUM(A2:A5).

(continued)

Table 1-1. (*continued*)

Characters	Name	Description
Space	Intersection operator	Creates a range from the intersection of two references. For example, =SUM(A2:A5 A3:D3) would result in =SUM(A3).
+	Addition	The operator to add values.
-	Subtract	The operator for subtracting values.
*	Multiply or asterisk	This symbol is most used as the multiply operator. It is also a wildcard character. It is used to replace unknown characters when performing partial text matches.
/	Divide	The operator to divide values.
%	Percent	Used in a formula to represent a number as a percentage.
>	Greater than	Logical operator to test if the first value is larger than the second value.
>=	Greater than or equal to	Logical operator to test if the first value is larger than or equal to the second value.
<	Less than	Logical operator to test if the first value is less than the second value.
<=	Less than or equal to	Logical operator to test if the first value is less than or equal to the second value.
	Not equal to	Logical operator to test if a value is not equal to another value.
{}	Array	Curly braces around a formula indicate an array formula. They are generated automatically by Excel on pressing **Ctrl + Shift + Enter**. For example, {=SUM(A2:A5*B2:B5)}.
{1,2,5} or {1;2;5}	Array of values	This could be values returned by part of a formula or entered as an array of constants. A comma is used to separate columns and a semicolon to separate rows.
" "	Double quotes	Denotes a text string.

(*continued*)

Table 1-1. (*continued*)

Characters	Name	Description
&	Ampersand	The concatenate operator. Used to join different text strings together. For example, =`"Sales total: "&SUM(A2:A5)`.
[ ]	Square brackets	Most used when referring to the column name of a table. For example, =`SUM(Sales[Total])`. Also used when referencing another workbook in a formula. For example, =`[Book1.xlsx]Sheet1!$C$6`. And this character is seen in the function tooltip to indicate an optional argument.
' '	Single quotes	Used in references to surround worksheet and workbook names that contain spaces. For example, =`'South Africa'!A3`.
!	Exclamation mark	Follows a sheet name in a formula and separates it from the grid reference. For example, =`Sheet1!A2`.
$	Absolute marker	Used to make parts of a cell reference absolute. For example, $A$2 or $A2.
#	Hash or pound symbol	Used to reference a spill range. For example, =`SUM(D2#)`.
@	Implicit intersection	Indicates that the data being referenced is on the same row. Most used when writing formulas in tables and you reference a cell on the same row. For example, =`[@Total]*0.1`.
.	Period	Used to reference information in a data type. For example, =`C3.Population`.
--	Double unary	Used to convert TRUE and FALSE to a 1 and 0.

Order of Calculation

File   order-of-calculation.xlsx

With so many operators and other characters, it is important to be aware of the order that a formula calculates.

An Excel formula is evaluated in the following order:

1. Range operations in the order of colon, space, and then comma

2. Converting values in the order of negation (Excel needs to convert a value entered as –5 from 5 to –5) followed by converting percentages (10% to 0.1)

3. Mathematical operations (exponentiation, followed by divide and multiply, then addition and subtraction)

4. Concatenation (the joining of text strings)

5. Comparison operations (=, <, >, <=, >=, <>)

Brackets or parentheses can be used to change the order of calculation. Let's see some examples.

Order of Range Operations

We have the data shown in Figure 1-3, and we want to sum the values for *hot dogs* and *chips* in *April* only.

	A	B	C	D	E	F
1		Jan	Feb	Mar	Apr	May
2	Pizza	159	217	60	166	287
3	Hot Dogs	262	297	209	135	173
4	Apple Juice	81	210	228	203	88
5	Chips	67	35	84	226	242
6	Grapefruit	271	50	216	160	187
7	Coffee	180	144	159	189	73
8						

Figure 1-3. *Data for the order of range operation examples*

The following SUM function is used. You can see that both the union (comma) and intersection (space) operators have been deployed.

```
=SUM(B3:F3,B5:F5 E2:E7)
```

This was done to sum the values in E3 and E5 only, as those cells are at the intersection of rows 3 and 5 (*hot dogs* and *chips*) and column E (*April*). However, we do not get the result that we wanted.

The range operator evaluates first, followed by the intersection operation, then the union operation, as detailed in the following. Figure 1-4 illustrates the intersection operation occurring before the union.

1. Evaluation of the ranges: {262,297,209,135,173},{67,35,84,22 6,242} {166;135;203;226;160;189}

2. Intersection of the two arrays in row 5 and column E: {67,35,84,226,242} {166;135;203;226;160;189}= 226

3. Summing the union of the array in row 3 and the resulting value of the intersection: SUM({262,297,209,135,173},226) = 1302

H3			× ✓ *fx*	=SUM(B3:F3,B5:F5 E2:E7)			
	A	B	C	D	E	F	G	H
1		Jan	Feb	Mar	Apr	May		
2	Pizza	159	217	60	166	287		Total
3	Hot Dogs	262	297	209	135	173		1302
4	Apple Juice	81	210	228	203	88		
5	Chips	67	35	84	226	242	2	
6	Grapefruit	271	50	216	160	187		
7	Coffee	180	144	159	189	73		
8								

Figure 1-4. *Intersection operation is evaluated before the union*

Brackets can be used to force the union operation to occur before the intersection, and then we get our desired result (Figure 1-5).

```
=SUM((B3:F3,B5:F5) E2:E7)
135 + 226 = 361
```

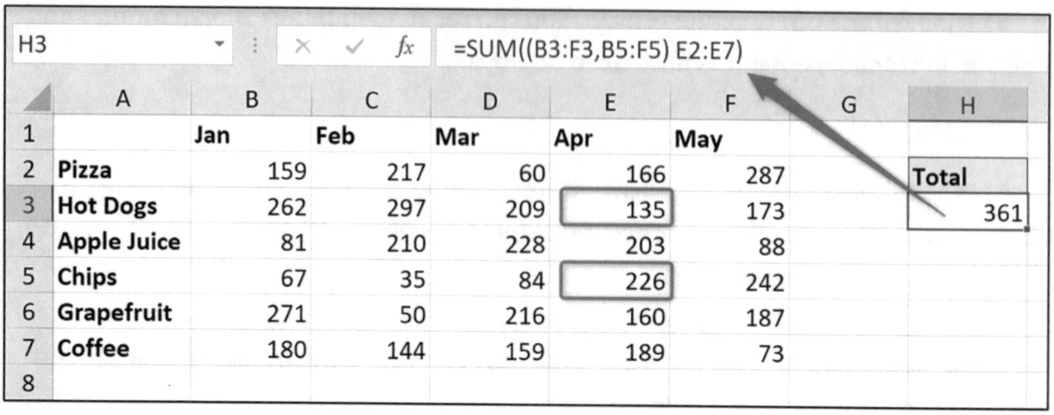

Figure 1-5. *Brackets to change the calculation order*

Now, it is unlikely that you will write a formula such as this. However, it does demonstrate the order of calculation in range operations. This could explain an incorrect result you get from a formula, maybe from the accidental use of spaces.

Order of Mathematical Operations

There is also an order to the mathematical operations. Division and multiplication are evaluated before addition and subtraction.

Let's see a simple example.

The result of the following formula is 53, because multiplication (10*5) occurs before addition (3+10):

=3+10*5

So, this formula is evaluated as 10 * 5 = 50, then 50 + 3 = 53.

If we needed the addition to occur first, that operation would be surrounded in brackets to change the order of calculation. The result of the following formula is 65:

=(3+10)*5

When writing complex formulas, not only do brackets change the order of calculation, but they also make the formula easier to read and digest by everyone.

Documenting formulas better is a rarely taught and underappreciated skill. It is important, especially if you are not the only one using the spreadsheet.

The Function Wizard

You may have used the Function Wizard before, probably in your early days of using Excel formulas. I personally do not use it, but I have friends who are advanced Excel users, and they love it.

It is a tool that helps you find and, more importantly, use a function. It provides a lot more information and assistance than you get when typing a formula into a cell.

You can open the Function Wizard quickly by pressing **Shift + F3** from the cell where you want to enter the formula.

It can also be opened by clicking the **Insert Function** button on the **Formulas** tab of the Ribbon or to the left of the Formula Bar (Figure 1-6). Starting a function through the menus of the function library will also trigger the Function Wizard.

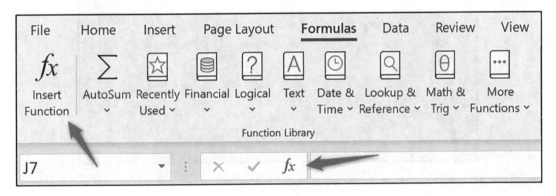

Figure 1-6. *How to open the Function Wizard*

After starting the wizard, you can find the function you need by either searching for it or by navigating through the different function categories (Figure 1-7).

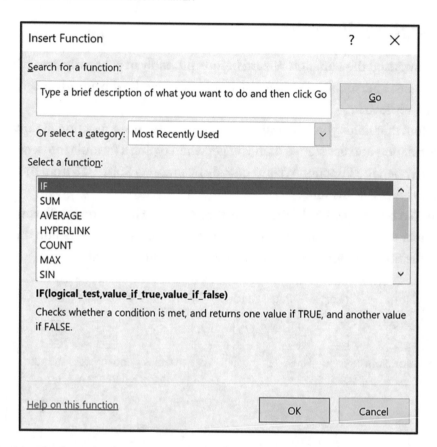

Figure 1-7. *Finding the function you want to use*

It really gets interesting when you get to the *Function Arguments* window. In Figure 1-8, the VLOOKUP function is shown with the different elements of the window detailed.

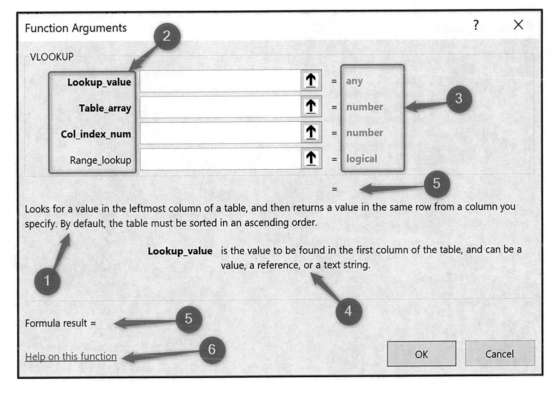

Figure 1-8. *VLOOKUP function in the Function Arguments window*

1. Description of the function you are using.

2. The function arguments. The names in bold are mandatory, and others are optional.

3. The data type expected from the argument. This part can be very useful. As you write the function, this area will show you the current value and alert you to errors.

4. Description of the active argument.

5. Formula result.

6. Link for extra help with how to use the function.

Figure 1-9 shows a completed VLOOKUP function. Notice the returned values next to each argument box and the formula result shown before you run the formula.

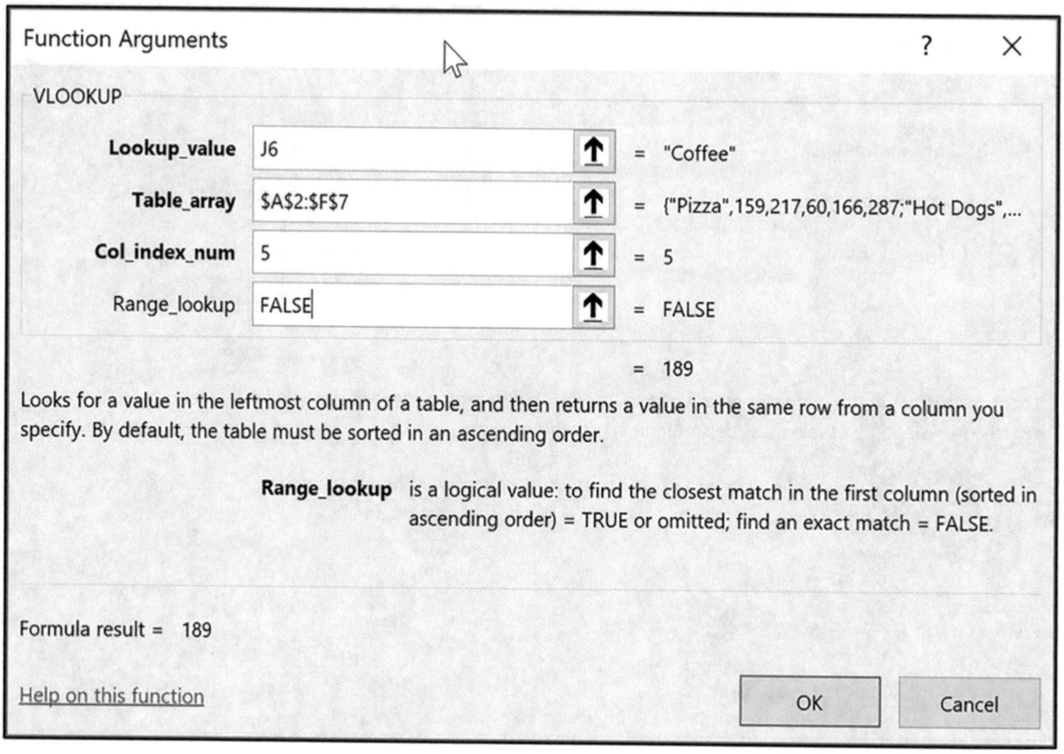

Figure 1-9. *Completed formula in the Function Arguments window*

Note   You can click any part of the formula in the Formula Bar to quickly switch the *Function Arguments* box to that area of the formula, and vice versa. This is great for navigating complex formulas in the wizard.

Cell Referencing

We have individual chapters dedicated to defined names, tables, and data type references. In this chapter, we will focus on different types of cell references in your Excel formulas.

Absolute References

File   absolute-references.xlsx

One of the biggest obstacles to learning formulas when people are just getting started is the understanding of an absolute reference.

Absolute references can be found in many places within a spreadsheet. They are often input by Excel itself when you select a range from within a feature such as Data Validation or defined names.

The use of absolute references is extremely important to understand. Let's look at when, why, and how to use absolute references.

Relative References Explained

In Figure 1-10, the formula =B4*E2 has been used in cell C4.

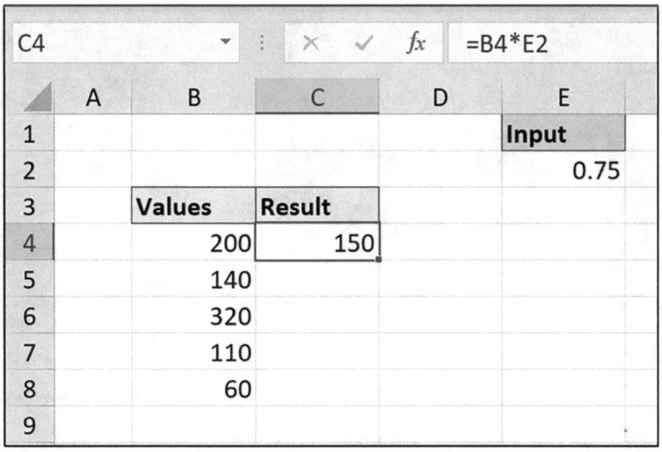

C4			▼	⋮	✕	✓	*fx*	=B4*E2	

◢	A	B	C	D	E
1					Input
2					0.75
3		Values	Result		
4		200	150		
5		140			
6		320			
7		110			
8		60			
9					

Figure 1-10. *Formula with relative references*

This multiplies the first value by the input cell in E2. This works great. But when the formula is filled down to range C5:C8, zeroes are returned as the result for the other values (Figure 1-11).

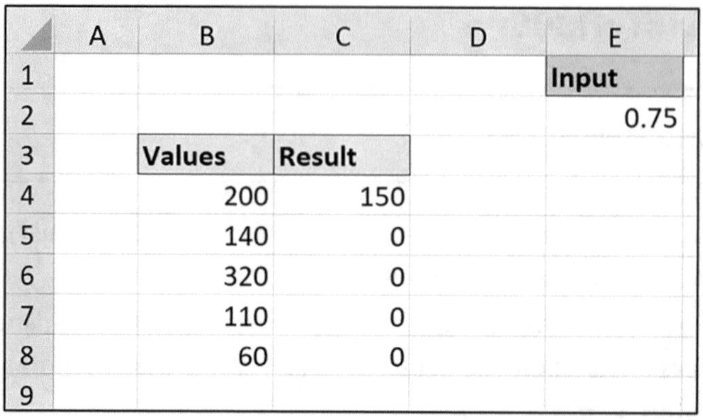

	A	B	C	D	E
1					**Input**
2					0.75
3		Values	Result		
4		200	150		
5		140	0		
6		320	0		
7		110	0		
8		60	0		
9					

Figure 1-11. *Zero is returned as the result for the other values*

The formula in cell C4 is using relative cell references. So, when the formula is filled down, both references change in conjunction to the formula.

In Figure 1-12, you can see the formula in cell C5 refers to the cells one cell below the original references.

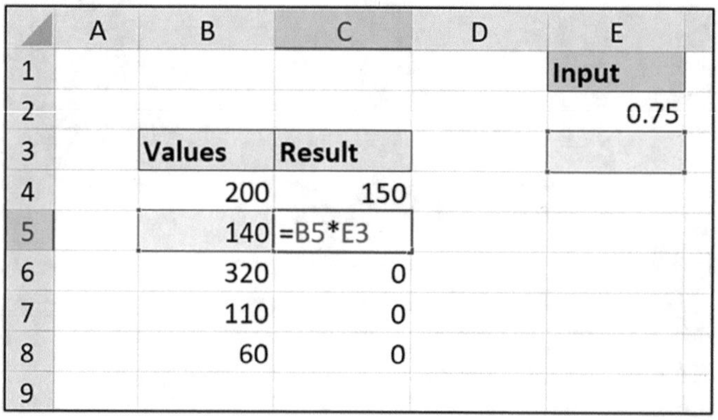

	A	B	C	D	E
1					**Input**
2					0.75
3		Values	Result		
4		200	150		
5		140	=B5*E3		
6		320	0		
7		110	0		
8		60	0		
9					

Figure 1-12. *Both cell references change*

Although the original formula was =B4*E2, what it is really calculating is the cell one column to the left multiplied by the cell two rows up and two columns to the right (Figure 1-13).

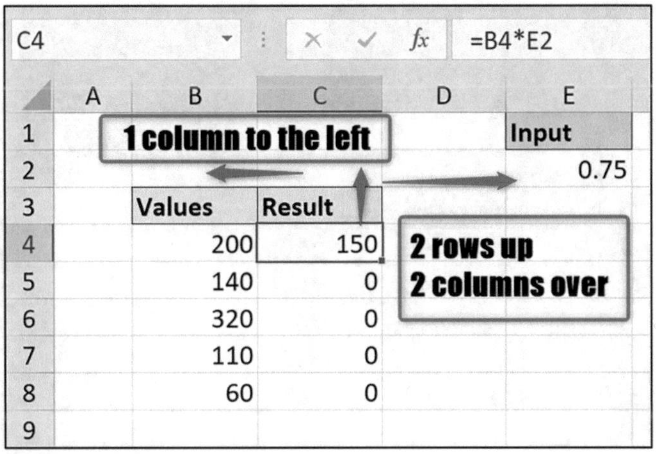

Figure 1-13. *Relative references explained*

This is no different to how we may provide directions to someone. For example, take the second left and in 50 meters take the next right. It is all relative to the starting position or starting cell in Excel's case.

This behavior is why they are called relative references.

The formula displays the cell address from the grid, making it easier to read and write. Although behind the scenes, this is not what is being used.

Making a Reference Absolute

In this example, we need the reference to cell E2 to be an absolute address instead of the relative reference. This will stop it from changing when the formula is filled down.

To make a reference absolute, dollar signs are added before the column letter and row number of the reference, that is, $E$2. You can do this by simply typing the dollar signs or with the **F4** key on your keyboard.

Figure 1-14 shows the reference to the input cell as an absolute reference. It no longer changes when the formula is filled, therefore returning the correct results.

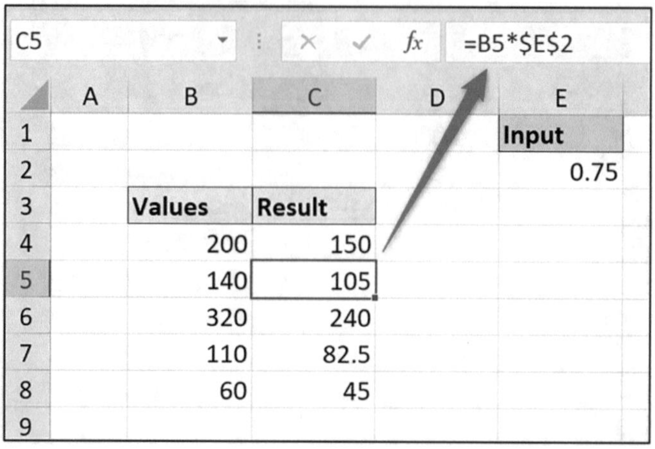

Figure 1-14. Absolute reference in an Excel formula

This reference is fully absolute and will not change if the formula is filled to the left, right, up, or down.

In this example, we are filling the formula down. Because of this, we only really need to make the row absolute. This cell reference is sufficient for the formula = E$2.

Note   Each time you press the **F4** key, it cycles through the different references available – $E$2, E$2, $E2, and E2.

Despite that being the case, most users will make a reference fully absolute unless there is a requirement otherwise.

Mixed References

A mixed reference is the term used when you make only the column or the row of a cell reference absolute.

Let's see an example where these mixed references come in helpful. In Figure 1-15, we want to complete the grid with the result of the times tables from 2 to 10.

▲	A	B	C	D	E	F	G	H	I	J
1		2	3	4	5	6	7	8	9	10
2	2									
3	3									
4	4									
5	5									
6	6									
7	7									
8	8									
9	9									
10	10									
11										

Figure 1-15. *Calculate times tables in Excel*

In cell B2, the formula =A2*B1 is used. But this does not work when the formula is filled down to B10 and across to column J (Figure 1-16).

B2		▼	:	×	✓	*fx*	=A2*B1			

▲	A	B	C	D	E	F	G	H	I	J
1		2	3	4	5	6	7	8	9	10
2	2	4	12	48	240	1440	10080	80640	725760	7257600
3	3	12	144	6912	1658880	2.39E+09	2.41E+13	1.94E+18	1.41E+24	1.02E+31
4	4	48	6912	47775744	7.93E+13	1.89E+23	4.56E+36	8.85E+54	1.25E+79	1.3E+110
5	5	240	1658880	7.93E+13	6.28E+27	1.19E+51	5.42E+87	4.8E+142	6E+221	#NUM!
6	6	1440	2.39E+09	1.89E+23	1.19E+51	1.4E+102	7.7E+189	#NUM!	#NUM!	#NUM!
7	7	10080	2.41E+13	4.56E+36	5.42E+87	7.7E+189	#NUM!	#NUM!	#NUM!	#NUM!
8	8	80640	1.94E+18	8.85E+54	4.8E+142	#NUM!	#NUM!	#NUM!	#NUM!	#NUM!
9	9	725760	1.41E+24	1.25E+79	6E+221	#NUM!	#NUM!	#NUM!	#NUM!	#NUM!
10	10	7257600	1.02E+31	1.3E+110	#NUM!	#NUM!	#NUM!	#NUM!	#NUM!	#NUM!
11										

Figure 1-16. *Relative reference goes horribly wrong*

Because we are filling the formula in two directions, we need to fix (or make absolute) the column or the row of each reference in the formula.

The formula =$A2*B$1 is used in Figure 1-17 and works perfectly.

B2		▾	:	×	✓	fx	=$A2*B$1				
	A	B	C	D	E	F	G	H	I	J
1		2	3	4	5	6	7	8	9	10
2	2	4	6	8	10	12	14	16	18	20
3	3	6	9	12	15	18	21	24	27	30
4	4	8	12	16	20	24	28	32	36	40
5	5	10	15	20	25	30	35	40	45	50
6	6	12	18	24	30	36	42	48	54	60
7	7	14	21	28	35	42	49	56	63	70
8	8	16	24	32	40	48	56	64	72	80
9	9	18	27	36	45	54	63	72	81	90
10	10	20	30	40	50	60	70	80	90	100
11										

Figure 1-17. Mixed references used to ensure correct results

In the first part of the formula, column A is made absolute to keep it on that column when the formula is filled over to column J. Yet, we need it to look at the numbers in the other rows of column A.

In the second part of the formula, row 1 is made absolute to stop it changing when the formula is filled down the row 10. Yet, we need the other numbers along row 1 to be used.

Sheet References

Files   worksheet-references.xlsx

When you reference data on other sheets in a formula, Excel writes the references for you. This is brilliant!

However, it is important to be fluent in the syntax used to reference data on other sheets, especially if you want to be an advanced Excel formula user.

If you were to reference cell A1 of a sheet named [Canada], the syntax would be

Canada!A1

The exclamation mark (!) always follows the sheet name.

Single quotations are used to enclose the sheet name if it includes spaces. So, if you referenced cell A1 of a sheet named [South Africa], the syntax would be

'South Africa'!A1

Note Cross-sheet references can be simplified by using defined names and tables. Both these topics are covered later in the book.

Let's see two examples of the SUM function being used to sum values from different worksheets. We will be using the [worksheet-references.xlsx] workbook for these examples.

The workbook contains attendance data on four different worksheets (Figure 1-18). These are [France], [South Africa], [Canada], and [Germany]. On each sheet, the attendance values are in range B2:B7.

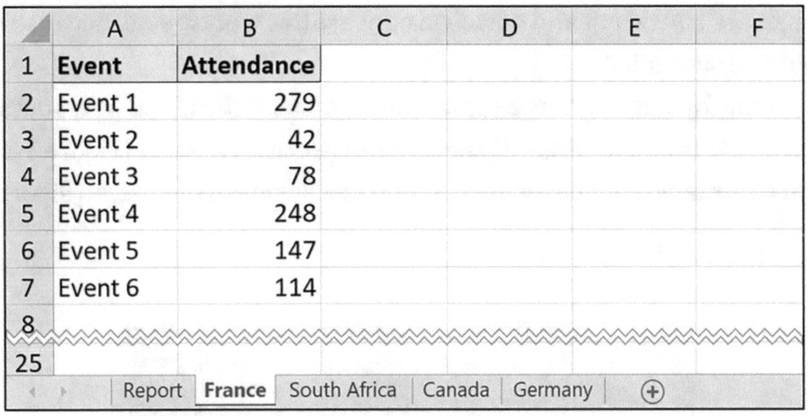

	A	B	C	D	E	F
1	**Event**	**Attendance**				
2	Event 1	279				
3	Event 2	42				
4	Event 3	78				
5	Event 4	248				
6	Event 5	147				
7	Event 6	114				
8						
25						

Figure 1-18. *Attendance data on four different worksheets*

The following formula is used in cell B3 of the [Report] sheet (Figure 1-19):

```
=SUM(France!B2:B7,'South Africa'!B2:B7,Canada!B2:B7,Germany!B2:B7)
```

It sums the values from range B2:B7 on each sheet. You can see the syntax described earlier, including the single quotes around the [South Africa] sheet.

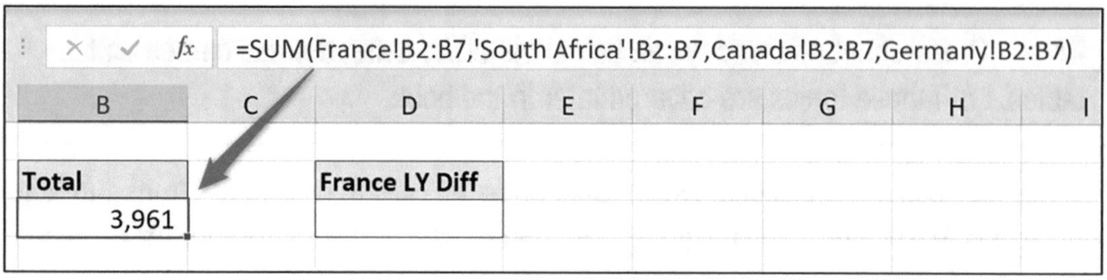

Figure 1-19. *Sum ranges from multiple worksheets*

In this example, the comma is used to separate each range used by the SUM function.

The ranges are consistent and occur on consecutive worksheets. Because of this, the formula could be simplified.

The following formula sums the same values but uses the range operator to sum the values in B2:B7 from the [France] sheet to the [Germany] sheet (Figure 1-20). The [France] and [Germany] sheets are the first and last sheets in the range (Figure 1-18).

```
=SUM(France:Germany!B2:B7)
```

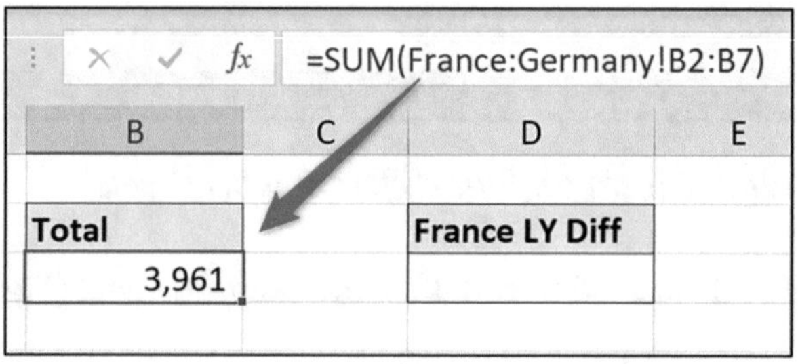

Figure 1-20. *Sum values from multiple sheets with the range operator*

This formula is more concise than the previous example. It also offers the advantage that any new sheet, if inserted in the range (between [France] and [Germany]), would also be included in the sum.

In this example, using sheets named [France] and [Germany] is quite arbitrary. So, a neat technique to deploy is to create "start" and "end" sheets that function as book ends for the sum formula. These sheets would be empty and have no purpose aside from containing the sheets involved in the sum range.

Protecting a workbook to prevent the accidental moving of sheets is also a good idea. The technique of summing a range of sheets is great, but it does have vulnerabilities also.

Workbook References

Files   worksheet-references.xlsx and France.xlsx

Just like with sheet references, Excel will write the reference for you when you select another workbook from a formula. However, it is important to be familiar with workbook references in Excel formulas.

If you referenced cell A1 on a sheet named [Report] of a workbook named [Sales. xlsx], the syntax would look like this:

```
='[Sales.xlsx]Report'!$A$1
```

If the [Sales.xlsx] workbook is closed, then the formula syntax would change to show the full file path:

```
'C:\Users\admin\Google Drive\Performance\[Sales.xlsx]Report'!$A$1
```

Let's see an example of a workbook reference in a formula. We will write a formula on the [worksheet-references.xlsx] workbook that references the [France] workbook.

The following formula is entered in cell D3 of the [Report] sheet (Figure 1-21). It calculates the difference between the sum of values on the [France] sheet of the current workbook and the sum of values on the [Last Year] sheet of the [France.xlsx] workbook.

```
=sum(France!$B$2:$B$7)-sum('[france.xlsx]Last Year'!$B$2:$B$7)
```

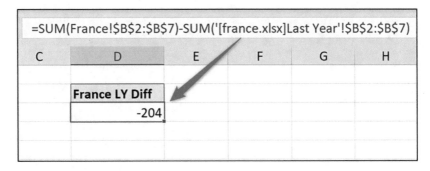

Figure 1-21. *Formula that sums values from another workbook*

Note   Many functions in Excel are able to retrieve data from a closed Excel workbook, such as SUM, AVERAGE, and INDEX, while others cannot, such as SUMIFS and OFFSET.

When you open a file that contains external references to other workbooks, it will probably greet you with a security message (Figure 1-22).

External links are disabled, by default, from updating automatically. Click **Enable Content** to update the links and see the changes in the current file.

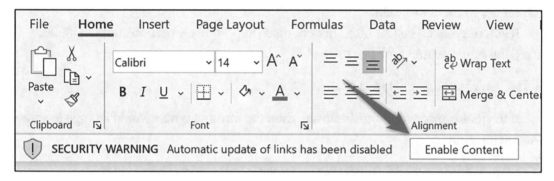

Figure 1-22. *Security warning to update external links*

You can change these settings by clicking **File ➤ Options ➤ Trust Center ➤ Trust Center Settings ➤ External Content** (Figure 1-23).

The default is to prompt the user for the update, which is why you receive the security message. This can be changed to enable or disable these updates.

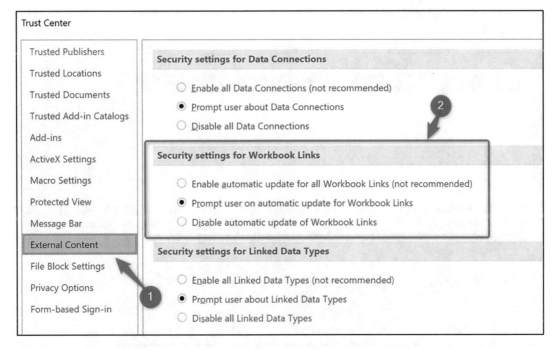

Figure 1-23. *Trust Center settings to disable or enable workbook links*

Figure 1-24 shows the *Edit Links* window, which is accessed by clicking **Data ➤ Edit Links**. In this window, you can view, update, and edit external links in a workbook.

The *Edit Links* window lists all external links in the workbook. You can see the location of the external files, and there are multiple controls on the right to update, change, and break the links.

When breaking a link to an external source, the formula is converted to the calculated value at the time the link was broken.

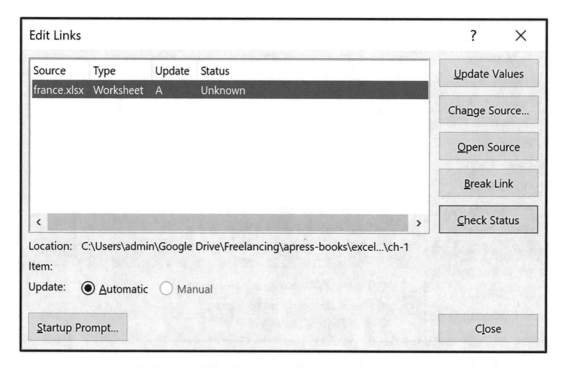

Figure 1-24. *Edit links in a workbook*

Calculating Percentages

File   percentages.xlsx

Calculating percentages is very commonplace in Excel, so I thought it would be good to include some quick examples.

Percentage of a Value

Let's start by finding the percentage of a value. The following formula returns 3% of the value in cell B3 (Figure 1-25):

=B3*3%

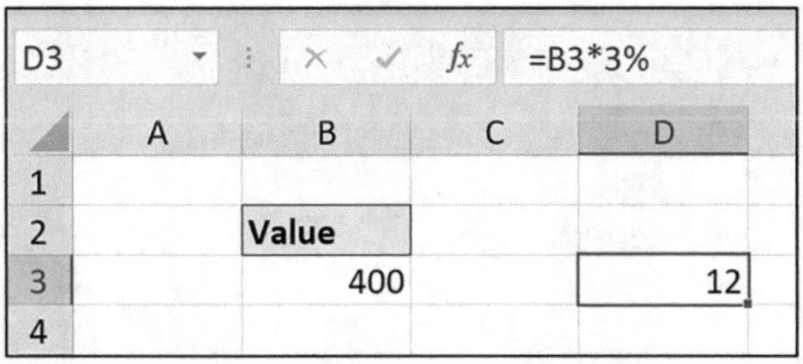

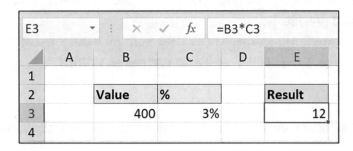

Figure 1-25. *Find 3% of the value in cell B3*

This is probably the most straightforward method. You could also use =B3*0.03.

It may also be the case that the percentage is a variable. In this scenario, we could reference a cell that contains that value (Figure 1-26).

=B3*C3

Figure 1-26. *Variable percentage of a value*

Percentage of a Total

The calculation for percentage of a total is value/total. You will then need to format the result as a percentage.

The following formula has been entered into cell D3 and then formatted as a percentage to one decimal place (Figure 1-27):

=B3/C3

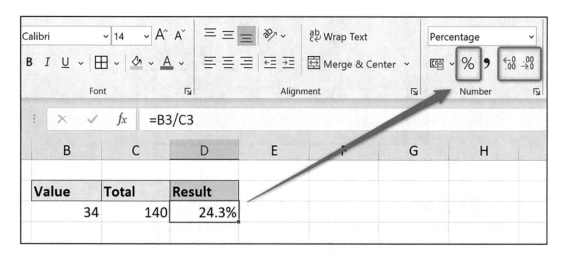

Figure 1-27. *Calculate percentage of total and then format as required*

Let's look at another example. This example is a nice reminder of the use of absolute references covered previously.

We want to return the percentage of total for multiple values. In cell G5, the following formula has been used and filled to range G6:G9 (Figure 1-28):

=F5/$G$2

Cell G2 is absolute to prevent it from changing when the formula is filled down.

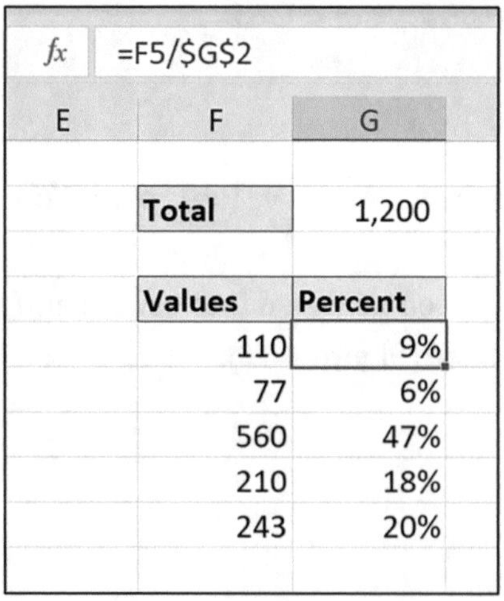

fx	=F5/$G$2	
E	F	G
	Total	1,200
	Values	Percent
	110	9%
	77	6%
	560	47%
	210	18%
	243	20%

Figure 1-28. *Percentage of total for multiple values*

Increase a Value by a Percentage

The following formula increases the value in cell B3 by the percentage in cell C3. You can see brackets being used to ensure the second operation occurs first (Figure 1-29).

```
=B3*(1+C3)
```

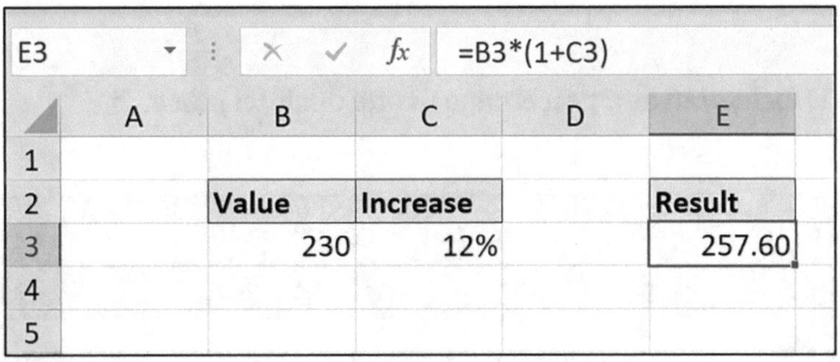

Figure 1-29. *Increase a value by a given percentage*

Decrease a Value by a Percentage

A similar technique can be used to decrease a value by a given percentage. The following formula is used to decrease the value in cell B3 by the percentage in cell C3 (Figure 1-30):

```
=B3*(1-C3)
```

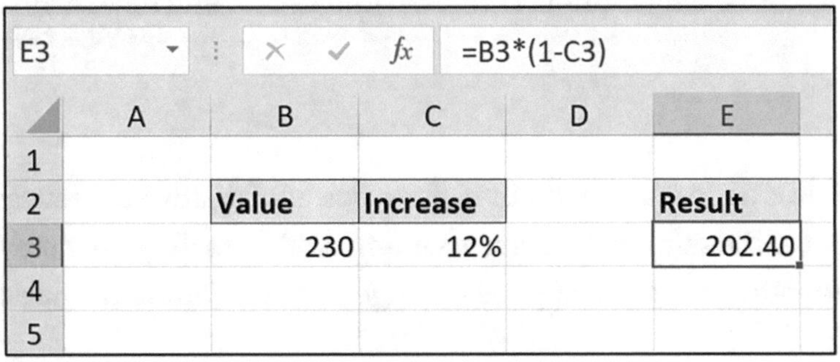

Figure 1-30. *Decrease a value by a given percentage*

Calculate Percentage Change

For the final examples, let's calculate the percentage change between two values. The following formula is entered in cell E3 to return the percentage change from the value last month to this month. Cell B3 contains the old value, and cell C3 contains the new value (Figure 1-31).

```
=(C3-B3)/B3
```

The result is formatted as a percentage to one decimal place.

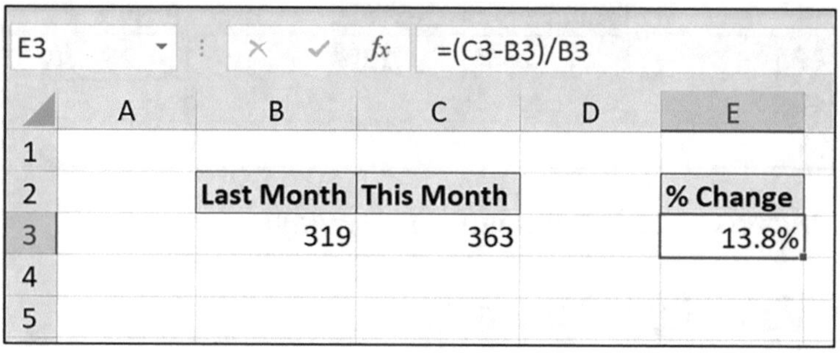

Figure 1-31. *Formula to calculate percentage change*

So, the value in cell C3 was a 13.8% increase on the value in cell B3.

Here is another example that calculates the percentage change monthly (Figure 1-32). The following formula is entered into cell C8 and filled across to cells D8:G8:

```
=(C7-B7)/B7
```

This example is a nice demonstration of the power of relative references. The formula references the sales of the current column and the sales of the previous column.

Custom formatting has been applied to range B8:G8 to format the negative values in red.

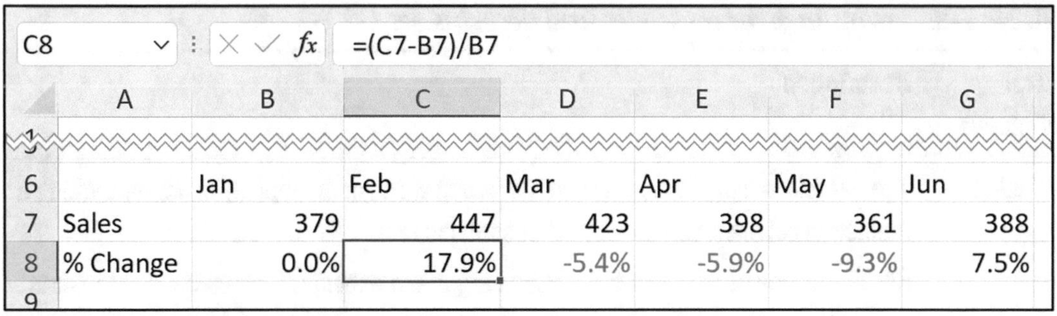

C8		⋮ × ✓ ƒx	=(C7-B7)/B7			

	A	B	C	D	E	F	G
6		Jan	Feb	Mar	Apr	May	Jun
7	Sales	379	447	423	398	361	388
8	% Change	0.0%	17.9%	-5.4%	-5.9%	-9.3%	7.5%
9							

Figure 1-32. *Percentage change monthly*

When Formulas Go Wrong

Excel formulas can and will go wrong. This can happen for many reasons. Let's explore the different types of errors you may encounter and some of the common reasons behind formulas that stop calculating.

Formula Errors

Formulas often return error messages when their expectations are not met. For example, multiplying a value by another cell that contains text will not work, so the #VALUE! error is returned.

Table 1-2 lists the different error messages you may come across when using Excel formulas. A description for each error is provided.

Table 1-2. *Formula error messages and description*

Error Message	Description
#VALUE!	The formula is using a data type in the wrong way. For example, you are performing a mathematical operation on a cell that contains text.
	Check the type of data that the function argument expects. Then check that the data type in the cell you referenced, or that you typed, matches the expected data type.
#REF!	A reference used by the formula is invalid.
	This is often caused when a reference that is being used by a formula is removed. For example, when a sheet that is being referenced in a formula is deleted.
	Another cause can be if the reference is out of range. For example, if a formula that uses a relative reference to seven cells above is copied into cell G3. G3 does not have seven cells above it, so the #REF! error is returned.
#N/A!	The familiar error commonly associated with lookup formulas.
	It is returned when the lookup formula cannot match the value you are looking for. This could be because the data types do not match, a typing mistake, or maybe the lookup value cell is empty.
#NAME!	The formula does not recognize a name used in the formula.
	This could be the name of the function, a defined name, table, or some other name.
	Other causes can be a missing bracket after a function name or missing double quotes around a text string.
#DIV/0!	Your formula has attempted to divide by zero or a blank cell.
#NULL!	A formula returns this error when the intersection operator (the space) is used incorrectly. If the ranges do not intersect, this error is returned.
	This is often caused when a space is accidentally used in a formula. Typically, a typing mistake when a space is entered instead of a comma or a colon.
#NUM!	This error is returned when the formula tries to use invalid numeric values.
	For example, entering symbols such as dollar signs when entering a numeric value, i.e., $1000. Symbols such as dollar signs have a specific role within formulas, so should not be used as part of an entered value.

(continued)

Table 1-2. (*continued*)

Error Message	Description
#SPILL!	This error occurs when a formula cannot spill its results. This is often due to another cell value blocking the spill range.
	A blue border is shown to visualize the spill range and help diagnose this formula error.
	To fix this, the value that is interfering with the spill range must be moved or deleted.
#CALC!	This error is returned when there is a calculation error in the array of a formula. For example, if an empty array is returned.
	This is often seen, though not uniquely found, with the FILTER function, when the conditions provided cannot be evaluated properly, typically when no results are returned by FILTER. The [if_empty] argument is provided to prevent the error in this scenario.
#FIELD!	This formula error is related to the rich data types in Excel.
	If the formula cannot access the required field from a data type, this error is returned.
#BLOCKED!	The formula cannot access a required resource.
	The solution depends on the resource you cannot access and why. Potential solutions include checking your Trust Center settings, privacy settings, or the connection settings to external workbooks.
#BUSY!	The formula is waiting for a required resource that's taking a long time to access.
	This is typically seen when accessing online data using linked data types, rendering images, or getting data from an external Excel workbook.

Automatic Error Checking

Excel performs specific checks in the background and will display a green triangle in the top-left corner of the cell if it has a query (Figure 1-33).

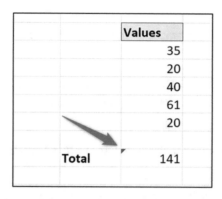

Figure 1-33. *Green triangle warning*

This does not mean that there is an error with your formula, but that Excel is querying something about it. Excel has a list of "error checking" rules, and the formula has failed one or more of these checks.

When you select the cell, a warning icon appears. Click the icon to see further information about the warning and a few options on dealing with it (Figure 1-34).

In this example, the formula is wrong. Cell D3 has been omitted from the SUM function by mistake.

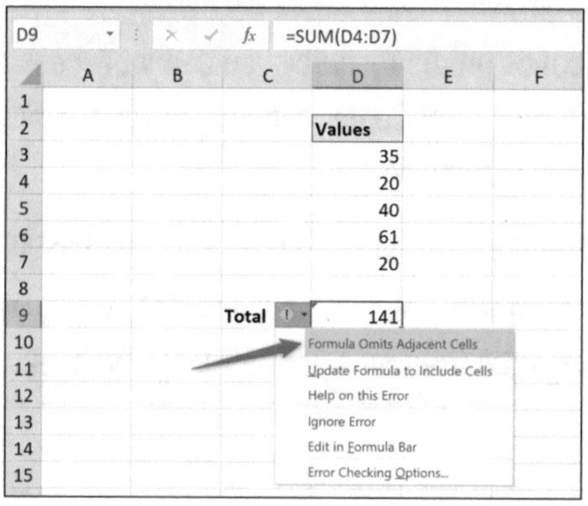

Figure 1-34. *Access information and options regarding the warning*

This can be fixed by editing the formula to include cell D3 in the range or by clicking the **Update Formula to Include Cells** option.

The options you see in this list are dependent upon the rule that the formula failed to clear.

You can turn off this background error checking or even turn off specific error checking rules. To do so, click **File ➤ Options ➤ Formulas** and change the required settings at the bottom of the window (Figure 1-35).

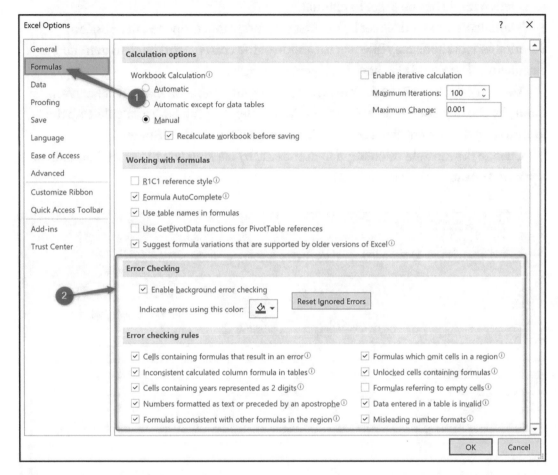

Figure 1-35. *Change error checking settings in the Excel options window*

Excel Formula Is Not Calculating

There are a few reasons to explain why a formula has stopped updating. Let's look at a few.

Formula Calculations Are Set to Manual

The most likely reason that your formulas do not calculate automatically is that the calculation mode has been set to manual.

The calculation mode is set by the first workbook that is opened in a session. So, another workbook may have set the mode of the current workbook to manual calculation. This could also have been set by a macro.

You can calculate all the formulas in the workbook, while in manual calculation mode, by clicking **Formulas ➤ Calculate Now** or by pressing **F9**. To calculate all the formulas on the current sheet only, click **Formulas ➤ Calculate Sheet**.

Change the formula calculation to automatic by clicking **Formulas ➤ Calculation Options ➤ Automatic** (Figure 1-36).

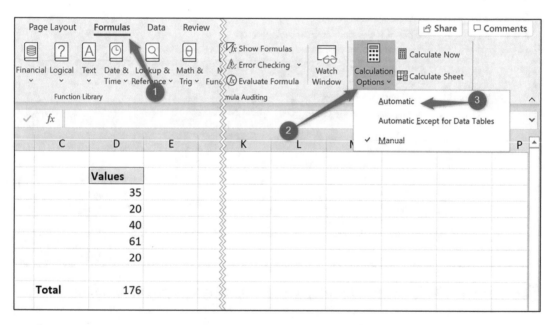

Figure 1-36. *Change formula calculation to automatic*

Show Formulas Is Switched On

When the Show Formulas feature is switched on, it is quite noticeable because the columns get wider to accommodate the formula text.

It is, however, another reason that stops your formulas from calculating (Figure 1-37). This feature can be switched on accidentally with the **Ctrl + '** (back quote symbol) keyboard shortcut.

To fix this issue, switch it off by pressing **Ctrl + '** or clicking **Formulas ➤ Show Formulas**.

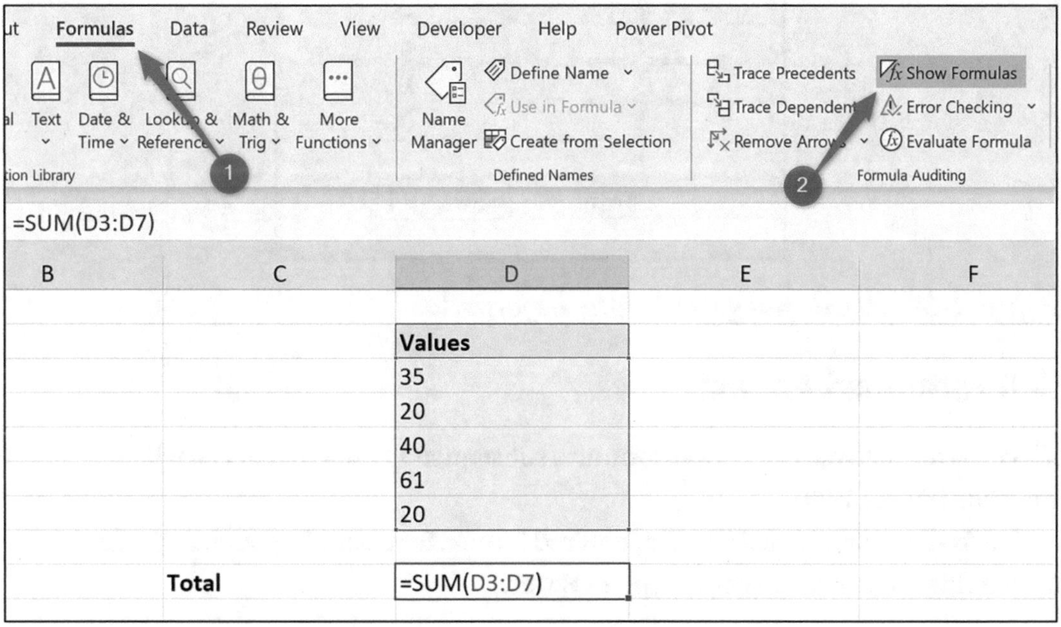

Figure 1-37. *Show Formulas feature is switched on*

Formula Is Stored As Text

Excel formulas can be inadvertently stored as text by typing a character before the equals of the formula.

In Figure 1-38, a space has been entered before the SUM function. The formula therefore does not calculate and is instead stored as text. Remove the character that is causing this issue (space in this example) to fix this issue.

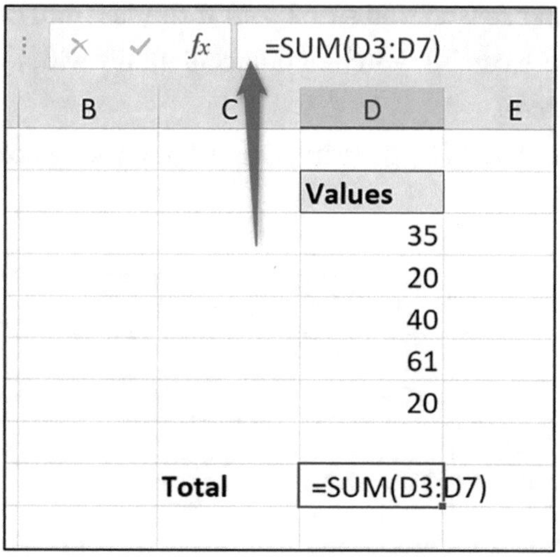

Figure 1-38. *Accidental space before the formula*

Cell Formatted As Text

If a cell is formatted as text, some formulas subsequently used in that cell will not calculate (Figure 1-39).

To fix the issue, change it to the required format, for example, general, number, accounting. Then edit the cell and press **Enter**.

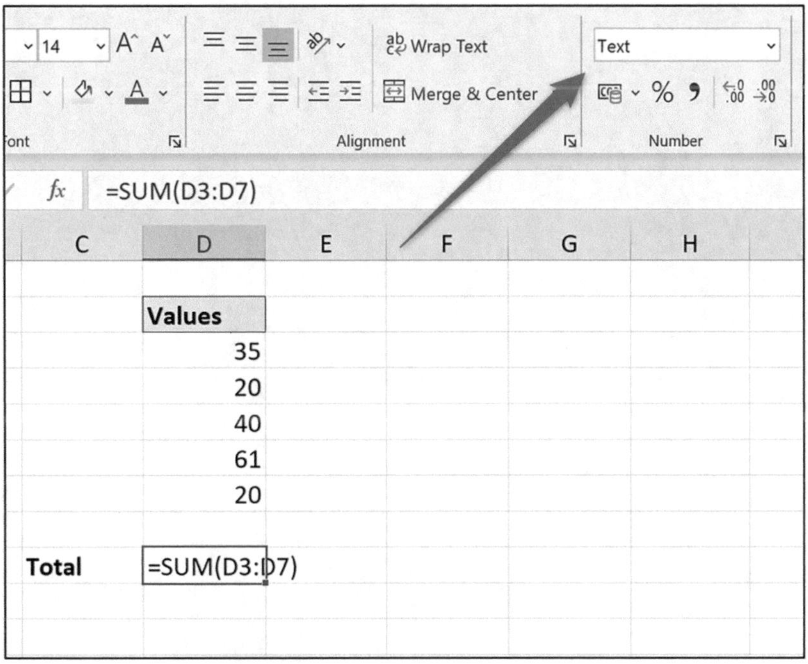

Figure 1-39. *Cell formatted as text before inputting a formula*

It is interesting that if the cell is formatted as text after the formula is entered, it continues to calculate.

Summary

This chapter provided a comprehensive primer on Excel formulas and their parts. It covered the important building blocks of formulas and functions including

- The different characters and the role that they play within formulas

- The order that a formula evaluates

- And different methods to reference other cells, worksheets, and workbooks, and how to work with them

We also covered the important task of identifying and handling errors and other issues that will occur with formulas.

In the next chapter, we will look at the logical functions in Excel including IF, SWITCH, AND, IFERROR, and more. These functions are incredibly useful and provide a logical (sorry! 😊) next step in our formula journey.

CHAPTER 2

Logical Functions

Logical functions are essential for the arsenal of any Excel user. They are the building blocks of many automated reports and Excel models.

They automate decision-making and perform specific actions based on the value of a cell or handle errors that may be expected.

The chapter begins with multiple examples of the quite brilliant IF function. This function is a gateway function for users going from a basic to intermediate level. But you will never stop using this effective little function.

We then proceed into more complex logical formula examples that perform multiple conditions, cover the powerful SWITCH function, and then combine logical formulas with Excel features such as charts and Conditional Formatting.

What Is TRUE and FALSE?

Logical tests normally evaluate to TRUE or FALSE. For example, 20>15 = TRUE. Although we are normally performing these binary decisions (and this chapter solely uses such examples), it is important to know that any numeric value except 0 evaluates to TRUE. This includes both positive and negative values.

In Figure 2-1, the following formula is used to return TRUE or FALSE dependent upon the value in column A. Only the 0, blank cell, and FALSE value return FALSE.

```
=IF(A2,TRUE,FALSE)
```

As mentioned, all examples in this chapter will be performing logical expressions that evaluate to 1 or 0, TRUE or FALSE. However, this feels like the ideal opportunity, as we begin to discuss logical functions, to state that any numeric value, except 0, evaluates to TRUE. We will see examples of this application later in the book.

© Alan Murray 2022
A. Murray, *Advanced Excel Formulas*, https://doi.org/10.1007/978-1-4842-7125-4_2

B2	⌄ ⋮	✕ ✓	*fx*	=IF(A2,TRUE,FALSE)

	A	B	C
1	**Values**	**TRUE/FALSE**	
2	3	TRUE	
3	-10	TRUE	
4	0	FALSE	
5	TRUE	TRUE	
6		FALSE	
7	FALSE	FALSE	
8	1	TRUE	

Figure 2-1. *All numeric values except 0 evaluate to TRUE*

The IF Function

Availability: All versions

File   if-function.xlsx

As mentioned, let's begin with the IF function.

The purpose of the IF function is to test a condition and then perform a different action or return a different value, dependent on the result of the test. If the result was TRUE, perform a specified action or return a specific value, and if FALSE, an alternative action or value will be returned.

The syntax of the IF function is

```
=IF(logical_test, [value_if_true], [value_if_false])
```

- **Logical test:** The condition to test. This can be anything that can be evaluated to TRUE or FALSE.

- **[Value if true]:** The action to perform if the result of the test is TRUE.

- **[Value if false]:** The action to perform if the result of the test is FALSE.

Example 1: Testing Numeric Values

Let's begin with an IF function example that tests a numeric value.

In this example, we want to apply a 5% discount on an order total, but only if the order total is greater than or equal to the value of 500.

In Figure 2-2, the following formula has been entered into cell C2:

```
=IF(B2>=500,B2*(1-5%),B2)
```

This formula tests the order total against the value of 500, and if the result is TRUE, it decreases the total by 5%. If it fails the test and returns FALSE, then the order total is kept the same.

C2	▾	⋮	×	✓	fx	=IF(B2>=500,B2*(1-5%),B2)	

	A	B	C	D
1	Customer	Total	Inc Discount	
2	Mario Pontes	711.00	675.45	
3	Daniel Tonini	450.00	450.00	
4	Hanna Moos	509.00	483.55	
5	Jaime Yorres	395.00	395.00	
6	José Pedro Freyre	683.00	648.85	
7	Carlos Hernández	340.00	340.00	
8	André Fonseca	442.00	442.00	
9				

Figure 2-2. *Formula to apply a 5% discount only if the total value is >=500*

Let's change this example by using cell values for the threshold to qualify for a discount and the percentage to apply as a discount.

The following formula has been entered into cell C2. It uses the values in cells F2 and F4, instead of fixed values (Figure 2-3):

```
=IF(B2>=$F$2,B2*(1-$F$4),B2)
```

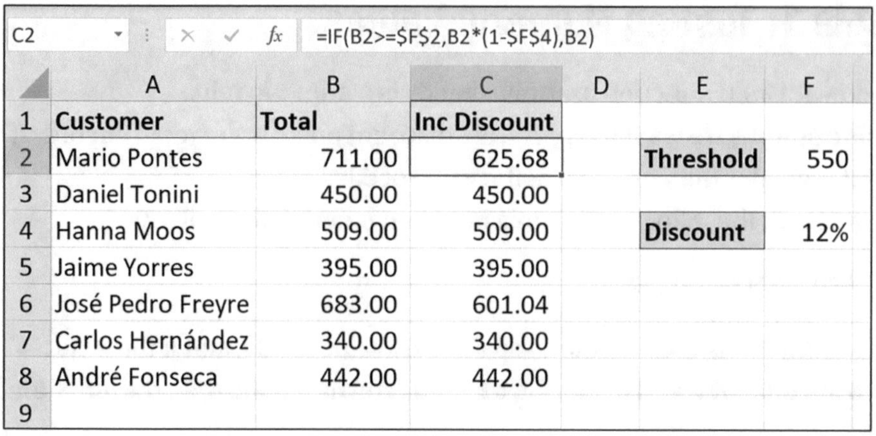

| C2 | ▾ | : | × | ✓ | fx | =IF(B2>=$F$2,B2*(1-$F$4),B2) |

	A	B	C	D	E	F
1	Customer	Total	Inc Discount			
2	Mario Pontes	711.00	625.68		Threshold	550
3	Daniel Tonini	450.00	450.00			
4	Hanna Moos	509.00	509.00		Discount	12%
5	Jaime Yorres	395.00	395.00			
6	José Pedro Freyre	683.00	601.04			
7	Carlos Hernández	340.00	340.00			
8	André Fonseca	442.00	442.00			
9						

Figure 2-3. *Cell values used for the threshold and discount percentage*

This time, the formula uses a different threshold value (550) and a different discount percentage (12%). You can see that *Hanna Moos* is not given a discount, but she did previously.

Example 2: Testing Text Values

Now, let's see an example of the IF function performing a logical test with text values.

In this example, we have customers with different levels of membership. Only those with an *Executive* membership level qualify for a 15% discount off the order total.

The following formula has been entered into cell D2 (Figure 2-4):

```
=IF(B2="Executive",C2*(1-15%),C2)
```

The double quotations have been used to denote a text string (written characters, not the name of an object such as another function or defined name).

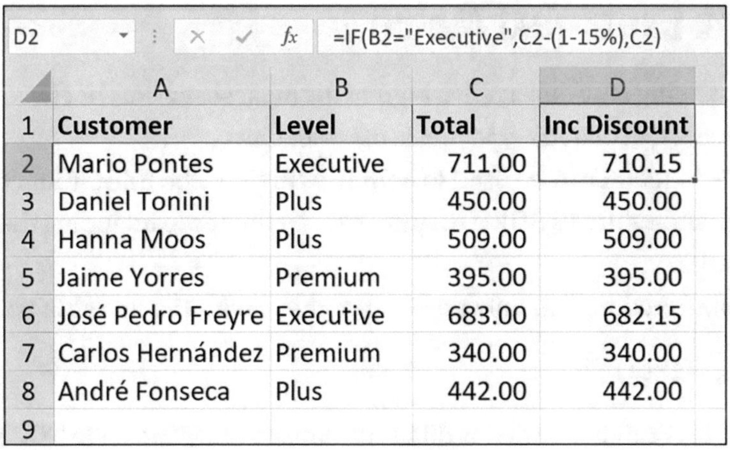

	A	B	C	D
				=IF(B2="Executive",C2-(1-15%),C2)
1	Customer	Level	Total	Inc Discount
2	Mario Pontes	Executive	711.00	710.15
3	Daniel Tonini	Plus	450.00	450.00
4	Hanna Moos	Plus	509.00	509.00
5	Jaime Yorres	Premium	395.00	395.00
6	José Pedro Freyre	Executive	683.00	682.15
7	Carlos Hernández	Premium	340.00	340.00
8	André Fonseca	Plus	442.00	442.00
9				

Figure 2-4. *IF function to apply a 15% discount for Executive-level customers*

The IF function is not case-sensitive when testing text values. In Figure 2-5, you can see that the IF function is undeterred by "executive" being in lowercase.

However, the text string must match perfectly. "Executive level," "Exxecutive," and " executive" (leading space) are not the same value.

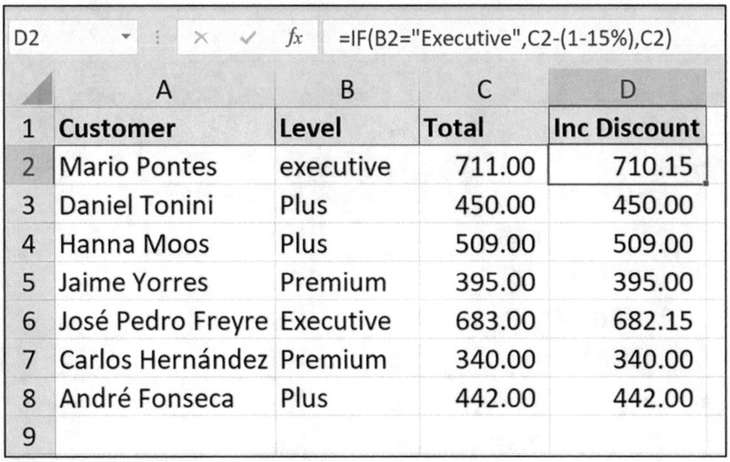

	A	B	C	D
				=IF(B2="Executive",C2-(1-15%),C2)
1	Customer	Level	Total	Inc Discount
2	Mario Pontes	executive	711.00	710.15
3	Daniel Tonini	Plus	450.00	450.00
4	Hanna Moos	Plus	509.00	509.00
5	Jaime Yorres	Premium	395.00	395.00
6	José Pedro Freyre	Executive	683.00	682.15
7	Carlos Hernández	Premium	340.00	340.00
8	André Fonseca	Plus	442.00	442.00
9				

Figure 2-5. *The IF function is case-insensitive*

Example 3: Exact Text Match

The IF function being case-insensitive is great for most scenarios, but let's see how you can make an exact text match – one that is case-sensitive.

The EXACT function can be used to help IF with this. The EXACT function compares two text strings and returns TRUE if they are exactly the same including the case and FALSE if they are not.

It is a simple function. You only need to provide it with the two strings:

```
=EXACT(Text1, Text2)
```

In Figure 2-6, column B contains different status codes. The code "XX" means you have been approved.

The following formula has been entered into cell C2 to display "Yes" if approved and "No" if not:

```
=IF(EXACT(B2,"XX"),"Yes","No")
```

In this formula, the EXACT function compares the content of cell B2 with the string "XX" to check that they are exactly the same. IF then returns the required result.

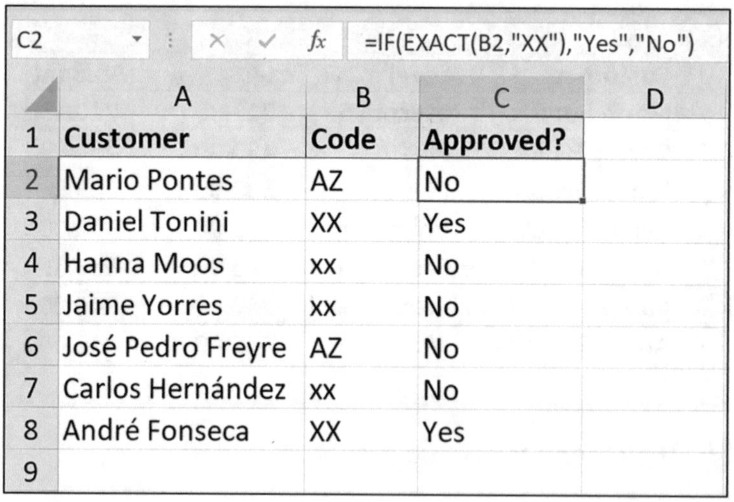

	A	B	C	D
	Customer	Code	Approved?	
1	Customer	Code	Approved?	
2	Mario Pontes	AZ	No	
3	Daniel Tonini	XX	Yes	
4	Hanna Moos	xx	No	
5	Jaime Yorres	xx	No	
6	José Pedro Freyre	AZ	No	
7	Carlos Hernández	xx	No	
8	André Fonseca	XX	Yes	
9				

C2 fx =IF(EXACT(B2,"XX"),"Yes","No")

Figure 2-6. *Exact text match with the IF function*

Example 4: Partial Text Match

In this example, we want to only match part of the text in a cell.

We have a list of booking references in column A and a two-character code which indicates how the booking was referred to us. There are two referral codes (EX = External and ME = Member). These two characters can appear anywhere in the booking reference string (Figure 2-7).

	A	B
1	**Booking Ref**	**Referral Type**
2	100EX23	
3	ME1900	
4	4EX3156	
5	400ME	
6	419ME	
7	2EX2918	
8	102EX87	

Figure 2-7. *Booking reference data with referral codes*

In column B, we want to return the referral type (External or Member) using the two-character code.

The IF function does not allow the use of wildcard characters like many other functions including VLOOKUP and COUNTIFS. You will see examples of these later in the book, but for now, we need an alternative approach for the IF function.

We will use the SEARCH function to search for the referral code in the booking reference and confirm if it is there or not. The purpose of the SEARCH function is to find text within another text string and return its position.

The SEARCH function takes three arguments:

```
=SEARCH(find_text, within_text, [start_num])
```

- **Find text:** What text you are searching for.

- **Within text:** Where you want to search for that text.

- **[Start num]:** What position (specified by index number) in the *within_text* string to begin the search. If omitted, it starts from the first character.

Figure 2-8 shows the SEARCH function returning the position of the referral code "EX" from the booking references in column A. If it is not found, the #VALUE! error is returned.

```
=SEARCH("EX",A2)
```

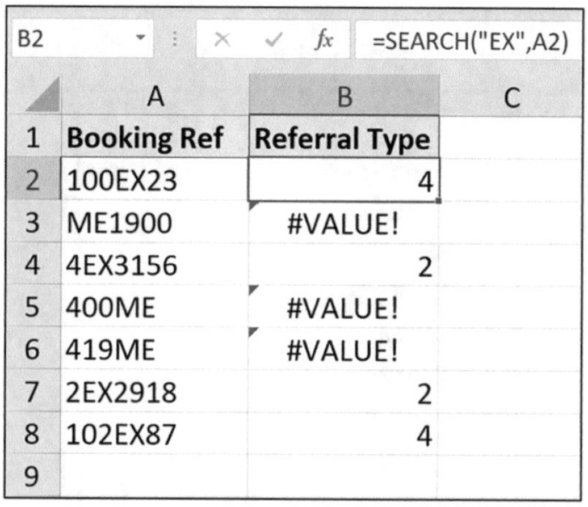

B2 =SEARCH("EX",A2)

	A	B	C
1	Booking Ref	Referral Type	
2	100EX23	4	
3	ME1900	#VALUE!	
4	4EX3156	2	
5	400ME	#VALUE!	
6	419ME	#VALUE!	
7	2EX2918	2	
8	102EX87	4	
9			

Figure 2-8. *SEARCH function used to test the referral code*

Note The FIND function could also be used. The difference between FIND and SEARCH is that FIND is case-sensitive and SEARCH is not. You will learn more about these in the Text functions chapter in the book.

So, the SEARCH function returns the position of the referral code "EX" if it is found. It returns the index number of the first character.

For the booking reference "100EX23" in cell A2, 4 is returned as "EX" begins from the fourth character in that reference.

We can then use the ISNUMBER function to convert this information to TRUE or FALSE. ISNUMBER checks whether a value is a number and returns TRUE if it is and FALSE if not.

Figure 2-9 shows the ISNUMBER function converting the search results into TRUE or FALSE.

```
=ISNUMBER(SEARCH("EX",A2))
```

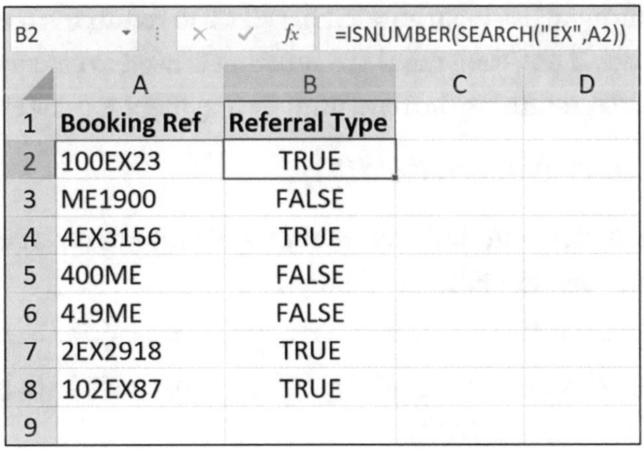

B2 =ISNUMBER(SEARCH("EX",A2))

	A	B	C	D
1	Booking Ref	Referral Type		
2	100EX23	TRUE		
3	ME1900	FALSE		
4	4EX3156	TRUE		
5	400ME	FALSE		
6	419ME	FALSE		
7	2EX2918	TRUE		
8	102EX87	TRUE		
9				

Figure 2-9. *ISNUMBER function to convert search results to TRUE and FALSE*

Finally, we can add the IF function to then take the decisive action of displaying "External" if the referral code "EX" is found and "Member" if not (Figure 2-10).

```
=IF(ISNUMBER(SEARCH("EX",A2)),"External","Member")
```

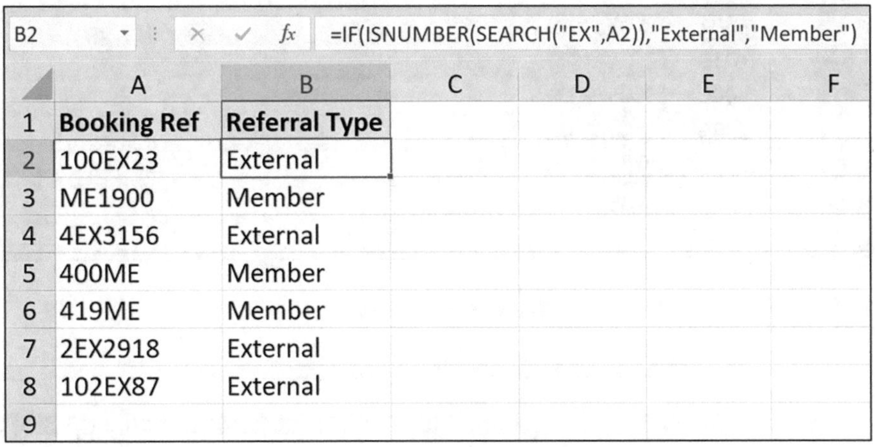

B2 =IF(ISNUMBER(SEARCH("EX",A2)),"External","Member")

	A	B	C	D	E	F
1	Booking Ref	Referral Type				
2	100EX23	External				
3	ME1900	Member				
4	4EX3156	External				
5	400ME	Member				
6	419ME	Member				
7	2EX2918	External				
8	102EX87	External				
9						

Figure 2-10. *IF function with a partial text match*

Example 5: Testing Date Values

Let's see an example of the IF function used to test date values. In this example, we want to easily identify invoice payments that are overdue.

The following formula has been entered in cell C2 to return the text "Late" if the due date is in the past. If not, then the DAYS function is used to calculate the difference between the two dates, returning the days until the payment is due (Figure 2-11).

```
=IF(B2<TODAY(),"Late",DAYS(B2,TODAY()))
```

The TODAY() function returns the current date. It requires no arguments. You must always enter the brackets after its name though.

Note   The dates are shown in dd/MM/yyyy format because I am based in the UK. Today's date is the 11/03/2021.

C2	▾ ⋮	× ✓	*fx*	=IF(B2<TODAY(),"Late",DAYS(B2,TODAY()))		
	A	B	C	D	E	F
1	Invoice	Due Date	Status			
2	939	13/04/2021	33			
3	869	07/03/2021	Late			
4	907	02/03/2021	Late			
5	1019	12/04/2021	32			
6	1449	15/03/2021	4			
7	1066	01/04/2021	21			
8	1330	30/03/2021	19			
9	909	09/03/2021	Late			
10						

Figure 2-11. *IF function to identify late payments*

Note   There are formulas in the [Due Date] column to automatically update these dates. The dates you see on your spreadsheet will be different to those shown in Figure 2-11. This ensures that you can follow along with the example and get the same results.

Example 6: Testing If a Cell Is Empty or Blank

There are two different methods to test if a cell is empty or blank. And I do make a distinction between those two words, because sometimes a cell may look blank, but it does contain something.

Let's look at an example; we have a list containing dates of approval for something. If they have not been approved yet, there is no date, and the cell is blank.

The following formula has been used in cell C2 of Figure 2-12 to input an empty string if the cell is blank, otherwise to calculate the days since approval:

```
=IF(ISBLANK(B2),"",TODAY()-B2)
```

C2	▼	⋮	×	✓	fx	=IF(ISBLANK(B2),"",TODAY()-B2)	
	A		B		C		D
1	Name		Approved		Days Since Approval		
2	Nick		16/02/2021		26		
3	Mark		09/03/2021		5		
4	Shelley						
5	Anne		08/03/2021		6		
6	Katrin						
7	Rene		06/02/2021		36		
8	Charlotte		16/02/2021		26		
9							

Figure 2-12. *IF function to test if a cell is blank or empty*

The ISBLANK function has been used to test if the cell is blank and return TRUE if so. Otherwise, it returns FALSE.

This could also have been achieved with the following formula:

```
=IF(B2="","",TODAY()-B2)
```

In this example, they both work. But what is the difference between an empty string ("") and the ISBLANK function?

Well, for the ISBLANK function to work, the cell must be completely blank. If a cell contains an empty string, like the ones in column C of Figure 2-12, then it is not completely blank.

When testing for an empty string, like in the second example, the cell needs to only be visually empty. If it contains an empty string returned by a formula, the cell is empty.

So, there is a difference between empty and blank.

If you wanted to test if a cell contained something, anything. So, it is not empty. The following formula could be used (Figure 2-13). The not equal to operator (<>) has been used:

```
=IF(B2<>"",TODAY()-B2,"")
```

C2	▾	:	✕	✓	fx	=IF(B2<>"",TODAY()-B2,"")	

	A	B	C	D
1	Name	Approved	Days Since Approval	
2	Nick	16/02/2021	26	
3	Mark	09/03/2021	5	
4	Shelley			
5	Anne	08/03/2021	6	
6	Katrin			
7	Rene	06/02/2021	36	
8	Charlotte	16/02/2021	26	
9				

Figure 2-13. *If a cell is not empty*

This formula can be used to test if the cell is not blank:

```
=IF(NOT(ISBLANK(B2)),TODAY()-B2,"")
```

The NOT function has been used to reverse the result of the ISBLANK function. We will see more on the NOT function soon.

Example 7: Return a Symbol or Emoji

It is easy to use a symbol or an emoji in an Excel formula. And these can have a great visual impact. We will look at both examples beginning with using a symbol.

There are many symbols available in Excel. For this example, we will use the thumbs up and thumbs down symbols on the list of student scores in Figure 2-14.

The passing score is 75. In column C, we will display the thumbs up symbol for any score of 75 or above. The thumbs down symbol will be displayed for the other scores.

	A	B	C
1	Name	Score	Result
2	Mandy	92	
3	John	69	
4	Ken	92	
5	Cristian	74	
6	Tanja	61	
7	Elizabeth	79	
8	Franck	93	
9			

Figure 2-14. *Exam score data for some students*

We will insert the symbols onto the worksheet first. Then write the IF function and copy and paste the symbols into the formula where we need them:

1. Click **Insert ➤ Symbols ➤ Symbol** to open the *Symbol* window.

2. Select **Wingdings** from the *Font* list.

3. Select the thumbs up symbol and click **Insert**. Then repeat for the thumbs down symbol (Figure 2-15).

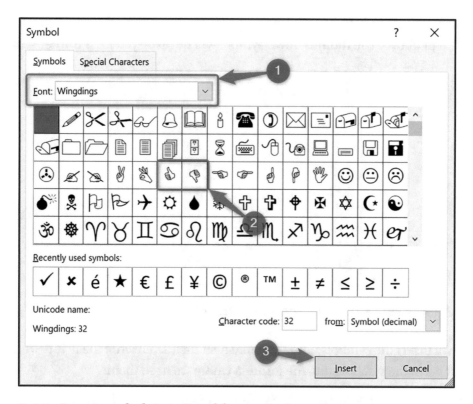

Figure 2-15. *Insert symbols into Excel for use in formulas*

The following formula has been entered into cell C2 (Figure 2-16). The symbols were copied and pasted from cell E2 into the *value if true* and *value if false* arguments between the double quotations.

```
=IF(B2>=75,"C","D")
```

This Wingdings font converts a character to a symbol. You can see that the thumbs up symbol is an uppercase C, and thumbs down is an uppercase D.

We could have simply typed these letters instead of copying and pasting the symbols. Not all symbols are that easy though, so copying and pasting avoids having to think about that.

Format the range of cells with the formula to the Wingdings font so that they are displayed correctly.

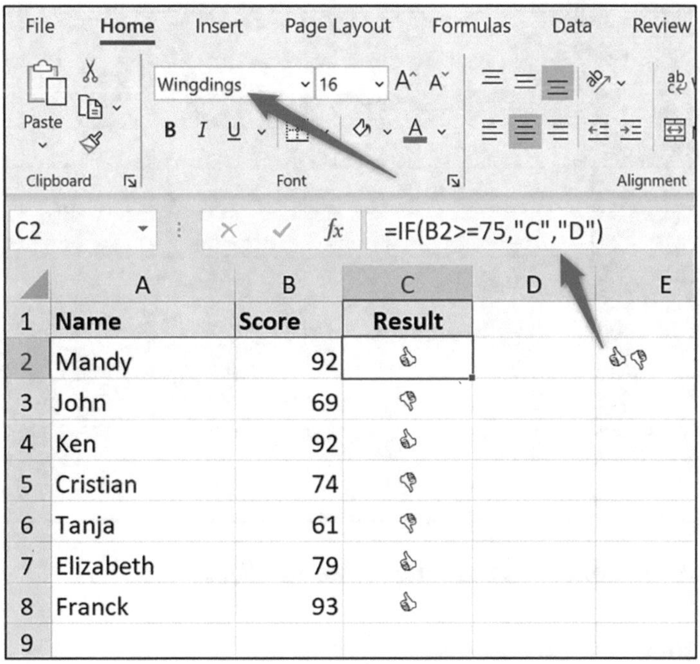

Figure 2-16. *Apply the Wingdings font to display the symbols correctly*

Conditional Formatting rules can then be applied to the range to format the thumbs up symbol in a green font and thumbs down in a red font. This has a great impact in distinguishing the symbols.

Click **Home ➤ Conditional Formatting ➤ Highlight Cells Rules ➤ Equal To**. Type an uppercase "C" and choose the formatting. Then repeat with "D" for the thumbs down symbol.

Figure 2-17 shows the thumbs down rule being set up.

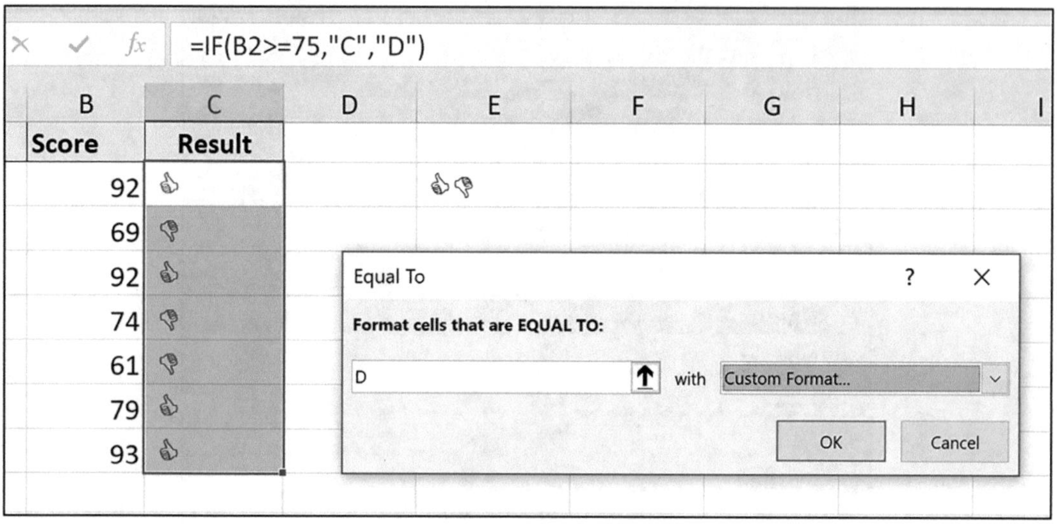

		fx	=IF(B2>=75,"C","D")						

B	C	D	E	F	G	H	I
Score	**Result**						
92	👍		👍👎				
69	👎						
92	👍						
74	👎						
61	👎						
79	👍						
93	👍						

Equal To   ?   ✕

Format cells that are EQUAL TO:

D	↑	with	Custom Format...	⌄

OK   Cancel

Figure 2-17. *Conditional Formatting for extra effect*

Figure 2-18 shows the final result.

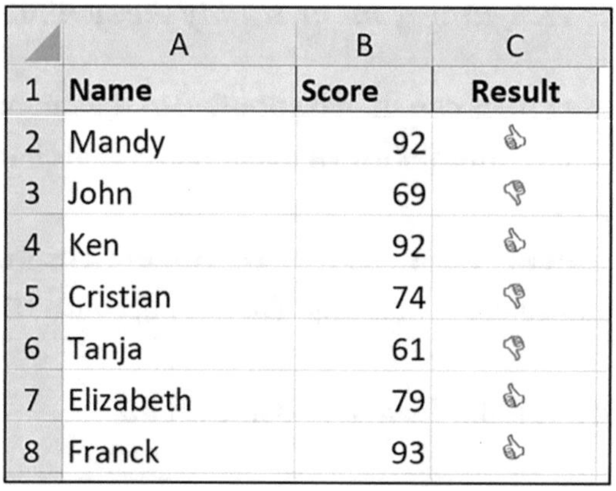

	A	B	C
1	**Name**	**Score**	**Result**
2	Mandy	92	👍
3	John	69	👎
4	Ken	92	👍
5	Cristian	74	👎
6	Tanja	61	👎
7	Elizabeth	79	👍
8	Franck	93	👍

Figure 2-18. *Thumbs up and thumbs down symbols based on score achieved*

Using an emoji in a formula is easier than using symbols. There are multiple ways of inserting emojis. These include

- From a website with an emoji library

- Using the touch keyboard

- Using the emoji keyboard

You can access the touch keyboard by clicking the icon on the Taskbar (Figure 2-19).

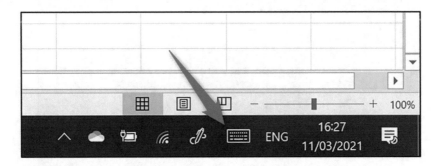

Figure 2-19. *Opening the touch keyboard*

You can then click the button to switch from letters to the emojis. There are many emojis to choose from, and they are organized in categories such as food and travel (Figure 2-20).

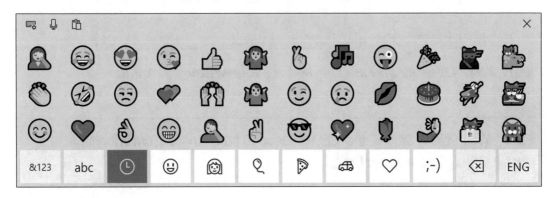

Figure 2-20. *Emojis on the touch keyboard*

This is great! But the easiest way is to use the emoji keyboard.

Type the IF function to the moment when you need to insert an emoji. Press the **Windows key + period (.)** to open the emoji keyboard (Figure 2-21).

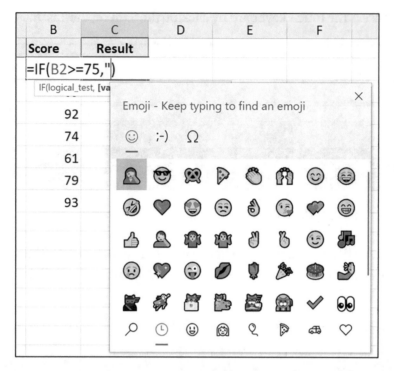

Figure 2-21. *Opening the emoji keyboard while writing a formula*

Note   When using emojis, the font will need to be changed from Wingdings to a normal writing font such as Calibri.

You can keep typing to search for an emoji or find one using the categories along the bottom of the keyboard. Click the emoji you want to use.

Press **Esc** to return to the formula and repeat the process if you need another emoji.

The following formula has been entered into cell C2 (Figure 2-22):

=IF(B2>=75,"😎","🧝‍♀️")

It uses two different emojis: one for the *value if true* and another for the *value if false*.

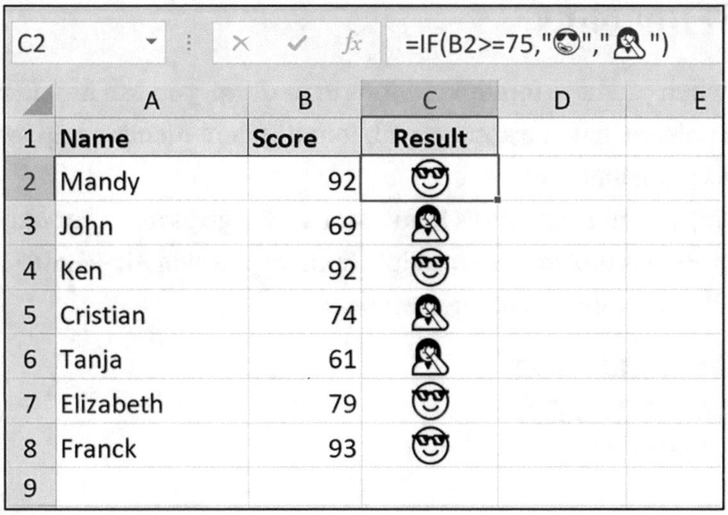

Figure 2-22. *Using emojis in an IF function*

The emojis are shown in black and white on the desktop version of Excel. But if you open the file in Excel online, they are shown in full color (Figure 2-23).

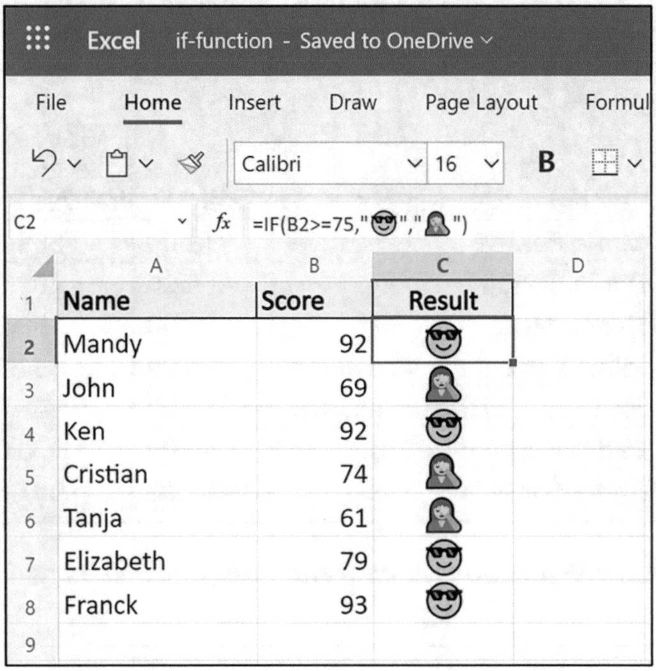

Figure 2-23. *Emojis in color on Excel online*

Nested IF Functions

On occasions when you have multiple actions to perform, you can nest IF functions.

In this example, we have customers with four different membership levels. Each level has different discount amounts.

The following formula uses three IF functions. This gives us three *value if true* actions. The formula is broken over multiple lines by pressing **Alt + Enter** to make it easier to read. Each IF function has its own line:

```
=IF(B2="Executive",C2*(1-20%),
IF(B2="Premium",C2*(1-15%),
IF(B2="Plus",C2*(1-10%),
C2*(1-5%))))
```

It tests each membership level in turn and applies the discount when required. A 5% discount is then given for the one remaining untested membership level, which is "Basic" in this case (Figure 2-24).

D2	▾ : × ✓ *fx*	=IF(B2="Executive",C2*(1-20%),
		IF(B2="Premium",C2*(1-15%),
		IF(B2="Plus",C2*(1-10%),
		C2*(1-5%))))	

	A	B	C	D
1	Customer	Level	Total	Inc Discount
2	Mario Pontes	Executive	711.00	568.80
3	Daniel Tonini	Plus	450.00	405.00
4	Hanna Moos	Plus	509.00	458.10
5	Jaime Yorres	Premium	395.00	335.75
6	José Pedro Freyre	Executive	683.00	546.40
7	Carlos Hernández	Basic	340.00	323.00
8	André Fonseca	Plus	442.00	397.80

Figure 2-24. *Nested IF functions to perform multiple different actions*

Note   Lookup functions such as VLOOKUP and XLOOKUP, both covered later in this book, are a great alternative to using nested IF functions.

IFS Function

Availability: Excel 2016, Excel 2019, Excel 2021, Excel for Microsoft 365, Excel for the Web, Excel 2019 for Mac, Excel 2021 for Mac, Excel for Microsoft 365 for Mac

---

File   ifs-function.xlsx

The IFS function was introduced to simplify the writing of nested IF formulas. This one function can handle multiple logical tests without the need to open several different IF functions.

This function requires a list of conditions and the value to return if that condition is met. It will return the value for the first condition that returns TRUE.

The syntax of the IFS function is

```
=IFS(logical_test1, value_if_true1, [logical_test2], [value_if_true2])
```

- **Logical test1:** The first condition to test. This can be anything that can be evaluated to TRUE or FALSE.

- **Value if true1:** The value to return if the result of the first test is TRUE.

- **[Logical test2]:** The second condition to test.

- **[Value if true2]:** The value to return if the result of the second test is TRUE.

The IFS function can accept up to 127 different conditions. But that is crazy!! Please do not use too many. There are better ways to do this.

You may have noticed that there is no *value if false* or *default value* argument. So, we will see how that affects the way we write our formula.

In this example, we have a list of student exam scores, and we need to grade them. The following formula assigns five different grades (Figure 2-25). Each grade is dependent on the score they achieved:

```
=IFS(B2>=90,"A",B2>=80,"B",B2>=70,"C",B2>=60,"D",B2<60,"E")
```

The last condition in the IFS function is used as an else condition. Because the function has no built-in *value if false* or *default value*, the B2<60 condition was written to return "E" if else.

| C2 | ▾ | ⋮ | × | ✓ | *fx* | =IFS(B2>=90,"A",B2>=80,"B",B2>=70,"C",B2>=60,"D", B2<60,"E") |

	A	B	C	D	E	F
1	Name	Score	Result			
2	Mandy	92	A			
3	John	69	D			
4	Ken	85	B			
5	Cristian	74	C			
6	Tanja	54	E			
7	Elizabeth	79	C			
8	Franck	93	A			
9						

Figure 2-25. *IFS function to grade the scores correctly*

The IFS function returns the value for the first condition that returns TRUE. So, in this example, the order of the conditions is important.

The following formula has the conditions in the reverse order and returns disastrous results:

```
=IFS(B2<60,"E",B2>=60,"D",B2>=70,"C",B2>=80,"B",B2>=90,"A")
```

In Figure 2-26, most grades are returned as D because they are >=60, and that is the first test that returns TRUE.

| C2 | ▾ | ⋮ | × | ✓ | *fx* | =IFS(B2<60,"E", B2>=60,"D",B2>=70,"C",B2>=80,"B",B2>=90,"A") |

	A	B	C	D	E	F
1	Name	Score	Result			
2	Mandy	92	D			
3	John	69	D			
4	Ken	85	D			
5	Cristian	74	D			
6	Tanja	54	E			
7	Elizabeth	79	D			
8	Franck	93	D			
9						

Figure 2-26. *IFS returns the value for the first test that returns TRUE*

If the value being tested does not match any of the listed criteria, then the #N/A error is returned. We will look at dealing with this in the "Handling Errors" section of this chapter.

The following formula uses nested IF functions to return the same results (Figure 2-27):

```
=IF(B2>=90,"A",IF(B2>=80,"B",IF(B2>=70,"C",IF(B2>=60,"D","E"))))
```

To be honest, IFS is not a big improvement. It simplifies the task for beginners as there is no need to open and close multiple IF functions.

However, the formulas are a similar size, and the lack of a *value if false* argument is a shame.

Note   The SWITCH function is a better way of handling multiple logical tests than both IFS and nested IFs.

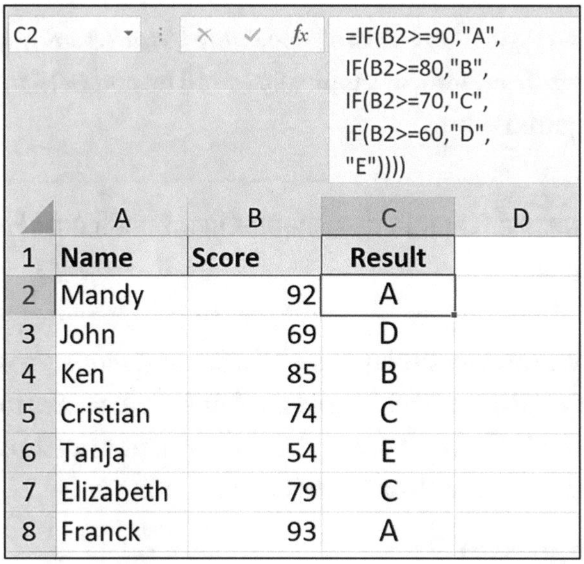

Figure 2-27. Nested IF functions to grade the scores

AND, OR, XOR, and NOT Functions

There are logical functions in Excel that will allow us to perform more than one logical test. Using these, we can construct more complex logic that extends beyond the capabilities of the IF function alone.

These functions are AND, OR, and XOR. There is also the NOT function that can be used to reverse the TRUE or FALSE values. Let's look at each one in turn with one or more examples of their use.

AND Function

Availability: All versions

The AND function tests multiple conditions and returns TRUE only if all the conditions are met.

Its syntax is

```
=AND(logical1, [logical2], ...)
```

Each argument is a logical test. There is no *value if true* or *value if false* argument with the AND function. Therefore, it is typically found nested in IF to take some required action or return a required value.

Note   It will also be used later in this chapter in a Conditional Formatting rule to test multiple cell values.

In this example, we want to display "Pass" if a student scores 70 or more in each of their exams. Otherwise, display "Fail." There are three exam scores to test.

The following formula has been entered in cell E2. It tests all three scores and returns TRUE only if all three scores are 70 or more (Figure 2-28):

```
=AND(B2>=70,C2>=70,D2>=70)
```

E2	▾	:	✕	✓	*fx*	=AND(B2>=70,C2>=70,D2>=70)

	A	B	C	D	E
1	Name	Exam 1	Exam 2	Exam 3	Result
2	Emily	57	80	64	FALSE
3	Andreas	91	60	69	FALSE
4	Jan	88	74	83	TRUE
5	Rachel	88	95	89	TRUE
6	Alexandra	89	71	74	TRUE
7	Jason	72	89	82	TRUE
8	Claire	55	74	93	FALSE
9	Tony	95	75	81	TRUE
10					

Figure 2-28. *AND function to test that three conditions are all met*

Returning TRUE or FALSE is not our end goal. So, once we are happy that our logic is working, we can wrap it in an IF function to return "Pass" or "Fail."

In Figure 2-29, the following formula has been entered into cell E2:

```
=IF(AND(B2>=70,C2>=70,D2>=70),"Pass","Fail")
```

E2	▾	:	✕	✓	*fx*	=IF(AND(B2>=70,C2>=70,D2>=70),"Pass","Fail")	

	A	B	C	D	E	F	G
1	Name	Exam 1	Exam 2	Exam 3	Result		
2	Emily	57	80	64	Fail		
3	Andreas	91	60	69	Fail		
4	Jan	88	74	83	Pass		
5	Rachel	88	95	89	Pass		
6	Alexandra	89	71	74	Pass		
7	Jason	72	89	82	Pass		
8	Claire	55	74	93	Fail		
9	Tony	95	75	81	Pass		
10							

Figure 2-29. *Return "Pass" only if all three cell values are >=70*

Let's look at another example. This time, the student needs to score 75 or more from the average of the three exam scores and score 70% or more on their coursework score.

The following formula is used in Figure 2-30 to display "Pass" or "Fail" using this criterion:

```
=IF(
AND(AVERAGE(B2:D2)>=75,E2>=70%),
"Pass","Fail")
```

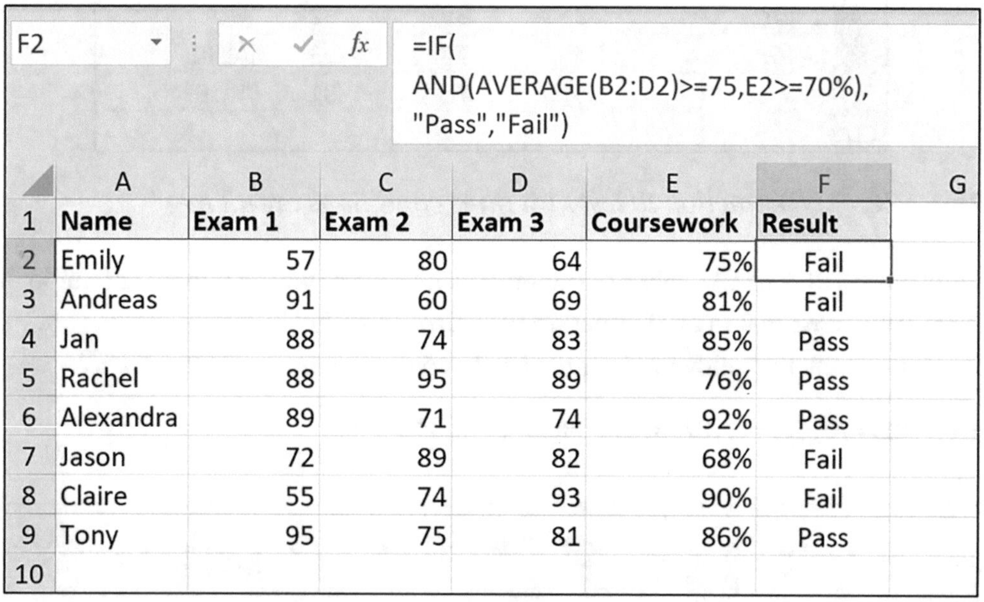

	A	B	C	D	E	F	G
	Name	Exam 1	Exam 2	Exam 3	Coursework	Result	
1							
2	Emily	57	80	64	75%	Fail	
3	Andreas	91	60	69	81%	Fail	
4	Jan	88	74	83	85%	Pass	
5	Rachel	88	95	89	76%	Pass	
6	Alexandra	89	71	74	92%	Pass	
7	Jason	72	89	82	68%	Fail	
8	Claire	55	74	93	90%	Fail	
9	Tony	95	75	81	86%	Pass	
10							

F2 ▾ ⋮ ✕ ✓ *fx* =IF(AND(AVERAGE(B2:D2)>=75,E2>=70%), "Pass","Fail")

Figure 2-30. *Second AND function example*

OR Function

Availability: All versions

The OR function tests multiple conditions and returns TRUE if one or more conditions are met. So, with the OR function, only one condition needs to be met to return TRUE.

The syntax for the OR function is

```
=OR(logical1, [logical2], ...)
```

Let's repeat the previous AND function example but using the OR function and changing the coursework pass mark to 80% (Figure 2-31):

```
=IF(
OR(AVERAGE(B2:D2)>=75,E2>=80%),
"Pass","Fail")
```

This formula returns a "Pass" for all students except "Emily." That is the only student to not meet at least one of the conditions.

	A	B	C	D	E	F
1	Name	Exam 1	Exam 2	Exam 3	Coursework	Result
2	Emily	57	80	64	75%	Fail
3	Andreas	91	60	69	81%	Pass
4	Jan	88	74	83	85%	Pass
5	Rachel	88	95	89	76%	Pass
6	Alexandra	89	71	74	92%	Pass
7	Jason	72	89	82	68%	Pass
8	Claire	55	74	93	90%	Pass
9	Tony	95	75	81	86%	Pass
10						

F2 — fx =IF(OR(AVERAGE(B2:D2)>=75,E2>=80%),"Pass","Fail")

Figure 2-31. OR function returning three extra "Pass" values

The OR function can be very useful when testing multiple text conditions in the same column.

Take this example; we distribute 5% of the sales value as a bonus to all staff from the "London" or "Paris" stores. But we distribute 8% of the sales value as a bonus to staff from any other store.

The following formula has been used in cell C2 of Figure 2-32. The ROUND function has also been used to round the value to 0 decimal places:

```
=ROUND(
IF(OR(A2="London",A2="Paris"),
B2*0.05,B2*0.08),
0)
```

C2	▾ : ✕ ✓ fx	=ROUND(IF(OR(A2="London",A2="Paris"), B2*0.05,B2*0.08), 0)		
	A	B	C	D
1	Store	Sales	Bonus	
2	Strasbourg	25,324	2,026	
3	Munich	49,105	3,928	
4	London	96,655	4,833	
5	Vienna	50,349	4,028	
6	Rotterdam	11,551	924	
7	Paris	72,016	3,601	
8				

Figure 2-32. *OR function to test multiple text values*

Let's now look at an example that combines both the AND and OR functions.

The following formula displays "Pass" if the student gets 90 or more in any of their exams and a score of 70% or more on their coursework. Otherwise, "Fail" is displayed (Figure 2-33):

```
=IF(AND(
OR(B2>=90,C2>=90,D2>=90),
E2>=70%),
"Pass","Fail")
```

F2	▼	:	×	✓	fx	=IF(AND(
						OR(B2>=90,C2>=90,D2>=90),
						E2>=70%),
						"Pass","Fail")

	A	B	C	D	E	F
1	Name	Exam 1	Exam 2	Exam 3	Coursework	Result
2	Emily	57	80	94	75%	Pass
3	Andreas	91	60	69	81%	Pass
4	Jan	88	74	83	85%	Fail
5	Rachel	88	95	89	76%	Pass
6	Alexandra	99	71	74	92%	Pass
7	Jason	72	89	82	68%	Fail
8	Claire	55	74	93	90%	Pass
9	Tony	95	75	81	86%	Pass

Figure 2-33. *AND and OR functions together*

XOR Function

Availability: Excel 2013, Excel 2016, Excel 2019, Excel 2021, Excel for Microsoft 365, Excel for the Web, all Excel for Mac versions

The XOR function performs "Exclusive Or" logic. It tests multiple conditions and returns TRUE if an odd number of conditions is met and FALSE if an even number of conditions is met.

The syntax for the XOR function is

```
=XOR(logical1, [logical2], ...)
```

In this example, we have organized two workshops and want to know who attended only one of the workshops. We cannot use OR logic because that returns TRUE if they attend one or more. We want to know if it was strictly just one attendance.

The following formula can be seen in Figure 2-34. It returns FALSE for "Emily" and "Alexandra" because they attended both. It also returns FALSE for "Claire" who did not attend either workshop.

```
=XOR(ISBLANK(B2),ISBLANK(C2))
```

| D2 | | × | ✓ | fx | =XOR(ISBLANK(B2),ISBLANK(C2)) | |

	A	B	C	D
1	Name	Workshop 1	Workshop 2	XOR
2	Emily	16/01/2021	06/03/2021	FALSE
3	Andreas		08/03/2021	TRUE
4	Jan		28/01/2021	TRUE
5	Rachel	06/03/2021		TRUE
6	Alexandra	13/03/2021	16/02/2021	FALSE
7	Jason		02/03/2021	TRUE
8	Claire			FALSE
9	Tony	05/03/2021		TRUE

Figure 2-34. *XOR function to test if strictly only one condition is met*

This can now be wrapped in an IF function to perform a required action. In this example, we have returned "Yes" and "No" (Figure 2-35):

```
=IF(XOR(ISBLANK(B2),ISBLANK(C2)),"Yes","No")
```

| D2 | | × | ✓ | fx | =IF(XOR(ISBLANK(B2),ISBLANK(C2)),"Yes","No") | |

	A	B	C	D	E
1	Name	Workshop 1	Workshop 2	XOR	
2	Emily	16/01/2021	06/03/2021	No	
3	Andreas		08/03/2021	Yes	
4	Jan		28/01/2021	Yes	
5	Rachel	06/03/2021		Yes	
6	Alexandra	13/03/2021	16/02/2021	No	
7	Jason		02/03/2021	Yes	
8	Claire			No	
9	Tony	05/03/2021		Yes	
10					

Figure 2-35. *XOR function nested within an IF function*

If you have a version of Excel without the XOR function, we can achieve this behavior with our own formula.

The following formula would also work in this example (Figure 2-36). It counts the numeric values in the range B2:C2 and then tests if an odd number is returned, with the ISODD function:

```
=IF(ISODD(COUNT(B2:C2)),"Yes","No")
```

	A	B	C	D
	fx	=IF(ISODD(COUNT(B2:C2)),"Yes","No")		
1	Name	Workshop 1	Workshop 2	XOR
2	Emily	16/01/2021	06/03/2021	No
3	Andreas		08/03/2021	Yes
4	Jan		28/01/2021	Yes
5	Rachel	06/03/2021		Yes
6	Alexandra	13/03/2021	16/02/2021	No
7	Jason		02/03/2021	Yes
8	Claire			No
9	Tony	05/03/2021		Yes

Figure 2-36. *Alternative formula for XOR logic using COUNT and ISODD*

In this example, we are testing if a cell is blank or is not blank. If your scenario is to test for a specific value, then use the COUNTIFS function (covered later in the book) instead of COUNT.

For example, if the criteria were the word "Yes," the following formula could be used for the logic test:

```
=ISODD(COUNTIFS(B2:C2,"Yes"))
```

NOT Function

Availability: All versions

The NOT function is used to test if a value is not equal to another. It is used to reverse the logical result of FALSE to TRUE or TRUE to FALSE.

The syntax for the NOT function is

```
=NOT(logical)
```

It requires just the one argument, the logical expression to reverse. Let's see a couple of examples of its use.

In this first example, we have a list of stores, and we want to group them into "Main" and "Satellite" sites.

The following formula is used in cell C2 (Figure 2-37). The OR function tests if the store is "London" or "Paris." Then the NOT function reverses the result to not equal those store names:

```
=IF(NOT(
OR(A2="London",A2="Paris")),
"Satellite","Main")
```

"Satellite" is displayed if the store is not "London" or "Paris." And if it is, then "Main" is displayed.

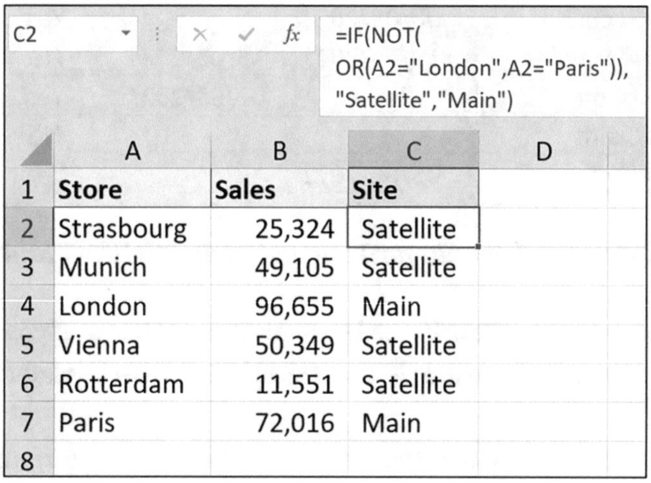

Figure 2-37. *NOT function reversing the result of an OR function*

Note   This example could have been achieved in a few different ways. These include using the not equal to operator (<>) with AND or switching the *value if true* and *value if false* values.

For this second example, we have a list of sales staff and the amount of upsells they have performed. They will receive a bonus based on 20% of their upsell value.

This formula tests if cell C2 is not blank. And if this is TRUE, it returns 20% of that value, and if it is FALSE, an empty string is returned (Figure 2-38):

```
=IF(NOT(ISBLANK(C2)),C2*0.2,"")
```

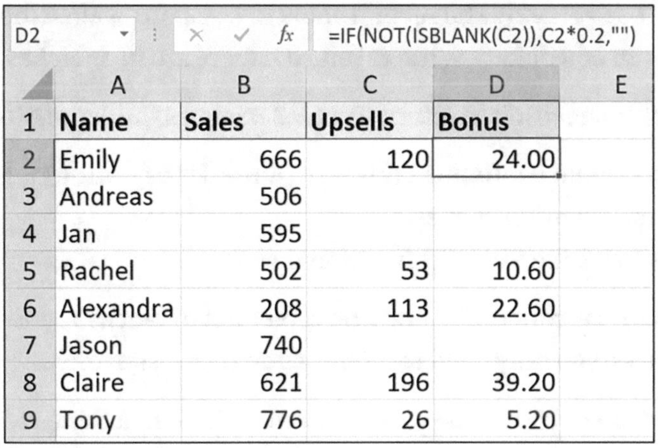
D2 =IF(NOT(ISBLANK(C2)),C2*0.2,"")

	A	B	C	D	E
1	**Name**	**Sales**	**Upsells**	**Bonus**	
2	Emily	666	120	24.00	
3	Andreas	506			
4	Jan	595			
5	Rachel	502	53	10.60	
6	Alexandra	208	113	22.60	
7	Jason	740			
8	Claire	621	196	39.20	
9	Tony	776	26	5.20	

Figure 2-38. *Testing if a cell is not blank*

The SWITCH Function

Availability: Excel 2019, Excel 2021, Excel for Microsoft 365, Excel for the Web, Excel 2019 for Mac, Excel 2021 for Mac, Excel for Microsoft 365 for Mac

---

File switch-function.xlsx

The SWITCH function was released in Excel 2019 and is superior to the IFS function and the technique of nesting IFs when you have a list of different values to return.

The SWITCH function tests an expression against a list of values and returns the result for the first matching value.

The syntax for SWITCH is

```
=SWITCH(expression, value1, result1, [default or value2], [result2] ...)
```

- **Expression:** An expression that returns a value. This can be a hardcoded value, a cell reference, or a formula. This value is compared to the list of values: value1, value2, and so on.
- **Value1:** The first value to be compared against the expression.
- **Result1:** The result to return if value1 matches the expression. This can be a value, range, or formula.

- **[Default or value2]:** The second value to compare against the expression or a default value to return if there are no matches.

- **[Result2]:** The result to return if value2 matches the expression.

The arguments would continue in this way [default or value3], [result3], and so on. SWITCH can test up to 126 values.

Advantages of using the SWITCH function include

- Its structure is concise. There is no repetition of brackets, and for most cases, you only need to reference an expression once.

- It provides a default value to return if there is no matching value. The IFS function does not have this option.

Let's see some examples to understand the SWITCH function better.

Example 1: Match Against a List of Text Values

In this example, we provide a discount to customers dependent on their membership level.

In Figure 2-39, the following formula has been used to test the value of cell B2 against the list of text values. It then performs the result returned by the first matching value.

```
=SWITCH(B2,
"Executive",C2*(1-20%),
"Premium",C2*(1-15%),
"Plus",C2*(1-10%),
C2*(1-5%))
```

A default value is used for the last argument to provide a 5% discount for any customers not on the "Executive," "Premium," or "Plus" levels. In this example, only the "Basic" level meets these requirements. The "Basic" level and its corresponding 5% discount could have been added into the formula for the value4 and result4 arguments instead.

If a default value is not provided, and the expression does not match any of the values, the #N/A error is returned.

D2	▾	:	×	✓	*fx*	=SWITCH(B2,
						"Executive",C2*(1-20%),
						"Premium",C2*(1-15%),
						"Plus",C2*(1-10%),
						C2*(1-5%))

	A	B	C	D
1	**Customer**	**Level**	**Total**	**Inc Discount**
2	Mario Pontes	Executive	711.00	568.80
3	Daniel Tonini	Plus	450.00	405.00
4	Hanna Moos	Plus	509.00	458.10
5	Jaime Yorres	Premium	395.00	335.75
6	José Pedro Freyre	Executive	683.00	546.40
7	Carlos Hernández	Basic	340.00	323.00
8	André Fonseca	Plus	442.00	397.80

Figure 2-39. *SWITCH function testing a list of text values*

This is the nested IF formula we used earlier for this same task:

```
=IF(B2="Executive",C2*(1-20%),
IF(B2="Premium",C2*(1-15%),
IF(B2="Plus",C2*(1-10%),
C2*(1-5%))))
```

There is no repetition of "IF(B2=" or the use of the two extra closing brackets at the end when using the SWITCH function.

If we were to achieve this task with the IFS function, it would look like this:

```
=IFS(B2="Executive",C2*(1-20%),
B2="Premium",C2*(1-15%),
B2="Plus",C2*(1-10%),
B2="Basic",C2*(1-5%))
```

There is no default value or *value if false* argument with IFS, so the test B2="Basic" was added to accommodate for that discount. It avoids the repetition of "IF(", but the "B2=" is still repeated.

When testing a list of possible values, SWITCH offers a more organized, concise, and clutter-free formula.

Example 2: Evaluate to TRUE

In the previous example, we tested for an exact match between the expression and the list of values. And that is the typical use of this function.

However, by entering TRUE as the expression, we can use logical operators such as >, <, >=, and <= for our values. We are then no longer restricted to exact matches.

In this example, we assign a grade to the student scores (Figure 2-40). TRUE is entered as the expression, and then for each value, we test cell B2 against the required score. "D" has been entered as the default value:

```
=SWITCH(TRUE,B2>=90,"A",B2>=80,"B",B2>=70,"C","D")
```

C2	▾	:	×	✓	*fx*	=SWITCH(TRUE, B2>=90,"A",B2>=80,"B",B2>=70,"C", "D")		
	A		B		C		D	E
1	**Name**		**Score**		**Result**			
2	Mandy		92		A			
3	John		69		D			
4	Ken		92		A			
5	Cristian		74		C			
6	Tanja		61		D			
7	Elizabeth		79		C			
8	Franck		93		A			

Figure 2-40. *SWITCH function with logical operators*

The order of the values is important as the SWITCH function returns the result for the first matching value.

Example 3: Match a Formula Result to the List of Values

So, we have seen examples of a cell reference and then TRUE being used for the expression of the SWITCH function. Now, let's see a formula.

In this example, the SWITCH function is used to calculate pay based on the day of the week and the number of hours worked (Figure 2-41). Saturday pays £18 an hour, Sunday pays £16.5 an hour, and every other day is £14 an hour.

```
=B2*SWITCH(WEEKDAY(A2,2),6,18,7,16.5,14)
```

The WEEKDAY function is used to return the day of the week as a number from the dates in column A. The 2 in the WEEKDAY function sets the week to begin on a Monday, so Monday is 1, Tuesday is 2, and so on.

Note   We have a chapter dedicated to date and time functions, so we will learn more about WEEKDAY and others later in this book.

The 6 (Saturday) and the 7 (Sunday) are used as values in the SWITCH function. 14 has been entered as the default value if the expression does not match 6 or 7.

The value returned by the SWITCH function is then multiplied by cell B2. Column B contains the hours worked.

C2				fx	=B2*SWITCH(WEEKDAY(A2,2),6,18,7,16.5,14)		
	A	B	C			D	E
1	Date	Hours	Pay				
2	01/03/2021	3	42.00				
3	02/03/2021	7.5	105.00				
4	09/03/2021	9	126.00				
5	05/03/2021	2	28.00				
6	11/03/2021	3.5	49.00				
7	15/03/2021	5	70.00				
8	07/03/2021	8.5	140.25				
9							

Figure 2-41. *SWITCH to calculate pay dependent upon the day of the week*

Example 4: Pick Formula from a Drop-Down List

In this example, we will use the SWITCH function to return the result of a function that is selected from a drop-down list.

In Figure 2-42, the following formula has been entered into cell C3:

```
=SWITCH(B3,
"Sum",SUM(F3:F14),
"Average",AVERAGE(F3:F14),
```

```
"Max",MAX(F3:F14),
"Min",MIN(F3:F14),
"")
```

Cell B3 contains a drop-down list with the options "Sum," "Average," "Max," and "Min." This cell is used as the expression and SWITCH matches the selected values against its list of values and returns the corresponding function.

An empty string ("") has been used for the default value. So, if a function is not selected from the drop-down, and that cell is blank, then cell C3 shows nothing.

| C3 | ▾ | ⋮ | ✕ | ✓ | *fx* | =SWITCH(B3,
"Sum",SUM(F3:F14),"Average",AVERAGE(F3:F14),
"Max",MAX(F3:F14),"Min",MIN(F3:F14),
"") |

◢	A	B	C	D	E	F	G	H
1								
2		Function	Result		Month	Visitors		
3		Max	1,462		January	1,012		
4					February	1,021		
5					March	1,047		
6					April	1,150		
7					May	1,180		
8					June	1,037		
9					July	1,321		
10					August	1,164		
11					September	1,429		
12					October	1,462		
13					November	1,027		
14					December	1,283		
15								

Figure 2-42. *SWITCH function to change formula from drop-down selection*

Handling Errors

File   error-handling.xlsx

Formula errors are not good, but many errors occur for logical reasons that can be expected. In these situations, we can use functions available in Excel to trap and handle these errors in an appropriate way.

IFERROR Function

Availability: All versions

The most used function for handling formula errors is the IFERROR function. The purpose of the IFERROR function is to check if a formula or cell value has evaluated to an error and, if so, take a different action that you specify.

The IFERROR function requires two arguments:

=IFERROR(value, value_if_error)

- **Value:** The value to check for an error. This can be a formula, cell reference, or logical expression.

- **Value if error:** The action to perform if an error is returned.

In this example, we have some training courses, and we measure the utilization for each course. This is the number of seats sold divided by the number of seats available.

In cell D2, the formula =C2/B2 is used (Figure 2-43). This produces the #DIV/0 error for courses C and D because we have not made any of those courses available yet this year. And you cannot divide by a zero or a blank cell.

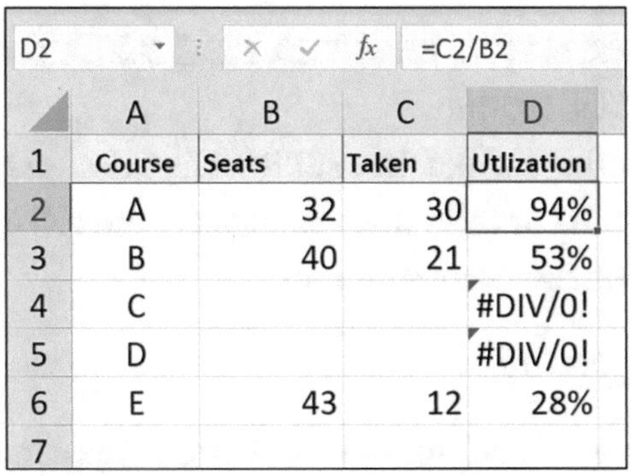

D2		⊽	:	× ✓	fx	=C2/B2

	A	B	C	D
1	Course	Seats	Taken	Utlization
2	A	32	30	94%
3	B	40	21	53%
4	C			#DIV/0!
5	D			#DIV/0!
6	E	43	12	28%
7				

Figure 2-43. *#DIV/0 error shown due to blank cells*

These errors are untidy and may cause further problems, so we want to handle them.

The following formula uses the IFERROR function to show an empty string if the utilization formula produces an error (Figure 2-44):

`=IFERROR(C2/B2,"")`

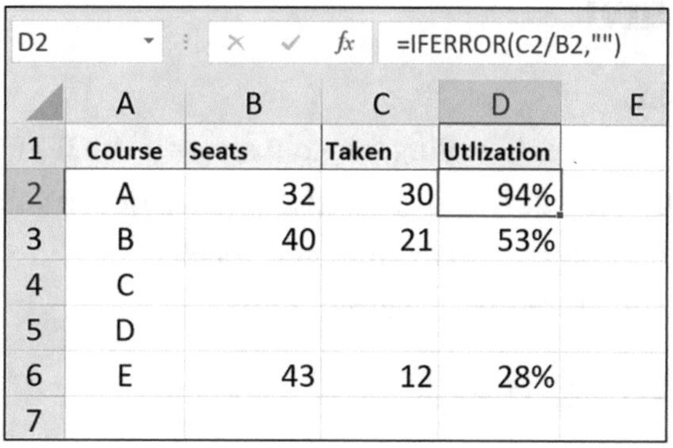

D2		⋮	×	✓	*fx*	=IFERROR(C2/B2,"")	
	A	B		C		D	E
1	Course	Seats		Taken		Utlization	
2	A	32		30		94%	
3	B	40		21		53%	
4	C						
5	D						
6	E	43		12		28%	
7							

Figure 2-44. *Return an empty string instead of the formula error*

Note   The IFERROR function is incredibly useful and will be seen in a few other formula examples throughout this book.

IFNA Function

Availability: Excel 2013, Excel 2016, Excel 2019, Excel 2021, Excel for Microsoft 365, Excel for the Web, all Excel for Mac versions

The IFNA function works just like the IFERROR function, except that it only takes alternative action if a formula or cell value evaluates to the #N/A error.

The IFNA function requires two arguments:

`=IFNA(value, value_if_error)`

- **Value:** The value to check for the #N/A error. This can be a formula, cell reference, or logical expression.

- **Value if na:** The action to perform if the #N/A error is returned.

In this example, we have used the IFS function to calculate a discount dependent upon the membership level of a customer (Figure 2-45).

We learned earlier that the IFS function does not have a built-in *default value* argument, and if none of its conditions are met, the #N/A error is returned.

This can be seen in cell D4 where a typo in cell B4 has generated the #N/A error from IFS.

```
=IFS(B2="Executive",C2*(1-20%),
B2="Premium",C2*(1-15%),
B2="Plus",C2*(1-10%),
B2="Basic",C2*(1-5%))
```

D2	▾ : × ✓ *fx*	=IFS(B2="Executive",C2*(1-20%), B2="Premium",C2*(1-15%), B2="Plus",C2*(1-10%), B2="Basic",C2*(1-5%))		
	A	B	C	D
1	Customer	Level	Total	Inc Discount
2	Mario Pontes	Executive	711.00	568.80
3	Daniel Tonini	Plus	450.00	405.00
4	Hanna Moos	Pluss	509.00	#N/A
5	Jaime Yorres	Premium	395.00	335.75
6	José Pedro Freyre	Executive	683.00	546.40
7	Carlos Hernández	Basic	340.00	323.00
8	André Fonseca	Plus	442.00	397.80
9				

Figure 2-45. *#N/A error caused by a typo on the "Plus" level*

To fix this, the IFNA function is introduced. In Figure 2-46, the IFNA function returns the more meaningful message of "Level not found" if the #N/A error occurs.

```
=IFNA(IFS(B2="Executive",C2*(1-20%),
B2="Premium",C2*(1-15%),
B2="Plus",C2*(1-10%),
B2="Basic",C2*(1-5%)),
"Level not found")
```

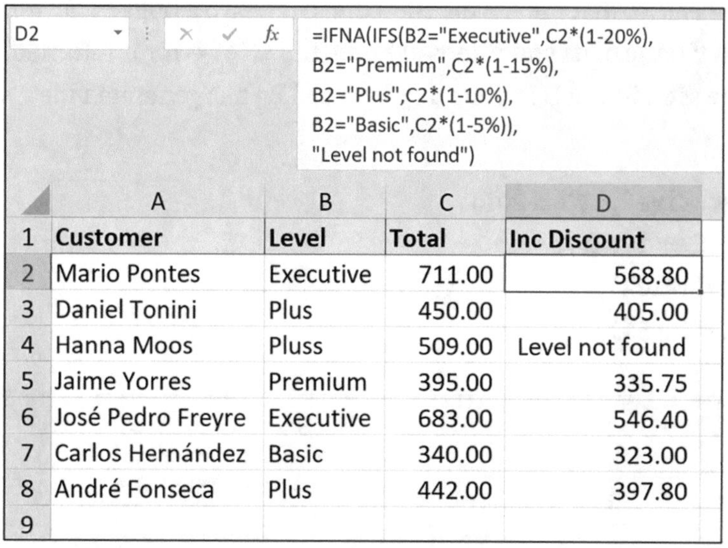

D2	▾	:	×	✓	fx	=IFNA(IFS(B2="Executive",C2*(1-20%), B2="Premium",C2*(1-15%), B2="Plus",C2*(1-10%), B2="Basic",C2*(1-5%)), "Level not found")

◢	A	B	C	D
1	Customer	Level	Total	Inc Discount
2	Mario Pontes	Executive	711.00	568.80
3	Daniel Tonini	Plus	450.00	405.00
4	Hanna Moos	Pluss	509.00	Level not found
5	Jaime Yorres	Premium	395.00	335.75
6	José Pedro Freyre	Executive	683.00	546.40
7	Carlos Hernández	Basic	340.00	323.00
8	André Fonseca	Plus	442.00	397.80
9				

Figure 2-46. *IFNA function to display a meaningful message on error*

Logical Functions with Excel Features

File   logical-formulas-with-excel-features.xlsx

All the formula examples in this chapter have been used on the worksheet. In each of the chapters of this book, I will also include examples of that chapter's formulas being used within Excel features.

So, let's see some examples of logical functions with Excel features.

Format Values That Meet a Goal

In this first example, we have some values for this month and the previous month (Figure 2-47). We want to use a Conditional Formatting rule to format the rows where the [This Month] values have improved since the previous month.

	A	B	C
1	Name	Last Month	This Month
2	Katrin	2,698	2,482
3	Michelle	2,714	2,816
4	Arthur	2,510	1,373
5	Mark	1,950	2,060
6	Brent	1,503	2,243
7	Jane	2,128	1,288
8	Celia	1,947	1,988

Figure 2-47. *Values for this month and the previous month*

1. Select range A2:C8.

2. Click **Home ➤ Conditional Formatting ➤ New Rule ➤ Use a formula to determine which cells to format**.

3. Enter the formula =$C2>$B2 into the *Format values where this formula is true box* provided (Figure 2-48).

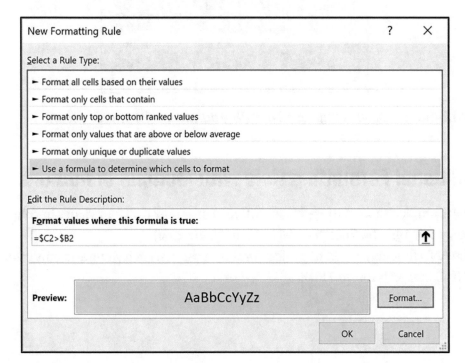

Figure 2-48. *Enter a formula for the Conditional Formatting rule*

4.   Click **Format** and choose the formatting you want.

5.   Click **OK**.

Figure 2-49 shows the rows with improved monthly values formatted with a green fill color.

The formula that we used did not require the use of the IF function. This is because the Conditional Formatting feature took the action. When we write a logical formula in a cell, we usually use IF for this job. Here, we just needed a formula that would return a True value.

The columns were made absolute in the formula, and it is important that the cell references used are for the first row of the selected range, row 2 in this example.

	A	B	C
1	Name	Last Month	This Month
2	Katrin	2,698	2,482
3	Michelle	2,714	2,816
4	Arthur	2,510	1,373
5	Mark	1,950	2,060
6	Brent	1,503	2,243
7	Jane	2,128	1,288
8	Celia	1,947	1,988
9			

Figure 2-49. *Rows with improved monthly values are formatted green*

Conditional Formatting Rule with Multiple Conditions

For this example, we want to apply formatting to cells only if all four values in columns B:E have values greater than or equal to 1500 (Figure 2-50).

The AND function would be perfect for this. It can test each value and only return TRUE if all four tests return TRUE.

	A	B	C	D	E
1	Name	Qtr 1	Qtr 2	Qtr 3	Qtr 4
2	Katrin	2,077	2,658	2,971	2,047
3	Michelle	1,051	3,877	3,736	3,821
4	Arthur	1,802	3,890	2,897	2,492
5	Mark	1,205	3,107	1,966	1,322
6	Brent	2,394	1,613	2,716	2,660
7	Jane	3,407	2,734	1,755	2,446
8	Celia	3,329	3,573	3,962	1,227
9					

Figure 2-50. *Values for each quarter must be >=1500*

1. Select range B2:E8 (we will not format the cells in the [Name] column).

2. Click **Home ➤ Conditional Formatting ➤ New Rule ➤ Use a formula to determine which cells to format**.

3. Enter the following formula into the *Format values where this formula is true* box provided (Figure 2-51):

   =AND($B2>=1500,$C2>=1500,$D2>=1500,$E2>=1500)

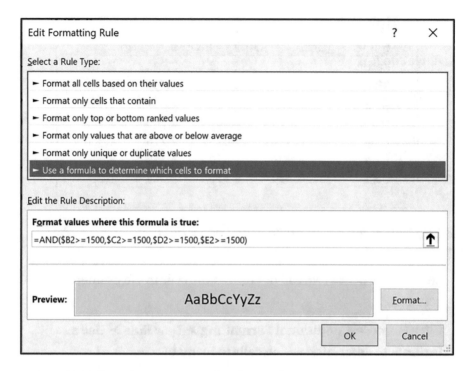

Figure 2-51. *AND function to test multiple conditions*

4. Click **Format** and choose the formatting you want.

5. Click **OK**.

Figure 2-52 shows the result of the Conditional Formatting rule.

	A	B	C	D	E
1	**Name**	**Qtr 1**	**Qtr 2**	**Qtr 3**	**Qtr 4**
2	Katrin	2,077	2,658	2,971	2,047
3	Michelle	1,051	3,877	3,736	3,821
4	Arthur	1,802	3,890	2,897	2,492
5	Mark	1,205	3,107	1,966	1,322
6	Brent	2,394	1,613	2,716	2,660
7	Jane	3,407	2,734	1,755	2,446
8	Celia	3,329	3,573	3,962	1,227
9					

Figure 2-52. *Rows formatted if all four quarters are >=1500*

Data Validation Rule Based on Another Cell Value

The Data Validation tool can be very useful for limiting mistakes on entering data. In this example, we will use a simple logical formula to test the value of a different cell to the one containing the validation rule.

Figure 2-53 shows an issues log with a column for the date the issue was resolved/completed and a column for the name of the staff member who resolved it.

We want to set up a Data Validation rule to stop someone from entering the [Handler] name if the [Completed] date has not been entered yet.

	A	B	C
1	Issue	Completed	Handler
2	1	10/03/2021	Chirag
3	2		
4	3	11/03/2021	Anne
5	4	15/06/2021	Tea
6	5		
7	6		
8	7	18/03/2021	Chandeep

Figure 2-53. *Issues log data for our Data Validation rule*

1. Select range C2:C8.

2. Click **Data ➤ Data Validation**.

3. On the *Settings* tab, select **Custom** from the *Allow* list.

4. Type =B2:B8<>"" into the *Formula* box (Figure 2-54).

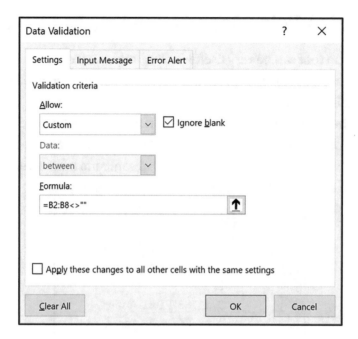

Figure 2-54. *Formula for a Data Validation rule*

5.   Click the **Error Alert** tab. Enter a *Title* and *Error Message* as shown
     in Figure 2-55.

Figure 2-55. *Helpful error alert when data is invalid*

6. Click **OK**.

If you attempt to enter a name into the [Handler] column without a [Completed] date, the validation rule is triggered, and the error alert is shown (Figure 2-56).

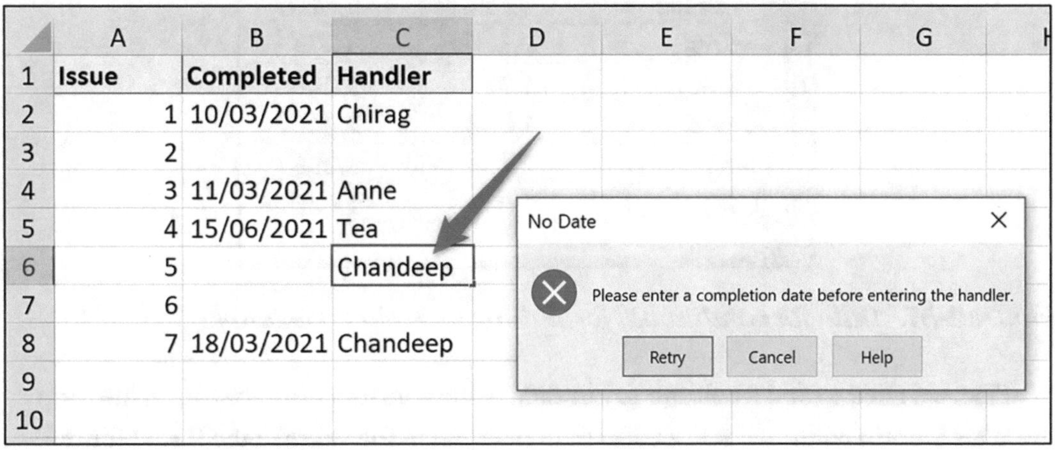

Figure 2-56. *Error shows when entering a handler without a completion date*

The formula in this example took advantage of the rule of implicit intersection.

Range C2:C8 was selected for the rule, and then the formula referenced range B2:B8. It is implied, in a technique such as this, that you require testing the cell on the same row of the two ranges. So, for cell C2, test cell B2, and for C3, test cell B3, and so on.

Conditional Formatting with Charts

Excel does not provide the built-in functionality to set conditional formatting rules to the data points of a chart. However, using logical formulas in a range, and a little Excel trickery, we can create a conditional formatting effect.

In this example, we have values for this month and last month (Figure 2-57). We want to create a column chart to display the values for this month only.

We then want to set a formatting rule to automatically change the color of the column if the values this month are greater than or equal to the previous month. So, to change the color of a column if the value has improved.

	A	B	C
1	Name	Last Month	This Month
2	Katrin	2,698	2,482
3	Michelle	2,714	2,816
4	Arthur	2,510	1,373
5	Mark	1,950	2,060
6	Brent	1,503	2,243
7	Jane	2,128	1,288
8	Celia	1,947	1,988
9			

Figure 2-57. *Data for conditional formatting with charts example*

First, we need to add a column to our data using a formula to show the value from the [This Month] column if it is greater than or equal to the value in the [Last Month] column. If it is not, show the #N/A error.

Column charts in Excel do not plot data if there is an error. So, this technique will show a column in the chart if the values have improved; otherwise, it will not.

The following formula is entered into cell D2 (Figure 2-58). The NA( ) function has been used to produce the #N/A error.

```
=IF(C2>=B2,C2,NA())
```

D2			×	✓	*fx*	=IF(C2>=B2,C2,NA())	

	A	B	C	D	E
1	Name	Last Month	This Month	Met Goal	
2	Katrin	2,698	2,482	#N/A	
3	Michelle	2,714	2,816	2816	
4	Arthur	2,510	1,373	#N/A	
5	Mark	1,950	2,060	2060	
6	Brent	1,503	2,243	2243	
7	Jane	2,128	1,288	#N/A	
8	Celia	1,947	1,988	1988	
9					

Figure 2-58. *Logical formula to show a value only if it is >= last month's value*

We will now create the column chart:

1. Select range A1:A8, hold the **Ctrl** key, and select range C1:D8 so
    that both ranges are selected.

2. Click **Insert ➤ Insert Column or Bar Chart ➤ Clustered Column**
    (Figure 2-59).

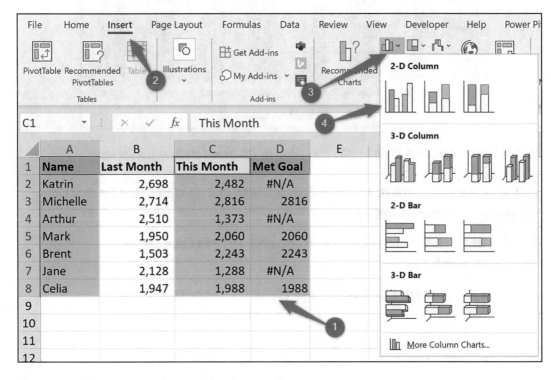

Figure 2-59. *Insert a clustered column chart*

The column chart is inserted. It shows all columns for the *This Month* data series,
but for the *Met Goal* data series, columns are only shown if the value met our IF function
criteria (Figure 2-60).

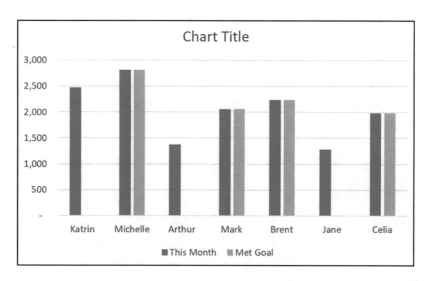

Figure 2-60. *Column chart with this month and met goal data series*

The final step is to overlap the two data series so that we cannot see the *Met Goal* data series as separate columns.

3. Right-click a *Met Goal* column and click **Format Data Series** (Figure 2-61).

4. Click the **Series Options** category from the *Format Data Series* pane.

5. Set the *Series Overlap* to **100%**.

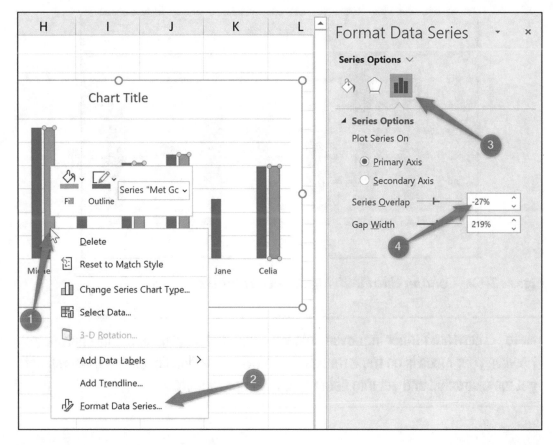

Figure 2-61. *Overlapping the data series*

6. The chart is completed (Figure 2-62). Format the columns to the colors you want to use and make any other necessary improvements.

If the values in columns B and C are changed, the chart will automatically update, including the color of the columns. So, this is a true conditional formatting effect for charts in Excel.

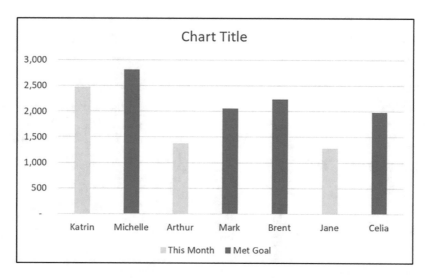

Figure 2-62. *Column chart with highlighted columns*

Note   There are further improvements we could certainly make to this chart. However, our focus is on the formulas that provide this functionality. So, we will not get too distracted and get into detail on chart improvements.

Dynamic Chart Data with SWITCH

In this example, we will make the data used by a column chart dynamic using the SWITCH function.

Figure 2-63 shows range A1:B7 with some values missing. There is a chart on the sheet that is using range A1:B7 as its source. And there is a drop-down list in cell D2 with options for "Chicago," "London," and "Munich." The cell currently has the value of "Munich."

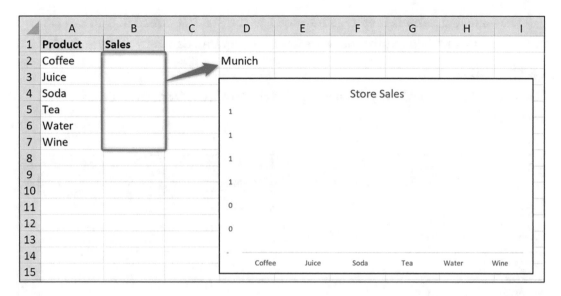

Figure 2-63. *Data for a dynamic chart using SWITCH*

There is another sheet in the workbook named [Chart Data]. That sheet contains three data ranges with product sales for "London," "Chicago," and "Munich" (Figure 2-64).

	A	B	C	D	E	F	G	H	I
1									
2		London			Chicago			Munich	
3									
4		**Product**	**Sales**		**Product**	**Sales**		**Product**	**Sales**
5		Coffee	556		Coffee	1,318		Coffee	1,560
6		Juice	1,512		Juice	1,356		Juice	1,938
7		Soda	1,541		Soda	1,037		Soda	1,645
8		Tea	1,139		Tea	706		Tea	1,356
9		Water	727		Water	869		Water	1,173
10		Wine	2,000		Wine	1,791		Wine	641
11									

Figure 2-64. *Three different data sets for SWITCH to return the sales values*

The goal is to use a formula in column B that returns the sales values for the data range chosen from the drop-down list in cell D2 of the [Chart 2] sheet.

The following formula is entered into cell B2. The SWITCH function uses cell D2 as its expression and then returns the value from the required data range (Figure 2-65):

```
=SWITCH($D$2,
"Chicago",'Chart Data'!F5,"London",'Chart Data'!C5,"Munich",'Chart
Data'!I5)
```

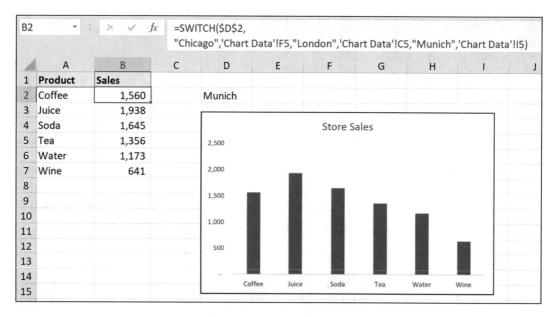

Figure 2-65.   *SWITCH function for a dynamic column chart*

The chart now looks great. And if you select a different store from the drop-down list, the chart updates.

Summary

In this chapter, we learned the best logical functions available in Excel including IF, AND, OR, IFERROR, and SWITCH.

These functions are incredibly useful and found in most spreadsheets. IF is the flagbearer for this category, but it is certainly not alone. Understanding how logical expressions evaluate is key for the upcoming chapters of this book. Many more examples await.

In the next chapter, we will dive into defining names in Excel. The ability to name values, ranges, formulas, and arrays provides many benefits for your formulas.

CHAPTER 3

Defined Names

In Excel, you can define names for ranges, arrays, constants, and formulas.

Most Excel users are familiar with named ranges. The ability to name a range makes our formulas easier to read and write.

However, the technique of defining names in Excel has special powers that many Excel users are unfamiliar with. You will see names being used at various points in this book to overcome Excel limitations.

This comprehensive chapter will cover all the fundamentals of defined names so that when they are used within formulas later in the book, you are well versed in handling them.

We will cover different methods of creating named ranges, how to use them in formulas, and a few tips and tricks for using names in Excel.

We will show how to find and edit existing names and see a basic example of creating a named formula.

Named Ranges

File   named-ranges.xlsx

As mentioned, you can define names for many things in Excel including constants, formulas, arrays, and tables (covered separately in the next chapter). However, when using names, we are often referring to named ranges.

This range can be a single cell, multiple cells, or even an entire row or column.

© Alan Murray 2022
A. Murray, *Advanced Excel Formulas*, https://doi.org/10.1007/978-1-4842-7125-4_3

Why Use Named Ranges?

There are a few reasons why you would use named ranges in Excel:

- More meaningful references

Using named ranges makes your formulas easier to read and write. Consider a reference to $G$4 vs. `CityTax`. The reference to `CityTax` is much simpler and more meaningful than a reference to the grid such as $G$4.

Named ranges can also be unique for an entire workbook. This makes referencing across worksheets simple and concise. They are also absolute by default, so a reference such as `'Master Sheet'!$G$4` can be simplified to `CityTax`.

- Faster formula creation

Named ranges appear as you write your formulas, making them faster to type and eliminating the need to click between sheets and scroll on a sheet to locate the cell(s) you want to reference.

We will cover a few tips for your named ranges shortly. These tips will make referencing these named ranges even faster and easier.

- Easy navigation

Naming ranges makes them easy to find, diagnose, and super quick to navigate to in a workbook. This chapter will show a few techniques to quickly find a named range.

- Special powers

Named ranges have always had a special power, and this is to link Excel features that cannot work together directly. You will see many examples of this throughout the book.

Define a Named Range with the Name Box

The quickest way to define a named range is to use the Name Box. Let's see how to do this and then use that name in a formula.

In the previous chapter, we saw the following formula. This IF function uses values from cells F2 and F4 (Figure 3-1):

```
=IF(B2>=$F$2,B2*(1-$F$4),B2)
```

Cell F2 is used as the threshold value in the *logical test*, and cell F4 stores the discount percentage that is used for the *value if true* behavior.

| C2 | ▾ | : | × | ✓ | fx | =IF(B2>=$F$2,B2*(1-$F$4),B2) |

	A	B	C	D	E	F
1	Customer	Total	Inc Discount			
2	Mario Pontes	711.00	625.68		Threshold	550
3	Daniel Tonini	450.00	450.00			
4	Hanna Moos	509.00	509.00		Discount	12%
5	Jaime Yorres	395.00	395.00			
6	José Pedro Freyre	683.00	601.04			
7	Carlos Hernández	340.00	340.00			
8	André Fonseca	442.00	442.00			
9						

Figure 3-1. *IF function using cell values*

Let's name both input cells to make the formula more meaningful:

1. Click cell F2.

2. Click in the Name Box and type "Threshold" (Figure 3-2).

3. Press **Enter**.

4. Repeat the steps to name cell F4 as "Discount".

Note   You must press **Enter** when confirming a name in the Name Box. Pressing Tab or clicking the sheet will not work.

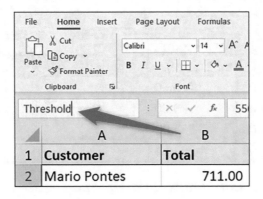

Figure 3-2. *Define a name using the Name Box*

You can check that the names have been created successfully by clicking the drop-down list arrow on the Name Box. Figure 3-3 shows both names listed along with an existing [lstProducts] name.

If you click a name in the list, it will take you to that named range.

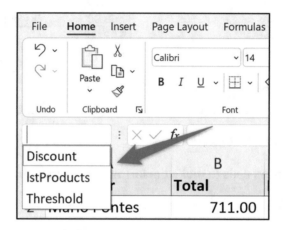

Figure 3-3. *Quickly check that the names were created successfully*

Using Named Ranges in Formulas

Let's now replace the cell references in the formula with references to the named ranges.

The easiest way to do this is to type the names when creating or editing a formula. Figure 3-4 shows our two named ranges being entered into the formula.

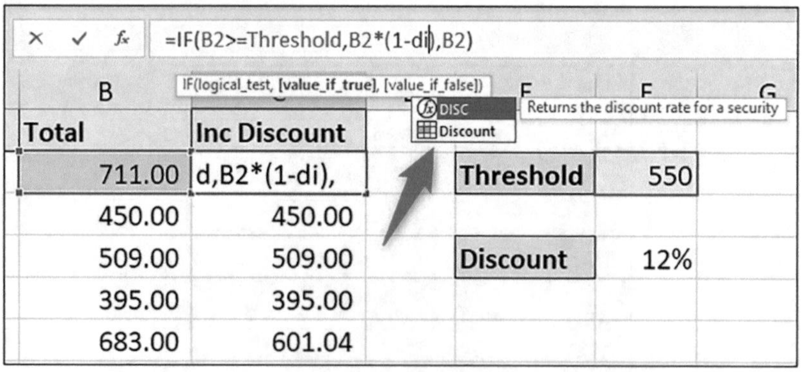

Figure 3-4. *Entering a named range into a formula*

As you type the name, a list appears that shows names of functions and ranges. You can identify a named range by the icon to the left of the name.

The following formula is easier to understand than the previous one that used references to the grid:

```
=IF(B2>=Threshold,B2*(1-Discount),B2)
```

Note   If you select a range that has been named from within a formula, the named range is returned. However, the grid reference is still understood, and any existing formulas or features that are using the grid reference will continue to work.

You can also insert a named range using a list on the Ribbon. This is especially helpful if you are unsure on the name that was assigned.

From within the formula where you want the name inserted

1.   Click **Formulas ➤ Use in Formula**.

2.   Click the name in the list (Figure 3-5).

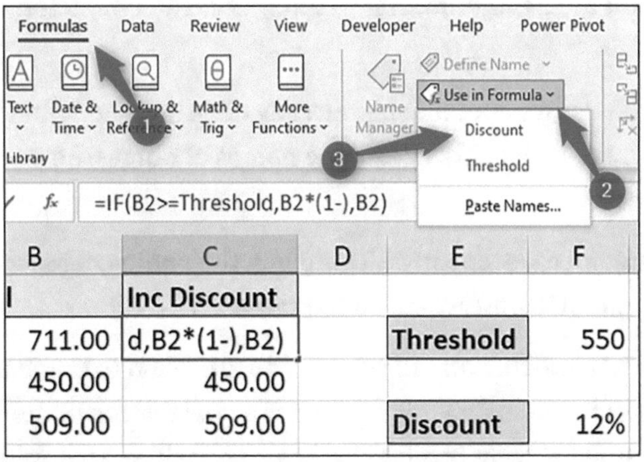

Figure 3-5. *Using a name in a formula from the Ribbon*

Another alternative is to press the keyboard shortcut **F3**. This opens the *Paste Name* window (Figure 3-6). Select the name to paste and click **OK**.

This window can also be opened by clicking **Paste Names** from the **Use in Formula** list on the Ribbon.

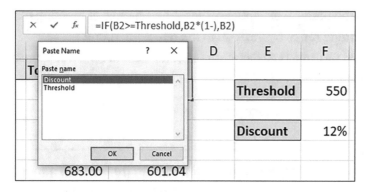

Figure 3-6. *Paste Name window in Excel*

Rules for Defining Names

There are a few rules to be aware of when defining names in Excel:

- A name can include numbers, but a name cannot begin with a number.

- You cannot use spaces in a name.

- Other invalid characters that cannot be used in a name include the /, &, %, and $. The underscore "_" and period "." characters are both allowed.

- You cannot use a name that has already been assigned, for example, a cell address such as D2 or existing names of ranges, formulas, macros, etc.

- Names are not case-sensitive. Therefore, the names rngSales, rngsales, and RNGSALES are all the same.

If you try to use a name that already exists, you are taken to that name. Quickly jumping to a range or macro using this method is a cool feature of the Name Box.

If you enter a name using an invalid character, you will see the message shown in Figure 3-7.

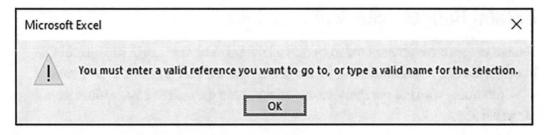

Figure 3-7. *Message when entering an invalid name*

Tips for Defining Names

Here are a few tips when creating a name:

- Use an underscore "_", period ".", or camel casing as an alternative to a space. For example, I like the camel casing approach and use names such as *thisYear*. A capital letter is used to denote a word change.

- Use a prefix for your names. You can use whatever prefix you like, just be consistent. Common prefixes include rng for range, fx for formula, lst for list, and tbl for table (discussed in the next chapter).

Benefits to using prefixes include that you can easily identify the type of name by its prefix, you can use the same name more than once because the prefix is different, and Excel will group them together, making it quick and easy to enter them (Figure 3-8).

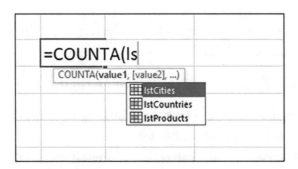

Figure 3-8. *Named ranges grouped due to the use of a prefix*

- You can also use a consistent suffix to a name.

You want your names to be quick to find and easy to understand. These are only ideas, and you should do what works for you.

Named Ranges with Multiple Cells

Named ranges are not restricted to single cell ranges. A named range can be multiple contiguous cells, a selection of non-contiguous cells, or even an entire row or column.

Continuing with the previous example, let's name the range of total values from range B2:B8:

1. Select range B2:B8.

2. Type "rngTotal" in the Name Box (Figure 3-9).

3. Press **Enter**.

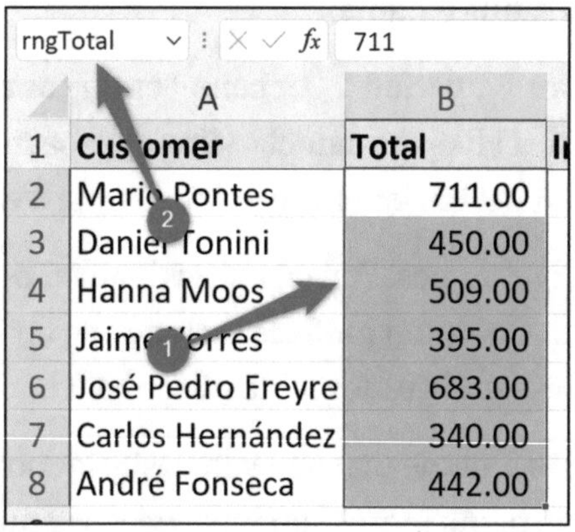

Figure 3-9. *Define a multicell named range*

The formula can now be rewritten to include the [rngTotal] name in place of the reference to the cells in range B2:B8:

```
=IF(rngTotal>=Threshold,rngTotal*(1-Discount),rngTotal)
```

Figure 3-10 shows the completed formula. It has spilled to the other cells in range C2:C8, and this is identified by the blue border.

This is a dynamic array, and this behavior will occur if you are using an Excel 2021, Excel for Microsoft 365 (Windows and Mac), or the Excel for the Web version. Dynamic arrays are covered in detail in Chapter 10.

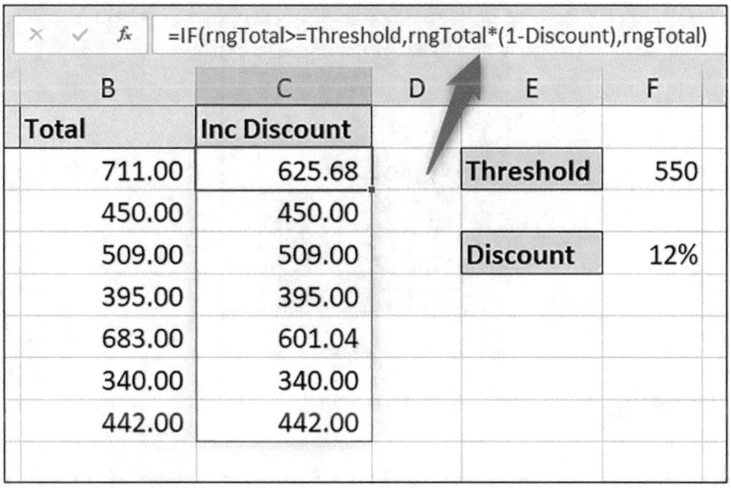

	B	C	D	E	F
	Total	Inc Discount			
	711.00	625.68		Threshold	550
	450.00	450.00			
	509.00	509.00		Discount	12%
	395.00	395.00			
	683.00	601.04			
	340.00	340.00			
	442.00	442.00			

Formula bar: `=IF(rngTotal>=Threshold,rngTotal*(1-Discount),rngTotal)`

Figure 3-10. Formula spills to the cells below when rngTotal is used

If you are using a non-dynamic array–enabled version of Excel, you will need to fill the formula down the range. It will not spill.

The IF function expects a single value, but multiple values were provided to it when using the [rngTotal] name, so the formula assumed the use of the value in the same row on the grid. This behavior is known as implicit intersection.

As an advanced Excel formula user, it is important to understand this behavior so that we can recognize it on spreadsheets. And there is a case that the formula is more meaningful when using the named range.

However, despite demonstrating this technique, it is not one that I would encourage. A better approach would be to format the range as a table and use the qualities of the table for the formula. Tables are discussed in the next chapter.

Named Range for a Drop-Down List

A common scenario for defining a multicell named range is when using it for the source of a drop-down list.

For this example, we have a list of products that has been named [lstProducts] (Figure 3-11). This can be found on the [Lists] sheet of the provided [named-ranges.xlsx] workbook.

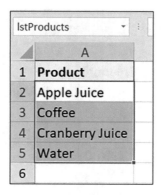

Figure 3-11. *Range of cells named lstProducts*

On the [Sales] worksheet, there is a SUMIFS function (covered later in the book) in cell F3 returning the total sales for the product entered in cell E3 (Figure 3-12).

We will create a drop-down list in cell E3 to ensure that the data entered is accurate. We will use the [lstProducts] defined name for the source of the list.

	A	B	C	D	E	F
1	Date	Product	Sales			
2	12/01/2021	Coffee	165		Product	Total
3	22/02/2021	Coffee	197		Water	112
4	04/02/2021	Apple Juice	142			
5	17/02/2021	Coffee	67			
6	12/02/2021	Water	35			
7	29/01/2021	Water	29			
8	16/01/2021	Apple Juice	143			
9	19/03/2021	Water	19			
10	18/02/2021	Cranberry Juice	127			
11	09/03/2021	Cranberry Juice	87			
12	30/01/2021	Water	29			
13	17/01/2021	Coffee	87			

Figure 3-12. *Sales data with a drop-down list required in cell E3*

1. Click cell E3.

2. Click **Data ➤ Data Validation**.

3. From the **Settings** tab, select **List** from the *Allow* list.

4. In the *Source* field, type "=lstProducts" (Figure 3-13). Click **OK**.

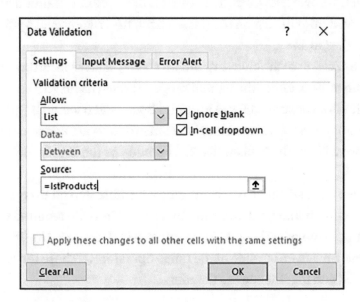

Figure 3-13. *Named range as the source for a Data Validation list*

Note   You can also use the **F3** shortcut when in the *Source* field to open the *Paste Name* window.

The drop-down list can then be used to easily select the required product (Figure 3-14).

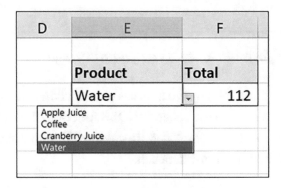

Figure 3-14. *Drop-down list of products*

Define a Dynamic Named Range

The products' drop-down list works great, but it is not dynamic. If products are added to the end or removed from the list on the [Lists] sheet, the [rngProducts] name will not automatically adjust in size.

Sure, there are clever techniques around this issue, such as inserting cells in the middle of the range. This forces the named range to adjust its height.

However, this is an advanced Excel formulas book, and it would be great if the named range automatically changed height when products are added or removed.

To do this, we will use the brilliant INDEX function as the source for the named range.

You do not get any assistance when entering a formula into an Excel window, so it is good practice to enter it into a cell first and then copy it into the required window.

The following formula has been entered into cell C2 (Figure 3-15). This uses two INDEX functions; one on either side of the range operator (:). These return the first and last cells in the list and together create the range.

```
=INDEX(Lists!$A:$A,2):INDEX(Lists!$A:$A,COUNTA(Lists!$A:$A))
```

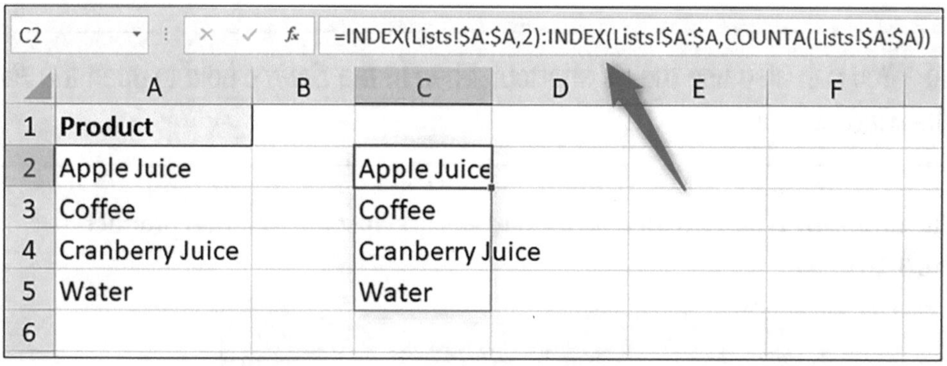

Figure 3-15. *INDEX formula to create a dynamic range*

The first INDEX function returns the address of the cell in row 2 of column A. Row 2 is entered as a constant value. In the second INDEX function, the COUNTA function is used to count the number of non-blank cells in column A. In this example, it successfully returns the address of the final non-blank cell.

> **Note**   The INDEX function is covered in depth in Chapter 11. If you are new
> to this function, you can jump to that chapter for an explanation on how this
> formula works.

I am using an Excel for Microsoft 365 version, so the values from the range are returned and spilled to the grid. You will not see this if you are using an older version of Excel; however, the formula works, so proceed with the next steps:

1. Copy the formula from the Formula Bar.

2. Click **Formulas ➤ Name Manager**.

3. Select the *lstProducts* name and click **Edit** (Figure 3-16).

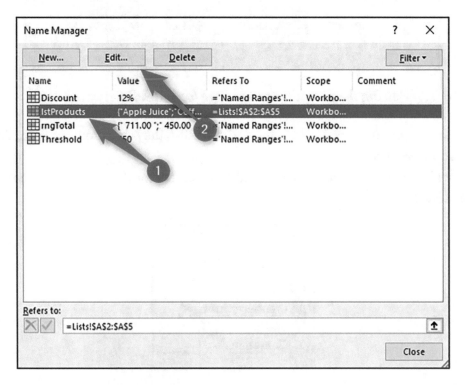

Figure 3-16. *Edit an existing named range*

4. Delete the contents of the *Refers to* field and paste in the formula (Figure 3-17). Click ***OK***.

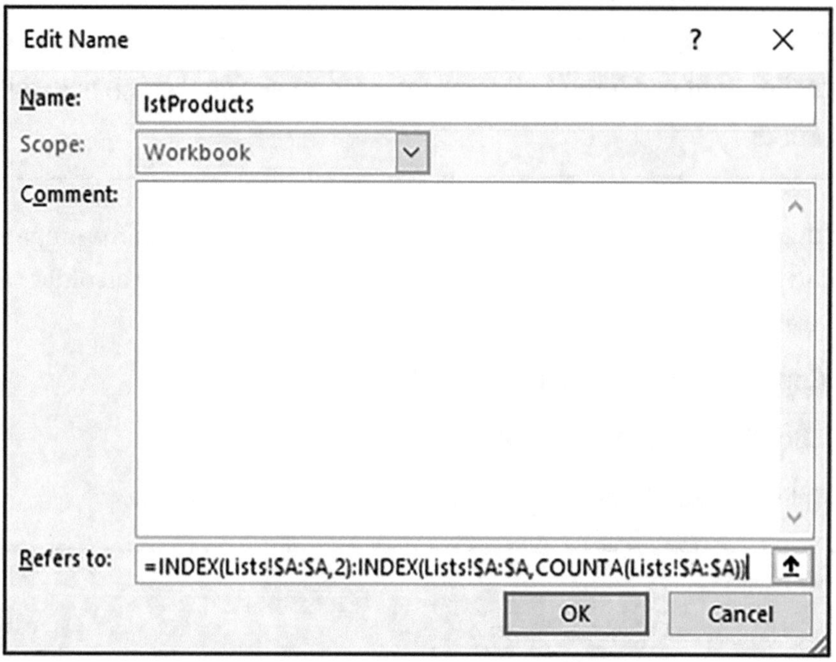

Edit Name
?
Name:
lstProducts
Scope:
Workbook
Comment:
Refers to:
=INDEX(Lists!$A:$A,2):INDEX(Lists!$A:$A,COUNTA(Lists!$A:$A))
OK
Cancel

***Figure 3-17.** Pasting the formula as the range for the defined name*

When new products are added to the end of the list, they are automatically included in the drop-down list.

Figure 3-18 shows "Orange Juice" added to the end of the list. This list can then be sorted in A-Z order.

A
B
1 Product
2 Apple Juice
3 Coffee
4 Cranberry Juice
5 Water
6 Orange Juice
7

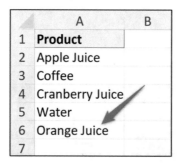

***Figure 3-18.** Adding a new product to the end of the list*

Figure 3-19 shows "Orange Juice" in the drop-down list after it was added to the source list on the [Lists] sheet, and the products were sorted in A-Z order.

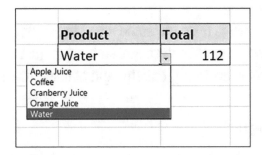

Figure 3-19. *Range automatically adjusts to include new products*

Note   Dynamic named ranges can also be created using a combination of tables and named ranges. We show an example of this in the next chapter.

Define Names with Create from Selection

Another way to create named ranges is to use the Create from Selection option. This is great for creating multiple named ranges at once.

In this example, we have the data shown in Figure 3-20. We have three levels that each apply a different discount.

We will name the cells in ranges G3, G4, and G5 using the values in the cells to their left (F3, F4, and F5). Then use a SWITCH function to subtract the necessary discount in column D.

	A	B	C	D	E	F	G
1	Customer	Level	Amount	Inc Discount			
2	Mario Pontes	Silver	129			Level	Discount
3	Daniel Tonini	Silver	191			Gold	15%
4	Hanna Moos	Bronze	224			Silver	10%
5	Jaime Yorres	Gold	254			Bronze	5%
6	José Pedro Freyre	Silver	219				
7	Carlos Hernández	Bronze	74				
8	André Fonseca	Bronze	233				
9							

Figure 3-20. *Data containing the level and discount to apply*

Note   The discount's range is on the same sheet to simplify the example. Named ranges default to having a workbook scope, so they are just as easy to access on other worksheets. That is another great strength of using them.

1. Select range F3:G5.

2. Click **Formulas ➤ Create from Selection** or press **Ctrl + Shift F3**.

3. The *Create Names from Selection* window appears and guesses where the values you want to use for the names are (Figure 3-21). Very often, this is correct, but you should check. ***Left column*** is selected in our example. This is correct. Click ***OK***.

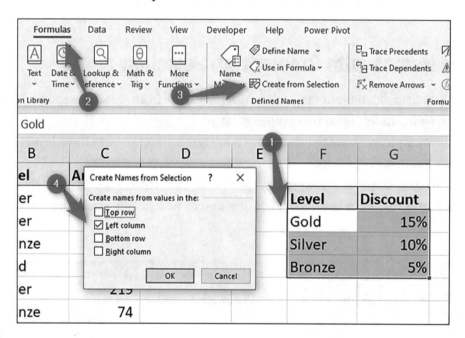

Figure 3-21. *Create multiple names at once with Create from Selection*

This creates three named ranges – *Gold, Silver,* and *Bronze.* Faster than creating them individually.

4. The following SWITCH function can be entered into cell D2 and filled down (Figure 3-22):

```
=C2*SWITCH(B2,"Gold",(1-Gold),"Silver",(1-Silver),
"Bronze",(1-Bronze))
```

The SWITCH function checks the level in column B against its list of values and returns the matching discount to be applied to the amount.

f_x	=C2*SWITCH(B2,"Gold",(1-Gold),"Silver",(1-Silver),"Bronze",(1-Bronze))						
	B	C	D	E	F	G	
	Level	Amount	Inc Discount				
	Silver	129	116.10		Level	Discount	
	Silver	191	171.90		Gold	15%	
	Bronze	224	212.80		Silver	10%	
	Gold	254	215.90		Bronze	5%	
	Silver	219	197.10				
	Bronze	74	70.30				
	Bronze	233	221.35				

Figure 3-22. *SWITCH function to apply the correct discount*

Scope of a Defined Name

The scope of a defined name is the location and general accessibility of the name. A name can either have workbook scope or worksheet scope:

- **Workbook**: The name is available to all sheets of a workbook. The name is unique across all sheets of the workbook and can easily be referenced using its name.

- **Worksheet**: The name is only unique and easily accessible within that specific worksheet.

The default scope of a named range is the workbook level, and all the names created so far in this chapter have had that scope.

Note   You can reference names with a worksheet scope from other sheets by preceding its name with the sheet name, for example, Sheet3!TotalSales. However, this is not encouraged, and the name should have been given workbook scope.

Let's look at how to create a named range with worksheet scope.

We have the data shown in Figure 3-23, with the following IF function in column C that calculates a 15% discount if the target in cell E3 is reached:

```
=IF(B2>=$E$3,B2*(1-15%),B2)
```

C2		× ✓ *fx*	=IF(B2>=$E$3,B2*(1-15%),B2)		
	A	B	C	D	E
1	Customer	Total	Inc Discount		
2	Mario Pontes	711.00	604.35		Target
3	Daniel Tonini	450.00	382.50		450
4	Hanna Moos	509.00	432.65		
5	Jaime Yorres	395.00	395.00		
6	José Pedro Freyre	683.00	580.55		
7	Carlos Hernández	340.00	340.00		
8	André Fonseca	442.00	442.00		

Figure 3-23.   IF function to apply discount if target is reached

We will create a named range for cell E3 with worksheet-level scope:

1.   Click cell E3.

2.   Click **Formulas ➤ Define Name**.

3.   In the *New Name* window (Figure 3-24), change the *Name* to "rngTarget".

4.   Change the *Scope* using the drop-down list provided from *Workbook* to **Scope and Constants** (this is the name of the worksheet). Click **OK**.

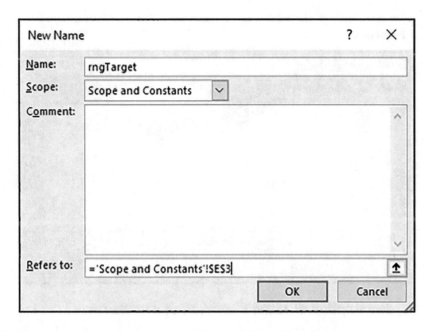

Figure 3-24. *Creating a new name with worksheet-level scope*

The rngTarget name can now be used instead of the $E$3 reference in the IF function (Figure 3-25). However, if you try and reference rngTarget from another worksheet, it will not be recognized.

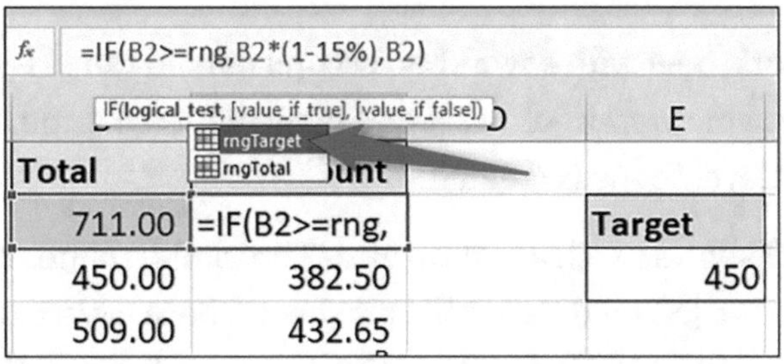

f_x	=IF(B2>=rng,B2*(1-15%),B2)		
	IF(logical_test, [value_if_true], [value_if_false]) ⅅ		E
Total	⊞ rngTarget ⊞ rngTotal ᵘnt		
711.00	=IF(B2>=rng,		Target
450.00	382.50		450
509.00	432.65		

Figure 3-25. *Using rngTarget in the IF function*

You cannot edit the scope of an existing named range. Figure 3-26 shows the *Edit Name* window and the scope option disabled.

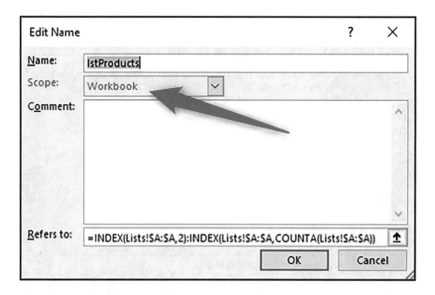

Figure 3-26. *Scope option disabled when editing a named range*

It is worth noting the behavior of names when sheets are copied in Excel. The behavior is often undesirable causing confusion and cluttered workbooks. Therefore, it is important to be familiar and understanding of what happens when sheets are copied.

The following lists the general behavior of names when sheets are copied within the same workbook or to another workbook:

- When a worksheet with a workbook scope named range is duplicated within the same workbook, a second name with the same name but worksheet level scope is created.

- Figure 3-27 shows two [Discount] and [Threshold] names caused by copying the [Named Ranges] worksheet. These new names have worksheet scope. This is shown in the [Scope] column of the *Name Manager* window. The name of the duplicated worksheet [Named Ranges (2)] is shown.

me Yorres

sé Pedro Freyre

rlos Hernández

ıdré Fonseca

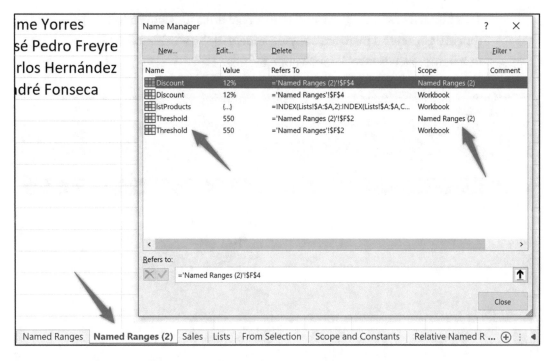

Figure 3-27. *Copied sheet creating duplicated names with worksheet scope*

- When a worksheet with a named range is copied to another Excel workbook, the name is copied along with the sheet. This applies to both workbook and worksheet scope named ranges.

  This is generally a good action as you probably require the named range in that workbook too. However, it is important to be aware of this behavior; otherwise, Excel files can get cluttered quickly with redundant names.

- When a workbook contains a named formula with workbook scope, and a worksheet is copied to another workbook, the named formula is also copied to the other workbook. However, the named formula links back to the workbook from which it was copied.

  Figure 3-28 shows the [lstproducts] name that we created using the INDEX formula. A worksheet was copied to another workbook, and this named formula was copied with it, but links back to the [named-ranges.xlsx] workbook.

This behavior is bad. Be careful of external links in a workbook that are generated by users copying sheets to the workbook. This only happens with workbook scope names.

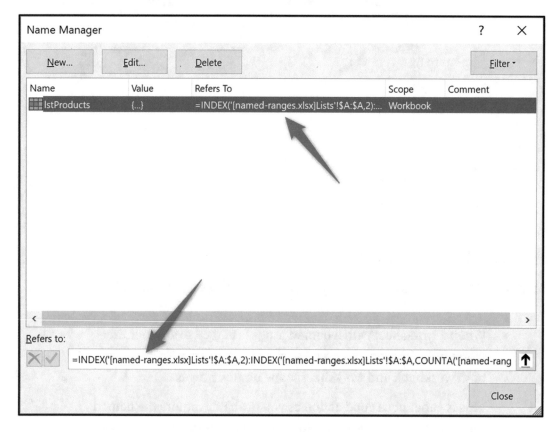

Figure 3-28. *External link caused by copying a name to another workbook*

Note   In Chapter 15, when LAMBDA functions are discussed, we will use the technique of copying ranges that contain formulas as a simple method to copy our custom named formulas to other workbooks.

Define a Named Constant

In addition to naming ranges, it is also possible to name constants. As its name suggests, a constant is a value that does not change, unless the named constant is edited.

So, it is not necessary to have a value on the worksheet to be able to assign a name to it.

This can help to free your worksheet from unnecessary clutter while enabling the ability to use meaningful names for values.

In a previous example, the following formula was used to apply a discount if a specified condition was met. A 15% discount is applied and is written into the formula:

```
=IF(B2>=rngTarget,B2*(1-15%),B2)
```

Let's create a named constant for that discount value:

1. Click **Formulas ➤ Define Name**.

2. In the *Name* field, enter "cstDiscount" (Figure 3-29).

3. In the *Refers to* field, enter "=0.15". Click **OK**.

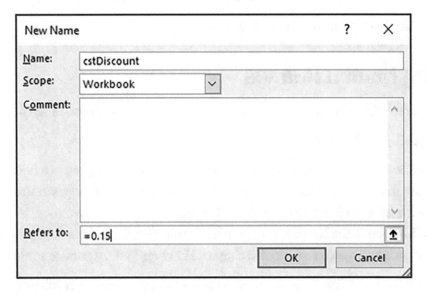

Figure 3-29. *Creating a named constant*

Note   The prefix *cst* has been used in the name to easily identify it as a constant. Remember, prefixes are optional, and you can use whatever you want. Other common prefixes for constants include *const* and *k*.

This named constant can now be used in the formula instead of typing 15% (Figure 3-30).

This constant has workbook scope. So, if the constant were changed to a different percentage in the future, all formulas that reference it would update.

This is more efficient than changing the percentage directly in all formulas it was written into.

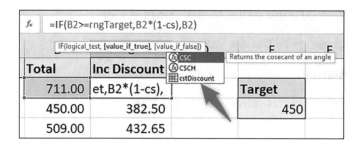

Figure 3-30. *Using a named constant in a formula*

Finding Named Ranges

There are a few different methods to easily find and jump to a named range in Excel:

- Using the Name Box

The Name Box provides a quick no-nonsense method of jumping to a named range. Click the list arrow on the end of the Name Box to list the named ranges in the current scope. Click a name to jump to that selected range.

Figure 3-31 shows the Name Box list activated from the [Lists] sheet. It lists the named ranges that we have created so far in this chapter. However, you may notice some absentees:

- *cstDiscount*: It only lists named ranges, so named constants will not appear in the list.

- *lstProducts*: This name is the dynamic named range created earlier using the INDEX formula. Names that use a formula as their source are not shown in the Name Box list.

- *rngTarget*: This name was created from the [Scope and Constants] worksheet with worksheet-level scope. Therefore, it is not visible from the Name Box list on the [Lists] sheet.

Figure 3-31. *Using the Name Box to find named ranges*

You can also navigate to these names by typing their names into the Name Box. This includes those that use a formula as their source such as [lstProducts].

This applies to grid references too. So, if you type D10000 into the Name Box and press **Enter**, you are taken to cell D10000. If you type A1 and press **Enter**, you are taken back to A1.

You can even take this further and enter ranges such as B2:D10 to select that range. You can include the sheet name in the range such as Sheet3!B2:D10. You can even enter R1C1 references such as R1C19 to jump to row 1 column 19.

Some of these tricks are not every day useful, but they are pretty cool, and you never know when they may come in handy.

- The *Go To* window

The *Go To* window provides another fast way to jump to a named range from anywhere within its scope.

Press **F5** on the keyboard to open the *Go To* window (Figure 3-32). Select the name you want to go to and click **OK**.

Note   You can also open the *Go To* window by pressing the **Ctrl + G** shortcut or by clicking **Home ➤ Find & Select ➤ Go To**.

Figure 3-32. *The Go To window listing named ranges*

Just like the Name Box, the *Go To* window only lists the names that are from a range. So, names that use a formula for their source, such as [lstProducts], are not listed.

Once you have followed a name, you can return to the previously active range quickly by pressing **F5** and then **Enter**.

This keyboard combination works because on following a range, the previously active range is listed first in the *Go To* window (Figure 3-33).

Figure 3-33. *Previous range listed in the Go To window*

Relative Named Ranges

Named ranges are absolute by default. And this makes sense as you are defining a specific area in the workbook.

However, it is possible to create relative named ranges in Excel. Let's see an example of how and why you would want to do this.

In Figure 3-34, the following formula has been entered in cell C3 and filled down. This formula calculates the percentage change between the current month and the previous month:

`=(B3-B2)/B2`

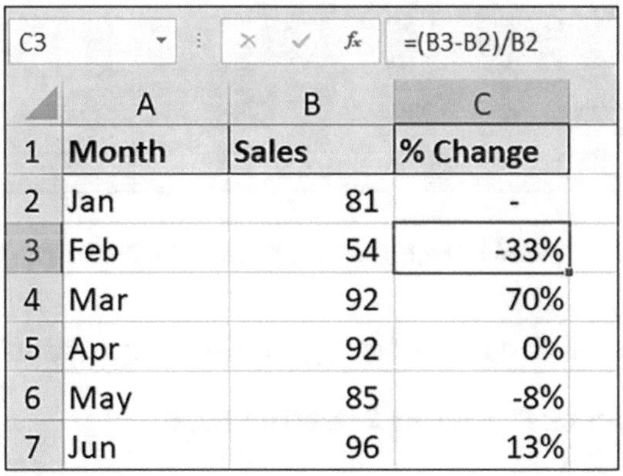

Figure 3-34. *Month on month percent change*

In this example, we will define names for both the cells used in the formula (B2 and B3). These references will be made relative so that when the formula is filled down, it uses the correct cells in context to the month:

1. Click cell C3.

2. Click **Formulas ➤ Define Name**.

3. Enter "PrevMonth" as the *Name* for the range (Figure 3-35).

4. Change the *Scope* to the worksheet. The worksheet we are using is named *Relative Named Range*. I do not want this name appearing on other sheets.

5. Enter a descriptive comment such as "Refers to the cell one row above and one column to the left." In this example, I do not think the name is descriptive enough and a comment is required.

6. In the *Refers to* field, change the cell on the end of the reference from $C$3 to B2. Click **OK**.

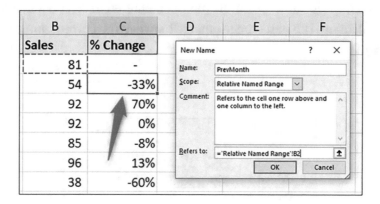

Figure 3-35. *Relative named range for the previous month*

Let's create another relative named range for the current month's value:

1. From cell C3, click **Formulas ➤ Define Name**.

2. Enter "CurrentMonth" for the *Name* (Figure 3-36).

3. Set the *Scope* to the current worksheet *Relative Named Range*.

4. Enter a descriptive comment such as "Refers to the cell in the current row and one column to the left."

5. In the *Refers to* field, change the cell on the end of the reference from $C$3 to B3. Click **OK**.

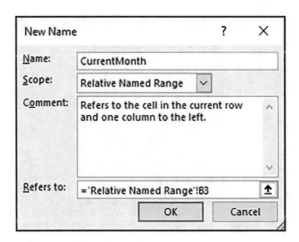

Figure 3-36. *Relative named range for the current month*

With both named ranges set up, we can now edit the formula to use them. Figure 3-37 shows the updated formula with C6 as the active cell. This shows the formula working perfectly, and it is more descriptive with the named ranges.

	A	B	C	D	E
1	Month	Sales	% Change		
2	Jan	81	-		
3	Feb	54	-33%		
4	Mar	92	70%		
5	Apr	92	0%		
6	May	85	-8%		
7	Jun	96	13%		

C6 formula: =(CurrentMonth-PrevMonth)/PrevMonth

Figure 3-37. *Percent change formula using the relative named ranges*

Named Formulas

In addition to naming ranges and constants in Excel, you can also create named formulas. We have actually already done an example of this – the dynamic named range using the INDEX function.

Now, that formula returned a range, so it was really still a named range. Let's see an example of a named formula that returns a value.

On the [Lists] worksheet, we have a list of products (Figure 3-38).

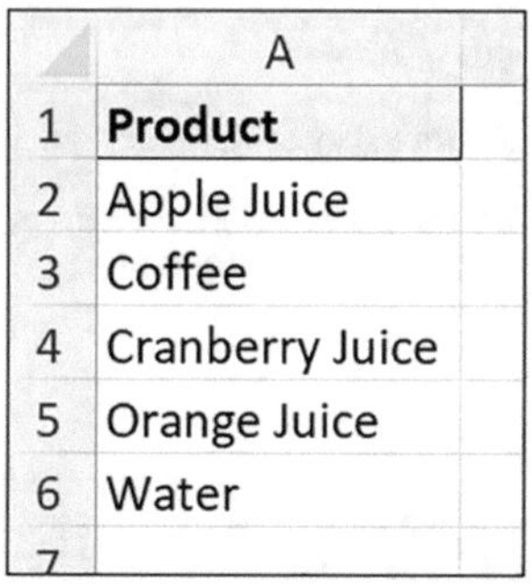

	A
1	**Product**
2	Apple Juice
3	Coffee
4	Cranberry Juice
5	Orange Juice
6	Water
7	

Figure 3-38. *List of products*

We want to return a count of the products so that we can use that result within other formulas in Excel.

Instead of writing a formula to return the result to the grid, we will write it in the *Refers to* field when defining a name:

1. Click any cell of the worksheet and enter the following formula. It is easier to write a formula in a cell first.

   ```
   =COUNTA(Lists!$A:$A)-1
   ```

2. Copy the formula text.

3. Click **Formulas ➤ Define Name**.

4. Enter "fCountProducts" as the *Name* for the formula (Figure 3-39).

5. Paste the formula into the *Refers to* field and click **OK**.

Figure 3-39. *Defining a named formula for count of products*

6. The formula can now be deleted from the cell it was written in.

This name can now be used in a cell, or within another formula, to always return the count of products.

This name was created with workbook scope, so it can be referenced easily from any worksheet (Figure 3-40).

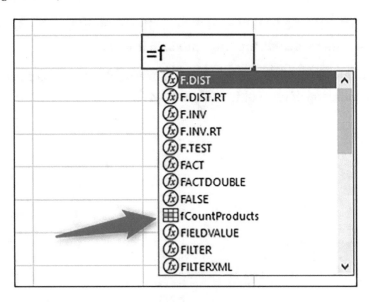

Figure 3-40. *Using the named formula in a cell*

Note   We will see more advanced examples of naming formulas in Chapter 15, when we explore the LET and LAMBDA functions of Excel.

Managing Names

The Name Manager in Excel makes it super simple to find, review, edit, and delete your names.

To open the Name Manager, click **Formulas ➤ Name Manager** or press **Ctrl + F3**.

The Name Manager lists all the names in the workbook (Figure 3-41). This includes the constants, tables, and named formulas.

It displays the current value (if possible) and shows what the name refers to and the scope of the name. Everything you need to know about a name is here. It truly is the name manager.

Edit a Name

Let's edit the [Threshold] name that we created at the beginning of the chapter. We want to make a simple edit to include the "rng" prefix in front of its name:

1.   From the *Name Manager,* select the "Threshold" name and click
     Edit at the top of the window (Figure 3-41).

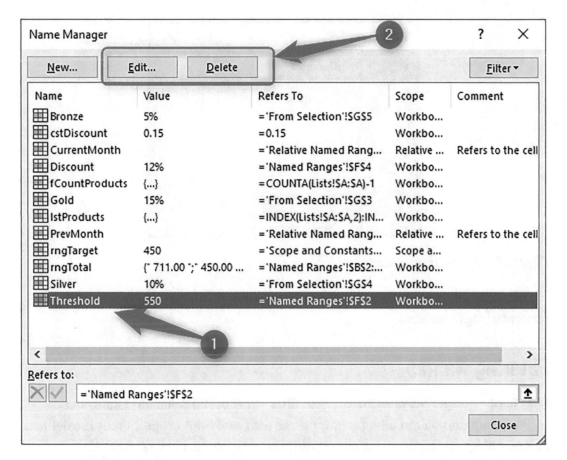

Figure 3-41. *Editing a name in the Name Manager*

2. Edit the *Name* to read "rngThreshold" (Figure 3-42). Click **OK**.

Note   You can also edit the *Refers to* and *Comment* fields, but note that the *Scope* of a name cannot be changed.

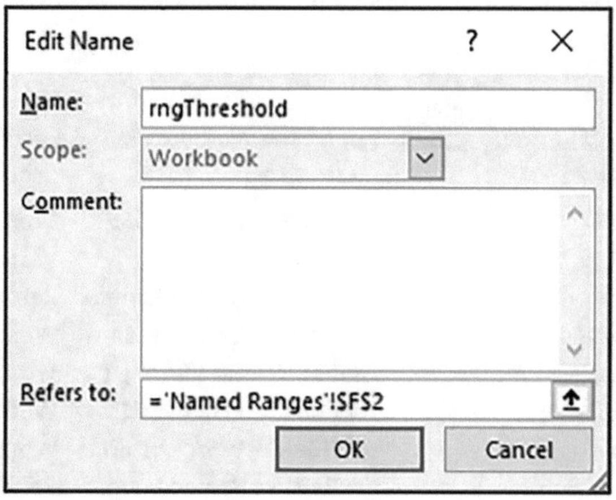

Figure 3-42. *Editing a name*

All formulas that reference the name [Threshold] will automatically update to reference [rngThreshold].

Filtering Names

The Name Manager provides an excellent filter – very useful if you have many names.

For example, you can filter for only names with workbook scope, or only the defined names and ignore the tables, or filter to only show names that have errors.

Figure 3-43 shows three of the names displaying the #REF! error. This is caused because the data that the names were using has been removed.

Click **Filter** in the top-right corner and click **Names with Errors** to only show these names.

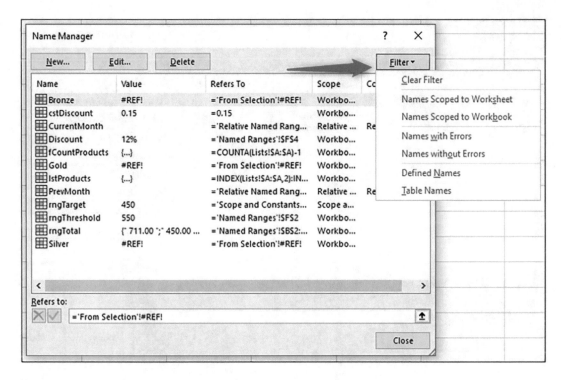

Figure 3-43. *Filtering names in the Name Manager*

When the names have been fixed, or you just want to return to seeing all the names, click **Filter ➤ Clear Filter** (Figure 3-44).

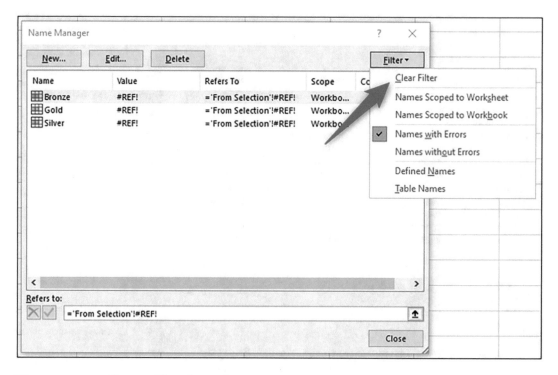

Figure 3-44. *Clear a filter from the Name Manager*

Print a List of the Names

You can also print a list of the names to the worksheet. This feature will only print names that have workbook scope.

Let's print the names to cell A2 of the [Print Names] worksheet:

1. Click cell A2.

2. Click **Formulas ➤ Use in Formula ➤ Paste Names** or press **F3**.

3. Click the **Paste List** button (Figure 3-45).

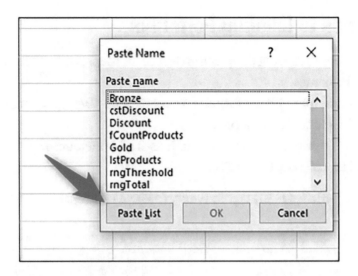

Figure 3-45. *Paste list of names*

The list of names is printed, including what they refer to (Figure 3-46).

	A	B
1	**Name**	**Refers to**
2	Bronze	='From Selection'!$G$5
3	cstDiscount	=0.15
4	Discount	='Named Ranges'!$F$4
5	fCountProducts	=COUNTA(Lists!$A:$A)-1
6	Gold	='From Selection'!$G$3
7	lstProducts	=INDEX(Lists!$A:$A,2):INDEX(Lists!$A:$A,COUNTA(Lists!$A:$A))
8	rngThreshold	='Named Ranges'!$F$2
9	rngTotal	='Named Ranges'!$B$2:$B$8
10	Silver	='From Selection'!$G$4

Figure 3-46. *List of names and what they refer to*

Note   This list is not dynamic and therefore will not update when names are added, removed, or changed.

Apply Names to Existing Formulas

If you define names after using them within formulas, there is a neat way to update these formulas with the names.

Let's use an example with the formula we used in the "Define Names with Create from Selection" section of this chapter.

The formula is shown in Figure 3-47, but it uses grid references and not the names that we defined for cells G3, G4, and G5.

```
=C2*SWITCH(B2,"Gold",(1-$G$3),"Silver",(1-$G$4),"Bronze",(1-$G$5))
```

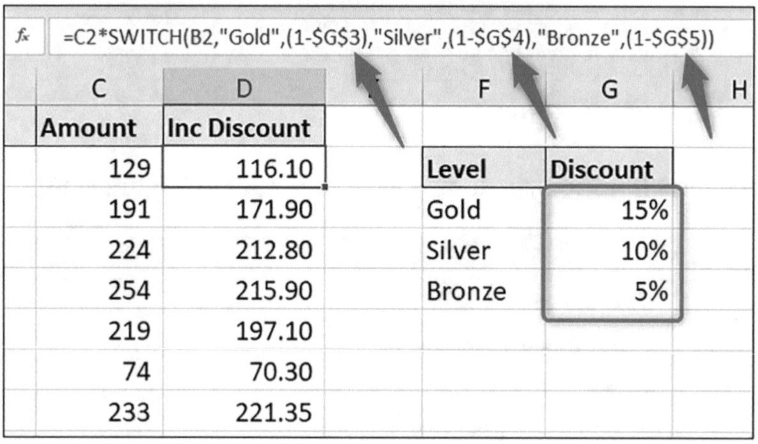

Figure 3-47. *SWITCH function using grid references*

To update the formulas with the names

1.   Click **Formulas** ➤ list arrow next to **Define Name** ➤ **Apply Names** (Figure 3-48).

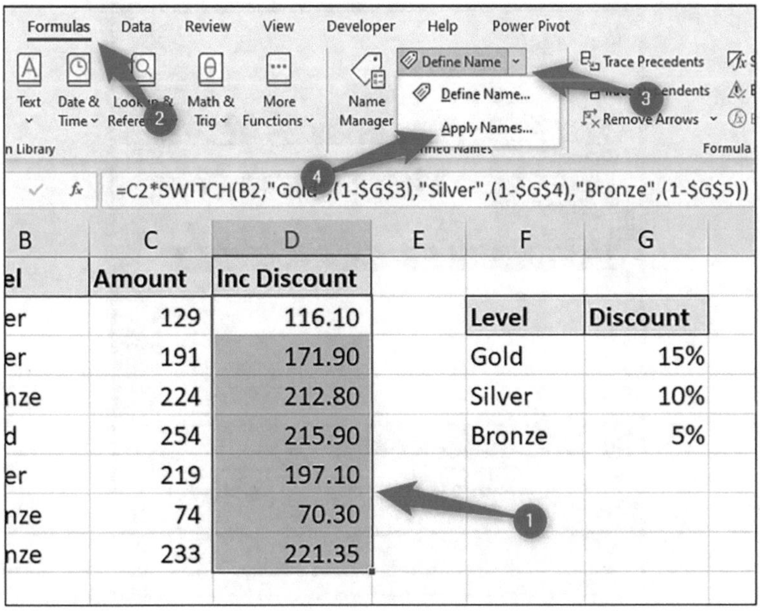

Figure 3-48. *Apply names to existing formulas with grid references*

2. Click the *Bronze, Gold,* and *Silver* names. Click **OK** (Figure 3-49).

Note The names will be applied to all formulas where they can match the name and grid reference in the entire worksheet.

Figure 3-49. *Applying names to a worksheet*

The *Ignore Relative/Absolute* option ensures that the name and grid are an exact match. If the grid reference is relative, but the named range is absolute, it will be ignored.

This is preferable, so we leave it checked. Changing relative references to absolute and vice versa at large scale does not sound good.

Summary

This chapter has provided a comprehensive understanding of defining names in Excel. We have covered the creation, application, and best practice of named ranges, formulas, and constants. We also saw how to work with existing names in an Excel workbook and how to find and manage the different types of names.

We will see names throughout this book. They will be used in different moments to simplify our formulas and to achieve tasks that would be difficult or not even possible without them.

In the next chapter, we will explore tables in Excel. Tables provide a way for us to work with structured data easier. They enable us to work beyond the grid and make referencing and analyzing Excel data more meaningful and simpler. Tables have been mentioned a few times in this chapter as they are also a named item and appear in the Name Manager. This makes tables a logical chapter to succeed the topic of defined names.

CHAPTER 4

You Need to Start Using Tables

When working with structured data in Excel, it should be formatted as a table. Tables are a feature in Excel that make managing and analyzing a group of related data much easier. A range of cells can be converted into a table at the click of a button.

Working with tables vs. cell ranges is to compare today's smartphone to a rotary dial telephone. The difference in the accessibility of the data, automation, and simplicity of use is remarkable. In fact, there are features in Excel such as Slicers and Power Query that require a range to be converted to a table.

Now, this does not mean that every range should be formatted as a table. There are dynamic arrays (covered in Chapter 10), which are their own thing. And single cell inputs for your models and reports. But when working with data structured as a list, there are many benefits from having it formatted as a table.

This chapter will focus on how tables improve how we write and work with formulas. We will not discuss the numerous other benefits of using tables including formatting, PivotTables, Power Query, and the data model.

In this chapter, we begin by explaining the many benefits of using tables. We then look at how to convert a range to a table and some best practice for using them.

Finally, we will see the correct and best ways to access data in a table when using formulas. It is outrageously fast and simple.

File   tables.xlsx

© Alan Murray 2022
A. Murray, *Advanced Excel Formulas*, https://doi.org/10.1007/978-1-4842-7125-4_4

Why Use Tables?

There are many reasons to use tables in Excel.

- Meaningful references

Tables provide a simple way to reference a range of cells. Compare a formula that references `tblLondonSales` vs. `London!$A$1:$G$1022`. The table reference is much easier to read and write than the worksheet reference.

References to elements of a table such as the header row or specific columns are also more meaningful. For example, a reference to the table headers would look like `tblLondonSales[#Headers]`, and the reference to a column named "Product" would look like `tblLondonSales[Product]`. This is far superior to references such as `London!$A$1:$G$1` or `London!$E:$E`.

- Super easy referencing in formulas

The ease at which you can access the different elements of a table is remarkable.

You can select the elements of a table in a similar way that you would select a range of cells, or you can type the reference.

I love typing the references myself. It is so fast and simple. Figure 4-1 shows Excel listing the elements of a table as you type, making it super simple to access from anywhere in the workbook.

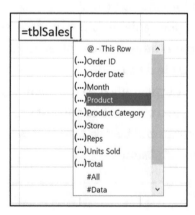

Figure 4-1. *Referencing table elements from a formula*

- Tables are dynamic.

When additional rows or columns are added to a table, it automatically expands. Therefore, any formulas that reference that table will use the updated range.

When using a range of cells on the grid such as A2:D10, you cannot be sure that your formulas are using the correct range when you or your colleagues add and remove data from that range. It is less reliable and more awkward to update, especially if many formulas are using that range.

Users will commonly use tricks such as referencing entire columns in a formula, such as, $E:$E, or inserting rows into the middle of a table instead of at the bottom. These tricks help to ensure that any rows added to the range are included in the formulas.

With tables, that behavior is unnecessary. Tables provide that single source of truth. If the table correctly contains all the data, then all formulas that reference the table's data are correct. They are much more reliable and easier to control.

- Additional functionality

Tables enable additional functionality that is not in the scope of this book. This extra functionality includes the power tools such as Power Query and Power Pivot, using Slicers and consistent formatting.

Format a Range As a Table

So, tables are fantastic. Let's look at how to convert a range into a table and then cover some essentials and best practices.

Creating a Table

In this example, we will use the data in range A1:C8 on the [Discounts] sheet (Figure 4-2).

	A	B	C
1	Customer	Total	Inc Discount
2	Mario Pontes	711.00	
3	Daniel Tonini	450.00	
4	Hanna Moos	509.00	
5	Jaime Yorres	395.00	
6	José Pedro Freyre	683.00	
7	Carlos Hernández	340.00	
8	André Fonseca	442.00	
9			

Figure 4-2. *Range of data that needs converting to a table*

To convert this range to a table

1. Click a cell within the range.

2. Click **Insert ➤ Table** or press **Ctrl + T**.

Note   You can also click **Home ➤ Format as Table** and click a style from the list.

---

3. In the *Create Table* window (Figure 4-3), check that the range is
    correct and that the *My table has headers* box is checked (there are
    headers in the first row of the range). Click **OK**.

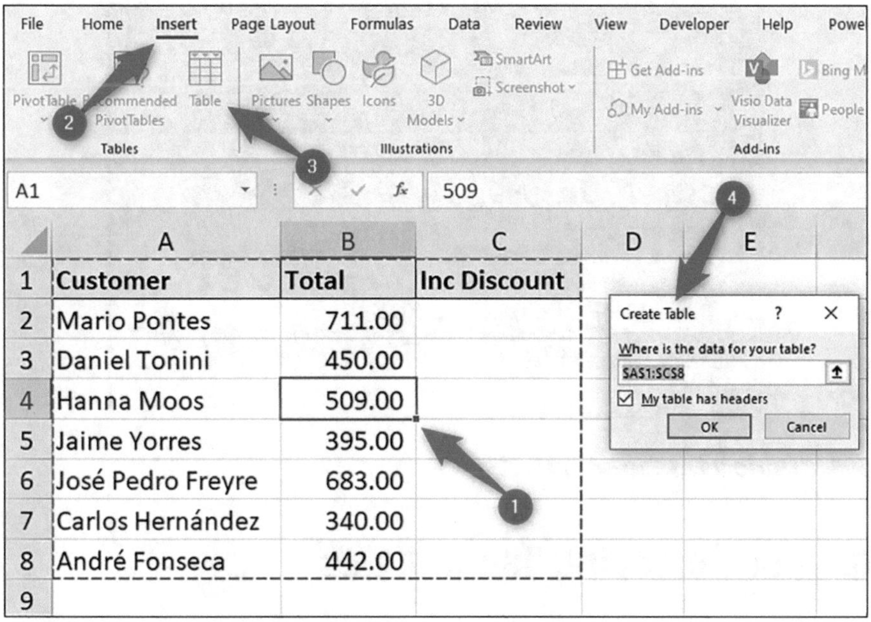

Figure 4-3. *Create a table from a range*

That's it! The range is now formatted as a table (Figure 4-4).

The default style is applied. This style keeps any existing formatting that was applied to the range, such as the orange fill color in the header row.

It applies the elements of the default table style to areas where no previous formatting was specified. This includes the blue banded rows, blue border, and white font in the header row.

In the bottom-right corner of the table is a blue resize handle (Figure 4-4). This identifies the last cell of a table and can be used to quickly resize it if necessary.

◢	A	B	C	D
1	Customer ▾	Total ▾	Inc Discount ▾	
2	Mario Pontes	711.00		
3	Daniel Tonini	450.00		
4	Hanna Moos	509.00		
5	Jaime Yorres	395.00		
6	José Pedro Freyre	683.00		
7	Carlos Hernández	340.00		
8	André Fonseca	442.00		
9				

Figure 4-4. *Table with the default style*

Changing or Removing Table Styles

You can easily change or remove the table style if you are not contented with the default style applied. You can even create your own styles, but we will not be looking at this in the book.

Personally, I like to remove the table style, so will demonstrate that:

1. Click a cell within the table.

2. Click **Table Design** and then the **More** button in the corner of the Styles gallery (Figure 4-5).

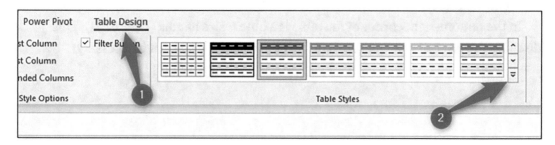

Figure 4-5. *More button of the Styles gallery*

3. The gallery expands. You can choose a different style, create your own, or clear the style. To clear a style, click **Clear** at the bottom of the gallery, or click the **None** option (Figure 4-6).

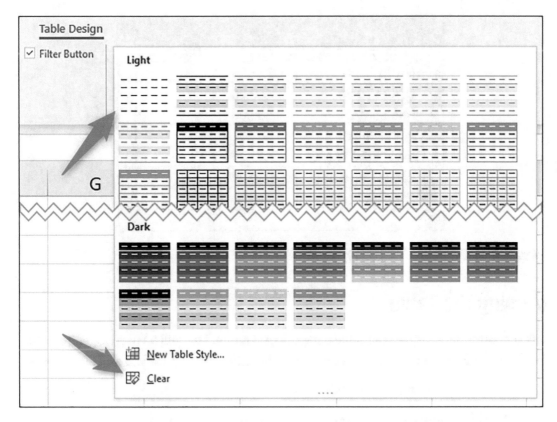

Figure 4-6. *Clear the table style*

In Figure 4-7, the table style has been removed. Although it does not have any new formatting applied, it is still formatted as a table.

You can see the blue resize handle in the bottom-right corner. Also, the **Table Design** tab appears when the table is active. These are two signs that the range is formatted as a table.

	A	B	C
1	Customer	Total	Inc Discount
2	Mario Pontes	711.00	
3	Daniel Tonini	450.00	
4	Hanna Moos	509.00	
5	Jaime Yorres	395.00	
6	José Pedro Freyre	683.00	
7	Carlos Hernández	340.00	
8	André Fonseca	442.00	
9			

Figure 4-7. *Table with no style applied*

Naming the Table

It is very important to give your table a meaningful name. This will be used to reference it from a formula, so you want it to be distinct to this table and easy for you and others to use.

1. Click a cell within the table.

2. Click **Table Design** and enter the name you want to use in the *Table Name* box (Figure 4-8). In this example, it has been named "tblCustomerSales".

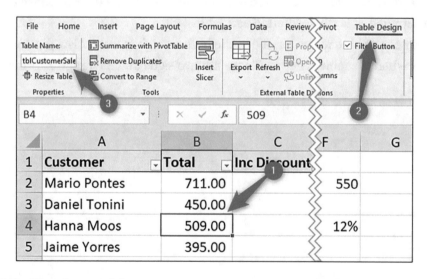

Figure 4-8. *Naming a table*

Note   The *tbl* prefix has been used to denote a table. This is optional but is a useful tip to easily distinguish tables from other names.

Working with Tables

When working with a workbook that contains tables, you may need to find, view, and edit these tables at some point.

The easiest way to view the tables in a workbook is through the *Name Manager*. There is even a filter in the *Name Manager* making it easy to only focus on the tables (Figure 4-9).

To open the *Name Manager*, click **Formulas ➤ Name Manager**.

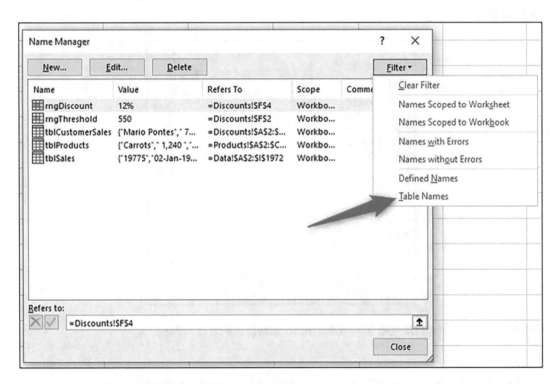

Figure 4-9. *Viewing tables in the Name Manager*

From the *Name Manager*, you can view all tables and see what they refer to.

The quickest way to navigate to a table in a workbook is either using the Name Box to the left of the Formula Bar (Figure 4-10).

Figure 4-10. *Using the Name Box to navigate to a table*

Or by pressing **F5** or **Ctrl + G** to open the *Go To* window (Figure 4-11). Select the table and click **OK**.

Figure 4-11. *Using the Go To window to navigate to a table*

Note These same methods can be used to navigate to named ranges and were covered in the previous chapter.

Table References in a Formula

This is an Excel formulas book, so we have now arrived at the exciting part. How do we reference the table and its elements from within a formula?

The Magic of @

Let's begin by using a formula that references a single cell of the table. We will use the [tblCustomerSales] table that was just created.

In cell C2, the following IF function has been used to calculate the discount on the customer totals, but only if they reach the threshold value (Figure 4-12):

```
=IF([@Total]>=rngThreshold,[@Total]*(1-rngDiscount),[@Total])
```

When clicking cell B2 while writing the formula, it is referenced as [@Total]. Total is the name of the column, the @ symbol refers to the same row within the table, and it is all enclosed in square brackets.

The names [rngThreshold] and [rngDiscount] refer to cells F2 and F4, respectively.

| C2 | ▾ | : | ✕ | ✓ | *fx* | =IF([@Total]>=rngThreshold,[@Total]*(1-rngDiscount),[@Total]) |

	A	B	C	D	E	F
1	Customer	Total	Inc Discount			
2	Mario Pontes	711.00	625.68		Threshold	550
3	Daniel Tonini	450.00	450.00			
4	Hanna Moos	509.00	509.00		Discount	12%
5	Jaime Yorres	395.00	395.00			
6	José Pedro Freyre	683.00	601.04			
7	Carlos Hernández	340.00	340.00			
8	André Fonseca	442.00	442.00			
9						

Figure 4-12. *IF function that references cells in the Total column*

This is a very meaningful reference. Using the column header [Total] has greater meaning than column B.

And what is extra cool is that every cell in the [Inc Discount] column (column C) contains the same formula. If we used a range, the formulas would all be a little different as they would reference B3, B4, B5, and so on.

Another awesome feature when writing formulas that refer to a single cell on the same row in a table is that they automatically fill down to the last row. No need to click and drag or double-click that fill handle.

Note   If you reference a single cell in a table on a different row to the active cell, then a grid reference is used. So, if you clicked on cell B3 while writing a formula in cell C2, then the reference to B3 is used. This is because there is no obvious relationship between two different rows of a table (rows 2 and 3 in this case) that Excel can recognize.

Let's see another example of the magic @ symbol in action. In this example, we have the table shown in Figure 4-13. This table is named [tblProducts].

We will write a formula in the [Percentage] column that calculates the percentage contribution that the sales of each product have made to the grand total.

	A	B	C
1	**Product**	**Total**	**Percentage**
2	Carrots	1,240	
3	Tomatoes	393	
4	Lettuce	1,096	
5	Strawberries	339	
6	Cucumber	781	
7	Cherries	1,300	
8			

Figure 4-13. *tblProducts showing product sales*

In cell C2, the following formula has been used (Figure 4-14):

```
=[@Total]/SUM([Total])
```

This formula includes a reference to a single product total, shown as [@Total], and a reference to the column, shown as [Total] (without the @ sign).

I think this is a good example of the use of the magic @ sign and how readable these formulas are when referencing table data.

When I read the @ symbol in my head, I like to say the word "this." So, the formula reads "this total divided by the sum of totals" to me.

The cells where the formula is input are formatted as a percentage. However, Excel appears to change the cell formatting when this formula is entered. So, you may be required to format the [Percentage] column as percentages again.

C2			× ✓ *fx*	=[@Total]/SUM([Total])
	A	B		C
1	Product	Total		Percentage
2	Carrots	1,240		24%
3	Tomatoes	393		8%
4	Lettuce	1,096		21%
5	Strawberries	339		7%
6	Cucumber	781		15%
7	Cherries	1,300		25%

Figure 4-14. *Percentage of column total*

One final thing to mention about referencing single cells in a table. If the column header contains a space, an extra set of square brackets is used to enclose the column name:

[@[Order Date]]

Referencing Table Elements

A table is made up of a few elements. These include the header row, total row, the columns, the data minus the headers, and everything (data and headers). We will see examples of referencing these different elements as we progress through the book.

You can reference these table elements by selecting or clicking with your mouse or by typing the reference directly into the formula. I am a big fan of typing table references. It is so fast and easy. Let's look at both methods.

For this example, we have a table on the [Data] sheet of the workbook named [tblSales]. A snapshot of this table is shown in Figure 4-15.

	A	B	C	D	E	F
1	Order ID	Order Date	Product	Store	Units Sold	Total
2	19775	02-Jan-19	Sausage Roll	Olympia	12	30
3	20684	03-Jan-19	Baguette	Olympia	40	112
4	20685	03-Jan-19	Baguette	Neptune Way	80	224
5	20686	03-Jan-19	Baguette	Bartholomew Drive	70	196
6	20687	03-Jan-19	Baguette	Bartholomew Drive	55	154
7	20688	03-Jan-19	Baguette	Longleaf Drive	18	50
8	20689	04-Jan-19	Chocolate Chip Muffin	Bartholomew Drive	8	11

Figure 4-15. *tblSales containing a list of orders*

On the [Report] worksheet, we will use the SUMIFS function (covered in Chapter 8) to sum the [Total] column for the sales of a specific product.

The following formula has been entered into cell C3 (Figure 4-16). It sums the [Total] column, only for sales of the product entered in cell B3.

```
=SUMIFS(tblSales[Total],tblSales[Product],B3)
```

The name of the table precedes the column name as we are referencing the column from outside of the table.

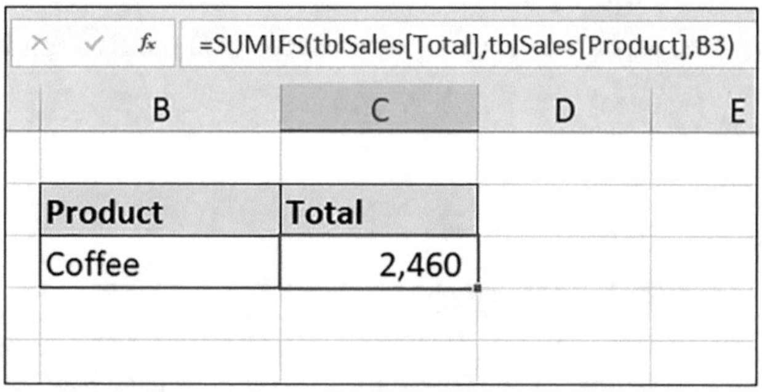

Figure 4-16. *SUMIFS function summing sales of coffee only*

To reference the columns, you can click the column header. This is great, but you must be careful.

Figure 4-17 shows the [Product] column of the table being clicked. The black arrow indicates that I am in the correct position to select the table's column.

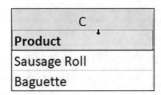

Figure 4-17. *Clicking a table column*

If you position the cursor a little too high, you may select the sheet column by mistake. Figure 4-18 shows the black arrow positioned on column C of the sheet and not the [Product] column of the table.

The sheet column header changes to a green fill to illustrate this. However, this is easy to miss during the excitement of writing formulas.

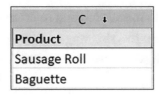

Figure 4-18. *Clicking a sheet column*

Note   You can also select the header row of a table and the entire table in a similar way. Be careful not to select the sheet row or column by mistake.

A better method could be to type the reference. Excel assists this process by providing a list of all table elements as you type. Figure 4-19 shows this list as I type the reference to the [Product] column in the SUMIFS function.

The list appears when the opening square bracket is typed.

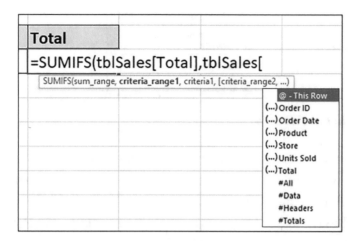

Figure 4-19. *List of table elements as you type a formula*

One final thing I would like to mention when referencing table elements, if you select a range of columns from a table, the range operator is included, and an extra set of square brackets is added to enclose the column range:

```
tblSales[[Product]:[Store]]
```

Make Table Column and Cell References Absolute

Single column table references such as [@Product] and [Product] are relative by default, just like references to cells on a worksheet such as B2. Unfortunately, it is a little more awkward to make table references absolute.

Let's see an example. We have the following SUMIFS function shown in Figure 4-20. It sums the [Total] column from [tblSales] for the product entered in cell E3 and the store in cell F2.

```
=SUMIFS(tblSales[Total],tblSales[Product],$E$3,tblSales[Store],F2)
```

This works great!

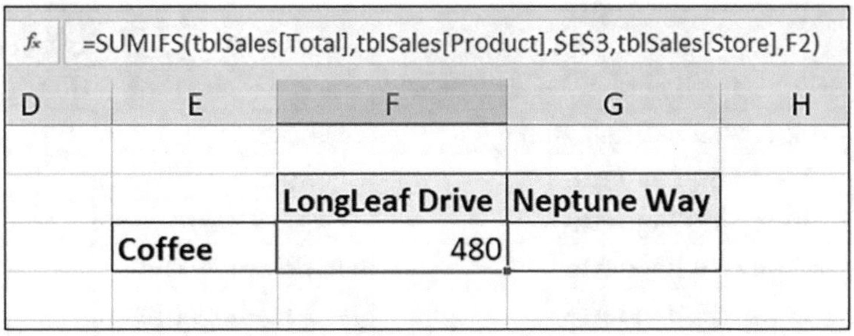

Figure 4-20. *SUMIFS function with table references*

When the formula is filled to cell G3 to the right by dragging the fill handle, the formula goes horribly wrong (Figure 4-21). The following is the resulting formula:

```
=SUMIFS(tblSales[Order ID],tblSales[Store],$E$3,tblSales[Units Sold],G2)
```

All three table column references have changed.

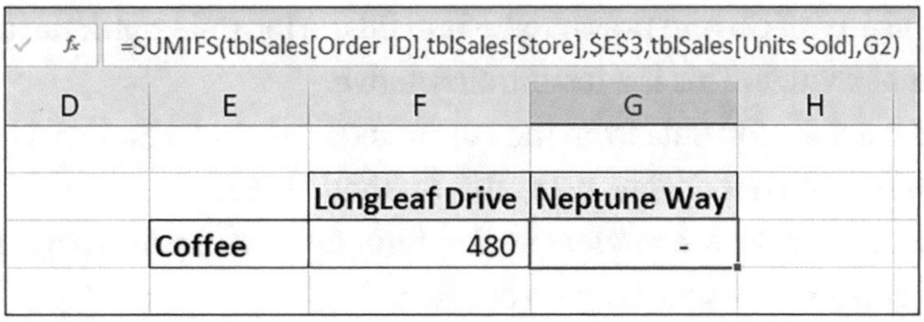

Figure 4-21. *All table column references have shifted to the right*

The columns of [tblSales] can be seen in Figure 4-22. The [Product] column has changed to [Store], the [Store] column changed to [Units Sold], and the [Total] column changed to [Order ID]. As it is the last column of the table, the reference shifted back to the first column.

153

	A	B	C	D	E	F
1	Order ID	Order Date	Product ➡	Store ➡	Units Sold	Total
2	19775	02-Jan-19	Sausage Roll	Olympia	12	30
3	20684	03-Jan-19	Baguette	Olympia	40	112
4	20685	03-Jan-19	Baguette	Neptune Way	80	224
5	20686	03-Jan-19	Baguette	Bartholomew Drive	70	196
6	20687	03-Jan-19	Baguette	Bartholomew Drive	55	154
7	20688	03-Jan-19	Baguette	Longleaf Drive	18	50
8	20689	04-Jan-19	Chocolate Chip Muffin	Bartholomew Drive	8	11
9	20690	04-Jan-19	Chocolate Chip Muffin	Neptune Way	40	56

Figure 4-22. *The columns of tblSales*

Now, there are a few ways to prevent this behavior.

One method is to copy or fill the formula using an alternative method to the classic drag of the fill handle.

You can click in cell G3 and press **Ctrl + R** to fill the formula right; the table references do not change. This is a terrific alternative.

Or you can copy the formula from the Formula Bar of cell F3 and paste it in cell G3. The table references do not change using this method either.

Finally, we could make the references absolute. To do this, you change the reference to a range and add an extra set of square brackets.

The following formula has been split onto two lines to make it more readable. All table column references have been made absolute.

```
=SUMIFS(tblSales[[Total]:[Total]],
tblSales[[Product]:[Product]],$E$3,tblSales[[Store]:[Store]],F2)
```

Figure 4-23 shows the SUMIFS function with absolute table references. When the formula is filled to the right by dragging the fill handle, the references no longer change.

Because the solution to make single column table references absolute is to convert the reference to a range, this means that when selecting multiple columns like the following formula, they are absolute by default, as those columns are already part of a range:

```
tblSales[[Product]:[Store]]
```

✓	*fx*	=SUMIFS(tblSales[[Total]:[Total]], tblSales[[Product]:[Product]],$E$3,tblSales[[Store]:[Store]],F2)		
D	E	F	G	H
		LongLeaf Drive	Neptune Way	
	Coffee	480	708	

Figure 4-23. *Absolute table references in a formula*

Fixing the table columns in the formula is a more reliable method. It provides protection against other users of the sheet who may copy the formula.

However, the formula is more awkward to read, so it is useful to know the alternative methods such as **Ctrl + R**. Different situations can warrant a different approach.

Making a table cell reference absolute is a familiar tale. To make a reference to a cell in a column named [Order ID] absolute, include the range operator and enclose it all in square brackets:

```
tblSales[@[Order ID]:[Order ID]]
```

Tables with Other Excel Features

Throughout this book, we will see examples of using formulas with other Excel features such as charts. If we are entering formulas within tables, it is important to understand how other Excel features work with tables.

Dynamic Lists

In the previous chapter, there was an example of creating a dynamic name using a formula. This name was then used as the source of a Data Validation list.

Tables are dynamic, so offer a wonderful alternative to this approach. Now, unfortunately tables do not work directly with Data Validation. You cannot enter a formula that uses the structured references of a table within a Data Validation rule directly. So, we will create a defined name for the table data and then use the name for the Data Validation list.

Figure 4-24 shows a list of products that has been formatted as a table named [tblProductList].

◢	A	B
1	**Products**	
2	Baguette	
3	Beer	
4	Blueberry Muffin	
5	Caramel Shortbread	
6	Chocolate Chip Muffin	
7	Coffee	
8	Cornish Pasty	
17	Sausage Roll	
18	Soup	
19	Tea	
20	Water	
21	Wine	
22		

Figure 4-24. *List of products formatted as a table named tblProductList*

To name the table data

1. Select the data range of the table, A2:A21.

2. Click **Formulas ➤ Define Name**.

3. Type "lstProducts" for the *Name* (Figure 4-25). Notice the table reference in the *Refers to* field.

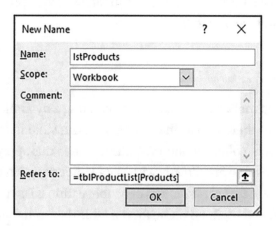

Figure 4-25. *Define a name for the list of products*

We can then use this name for the source of the Data Validation list. Because the name understands the table, it works as a translator between the table and Data Validation features of Excel.

Let's use the list for cell B3 of the [Report] sheet:

1. Click cell B3.

2. Click **Data ➤ Data Validation**.

3. From the **Settings** tab, click the *Allow* list and select **List**.

4. Type "=lstProducts" in the *Source* field and click **OK** (Figure 4-26).

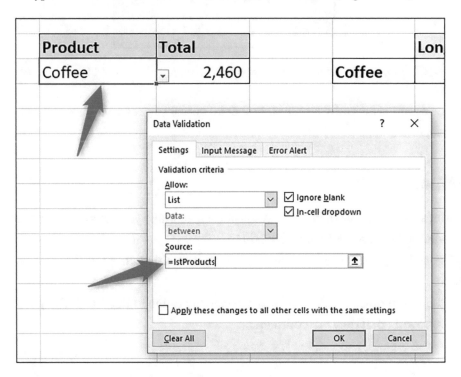

Figure 4-26. *Data Validation list using the defined name as its source*

The Data Validation list is set up (Figure 4-27).

If more products are added to [tblProductList], they are automatically included in the Data Validation list.

There have been some major improvements made to Data Validation in recent months. So, at the time of writing this book, although we cannot directly use a Data Validation list from table data on another sheet, it may be a functional feature in modern Excel versions soon.

Such advancements will only be available to Excel for Microsoft 365 (Windows and Mac) and Excel for the Web, meaning this technique of using defined names is still very applicable.

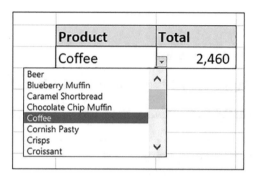

Figure 4-27. *Dynamic drop-down list of products*

Defined names have always had this special power to get two different Excel features working together.

Dynamic Charts

Using tables as the source of charts is a simple way to make your charts automatically update when new data is added to the table.

In Figure 4-28, we have a line chart that is using a table named [tblMonthlySales] as its source.

The table is in range A1:B6, and you can see that range highlighted when the chart is selected, showing that they are connected.

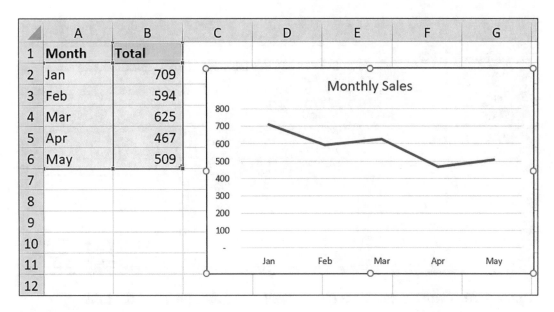

Figure 4-28. *Line chart using table data*

If we look at the chart data though, it does not reference the table that it is connected to.

Select the chart and click **Chart Design ➤ Select Data**.

In the *Chart data range* field (Figure 4-29), the chart source is shown as

=Chart!$A$1:$B$6

Although it does not directly mention [tblMonthlySales], it is connected to it. This is a little confusing, but you get used to it.

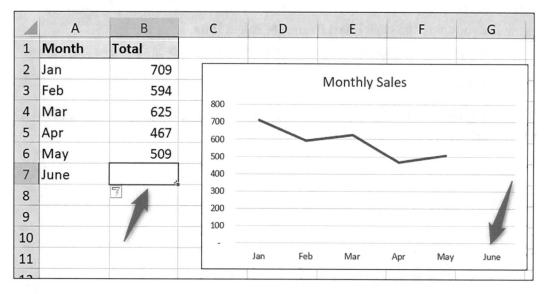

Figure 4-29. *Chart range is shown as a cell range despite using the table*

Because the range that the chart is using for its source is formatted as a table, when new data is added, the chart automatically updates (Figure 4-30).

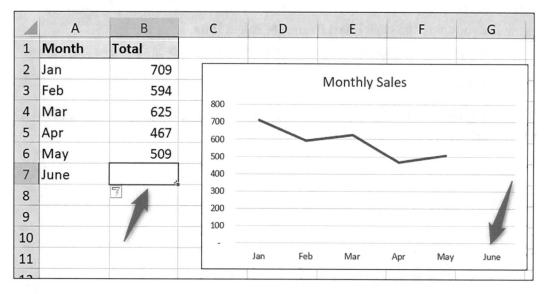

Figure 4-30. *Chart updates automatically when data is added to the table*

Tables are an incredible feature of Excel, and many of the formula examples in this book will be using table references.

Summary

In this chapter, we learned how tables help us to manage and analyze structured data in Excel. We also learned how to effectively reference table data within formulas.

In the next chapter, we will learn the text functions in Excel. These functions enable us to split, extract, join, and format text. They are very useful, and we have many to discuss, so let's start.

CHAPTER 5

Manipulating Text

I have always enjoyed using formulas to manipulate text in Excel. Solving the puzzle of extracting, joining, and shaping text to our requirements is very exciting. They are some of my most enjoyable formulas to use and teach.

Excel contains over 30 functions for manipulating text. We will cover many of the most useful text functions in this chapter. These include LEFT, TEXT, TRIM, FIND, SUBSTITUTE, TEXTJOIN, and many more. We will also cover the new text functions released in 2022 – TEXTAFTER, TEXTBEFORE, and TEXTSPLIT.

In this chapter, we will use formulas to extract, combine, replace, and convert text. There is a lot of content in this chapter, so let's get started.

File   text-functions.xlsx

Extract Characters from a Text String

There are three functions in Excel that are used to extract a specified number of characters from a text string – LEFT, RIGHT, and MID. The one you use depends on the position of the characters you need to extract.

Let's begin with some simple extraction tasks and then progress to more complex examples. The more complex examples will require some help from additional text functions.

Figure 5-1 shows the sample data we will use for the simple examples.

© Alan Murray 2022
A. Murray, *Advanced Excel Formulas*, https://doi.org/10.1007/978-1-4842-7125-4_5

The text strings in column A are made up of three different sections. Each section identifies an element of a transaction, and we need to extract each one for analysis.

In a typical business scenario, the first three digits could be a client reference, middle two numbers the order ID, and the last letter could be the store code.

	A	B	C	D
1	Reference	LEFT	RIGHT	MID
2	THJ-34-D			
3	KHL-59-B			
4	ANN-61-D			
5	PVQ-33-K			
6	THJ-28-B			
7	PVQ-90-C			
8	ASD-12-K			

Figure 5-1. *Sample data for simple text extractions*

LEFT and RIGHT

Availability: All versions

The LEFT and RIGHT functions are used to extract characters from the start and end of a text string.

The functions have the same arguments. Their syntaxes are

```
=LEFT(text, [num_chars])
```

and

```
=RIGHT(text, [num_chars])
```

- **Text:** The text containing the characters you want to extract

- **[Num chars]:** The number of characters you want to extract

In Figure 5-2, the following formula has been used in column B to extract the first three characters (client reference) from the text in column A:

```
=LEFT(A2,3)
```

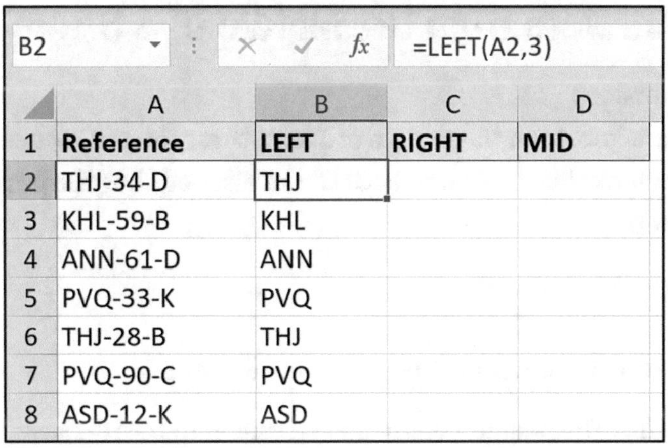

B2	▾	⋮	×	✓	fx	=LEFT(A2,3)	

◢	A	B	C	D
1	**Reference**	**LEFT**	**RIGHT**	**MID**
2	THJ-34-D	THJ		
3	KHL-59-B	KHL		
4	ANN-61-D	ANN		
5	PVQ-33-K	PVQ		
6	THJ-28-B	THJ		
7	PVQ-90-C	PVQ		
8	ASD-12-K	ASD		

Figure 5-2. *LEFT function to extract the first three characters*

The RIGHT function is then used to extract the last character (store code) from column A (Figure 5-3):

=RIGHT(A2,1)

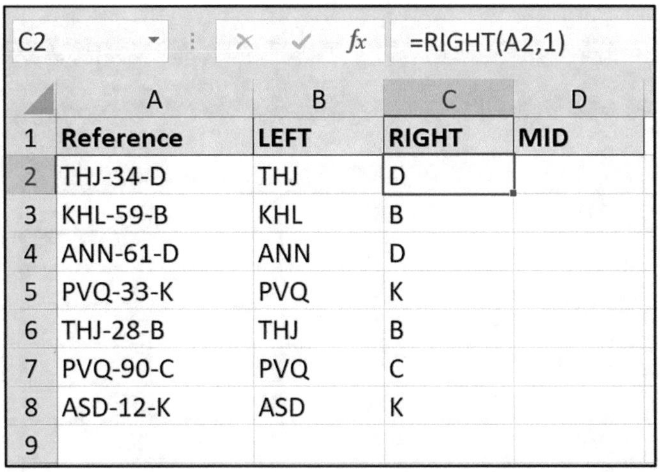

C2	▾	⋮	×	✓	fx	=RIGHT(A2,1)	

◢	A	B	C	D
1	**Reference**	**LEFT**	**RIGHT**	**MID**
2	THJ-34-D	THJ	D	
3	KHL-59-B	KHL	B	
4	ANN-61-D	ANN	D	
5	PVQ-33-K	PVQ	K	
6	THJ-28-B	THJ	B	
7	PVQ-90-C	PVQ	C	
8	ASD-12-K	ASD	K	
9				

Figure 5-3. *RIGHT function to extract the last character*

Extract Characters from the Middle of a String

Availability: All versions

To extract characters from the middle of a text string, the MID function is used. The MID function looks like LEFT and RIGHT, but also requires the position of the first character to extract:

```
=MID(text, start_num, num_chars)
```

- **Text:** The text containing the characters to extract

- **Start num:** The position of the first character in the text string you want to extract

- **Num chars:** The number of characters to extract

The following formula is used to extract the middle two numbers from the reference (Figure 5-4). It extracts two characters, starting from the fifth character in the string:

```
=MID(A2,5,2)
```

D2	▾ : × ✓ ƒx	=MID(A2,5,2)	
	A	B	C	D
1	Reference	LEFT	RIGHT	MID
2	THJ-34-D	THJ	D	34
3	KHL-59-B	KHL	B	59
4	ANN-61-D	ANN	D	61
5	PVQ-33-K	PVQ	K	33
6	THJ-28-B	THJ	B	28
7	PVQ-90-C	PVQ	C	90
8	ASD-12-K	ASD	K	12
9				

Figure 5-4. *Extract characters from the middle of a text string*

FIND and SEARCH for Irregular Strings

Availability: All versions

The first examples of the LEFT, MID, and RIGHT functions relied on a fixed number of characters to extract and a fixed position of the first character. Sometimes, you may need to extract from an irregular text string.

In these situations, the characters you want to extract are typically separated by a delimiter. For example, in the text THJ-34-D, the "-" is separating the different parts of the text and is known as the delimiter.

The FIND and SEARCH functions of Excel are great for working with irregular strings. They can be used to locate the position of a delimiter and therefore help to determine the first character and/or number of characters to extract.

The purpose of these functions is to return the position of a text string within another text string. The only difference between the FIND and SEARCH functions is that FIND is case-sensitive and SEARCH is not.

Their syntaxes are

```
=FIND(find_text, within_text, [start_num])
```

and

```
=SEARCH(find_text, within_text, [start_num])
```

- **Find text:** The text you want to find and return the position of.

- **Within text:** The text that you are searching within.

- **[Start num]:** The position within the text to begin the search. This is an optional argument, and if omitted, it searches from the first character of the *within_text* string.

Example 1: Extract Characters Before a Delimiter

In this example, we want to extract characters from the beginning of a string, so we will use the LEFT function. However, the number of characters to extract is irregular. A delimiter signifies the end of the characters that we need.

In the following formula (Figure 5-5), the SEARCH function is used to return the position of the "-" delimiter. One is then subtracted from this value to get the position of the character before the delimiter (last character of the text to extract):

```
=LEFT(A2,SEARCH("-",A2)-1)
```

B2	▼	:	×	✓	*fx*	=LEFT(A2,SEARCH("-",A2)-1)		

	A	B	C	D	E
1	**Reference**	**Before**	After		
2	CARV-59	CARV			
3	ARB-12	ARB			
4	FY-528	FY			
5	WOOD-2	WOOD			
6	PEX-49	PEX			
7	MA-210	MA			

Figure 5-5. *Extract characters before a delimiter*

Example 2: Extract Characters After a Delimiter

In this example, we use the RIGHT function to extract the numbers from the end of the text in column A (Figure 5-6). The number of characters is irregular, and we need the delimiter to identify the number of characters to extract.

To calculate the number of characters to extract, we will subtract the position of the delimiter from the total number of characters in the cell.

The LEN function is used to return the total number of characters in a cell. We will see more examples of the LEN function shortly.

```
=RIGHT(A2,LEN(A2)-FIND("-",A2))
```

C2	▼	:	×	✓	*fx*	=RIGHT(A2,LEN(A2)-FIND("-",A2))		

	A	B	C	D	E	F
1	**Reference**	**Before**	**After**			
2	CARV-59	CARV	59			
3	ARB-12	ARB	12			
4	FY-528	FY	528			
5	WOOD-2	WOOD	2			
6	PEX-49	PEX	49			
7	MA-210	MA	210			

Figure 5-6. *Extract characters after a delimiter*

In this example, the FIND function was used to return the position of the "-"
delimiter. It makes no difference if you use the FIND or SEARCH function as the case of
the delimiter is not important in this example.

Example 3: Combining LEFT and RIGHT

It can sometimes be useful to combine the LEFT and RIGHT functions together. One
function can work off the string provided by the other.

In this example, we want to return the characters between the brackets. These
characters are the last characters in the cell, except for the closing bracket. They are also
a regular length of three characters.

In the following formula (Figure 5-7), the RIGHT function is used to extract the
last four characters. This is passed to the LEFT function to then return the first three
characters from that string:

`=LEFT(RIGHT(A2,4),3)`

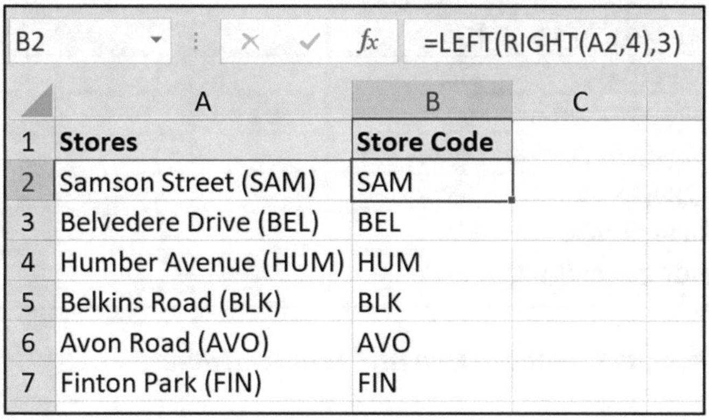

Figure 5-7. *LEFT and RIGHT working together*

Example 4: Extract Text Between Two Characters

Let's look at two examples of extracting text between two characters. In the first example,
the characters are different. And in the second example, we will extract text from
between two identical characters.

The following formula has been used in Figure 5-8. The formula has been split over multiple lines to distinguish the three parts of the MID function easier:

```
=MID(A2,
SEARCH("(",A2)+1,
SEARCH(")",A2)-SEARCH("(",A2)-1)
```

The first SEARCH function finds the position of the first character to extract. This is one character after the opening bracket.

To calculate the number of characters to extract, the position of the opening bracket is subtracted from the position of the closing bracket, then another one is subtracted.

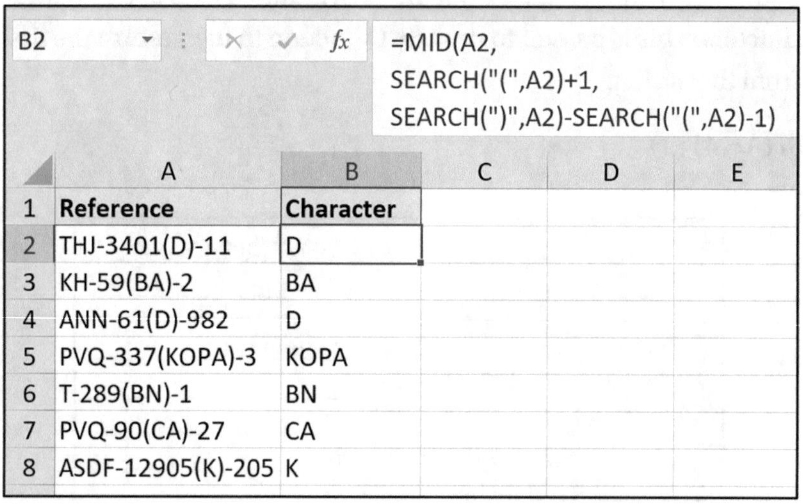

	A	B	C	D	E
	Reference	Character			
1	Reference	Character			
2	THJ-3401(D)-11	D			
3	KH-59(BA)-2	BA			
4	ANN-61(D)-982	D			
5	PVQ-337(KOPA)-3	KOPA			
6	T-289(BN)-1	BN			
7	PVQ-90(CA)-27	CA			
8	ASDF-12905(K)-205	K			

B2 — fx =MID(A2,
SEARCH("(",A2)+1,
SEARCH(")",A2)-SEARCH("(",A2)-1)

Figure 5-8. Extract text between two different characters

When the two characters to extract between are identical, the formula is a little more complex.

The following formula is shown in Figure 5-9:

```
=MID(A2,
SEARCH("-",A2)+1,
SEARCH("-",A2,SEARCH("-",A2)+1)-SEARCH("-",A2)-1)
```

This formula is actually very similar to the previous one. The exception is with the second SEARCH function on the last line.

This SEARCH function is nested within another to find the second occurrence of a hyphen "-". It is nested within the *start num* argument of the other SEARCH to instruct it to look for the "-" after the first instance of a "-".

So, the final line of the formula reads the position of the second "-", minus position of the first "-", and then minus one. This returns the number of characters to extract.

B2	f_x	=MID(A2, SEARCH("-",A2)+1, SEARCH("-",A2,SEARCH("-",A2)+1)-SEARCH("-",A2)-1)

	A	B	C	D	E	F	G
1	Reference	Character					
2	7-CARV-59	CARV					
3	197-ARB-12	ARB					
4	5512-FY-528	FY					
5	094-WOOD-2	WOOD					
6	6-PEX-49	PEX					
7	93373-MA-210	MA					
8							

Figure 5-9. *Extract text between two identical characters*

To help understand complex formulas such as this, a great technique is to select an element of a formula and press the **F9** key to calculate just that part. This helps you step through the formula in its parts, instead of its entirety.

In the following final formula line, this technique has been used to return the result of the nested SEARCH only. This result is shown in bold text:

SEARCH("-",A2,**2**+1)-SEARCH("-",A2)-1)

Press **Esc** when finished so that the formula remains intact. Otherwise, the results are stored instead of the formula.

Example 5: Extract Number from a Text String

For our final examples of working with FIND and SEARCH, we will extract a number from text when there is no delimiter.

In Figure 5-10, the references contain a combination of text and numbers. In this example, the numbers follow the text, but we will also see an example where the numbers precede the text.

	A	B
1	Reference	Number
2	CARV59	
3	ARB12	
4	FY528	
5	WOOD2	
6	PEX49	
7	MA210	
8		

Figure 5-10. *References that contain a combination of text and numbers*

As with all the examples so far, a key task is to locate the beginning and/or end of the characters to extract. Once this is known, the LEFT, RIGHT, or MID functions can be used for extraction.

The following formula is used to return the position of the first number in cell A2. This is shown in Figure 5-11.

```
=MIN(FIND({0,1,2,3,4,5,6,7,8,9},A2&"0123456789"))
```

	A	B
1	Reference	Number
2	CARV59	5
3	ARB12	4
4	FY528	3
5	WOOD2	5
6	PEX49	4
7	MA210	3
8		

Figure 5-11. *Return the position of the number in the string*

This formula uses the FIND function to find all occurrences of numbers in cell A2. The numbers 0–9 are entered as an array constant by enclosing them in the curly braces.

The reason we search for all the numbers is because we do not know which numbers are in the cell.

If a number is not found, the FIND function returns the #VALUE! error. To prevent this, the string containing all numbers is appended to the value in cell A2. This part of the formula is shown in bold as follows:

```
=MIN(FIND({0,1,2,3,4,5,6,7,8,9},A2&"0123456789"))
```

The FIND function returns an array containing the position of all ten numbers 0–9. This result is shown as follows:

```
=MIN({7,8,9,10,11,5,13,14,15,6})
```

Because the formula returns the position of all the numbers, the MIN function is used to return the smallest value in the array (the first number). In this example, it is number 5, which coincidentally is in position 5 of cell A2.

To return the numbers from the references, the following formula is used. This is shown in Figure 5-12.

```
=RIGHT(A2,
LEN(A2)-MIN(FIND({0,1,2,3,4,5,6,7,8,9},A2&"0123456789"))+1
)
```

This formula uses the same technique used in example 2. To calculate the number of characters to return, the position of the first number is subtracted from the total number of characters in the cell. The +1 is added to extract the first number too. For example, there are six characters in cell A2, minus the position of the first number (position 5) equals one. Then add one to this result to include that first number. Cell A2 contains two numbers.

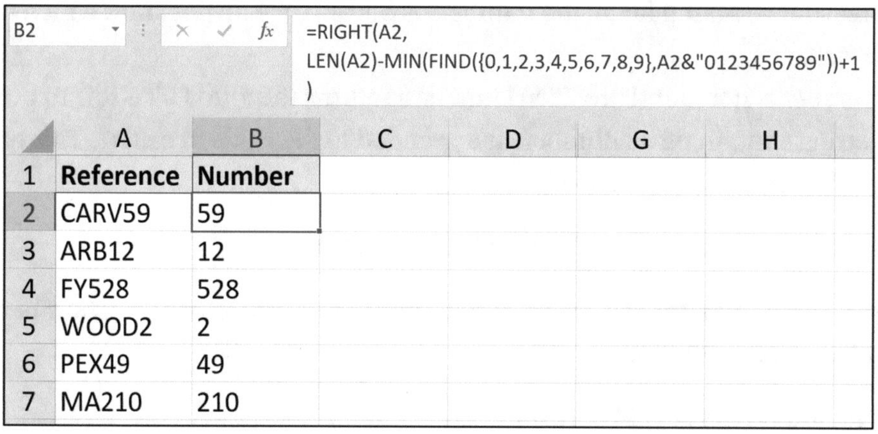

B2 =RIGHT(A2,
LEN(A2)-MIN(FIND({0,1,2,3,4,5,6,7,8,9},A2&"0123456789"))+1
)

	A	B	C	D	G	H
1	**Reference**	**Number**				
2	CARV59	59				
3	ARB12	12				
4	FY528	528				
5	WOOD2	2				
6	PEX49	49				
7	MA210	210				

Figure 5-12. *Extract the numbers from the end of a string*

If you wanted to extract the letters at the start of the references, you can use the following formula (Figure 5-13):

```
=LEFT(A2,
MIN(FIND({0,1,2,3,4,5,6,7,8,9},A2&"0123456789"))-1
)
```

The same formula is used to return the position of the first number. But this time we use the technique shown in example 1 to extract the characters before the found character.

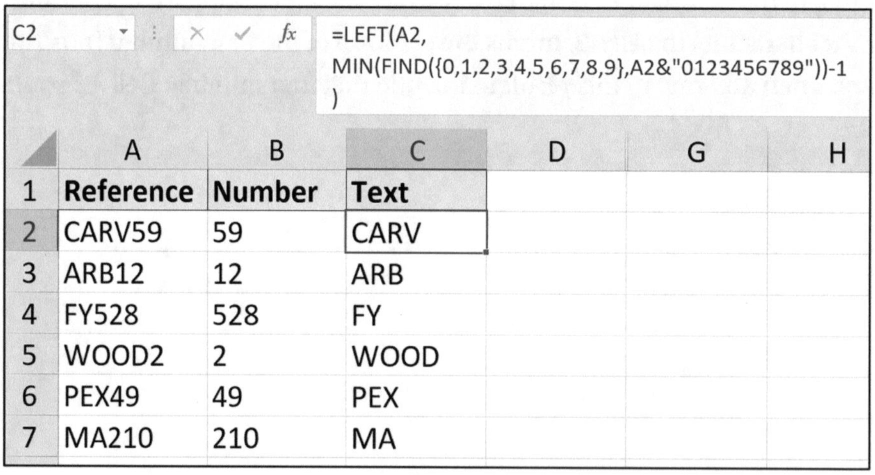

C2 =LEFT(A2,
MIN(FIND({0,1,2,3,4,5,6,7,8,9},A2&"0123456789"))-1
)

	A	B	C	D	G	H
1	**Reference**	**Number**	**Text**			
2	CARV59	59	CARV			
3	ARB12	12	ARB			
4	FY528	528	FY			
5	WOOD2	2	WOOD			
6	PEX49	49	PEX			
7	MA210	210	MA			

Figure 5-13. *Extract the letters from the start of a string*

In an example when the numbers precede the text (Figure 5-14), we can reverse the formula that returns the position of the numbers to return the position of the letters.

E	F
Reference	**Number**
2BGH	
4156HJ	
23J	
119SSS	
92DCQ	
8LC	

Figure 5-14. *References that contain numbers before text*

The following formula looks a little crazy; however, it is the same as before but looking for letters instead. This formula will return the position of the first letter:

```
MIN(SEARCH({"a","b","c","d","e","f","g","h","I","j","k","l","m","n","o","p",
"q","r","s","t","u","v","w","x","y","z"},
E2&"abcdefghijklmnopqrstuvwxyz"))
```

It is flexible, so if you were only looking for specific letters, you would only need to include them. They would be included in the array of letters you are looking for and the string that is appended to the value of cell E2.

This formula can be nested within the LEFT function to return the numbers at the start of the string (Figure 5-15):

```
=LEFT(E2,
MIN(SEARCH({"a","b","c","d","e","f","g","h","I","j","k","l","m","n","o",
"p","q","r","s","t","u","v","w","x","y","z"},
E2&"abcdefghijklmnopqrstuvwxyz"))-1
)
```

```
=LEFT(E2,
MIN(SEARCH({"a","b","c","d","e","f","g","h","I","j","k","l","m","n","o","p","q","r","s","t","u","v","w","x","y","z"},
E2&"abcdefghijklmnopqrstuvwxyz"))-1
)
```

C	D	E	F	G	H	I	J	K	L	M
		Reference	Number							
		2BGH	2							
		4156HJ	4156							
		23J	23							
		119SSS	119							
		92DCQ	92							
		8LC	8							

Figure 5-15. *Extract the numbers from the start of the string*

It could also be used as before to extract the text at the end of the references, if required.

Note This formula used the SEARCH function, so the case of the letters did not matter. If the FIND function was used, the letter would need to have matched the case it was entered into the formula. This was lowercase in the example.

Change the Case of Text

Availability: All versions

There are three functions in Excel for changing the case of text – UPPER, LOWER, and PROPER. They are very simple to use and follow the same syntax.

Each of the functions asks only one argument – the text to convert. The following syntax is for the UPPER function but applies to all three functions, as you only need to change the function name:

`=UPPER(text)`

In the following example, we have a list of country names and need to correct their case to proper case. In this case, the first letter is in uppercase, and the remaining letters are lowercase.

The following formula is used in column B to convert the names to proper case (Figure 5-16):

=PROPER(A2)

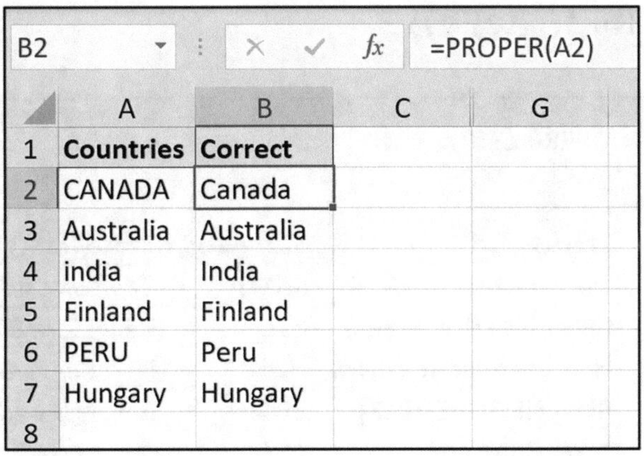

B2	▼ :	× ✓	fx	=PROPER(A2)	

	A	B	C	G
1	**Countries**	**Correct**		
2	CANADA	Canada		
3	Australia	Australia		
4	india	India		
5	Finland	Finland		
6	PERU	Peru		
7	Hungary	Hungary		
8				

Figure 5-16. *Convert text to proper case*

As you can see, these functions are very simple to use. So, let's use them with other functions we learned earlier.

In this example (Figure 5-17), the UPPER function is used to convert text to uppercase. The text being converted is extracted from between the brackets using the LEFT and RIGHT combination we saw earlier:

=UPPER(LEFT(RIGHT(D2,4),3))

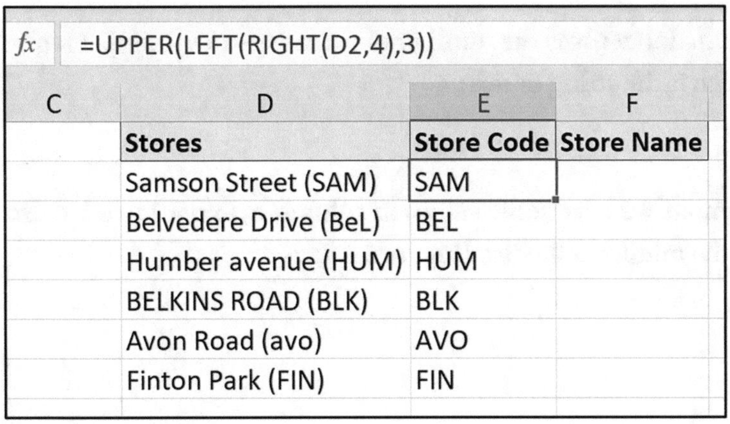

fx	=UPPER(LEFT(RIGHT(D2,4),3))		

C	D	E	F
	Stores	**Store Code**	**Store Name**
	Samson Street (SAM)	SAM	
	Belvedere Drive (BeL)	BEL	
	Humber avenue (HUM)	HUM	
	BELKINS ROAD (BLK)	BLK	
	Avon Road (avo)	AVO	
	Finton Park (FIN)	FIN	

Figure 5-17. *Convert extracted text to uppercase*

Continuing with the same data, the PROPER function is then used to convert the store name to proper case (Figure 5-18).

This formula converts the text that is extracted before the opening bracket using a typical LEFT and FIND combination:

`=PROPER(LEFT(D2,FIND("(",D2)-2))`

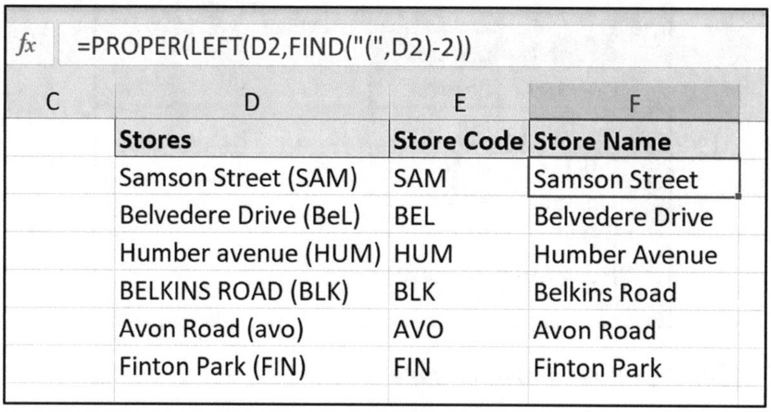

fx	=PROPER(LEFT(D2,FIND("(",D2)-2))		
C	D	E	F
	Stores	**Store Code**	**Store Name**
	Samson Street (SAM)	SAM	Samson Street
	Belvedere Drive (BeL)	BEL	Belvedere Drive
	Humber avenue (HUM)	HUM	Humber Avenue
	BELKINS ROAD (BLK)	BLK	Belkins Road
	Avon Road (avo)	AVO	Avon Road
	Finton Park (FIN)	FIN	Finton Park

Figure 5-18. *Convert extracted text to proper case*

The LEN Function

Availability: All versions

We have used the LEN function in this book already to assist us in extracting an irregular number of characters from a string. Let's give it a special focus and see another example.

The LEN function returns the number of characters in a string. It requires only one argument, which is the string or text:

`=LEN(text)`

In this example, we have some values in column A, and we need to extract the number from the middle of the text (Figure 5-19).

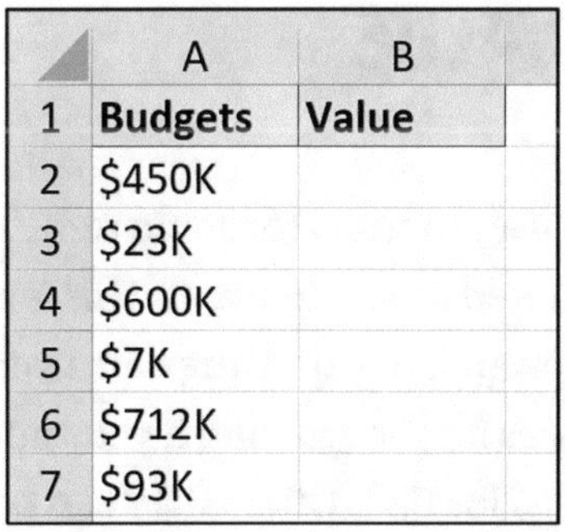

	A	B
1	**Budgets**	**Value**
2	$450K	
3	$23K	
4	$600K	
5	$7K	
6	$712K	
7	$93K	

Figure 5-19. *Values bookended by different text characters*

The values have a character at each end of the string that is not required. The number has a fixed starting position of the second character, but an irregular length.

To calculate the number of characters in the value, we will use LEN to calculate the total number of characters in the string and minus two. This will work as we need all characters except two ($ and K).

The following formula is used in column B (Figure 5-20):

```
=MID(A2,2,LEN(A2)-2)
```

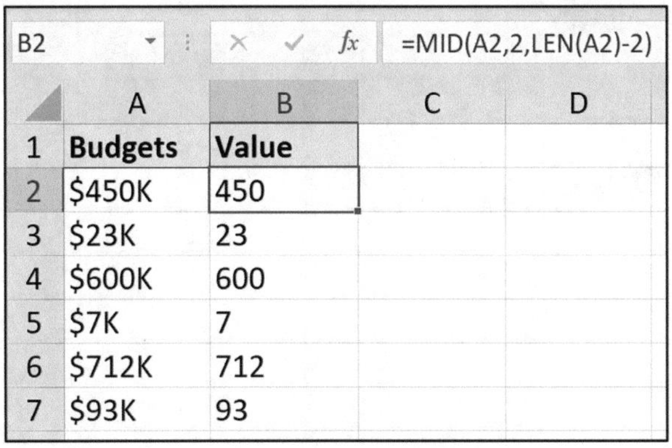

B2	▾ : × ✓ *fx*	=MID(A2,2,LEN(A2)-2)		
	A	B	C	D
1	**Budgets**	**Value**		
2	$450K	450		
3	$23K	23		
4	$600K	600		
5	$7K	7		
6	$712K	712		
7	$93K	93		

Figure 5-20. *Values extracted with MID and LEN*

Convert Text to a VALUE

Availability: All versions

If you have been a regular user of Excel for some time, I'm confident you have experienced numbers being stored as text in Excel. This is a common occurrence especially when copying and pasting or exporting data from other programs.

There are various techniques for recognizing if your numbers have been stored as text, including functions such as ISTEXT. Often, they can be identified easier than that.

Firstly, Excel stores text on the left of a cell and numbers on the right. This is only a clue, as anyone could easily format your numbers to align left and vice versa. But this is often adequate.

Another quick approach is to select the range and look to the quick calculations in the Status Bar (Figure 5-21). If Excel does not sum the values, they must be stored as text.

To convert text values to numeric values using a formula, the VALUE function can be used. This is a simple function that only requires the text to convert:

=VALUE(text)

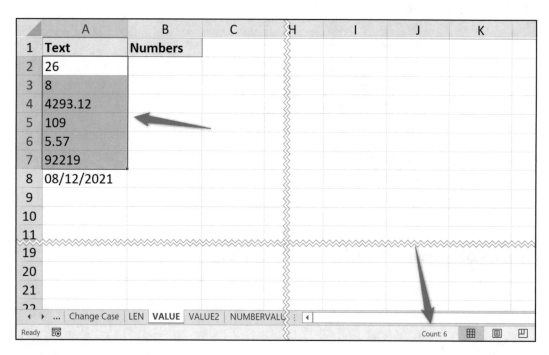

Figure 5-21. *Numbers being stored as text*

The following formula is used in column B to convert the text values to numeric values (Figure 5-22). The necessary formatting can then be applied to the range.

=VALUE(A2)

In this example, you can see that the VALUE function even converted the date in cell A8 to a serial number and handled the values containing decimal points.

Note   The VALUE function recognized the decimal points as my locale is the UK, and the decimal separator used here is the point. The NUMBERVALUE function allows you to specify a decimal separator, so this is better for numbers outside of your locale.

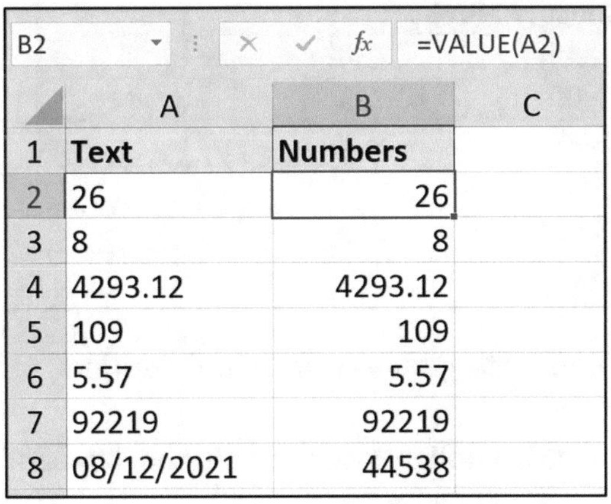

B2		⋮	×	✓	*fx*	=VALUE(A2)	

	A	B	C
1	Text	Numbers	
2	26	26	
3	8	8	
4	4293.12	4293.12	
5	109	109	
6	5.57	5.57	
7	92219	92219	
8	08/12/2021	44538	

Figure 5-22. *VALUE used to convert the text to numbers*

Using the VALUE function to convert text to numbers is useful, but in a scenario like this, there are many non-formula approaches that may have been quicker and more useful.

Note   Other techniques to convert text values to numbers quickly include Text to Columns and Paste Special.

The VALUE function truly excels when converting formula results to numeric values.

There have been a few examples in this chapter when we have extracted numbers from cell values. Because text functions such as LEFT, RIGHT, and MID have been used, the result is stored as text.

Now, not all numbers need to be converted to numbers. Examples of this include street numbers, phone numbers, and IP numbers. However, if you require the result to be a number, the VALUE function can be used to convert them.

In Figure 5-23, the VALUE function is wrapped around the MID function to convert the monetary value to a number:

```
=VALUE(MID(A2,2,LEN(A2)-2))
```

B2	▼	:	×	✓	fx	=VALUE(MID(A2,2,LEN(A2)-2))		
	A		B		C	D		E
1	**Budgets**		**Value**					
2	$450K		450					
3	$23K		23					
4	$600K		600					
5	$7K		7					
6	$712K		712					
7	$93K		93					

Figure 5-23. *VALUE converting the results of a formula*

This number represents US dollars and is also in the thousands. Custom number formatting can be used to present it correctly. Or the result could be multiplied by 1000 to get the true number:

```
=VALUE(MID(A2,2,LEN(A2)-2))*1000
```

The NUMBERVALUE Function

Availability: Excel 2013, Excel 2016, Excel 2019, Excel 2021, Excel for Microsoft 365 and Excel for the Web, Excel for Mac 2011, Excel 2016 for Mac, Excel 2019 for Mac, Excel 2021 for Mac, Excel for Microsoft 365 for Mac

The NUMBERVALUE function converts text to a value just like the VALUE function. However, it has a special power. It can convert text to a number in a locale-dependent manner.

This means that the NUMBERVALUE function can be used to convert values that are using a different decimal separator to the one specified in the settings of Excel.

The decimal and thousand separators are determined by your computer's regional settings but can be manually changed within the Excel options, if you often handle data outside of the regional standard.

Excel will not recognize a value as a numeric value if it contains a different decimal separator to the one set within the Excel options. But with NUMBERVALUE, we can convert the decimal and thousand separators to the correct ones.

The NUMBERVALUE function asks for three arguments, although only one is mandatory:

```
=NUMBERVALUE(text, [decimal_separator], [group_separator])
```

- **Text:** The text that you want to convert.

- **[Decimal separator]:** The character used in the text as the decimal separator. If omitted, the locale's decimal separator is used.

- **[Group separator]:** The character used in the text as the group separator. If omitted, the group separator of the locale is used.

In Figure 5-24, column A contains values that use the comma as a decimal separator and the point as the group separator (thousand separator). This is different to my locale settings, so the VALUE function fails to convert them correctly.

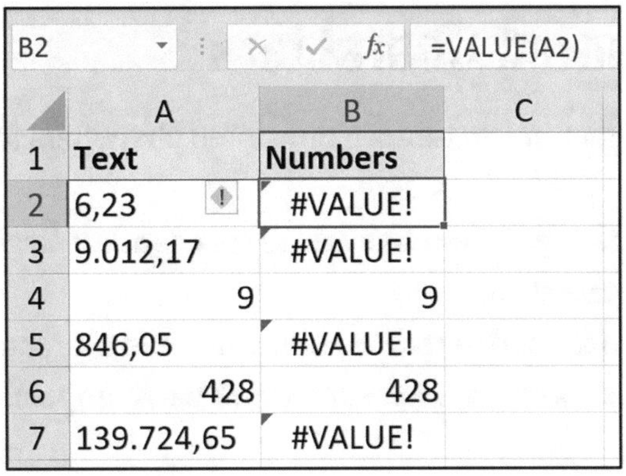

Figure 5-24. *VALUE function fails to recognize the text as a number*

The following formula correctly converts the text values (Figure 5-25). It specifies the decimal and group separators used by the values in column A:

=NUMBERVALUE(A2,",",".")

Note   The Text to Columns feature of Excel can also convert values from other locales. NUMBERVALUE is best deployed to convert the results of formulas or to automate the conversion task.

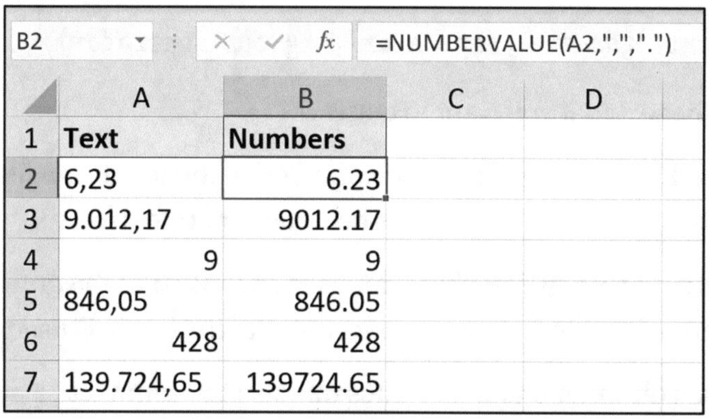

B2		:	×	✓	*fx*	=NUMBERVALUE(A2,",",".")	
	A		B		C	D	
1	Text		Numbers				
2	6,23		6.23				
3	9.012,17		9012.17				
4		9	9				
5	846,05		846.05				
6		428	428				
7	139.724,65		139724.65				

Figure 5-25. NUMBERVALUE with separators specified

Remove Unwanted Characters

Excel has two general functions to remove unwanted characters from a text string. These are TRIM and CLEAN.

The TRIM function is used to remove excess spaces at the beginning, end, or between the words of a text string.

The CLEAN function is used to remove non-printable characters such as line breaks and other characters that appear sometimes when importing data from other applications.

Note   The SUBSTITUTE function is discussed soon. This function is great for removing specific characters. It is more versatile than TRIM and CLEAN.

The TRIM Function

Availability: All versions

Extra spaces in cell values are not an uncommon issue. And because a space is not a visible character, they can be awkward to identify.

The TRIM function performs the very useful and simple job of removing these extra spaces. It will remove spaces before and after the text. It will also remove any extra spaces between each word of the text value, ensuring that there are only single spaces between words.

The TRIM function accepts only one argument. This is the text value to remove extra spaces from:

```
=TRIM(text)
```

In Figure 5-26, column A contains names with erroneous spaces. There is an extra space after the value "Patrick Benson" in cell A2. There are also more notable extra spaces before "Shelley Hopkins" in cell A3 and between the words of "David Carter" in cell A5.

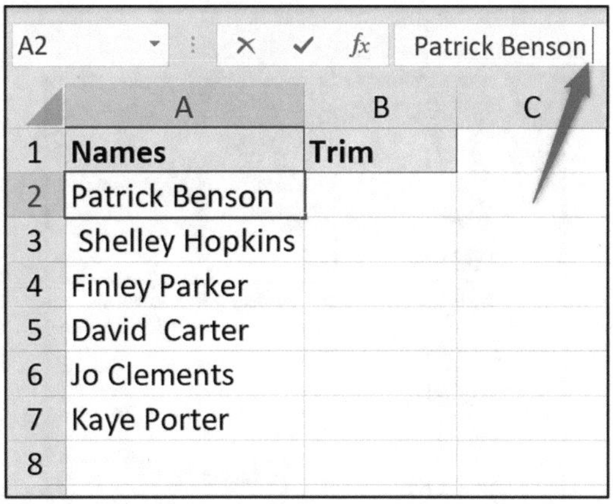

Figure 5-26. *Cell values with erroneous spaces*

The following formula is used in column B to remove these erroneous spaces (Figure 5-27):

```
=TRIM(A2)
```

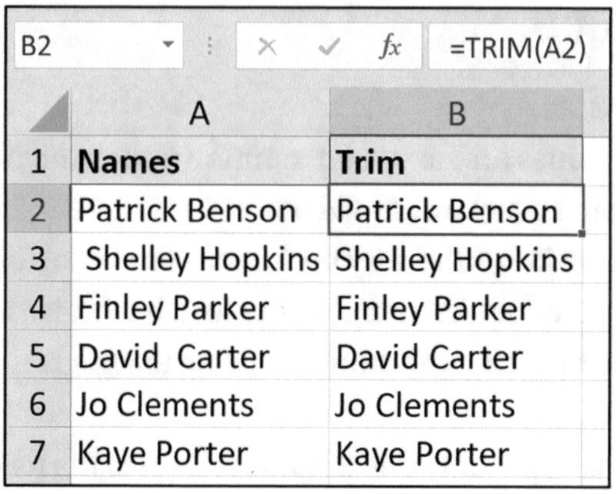

Figure 5-27. *Spaces removed with TRIM*

As with the VALUE function, TRIM is often used with other functions to aid the extraction of characters or some other task.

In Figure 5-28, extra trailing spaces on the end of the values in column D are causing the RIGHT function in the following formula to return incorrect results:

```
=RIGHT(D2,2)
```

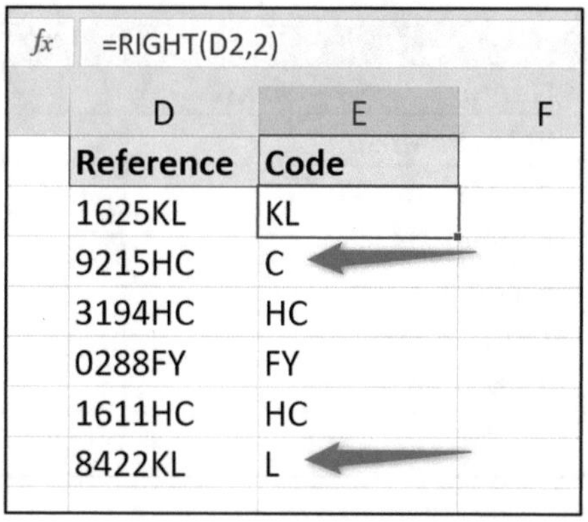

Figure 5-28. *Spaces causing incorrect RIGHT function results*

The TRIM function can be nested within RIGHT to provide a clean text value. The following formula is used in Figure 5-29:

```
=RIGHT(TRIM(D2),2)
```

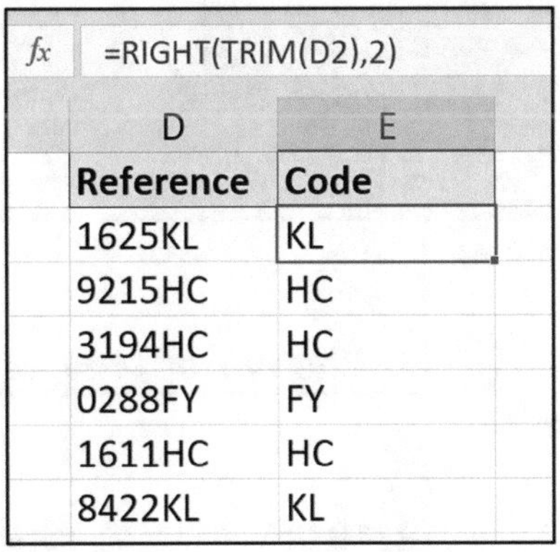

fx	=RIGHT(TRIM(D2),2)

D	E
Reference	**Code**
1625KL	KL
9215HC	HC
3194HC	HC
0288FY	FY
1611HC	HC
8422KL	KL

Figure 5-29. *TRIM providing RIGHT with clean text*

The CLEAN Function

Availability: All versions

The CLEAN function cleans the cell of non-printable characters. It was designed to remove the first 32 non-printable characters from the 7-bit ASCII code.

The CLEAN function has limitations and cannot remove all non-printable characters that may find their way into your Excel data. Most notably, there are characters in the Unicode character set that it cannot remove.

The CLEAN function accepts only one argument, the text value to be cleaned:

=CLEAN(text)

In Figure 5-30, we have addresses in column A that contain line breaks. The following CLEAN function has been used in column B to remove the line breaks from the cell values:

=CLEAN(A2)

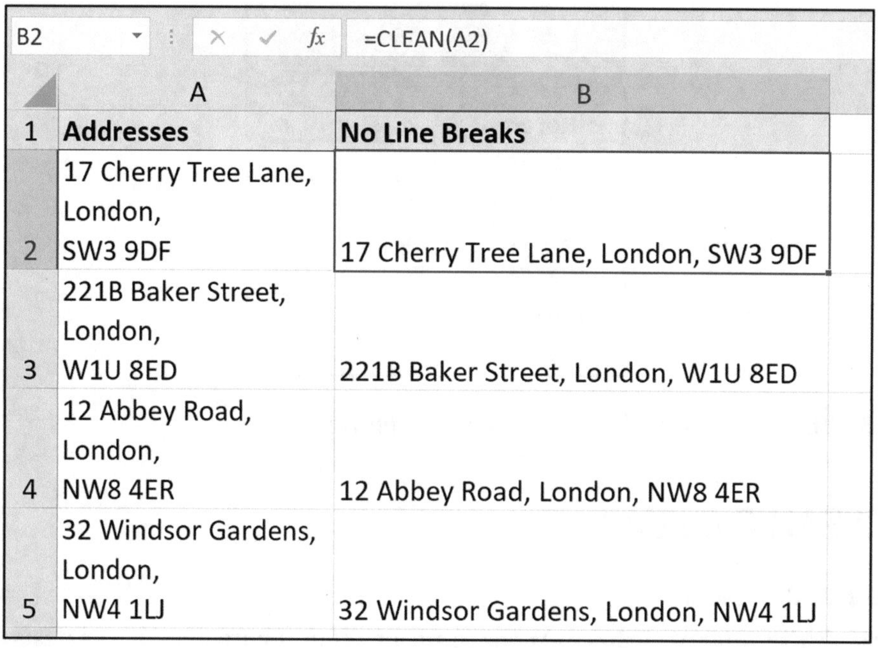

B2	▾	:	×	✓	*fx*	=CLEAN(A2)	

◢	A	B
1	**Addresses**	**No Line Breaks**
2	17 Cherry Tree Lane, London, SW3 9DF	17 Cherry Tree Lane, London, SW3 9DF
3	221B Baker Street, London, W1U 8ED	221B Baker Street, London, W1U 8ED
4	12 Abbey Road, London, NW8 4ER	12 Abbey Road, London, NW8 4ER
5	32 Windsor Gardens, London, NW4 1LJ	32 Windsor Gardens, London, NW4 1LJ

Figure 5-30. *CLEAN removing line breaks from cell values*

Removing line breaks is a classic use of the CLEAN function. Let's see a second example where data has been imported from another source and some undesirable characters have appeared with our data.

In Figure 5-31, a rectangle is shown as Excel cannot correctly display a non-printable character.

The following formula is used to remove these characters:

=CLEAN(D2)

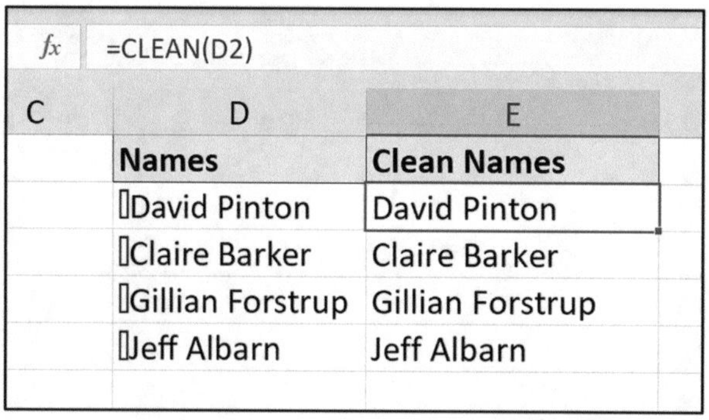

fx		=CLEAN(D2)	
C	D	E	
	Names	**Clean Names**	
	▯David Pinton	David Pinton	
	▯Claire Barker	Claire Barker	
	▯Gillian Forstrup	Gillian Forstrup	
	▯Jeff Albarn	Jeff Albarn	

Figure 5-31. *Remove undesired characters with CLEAN*

SUBSTITUTE and REPLACE Functions

In Excel, there are two functions that can be used to replace existing text within a text string, with different text. These functions are often used to replace, or remove, undesired characters.

These functions are REPLACE and SUBSTITUTE. We will look at both with examples. The SUBSTITUTE function is very useful indeed and has a special power that makes it useful when combined with other functions.

The REPLACE Function

Availability: All versions

The REPLACE function is used to replace text that occurs at a specific position within a text string.

The REPLACE function is similar in its structure to MID but will replace text instead of extracting it. Like MID, it requires the position of the text as an index number and the number of characters to replace.

The syntax of the REPLACE function is as follows. All arguments are mandatory:

```
=REPLACE(old_text, start_num, num_chars, new_text)
```

- **Old text:** The text for which you want to replace characters

- **Start num:** The position of the first character in *old_text* that you want to replace

- **Num chars:** The number of characters to replace

- **New text:** The text that will replace the characters in *old_text*

The REPLACE function can be used to remove characters that you do not need. This offers an alternative to extracting the text that you do need.

In Figure 5-32, the following REPLACE function is used to remove the two middle numbers and one of the hyphen delimiters:

```
=REPLACE(A2,4,3,"")
```

It removes the three characters from the fourth position in the string and replaces it with nothing.

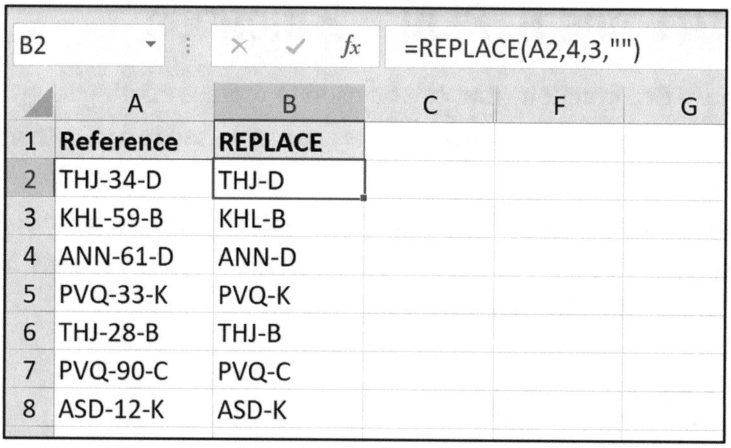

| B2 | ▼ | : | × | ✓ | f_x | =REPLACE(A2,4,3,"") | | |

	A	B	C	F	G
1	**Reference**	**REPLACE**			
2	THJ-34-D	THJ-D			
3	KHL-59-B	KHL-B			
4	ANN-61-D	ANN-D			
5	PVQ-33-K	PVQ-K			
6	THJ-28-B	THJ-B			
7	PVQ-90-C	PVQ-C			
8	ASD-12-K	ASD-K			

Figure 5-32. *Simple REPLACE example*

This next example (Figure 5-33) shows an alternative approach to handling the example from the LEN chapter earlier. The earlier example is simpler, I think. However, this offers a more complex example to show where REPLACE could come in helpful to you.

The following formula has a REPLACE function nested within another:

=VALUE(REPLACE(REPLACE(D2,LEN(D2),1,""),1,1,""))

The nested REPLACE removes the final character (K) in the string. This result is passed to the other REPLACE, which then removes the first character ($). VALUE then converts the result to a numeric value.

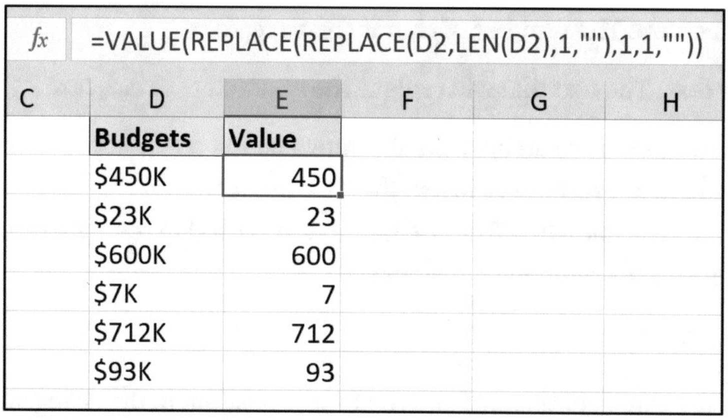

| f_x | =VALUE(REPLACE(REPLACE(D2,LEN(D2),1,""),1,1,"")) | | | | |

C	D	E	F	G	H
	Budgets	**Value**			
	$450K	450			
	$23K	23			
	$600K	600			
	$7K	7			
	$712K	712			
	$93K	93			

Figure 5-33. *Nested REPLACE functions to clean text*

The SUBSTITUTE Function

Availability: All versions

The SUBSTITUTE function will replace, or substitute, specific text in a string with different text. So, the REPLACE function replaces text at a specific position within a string, while SUBSTITUTE will find and replace specific text.

The SUBSTITUTE function can work with a specific instance of the text it is asked to replace, for example, the second or third instance. This feature of SUBSTITUTE is very valuable.

Another important note about the SUBSTITUTE function is that it is case-sensitive. So, it is necessary for the case of the *old text* and *new text* to match exactly. The UPPER, LOWER, and PROPER functions discussed earlier can prove useful in ensuring that the text in these two arguments match case.

The syntax for the SUBSTITUTE function is

```
=SUBSTITUTE(text, old_text, new_text, [instance_num])
```

- **Text:** The text for which you want to substitute characters.

- **Old text:** The text that you want to replace.

- **New text:** The text that you want to replace *old_text* with.

- **[Instance num]:** This is the instance of *old_text* that you want to replace. This is an optional argument. If not specified, all instances of *old_text* are replaced.

Example 1: Simple SUBSTITUTE Example

Let's see a simple example of the SUBSTITUTE function in action before we move on to more advanced examples.

The following formula substitutes the text "London" in the references with the text "LDN" (Figure 5-34):

```
=SUBSTITUTE(A2,"London","LDN")
```

This formula replaces all instances of the text "London" with "LDN," so the optional *instance_num* argument was not needed.

B2	▾	:	×	✓	fx	=SUBSTITUTE(A2,"London","LDN")		

◢	A	B	C	D
1	**Reference**	**Corrected**		
2	72814/London	72814/LDN		
3	891/London	891/LDN		
4	1928/London	1928/LDN		
5	9182/London	9182/LDN		
6	45502/London	45502/LDN		

Figure 5-34. *Simple SUBSTITUTE formula replacing all instances of text*

This demonstrates the basic idea of SUBSTITUTE and how it differs from REPLACE. In this example, the text "London" was at different positions in the references. However, functions such as FIND or SEARCH were not required because we could look for the specific text "London."

Let's take it a step further and replace two text strings in one formula. The following formula has one SUBSTITUTE nested within another (Figure 5-35):

```
=SUBSTITUTE(SUBSTITUTE(D2,"London","LDN"),"Manchester","MCR")
```

The nested SUBSTITUTE replaces the "London" text with "LDN." Then this is passed to the outer SUBSTITUTE to replace the "Manchester" text with "MCR."

fx	=SUBSTITUTE(SUBSTITUTE(D2,"London","LDN"),"Manchester","MCR")			

C	D	E	F	G
	Reference	**Corrected**		
	72814/Manchester	72814/MCR		
	891/London	891/LDN		
	1928/London	1928/LDN		
	9182/Manchester	9182/MCR		
	45502/London	45502/LDN		

Figure 5-35. *Nested SUBSTITUTE to replace two different text strings*

The SUBSTITUTE function is case-sensitive, and if you wanted to ensure that the *old text* and *new text* values were of matching case, the following formula could be used (Figure 5-36):

```
=UPPER(
SUBSTITUTE(PROPER(SUBSTITUTE(PROPER(D2),"London","LDN")),"Manchester",
"MCR")
)
```

This formula uses the PROPER function around the reference to D2 and around the nested SUBSTITUTE function. This ensured that the values "London" and "Manchester" were of the correct case ready to be found and substituted.

The UPPER function was applied at the final step to convert the "Ldn" value back to uppercase, as the PROPER function had temporarily converted it when using the outer SUBSTITUTE to match "Manchester."

=UPPER(SUBSTITUTE(PROPER(SUBSTITUTE(PROPER(D2),"London","LDN")),"Manchester","MCR"))				
D	**E**	**F**	**G**	**H**
Reference	**Corrected**			
72814/Manchester	72814/MCR			
891/London	891/LDN			
1928/London	1928/LDN			
9182/Manchester	9182/MCR			
45502/London	45502/LDN			

Figure 5-36. *Using UPPER and PROPER to work around case sensitivity*

Example 2: Count the Number of Words in a Cell

In this next example, we want to count the number of words in a cell. This is useful for analysis of keywords and other metadata.

The SUBSTITUTE function greatly assists us in this task. Really, our goal is to count the number of spaces and then plus one to that result. The count of words will be one more than the count of spaces.

In Figure 5-37, the following formula is entered in column B:

```
=LEN(TRIM(A2))-LEN(SUBSTITUTE(A2," ",""))+1
```

The first LEN function returns the number of characters in a cell. The TRIM function is added to remove any erroneous spaces.

The second LEN function returns the number of characters once the spaces between each word have been removed. SUBSTITUTE removes the spaces from the text.

The difference between the result of the first LEN calculation and the second returns the number of spaces there are in the cell. One is added to this total to count the number of words.

B2		f_x	=LEN(TRIM(A2))-LEN(SUBSTITUTE(A2," ",""))+1		
	A		B	C	D
1	Words		Number		
2	Excel Formulas and Functions		4		
3	Apress Book Publications		3		
4	Computergaga		1		
5	The SUBSTITUTE Function is awesome		5		
6	I love Excel, it is fun		6		
7	Advanced Excel formulas		3		
8					

Figure 5-37. *Count the number of words in a cell*

Example 3: Use the Instance Number to Extract Text

The *instance num* argument of the SUBSTITUTE function is a special weapon. It has been very useful for me over the years when manipulating data in Excel.

In Figure 5-38, there is a list of URLs, and we want to extract the text from the period " ." to the third slash "/". This is the domain without the www part.

	A	B
1	URL	Site
2	https://www.google.co.uk/	
3	https://www.computergaga.com/	
4	https://www.bbc.co.uk/	
5	https://www.microsoft.com/en-gb	
6	https://www.apress.com/gb	
7		

Figure 5-38. *List of URLs*

The following formula achieves this objective (Figure 5-39). It has been split over multiple lines to make it easier to read:

```
=MID(A2,
SEARCH(".",A2)+1,
SEARCH("@",SUBSTITUTE(A2,"/","@",3))
   -SEARCH(".",A2)-1)
```

The first SEARCH function is performing the simple task of finding the first character after the period ".". This is the beginning of the text to extract.

The third argument of MID to return the number of characters to extract is more complex:

1. The SUBSTITUTE function replaces the third occurrence of a slash "/" with an "@".

2. The SEARCH function searches for the "@" within the results of the SUBSTITUTE function and returns its position.

3. Then the position of the period "." is subtracted from that. And another one is also subtracted.

B2	▾	:	×	✓	fx	=MID(A2, SEARCH(".",A2)+1, SEARCH("@",SUBSTITUTE(A2,"/","@",3)) -SEARCH(".",A2)-1)

	A	B	C
1	URL	Site	
2	https://www.google.co.uk/	google.co.uk	
3	https://www.computergaga.com/	computergaga.com	
4	https://www.bbc.co.uk/	bbc.co.uk	
5	https://www.microsoft.com/en-gb	microsoft.com	
6	https://www.apress.com/gb	apress.com	
7			

Figure 5-39. *Extract the domain from a list of URLs*

Example 4: Return Text After the Last Delimiter

Following on from the previous example, you may not always know the instance number
of the character. You may only know its position relative to the text, for example, the final
instance or penultimate instance.

In this example, we will return the text after the final instance of the delimiter. I often
refer to this as a reverse FIND or SEARCH function as we are searching for the character
right to left instead of left to right.

In Figure 5-40, there is a list of web page addresses, and we want to extract the text
after the last slash "/".

	A	B
1	URL	Page
2	https://www.apress.com/gb/book/9781484264669	
3	https://www.computergaga.com/online-courses	
4	https://www.bbc.co.uk/news/technology	
5	https://techcommunity.microsoft.com/t5/excel-blog/bg-p/ExcelBlog	
6	https://www.howtogeek.com/author/alanmurray	
7	https://techcommunity.microsoft.com/t5/excel/bd-p/ExcelGeneral	
8		

Figure 5-40. *List of web page addresses*

The following formula (Figure 5-41) uses the RIGHT function to extract the final text in each of the values of column A:

```
=RIGHT(A2,LEN(A2)-FIND("*",
    SUBSTITUTE(A2,"/","*",
      LEN(A2)-LEN(SUBSTITUTE(A2,"/","")))
))
```

Let's break this formula down. The first task was to return the total instances of the slash "/" in the text. That is performed by the following part of the formula:

```
LEN(A2)-LEN(SUBSTITUTE(A2,"/",""))
```

You may recognize this, as it is very similar to the technique we used in example 2 to count the number of words in a cell.

We then added to this formula to replace the final instance of the slash "/" with an asterisk "*". This uniquely flags that character ready for the next task:

```
SUBSTITUTE(A2,"/","*",
    LEN(A2)-LEN(SUBSTITUTE(A2,"/","")))
```

	A	B
1	URL	Page
2	https://www.apress.com/gb/book/9781484264669	9781484264669
3	https://www.computergaga.com/online-courses	online-courses
4	https://www.bbc.co.uk/news/technology	technology
5	https://techcommunity.microsoft.com/t5/excel-blog/bg-p/ExcelBlog	ExcelBlog
6	https://www.howtogeek.com/author/alanmurray	alanmurray
7	https://techcommunity.microsoft.com/t5/excel/bd-p/ExcelGeneral	ExcelGeneral
8		

Formula bar: B2   fx   =RIGHT(A2,LEN(A2)-FIND("*",
    SUBSTITUTE(A2,"/","*",
      LEN(A2)-LEN(SUBSTITUTE(A2,"/","")))
))

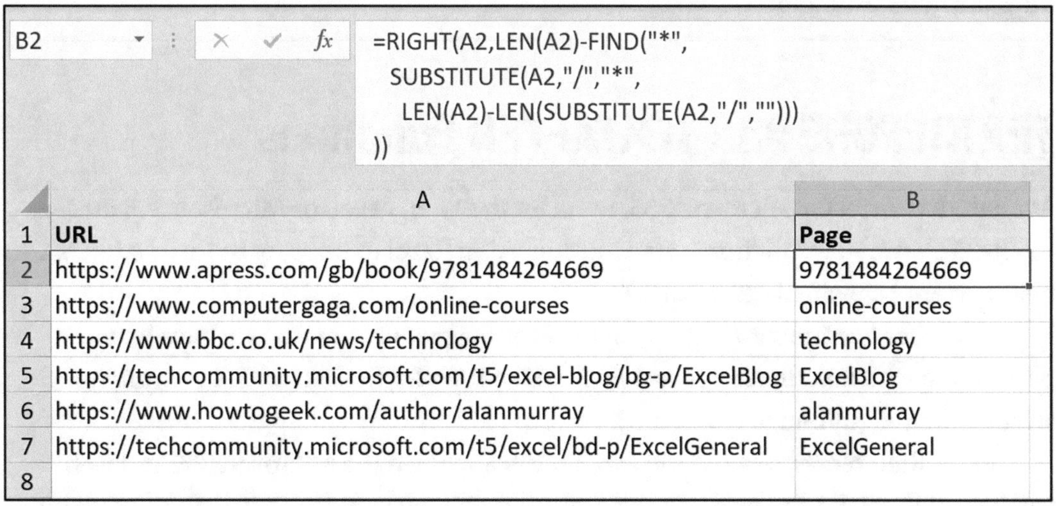

Figure 5-41. *Formula to extract the text after the final delimiter*

Now, we can extract the text after the final slash "/" with the RIGHT, LEN, and FIND function combination. The ??? in the following formula represents the formula from the previous step:

```
=RIGHT(A2,LEN(A2)-FIND("*",
    ???
))
```

FIND returns the position of the "*" flag we set in the previous step, and this is subtracted from the total number of characters returned by LEN.

RIGHT then performs the simple task of returning this number of characters from the end of the text strings in column A.

Note   The FIND function has been used to find the asterisk "*" in this example. If the SEARCH function was used, it would return the wrong results as it treats the "*" as a wildcard character.

To avoid this, precede it with a tilde, for example, "~*", to treat the asterisk as a character, or substitute the slash with a different character such as the "@" like the previous example.

TEXTBEFORE and TEXTAFTER Functions

Availability: Excel for Microsoft 365, Excel for the Web, Excel for Microsoft 365 for Mac

In 2022, two new functions were introduced in Excel to simplify the extraction of text before or after specified delimiters.

With these two functions, many of the formula gymnastics that we have been performing with functions such as LEFT, MID, SEARCH, SUBSTITUTE, etc., are no longer required (although it was fun).

Due to their recent release, they are only available in the Microsoft 365 and web versions of Excel. So, the previous examples are still relevant for compatibility with older versions of Excel.

As their names suggest, TEXTBEFORE will extract the text before a specified delimiter, and TEXTAFTER will extract the text after a specified delimiter.

The syntaxes for the two functions are as follows:

```
=TEXTBEFORE(text, delimiter, [instance_num], [match_mode], [match_end],
[if_not_found])
```

and

```
=TEXTAFTER(text, delimiter, [instance_num], [match_mode], [match_end], [if_
not_found])
```

- **Text:** The text from which you want to extract specific text. This can be entered as a string or be a reference to a range.

- **Delimiter:** The character or text that marks the point before (TEXTAFTER) or after (TEXTBEFORE) which you want to extract.

- **[Instance num]:** The instance number of the delimiter text that marks the point of extraction. For example, enter 2 for the second occurrence of the delimiter. Enter a negative number to search for the delimiter from the end.

- **[Match mode]:** Specify if you want the delimiter match to be case-sensitive. Enter 0 for case-sensitive or 1 for case-insensitive. By default, a case-sensitive match is done.

- **[Match end]:** Specify if you want to treat the end of the text string as a wildcard match. By default, there must be an exact match for the delimiter text or the #N/A error is returned. Enter 0 to specify an exact match of the delimiter or 1 to specify the match to end feature.

- **[If not found]:** The value to return if no match is found. Otherwise, the #N/A error is returned.

Example 1: Text Before or After the First Delimiter

Let's begin with some simple examples of the TEXTBEFORE and TEXTAFTER functions extracting text when there is a single unique instance of a delimiter.

In Figure 5-42, the following formula extracts the text before the "-" delimiter. This is a very simple formula that requires the two mandatory arguments of *text* and *delimiter* only. Much easier than the LEFT and FIND combination used in a previous example to achieve this task.

`=TEXTBEFORE(A2,"-")`

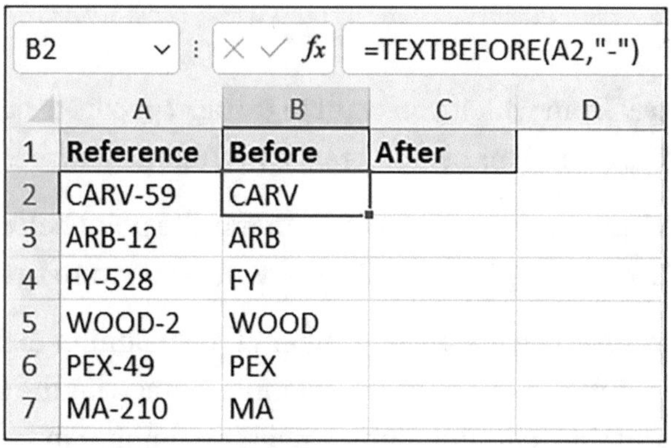

B2	⌄	⋮	× ✓	*fx*	=TEXTBEFORE(A2,"-")

	A	B	C	D
1	Reference	Before	After	
2	CARV-59	CARV		
3	ARB-12	ARB		
4	FY-528	FY		
5	WOOD-2	WOOD		
6	PEX-49	PEX		
7	MA-210	MA		

Figure 5-42. *TEXTBEFORE to extract text before the first delimiter*

In Figure 5-43, the following formula uses TEXTAFTER to extract all characters after the "-" delimiter:

`=TEXTAFTER(A2,"-")`

This is a neat alternative to the combination of the RIGHT, LEN, and FIND functions used earlier in this chapter to extract characters after a delimiter.

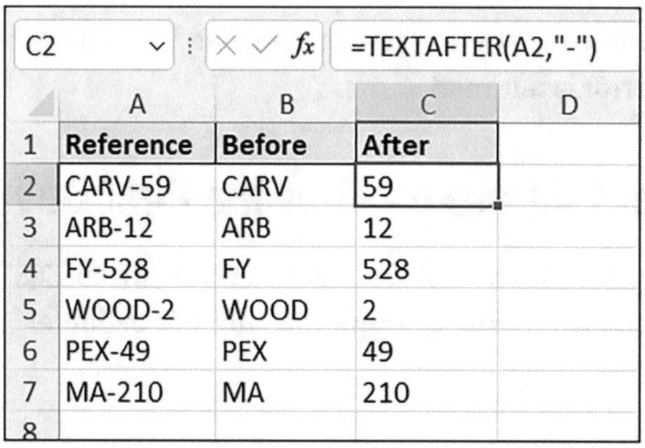

C2	⌄	⋮	× ✓	*fx*	=TEXTAFTER(A2,"-")

	A	B	C	D
1	Reference	Before	After	
2	CARV-59	CARV	59	
3	ARB-12	ARB	12	
4	FY-528	FY	528	
5	WOOD-2	WOOD	2	
6	PEX-49	PEX	49	
7	MA-210	MA	210	
8				

Figure 5-43. *TEXTAFTER to extract text after the first delimiter*

Example 2: Specify an Instance Number

The *instance number* argument of the two functions is very useful when a delimiter occurs multiple times within a string. And both functions allow searching for the delimiter from the end of the string, in addition to a typical approach of searching from the start.

In Figure 5-44, the following formula uses the TEXTAFTER function to return the text after the second instance of the "-" delimiter:

=TEXTAFTER(A2,"-",2)

Note   As shown earlier in this chapter, the SUBSTITUTE function can be used to help extract text before or after a specific instance of a delimiter. This is important for Excel versions without the TEXTBEFORE and TEXTAFTER functions.

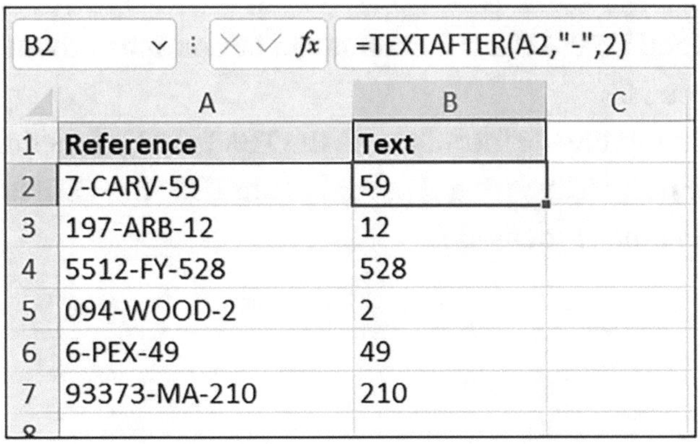

B2	∨ : × ✓ fx	=TEXTAFTER(A2,"-",2)	
	A	B	C
1	Reference	Text	
2	7-CARV-59	59	
3	197-ARB-12	12	
4	5512-FY-528	528	
5	094-WOOD-2	2	
6	6-PEX-49	49	
7	93373-MA-210	210	

Figure 5-44. *TEXTAFTER the second instance of the delimiter*

In the following formula, shown in Figure 5-45, –1 has been entered for the *instance number* argument of TEXTAFTER to extract the text after the last instance of the "/" delimiter (first instance of the delimiter when searching from the end of the string):

=TEXTAFTER(A2,"/",-1)

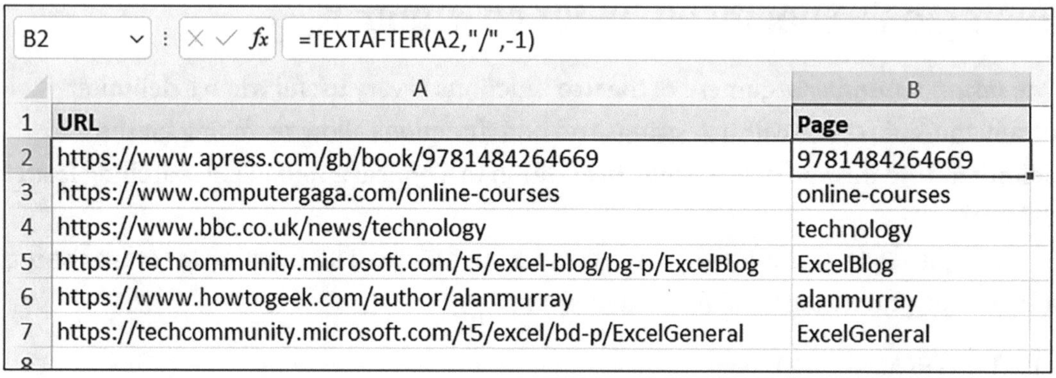

| B2 | ⌄ | : | × ✓ *fx* | =TEXTAFTER(A2,"/",-1) | | |

	A	B
1	URL	Page
2	https://www.apress.com/gb/book/9781484264669	9781484264669
3	https://www.computergaga.com/online-courses	online-courses
4	https://www.bbc.co.uk/news/technology	technology
5	https://techcommunity.microsoft.com/t5/excel-blog/bg-p/ExcelBlog	ExcelBlog
6	https://www.howtogeek.com/author/alanmurray	alanmurray
7	https://techcommunity.microsoft.com/t5/excel/bd-p/ExcelGeneral	ExcelGeneral
8		

Figure 5-45. *TEXTAFTER with instance number from the end of string*

The ability to search from the end of the string made it simple to find the last occurrence of the delimiter and extract the web page from the URLs.

Example 3: Extract Text Between Two Characters

The TEXTBEFORE and TEXTAFTER functions can be combined to extract the text between two characters.

In Figure 5-46, the following formula uses the TEXTAFTER function to extract the text after the "(" delimiter. This string is passed to the TEXTBEFORE function to then extract the text before the ")" delimiter:

```
=TEXTBEFORE(
TEXTAFTER(A2,"("),
")")
```

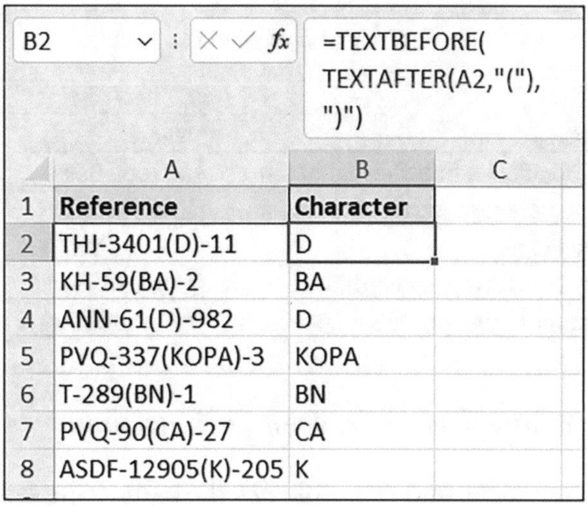

| B2 | ⌄ | : | × ✓ *fx* | =TEXTBEFORE(TEXTAFTER(A2,"("), ")") |

	A	B	C
1	Reference	Character	
2	THJ-3401(D)-11	D	
3	KH-59(BA)-2	BA	
4	ANN-61(D)-982	D	
5	PVQ-337(KOPA)-3	KOPA	
6	T-289(BN)-1	BN	
7	PVQ-90(CA)-27	CA	
8	ASDF-12905(K)-205	K	

Figure 5-46. *Extracting the text between two characters*

In this example, the delimiter characters were unique. If they were duplicated within the string, the *instance number* argument could have been used.

Example 4: Using Match End and If Not Found

There are two different methods available with the TEXTBEFORE and TEXTAFTER functions to handle scenarios when the delimiter being searched is not found. They are the *match end* and *if not found* arguments.

Figure 5-47 shows a formula being used to extract a person's name from a cell containing a person's name and email address separated by a semicolon (;). The TEXTBEFORE function is used as the name occurs before the ";" delimiter.

In cell B4, the #N/A error is returned because the ";" delimiter could not be found.

```
=TEXTBEFORE(A2,";")
```

B2	⌄ ⋮ ✕ ✓ *fx*	=TEXTBEFORE(A2,"; ")	

	A	B
1	**Name & Email**	**Name**
2	Melody Bailie; m.bailie@gts.com	Melody Bailie
3	Eddie Parker; e.parker@gts.com	Eddie Parker
4	Faye Evans	#N/A
5	Leigh Shaverin; l.shaverin@gts.com	Leigh Shaverin
6	Heather Bowen; h.bowen@gts.com	Heather Bowen
7		

Figure 5-47. *Error returned when the delimiter is not found*

Obviously, this is not ideal, and we would like the name to be returned despite the missing semicolon.

In Figure 5-48, the *match end* feature of TEXTBEFORE has been specified by entering a 1 for the fifth argument. The *instance number* and *match mode* arguments have been omitted.

```
=TEXTBEFORE(A2,";",,,1)
```

Enabling *match end* specifies that the end of the text string is used as a delimiter if the delimiter is not found. In this example, the formula continues to successfully return the person's name when the email address is omitted.

B2	⌄ ⋮ ✕ ✓ *fx*	=TEXTBEFORE(A2,"; ",,,1)	

	A	B
1	**Name & Email**	**Name**
2	Melody Bailie; m.bailie@gts.com	Melody Bailie
3	Eddie Parker; e.parker@gts.com	Eddie Parker
4	Faye Evans	Faye Evans
5	Leigh Shaverin; l.shaverin@gts.com	Leigh Shaverin
6	Heather Bowen; h.bowen@gts.com	Heather Bowen
7		

Figure 5-48. *Using match end with TEXTBEFORE*

In a second example of *match end* being used, Figure 5-49 shows the #N/A error being returned when searching for the second instance of the hyphen delimiter, and it is missing from the string.

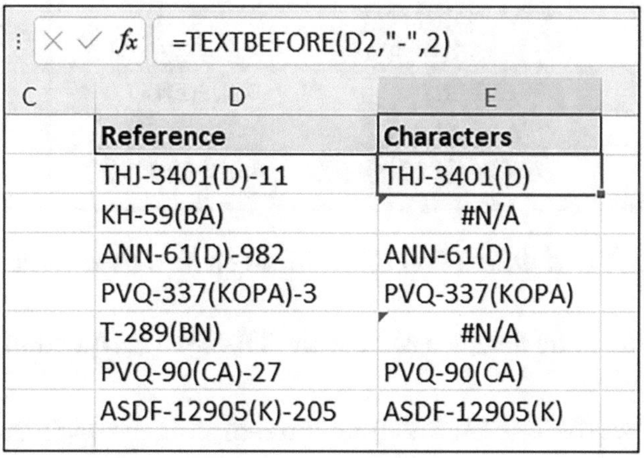

=TEXTBEFORE(D2,"-",2)

C	D	E
	Reference	Characters
	THJ-3401(D)-11	THJ-3401(D)
	KH-59(BA)	#N/A
	ANN-61(D)-982	ANN-61(D)
	PVQ-337(KOPA)-3	PVQ-337(KOPA)
	T-289(BN)	#N/A
	PVQ-90(CA)-27	PVQ-90(CA)
	ASDF-12905(K)-205	ASDF-12905(K)

Figure 5-49. Error returned when the second hyphen is missing

When the hyphen delimiter is missing, the end of the string can be used as an alternative delimiter. So, this is another example where the *match end* argument can be applied successfully.

Figure 5-50 shows the following formula extracting the text before the second hyphen delimiter, whether it is present or not:

=TEXTBEFORE(D2,"-",2,,1)

: × ✓ *fx*	=TEXTBEFORE(D2,"-",2,,1)	

C	D	E
	Reference	**Characters**
	THJ-3401(D)-11	THJ-3401(D)
	KH-59(BA)	KH-59(BA)
	ANN-61(D)-982	ANN-61(D)
	PVQ-337(KOPA)-3	PVQ-337(KOPA)
	T-289(BN)	T-289(BN)
	PVQ-90(CA)-27	PVQ-90(CA)
	ASDF-12905(K)-205	ASDF-12905(K)

Figure 5-50. *Match end with TEXTBEFORE to ensure successful extraction*

Keeping with this same data, we will use the TEXTAFTER function to extract the text after the second hyphen.

Figure 5-51 shows the TEXTAFTER function returning the #N/A error when the second hyphen delimiter does not exist in the string.

```
=TEXTAFTER(D2,"-",2)
```

: × ✓ *fx*	=TEXTAFTER(D2,"-",2)	

C	D	E
	Reference	**Version**
	THJ-3401(D)-11	11
	KH-59(BA)	#N/A
	ANN-61(D)-982	982
	PVQ-337(KOPA)-3	3
	T-289(BN)	#N/A
	PVQ-90(CA)-27	27
	ASDF-12905(K)-205	205

Figure 5-51. *Error with TEXTAFTER due to missing delimiter*

The *match end* argument can also be used with TEXTAFTER (Figure 5-52). In this example, it has been used to suppress the error, because if the delimiter does not exist, then there is no text to extract:

```
=TEXTAFTER(D2,"-",2,,1)
```

		=TEXTAFTER(D2,"-",2,,1)	

C	D	E
	Reference	**Version**
	THJ-3401(D)-11	11
	KH-59(BA)	
	ANN-61(D)-982	982
	PVQ-337(KOPA)-3	3
	T-289(BN)	
	PVQ-90(CA)-27	27
	ASDF-12905(K)-205	205

Figure 5-52. *Match end applied with the TEXTAFTER function*

Let's imagine that the number after the second hyphen represents a version, and if the second hyphen does not exist, it means that it is the first version. So, instead of returning an empty string using the *match end* argument, we would prefer to return the value "1".

In this scenario, using the *if not found* argument would be the better approach, as it allows us to return an alternative value.

In Figure 5-53, the following formula is used to return "1" if the second hyphen delimiter is not found. Otherwise, TEXTAFTER will extract the text as usual:

```
=TEXTAFTER(D2,"-",2,,,1)
```

This formula looks very similar to the previous one. But note that the 1 is entered in the sixth argument (*if not found*) and not the fifth (*match end*).

		=TEXTAFTER(D2,"-",2,,,1)	

C	D	E
	Reference	**Version**
	THJ-3401(D)-11	11
	KH-59(BA)	1
	ANN-61(D)-982	982
	PVQ-337(KOPA)-3	3
	T-289(BN)	1
	PVQ-90(CA)-27	27
	ASDF-12905(K)-205	205

Figure 5-53. *If not found argument used to return an alternative value*

The TEXTSPLIT Function

Availability: Excel for Microsoft 365, Excel for the Web, Excel for Microsoft 365 for Mac

Another new function released in 2022, and therefore only available on Microsoft 365 and the web versions of Excel, is TEXTSPLIT. This function has been eagerly anticipated by Excel users.

The TEXTSPLIT function splits text into multiple columns and/or rows at each instance of specified delimiters.

At its core, it is a formula alternative to the Text to Columns feature of Excel. The two are not directly comparable as they both contain some functionality that the other does not. But conceptually, it is the case.

Note   TEXTSPLIT is an array function. The topic of dynamic arrays is not covered in detail until Chapter 10. However, it was logical to cover TEXTSPLIT at this point in the book. If you are not familiar with dynamic arrays in Excel, jump to Chapter 10 for a quick read through the basics.

This is the syntax for the TEXTSPLIT function:

```
=TEXTSPLIT(text, col_delimiter, [row_delimiter], [ignore_empty], [match_
mode], [pad_with])
```

- **Text:** The text that you want to split.

- **Col delimiter:** The character or text that determines where to split into columns. An array containing multiple delimiters can be used. This argument is optional. If omitted, a row delimiter must be provided.

- **[Row delimiter]:** The character or text that determines where to split into rows. An array containing multiple delimiters can be used. If omitted, a column delimiter must be provided.

- **[Ignore empty]:** Specify if you want to return a blank cell when two delimiters are consecutive. Enter FALSE to return the blank cell or TRUE to ignore the empty string and not return the blank cell. By default, the blank cell is returned.

- **[Match mode]:** Specify if you want the delimiter match to be case-sensitive. Enter 0 for case-sensitive or 1 for case-insensitive. By default, a case-sensitive match is done.

- **[Pad with]:** When data is missing, the #N/A error is returned to pad the cells that are missing data. Enter an alternative value to pad with to replace the #N/A error.

Example 1: Simple TEXTSPLIT

Let's start with a simple example of TEXTSPLIT in action. In Figure 5-54, the following formula is entered in cell B2 and filled down the cells in range B3:B7:

```
=TEXTSPLIT(A2,"-")
```

It splits the references in range A2:A7 at each occurrence of the hyphen (-) delimiter. An array three columns wide is returned as there are two delimiters.

	A	B	C	D
B2			fx	=TEXTSPLIT(A2,"-")

	A	B	C	D
1	Reference	First	Second	Third
2	7-CARV-59	7	CARV	59
3	197-ARB-12	197	ARB	12
4	5512-FY-528	5512	FY	528
5	094-WOOD-2	094	WOOD	2
6	6-PEX-49	6	PEX	49
7	93373-MA-210	93373	MA	210

Figure 5-54. *Simple TEXTSPLIT across columns with a single delimiter*

Example 2: Using Multiple Column Delimiters

You can specify multiple column, or row, delimiters in the TEXTSPLIT function. The delimiters must be entered in an array.

In Figure 5-55, the following formula is entered in cell B2. It specifies three delimiters: the hyphen "-", opening bracket "(", and the closing bracket ")".

```
=TEXTSPLIT(A2,{"-","(",")"})
```

B2	v : X ✓ *fx*	=TEXTSPLIT(A2,{"-","(",")"})				
	A	B	C	D	E	F
1	Reference	First	Second	Third	Fourth	
2	THJ-3401(D)-11	THJ	3401	D		11
3	KH-59(BA)-2	KH	59	BA		2
4	ANN-61(D)-982	ANN	61	D		982
5	PVQ-337(KOPA)-3	PVQ	337	KOPA		3
6	T-289(BN)-1	T	289	BN		1
7	PVQ-90(CA)-27	PVQ	90	CA		27
8	ASDF-12905(K)-205	ASDF	12905	K		205

Figure 5-55. *Multiple column delimiters with TEXTSPLIT*

In Figure 5-55, the TEXTSPLIT function returned an array of five columns. We only require four columns of values, but five were returned due to the consecutive delimiters of the closing bracket ")" followed by the hyphen "-" near the end of the string.

To prevent the blank cell from being returned, the *ignore empty* argument can be enabled within TEXTSPLIT.

In the following formula, TRUE has been entered in the fourth argument (*ignore empty*) to ignore the empty string caused by the consecutive delimiters (Figure 5-56). The *row delimiter* argument has been omitted.

```
=TEXTSPLIT(A2,{"-","(",")"},,TRUE)
```

B2	v : X ✓ *fx*	=TEXTSPLIT(A2,{"-","(",")"},,TRUE)			
	A	B	C	D	E
1	Reference	First	Second	Third	Fourth
2	THJ-3401(D)-11	THJ	3401	D	11
3	KH-59(BA)-2	KH	59	BA	2
4	ANN-61(D)-982	ANN	61	D	982
5	PVQ-337(KOPA)-3	PVQ	337	KOPA	3
6	T-289(BN)-1	T	289	BN	1
7	PVQ-90(CA)-27	PVQ	90	CA	27
8	ASDF-12905(K)-205	ASDF	12905	K	205

Figure 5-56. *Ignore empty option to prevent the creation of blank cells*

Example 3: Splitting Across Rows (and Columns)

For the TEXTSPLIT function, you can enter either a column or row delimiter. You may even require both. Let's see some examples of this.

In Figure 5-57, we have a cell that contains the details of four different people. For each person, we have a name and an email address.

The detail of each person is delimited by a semicolon and space "; ". And the email address for each person is enclosed by a space and opening bracket " (" to the left, and a closing bracket ")" to the right.

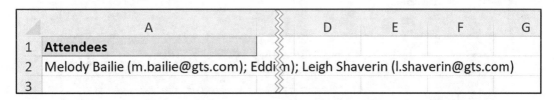

Figure 5-57.   *Data to be split across rows and columns*

In Figure 5-58, the following formula is entered in cell A5 to return each person's details on a separate row. The *column delimiter* was omitted, and the semicolon and space "; " were entered for the *row delimiter*:

```
=TEXTSPLIT(A2,,"; ")
```

A5	⌄ : × ✓ *fx*	=TEXTSPLIT(A2,,"; ")	
	A		B
1	**Attendees**		
2	Melody Bailie (m.bailie@gts.com); Eddie Parker (e.parker@		
3			
4	**Name**		**Email**
5	Melody Bailie (m.bailie@gts.com)		
6	Eddie Parker (e.parker@gts.com)		
7	Faye Evans (f.evans@gts.com)		
8	Leigh Shaverin (l.shaverin@gts.com)		
9			

Figure 5-58.   *Using the row delimiter with TEXTSPLIT*

This nicely demonstrates that you are not required to specify a column delimiter; however, in this example we do want to split the name and email address into separate columns.

In the following formula (Figure 5-59), the space and opening bracket " (" and the closing bracket ")" delimiters were entered in an array for the *column delimiter*:

```
=TEXTSPLIT(A2,{" (",")"},"; ",TRUE)
```

TRUE was stated for the *ignore empty* argument to prevent a blank cell being created in a third column. This is caused by the consecutive closing bracket ")" and semicolon and space "; " delimiters.

A5	▼ : × ✓ *fx*	=TEXTSPLIT(A2,{" (",")"},"; ",TRUE)	
	A		B
1	**Attendees**		
2	Melody Bailie (m.bailie@gts.com); Eddie Parker (e.parker@gts.com); Faye		
3			
4	**Name**		**Email**
5	Melody Bailie		m.bailie@gts.com
6	Eddie Parker		e.parker@gts.com
7	Faye Evans		f.evans@gts.com
8	Leigh Shaverin		l.shaverin@gts.com
9			

Figure 5-59. TEXTSPLIT with column and row delimiters specified

Example 4: Handling Missing Data

If data is missing, the #N/A error is returned. This is helpful when identifying problems with your data. Figure 5-60 shows the following formula returning the #N/A error in cell B6 due to the missing email address for "Eddie Parker":

```
=TEXTSPLIT(A2,{" (",")"},"; ",TRUE)
```

A5	⌄	⋮	× ✓ *fx*	=TEXTSPLIT(A2,{" (",")"},"; ",TRUE)

	A	B
1	**Attendees**	
2	Melody Bailie (m.bailie@gts.com); Eddie Parker (); Faye Evans (f.evans@gts	
3		
4	**Name**	**Email**
5	Melody Bailie	m.bailie@gts.com
6	Eddie Parker	#N/A
7	Faye Evans	f.evans@gts.com
8	Leigh Shaverin	l.shaverin@gts.com
9		

Figure 5-60. *Error returned due to missing data*

Using the *pad with* argument of TEXTSPLIT, we can return an alternative value to the #N/A error.

The following formula (Figure 5-61) uses the *pad with* argument to return an empty string instead of the error. The *match mode* argument has been omitted.

```
=TEXTSPLIT(A2,{" (",")"},"; ",TRUE,,"")
```

A5	⌄	⋮	× ✓ *fx*	=TEXTSPLIT(A2,{" (",")"},"; ",TRUE,,"")

	A	B
1	**Attendees**	
2	Melody Bailie (m.bailie@gts.com); Eddie Parker (); Faye Evans (f.evans@gts	
3		
4	**Name**	**Email**
5	Melody Bailie	m.bailie@gts.com
6	Eddie Parker	
7	Faye Evans	f.evans@gts.com
8	Leigh Shaverin	l.shaverin@gts.com
9		

Figure 5-61. *Empty string added for the pad with argument to suppress errors*

Combine Text into One Cell

There are multiple functions in Excel that can be used to combine text from multiple ranges, arrays, or strings into one.

This has always been a popular task for Excel users, and with recent advances in the Excel function library and in how Excel handles arrays (Chapter 10), this has become easier and possibly in even higher demand.

Let's have a look at the different functions to combine values into one cell – CONCATENATE, CONCAT, and TEXTJOIN – and how they differ from each other.

The CONCATENATE Function

Availability: All versions

The original function for combining cell values and strings into one is CONCATENATE. It is possibly the most well-known text function in Excel, and I still remember the day (many moons ago) when I first learned it.

The CONCATENATE function prompts you for each of the text strings or cell values that you want to join:

```
=CONCATENATE(text1, [text2], [text3], ...)
```

In Excel 2019, CONCATENATE was replaced by a function named CONCAT. CONCAT can do everything CONCATENATE does, plus it can handle ranges of values, which CONCATENATE cannot.

When you enter CONCATENATE into a cell in a version of Excel 2016 or later, you see the compatibility sign next to its name (Figure 5-62).

Now, do not let that mislead you. Many functions have been replaced over the years and left in Excel for compatibility purposes. CONCATENATE joins that list. It is still very important to understand as it remains an extremely popular function and can be found in millions of spreadsheets around the world.

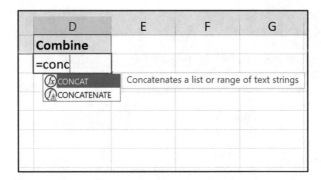

Figure 5-62. *CONCATENATE with compatibility sign*

In the following formula (Figure 5-63), CONCATENATE is used to join the values from three cells into one:

=CONCATENATE(A2,B2,C2)

No delimiter is used to separate the combined values.

D2	▼	⋮	×	✓	*fx*	=CONCATENATE(A2,B2,C2)	

	A	B	C	D	E
1	Part 1	Part 2	Part 3	Combine	
2	TY	9009	S	TY9009S	
3	DF	2652	L	DF2652L	
4	CQ	2131	S	CQ2131S	
5	PD	2637	M	PD2637M	
6	DF	4444	R	DF4444R	
7	CQ	7235	L	CQ7235L	

Figure 5-63. *Combine multiple strings into one with CONCATENATE*

To add delimiters between each part of the text, we will enter them as text enclosed in the double quotations.

In the following formula (Figure 5-64), a hyphen "-" has been used as a delimiter:

=CONCATENATE(A2,"-",B2,"-",C2)

You can enter any text you want within the double quotations to be included in the combined text string. CONCATENATE can handle up to 255 different strings or cell values, so there is more than enough for any scenario.

D2		▾	:	×	✓	fx	=CONCATENATE(A2,"-",B2,"-",C2)		

◢	A	B	C	D	E	F
1	**Part 1**	**Part 2**	**Part 3**	**Combine**		
2	TY	9009	S	TY-9009-S		
3	DF	2652	L	DF-2652-L		
4	CQ	2131	S	CQ-2131-S		
5	PD	2637	M	PD-2637-M		
6	DF	4444	R	DF-4444-R		
7	CQ	7235	L	CQ-7235-L		
8						

Figure 5-64. *Concatenate cell values with delimiters*

Let's see another example; this time, CONCATENATE is being used to change how a name is displayed. This demonstrates its flexibility.

In the following formula (Figure 5-65), the name is displayed as last name followed by the first name and delimited by a comma and space:

```
=CONCATENATE(G2,", ",F2)
```

	fx	=CONCATENATE(G2,", ",F2)	
E	F	G	H
	First Name	**Last Name**	**Combine**
	Frederick	De Santos	De Santos, Frederick
	Carl	Edwards	Edwards, Carl
	Mary	Brown	Brown, Mary
	Lucy	Fox	Fox, Lucy
	Alphonso	Garcia	Garcia, Alphonso
	Emily	Marshall	Marshall, Emily

Figure 5-65. *Reverse names with CONCATENATE*

For our final CONCATENATE example, we will see how to add line breaks into a text string. To do this, we will use the CHAR function with character code 10 – the line break character (character 13 on a Mac).

In Figure 5-66, we have a list of people and their top three preferred locations for something in columns L, M, and N.

The following formula lists these locations in order and concatenates the number and the line break to split each choice on separate lines:

=CONCATENATE("1. ",L2,CHAR(10),"2. ",M2,CHAR(10),"3. ",N2)

When using CHAR(10) in a CONCATENATE formula, you will need to apply wrap text to the cell(s) to split them onto separate lines.

fx	=CONCATENATE("1. ",L2,CHAR(10),"2. ",M2,CHAR(10),"3. ",N2)					
	J	K	L	M	N	O
	First Name	Last Name	First	Second	Third	List
	Frederick	De Santos	London	Dartford	Guildford	1. London 2. Dartford 3. Guildford
	Carl	Edwards	Manchester	Preston	Bury	1. Manchester 2. Preston 3. Bury
	Mary	Brown	Guildford	London	Eastbourne	1. Guildford 2. London 3. Eastbourne

Figure 5-66. *Inserting line breaks with CHAR(10)*

The Ampersand Character

Availability: All versions

An alternative to using the CONCATENATE function is to use the concatenate operator – the ampersand (&).

In the following formula (Figure 5-67), we repeat the example of reversing the names in columns F and G and delimiting them by a comma and space.

f_x	=G2&", "&F2		
E	**F**	**G**	**H**
	First Name	Last Name	Combine
	Frederick	De Santos	De Santos, Frederick
	Carl	Edwards	Edwards, Carl
	Mary	Brown	Brown, Mary
	Lucy	Fox	Fox, Lucy
	Alphonso	Garcia	Garcia, Alphonso
	Emily	Marshall	Marshall, Emily

Figure 5-67. *Reversing the names with the ampersand*

You may have a preference as to whether you use the function or the operator. It is important to understand both, so that you can read and edit formulas that you inherit from other spreadsheet warriors.

The CONCAT Function

Availability: Excel 2016, Excel 2019, Excel 2021, Excel for Microsoft 365, Excel for the Web, Excel 2016 for Mac, Excel 2019 for Mac, Excel 2021 for Mac, Excel for Microsoft 365 for Mac

The CONCAT function was introduced in Excel 2016 to replace the CONCATENATE function. It works in the same way and with the added power of being able to work with ranges.

The syntax for CONCAT is

```
=CONCAT(text1, [text2],...)
```

- **Text:** The text or range of text values that you want to combine into a single text string

If we return to the first CONCATENATE example, when we combined values from multiple cells without delimiters, CONCAT performs this with just one text argument (Figure 5-68):

```
=CONCAT(A2:C2)
```

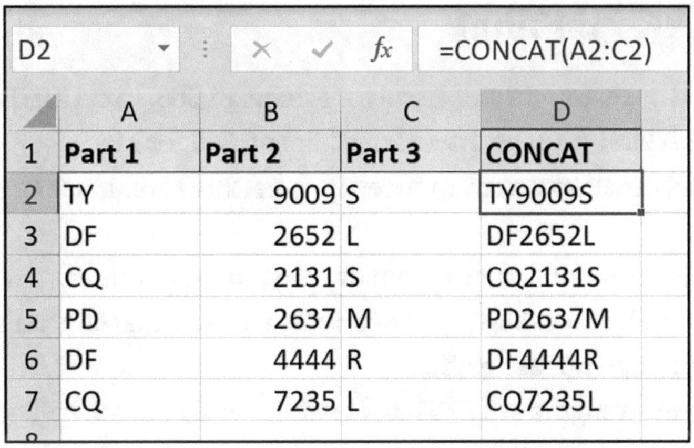

D2 =CONCAT(A2:C2)

	A	B	C	D
1	Part 1	Part 2	Part 3	CONCAT
2	TY	9009	S	TY9009S
3	DF	2652	L	DF2652L
4	CQ	2131	S	CQ2131S
5	PD	2637	M	PD2637M
6	DF	4444	R	DF4444R
7	CQ	7235	L	CQ7235L

***Figure 5-68.** CONCAT function working with a range of values*

This extra skill that CONCAT has over CONCATENATE can come in useful, but it cannot handle delimiters between the different text values of a range neatly. For that job, we will look at the TEXTJOIN function next.

If we did require the delimiters between each of the values, we would use CONCAT in the same way that we used CONCATENATE (Figure 5-69):

```
=CONCAT(A2,"-",B2,"-",C2)
```

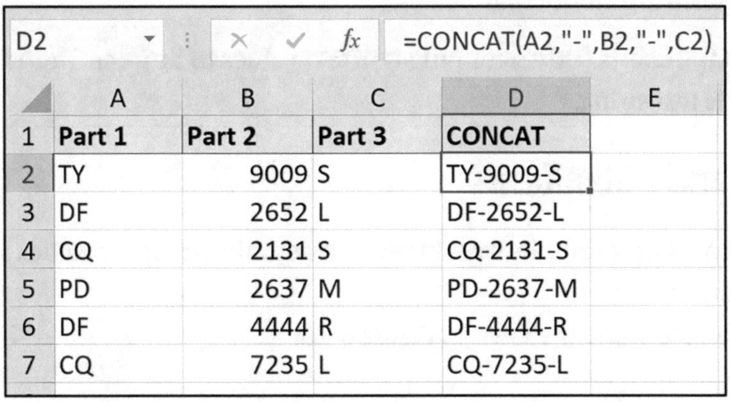

D2 =CONCAT(A2,"-",B2,"-",C2)

	A	B	C	D	E
1	Part 1	Part 2	Part 3	CONCAT	
2	TY	9009	S	TY-9009-S	
3	DF	2652	L	DF-2652-L	
4	CQ	2131	S	CQ-2131-S	
5	PD	2637	M	PD-2637-M	
6	DF	4444	R	DF-4444-R	
7	CQ	7235	L	CQ-7235-L	

***Figure 5-69.** CONCAT with delimiters*

The TEXTJOIN Function

Availability: Excel 2019, Excel 2021, Excel for Microsoft 365, Excel for the Web, Excel 2019 for Mac, Excel 2021 for Mac, Excel for Microsoft 365 for Mac

The TEXTJOIN function was introduced in Excel 2019 and is a fantastic addition to Excel.

It enables us to specify a delimiter, can handle ranges of values, and has an option to ignore empty cells in a range. So, it contains some features that can make it more useful than CONCAT, although not as flexible.

One of the great strengths of TEXTJOIN is when working with spilled ranges. We discuss dynamic arrays and spilled ranges in detail Chapter 10, but we will see an example of TEXTJOIN and arrays soon.

The following is the syntax of the TEXTJOIN function:

```
=TEXTJOIN(delimiter, ignore_empty, text1, [text2], ...)
```

- **Delimiter:** The character to insert between the different text values.

- **Ignore empty:** Would you like to ignore empty values. Enter TRUE to ignore the empty values and FALSE to include them in the resulting string. This is an optional argument, and if omitted, TRUE is applied to ignore the empty cells.

- **Text1, [text2]:** The text or ranges of text values to be joined into a single text string.

TEXTJOIN and Delimiters

For the first TEXTJOIN example, we will use it to combine multiple values separated by the same delimiter.

The following formula is shown in Figure 5-70:

```
=TEXTJOIN("-",,A2:C2)
```

We saw examples of CONCATENATE and CONCAT combine these same values earlier. With TEXTJOIN, the hyphen "-" delimiter needs only to be stated once, and the range of cells is used instead of individual cell referencing – a cleaner alternative to CONCAT.

The second argument has been omitted. This means that blank cells would be excluded from the results, if we had any.

| D2 | ▼ | ⋮ | × | ✓ | f_x | =TEXTJOIN("-",,A2:C2) |

	A	B	C	D	E
1	Part 1	Part 2	Part 3	TEXTJOIN	
2	TY	9009	S	TY-9009-S	
3	DF	2652	L	DF-2652-L	
4	CQ	2131	S	CQ-2131-S	
5	PD	2637	M	PD-2637-M	
6	DF	4444	R	DF-4444-R	
7	CQ	7235	L	CQ-7235-L	

Figure 5-70. *TEXTJOIN handling delimiters with ease*

TEXTJOIN and Empty Values

Let's now see an example of the TEXTJOIN function ignoring empty values in a range that it is asked to combine.

In Figure 5-71, the following formula is used to combine the different parts of these UK addresses. There are blank cells in the range to combine, as those values are not required in the address. TRUE is entered for the second argument to ignore the empty values:

```
=TEXTJOIN(", ",TRUE,F2:J2)
```

=TEXTJOIN(", ",TRUE,F2:J2)

F	G	H	I	J	K
Address 1	Address 2	City	County	Postcode	Full Address
14 Kings Avenue		Warwick	Warwickshire	CV31 8OE	14 Kings Avenue, Warwick, Warwickshire, CV31 8OE
211 King's Mall	Davy Street	London		WC1A 5RD	211 King's Mall, Davy Street, London, WC1A 5RD
5 Finsbury Drive	Kesgrave	Ipswich	Suffolk	IP5 9NX	5 Finsbury Drive, Kesgrave, Ipswich, Suffolk, IP5 9NX
90 Cannon Street		London		EC2 8IF	90 Cannon Street, London, EC2 8IF
Crown House	83 Herald Avenue	Salcombe	Devon	TQ7 1GY	Crown House, 83 Herald Avenue, Salcombe, Devon, TQ7 1GY

Figure 5-71. *TEXTJOIN function excluding empty values*

We saw in the previous example that if the *ignore empty* argument is omitted, the empty values are ignored. So, the following formula also works:

```
=TEXTJOIN(", ",,F2:J2)
```

Although it is not our objective in this example, let's see what the results would look like if the empty values were included.

The following formula specifies FALSE for the *ignore empty* argument, therefore including the empty values (Figure 5-72):

```
=TEXTJOIN(", ",FALSE,F2:J2)
```

You can see that there are duplicated commas in the address ranges that contained blank cells.

=TEXTJOIN(", ",FALSE,F2:J2)					
F	G	H	I	J	K
Address 1	Address 2	City	County	Postcode	Full Address
14 Kings Avenue		Warwick	Warwickshire	CV31 8OE	14 Kings Avenue, , Warwick, Warwickshire, CV31 8OE
211 King's Mall	Davy Street	London		WC1A 5RD	211 King's Mall, Davy Street, London, , WC1A 5RD
5 Finsbury Drive	Kesgrave	Ipswich	Suffolk	IP5 9NX	5 Finsbury Drive, Kesgrave, Ipswich, Suffolk, IP5 9NX
90 Cannon Street		London		EC2 8IF	90 Cannon Street, , London, , EC2 8IF
Crown House	83 Herald Avenue	Salcombe	Devon	TQ7 1GY	Crown House, 83 Herald Avenue, Salcombe, Devon, TQ7 1GY

Figure 5-72. *TEXTJOIN with empty values included*

TEXTJOIN and Arrays

TEXTJOIN can combine the values from arrays with ease, which makes it especially useful in modern Excel.

In Figure 5-73, we have a table named [Offices] that contains a list of office locations and the continent they are located in. Column D contains a distinct list of the continents, and we want to list all the offices for each continent in the cells of column E separated by a comma and a space.

	A	B	C	D	E
1	**Continent**	**Office**		**Continent**	**Offices**
2	Europe	Brussels		Africa	
3	North America	Chicago		Asia	
4	Asia	Delhi		Europe	
5	Africa	Laos		North America	
6	Europe	London			
7	Europe	Reykjavik			
8	North America	Toronto			
9	Europe	Zurich			
10					

Figure 5-73. *Combine the offices for each continent into a single cell*

The following formula uses an IF function to only return the offices for the continent specified in that row, otherwise return an empty value. These offices are returned in an array which TEXTJOIN combines into a single cell and ignores the empty values (Figure 5-74).

```
=TEXTJOIN(", ",,IF(Offices[Continent]=D2,Offices[Office],""))
```

E2	▼	:	×	✓	*fx*	=TEXTJOIN(", ",,IF(Offices[Continent]=D2,Offices[Office],""))

	A	B	C	D	E
1	**Continent**	**Office**		**Continent**	**Offices**
2	Europe	Brussels		Africa	Laos
3	North America	Chicago		Asia	Delhi
4	Asia	Delhi		Europe	Brussels, London, Reykjavik, Zurich
5	Africa	Laos		North America	Chicago, Toronto
6	Europe	London			
7	Europe	Reykjavik			
8	North America	Toronto			
9	Europe	Zurich			
10					

Figure 5-74. *Combining values from an array with TEXTJOIN*

> **Note**   If you are using a version of Excel that is not Excel for Microsoft 365, Excel 2021, or Excel for the Web, you will need to press Ctrl + Shift + Enter to run the formula instead of just Enter.
>
> This is an array formula, and handling arrays was only built into Excel after the 2019 version. Curly braces will be added around the formula if you press Ctrl + Shift + Enter.

The TEXT Function

Availability: All versions

The TEXT function is used to convert a value to text but apply a specific number format, such as a date in dd/mm/yyyy format, or display a text value as Euros with no decimal places.

This function is great for creating summary statements and other labels for your Excel reports and dashboards.

This is the syntax for the TEXT function:

```
=TEXT(value, format_text)
```

- **Value:** The number that you want to format.

- **Format text:** The number format enclosed in double quotes that you want to apply. The format code is similar to that used for number formatting in the *Format Cells* window.

In the following example (Figure 5-75), the TEXT function has formatted the number in cell A2 to display a thousand separator with zero decimal places:

```
=TEXT(A2,"#,#")
```

B2	▼	⋮	×	✓	f_x	=TEXT(A2,"#,#")

◢	A	B	C
1	Number	Text Format	
2	25781.63	25,782	

Figure 5-75. *Text formatted as a number using the TEXT function*

The format codes used to format values with the TEXT function are similar to those used to format values in the *Format Cells* window. If these are new to you, it may be worthwhile familiarizing yourself with the commonly used symbols.

You can view the format code for a formatted value in the *Type* field of the **Custom** category on the *Number* tab of *Format Cells* (Figure 5-76). You can copy the code from here and paste it into the TEXT function. So, a nice tip is to format the value in a cell how you want and then copy and paste the code into the function.

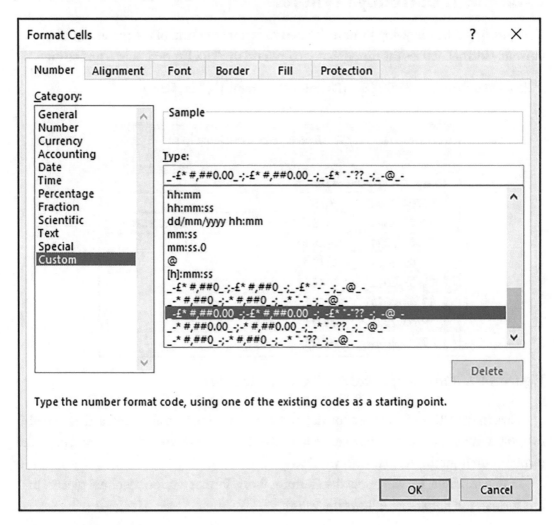

Figure 5-76. *Format codes shown in the Format Cells window*

Taking things up a notch from the previous example, the TEXT function is often given the result of a formula to format and is often combined with an ampersand or the CONCAT function to create a string of text.

Let's see some examples of the TEXT function used in this manner and how it can be used to format different numeric values such as currencies and date formats.

Example 1: Currency Formats

In Figure 5-77, the following formula is used to format the sum of the payments in a currency format. It uses the ampersand to append the TEXT function to a text string:

```
="Payments total: "&TEXT(SUM(Payments[Payment]),"£#,##0")
```

f_x	="Payments total: "&TEXT(SUM(Payments[Payment]),"£#,##0")		

	D	E	F	G
	Date	Payment		
	06/01/2021	3,155		
	12/01/2021	4,930		Payments total: £34,459
	22/01/2021	5,685		
	10/02/2021	2,168		
	04/03/2021	5,464		
	12/03/2021	5,034		
	19/03/2021	4,123		
	27/03/2021	3,900		

Figure 5-77. Currency format applied to a text value

I live in the UK, so applying a format in pounds sterling is straightforward. If I need to apply a different currency format, I can utilize the tip I mentioned earlier and copy the format code from the *Format Cells* window.

In this example, we will apply the German Euros format without decimal places. In this format, the Euros sign follows the value:

1. Open the *Format Cells* window and click **Accounting** in the *Category* list.

2. Select € **German (Germany)** from the *Symbol* list and specify **0** decimal places (Figure 5-78).

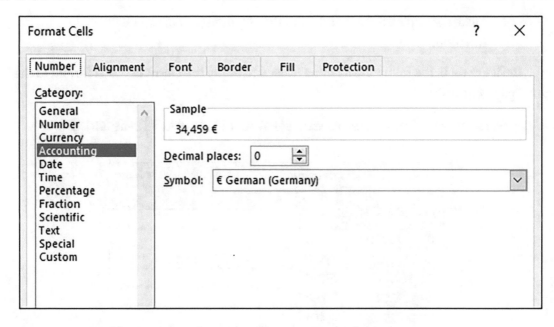

Figure 5-78. *Formatting values in a German Euros format*

3. Click **Custom** in the *Category* list and copy the format code from the *Type* field (Figure 5-79). In this example, I'm only copying the part of the code that is needed.

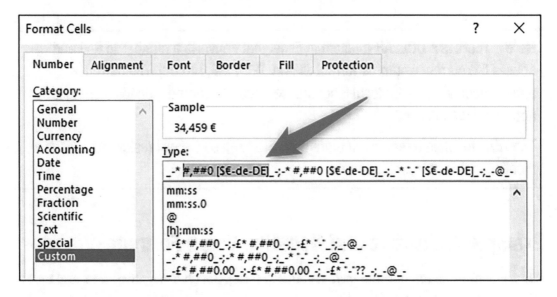

Figure 5-79. *Copy the format code for the TEXT function*

4. Paste the copied format code into the required part of the TEXT function.

In Figure 5-80, the following formula is used to apply the German Euros format to the total payments value:

```
="Payments total: "&TEXT(SUM(Payments[Payment]),"#,##0 [$€-de-DE]")
```

	fx	="Payments total: "&TEXT(SUM(Payments[Payment]),"#,##0 [$€-de-DE]")		
	D	**E**	**F**	**G**
	Date	**Payment**		
	06/01/2021	3,155		
	12/01/2021	4,930		Payments total: 34,459 €
	22/01/2021	5,685		
	10/02/2021	2,168		
	04/03/2021	5,464		
	12/03/2021	5,034		
	19/03/2021	4,123		
	27/03/2021	3,900		

Figure 5-80. *Using the format code in the TEXT function*

Note   There is a DOLLAR function in Excel that converts a number to text and applies the currency number format $#,##0.00_);($#,##0.00). The currency applied depends on your local language settings. So, for me, pounds sterling is applied when it is used.

The TEXT function offers much more than DOLLAR, so we will resign DOLLAR to a mention in this note, and no more.

Example 2: Positive and Negative Value Formats

When creating custom number format codes in Excel, positive, negative, zero, and text values can be displayed differently.

Each format is separated by a semicolon ";" when creating the format codes. Positive values are first, then negative values, then zero values, and finally text values.

In Figure 5-81, the following formula displays negative values with a negative sign. The positive and negative value formats are separated by a semicolon. No format is specified for zero values:

```
=CONCAT("The monthly variance is ",TEXT(J2-I2,"#,#;-#,#"))
```

The CONCAT function has been used to combine the string in this example instead of the ampersand.

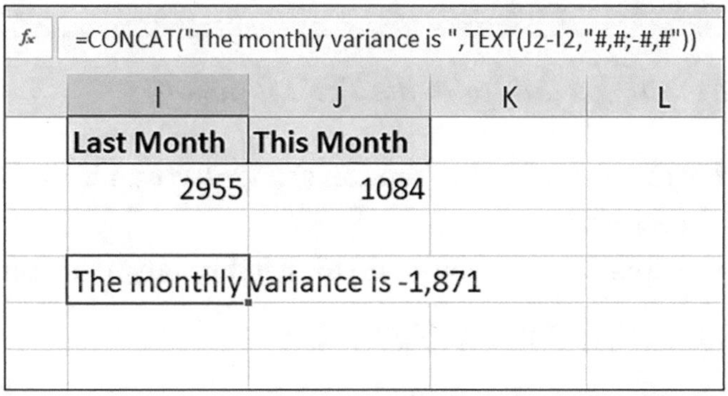

f_x	=CONCAT("The monthly variance is ",TEXT(J2-I2,"#,#;-#,#"))		
	I	J	K	L
	Last Month	**This Month**		
	2955	1084		
	The monthly variance is -1,871			

Figure 5-81. Different formats for positive and negative values

Example 3: Date Formats

Let's see an example of the TEXT function formatting date values. The following formula uses the MAX function to return the most recent date. TEXT then formats this in a dd/mm/yyyy format (Figure 5-82):

```
="Last Transaction date: "&TEXT(MAX(Payments[Date]),"dd/mm/yyyy")
```

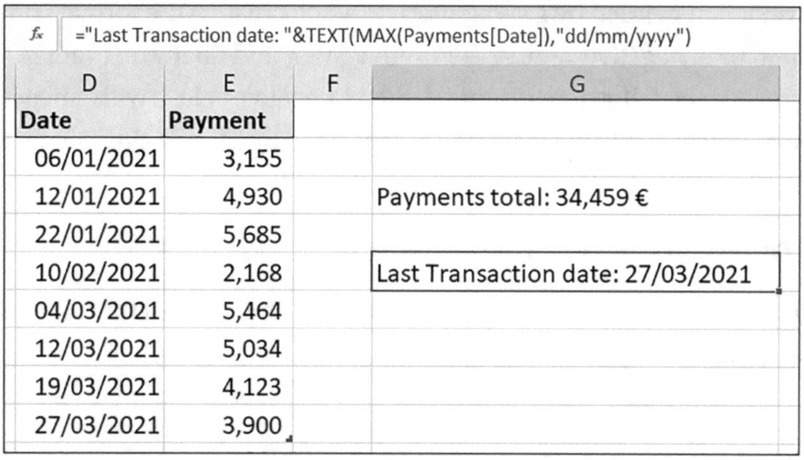

f_x	="Last Transaction date: "&TEXT(MAX(Payments[Date]),"dd/mm/yyyy")

	D	E	F	G
	Date	**Payment**		
	06/01/2021	3,155		
	12/01/2021	4,930		Payments total: 34,459 €
	22/01/2021	5,685		
	10/02/2021	2,168		Last Transaction date: 27/03/2021
	04/03/2021	5,464		
	12/03/2021	5,034		
	19/03/2021	4,123		
	27/03/2021	3,900		

Figure 5-82. *Formatting a date with the TEXT function*

Date formats are easy to work with. You can change the number and order of the d's, m's, and y's to get the format you want.

Here are some alternative ways you could format the date in the last example:

- **Text**: "mm/dd/yyyy" **Result**: 03/27/2021

- **Text**: "dd mmm yyyy" **Result**: 27 Mar 2021

- **Text**: "ddd dd mmm yyyy" **Result**: Sat 27 Mar 2021

- **Text**: "yyyy-mm-dd" **Result**: 2021-03-27

Repeating a Character – REPT Function

Availability: All versions

The REPT function repeats text a given number of times. It is often used to repeat a character in a cell.

Now this might not seem that useful, and you may be wondering why on earth someone would need to do this. That's ok. I thought the same.

The REPT function is typically used to create in-cell charts that work nicely on your Excel reports. You can get creative with the different symbols and other characters in Excel to create some very nice visuals.

The syntax of the REPT function is

```
=REPT(text, number_times)
```

- **Text:** The text to be repeated

- **Number times:** The number of times to repeat the text

In Figure 5-83, the REPT function has been used to repeat the star symbol for the number of star ratings of each site.

The following formula was entered into the cell:

```
=REPT("★",B2)
```

This was changed to the following formula as shown in the image. The symbol is changed dependent upon the font being used:

```
=REPT("«",B2)
```

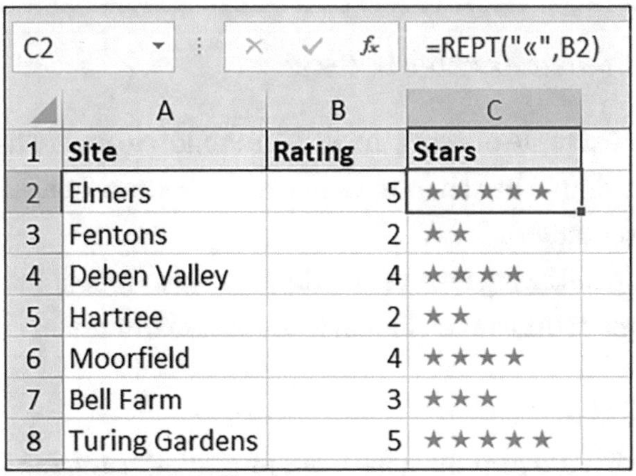

	A	B	C
1	Site	Rating	Stars
2	Elmers	5	★ ★ ★ ★ ★
3	Fentons	2	★ ★
4	Deben Valley	4	★ ★ ★ ★
5	Hartree	2	★ ★
6	Moorfield	4	★ ★ ★ ★
7	Bell Farm	3	★ ★ ★
8	Turing Gardens	5	★ ★ ★ ★ ★

C2   fx   =REPT("«",B2)

Figure 5-83. *Star rating system created with REPT*

To insert the star symbol, it was first inserted to a cell on the worksheet from the *Symbol* window (Figure 5-84). Click **Insert ➤ Symbol** to access the *Symbol* window. This was then cut and pasted into the REPT function as shown before.

The cells containing the formula were then formatted in the Wingdings font to display the star symbol correctly and formatted in a gold font color.

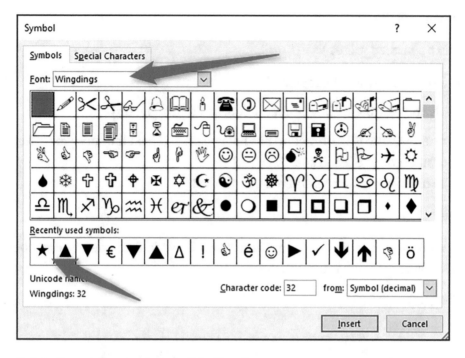

Figure 5-84. *Insert the star symbol in Excel*

Let's see another example of using the REPT function to create in-cell charts. This time, we will create a simple bar chart to visualize the volume of upsells achieved by different sales representatives.

In Figure 5-85, the following formula has been used to repeat the pipe or vertical bar symbol "|" the number of times specified in the Upsells column:

```
=REPT("|",F2)
```

The cells containing the formula have been formatted using the *Playbill* font. This font looks great for these in-cell charts. The gray font color was also applied.

Because these charts are created by repeating characters and using fonts, they are very open to get creative. For example, you can apply Conditional Formatting rules to change font colors if values pass specified thresholds. These give them more potential than Sparklines or the Data Bars of Conditional Formatting.

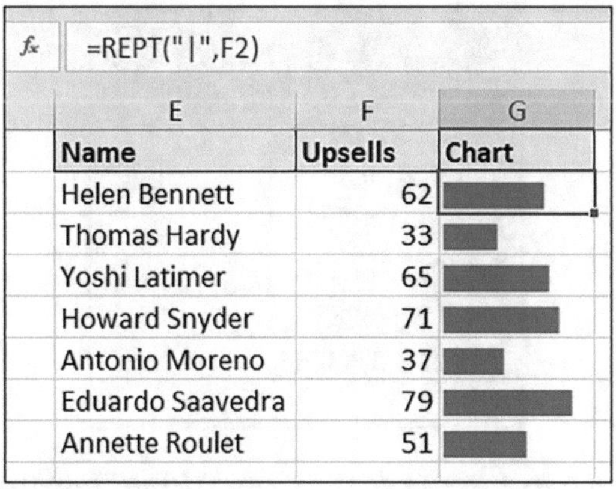

		=REPT("|",F2)

E	F	G
Name	Upsells	Chart
Helen Bennett	62	
Thomas Hardy	33	
Yoshi Latimer	65	
Howard Snyder	71	
Antonio Moreno	37	
Eduardo Saavedra	79	
Annette Roulet	51	

Figure 5-85. *Creating in-cell charts using the REPT function*

Note   If the values to repeat are very large, for example, 1562, you do not want to repeat a character this many times in a cell. To work with this, divide each value by a consistent number. So, the 1562 and other values in that column could all be divided within the REPT function by 10.

Text Functions with Other Excel Features

Let's see examples of how some of the text functions described in this chapter could be used with other Excel features.

Conditional Formatting Rules – Last Character Equals

In this example, we have some codes and want to format those that are external. These are identified by the "E" as the last character in the code (Figure 5-86).

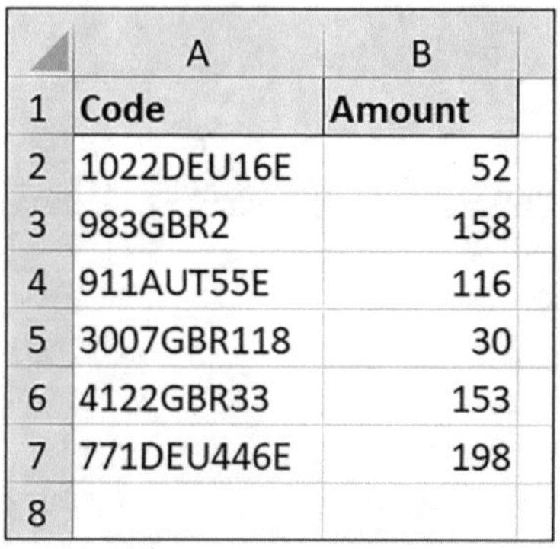

▲	A	B	
1	Code	Amount	
2	1022DEU16E	52	
3	983GBR2	158	
4	911AUT55E	116	
5	3007GBR118	30	
6	4122GBR33	153	
7	771DEU446E	198	
8			

Figure 5-86. *Codes we want to apply the Conditional Formatting rule to*

Conditional Formatting in Excel has a built-in "Text that Contains" rule. This can be useful for partial text matches.

However, it does not help us in this example as we may have codes with an "E" in another position in the code. We specifically want to test only the final character:

1. Select range A2:B7.

2. Click **Home ➤ Conditional Formatting ➤ New Rule ➤ Use a formula to determine which cells to format**.

3. Enter the following formula into the *Format values where this formula is true:* box (Figure 5-87):

    ```
    =RIGHT($A2,1)="E"
    ```

This formula uses the RIGHT function to extract the final character for evaluation. The column is made absolute as we have selected two columns in the range to format but need to focus only on the code column for testing.

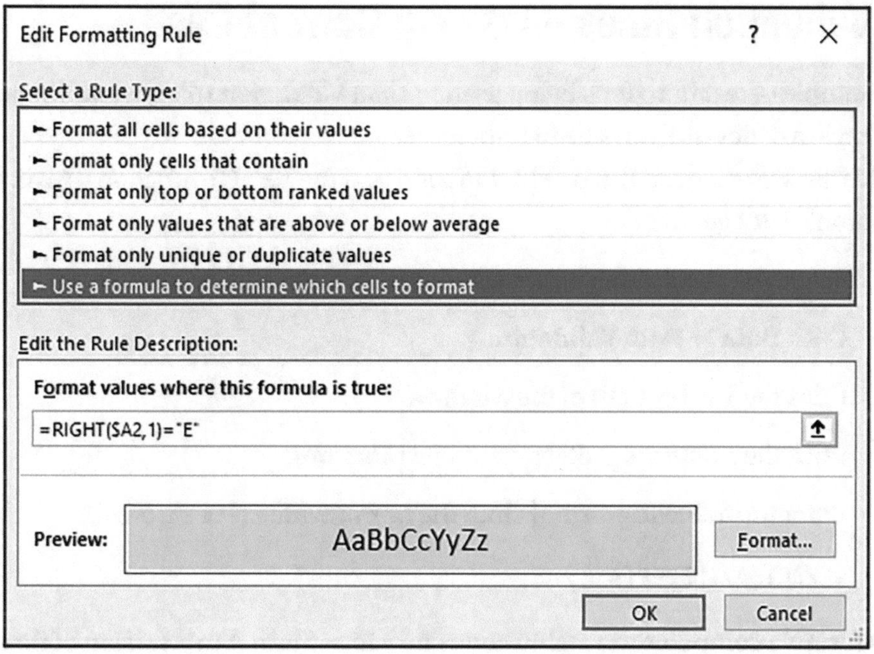

Figure 5-87. *RIGHT function in a Conditional Formatting rule*

4. Click **Format** and specify the formatting you want to apply.

5. Click **OK**.

The Conditional Formatting rule is applied to the range (Figure 5-88). All codes with an "E" as the final character have been formatted.

Figure 5-88. *Conditional Formatting applied to the range*

Data Validation Rules – Forcing Correct Case

For an example of text functions being used in Data Validation rules, we will validate the entry of region codes to always be in uppercase.

To do this, we will need the UPPER function and the EXACT function – two awesome text functions. Let's get to it:

1. Select the range that you want to apply the Data Validation rule to.

2. Click **Data ➤ Data Validation**.

3. Click the **Settings** tab of the window.

4. Click the *Allow* drop-down and select **Custom**.

5. Enter the following formula into the box provided (Figure 5-89):

    ```
    =EXACT(A2,UPPER(A2))
    ```

This formula compares the region code entry in column A to a version of that entry converted to uppercase. These entries must be the same to pass the validation criteria.

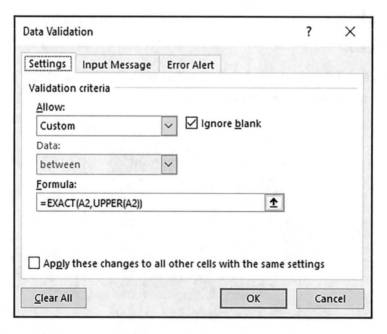

Figure 5-89. *EXACT and UPPER in a Data Validation rule*

6. Click the **Error Alert** tab and enter a meaningful *Title* and *Error message* to appear if a user enters a region code that is not in uppercase (Figure 5-90).

7. Click **OK**.

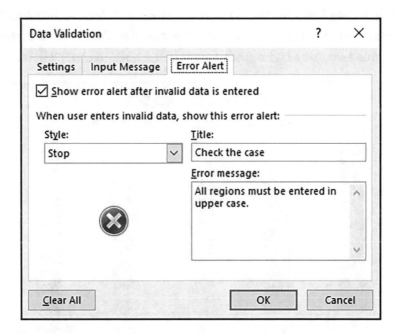

Figure 5-90. *Setting an error alert for a rule*

In Figure 5-91, the Data Validation rule was applied to the cells in range A2:A5. The error message is shown if an entry is not in uppercase.

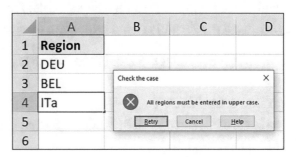

Figure 5-91. *Non-uppercase entries being prevented*

Dynamic Labels for Charts

The TEXT function is fantastic for creating more meaningful labels on your Excel charts. You can go beyond the standard labeling used by many and provide more information to the readers.

The chart in Figure 5-92 makes full use of the chart title by providing the month's total revenue and the monthly sales variance to the reader. This extra richness of information is one example of taking advantage of the built-in chart labels.

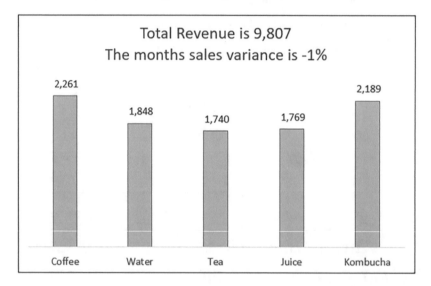

Figure 5-92. *Column chart with a chart title providing more information*

To create this title, the following formula was entered into cell D1 of the worksheet (Figure 5-93). It works with the data in the [Product_Sales] table. This formula may look intense, but it is not difficult. All the formulas used have been discussed in the book.

```
="Total Revenue is "&TEXT(SUM(Product_Sales[This Month]),"#,#")
&CHAR(10)&
"The months sales variance is "&TEXT(
    (SUM(Product_Sales[This Month])-SUM(Product_Sales[Last Month]))/
    SUM(Product_Sales[Last Month]),
    "0%;-0%")
```

There are two TEXT functions: one to display the revenue correctly and another for the percentage variance. The CHAR function is also used here to create the line break (character 10 for Windows and 13 for Mac).

Cell D1 has had text wrapping applied to look neater for the image. It is not required for chart titles.

	A	B	C	D
1				Total Revenue is 9,807 The months sales variance is -1%
2	Product	Last Month	This Month	
3	Coffee	2,445	2,261	
4	Water	2,533	1,848	
5	Tea	1,518	1,740	
6	Juice	1,807	1,769	
7	Kombucha	1,647	2,189	
8				

Figure 5-93. *Chart title created in a cell of the worksheet*

The chart title is then linked to cell D1. To do this, click the chart title, type = in the Formula Bar, then click cell D1, and press Enter (Figure 5-94).

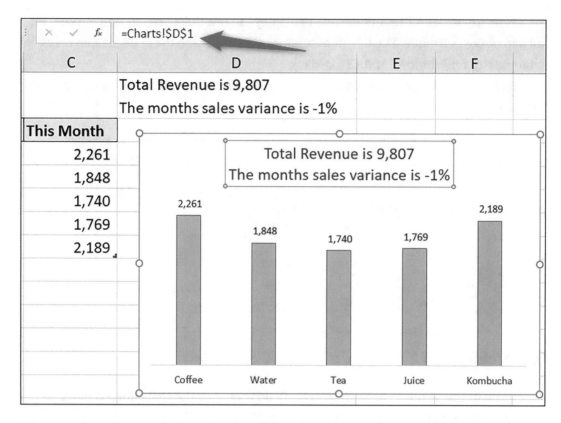

Figure 5-94. *Chart title linked to a cell for creative labeling*

Note   Typically, this formula would be hidden by entering it on a different sheet to the chart or in a hidden column. It is displayed here only to show the mechanics of the technique easier.

Summary

In this chapter, we covered the text functions of Excel, and, wow, there are many of them. These functions make it easy to extract, clean, split, combine, and convert text in Excel.

In the next chapter, it is time (sorry 😊) for the date and time functions in Excel. It is another extensive chapter, jam-packed with formula goodness.

You will first learn the fundamentals of dates and time in Excel. It is very important that this is understood to ensure correct and effective formulas with dates and times in Excel. The chapter then progresses through many functions, supported by many practical examples of their use.

CHAPTER 6

Working with Dates and Time

It is almost inevitable that you will work with dates and time in Excel, regardless of your job role or profession. Excel contains more than 20 awesome functions for you to perform the date and time calculations that you need.

This chapter begins with a guide to how dates and time work in Excel. It is very important that we understand the calendar system of Excel before we begin writing our formulas.

We then proceed into explanations of the most used date and time functions with examples using them to solve a myriad of typical business tasks.

Note   I am based in the UK, so all dates shown are entered in a dd/mm/yyyy format unless specified otherwise. I will often refer to dates using the month name, for example, 1st September 2021, to avoid any confusion with translation.

Understanding Dates and Time

File   dates-and-time.xlsx

Working with dates and time in Excel can certainly get interesting. To effectively work with the formulas of Excel, we must first understand how dates and time are stored.

© Alan Murray 2022
A. Murray, *Advanced Excel Formulas*, https://doi.org/10.1007/978-1-4842-7125-4_6

Dates and the Calendar System in Excel

Dates in Excel are stored as numbers. These numbers are known as serial numbers. You will often see this term when using the functions of Excel. Figure 6-1 shows a reference to a serial number in the description of the WORKDAY function.

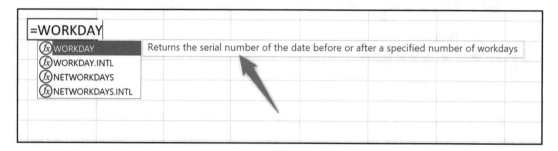

Figure 6-1. *Serial number mentioned in the WORKDAY function description*

When a date is entered into Excel, it is converted to a serial number based on the 1900 date system and formatted as a date. The 1900 date system begins on 1st January 1900. For Excel, this is the beginning of time. All dates are a sequential number beginning from this date.

So, 1st January 1900 is the serial number 1 and the date 2nd September 2021 is the serial number 44441. This is shown in Figure 6-2. The values are formatted in a general format to display the serial number.

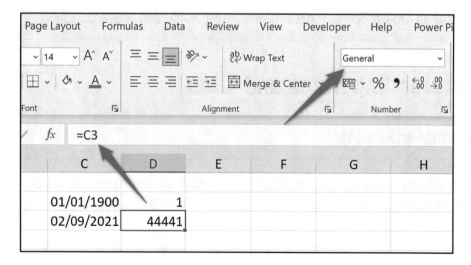

Figure 6-2. *The serial number of dates shown in Excel*

Excel actually supports two different date systems, the 1900 date system and 1904 date system. The 1904 date system starts on 1st January 1904.

The 1900 date system is the default, so we do not need to concern ourselves with the 1904 date system, although we will see an example of its use later in this chapter.

Note   Windows and Mac Excel now have the same date system, but Excel 2008 for Mac and earlier Excel for Mac versions used the 1904 date system as the default.

Calculate the Difference Between Two Dates

As dates are stored as serial numbers, calculating the difference between two dates is a simple case of subtracting one from the other.

In Figure 6-3, the following formula is used to return the difference between the dates in cells A2 and B2:

=B2-A2

C2		:	×	✓	*fx*	=B2-A2	
	A		B		C		
1	**Start Date**		**End Date**		**Difference**		
2	03/08/2021		10/09/2021		38		
3							

Figure 6-3. *Calculating the difference between two dates*

Days begin at midnight, so when calculating the date difference in this example, the day of 10/09/2021 (10th September 2021) is not included.

There is also a DAYS function in Excel that achieves this task. The DAYS function takes two arguments – the start date and the end date:

=DAYS(end_date, start_date)

This function performs the same calculation of end date – start date. Figure 6-4 shows the DAYS function returning the same result.

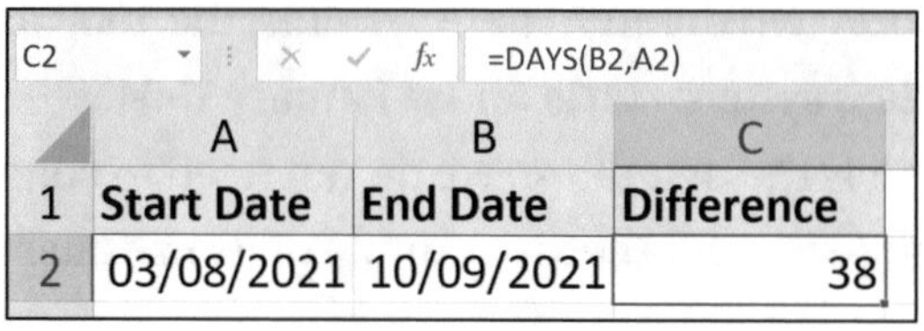

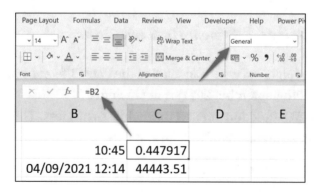

Figure 6-4. *Date difference using the DAYS function*

Note   If you enter the start and end dates in the incorrect order (start date first), you will receive a negative value as the result.

Time in Excel

So, a date in Excel is referred to as a serial number and represents the value of 1. Time is part of a day, so it is represented as a decimal value.

For example, the time 06:00 is 25% of a day, or the value 0.25 in Excel, while the time 14:00 is 0.58 (rounded to two decimal places).

Now, I do not recommend telling your colleagues in the office that the time is 0.58. You may find yourself excluded from the tea round (is that just a British thing?).

These values would be formatted as time so that they are understood. However, it is very important that we understand how time is stored in Excel when using formulas.

Figure 6-5 shows the general format of cells containing time and also date and time.

Figure 6-5. *Time and date and time shown in a general format*

The method for entering the time can depend on your regional settings. In the UK, the colon ":" is used to separate hours, minutes, and seconds, for example, 08:30 or 09:35:12.

Other delimiters such as using a period or dot "." to separate the hours, minutes, and seconds would not be accepted in the UK regional settings. However, they may be allowed in other regions.

Calculate the Difference in Two Times

As with dates, the difference in two times can be calculated by simply subtracting the start time from the end time.

The following formula has been used to calculate the duration in Figure 6-6:

=B2-A2

We will see further calculations with time later in this chapter. This includes calculating time difference across dates and when the duration is over 24 hours.

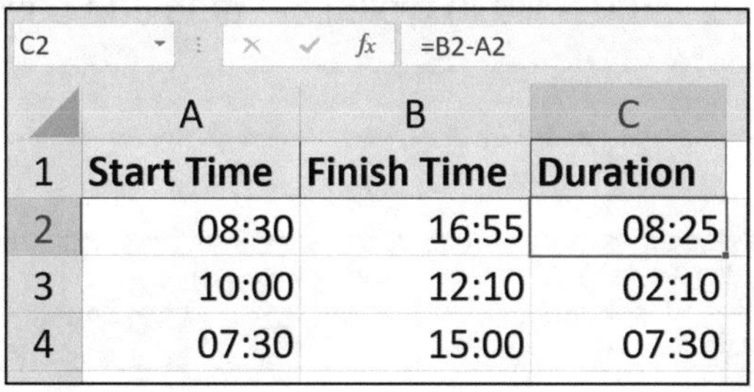

C2		× ✓ *fx*	=B2-A2	
	A	B	C	
1	Start Time	Finish Time	Duration	
2	08:30	16:55	08:25	
3	10:00	12:10	02:10	
4	07:30	15:00	07:30	

Figure 6-6. *Calculating the difference in two times*

The TODAY and NOW Functions

Availability: All versions

The TODAY function in Excel returns the current date, while the NOW function returns the current date and time. The results of these formulas will update every time the worksheet calculates.

These functions are useful if you need to display the current date or date-time in a cell or perform calculations that require the current date or current date and time.

The syntax of these functions is super simple, as they require no arguments. The syntax for the TODAY function is

=TODAY()

And the syntax for the NOW function is

=NOW()

The functions will return the date and time information from the system clock of your computer. Figure 6-7 shows the TODAY and NOW functions returning values to a cell for display.

When using Excel for the Web, the date and time information is taken from the regional settings of where the workbook is located. Ensure your regional settings in OneDrive, the SharePoint site, or wherever the workbook may be stored are correct when using these functions.

Note   The current date can be entered quickly in Excel with the **Ctrl + ;** keyboard shortcut. This is a faster alternative to typing the date and does not update like the TODAY function does.

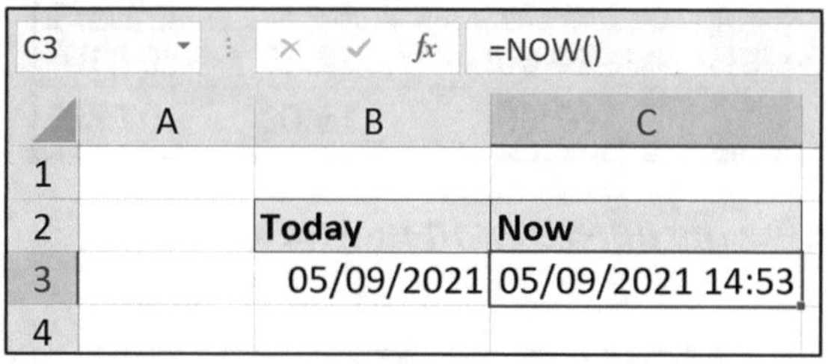

C3	▾ ⋮	✕ ✓ *fx*	=NOW()
	A	B	C
1			
2		Today	Now
3		05/09/2021	05/09/2021 14:53
4			

Figure 6-7. *TODAY and NOW functions displaying values in a cell*

The TODAY function is useful for calculations that require the current date, for example, calculating the number of days until a deadline or due date. The results would need to update with time.

The following formula is used in Figure 6-8 to calculate the number of days until the due date of a payment:

=F3-TODAY()

	ID	Due	No of Days
	CV352	30/09/2021	25
	CV729	21/09/2021	16
	CV023	08/09/2021	3
	CV647	20/09/2021	15

Figure 6-8. *Calculating the number of days until a due date*

Note The result may be returned in a date format. Strange, but true. To correct this, format the cell in the General format.

Convert Text to Date

The method for entering dates into Excel depends on your regional settings. I am based in the UK, so entering the date delimited by a slash "/" or a hyphen "-" is accepted, for example, 04/09/2021 or 04-09-2021. These are entered in the dd/mm/yyyy format. The name of a month can also be used, for example, 04 September 2021.

I would not be able to enter a date in the structure 04.09.2021 (although it can be formatted that way). It would be stored as text. However, in regions such as Germany, that structure would be accepted.

In the modern world, with data coming from a large variety of sources, dates can appear in a workbook in all shapes and sizes. When your Excel cannot translate a date as a date, you will need to convert it. We cannot work with the data until it is cleaned.

There are two main functions for this, DATEVALUE and DATE.

Note This is an Excel formulas book, so our focus is on formula solutions. They are often the perfect solution, as they are automated and can be combined with other functions. However, the Text to Columns and Power Query tools of Excel are also good options for converting date values.

The DATEVALUE Function

Availability: All versions

The purpose of the DATEVALUE function is to convert dates stored as text into dates. Or to be more specific, it converts them to their serial number, and then you would apply a date format to present them correctly.

The DATEVALUE function requires one argument – the date that is currently in a text format:

```
=DATEVALUE(date_text)
```

The following formula is used in Figure 6-9 to convert the text dates into serial numbers. A variety of date structures have been entered in column A to demonstrate the effectiveness of DATEVALUE in recognizing them.

```
=DATEVALUE(A2)
```

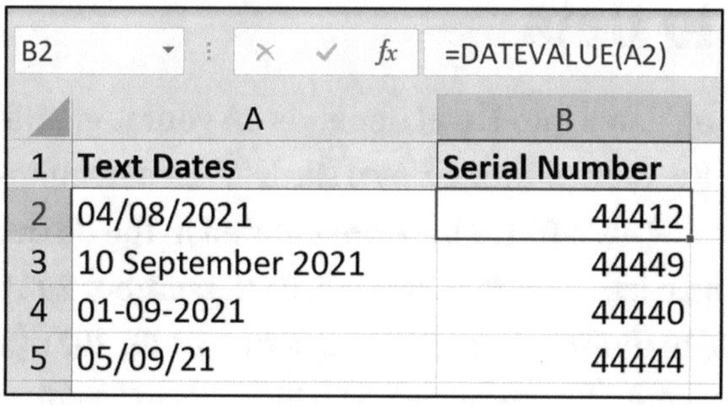

Figure 6-9. *DATEVALUE converting text dates to serial numbers*

If the year is omitted from the text date, then the DATEVALUE function will apply the current year to the converted date. Figure 6-10 shows some examples of the DATEVALUE function doing this.

Note that the serial numbers match those shown in Figure 6-9.

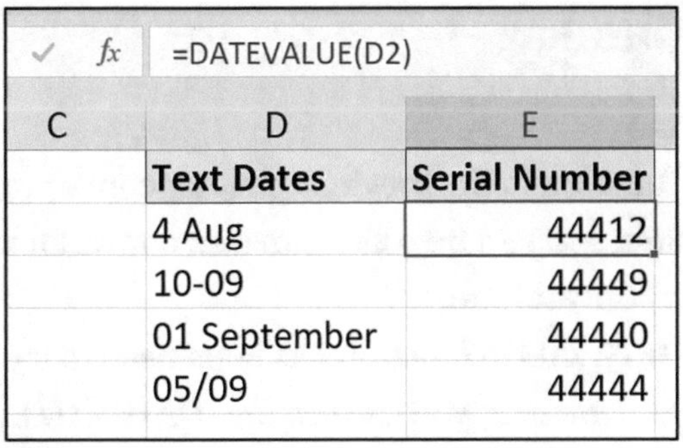

	fx	=DATEVALUE(D2)	
C	D		E
	Text Dates		**Serial Number**
	4 Aug		44412
	10-09		44449
	01 September		44440
	05/09		44444

Figure 6-10. *Converting text dates that are missing the year*

Now, you can also convert the text dates by using them in a simple mathematical operation. The DATEVALUE function is unnecessary.

The following formula also achieves the required task (Figure 6-11):

=A2*1

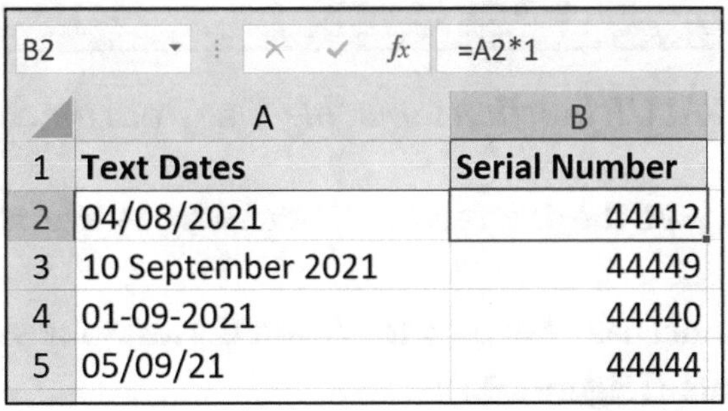

B2	▼ : × ✓ fx	=A2*1
	A	B
1	**Text Dates**	**Serial Number**
2	04/08/2021	44412
3	10 September 2021	44449
4	01-09-2021	44440
5	05/09/21	44444

Figure 6-11. *Converting text dates with a multiply operation*

I am demonstrating this to show what is possible and not to downplay the use of the DATEVALUE function. The better approach is probably to use DATEVALUE, especially if others are using your spreadsheets. It is much more descriptive to others who are trying to understand what that formula does.

The VALUE Function

Availability: All versions

We saw the VALUE function in the previous chapter converting text to numeric values. It is worth mentioning again here as it can also convert text to date but has the additional ability to also convert time.

In Figure 6-12, the DATEVALUE function has been used to try and convert text values into date and time values. However, you can see that DATEVALUE strips the time from the result.

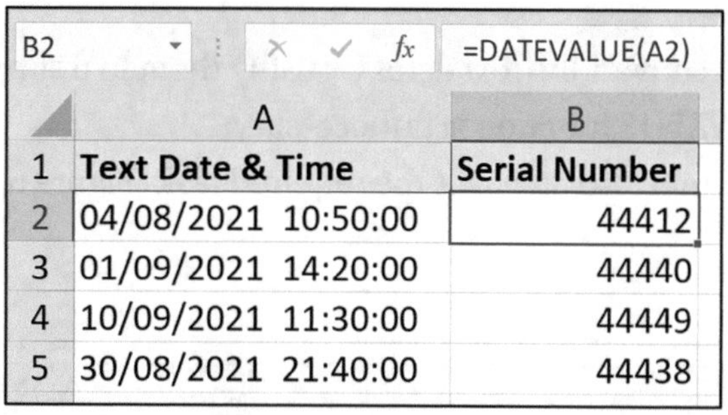

B2		×	✓	fx	=DATEVALUE(A2)

	A	B
1	Text Date & Time	Serial Number
2	04/08/2021 10:50:00	44412
3	01/09/2021 14:20:00	44440
4	10/09/2021 11:30:00	44449
5	30/08/2021 21:40:00	44438

Figure 6-12.   DATEVALUE function removing time from the converted text values

This is good if you want the time removed. Otherwise, let's turn to the VALUE function.

The following formula has been used to convert the text values into the serial number for date and time (Figure 6-13):

=VALUE(A2)

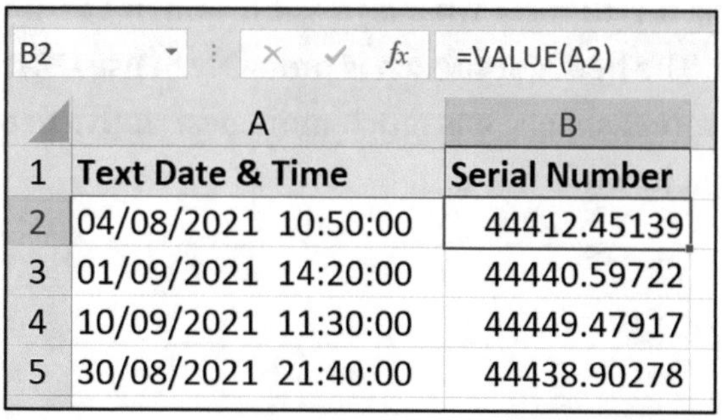

B2		×	✓	fx	=VALUE(A2)

	A	B
1	Text Date & Time	Serial Number
2	04/08/2021 10:50:00	44412.45139
3	01/09/2021 14:20:00	44440.59722
4	10/09/2021 11:30:00	44449.47917
5	30/08/2021 21:40:00	44438.90278

Figure 6-13.   VALUE function converts text values to date and time

The cell values can then be formatted to present the date and time correctly. Excel does not have a date and time number category, so it requires finding or creating a custom number format:

1. Select the range to format.

2. Open the *Format Cells* window by pressing **Ctrl + 1** or by right-clicking the selected range and clicking **Format Cells**.

3. Click the **Custom** category and then scroll through the list of formats to find a date and time format to use (Figure 6-14).

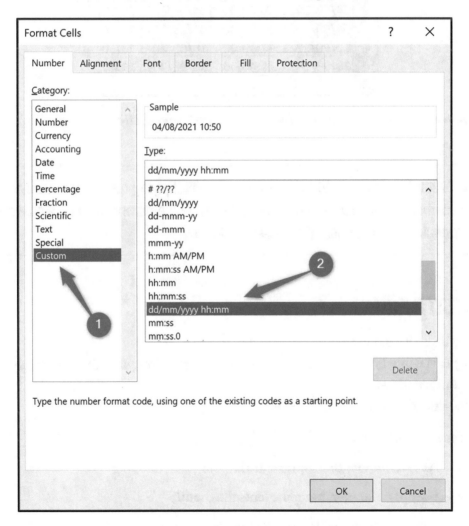

Figure 6-14. *Formatting values as date and time*

Performing a mathematical operation on the text values works again as an alternative method of converting them to date and time values. With this formula, Excel automatically applies a date and time format (Figure 6-15):

=A2*1

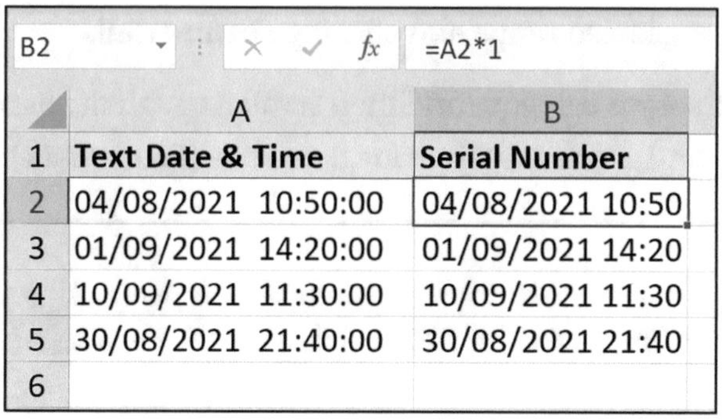

B2	▾	⋮	✕	✓	*fx*	=A2*1

	A	B
1	Text Date & Time	Serial Number
2	04/08/2021 10:50:00	04/08/2021 10:50
3	01/09/2021 14:20:00	01/09/2021 14:20
4	10/09/2021 11:30:00	10/09/2021 11:30
5	30/08/2021 21:40:00	30/08/2021 21:40
6		

Figure 6-15. *Converting text values to date and time easily*

Note   Although I demonstrate the example of multiplying the text values by one, other mathematical operations that do not change the number's value also work. For example, you could use A2/1, A2+0, or A2-0.

The DATE Function

Availability: All versions

The DATE function returns the serial number that represents a date from a given year, month, and day.

The syntax of the DATE function is

=DATE(year, month, day)

- **Year:** A number that represents the year

- **Month:** A number that represents the month

- **Day:** A number that represents the day

The DATEVALUE and VALUE functions are great when the text value is structured as a date. However, that is not always the case.

Another common structure is to receive date values in the structure yyyymmdd. This may be stored as a text value or a numeric value. It does not matter; the DATE function along with some text functions from the previous chapter can fix this.

The following formula creates a date from the number values in column A (Figure 6-16). It uses the LEFT, MID, and RIGHT functions to extract the different parts of the number that correspond to the year, month, and day:

```
=DATE(LEFT(A2,4),MID(A2,5,2),RIGHT(A2,2))
```

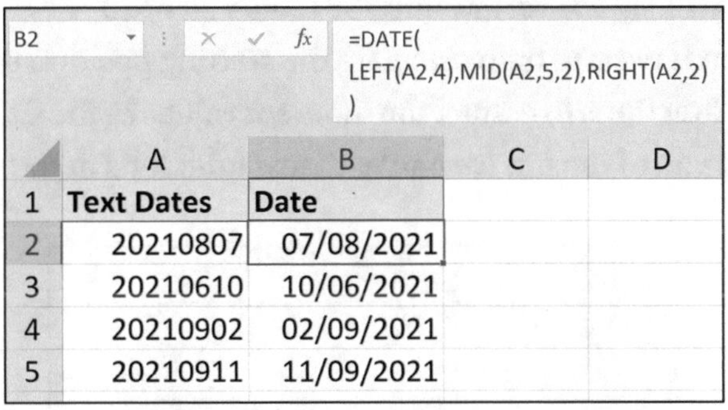
B2 =DATE(LEFT(A2,4),MID(A2,5,2),RIGHT(A2,2))

	A	B	C	D
1	Text Dates	Date		
2	20210807	07/08/2021		
3	20210610	10/06/2021		
4	20210902	02/09/2021		
5	20210911	11/09/2021		

***Figure 6-16.** DATE function creating a date from a number*

Another scenario could be that the day, month, and year values are in different columns, when you import data from another source. This is a perfect scenario for the DATE function.

The following formula is shown in Figure 6-17:

```
=DATE(F2,E2,D2)
```

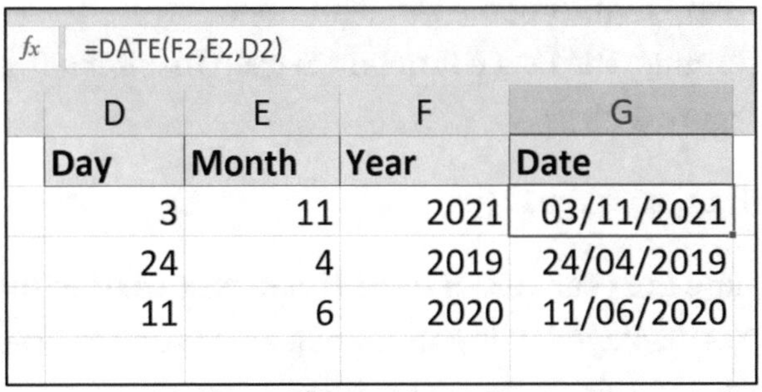
=DATE(F2,E2,D2)

D	E	F	G
Day	Month	Year	Date
3	11	2021	03/11/2021
24	4	2019	24/04/2019
11	6	2020	11/06/2020

***Figure 6-17.** Creating a date from three separate values*

And for a final example, the date can sometimes form part of a reference. I have a client I have worked with for years who store booking references in the format "21-08-02 AM." This represents 2nd August 2021 with only two digits used to represent the year.

The following formula can be used to extract the values and create the date from the booking reference (Figure 6-18):

```
=DATE(
"20"&LEFT(I2,2),MID(I2,4,2),MID(I2,LEN(I2)-4,2)
)
```

This formula concatenates the "20" to the two digits of the year to create the full year. Without this, it would likely convert 21 into 1921, instead of 2021.

The LEN function is used to help calculate the starting position of the day value.

Using these text functions to extract the different values of the date for the DATE function will remind you of the fun we had with text functions in the previous chapter.

	fx	=DATE("20"&LEFT(I2,2),MID(I2,4,2),MID(I2,LEN(I2)-4,2))		
H	I	J	K
	Booking Ref	**Date**	
	21-08-20 AM	20/08/2021	
	21-10-02 CB	02/10/2021	
	22-01-10 BH	10/01/2022	

Figure 6-18. *Extract and create a date from a booking reference*

So, the DATE function is a great function for converting values into a date. Another scenario for its use is to enter fixed dates into formulas. You cannot type dates directly into formulas due to Excel requiring the serial number.

In the following formula, the DATE function is used to enter a fixed date for the IF function condition (Figure 6-19):

```
=IF(A2<DATE(2021,9,1),2021,2022)
```

The formula displays the year 2021 if the cell values are earlier than 1st September 2021; otherwise, 2022 is displayed. It is common in areas such as academics, finances, and sporting seasons to have years that span different years.

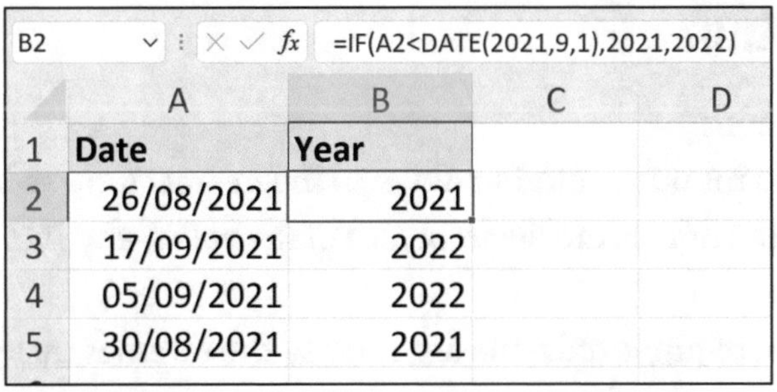

B2 =IF(A2<DATE(2021,9,1),2021,2022)

	A	B	C	D
1	Date	Year		
2	26/08/2021	2021		
3	17/09/2021	2022		
4	05/09/2021	2022		
5	30/08/2021	2021		

***Figure 6-19.** Using DATE to enter a fixed date into a formula*

Extract Date from a Date-Time Stamp

Often, when getting data from other sources such as a database, you will receive the date and time information.

There are several ways that you can extract the date from the date-time stamp if the time is not required.

We have already seen that the DATEVALUE function can achieve this with text values (Figure 6-12), but it wouldn't work with values that are recognized as date and time. In this instance, the DATEVALUE function returns the #VALUE! error (Figure 6-20).

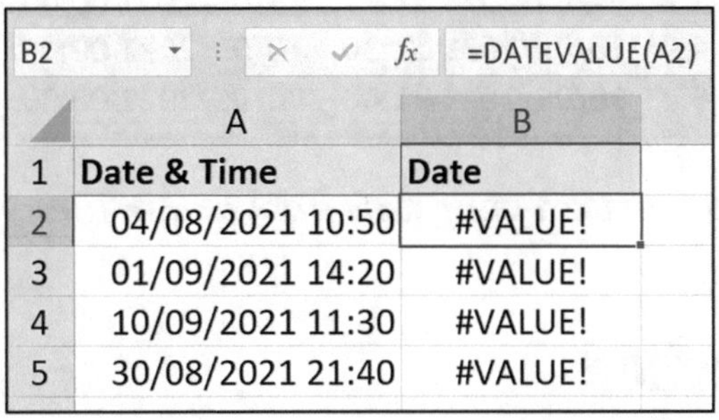

B2 =DATEVALUE(A2)

	A	B
1	Date & Time	Date
2	04/08/2021 10:50	#VALUE!
3	01/09/2021 14:20	#VALUE!
4	10/09/2021 11:30	#VALUE!
5	30/08/2021 21:40	#VALUE!

***Figure 6-20.** #VALUE! error returned by the DATEVALUE function*

To extract the date only from date-time values, we can use the INT or TRUNC functions.

The INT Function

Availability: All versions

The INT function rounds a number down to the nearest integer. This is perfect for the task at hand, as the time is the decimal part of the value, and INT will effectively nullify that.

The INT function requires only one argument – the number that you want to round:

```
=INT(number)
```

In Figure 6-21, the INT function is used to round the date-time values down to the nearest integer or date. The cells require a date-only format to remove the time from the display of the values.

```
=INT(A2)
```

B2	fx	=INT(A2)	
	A	**B**	
1	**Date & Time**	**Date**	
2	04/08/2021 10:50	04/08/2021 00:00	
3	01/09/2021 14:20	01/09/2021 00:00	
4	10/09/2021 11:30	10/09/2021 00:00	
5	30/08/2021 21:40	30/08/2021 00:00	

Figure 6-21. *INT function extracting date from a date-time value*

The TRUNC Function

Availability: All versions

The TRUNC function removes the decimal part of a number leaving only the integer. Once again, this is perfect for the task of removing the time from a date-time value.

The syntax for the TRUNC function has two arguments:

```
=TRUNC(number,[num_digits])
```

- **Number:** The number to truncate.

- **[Num digits]:** A number to specify the precision of truncation. If omitted, 0 is used to remove the decimal part of the number.

The TRUNC function does not round values like INT and other functions. It simply chops the numbers off at the specified precision.

In this scenario of extracting a date from a date-time stamp, it makes no difference if you use INT or TRUNC, the result is the same.

The following formula strips the time from the date-time values in column A (Figure 6-22). Once again, a date-only format would need to be applied to remove the display of the time.

```
=TRUNC(A2)
```

	A	B
	Date & Time	Date
1	Date & Time	Date
2	04/08/2021 10:50	04/08/2021 00:00
3	01/09/2021 14:20	01/09/2021 00:00
4	10/09/2021 11:30	10/09/2021 00:00
5	30/08/2021 21:40	30/08/2021 00:00

B2 ▾ : × ✓ *fx* =TRUNC(A2)

Figure 6-22. *TRUNC function extracting date from a date-time value*

Note   Although the official description of TRUNC is that it removes the decimal part of a number, this is only its default behavior.

For example, if you have a value of 728.91 in cell A2 and you use the formula =TRUNC(A2,-1), the value returned is 720 as it truncates one position to the left of the decimal. Or, if the formula was =TRUNC(A2,1), the value returned is 728.9 as it truncates to one position to the right of the decimal.

Extract Time from a Date-Time Stamp

To extract the time from a date-time stamp, we need to extract the decimal part of the value.

There are a few techniques for this. For example, we could subtract the extracted date part from the value (Figure 6-23). This would leave us with only the time element.

```
=A2-TRUNC(A2)
```

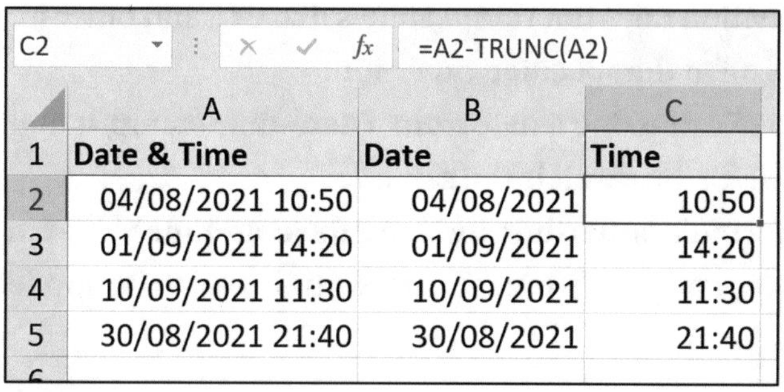

C2	▾	:	×	✓	*fx*	=A2-TRUNC(A2)

	A	B	C
1	Date & Time	Date	Time
2	04/08/2021 10:50	04/08/2021	10:50
3	01/09/2021 14:20	01/09/2021	14:20
4	10/09/2021 11:30	10/09/2021	11:30
5	30/08/2021 21:40	30/08/2021	21:40

Figure 6-23. *Extracting the time by subtracting the date element*

Let's look at how to extract the time element with the MOD function.

The MOD Function

Availability: All versions

The MOD function returns the remainder after dividing a number by a specified divisor. It requires two arguments – the number and the divisor:

```
=MOD(number, divisor)
```

- **Number:** The number to divide

- **Divisor:** The number that you want to divide the given number

In Figure 6-24, the MOD function is used to extract the time by dividing the date-time value by one:

```
=MOD(A2,1)
```

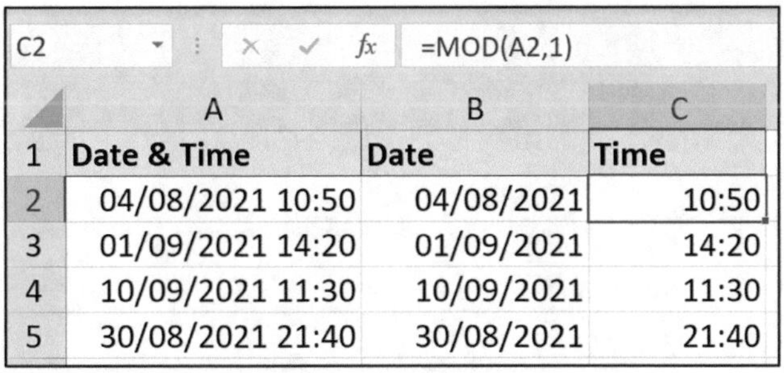

Figure 6-24. *Extracting the time with the MOD function*

After extracting the time using this method, you may need to format the cells to show the time only:

1. Select the cells to format.

2. Open the *Format Cells* window by right-clicking and click **Format Cells** or press **Ctrl + 1**.

3. On the *Number* tab, click **Custom** and then select the time format from the list (Figure 6-25). The *Custom* category has been used instead of time to specify only hours and minutes.

Note   The MOD function is a really cool function. I have personally utilized it over the years in several creative ways including to sum the values from every nth row.

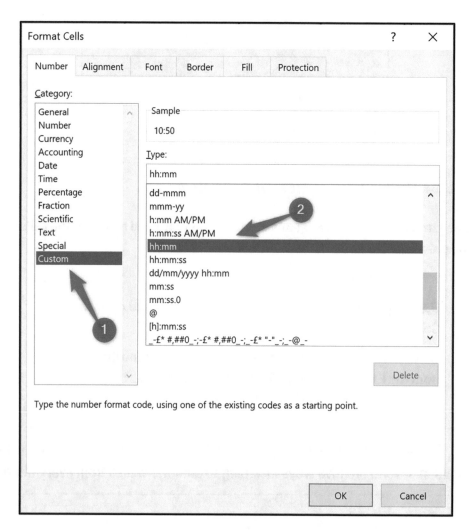

Figure 6-25. *Formatting the values to show time only in hours and minutes*

The YEAR, MONTH, and DAY Functions

Availability: All versions

The YEAR, MONTH, and DAY functions are simple, yet very useful. They each extract their relevant part from a given date. Year will extract the year and so on.

Each function requires only the date in which to extract their part from. This could be a cell value, entered text, or the result of a function such as TODAY.

```
=YEAR(serial_number)
```

In Figure 6-26, the YEAR, MONTH, and DAY functions have each been used to extract their element from the dates in column A.

The formula to extract the year is shown in the image. The MONTH and DAY functions are written the same.

```
=YEAR(A2)
```

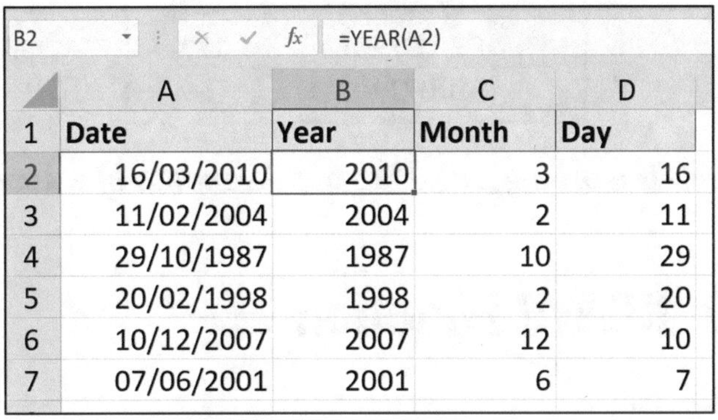

	A	B	C	D
1	Date	Year	Month	Day
2	16/03/2010	2010	3	16
3	11/02/2004	2004	2	11
4	29/10/1987	1987	10	29
5	20/02/1998	1998	2	20
6	10/12/2007	2007	12	10
7	07/06/2001	2001	6	7

Figure 6-26. *YEAR, MONTH, and DAY functions*

This example demonstrates how the functions work but is not a hugely practical example. We will see these functions being used later in this chapter to help calculate financial years and quarters. This will provide a greater insight to their use.

Let's see another quick example before we leave them though. These functions can be used to extract part of a date for another function to use, for example, the IF function.

In this example, we want to apply a different rate dependent upon the time of the year. Dates from September onward require a different rate to other times of the year.

The following formula (Figure 6-27) uses the MONTH function to extract the month of the date so that the IF function can test it and apply the required rate of 11% or 9%:

```
=IF(MONTH(F2>=9,11%,9%)
```

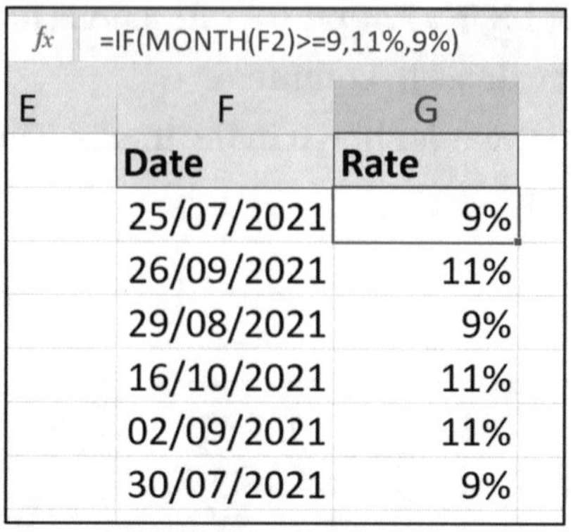

fx	=IF(MONTH(F2)>=9,11%,9%)	
E	F	G
	Date	**Rate**
	25/07/2021	9%
	26/09/2021	11%
	29/08/2021	9%
	16/10/2021	11%
	02/09/2021	11%
	30/07/2021	9%

Figure 6-27. MONTH working with IF to test the month of a date

The NETWORKDAYS Function

Availability: All versions

The NETWORKDAYS function returns the number of whole workdays between two dates. Weekends (Saturday and Sunday) are excluded, and an argument is provided to specify additional non-working days that you want excluded.

This function is great for calculating the number of days worked on a task or project.

The following is the syntax of the NETWORKDAYS function:

```
=NETWORKDAYS(start_date, end_date, [holidays])
```

- **Start date:** The start date to be used in the calculation.

- **End date:** The end date to be used in the calculation.

- **[Holidays]:** A range or array of dates that are considered non-working days. These could be national holidays or any other reason that the date is non-working. This is an optional argument.

It is important to note that the NETWORKDAYS function returns the number of whole workdays between two dates (Figure 6-28).

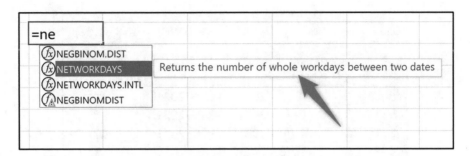

Figure 6-28. *NETWORKDAYS counts whole workdays*

Figure 6-29 shows the number of days difference between the two dates in cells G2 and H2. The formula in cell I2 is a simple =H2-G2 date difference calculation.

The NETWORKDAYS function in cell J2 returns a different result as both dates in the formula are working days, and NETWORKDAYS returns the number of whole workdays.

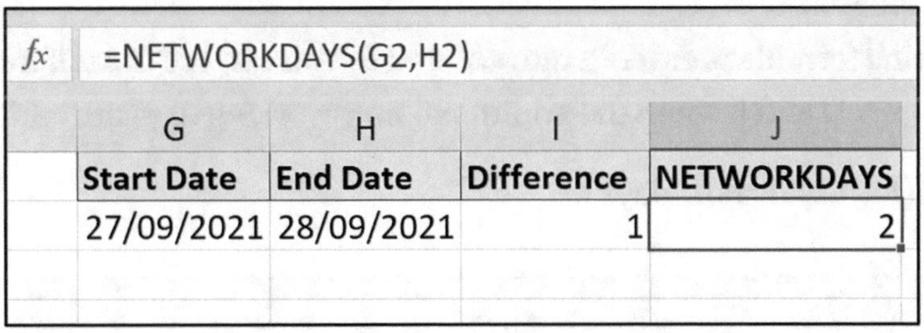

fx	=NETWORKDAYS(G2,H2)		
G	H	I	J
Start Date	**End Date**	**Difference**	**NETWORKDAYS**
27/09/2021	28/09/2021	1	2

Figure 6-29. *NETWORKDAYS returning a different result*

Calculate the Working Days Difference Between Two Dates

Let's see a practical example of the NETWORKDAYS function. In this example, we need to calculate the number of days worked on the tasks of a project.

The following formula is entered into column D (Figure 6-30). This formula omits the *Holidays* argument, so only weekend dates are excluded from the calculation:

```
=NETWORKDAYS(B2,C2)
```

D2 =NETWORKDAYS(B2,C2)

	A	B	C	D
1	**Task**	**Start**	**Finish**	**Days**
2	Task A	09/06/2021	14/06/2021	4
3	Task B	08/06/2021	19/06/2021	9
4	Task C	20/06/2021	13/07/2021	17
5	Task D	10/07/2021	12/07/2021	1
6	Task E	13/07/2021	30/07/2021	14
7	Task F	03/08/2021	08/08/2021	4

***Figure 6-30.** Calculating working days difference with NETWORKDAYS*

Let's specify additional non-working days for the formula to exclude. In Figure 6-31, the additional non-working dates have been entered into range L2:L6 and have been named [rngHolidays].

The following formula is entered into column E. You can see the difference in the results of columns D and E when the additional non-working days are added.

```
=NETWORKDAYS(B2,C2,rngHolidays)
```

E2 =NETWORKDAYS(B2,C2,rngHolidays)

	A	B	C	D	E	F	K	L
1	**Task**	**Start**	**Finish**	**Days**	**Inc Holidays**			**Holidays**
2	Task A	09/06/2021	14/06/2021	4	3			11/06/2021
3	Task B	08/06/2021	19/06/2021	9	7			15/06/2021
4	Task C	20/06/2021	13/07/2021	17	17			19/07/2021
5	Task D	10/07/2021	12/07/2021	1	1			05/08/2021
6	Task E	13/07/2021	30/07/2021	14	13			06/08/2021
7	Task F	03/08/2021	08/08/2021	4	2			
8								

***Figure 6-31.** NETWORKDAYS with additional non-working days*

The NETWORKDAYS.INTL Function

The NETWORKDAYS.INTL function performs the same role as NETWORKDAYS but with an additional argument to specify custom weekend parameters.

The following is the syntax of the NETWORKDAYS.INTL function. The custom weekend is the third argument:

```
=NETWORKDAYS.INTL(start_date, end_date, [weekend], [holidays])
```

Figure 6-32 shows the weekend options list provided by the *weekend* argument of NETWORKDAYS.INTL.

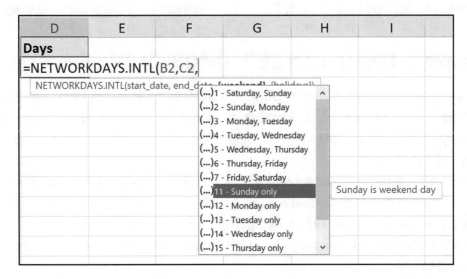

Figure 6-32. *The weekend options in the NETWORKDAYS.INTL function*

Let's use the NETWORKDAYS.INTL function on the same range of dates and apply the Sunday only option for the weekend. This is known as option 11, as shown in Figure 6-32.

The following formula is used in column D to calculate the working days difference between two dates (Figure 6-33). It also uses the [rngHolidays] named range for additional non-working days to exclude:

```
=NETWORKDAYS.INTL(B2,C2,11,rngHolidays)
```

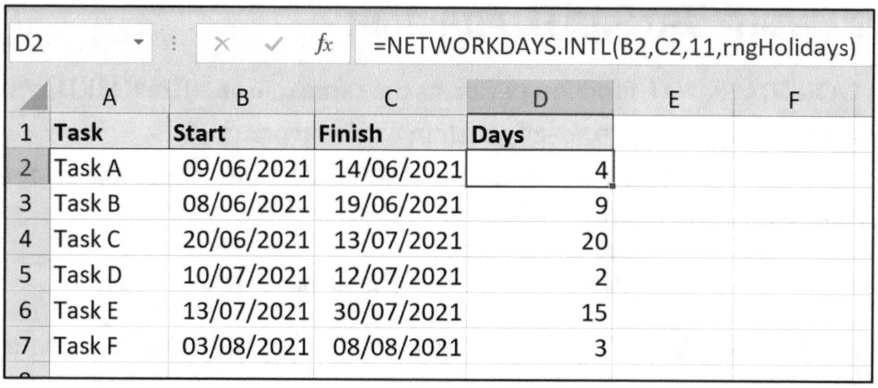

Figure 6-33. NETWORKDAYS.INTL with the Sunday only weekend option applied

Example 1: Customized NETWORKDAYS.INTL Function

The *weekend* argument of the NETWORKDAYS.INTL function can be customized to specify which days of the week are working and which are non-working. This provides much more flexibility in specifying non-working days than are offered by the *weekend* argument's list of options.

The *weekend* argument can be entered as a text string of seven 1s and 0s. The first character represents a Monday and the other six for the remaining days of the week. A 1 is entered to indicate a non-working day, and a 0 is entered for a working day.

The following formula specifies that only Monday-Thursday are working days (Figure 6-34):

```
=NETWORKDAYS.INTL(B2,C2,"0000111")
```

With this customization of the NETWORKDAYS.INTL function, it is easy to specify that you may only work on a project on Mondays and Tuesdays ("0011111") or that you may work Saturday only ("1111101") on a specific task.

The *holidays* argument can still be used for additional non-working days such as state holidays or interference by bad weather.

	A	B	C	D	E	F
1	Task	Start	Finish	Days		
2	Task A	09/06/2021	14/06/2021	3		
3	Task B	08/06/2021	19/06/2021	7		
4	Task C	20/06/2021	13/07/2021	14		
5	Task D	10/07/2021	12/07/2021	1		
6	Task E	13/07/2021	30/07/2021	11		
7	Task F	03/08/2021	08/08/2021	3		

D2 fx =NETWORKDAYS.INTL(B2,C2,"0000111")

Figure 6-34. Specifying a working week of Monday-Thursday

Example 2: Conditional Holiday Ranges

Creating customized weekend parameters and specifying holiday ranges is great for accurate working days difference calculation. However, you may require different parameters or holiday ranges dependent upon a location or an individual.

Take this example where we have two holiday ranges to cater for two different locations (Figure 6-35). Each range has a defined name assigned to it – [rngLocation1] and [rngLocation2].

	A	B
1	Location 1	Location 2
2	13/06/2021	19/06/2021
3	15/07/2021	21/06/2021
4	04/08/2021	02/07/2021
5		26/07/2021
6		29/07/2021

Figure 6-35. Different non-working days by location

The following formula uses the SWITCH function (discussed in Chapter 2) to test the location in column B and provide the required *holiday* range (Figure 6-36):

```
=NETWORKDAYS(C2,D2,
SWITCH(B2,"Location 1",rngLocation1,"Location 2",rngLocation2)
)
```

E2	▾	:	✕	✓	*fx*	=NETWORKDAYS(C2,D2, SWITCH(B2,"Location 1",rngLocation1,"Location 2",rngLocation2))

	A	B	C	D	E	F
1	Task	Location	Start	Finish	Days	
2	Task A	Location 1	09/06/2021	14/06/2021	4	
3	Task B	Location 1	08/06/2021	19/06/2021	9	
4	Task C	Location 2	20/06/2021	13/07/2021	15	
5	Task D	Location 1	10/07/2021	12/07/2021	1	
6	Task E	Location 2	13/07/2021	30/07/2021	12	
7	Task F	Location 1	03/08/2021	08/08/2021	3	

Figure 6-36. *Conditional holiday range with NETWORKDAYS*

The SWITCH function can handle many more than two criteria if required. And this same approach can be used to apply a conditional *weekend* parameter with NETWORKDAYS.INTL (Figure 6-37):

```
=NETWORKDAYS.INTL(C2,D2,
SWITCH(B2,"Location 1","0100111","Location 2","1111000")
)
```

E2	▾	:	✕	✓	*fx*	=NETWORKDAYS.INTL(C2,D2, SWITCH(B2,"Location 1","0100111","Location 2","1111000"))

	A	B	C	D	E	F
1	Task	Location	Start	Finish	Days	
2	Task A	Location 2	09/06/2021	14/06/2021	3	
3	Task B	Location 1	08/06/2021	19/06/2021	5	
4	Task C	Location 2	20/06/2021	13/07/2021	10	
5	Task D	Location 1	10/07/2021	12/07/2021	1	
6	Task E	Location 2	13/07/2021	30/07/2021	7	
7	Task F	Location 1	03/08/2021	08/08/2021	2	

Figure 6-37. *Conditional weekend parameters with NETWORKDAYS.INTL*

The first example utilizes defined holiday ranges, and the second example works with entered strings to specify the working and non-working days.

For a final example, we imagine that the non-working days are entered in a single list and that there are more than just the two locations. Figure 6-38 shows this list formatted as a table named [tblNonWorking].

Location	Date	Reason
Ashford	24/06/2021	Holiday
Salisbury	27/06/2021	Site closed
Bedford	05/07/2021	Holiday
Bedford	06/07/2021	Work re-scheduled
Salisbury	23/07/2021	Site closed
Bedford	23/07/2021	Low staff levels
Salisbury	28/07/2021	Site closed
Ashford	29/07/2021	Site closed

Figure 6-38. *Table of non-working days by location*

The following formula uses the NETWORKDAYS function along with a function named FILTER (Figure 6-39). The FILTER function filters the table to return only the non-working dates for the specified location.

E2   fx   =NETWORKDAYS(C2,D2,
FILTER(tblNonWorking[Date],tblNonWorking[Location]=B2,0)
)

	A	B	C	D	E	F	G
1	Task	Location	Start	Finish	Days		
2	Task A	Bedford	09/06/2021	14/06/2021	4		
3	Task B	Ashford	08/06/2021	19/06/2021	9		
4	Task C	Ashford	20/06/2021	13/07/2021	16		
5	Task D	Salisbury	10/07/2021	12/07/2021	1		
6	Task E	Bedford	13/07/2021	30/07/2021	13		
7	Task F	Salisbury	03/08/2021	08/08/2021	4		

Figure 6-39. *FILTER function returning the non-working dates for NETWORKDAYS*

> **Note**   The FILTER function is covered in detail in Chapter 13. It is only available in Excel for Microsoft 365, Excel 2021, and Excel for the Web.

Example 3: Number of Fridays Between Two Dates

A unique use of the customized weekend parameter in NETWORKDAYS.INTL, shown in example 1, is to count the number of instances of a specific weekday between two dates. In this example, we will count the number of Fridays, but it could be any weekday or weekdays.

The following formula counts the occurrences of Fridays between the dates in cells A2 and B2 (Figure 6-40):

```
=NETWORKDAYS.INTL(A2,B2,"1111011")
```

	A	B	C	D
	Start Date	End Date	No of Fridays	
1				
2	07/09/2021	15/09/2021	1	
3	30/09/2021	12/10/2021	2	
4	11/09/2021	16/09/2021	0	
5	08/09/2021	19/09/2021	2	
6	16/09/2021	08/10/2021	4	
7	26/09/2021	12/10/2021	2	

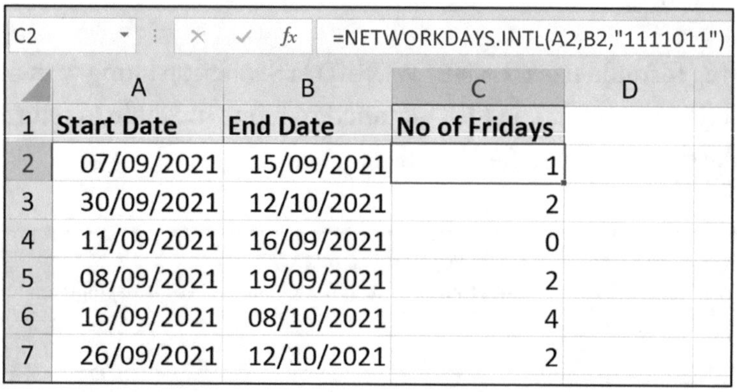

C2 — =NETWORKDAYS.INTL(A2,B2,"1111011")

Figure 6-40. *Formula to count the number of Fridays between two dates*

This can also be achieved using the *weekend* parameters provided with the NETWORKDAYS.INTL function. Option 16 is the Friday only option.

The formula in Figure 6-41 also returns the count of Fridays between two dates. A 1 is added at the end of the formula, as the NETWORKDAYS functions always return an extra day, due to their count of whole days:

```
=B2-A2-NETWORKDAYS.INTL(A2,B2,16)+1
```

| D2 | ▾ | : | × | ✓ | *fx* | =B2-A2-NETWORKDAYS.INTL(A2,B2,16)+1 |

	A	B	C	D
1	Start Date	End Date	No of Fridays	No of Fridays 2
2	07/09/2021	15/09/2021	1	1
3	30/09/2021	12/10/2021	2	2
4	11/09/2021	16/09/2021	0	0
5	08/09/2021	19/09/2021	2	2
6	16/09/2021	08/10/2021	4	4
7	26/09/2021	12/10/2021	2	2

Figure 6-41. *Using the Friday only weekend option with NETWORKDAYS.INTL*

The provided *weekend* options are limited. The text string offers more flexibility if you need multiple days, for example, Mondays and Thursdays between two dates.

The YEARFRAC Function

Availability: All versions

The YEARFRAC function returns the number of years and its fraction from a given start and end date. This can be very useful when calculating ages, proportions for annual benefits such as entitled leave, or financial interest between two dates.

It requires only the two dates with which to calculate the difference as a fraction. There is also an optional argument to specify the type of day count to use:

```
=YEARFRAC(start_date, end_date, [basis])
```

- **Start date:** The start date for the calculation.

- **End date:** The end date for the calculation.

- **[Basis]:** A number that represents the day count basis (Figure 6-42). If omitted, 0 is used to apply the US (NASD) 30/360 basis. This means that each month of the year has 30 days.

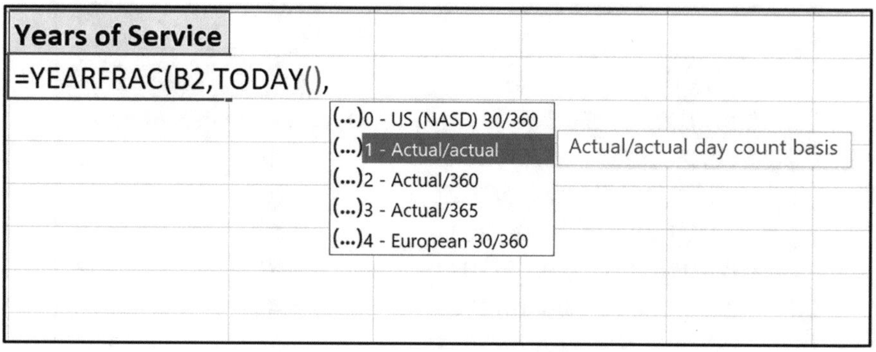

Figure 6-42. *Day count basis options in YEARFRAC*

The YEARFRAC function is great for calculating the number of years between two dates. And a great example for this task is calculating the age of someone or something.

Excel does not have a worksheet function to calculate age. This is quite a surprising omission. However, YEARFRAC makes it easy.

In Figure 6-43, the following YEARFRAC function is entered in column C. It returns the number of years with decimals to represent the proportion of the year that has passed between the date in column B and today's date:

```
=YEARFRAC(B2,TODAY(),1)
```

The day count basis has been specified as 1; this is the actual day count basis. So, it uses the actual number of days in each month. This is the most common basis to use. The other options apply for specific business uses.

The TRUNC function can be added to the formula to remove the decimal part of the value and display the number of years only (Figure 6-43):

```
=TRUNC(YEARFRAC(B2,TODAY(),1))
```

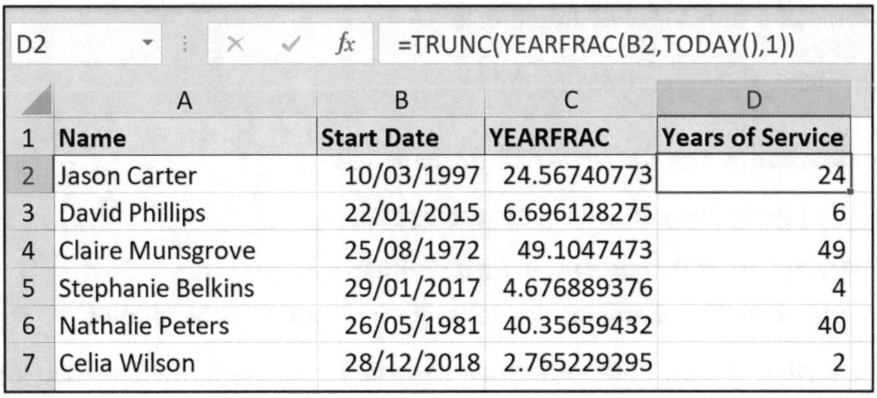

D2			f_x	=TRUNC(YEARFRAC(B2,TODAY(),1))	

	A	B	C	D
1	**Name**	**Start Date**	**YEARFRAC**	**Years of Service**
2	Jason Carter	10/03/1997	24.56740773	24
3	David Phillips	22/01/2015	6.696128275	6
4	Claire Munsgrove	25/08/1972	49.1047473	49
5	Stephanie Belkins	29/01/2017	4.676889376	4
6	Nathalie Peters	26/05/1981	40.35659432	40
7	Celia Wilson	28/12/2018	2.765229295	2

Figure 6-43. *Calculating years of service with YEARFRAC*

Equally, the fractional part of the result could have been used to calculate proportional interest.

The DATEDIF Function

Availability: All versions

The DATEDIF function calculates the difference between two dates in a specified unit such as years, months, or days.

The DATEDIF function is unique in that it is undocumented in Excel. When you type the DATEDIF function in Excel, no information is provided (Figure 6-44).

It remains for compatibility with older workbooks from Lotus 1-2-3. However, it can still come in useful.

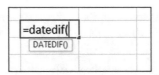

Figure 6-44. *DATEDIF function with no arguments showing*

The syntax for the DATEDIF function is

```
=DATEDIF(start_date, end_date, unit)
```

- **Start date:** The start date of the calculation.

- **End date:** The end date of the calculation.

- **Unit:** Letters that represent the unit difference that you want to calculate. The characters must be entered within double quotes.

The following lists the units and details the calculation performed by each unit entry.

- **"Y":** The difference in complete years

- **"M":** The difference in complete months

- **"D":** The difference in days

- **"MD":** The difference in days, ignoring years and months

- **"YM":** The difference in months, ignoring years and days

- **"YD":** The difference in days, ignoring years

Figure 6-45 shows examples of DATEDIF performing the more common unit entries. Excel does not have a function for months difference, so the calculation of months difference and months difference ignoring years is of special interest.

The following formula is entered into cell G2. Notice the result of 11. The difference between 10th March and 9th March is one day short of 12 months.

```
=DATEDIF(B2,C2,"ym")
```

G2		×	✓	fx	=DATEDIF(B2,C2,"ym")		
	A	B	C	D	E	F	G
1	Name	Start Date	End date	y	m	d	ym
2	Jason Carter	10/03/1997	09/03/2021	23	287	8765	11
3	David Phillips	22/01/2015	10/06/2017	2	28	870	4
4	Claire Munsgrove	25/08/1972	10/11/2006	34	410	12495	2
5	Stephanie Belkins	29/01/2017	13/12/2018	1	22	683	10
6	Nathalie Peters	26/05/1981	19/06/1991	10	120	3676	0
7	Celia Wilson	28/12/2018	04/05/2020	1	16	493	4

Figure 6-45. *DATEDIF function examples*

Note   Microsoft does not recommend the use of the "MD" unit. This is because it can produce an inaccurate result when calculating the remaining days after the last completed month. It is also why an example is omitted from this book.

DATEDIF function results can be combined to calculate the date difference in a string such as the number of years and months.

The following formula combines the results of two DATEDIF functions (Figure 6-46), one for the years difference and another for months difference, ignoring years. Text is added to present the result nicely:

```
=DATEDIF(J2,K2,"y")&" years, "&DATEDIF(J2,K2,"ym")&" months"
```

An IF function or an alternative can be added to prevent the display of results such as the 0 months in cell L6.

	fx	=DATEDIF(J2,K2,"y")&" years, "&DATEDIF(J2,K2,"ym")&" months"		

H	I	J	K	L	M
	Name	**Start Date**	**End date**	**Difference**	
	Jason Carter	10/03/1997	09/03/2021	23 years, 11 months	
	David Phillips	22/01/2015	10/06/2017	2 years, 4 months	
	Claire Munsgrove	25/08/1972	10/11/2006	34 years, 2 months	
	Stephanie Belkins	29/01/2017	13/12/2018	1 years, 10 months	
	Nathalie Peters	26/05/1981	19/06/1991	10 years, 0 months	
	Celia Wilson	28/12/2018	04/05/2020	1 years, 4 months	

Figure 6-46. *Date difference in years and months*

The WORKDAY Function

Availability: All versions

The WORKDAY function is used to return the date a given number of workdays in the future or before a specified date. This function is very useful for calculating due dates, such as estimated task completion dates or expected delivery dates.

The WORKDAY function works in a similar way to the NETWORKDAYS function that we covered earlier. Weekend dates are excluded from the calculation, and there is an optional *Holidays* argument, where a range of additional dates to exclude can be provided.

```
=WORKDAY(start_date, days, [holidays])
```

- **Start date:** The start date for the calculation.

- **Days:** The number of working days before or after the start date. Enter a negative value for days before the start date and a positive number for days after the start date.

- **[Holidays]:** An optional argument that specifies additional non-working dates to be excluded from the calculation. They can be provided as a range of dates on a worksheet or an array returned by another function such as FILTER or XLOOKUP.

Let's see some examples of the WORKDAY function in action.

Calculate a Due Date from a Starting Date

In this example, we have a list of tasks and their duration in working days. Based on this duration, we will use the WORKDAY function to calculate the estimated due dates.

In Figure 6-47, the following formula is entered into column D. This is a simple WORKDAY function to exclude weekends only from the calculation:

```
=WORKDAY(B2,C2)
```

	A	B	C	D
	Name	Start Date	Duration	End date
1				
2	Task 1	25/08/2021	7	03/09/2021
3	Task 2	04/09/2021	3	08/09/2021
4	Task 3	09/08/2021	5	16/08/2021
5	Task 4	03/09/2021	18	29/09/2021
6	Task 5	19/08/2021	11	03/09/2021
7	Task 6	10/08/2021	1	11/08/2021

D2 =WORKDAY(B2,C2)

Figure 6-47. *Calculating estimated due dates for a list of tasks*

Additional non-working dates can be specified by referencing a range containing the dates, as shown in Figure 6-48:

```
=WORKDAY(B2,C2,$F$2:$F$4)
```

D2		⋮	×	✓	fx	=WORKDAY(B2,C2,$F$2:$F$4)		

	A	B	C	D	E	F
1	Name	Start Date	Duration	End date		Exclude
2	Task 1	25/08/2021	7	07/09/2021		27/08/2021
3	Task 2	04/09/2021	3	09/09/2021		12/08/2021
4	Task 3	09/08/2021	5	17/08/2021		06/09/2021
5	Task 4	03/09/2021	18	30/09/2021		
6	Task 5	19/08/2021	11	07/09/2021		
7	Task 6	10/08/2021	1	11/08/2021		

Figure 6-48. *WORKDAY function including a holidays range*

Remember, the WORKDAY function can also return a date a specified number of working days in the past. To do this, a negative value would be entered for the *Days* argument.

Although a less common scenario, the WORKDAY function could be used to calculate the start date from a given end date and number of working days.

The WORKDAY.INTL Function

Along with the WORKDAY function, there is also a WORKDAY.INTL function. This is a more flexible alternative to WORKDAY.

It can be used to customize the weekend parameter using a list of predefined options or to specify the working days of a week by entering a string of seven 1s and 0s.

The syntax of WORKDAY.INTL is

```
=WORKDAY.INTL(start_date, days, [weekend], [holidays])
```

The list of weekend options is the same as that provided by the NETWORKDAYS. INTL function (Figure 6-49).

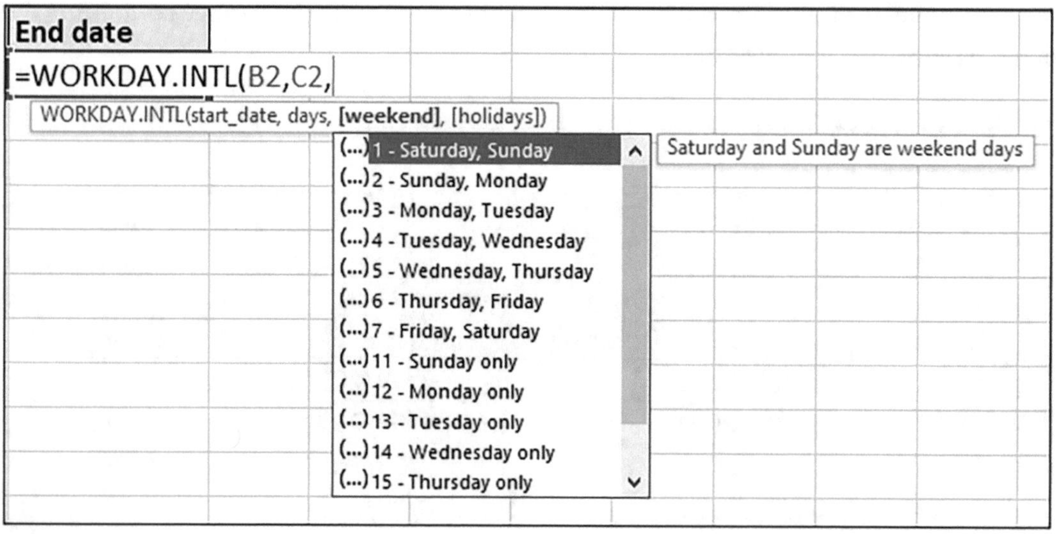

Figure 6-49. *Weekend options with WORKDAY.INTL*

In the following formula (Figure 6-50), option 11 for Sunday only is specified. The additional range of dates supplied in range F2:F4 is also excluded from the calculation:

```
=WORKDAY.INTL(B2,C2,11,$F$2:$F$4)
```

D2			fx	=WORKDAY.INTL(B2,C2,11,$F$2:$F$4)		
	A	B	C	D	E	F
1	Name	Start Date	Duration	End date		Exclude
2	Task 1	25/08/2021	7	03/09/2021		27/08/2021
3	Task 2	04/09/2021	3	09/09/2021		12/08/2021
4	Task 3	09/08/2021	5	16/08/2021		06/09/2021
5	Task 4	03/09/2021	18	25/09/2021		
6	Task 5	19/08/2021	11	02/09/2021		
7	Task 6	10/08/2021	1	11/08/2021		

Figure 6-50. *NETWORKDAYS.INTL function used to specify Sunday only*

You can go beyond the standard options provided with WORKDAY.INTL by entering a text string of seven 1s and 0s. This provides us with a way of specifying whatever working week we require.

The first day in the string is a Monday. A 1 indicates a non-working day, and a 0 is a working day.

In Figure 6-51, the formula specifies that only Tuesday, Wednesday, Thursday, and Friday are working days. The three dates in range F2:F4 are also excluded again:

```
=WORKDAY.INTL(B2,C2,"1000011",$F$2:$F$4)
```

	A	B	C	D	E	F
	Name	Start Date	Duration	End date		Exclude
1						
2	Task 1	25/08/2021	7	08/09/2021		27/08/2021
3	Task 2	04/09/2021	3	09/09/2021		12/08/2021
4	Task 3	09/08/2021	5	18/08/2021		06/09/2021
5	Task 4	03/09/2021	18	06/10/2021		
6	Task 5	19/08/2021	11	09/09/2021		
7	Task 6	10/08/2021	1	11/08/2021		

D2 `=WORKDAY.INTL(B2,C2,"1000011",$F$2:$F$4)`

Figure 6-51. *Entering a text string for the weekend argument of WORKDAY.INTL*

Note   The conditional holiday ranges and weekend options demonstrated in the section "The NETWORKDAYS Function" of this chapter can also be applied here to WORKDAY and WORKDAY.INTL.

Calculate First Working Day of a Month

It can be useful in some data analysis scenarios to calculate the next working day from specific date. In this example, we will return the first working day for the months of the year.

Figure 6-52 shows the names of the months in column H. However, each cell contains a date for the first day of each month; they are just formatted to show month name only.

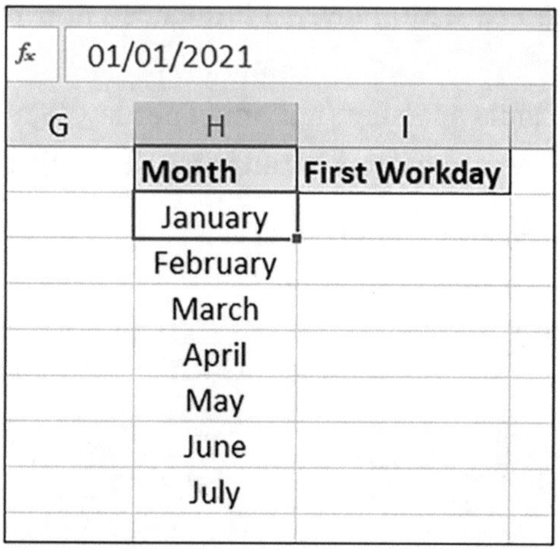

fx	01/01/2021	
G	**H**	**I**
	Month	**First Workday**
	January	
	February	
	March	
	April	
	May	
	June	
	July	

Figure 6-52. *Dates presented as a month name*

The following formula uses the WORKDAY.INTL function to specify a working week of Monday-Thursday and adds one working day to the date returned by the DATE function (Figure 6-53):

```
=WORKDAY.INTL(DATE(YEAR(H2),MONTH(H2),0),1,"0000111")
```

The DATE function creates a date from the same year and month as the date in column H, but for day 0. The formula therefore returns the first working day for that month.

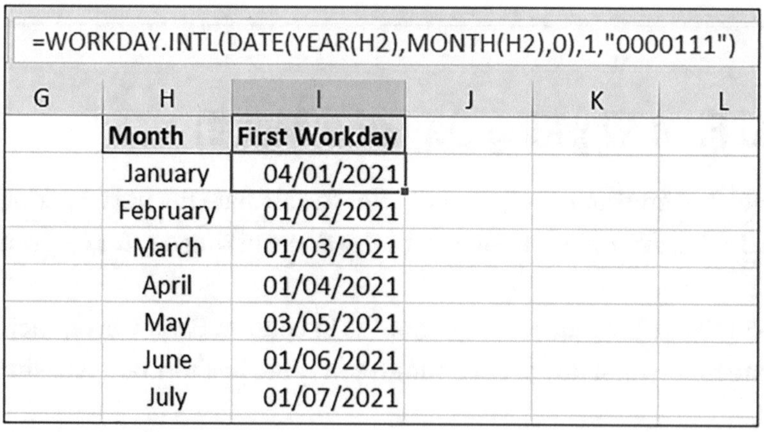

=WORKDAY.INTL(DATE(YEAR(H2),MONTH(H2),0),1,"0000111")					
G	**H**	**I**	**J**	**K**	**L**
	Month	**First Workday**			
	January	04/01/2021			
	February	01/02/2021			
	March	01/03/2021			
	April	01/04/2021			
	May	03/05/2021			
	June	01/06/2021			
	July	01/07/2021			

Figure 6-53. *Calculating the first working day of a month*

We will see how to calculate the last working day of a month, when we visit the EOMONTH function next.

EDATE and EOMONTH

Availability: All versions

The EDATE and EOMONTH functions return a date a specified number of months ahead or prior to an origin date. EDATE returns a date with the same day of the month as the origin date, and EOMONTH returns a date with the last day of the month.

Both functions require the same two arguments – the start date and the number of months to shift the date:

```
=EDATE(start_date, months)
```

or

```
=EOMONTH(start_date, months)
```

- **Start date:** The start date for the calculation.

- **Months:** The number of months after or before the start date that you would like to offset the date. Enter a positive number to return a future date and a negative number to return a past date.

Calculate Contract End Dates

These functions are perfect for calculating future end dates such as contract finish dates.

Use EDATE if the end date is the same day of the month as the start date and EOMONTH if you need the last day of the month for the end date.

In Figure 6-54, the following formula uses the EDATE function to return the date 12 months from the start date:

```
=EDATE(B2,12)
```

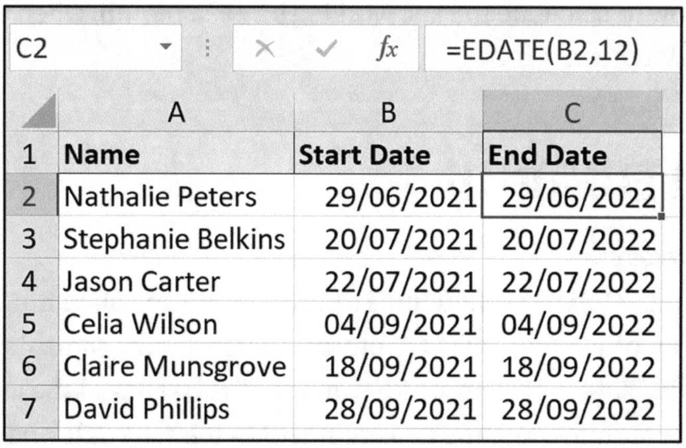

C2 =EDATE(B2,12)

	A	B	C
1	Name	Start Date	End Date
2	Nathalie Peters	29/06/2021	29/06/2022
3	Stephanie Belkins	20/07/2021	20/07/2022
4	Jason Carter	22/07/2021	22/07/2022
5	Celia Wilson	04/09/2021	04/09/2022
6	Claire Munsgrove	18/09/2021	18/09/2022
7	David Phillips	28/09/2021	28/09/2022

Figure 6-54. *EDATE returning the date 12 months from the start date*

And in Figure 6-55, the EOMONTH function has been used. This time, the contract is 18 months long, and notice that the EOMONTH function returns the last day of the month:

```
=EOMONTH(B2,18)
```

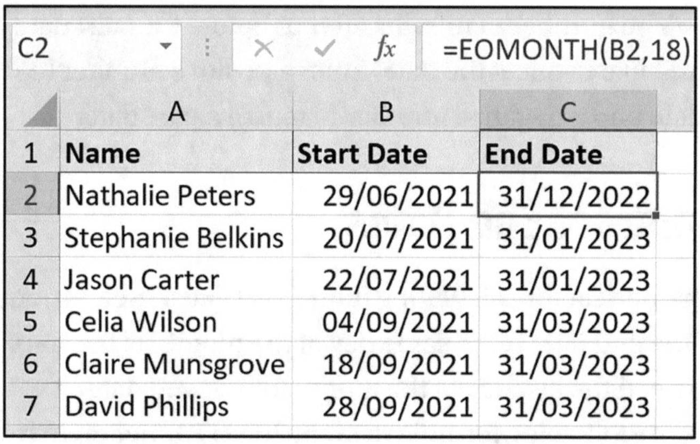

C2 =EOMONTH(B2,18)

	A	B	C
1	Name	Start Date	End Date
2	Nathalie Peters	29/06/2021	31/12/2022
3	Stephanie Belkins	20/07/2021	31/01/2023
4	Jason Carter	22/07/2021	31/01/2023
5	Celia Wilson	04/09/2021	31/03/2023
6	Claire Munsgrove	18/09/2021	31/03/2023
7	David Phillips	28/09/2021	31/03/2023

Figure 6-55. *EOMONTH returning the contract end date in 18 months' time*

Last Day of a Month

Instead of calculating a date a specified number of months into the future, maybe you want to return the date of the last day of a given month.

The following formula uses a 0 for the *months* argument to return the date on the last day of the month for the return date in column F (Figure 6-56):

`=EOMONTH(F2,0)`

The following formula is entered in column H to calculate the number of days for the hired item. A 1 is added to the days difference as I wanted to include full days in the result:

`=DAYS(G2,F2)+1`

fx	=EOMONTH(F2,0)		
E	**F**	**G**	**H**
Reference	Hire Date	Return Date	Days Hired
12-JB	27/01/2021	31/01/2021	5
45-NS	17/02/2021	28/02/2021	12
091-OB	15/05/2021	31/05/2021	17
72-UH	21/10/2021	31/10/2021	11
32-PL	08/10/2021	31/10/2021	24
116-XF	17/02/2021	28/02/2021	12

Figure 6-56. *Calculating the last day of a given month*

Number of Days in a Month

In a variation to the previous formula, maybe you do not want to return the date, but simply "how many days are in the month of a given date?".

To do this, the DAY function is combined with EOMONTH (Figure 6-57):

`=DAY(EOMONTH(J2,0))`

fx	=DAY(EOMONTH(J2,0))	
I	**J**	**K**
	Date	**No of Days**
	14/04/2021	30
	27/08/2021	31
	14/10/2021	31
	11/02/2021	28
	03/11/2021	30
	11/07/2021	31

Figure 6-57. *Returning the number of days in a given month*

Last Working Day of a Month

By using the WORKDAY function and the EOMONTH function together, we can calculate the last working day of a month.

The following formula (Figure 6-58) returns the first day of the following month by adding 1 to the EOMONTH function result. WORKDAY then returns the date of the previous working day by using –1 in its *months* argument:

```
=WORKDAY(EOMONTH(M2,0)+1,-1)
```

fx	=WORKDAY(EOMONTH(M2,0)+1,-1)		
L	**M**	**N**	**O**
	Date	**Last Working Day**	
	14/04/2021	30/04/2021	
	27/08/2021	31/08/2021	
	14/10/2021	29/10/2021	
	11/02/2021	26/02/2021	
	03/11/2021	30/11/2021	
	11/07/2021	30/07/2021	

Figure 6-58. *Calculating the last working day of a month*

First Working Day of Next Month

Following the previous example, returning the first working day of the next month may appear straightforward. Once again, the WORKDAY and EOMONTH functions are combined.

EOMONTH returns the date for the last day of the given month, and the WORKDAY function then returns the first working day after that date (Figure 6-59):

```
=WORKDAY(EOMONTH(M2,0), 1)
```

fx	=WORKDAY(EOMONTH(M2,0),1)		

L	M	N	O
	Date	**Last Working Day**	**First Working Day**
	14/04/2021	30/04/2021	03/05/2021
	27/08/2021	31/08/2021	01/09/2021
	14/10/2021	29/10/2021	01/11/2021
	11/02/2021	26/02/2021	01/03/2021
	03/11/2021	30/11/2021	01/12/2021
	11/07/2021	30/07/2021	02/08/2021

Figure 6-59. *Returning the first working day of the next month*

Note   The last two examples using WORKDAY were based on a working week of Monday-Friday. Remember, the working week can easily be customized to our requirements.

Returning Week Numbers

A common task in Excel is to return the week number for the year (calendar or fiscal), a project, or some other timeline.

Excel provides a couple of functions to calculate week numbers for years. For other scenarios, we can combine functions or be a little creative with our formulas.

The WEEKNUM Function

Availability: All versions

The WEEKNUM function returns the week number in the year. By default, it begins with the week that contains 1st January, but it can also return the week number according to the ISO 8601 standard.

The syntax for the WEEKNUM function is

```
=WEEKNUM(serial_number, [return_type])
```

- **Serial number:** The date for the calculation.

- **[Return type]:** A number that determines which day the week begins. By default, the week begins on a Sunday.

There are two systems for the return type. These are shown in Figure 6-60.

- **System 1:** The week containing 1st January is the first week of the year. You can specify on which day the week begins.

- **System 2:** This system uses the methodology specified in ISO 8601. This is a universal standard for communicating dates internationally, removing any confusion. The week containing the first Thursday is week 1. Only *return type* 21 is used for this system.

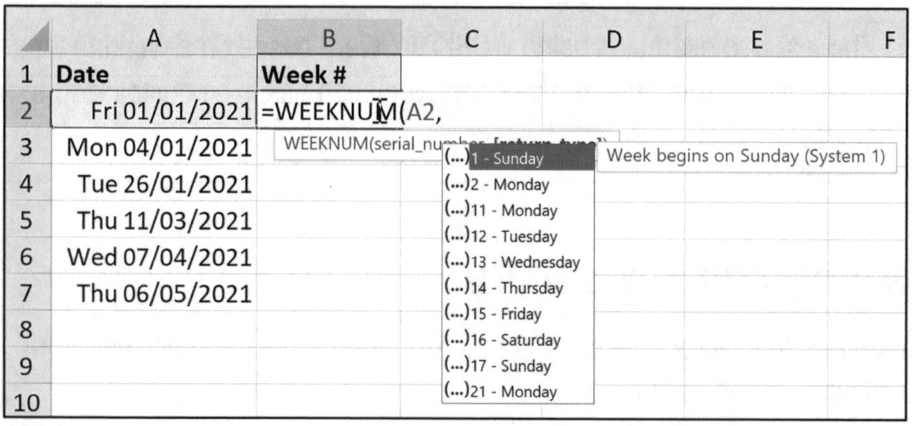

Figure 6-60. *Return type options with WEEKNUM*

In Figure 6-61, the WEEKNUM function is using the default return type – week begins on a Sunday:

```
=WEEKNUM(A2)
```

The date of 4th January 2021 has been identified as week 2, because week 2 begins on Sunday 3rd January 2021.

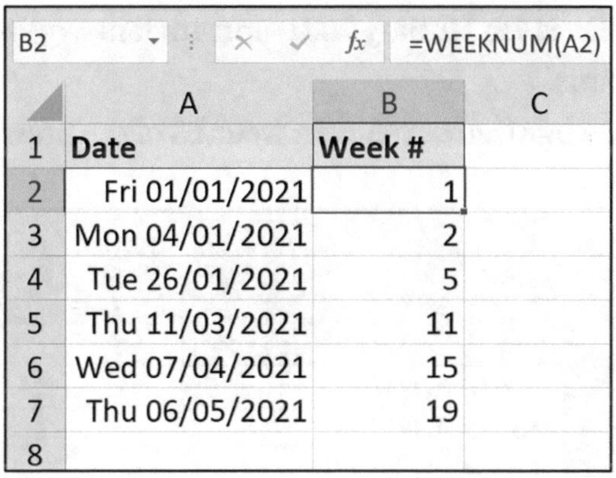
B2 =WEEKNUM(A2)

	A	B	C
1	Date	Week #	
2	Fri 01/01/2021	1	
3	Mon 04/01/2021	2	
4	Tue 26/01/2021	5	
5	Thu 11/03/2021	11	
6	Wed 07/04/2021	15	
7	Thu 06/05/2021	19	
8			

Figure 6-61. *WEEKNUM using the default return type*

The following formula specifies that Friday is the first day of the week. This is return type 15 (Figure 6-62):

```
=WEEKNUM(A2,15)
```

In this example, 4th January 2021 is identified as being in week number 1 of the year. Week 2 does not begin until Friday 8th January 2021.

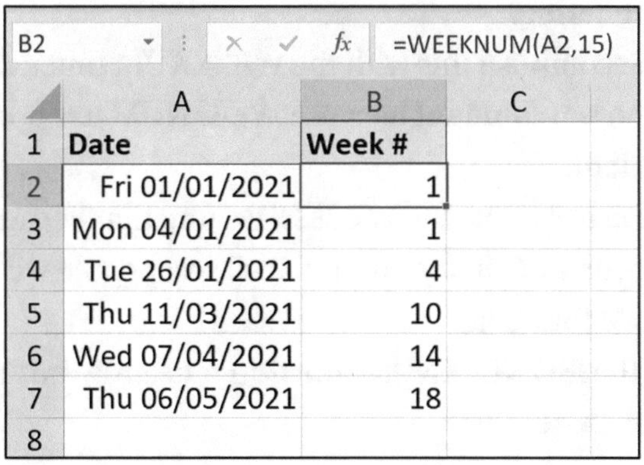
B2 =WEEKNUM(A2,15)

	A	B	C
1	Date	Week #	
2	Fri 01/01/2021	1	
3	Mon 04/01/2021	1	
4	Tue 26/01/2021	4	
5	Thu 11/03/2021	10	
6	Wed 07/04/2021	14	
7	Thu 06/05/2021	18	
8			

Figure 6-62. *WEEKNUM with the start of a week set as a Friday*

Let's now see the WEEKNUM function applying the ISO standard for week numbering. The following formula specifies the return type of 21 (Figure 6-63):

```
=WEEKNUM(A2,21)
```

The ISO 8601 standard defines the first week of a year as the week that contains the first Thursday. An ISO week begins on a Monday.

4th January 2021 is recognized as the first date of the first week of the year. This is because the first Thursday is 7th January 2021, and 4th January 2021 is the beginning of that week by ISO standards.

1st January 2021 is recognized as being in week 53 of the previous year.

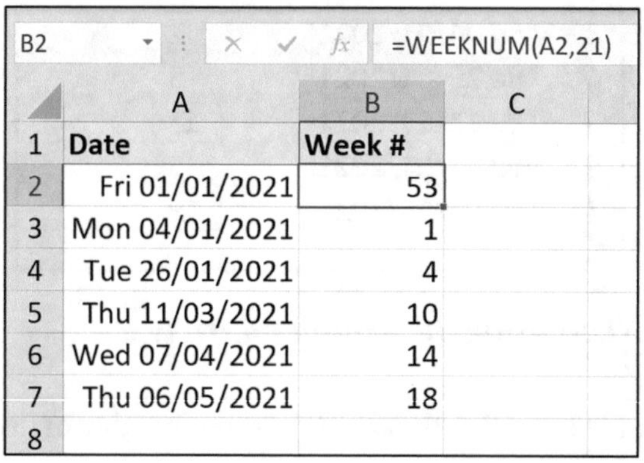

Figure 6-63. *WEEKNUM using the ISO standard for week numbering*

What Is ISOWEEKNUM?

The ISOWEEKNUM function returns the week number of the year as defined by the ISO standards for week numbering.

But didn't we just accomplish this with the WEEKNUM function? Yes, we did. The ISOWEEKNUM function is redundant because WEEKNUM has option 21 that defines the use of the ISO standard.

However, I prefer the use of the ISOWEEKNUM function because its name is more descriptive than a function that defines option 21. Most people will not know what 21 means in the WEEKNUM function.

Figure 6-64 shows the ISOWEEKNUM function returning the week numbers as defined by the ISO 8601 standards:

```
=ISOWEEKNUM(A2)
```

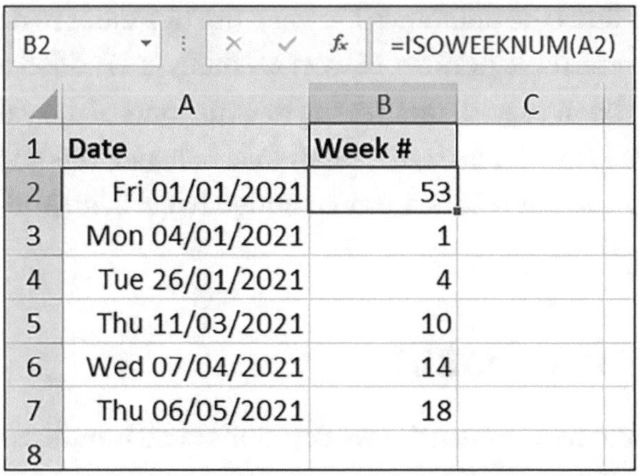

B2 =ISOWEEKNUM(A2)

	A	B	C
1	Date	Week #	
2	Fri 01/01/2021	53	
3	Mon 04/01/2021	1	
4	Tue 26/01/2021	4	
5	Thu 11/03/2021	10	
6	Wed 07/04/2021	14	
7	Thu 06/05/2021	18	
8			

Figure 6-64. *ISOWEEKNUM function returning week numbers*

Return the Week Number for Any Given Date

Instead of returning the week number in the year, you may want to calculate the week number in a project, fiscal cycle, or maternity period. For this, we can write a simple little formula.

In Figure 6-65, the following formula has been entered into cell J2 to return the number of weeks since the date in cell F2:

```
=TRUNC((I2-$F$2)/7+1)
```

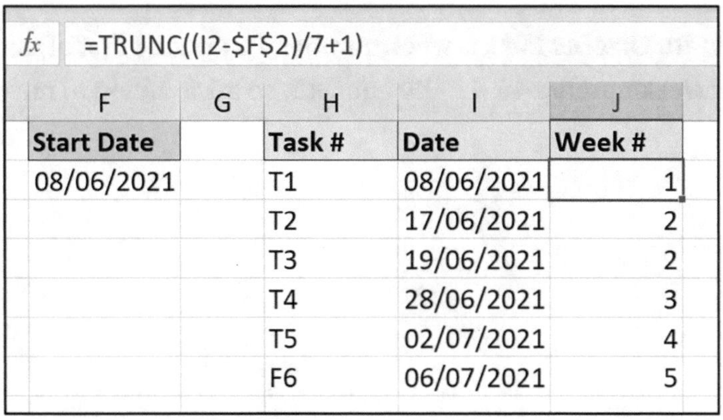

fx =TRUNC((I2-$F$2)/7+1)

F	G	H	I	J
Start Date		Task #	Date	Week #
08/06/2021		T1	08/06/2021	1
		T2	17/06/2021	2
		T3	19/06/2021	2
		T4	28/06/2021	3
		T5	02/07/2021	4
		F6	06/07/2021	5

Figure 6-65. *Returning the week number from any given date*

The formula first finds the difference between the two dates in days. This result is then divided by 7 to return the number of weeks. Finally, 1 is added to the result. The TRUNC function has been used to remove the decimal part of the value.

So, for the date of 17th June 2021, the difference between this and the start date is 9. When divided by 7, the result is 1.28. 1 is then added to get 2.28. And TRUNC strips of the decimals.

Week Number in a Month

Another scenario could be to return the week number in a month instead of years. The WEEKNUM, or ISOWEEKNUM, function can be used within a formula to calculate the week number within a month.

The following formula uses two WEEKNUM functions (Figure 6-66). Using the date in column L, the first returns the week number in the year, and the second returns the year's week number for the first day of that month.

The latter is subtracted from the former, therefore nullifying the year leading up to the first of that month. 1 is added to return the week number in the month.

```
=WEEKNUM(L2,2)-
WEEKNUM(DATE(YEAR(L2),MONTH(L2),1),2)
+1
```

The WEEKNUM function is using return type 2. This defines Monday as the first day of the week.

For example, 4th October 2021 is week number 41, and the first of that month (1st October 2021) is week number 40. 41 – 40 equals 1, so a 1 is added to return week 2 of that month.

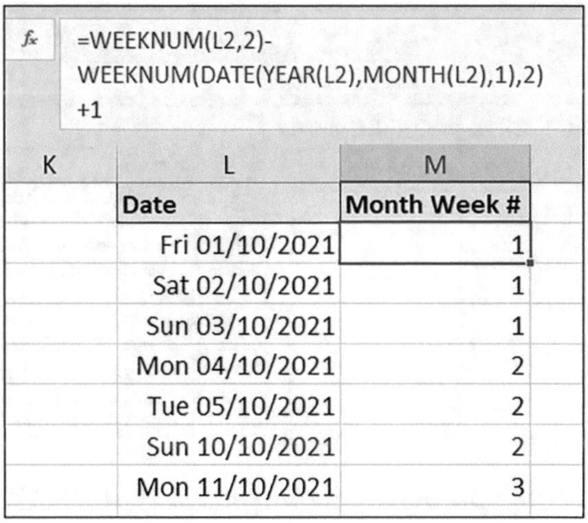

f_x	=WEEKNUM(L2,2)- WEEKNUM(DATE(YEAR(L2),MONTH(L2),1),2) +1

K	L	M
	Date	**Month Week #**
	Fri 01/10/2021	1
	Sat 02/10/2021	1
	Sun 03/10/2021	1
	Mon 04/10/2021	2
	Tue 05/10/2021	2
	Sun 10/10/2021	2
	Mon 11/10/2021	3

Figure 6-66. *Returning the week number within a month*

The WEEKDAY Function

Availability: All versions

The WEEKDAY function returns the day of the week of a given date. The day of the week is returned as an index number.

The function prompts for two arguments – the date and on which days a week begins and ends:

=WEEKDAY(serial_number, [return_type])

- **Serial number:** The date of which to return the weekday.

- **[Return type]:** A number that determines which day the week begins. By default, the week begins on a Sunday. So, Sunday = 1 and Saturday = 7.

The week can begin on any day of the week, and the list of options is provided as you type the formula (Figure 6-67).

	A	B	C	D	E
1	**Date**	**Weekday**			
2	Sun 24/01/2021	=WEEKDAY(A2,			
3	Tue 16/03/2021	WEEKDAY(serial_number, [return_type])			
4	Fri 09/04/2021		(...) 1 - Numbers 1 (Sunday) through 7 (Saturday)		
5	Mon 26/04/2021		(...) 2 - Numbers 1 (Monday) through 7 (Sunday)		
6	Mon 05/07/2021		(...) 3 - Numbers 0 (Monday) through 6 (Sunday)		
7	Sat 18/09/2021		(...) 11 - Numbers 1 (Monday) through 7 (Sunday)		
8			(...) 12 - Numbers 1 (Tuesday) through 7 (Monday)		
9			(...) 13 - Numbers 1 (Wednesday) through 7 (Tuesday)		

(...) 14 - Numbers 1 (Thursday) through 7 (Wednesday)
(...) 15 - Numbers 1 (Friday) through 7 (Thursday)
(...) 16 - Numbers 1 (Saturday) through 7 (Friday)
(...) 17 - Numbers 1 (Sunday) through 7 (Saturday)

Figure 6-67. *Return type options available for the WEEKDAY function*

In Figure 6-68, the WEEKDAY function is used to return the day of the week for the dates entered in column A. Return type 2 has been used. This specifies the start of the week as Monday, so Monday = 1 and Sunday = 7.

B2	▼ :	× ✓ *fx*	=WEEKDAY(A2,2)

	A	B	C
1	**Date**	**Weekday**	
2	Sun 24/01/2021	7	
3	Tue 16/03/2021	2	
4	Fri 09/04/2021	5	
5	Mon 26/04/2021	1	
6	Mon 05/07/2021	1	
7	Sat 18/09/2021	6	

Figure 6-68. *WEEKDAY function returning the day of week as a number*

The dates in column A of Figure 6-68 have been formatted to show the day of week name so that we may see the accuracy of the formula easily. It is not necessary for the formula.

Rate of Pay Determined by Day of Week

Let's now see a practical example of using the WEEKDAY function. In this example, we would like to apply a rate of pay that is dependent on the day of week when the hours were worked.

In this example, the staff will receive an increase in pay when they work on a Saturday or a Sunday. By setting the WEEKDAY function to return type 2, Monday = 1 and Sunday = 7, we can easily identify a Saturday or Sunday as their index number would be greater than 5.

The following formula (Figure 6-69) uses a simple IF function to test if the result of the WEEKDAY function is >5. It multiplies the hours worked by the Sat-Sun rate if it is, and multiplies the hours worked by the Mon-Fri rate if not:

```
=IF(WEEKDAY(D2,2)>5,E2*$I$3,E2*$I$2)
```

	fx	=IF(WEEKDAY(D2,2)>5,E2*$I$3,E2*$I$2)						
	D	E	F	G	H	I	
	Date	**Hours Worked**	**Pay**				
	Sun 24/01/2021	8	104.00		**Mon-Fri**	9.50	
	Tue 16/03/2021	6	57.00		**Sat-Sun**	13.00	
	Fri 09/04/2021	9	85.50				
	Mon 26/04/2021	7	66.50				
	Mon 05/07/2021	5	47.50				
	Sat 18/09/2021	7	91.00				

Figure 6-69. Applying a different rate of pay dependent on the day of week worked

---

Note   The WEEKDAY function is not required for tasks such as displaying the day of week name or sorting by day of week. The display of the weekday name in a cell can be achieved with some simple number formatting, and sorting by day of week in Excel is typically achieved using Custom Lists.

Calculating Financial Years and Quarters

For many countries, the financial year (also known as the fiscal year or business year) does not run from January-December, but from alternative start and end dates.

Let's explore how we can calculate time periods such as financial years and quarters for some of the different financial years in operation in countries across the globe.

Fiscal Years

We will calculate the financial years for three different countries (India, Australia, and the UK) to get an understanding for the techniques involved. We will display the financial year as FY YYYY-YYYY, for example, FY 2021-2022.

Let's dive into the formulas used for each calculation. The results for all three formulas are shown in Figure 6-70.

Indian Financial Year

The Indian financial year starts on 1st April and ends on 31st March. The following formula uses an IF function to test if the month of the date is later than March.

If it is, a text string is created from the current year to the next year. And if not, a text string is built from the previous year to the current year.

```
=IF(MONTH(A2)>3,
"FY "&YEAR(A2)&"-"&YEAR(A2)+1,
"FY "&YEAR(A2)-1&"-"&YEAR(A2)
)
```

Australian Financial Year

The Australian financial year runs from 1st July to 30th June of the following year.

This is similar to the Indian financial year, so requires only a simple adjustment. We will change the IF function to test if the month of the date is greater than 6, instead of the 3 we used for the Indian financial year.

```
=IF(MONTH(A2)>6,
"FY "&YEAR(A2)&"-"&YEAR(A2)+1,
"FY "&YEAR(A2)-1&"-"&YEAR(A2)
)
```

UK Financial Year

The financial year of the UK starts on 6th April and ends on 5th April. So, testing the month number of the date is not enough.

The following formula uses the DATE function to create a date from the year of the date being tested, month of April, and day six. If the date is later than 6th April of that year, then the financial year is that year to the following year. Otherwise, it is the previous year to the year of the date.

```
=IF(A2>DATE(YEAR(A2),4,5),
"FY "&YEAR(A2)&"-"&YEAR(A2)+1,
"FY "&YEAR(A2)-1&"-"&YEAR(A2)
)
```

	A	B	C	D
1	Date	India	Australia	UK
2	01/01/2021	FY 2020-2021	FY 2020-2021	FY 2020-2021
3	01/04/2021	FY 2021-2022	FY 2020-2021	FY 2020-2021
4	06/04/2021	FY 2021-2022	FY 2020-2021	FY 2021-2022
5	01/11/2021	FY 2021-2022	FY 2021-2022	FY 2021-2022
6	01/03/2022	FY 2021-2022	FY 2021-2022	FY 2021-2022
7	06/04/2022	FY 2022-2023	FY 2021-2022	FY 2022-2023
8	01/07/2022	FY 2022-2023	FY 2022-2023	FY 2022-2023

Figure 6-70. *Financial year formulas for India, Australia, and the UK*

Fiscal Quarters

The simplest way to calculate quarters for different company financial years is to use the CHOOSE function in Excel. So, we will start with an example using the CHOOSE function and then demonstrate an alternative method.

CHOOSE returns a value from a list of values based on an index number. This makes it perfect for quarter calculation. We can extract the month number from a date and use that as the index value to return the required quarter from a list.

Note   The CHOOSE function is explained in detail in Chapter 11.

Let's look at two different fiscal quarter formulas using CHOOSE. The results of both formulas are shown in Figure 6-71.

This first formula calculates the quarters for a year beginning on 1st April. The MONTH function returns the month number of the date in F2. CHOOSE then returns the number from its list that matches the month number. The string "Q" is added as a prefix to the quarter number:

```
="Q"&CHOOSE(MONTH(F2),4,4,4,1,1,1,2,2,2,3,3,3)
```

This second formula calculates the quarters for a year beginning on 1st October:

```
="Q"&CHOOSE(MONTH(F2),2,2,2,3,3,3,4,4,4,1,1,1)
```

		X ✓ fx	="Q"&CHOOSE(MONTH(F2),4,4,4,1,1,1,2,2,2,3,3,3)	
E	F	G	H	I
	Date	**1st April**	**1st October**	
	01/04/2021	Q1	Q3	
	01/06/2021	Q1	Q3	
	01/07/2021	Q2	Q4	
	01/11/2021	Q3	Q1	
	01/02/2022	Q4	Q2	
	01/04/2022	Q1	Q3	
	01/08/2022	Q2	Q4	

Figure 6-71. *Fiscal quarter calculations with CHOOSE*

In this second method, shown in Figure 6-72, the following formula uses a combination of the EDATE and CEILING functions along with a few mathematical operations. This first formula returns the fiscal quarter for a year beginning in April:

```
="Q"&CEILING(MONTH(EDATE(F2,-3)),3)/3
```

And the following formula returns the fiscal quarter for a year beginning in October:

```
="Q"&CEILING(MONTH(EDATE(F2,-9)),3)/3
```

Let's dive into how these formulas work.

	fx	="Q"&CEILING(MONTH(EDATE(F2,-3)),3)/3		

E	F	G	H	I
	Date	**1st April**	**1st October**	
	01/04/2021	Q1	Q3	
	01/06/2021	Q1	Q3	
	01/07/2021	Q2	Q4	
	01/11/2021	Q3	Q1	
	01/02/2022	Q4	Q2	
	01/04/2022	Q1	Q3	
	01/08/2022	Q2	Q4	

Figure 6-72. *Fiscal quarter calculations with CEILING and EDATE*

The EDATE function is used to offset the date a specified number of months. The number of months to offset is dependent upon the first month of the fiscal year.

The number of months to offset is one less than the first month number of the fiscal year. If the year starts in April (4), then EDATE returns the date three months prior. And if the year starts in October (10), then EDATE returns the date nine months prior.

The MONTH function extracts the month number from the date returned by EDATE. The purpose of the CEILING function is to round a number up to a given multiple. In these formulas, CEILING rounds the month number up to the multiple of 3. And this result is divided by 3 to return the fiscal quarter.

Let's see an example in action. We have the date of 1st July 2021 in cell F4. When returning the fiscal quarter for a year beginning in April, the EDATE function returns the date three months prior, so 1st April 2021 is returned. MONTH returns number 4 and CEILING rounds this up to a multiple of 3, which is 6. Then 6 divided by 3 is 2. The result is Q2.

For the same date but the fiscal year beginning in the month of October, EDATE returns the date nine months prior to 1st July 2021. The result is 1st October 2020. MONTH extracts the number 10, and CEILING rounds this value up to 12 (multiple of 3). 12 divided by 3 is 4, so the result is Q4.

An advantage of this formula over CHOOSE is that the number of months to offset by EDATE could be linked to a cell and be made more dynamic. It is nice to have different formula options. You can choose (😀) your preference.

Note   The CEILING function is used for the rounding task in these formulas. This function is compatible with all Excel versions. In a formula example shortly, the CEILING.MATH function (an updated version of CEILING) will be used.

Working with Time

At the beginning of this chapter, we defined how time is stored in Excel and how it is structured. We also performed some simple calculations to find the difference between two times.

Let's now dive into further important techniques to know when working with time in Excel.

Convert Text to Time

When receiving data from different sources, data does not always come in the format that we require.

To perform calculations and analysis on time data, it is imperative that Excel recognizes it as time. There are two main functions in Excel to convert text values into correct time values – TIMEVALUE and TIME.

The TIMEVALUE Function

Availability: All versions

The TIMEVALUE function returns the time that is represented by text. It is quite simply the time alternative to the DATEVALUE function discussed earlier.

It requires only one argument, and that is the text representation of time that needs to be converted:

```
=TIMEVALUE(time_text)
```

In Figure 6-73, the following formula is used to convert the different text representations of time. Notice that TIMEVALUE only returns the time part of the date-time value in cell A5.

```
=TIMEVALUE(A2)
```

The values are displayed in their raw state – a decimal value representing the time of day. They need to be formatted as time to become readable.

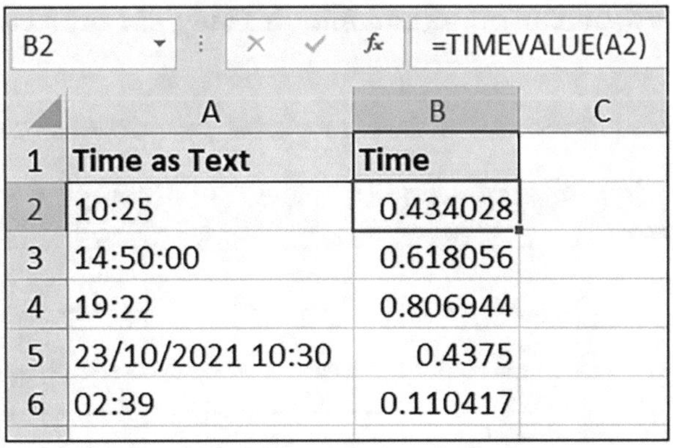

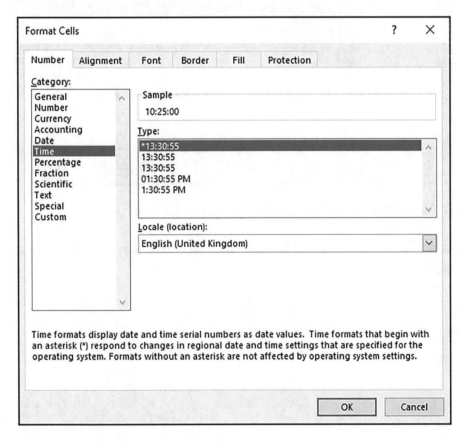

| B2 | ▾ | : | × | ✓ | fx | =TIMEVALUE(A2) |

▲	A	B	C
1	**Time as Text**	**Time**	
2	10:25	0.434028	
3	14:50:00	0.618056	
4	19:22	0.806944	
5	23/10/2021 10:30	0.4375	
6	02:39	0.110417	

Figure 6-73. *TIMEVALUE function converting text to time*

When formatting time, the standard time formatting options all assume that you want to present time to the granularity of seconds (Figure 6-74).

Figure 6-74. *Time formatting options all include seconds*

If you want a time format of hours and minutes only, specify a custom format (Figure 6-75).

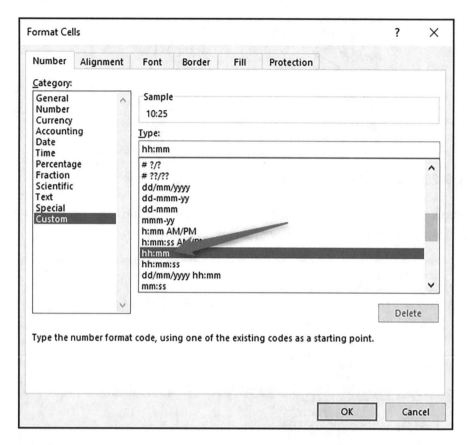

Figure 6-75. *Formatting time to show hours and minutes only*

The results of the TIMEVALUE function are now exactly as we expected them (Figure 6-76).

Figure 6-76. TIMEVALUE results correctly formatted

The TIMEVALUE function can only convert time that is stored as text. If the value you ask it to convert is not text, the #VALUE! error is returned.

Times stored as text can also be converted to time by using the VALUE function or by using a simple mathematical calculation that does not change the cell value.

Figure 6-77 shows the VALUE function converting the same text values. Notice that the VALUE function returns the date and time from the date-time value in cell A5. TIMEVALUE only returned the time. The better method depends on whether you want the date included or not.

=VALUE(A2)

Figure 6-77. VALUE function converting text values into time

In Figure 6-78, the same conversion has been achieved using the following formula. Any mathematical calculation that does not change the cell value can be used to convert text to number.

=A2+0

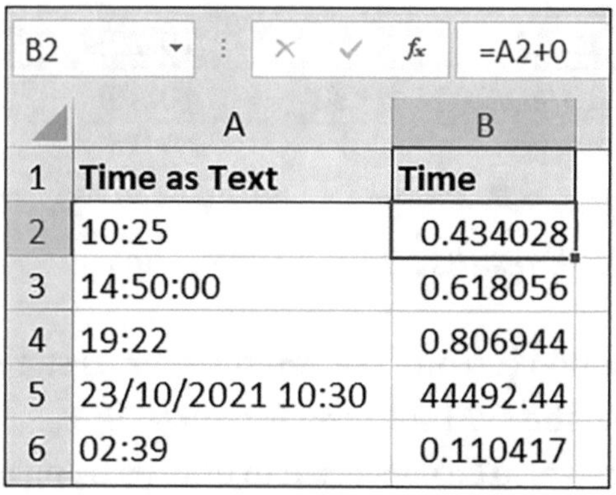

B2	▾	⋮	✕	✓	fₓ	=A2+0

◢	A	B
1	Time as Text	Time
2	10:25	0.434028
3	14:50:00	0.618056
4	19:22	0.806944
5	23/10/2021 10:30	44492.44
6	02:39	0.110417

Figure 6-78. *Simple mathematical operation to convert text to time*

The TIME Function

Availability: All versions

The TIME function returns the decimal value that represents a time from a given hour, minute, and second.

This function is ideal when you need to convert to time from its different parts. For example, the hour, minute, and second may be in different columns on a sheet or extracted by different text functions from a value.

The TIME function requires three arguments – hour, minute, and second. All arguments are mandatory:

=TIME(hour, minute, second)

If the cell that the TIME result is returned to is formatted as General, a time format is automatically applied. This format can be changed or applied in advance.

In the first example of the TIME function (Figure 6-79), the hours and minutes in the text values are separated by a period, or dot. My UK regional settings do not recognize these values as a legitimate time format; therefore, the TIMEVALUE function would not convert them. It produces the #VALUE! error instead.

The following formula uses the LEFT and RIGHT functions to extract the hour and minute from the value. These are passed to the TIME function to create the time value.

The second is a mandatory argument, so a 0 is entered. Although it is not shown in the initial value or the result, the TIME function demands it.

```
=TIME(LEFT(D2,2),RIGHT(D2,2),0)
```

f_x	=TIME(LEFT(D2,2),RIGHT(D2,2),0)	
C	D	E
	Time as Text	Time
	10.25	10:25 AM
	14.50	2:50 PM
	19.22	7:22 PM
	10.30	10:30 AM
	02.39	2:39 AM

Figure 6-79. *TIME function converting time stored as text*

Although this section is about converting text to time, it is worthwhile seeing an example of time being stored as an incorrect numeric value.

In this example, a spreadsheet has been generated from an export, and the time values contain the period or dot separator again. However, this time, my regional settings have forced Excel to assume that the dot is the decimal separator.

Because of this, they have been stored as incorrect numeric values. The following formula has been used to convert them to the correct time (Figure 6-80):

```
=TIME(
    LEFT(G2,FIND(".",G2)-1),
    IF(
        LEN(RIGHT(G2,LEN(G2)-FIND(".",G2)))=1,
        RIGHT(G2,LEN(G2)-FIND(".",G2))&"0",
        RIGHT(G2,LEN(G2)-FIND(".",G2))),
    0)
```

The number of digits for the *hour* and *minute* is irregular, so the FIND and LEN functions are used to help calculate the number of digits in each part of the time value.

```
 ✓  fx   =TIME(
            LEFT(G2,FIND(".",G2)-1),
            IF(
               LEN(RIGHT(G2,LEN(G2)-FIND(".",G2)))=1,
               RIGHT(G2,LEN(G2)-FIND(".",G2))&"0",
               RIGHT(G2,LEN(G2)-FIND(".",G2))),
            0)
```

F	G	H	I
	Time as Number	Time	
	10.25	10:25 AM	
	14.5	2:50 PM	
	19.22	7:22 PM	
	10.3	10:30 AM	
	2.39	2:39 AM	

Figure 6-80. *TIME fixing incorrect numeric values*

Note   Text functions such as FIND and LEN are covered in detail in Chapter 5.

For the *minute* argument of TIME, an IF function is nested to test if the number of characters representing the minute is only one character, for example, 14.5. If it is, then a "0" is appended to the minute string. So, 14.5 would become 14.50; otherwise, instead of being converted to 14:50, it would become 14:05.

In this formula, the calculation to return the minute is used three times. In Chapter 15, we will cover the LET function. This function helps us to create more efficient and meaningful formulas, and this formula is a good use case for LET (available in Excel for Microsoft 365, Excel 2021, and Excel for the Web versions only).

The following is an adapted version of the formula including the LET function (Figure 6-81). The hour and minute calculations are stored as variables named *hour* and *minute* and then used in the final calculation:

```
=LET(
hour,LEFT(G2,FIND(".",G2)-1),
minute,RIGHT(G2,LEN(G2)-FIND(".",G2)),
TIME(hour,IF(LEN(minute)=1,minute&"0",minute),0)
)
```

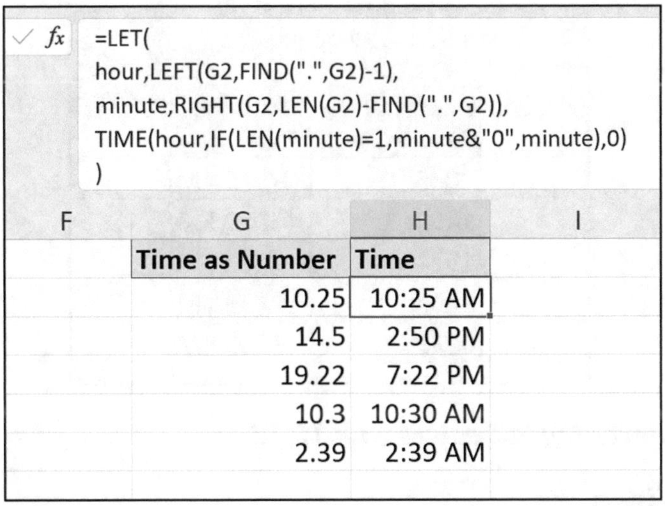

```
√  fx   =LET(
        hour,LEFT(G2,FIND(".",G2)-1),
        minute,RIGHT(G2,LEN(G2)-FIND(".",G2)),
        TIME(hour,IF(LEN(minute)=1,minute&"0",minute),0)
        )
```

F	G	H	I
	Time as Number	**Time**	
	10.25	10:25 AM	
	14.5	2:50 PM	
	19.22	7:22 PM	
	10.3	10:30 AM	
	2.39	2:39 AM	

Figure 6-81. Convert decimal number to time including the LET function

---

Note   The TEXTBEFORE and TEXTAFTER functions, available in modern Excel and covered in Chapter 5, could also have been used to simplify the formula. However, the original formula is compatible for all Excel versions.

For the final TIME function example, we see another common representation of time, which is to display the hours and minutes without any separator (Figure 6-82). The values are stored by text in Excel and need converting.

The following formula is the same as the first TIME formula example. Once again, it achieves the objective of converting the text values to time:

```
=TIME(LEFT(J2,2),RIGHT(J2,2),0)
```

fx	=TIME(LEFT(J2,2),RIGHT(J2,2),0)		
I	J	K	L
	Time as Text	Time	
	1025	10:25 AM	
	1450	2:50 PM	
	1922	7:22 PM	
	1030	10:30 AM	
	0239	2:39 AM	

Figure 6-82. *Converting text values with TIME*

Rounding Time

There may be situations when you need to round time values. Time can be rounded to any multiple of significance – hour, 30 minutes, 15 minutes, etc.

There are three key functions for rounding time: MROUND, CEILING.MATH, and FLOOR.MATH. Let's quickly cover how each of these functions operates before we see them in practice rounding time.

MROUND, CEILING.MATH, and FLOOR.MATH

The MROUND, CEILING.MATH, and FLOOR.MATH functions all round values to a multiple of significance. The function you use depends on how you wish to round.

The MROUND function rounds up or down to the nearest multiple. It requires the number to round and the multiple to round to:

```
=MROUND(number, multiple)
```

The CEILING.MATH function always rounds up to the nearest multiple. It also requires the number to round and the multiple of significance.

There is also an optional *Mode* argument to specify how to round negative values. Because time is rarely negative, we will omit this argument from these examples.

```
=CEILING.MATH(number, [significance], [mode])
```

The FLOOR.MATH function always rounds down to the nearest multiple. Its syntax is the same as CEILING.MATH:

```
=FLOOR.MATH(number, [significance], [mode])
```

Note   The CEILING.MATH and FLOOR.MATH functions were first released with Excel 2013 as improved functions to their predecessors – CEILING and FLOOR. If you use a version before Excel 2013, the CEILING and FLOOR functions work perfectly well too.

Round Time to the Nearest Hour

In Figure 6-83, the three functions have each been used to round time to the nearest hour.

The following MROUND function is used in column B to round time up or down to the nearest hour:

```
=MROUND(A2,"1:00")
```

The CEILING.MATH function is entered in column C to force the value to round up to the next hour:

```
=CEILING.MATH(A2,"1:00")
```

The FLOOR.MATH function is entered in column D to force the value to round down to the previous hour:

```
=FLOOR.MATH(A2,"1:00")
```

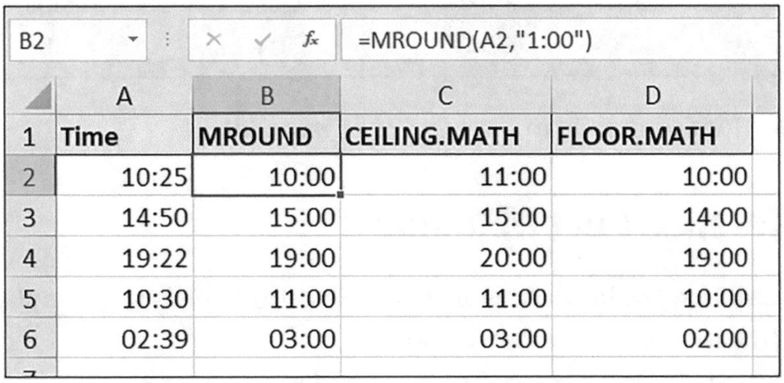

B2	▾	:	×	✓	*fx*	=MROUND(A2,"1:00")	

◢	A	B	C	D
1	Time	MROUND	CEILING.MATH	FLOOR.MATH
2	10:25	10:00	11:00	10:00
3	14:50	15:00	15:00	14:00
4	19:22	19:00	20:00	19:00
5	10:30	11:00	11:00	10:00
6	02:39	03:00	03:00	02:00

Figure 6-83. *Rounding time to the nearest hour*

Round Time to the Nearest 15 Minutes

Figure 6-84 shows further examples of these three functions rounding time values. In these examples, time is rounded to the nearest 15 minutes.

The following MROUND function is entered in column B to round up or down to the nearest 15 minutes:

```
=MROUND(A2,"00:15")
```

The CEILING.MATH function is used in column C to round up to the next 15 minutes:

```
=CEILING.MATH(A2,"00:15")
```

The FLOOR.MATH function is used in column D to round down to the nearest multiple of 15 minutes:

```
=FLOOR.MATH(A2,"00:15")
```

C2	▼	:	×	✓	*fx*	=CEILING.MATH(A2,"00:15")	

	A	B	C	D
1	Time	MROUND	CEILING.MATH	FLOOR.MATH
2	10:25	10:30	10:30	10:15
3	14:50	14:45	15:00	14:45
4	19:22	19:15	19:30	19:15
5	10:30	10:30	10:30	10:30
6	02:39	02:45	02:45	02:30

Figure 6-84. *Rounding time to the nearest 15 minutes*

Time Difference Past Midnight

Calculating the difference between two times in Excel is actually very simple. It is the formatting of the results that can be frustrating.

When the time difference is over 24 hours, the formatting can be even more tricky. In Figure 6-85, the results of the formula =G2-F2 are shown in column H.

These results are correct, but they need to be presented more effectively.

f_x	=G2-F2		
	F	G	H
	Start Time	**Finish Time**	**Duration**
	09/10/2021 08:30	09/10/2021 16:30	0.333333333
	12/09/2021 22:00	15/09/2021 06:00	2.333333333
	20/09/2021 21:00	21/09/2021 04:00	0.291666667
	22/09/2021 07:00	27/09/2021 01:00	4.75
	24/09/2021 09:30	24/09/2021 17:30	0.333333333

Figure 6-85. *Time difference in General format*

Some of the durations span multiple days, so let's format the cell values to be presented in the format "x days, x hours," for example, 2 days, 13 hours.

1. Select the range H2:H6 and press **Ctrl + 1** to open the *Format Cells* window.

2. On the *Number* tab, click the **Custom** category.

3. Type the following into the *Type* field (Figure 6-86):

   d "days," h "hours"

4. Click **OK**.

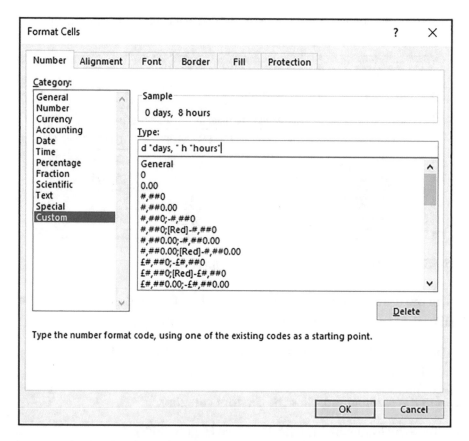

Figure 6-86. *Applying custom formatting to show days and hours*

The duration values are now more legible (Figure 6-87). Custom formatting is an incredibly powerful tool in Excel, and it can be used to format values exactly how we want.

In this example, the results are shown in days and hours. You could also show minutes if required or the results as just the total hours, which we will look at next.

F	G	H
Start Time	**Finish Time**	**Duration**
09/10/2021 08:30	09/10/2021 16:30	0 days, 8 hours
12/09/2021 22:00	15/09/2021 06:00	2 days, 8 hours
20/09/2021 21:00	21/09/2021 04:00	0 days, 7 hours
22/09/2021 07:00	27/09/2021 01:00	4 days, 18 hours
24/09/2021 09:30	24/09/2021 17:30	0 days, 8 hours

Figure 6-87. *Time difference formatted in days and hours*

You may notice in the duration results that three of the five results do not exceed 24 hours.

So, let's set a condition in our formatting rule to format the results that are over 24 hours in the format "x days, x hours" and results less than 24 hours in the format "x hours."

Select the range H2:H6 and open *Format Cells* to edit the existing custom number formatting code.

Replace the code with the following number formatting code (Figure 6-88). The condition is enclosed in square brackets [>1], and a semicolon is used to separate the different formats:

```
[>1] d "days," h "hours";h "hours"
```

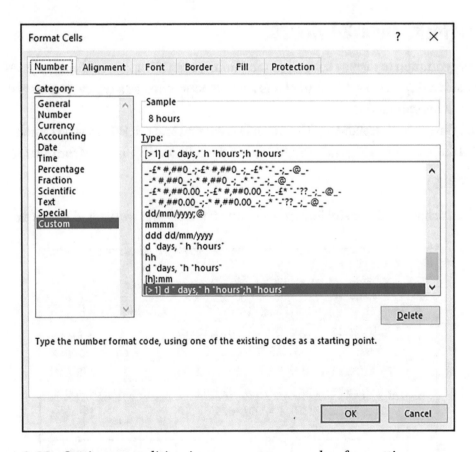

Figure 6-88. *Setting a condition in your custom number formatting*

The results of this conditional number formatting rule are shown in Figure 6-89. This is a cool technique demonstrating a little of what is possible with custom number formatting.

F	G	H
Start Time	Finish Time	Duration
09/10/2021 08:30	09/10/2021 16:30	8 hours
12/09/2021 22:00	15/09/2021 06:00	2 days, 8 hours
20/09/2021 21:00	21/09/2021 04:00	7 hours
22/09/2021 07:00	27/09/2021 01:00	4 days, 18 hours
24/09/2021 09:30	24/09/2021 17:30	8 hours

Figure 6-89. *Formatting to display hours only when less than 24 hours*

Sum Hours over 24 Hours

It is very common to display a result as total hours, even if it spans multiple days. After all, what is a day? Is a day 24 hours? Or is it 8 or 9 hours such as a typical business day? It is open to interpretation.

In Figure 6-90, the following SUM formula is entered into cell H8. Excel has automatically applied the same formatting rule that is used on the cells used by the SUM formula:

`=SUM(H2:H6)`

This is clever and a useful format. However, it is not what we wanted in this example.

fx	=SUM(H2:H6)		
	F	G	H
	Start Time	Finish Time	Duration
	09/10/2021 08:30	09/10/2021 16:30	8 hours
	12/09/2021 22:00	15/09/2021 06:00	2 days, 8 hours
	20/09/2021 21:00	21/09/2021 04:00	7 hours
	22/09/2021 07:00	27/09/2021 01:00	4 days, 18 hours
	24/09/2021 09:30	24/09/2021 17:30	8 hours
			8 days, 1 hours

Figure 6-90. *Sum of total hours with the same days and hours formatting*

There is a special formatting trick to display the total hours that exceed 24 hours in Excel. That trick is to enclose the "h" within square brackets.

An "h" without square brackets will only display the remaining hours past a multiple of 24 hours.

Let's format all the duration values to show total hours only:

1. Select range H2:H6 and cell H8 and press **Ctrl + 1** to open the *Format Cells* window.

2. On the *Number* tab, click the **Custom** category.

3. Type the following into the *Type* field:

   [h] "hours"

4. Click **OK**.

Figure 6-91 shows the total hours displayed in all cells.

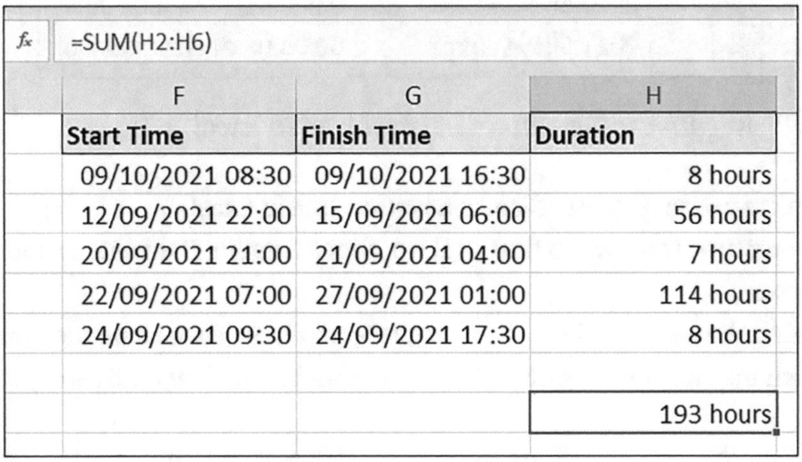

	F	G	H
f_x	=SUM(H2:H6)		
	Start Time	**Finish Time**	**Duration**
	09/10/2021 08:30	09/10/2021 16:30	8 hours
	12/09/2021 22:00	15/09/2021 06:00	56 hours
	20/09/2021 21:00	21/09/2021 04:00	7 hours
	22/09/2021 07:00	27/09/2021 01:00	114 hours
	24/09/2021 09:30	24/09/2021 17:30	8 hours
			193 hours

Figure 6-91. *Formatting time to show hours over 24*

Handling Negative Time

Excel cannot display negative time, so this can create a problem if you need them. Fortunately, there are always workarounds for problems such as this.

In Figure 6-92, we have the London Marathon finish times for the men's category for the last six years. In column D, a formula is calculating the time difference compared to the previous year.

Every year when the finish time is faster than the previous year, a negative time difference is returned, and Excel cannot display the time value, displaying ##### instead.

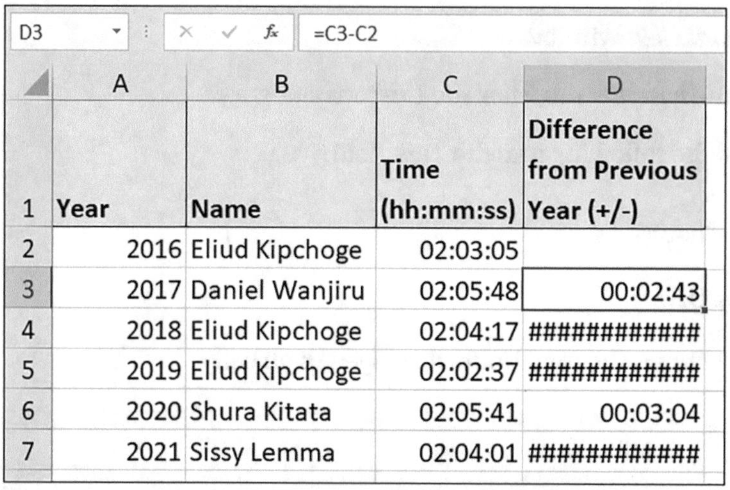

	A	B	C	D
			Time	Difference from Previous
1	Year	Name	(hh:mm:ss)	Year (+/-)
2	2016	Eliud Kipchoge	02:03:05	
3	2017	Daniel Wanjiru	02:05:48	00:02:43
4	2018	Eliud Kipchoge	02:04:17	############
5	2019	Eliud Kipchoge	02:02:37	############
6	2020	Shura Kitata	02:05:41	00:03:04
7	2021	Sissy Lemma	02:04:01	############

Figure 6-92. *Negative times cannot be displayed in Excel*

Let's look at two methods to display negative time in Excel.

The first method is to switch the Excel workbook from its 1900 date system to the 1904 date system.

This will fix the negative dates; however, be careful, because changing the date system will change any existing dates in the workbook. The dates will be adjusted by four years.

In this example, we do not have any dates, so it is not an issue:

1. Click **File ➤ Options ➤ Advanced**.

2. In the *When calculating this workbook* section, check the **Use 1904 date system** box (Figure 6-93).

3. Click **OK**.

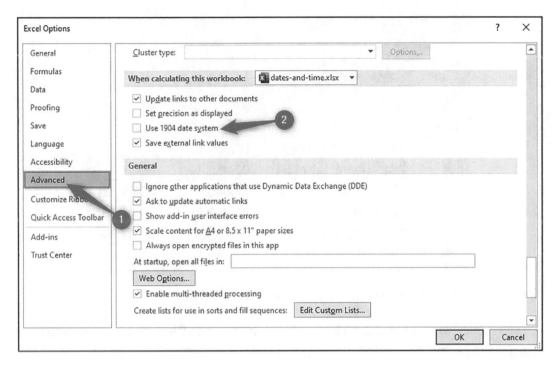

Figure 6-93. *Switching to the 1904 date system*

The negative times are now displayed correctly (Figure 6-94). If you notice this causes a problem with dates on your spreadsheet, you can easily come back to the Excel options and turn off the 1904 date system.

The results are also still numeric values. This is useful if you need to perform further calculations on them. The next approach will convert them to text to display them correctly.

Further formatting of the time values could be applied to hide the hours and display the negative values in a different color to highlight them. However, this is not the focus of this task, so let's move on to the second method.

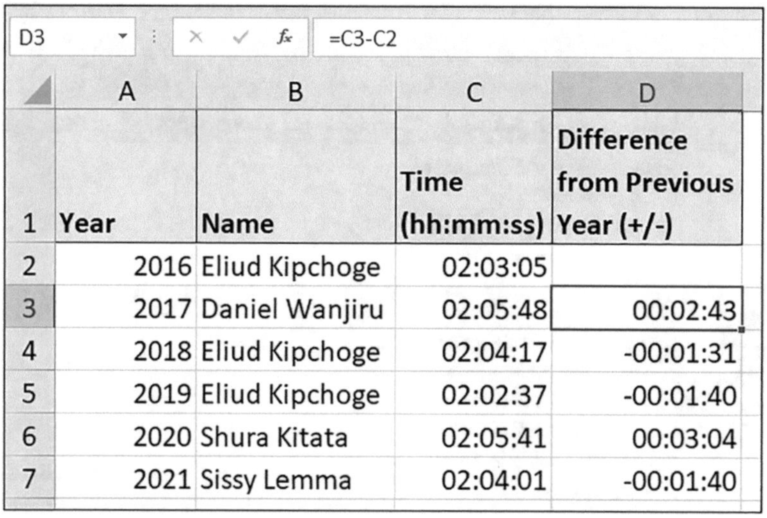

D3	▾	:	×	✓	f_x	=C3-C2	

◢	A	B	C	D
1	Year	Name	Time (hh:mm:ss)	Difference from Previous Year (+/-)
2	2016	Eliud Kipchoge	02:03:05	
3	2017	Daniel Wanjiru	02:05:48	00:02:43
4	2018	Eliud Kipchoge	02:04:17	-00:01:31
5	2019	Eliud Kipchoge	02:02:37	-00:01:40
6	2020	Shura Kitata	02:05:41	00:03:04
7	2021	Sissy Lemma	02:04:01	-00:01:40

Figure 6-94. *Negative times displayed correctly in Excel*

The second method uses the TEXT function (covered in Chapter 5) to display the negative time values as text, but in a time format.

We will also take this opportunity to hide the hours from the results, as a marathon finish time will never be more than 60 minutes improved on a previous year.

In Figure 6-95, the following formula is entered in cell D3. An IF function tests if the result is positive and performs the required TEXT function based on the result:

```
=IF(C3-C2>=0,
TEXT(C3-C2,"mm:ss"),
TEXT(ABS(C3-C2),"-mm:ss")
)
```

The ABS function removes the sign from the result of C3-C2. So, a negative value is converted to positive for the TEXT function to use.

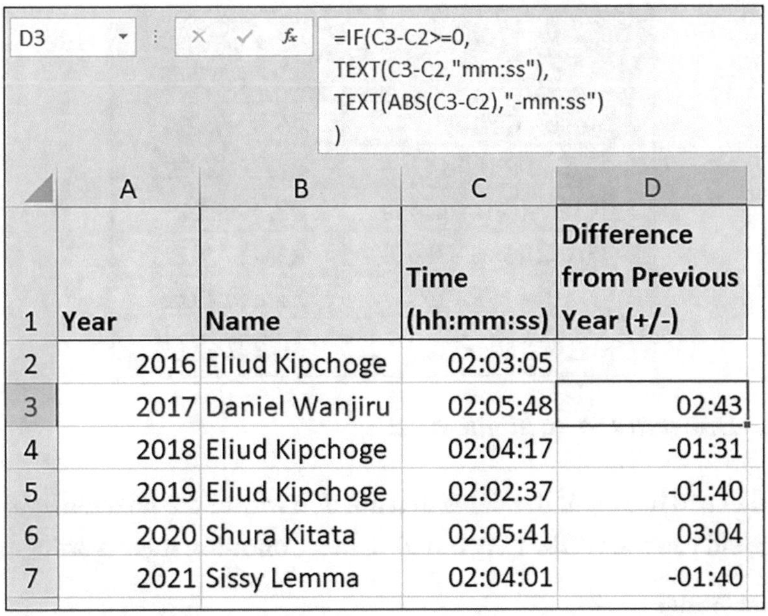

| D3 | ▾ : × ✓ fx | =IF(C3-C2>=0,
TEXT(C3-C2,"mm:ss"),
TEXT(ABS(C3-C2),"-mm:ss")
) |

	A	B	C	D
1	Year	Name	Time (hh:mm:ss)	Difference from Previous Year (+/-)
2	2016	Eliud Kipchoge	02:03:05	
3	2017	Daniel Wanjiru	02:05:48	02:43
4	2018	Eliud Kipchoge	02:04:17	-01:31
5	2019	Eliud Kipchoge	02:02:37	-01:40
6	2020	Shura Kitata	02:05:41	03:04
7	2021	Sissy Lemma	02:04:01	-01:40

Figure 6-95. *Formula to display negative time values*

Date and Time Functions with Other Excel Features

Let's now see a few practical examples of date and time functions being used with other Excel features.

Highlight Approaching Due Dates

A common requirement in Excel is to track due dates. These could be payments that are due, contracts expiring, or deadlines of project tasks.

With the array of date functions available in Excel, we can set almost any conditions we may need. Let's see a few examples.

Figure 6-96 shows a simple list that contains some due dates.

	A	B	
1	**Name**	**Due Date**	
2	Jason Carter	15/11/2021	
3	David Phillips	27/10/2021	
4	Claire Munsgrove	03/12/2021	
5	Stephanie Belkins	21/11/2021	
6	Nathalie Peters	31/10/2021	
7	Celia Wilson	10/11/2021	

Figure 6-96. *Due dates to be highlighted*

We would like to highlight the dates that are due within the next ten working days. For this, we could use the WORKDAY function in a Conditional Formatting rule:

1. Select range B2:B7.

2. Click **Home ➤ Conditional Formatting ➤ Highlight Cells Rules ➤ Less Than**.

3. Enter the following formula into the *Format cells that are LESS THAN:* box (Figure 6-97):

   =WORKDAY(TODAY(),10)

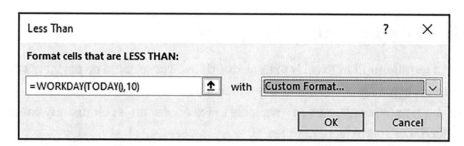

Figure 6-97. *Rule to format dates due within the next ten working days*

This formula is returning the date ten working days from today's date. This is a simple example that only excludes weekend dates from its calculation. We saw more advanced uses of WORKDAY earlier in this chapter.

4. Specify the cell formatting from the list and click **OK**.

Figure 6-98 shows two dates being identified as due within the next ten working days.

	A	B
1	Name	Due Date
2	Jason Carter	15/11/2021
3	David Phillips	27/10/2021
4	Claire Munsgrove	03/12/2021
5	Stephanie Belkins	21/11/2021
6	Nathalie Peters	31/10/2021
7	Celia Wilson	10/11/2021

Figure 6-98. *Two dates identified as being due soon*

Note   You will see different dates and possibly different results to what are shown in the images. The dates are calculated by a formula to remain current, and the results of WORKDAY are based on the TODAY function and so are determined by the date that you read and practice this.

You can add multiple Conditional Formatting rules to cells, so let's add another rule to highlight due dates that occur between the next 10 and 20 working days:

1. Select range B2:B7.

2. Click **Home ➤ Conditional Formatting ➤ Highlight Cells Rules ➤ Between**.

3. Enter the following formulas into the two *Format cells that are BETWEEN:* boxes (Figure 6-99):

    =WORKDAY(TODAY(),10)

and

    =WORKDAY(TODAY(),20)

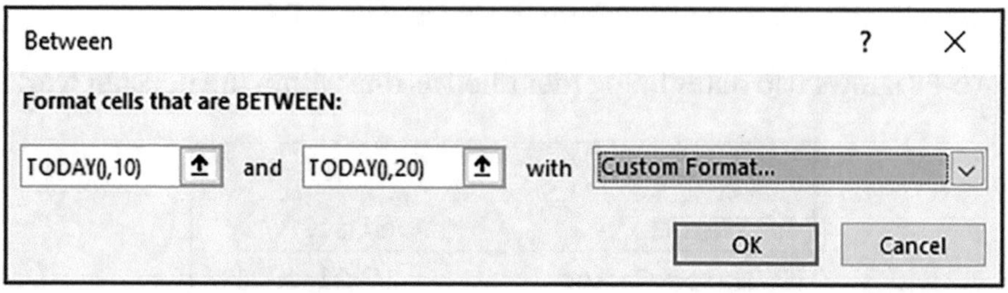

Figure 6-99. *Rule for dates due between the next 10 and 20 working days*

Unfortunately, this window is not resizable, so the full formulas could not be shown in the image.

Note   When editing formulas in Excel windows, be careful of the active cell mode. Using the cursor arrows on the keyboard while in "Point" mode causes chaos in your formula. The different cell modes of Excel were explained in Chapter 1.

---

4.   Specify the cell formatting from the list and click **OK**.

Figure 6-100 shows two rules active in the range of due dates. Dates within the next 10 working days and dates within the next 20 working days are both being highlighted independently.

	A	B
1	Name	Due Date
2	Jason Carter	15/11/2021
3	David Phillips	27/10/2021
4	Claire Munsgrove	03/12/2021
5	Stephanie Belkins	21/11/2021
6	Nathalie Peters	31/10/2021
7	Celia Wilson	10/11/2021

Figure 6-100. *Two formatting rules highlighting due dates*

Highlight Dates Due Within the Next Month

Let's add one more quick Conditional Formatting example, as an opportunity to recap on another function we saw in this chapter. That function is EDATE.

In this example, we want to highlight the dates due within the next month. This is often done by testing if a date is within the next 30 days. And this method is often sufficient, because we just want to bring the date to our attention and the result does not need to be that precise.

However, by using the EDATE function, we can test if a date is within the next month more accurately:

1. Select range B2:B7.

2. Click **Home ➤ Conditional Formatting ➤ Highlight Cells Rules ➤ Less Than**.

3. Enter the following formula into the *Format cells that are LESS THAN:* box (Figure 6-101):

    =EDATE(TODAY(),1)

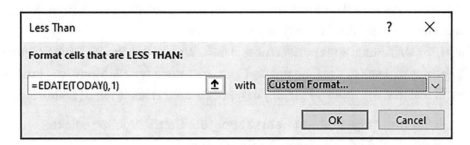

Figure 6-101. *Rule to format due dates within the next month*

The EDATE function returns the date in exactly one month's time. Remember, the EDATE function can also return previous dates if you needed to highlight dates with the last month, last three months, etc.

4. Specify the cell formatting from the list and click **OK**.

Figure 6-102 shows all except one date in the list occur within the next month.

	A	B
1	Name	Due Date
2	Jason Carter	15/11/2021
3	David Phillips	27/10/2021
4	Claire Munsgrove	03/12/2021
5	Stephanie Belkins	21/11/2021
6	Nathalie Peters	31/10/2021
7	Celia Wilson	10/11/2021

Figure 6-102. *All except one date occur within the next month*

Data Validation Rules – Prevent Weekend Entries

As an example of date functions being used in Data Validation rules, let's prevent the entry of weekend dates in a cell.

In this example, we will assume the weekend to be Saturday and Sunday; however, this can easily be customized for any day(s) of the week.

The WEEKDAY function is perfect for this task. We will use the WEEKDAY function to identify the day of week of the date entered and use return type 2, Monday = 1 to Sunday = 7. We will test that the index of the day of week entered is less than 6 (before Saturday):

1. Select the range that you want to apply the Data Validation rule to. Range E2:E6 has been used for this example.

2. Click **Data ➤ Data Validation**.

3. Click the **Settings** tab of the window.

4. Click the *Allow* drop-down and select **Custom**.

5. Enter the following formula into the box provided (Figure 6-103):

    `=WEEKDAY(E2,2)<6`

In the formula, cell E2 has been used. This must be the first cell of the selected range.

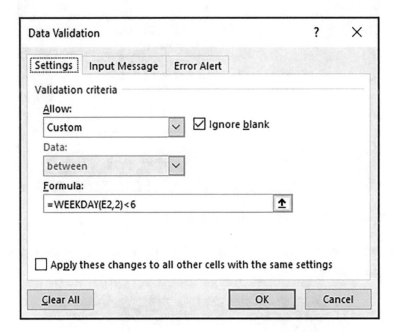

Figure 6-103. *Validation rule to prevent entry of weekend dates*

6. Click the **Error Alert** tab and enter a meaningful *Title* and *Error message* to appear if a user enters a date that is a Saturday or Sunday (Figure 6-104).

7. Click **OK**.

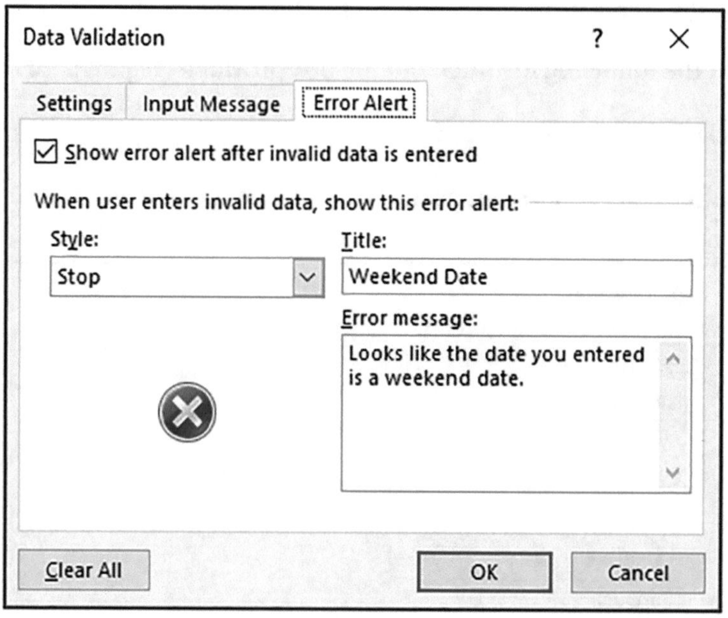

Data Validation   ?   ✕

Settings | Input Message | Error Alert

☑ Show error alert after invalid data is entered

When user enters invalid data, show this error alert:

Style: Title:

Stop   ∨   Weekend Date

                                Error message:

                                Looks like the date you entered   ∧
                                is a weekend date.

            ✕

                                                           ∨

Clear All   OK   Cancel

Figure 6-104. *Customized error alert for users*

The Data Validation rule is set. In Figure 6-105, the error alert is shown because 24th October 2021 is a Sunday.

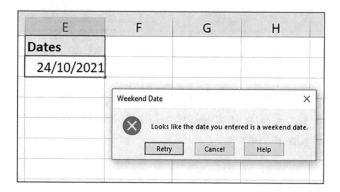

Figure 6-105. *Invalid date entry being rejected by the validation rule*

Summary

In this chapter, we learned the most useful date and time functions in Excel supported with numerous examples of their application in the "real world."

The chapter began with a detailed explanation of how dates and times are stored in Excel and how to effectively enter, convert, and extract dates and times. This topic is often misunderstood by Excel users, yet it is so critical to the performance of your calculations.

We then embarked on a tour of many different functions including WORKDAY, NETWORKDAYS.INTL, EDATE, and TIME. We performed many formulas including to find working days, return fiscal months and quarters, and return week numbers in a year or from a specific start date.

This chapter was very comprehensive and should act as a guide to refer to whenever you need a particular date or time calculation.

In the next chapter, we will learn the VLOOKUP function in Excel. This notorious function is extremely useful and is one of the most commonly used functions in Excel. Because of this, an entire chapter is dedicated to it.

You will learn how to use the VLOOKUP function including some insider tricks to make it more powerful, flexible, and dynamic. You will also understand common mistakes that users make and should be avoided.

CHAPTER 7

The Infamous VLOOKUP Function

VLOOKUP is one of the most used functions in Excel. Almost anyone who has used Excel for a certain number of years would have heard of VLOOKUP and has likely written one or two.

This function is often considered a benchmark in a user's Excel development – that moment when they step into the intermediate level of Excel formula skills. I will never forget the days when I was first learning VLOOKUP – a wild mixture of confusion, fun, and excitement.

In recent years, with the development of the new array engine in Excel (Chapter 10) and with new functions such as XLOOKUP and FILTER, the position of VLOOKUP as the number 1 lookup function of Excel is beginning to get a little shaky.

Make no mistake though. This function is incredibly useful, very popular (used in millions of spreadsheets worldwide), and therefore important for an Excel formula jedi to master.

VLOOKUP is available in all versions of Excel, so is reliable when sharing spreadsheets to staff across different offices or to users external to your organization.

In this chapter, we will begin with the basics of VLOOKUP and learn how to write the two different types of lookups (exact match and range lookup). We will learn some neat VLOOKUP tricks and understand common reasons to why things go wrong.

As the chapter progresses, we will see more advanced uses of VLOOKUP including using multiple lookup criteria and returning a specific instance of a value.

File   vlookup.xlsx

© Alan Murray 2022
A. Murray, *Advanced Excel Formulas*, https://doi.org/10.1007/978-1-4842-7125-4_7

Introduction to VLOOKUP

Availability: All versions

The name VLOOKUP stands for vertical lookup. It looks for a value, within a table, and returns a value from the same row but from a different column in the table.

The VLOOKUP function always looks for a value in the first column of the table in which it is told to search.

There are many reasons VLOOKUP is used. The most common use is to look up values in another table to combine them into one main table. This table would then be used for the analysis such as a PivotTable.

Other reasons include to compare two lists for differences, automate data entry on a spreadsheet, and fetch values from a lookup table for use in calculations, for example, a lookup table of different tax rates by city.

VLOOKUP asks for four pieces of information:

```
=VLOOKUP(lookup_value, table_array, col_index_num, [range_lookup])
```

- **Lookup value:** The value you are looking for.

- **Table array:** The table or range that you are looking and returning from.

- **Col index num:** The number of the column containing the value you want to return. This is the column number within the *table array*, not the worksheet.

- **[Range lookup]:** A logical value (TRUE or FALSE) to specify whether you are looking in ranges of values or not. This is an optional argument.

  TRUE is used to request a range lookup (also known as an approximate match). This is the default option. FALSE is used to specify an exact match.

VLOOKUP for an Exact Match

The most common form of VLOOKUP is to perform an exact match. This means that you are looking for a unique value such as a product code, booking reference, or an employee ID.

In this first example, we have a table named [tblTiers] that contains the prices for different membership tiers (Figure 7-1).

We have a table of customers and the membership tier they are enrolled in. We want to use VLOOKUP to return the price for each customer's membership.

	A	B	C
1			
2		Tier	Price
3		Blue	30
4		Bronze	45
5		Silver	55
6		Gold	80
7		Executive	140
8			

Figure 7-1. *Lookup table with tier prices*

Note   Although the second argument of VLOOKUP is named *table array* and this example uses a table, it should be noted that it does not need to be a table. It could be a range such as $B$2:$C$7, a named range, or an array returned by another function.

In Figure 7-2, the following formula is used in column C to return the membership price for each customer:

```
=VLOOKUP([@Membership],tblTiers,2,FALSE)
```

There are a few points of interest in this first VLOOKUP formula:

- VLOOKUP looks vertically down the first column of a given table. In this example, that is the [Tier] column of the [tblTiers] table.

- FALSE is used to specify an exact match in the final argument.

- The tiers in [tblTiers] are in ascending order by the [Price] column and not by [Tier]. This demonstrates that when performing an exact match, the *table array* does not need to be ordered by its first column.

- The column index number is 2. [Price] is the second column in the [tblTiers] table.

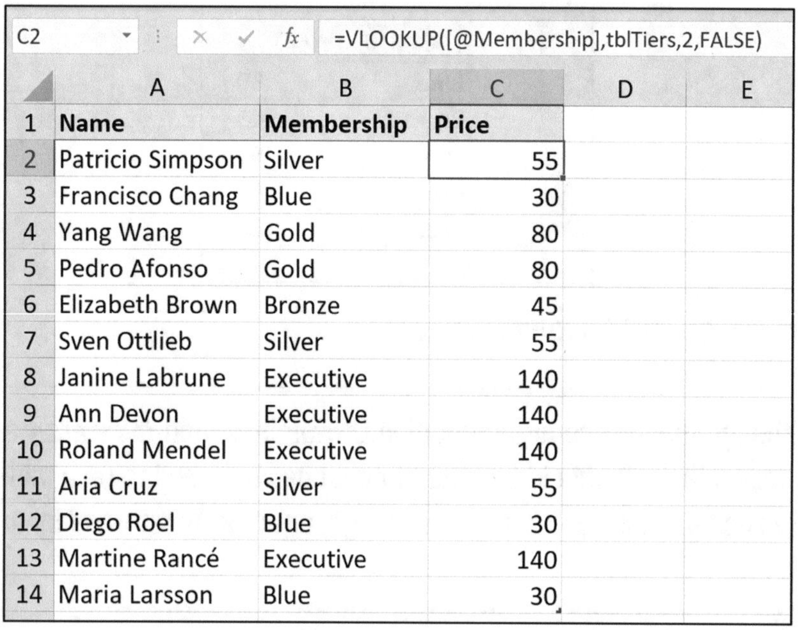

	A	B	C	D	E
			=VLOOKUP([@Membership],tblTiers,2,FALSE)		
1	Name	Membership	Price		
2	Patricio Simpson	Silver	55		
3	Francisco Chang	Blue	30		
4	Yang Wang	Gold	80		
5	Pedro Afonso	Gold	80		
6	Elizabeth Brown	Bronze	45		
7	Sven Ottlieb	Silver	55		
8	Janine Labrune	Executive	140		
9	Ann Devon	Executive	140		
10	Roland Mendel	Executive	140		
11	Aria Cruz	Silver	55		
12	Diego Roel	Blue	30		
13	Martine Rancé	Executive	140		
14	Maria Larsson	Blue	30		

Figure 7-2. VLOOKUP to return the price for each membership

Note   For the *range lookup* argument, a 0 can be entered to request an exact match instead of False, and a 1 can be entered to specify a range lookup instead of True.

VLOOKUP for a Range Lookup

The second type of lookup that you can perform with VLOOKUP is a range lookup. With this type of lookup, you are looking within ranges of values. For example, these could be date or time ranges or other values such as exam scores, amounts spent, or some other performance value.

This type of lookup, although not as commonplace as an exact match lookup, can be very useful. Let's see two examples.

In the first example, we have the lookup table shown in Figure 7-3. The first column contains a range of quantity values. We have a table of orders and want to look up the quantity ordered and return the earned discount.

When performing a range lookup (also known as an approximate match), it is essential that the first column of the lookup table is in ascending order.

VLOOKUP will match the value to the closest value less than the one searched for. So, for example, if we were looking for a quantity of 49 in the lookup table of Figure 7-3, the discount of 3% is returned, as 15 is the closest match less than 49.

	A	B
1	Qty	Discount
2	0	0.0%
3	15	3.0%
4	50	5.0%
5	65	7.5%
6	90	10.0%
7	100	11.5%
8		

Figure 7-3. *Range of quantities and discounts to look up*

The following formula has been used in Figure 7-4 to return the discount earned:

```
=VLOOKUP(B2,'Range Lookup Data'!$A$2:$B$7,2,TRUE)
```

Things to note in this formula include

- The lookup range is not formatted as a table, so has been referenced in the formula as `'Range Lookup Data'!$A$2:$B$7`.

This shows that the lookup table does not need to be in an Excel table; however, the use of tables is an improvement over the range that includes a worksheet name and absolute cell references.

- TRUE has been entered for the *range lookup* argument to specify an approximate match.

This argument is named *range lookup*, as it is asking you if you are looking in ranges or not. In this example, the answer is true; yes, we are looking in ranges of values. Remember, we could also type 1, or omit a response, as TRUE is the default lookup type.

D2			fx	=VLOOKUP(B2,'Range Lookup Data'!$A$2:$B$7,2,TRUE)		
	A	B	C	D	E	F
1	ID	Qty	Total	Discount	Minus Disc	
2	A288	63	504	5.0%	478.80	
3	A123	70	490	7.5%	453.25	
4	A781	20	100	3.0%	97.00	
5	A186	77	539	7.5%	498.58	
6	A210	31	124	3.0%	120.28	
7	A189	5	25	0.0%	25.00	
8	A515	64	384	5.0%	364.80	
9	A692	101	505	11.5%	446.93	
10	A417	45	180	3.0%	174.60	

Figure 7-4. *VLOOKUP returning the appropriate discount of each quantity ordered*

In the second example, the lookup table in Figure 7-5 contains date ranges in its first column. In the second column of the table is a tax rate that changes at specific dates. This table is named [tblRates].

E	F
Date Range	**Rate**
10/03/2021	2.2%
22/07/2021	5.1%
01/10/2021	8.0%

Figure 7-5. *Lookup table with date ranges and tax rates*

In Figure 7-6, the following VLOOKUP formula is used to return the necessary rate:

`=VLOOKUP(H2,tblRates,2)`

In this formula, the *range lookup* argument is omitted. The default result of the range lookup argument is True, so this is fine.

fx	=VLOOKUP(H2,tblRates,2)		
F	G	H	I
	Ref	**Date**	**Rate**
	BY78	23/07/2021	5.1%
	BY197	12/03/2021	2.2%
	BY88	16/07/2021	2.2%
	BY42	30/12/2021	8.0%
	BY90	08/06/2021	2.2%
	BY9	09/11/2021	8.0%

Figure 7-6. *Returning the tax rate dependent upon the date of transaction*

Column Index Number Tricks

In the examples demonstrated so far, the lookup tables have been small, and the *column index number* has always been 2. When looking up data in larger tables, counting to find the correct column index number can be frustrating.

There are a few tricks that we can deploy to save having to count to find the required column index number. These tricks also work in making our VLOOKUP formulas more durable, as when typing the number directly into the formula, it can easily be broken by someone inserting or deleting a column.

Another mistake can be that a user did not count hidden columns when finding the column index number.

Trick 1: The COLUMN Function

Availability: All versions

The COLUMN function returns the column number of a given reference. This reference can be a cell, table column, or a named range. It returns the column number of the sheet, for example, column D is column number 4.

The COLUMN function only asks for the reference from which to return the column number. This is an optional argument. If omitted, the column number of cell where the formula resides is returned.

```
=COLUMN([reference])
```

This function is ideal for the task of preventing having to find the column number in the lookup table ourselves. We can just reference the column of the lookup table that we want, and COLUMN returns its index number.

In Figure 7-7, we have a table named [tblReps] containing data about our sales representatives. We will use a VLOOKUP function to return the data from the [Status] column to another table.

	A	B	C	D	E	F
1	ID	Sales Rep	Age	Manager	Status	Years
2	3156	Trudy Andrews	43	Bernardo Batista	Gold	11
3	1815	Georgia Keegan	21	Isabel de Castro	Red	2
4	1229	Christopher Hartley	26	Carly Ferdinand	Red	11
5	3992	Paul Beechcroft	19	Marie Bertrand	Gold	3
6	3463	Cyndy Bloom	34	Guillermo Fernández	Red	12
7	1841	Audrey White	53	Lúcia Carvalho	Blue	10
8	3740	Elizabeth Kendrick	35	Georg Pipps	Red	12
9	2092	Simon James	34	Liz Evans	Blue	2
10	1571	Samantha Cavalho	48	Henriette Pfalzheim	Gold	9

Figure 7-7. *Sales representative data*

The following formula is used in Figure 7-8 to return the status data. A similar formula was also used in cell F2 to return the rep name.

```
=VLOOKUP(E2,tblReps,COLUMN(tblReps[Status]),0)
```

The COLUMN function is provided with the [Status] column of the table. This makes it very simple to provide a column number to VLOOKUP, as referencing columns in a table is fast and easy. This technique was covered in Chapter 4.

Remember, the column number returned is the column number of the worksheet, not the table.

As this lookup table (Figure 7-7) starts in column A, the worksheet column and the table column are the same number, so it is not a problem. However, let's explore an alternative scenario.

			fx	=VLOOKUP(E2,tblReps,COLUMN(tblReps[Status]),0)		

D	E	F	G	H	I
Store	Rep ID	Rep Name	Rep Status	Units Sold	Total
North	1229	Christopher Hartley	Red	7	325.27
West	3740	Elizabeth Kendrick	Red	3	378.00
East	1571	Samantha Cavalho	Gold	13	272.09
West	1815	Georgia Keegan	Red	15	252.27
South	1571	Samantha Cavalho	Gold	21	139.45
West	3740	Elizabeth Kendrick	Red	29	363.02
North	3740	Elizabeth Kendrick	Red	13	100.70

Figure 7-8. *COLUMN function used to prevent entering the column number*

In Figure 7-9, the [tblReps] table now begins in column C. So, the [Status] column is the fifth column of [tblReps], but the seventh column of the worksheet.

For the COLUMN function to work, we will need to subtract two from its result to account for columns A and B not being used by the table.

	A	B	C	D	E	F	G	H
1			ID	Sales Rep	Age	Manager	Status	Years
2			3156	Trudy Andrews	43	Bernardo Batista	Gold	11
3			1815	Georgia Keegan	21	Isabel de Castro	Red	2
4			1229	Christopher Hartley	26	Carly Ferdinand	Red	11
5			3992	Paul Beechcroft	19	Marie Bertrand	Gold	3
6			3463	Cyndy Bloom	34	Guillermo Fernández	Red	12
7			1841	Audrey White	53	Lúcia Carvalho	Blue	10
8			3740	Elizabeth Kendrick	35	Georg Pipps	Red	12
9			2092	Simon James	34	Liz Evans	Blue	2
10			1571	Samantha Cavalho	48	Henriette Pfalzheim	Gold	9
11								

Figure 7-9. *Lookup table beginning from column C*

In the following formula, minus 2 is entered after the COLUMN function (Figure 7-10):

```
=VLOOKUP(E2,tblReps,COLUMN(tblReps[Status])-2,0)
```

	D	E	F	G	H	I
fx	=VLOOKUP(E2,tblReps,COLUMN(tblReps[Status])-2,0)					
	Store	Rep ID	Rep Name	Rep Status	Units Sold	Total
	North	1229	Christopher Hartley	Red	7	325.27
	West	3740	Elizabeth Kendrick	Red	3	378.00
	East	1571	Samantha Cavalho	Gold	13	272.09
	West	1815	Georgia Keegan	Red	15	252.27
	South	1571	Samantha Cavalho	Gold	21	139.45
	West	3740	Elizabeth Kendrick	Red	29	363.02
	North	3740	Elizabeth Kendrick	Red	13	100.70

Figure 7-10. VLOOKUP function with COLUMN to fetch the column number

If someone were to insert another column, or remove a column, before the start of the table, our formula would fail. The subtraction of 2 would no longer be relevant.

For a more robust version of this formula, we want to dynamically return the column number of the column directly before the table, 2 in the previous example. To do this, the COLUMN function will be used to return the sheet's column number of the first column of the table. One will be subtracted from this to return the column number that precedes the start of the table.

The following formula is entered in cell G2 (Figure 7-11). The calculation to return the start column is enclosed in brackets to calculate first.

```
=VLOOKUP(E2,tblReps,COLUMN(tblReps[Status])-(COLUMN(tblReps[ID])-1),0)
```

| | | | fx | =VLOOKUP(E2,tblReps,COLUMN(tblReps[Status])-(COLUMN(tblReps[ID])-1),0) |

C	D	E	F	G	H	I
Product Name	Store	Rep ID	Rep Name	Rep Status	Units Sold	Total
Beer	North	1229	Christopher Hartley	Red	7	325.27
Orange Juice	West	3740	Elizabeth Kendrick	Red	3	378.00
Wine	East	1571	Samantha Cavalho	Gold	13	272.09
Coffee	West	1815	Georgia Keegan	Red	15	252.27
Beer	South	1571	Samantha Cavalho	Gold	21	139.45
Beer	West	3740	Elizabeth Kendrick	Red	29	363.02
Water	North	3740	Elizabeth Kendrick	Red	13	100.70

Figure 7-11. *More robust version of VLOOKUP with the COLUMN function*

Trick 2: The COLUMNS Function

Availability: All versions

The COLUMNS function returns the number of columns in a given reference or array. This could be a reference to a range of cells, a table, a named range, or an array formula.

The COLUMNS function only requires the array for which to return the total number of columns:

```
=COLUMNS(array)
```

This function is very useful when the column number you require is at the end or a specific number of columns from the end of a reference or array.

In Figure 7-12, we have a table named [tblMonthly] that contains monthly performance values for staff. We require a VLOOKUP to return the last month's performance. This will always be the final column in the table (currently May-21).

The COLUMNS function will be perfect for this task, as every month the table will expand with another column when a new month is added. The COLUMNS function will always return the number of columns in the table, that is, the final column number.

So, this will always be correct even when the table expands. Much better than counting columns or having to update the column number manually each month.

	A	B	C	D	E	F	G
1	ID	Name	Jan-21	Feb-21	Mar-21	Apr-21	May-21
2	SD270	Bernardo Batista	3,763	3,185	2,260	2,329	1,932
3	SD100	Isabel de Castro	3,515	3,656	3,931	1,493	3,323
4	SD461	Carly Ferdinand	3,786	1,597	3,224	3,767	2,891
5	SD155	Marie Bertrand	3,903	1,453	2,821	2,844	1,301
6	SD384	Guillermo Fernández	4,003	3,895	1,570	1,668	2,195
7	SD422	Lúcia Carvalho	2,969	3,646	3,140	2,954	2,289
8	SD64	Liz Evans	1,306	1,217	2,159	3,595	2,630
9	SD397	Henriette Pfalzheim	2,678	2,091	2,154	1,981	2,842

Figure 7-12. *Table with staff monthly performance*

In Figure 7-13, the following VLOOKUP formula is used to return the monthly total for each staff member. The COLUMNS function is used for the *column index number* argument to return the final column number from [tblMonthly].

```
=VLOOKUP(A2,tblMonthly,COLUMNS(tblMonthly),FALSE)
```

D2		▾ ⋮	✕ ✓	fx	=VLOOKUP(A2,tblMonthly,COLUMNS(tblMonthly),FALSE)

	A	B	C	D	E
1	ID	Name	Region	Monthly Total	
2	SD100	Isabel de Castro	North	3,323	
3	SD155	Marie Bertrand	South	1,301	
4	SD270	Bernardo Batista	South	1,932	
5	SD384	Guillermo Fernández	East	2,195	
6	SD397	Henriette Pfalzheim	East	2,842	
7	SD422	Lúcia Carvalho	East	2,289	
8	SD461	Carly Ferdinand	North	2,891	
9	SD64	Liz Evans	North	2,630	

Figure 7-13. *COLUMNS function used to return the final column's data*

If the required column number was a specified number of columns from the end, this number could be subtracted from the COLUMNS result. For example, the following formula would return the previous month's value:

```
COLUMNS(tblMonthly)-1
```

Note There are also ROW and ROWS functions in Excel to perform the equivalent tasks but for rows instead of columns. We will see ROWS later in this book.

Trick 3: Using an Index Row

Another technique that you may come across is the creation of an index row. This is a row where the column index numbers of the table are entered and then referenced in the VLOOKUP.

Figure 7-14 shows an index row set up above a lookup table. Notice that the lookup table range begins in column B, but the column is indexed as column 1, ready for VLOOKUP. This lookup range is on a sheet named [Index Row Data].

This row is often hidden once the formulas are created, to avoid accidental damage and to remove clutter.

B	C	D	E	F	G
1	2	3	4	5	6
ID	Sales Rep	Age	Manager	Status	Years
3156	Trudy Andrews	43	Bernardo Batista	Gold	11
1815	Georgia Keegan	21	Isabel de Castro	Red	2
1229	Christopher Hartley	26	Carly Ferdinand	Red	11
3992	Paul Beechcroft	19	Marie Bertrand	Gold	3
3463	Cyndy Bloom	34	Guillermo Fernández	Red	12
1841	Audrey White	53	Lúcia Carvalho	Blue	10
3740	Elizabeth Kendrick	35	Georg Pipps	Red	12
2092	Simon James	34	Liz Evans	Blue	2
1571	Samantha Cavalho	48	Henriette Pfalzheim	Gold	9

Figure 7-14. *Lookup table with an index row*

In Figure 7-15, the following formula is used to return the data from the [Status] column. It references cell F1 of the [Index Row Number] sheet to return the required column index number.

```
=VLOOKUP(E2,'Index Row Data'!$B$3:$G$11,'Index Row Data'!$F$1,0)
```

fx	=VLOOKUP(E2,'Index Row Data'!$B$3:$G$11,'Index Row Data'!$F$1,0)

	D	E	F	G	H	I
	Store	Rep ID	Rep Name	Rep Status	Units Sold	Total
	North	1229	Christopher Hartley	Red	7	325.27
	West	3740	Elizabeth Kendrick	Red	3	378.00
	East	1571	Samantha Cavalho	Gold	13	272.09
	West	1815	Georgia Keegan	Red	15	252.27
	South	1571	Samantha Cavalho	Gold	21	139.45
	West	3740	Elizabeth Kendrick	Red	29	363.02
	North	3740	Elizabeth Kendrick	Red	13	100.70

Figure 7-15. *VLOOKUP referring to a cell value to return the column index number*

Referring to a cell value in this manner is another trick to avoid counting the columns of your larger lookup tables.

It is not as durable as using the COLUMN function can be, but it is very simple to set up and utilize.

Note   Another technique is to use the MATCH function to find and return the required column number. We will see this technique in Chapter 11, when we explore more lookup functions in Excel.

Reasons Why VLOOKUP Is Not Working

There are a few reasons why your VLOOKUP is not working. Let's explore some of the common reasons along with their solutions.

Lookup Column Must Be the First Column

VLOOKUP looks for a value down the first column of a given range or array. If the column you need to look in is not the first (or leftmost) column of the *table array*, VLOOKUP will not find a match.

In Figure 7-16, the following VLOOKUP is returning the #N/A error as it cannot find a match for the ID value entered in cell B3. The lookup column is the second column of the range provided for the *table array* argument, $B$6:$E$9, and not the first column.

```
=VLOOKUP(B3,$B$6:$E$9,4,FALSE)
```

	B	C	D	E
		fx	=VLOOKUP(B3,$B$6:$E$9,4,FALSE)	
	ID	Salary		
	1841	#N/A		
	Name	ID	Dept	Salary
	Paul Beechcroft	3992	IT	33,500
	Cyndy Bloom	3463	HR	40,000
	Audrey White	1841	Finance	32,000
	Elizabeth Kendrick	3740	IT	58,000

Figure 7-16. *The lookup column needs to be the first column*

This can be fixed by reordering the columns of the lookup table so that the ID column is first or by using a different formula to VLOOKUP, such as XLOOKUP or the INDEX-MATCH function combination.

Another fix in this example is that you do not need to select all the columns of a table or range, only the ones that you need.

The following VLOOKUP formula uses the range $C$6:$E$9 for the lookup table (Figure 7-17). So, VLOOKUP now looks down column C and finds a match. Then it returns from column 3, as the salary is the third column of range $C$6:$E$9.

```
=VLOOKUP(B3,$C$6:$E$9,3,FALSE)
```

		fx	=VLOOKUP(B3,$C$6:$E$9,3,FALSE)

B	C	D	E
ID	Salary		
1841	32,000		
Name	ID	Dept	Salary
Paul Beechcroft	3992	IT	33,500
Cyndy Bloom	3463	HR	40,000
Audrey White	1841	Finance	32,000
Elizabeth Kendrick	3740	IT	58,000

Figure 7-17. VLOOKUP now works with an adjusted table array

Data Type of the Values Must Match

This issue causes problems even for regular users of VLOOKUP. The data type of the lookup value and the value it finds must match, not just its value.

This issue commonly occurs when the table array is an export from an external source, and the numeric values are stored as text. However, the lookup value is a number.

In Figure 7-18, the lookup value in cell G3 is numeric, but the values in range $G$6:$G$9 are text values. You see their different alignment in the cells. VLOOKUP returns the #N/A error as it cannot match the lookup value.

	fx	=VLOOKUP(G3,$G$6:$J$9,4,FALSE)

G	H	I	J
ID	Salary		
3463	#N/A		
ID	Dept	Name	Salary
3992	IT	Paul Beechcroft	33,500
3463	HR	Cyndy Bloom	40,000
1841	Finance	Audrey White	32,000
3740	IT	Elizabeth Kendrick	58,000

Figure 7-18. VLOOKUP not working due to problem with the data type

The fix is to convert either the lookup value to text or the values in the lookup column to numbers. Which side you convert depends on what the value should be – text or number.

Figure 7-19 shows the values in G6:G9 converted to numbers and the VLOOKUP now working.

The Text to Columns command in Excel provides a quick way to convert text to numbers. You need only to select the values, click **Data ➤ Text to Columns** and then click **Finish** to close the window for a quick conversion.

We did discuss functions such as VALUE in Chapter 5 that will perform this task also.

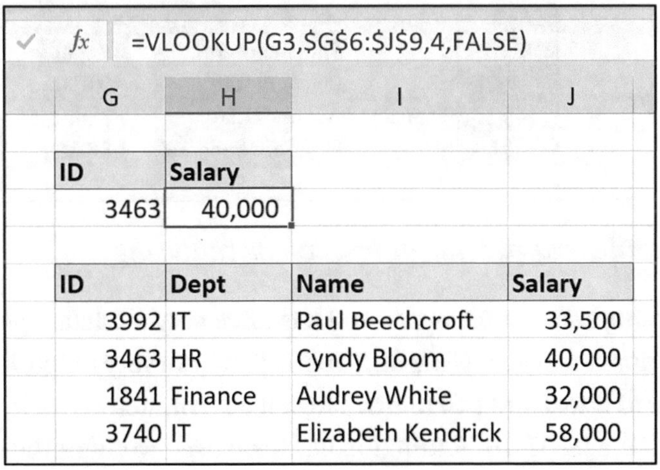

	fx	=VLOOKUP(G3,$G$6:$J$9,4,FALSE)		
	G	H	I	J
	ID	Salary		
	3463	40,000		
	ID	Dept	Name	Salary
	3992	IT	Paul Beechcroft	33,500
	3463	HR	Cyndy Bloom	40,000
	1841	Finance	Audrey White	32,000
	3740	IT	Elizabeth Kendrick	58,000

Figure 7-19. *ID values are converted to numbers and the VLOOKUP works*

This issue can be confusing and difficult to detect. Figure 7-20 shows the numeric values in range G6:G9 selected. They are left aligned and have a text format applied, so do not appear as numbers.

However, the VLOOKUP function is working, as the data type of cell G3 and the values in range G6:G9 do match.

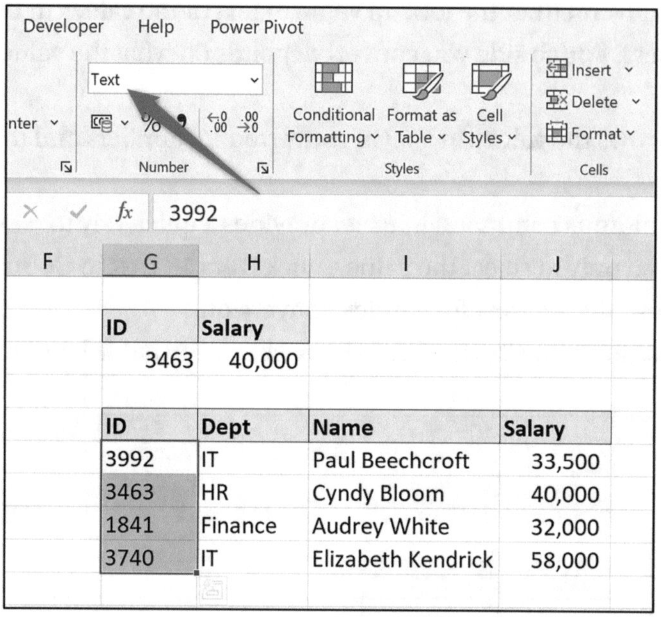

Figure 7-20. *Numbers appearing as text can be confusing*

When diagnosing issues such as this and it is unclear what data type a value is, the information functions such as ISNUMBER and ISTEXT are very helpful. They check if a value is a number or is text and will return TRUE if it is a match.

In Figure 7-21, the ISNUMBER function has been used to check the values in the original problem. The formula in cell I3 has confirmed that the value in cell G3 is a number, but the formulas in range K6:K9 show that the values in G6:G9 are not numbers.

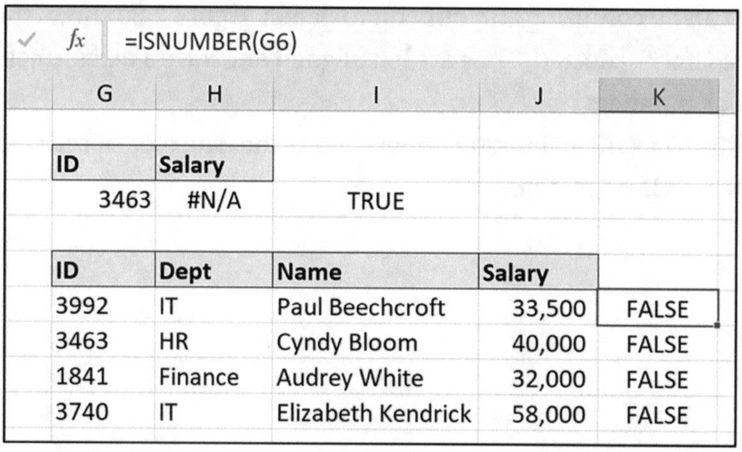

Figure 7-21. *ISNUMBER function confirming the data type of values*

Exact Match Has Not Been Specified

This is a common mistake for users that are new to using VLOOKUP. So, keep an eye out for this on spreadsheets set up by others that include VLOOKUP.

The final argument of VLOOKUP is *range lookup*. This argument is confusing when you are getting started with this function, it is optional, and TRUE is the default. These three factors seem to lead to the argument being missed or ignored.

If you require an exact match but do not specify one, you run the risk of having the wrong results and errors returned.

In Figure 7-22, the final argument is omitted when an exact match is required. You can see the incorrect result for ID 3992 in cell C6. There is also an error in cell C3 for ID 1841.

The values in the lookup table are not in ascending order by the first column, which is a requirement when performing range lookups. This is causing the chaos.

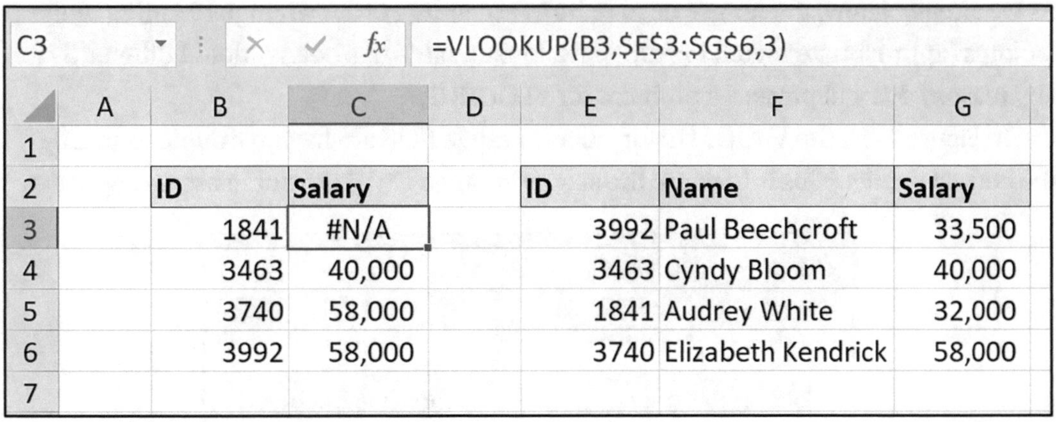

C3	▼	:	×	✓	*fx*	=VLOOKUP(B3,$E$3:$G$6,3)		
	A	B	C	D	E	F	G
1							
2		ID	Salary		ID	Name	Salary
3		1841	#N/A		3992	Paul Beechcroft	33,500
4		3463	40,000		3463	Cyndy Bloom	40,000
5		3740	58,000		1841	Audrey White	32,000
6		3992	58,000		3740	Elizabeth Kendrick	58,000
7							

Figure 7-22. *VLOOKUP returning incorrect results and errors*

The fix for this problem is simple. An exact match needs to be specified for this VLOOKUP by entering FALSE or 0 in the final argument (Figure 7-23).

C3	▾	:	×	✓	fx	=VLOOKUP(B3,$E$3:$G$6,3,0)

	A	B	C	D	E	F	G
1							
2		ID	Salary		ID	Name	Salary
3		1841	32,000		3992	Paul Beechcroft	33,500
4		3463	40,000		3463	Cyndy Bloom	40,000
5		3740	58,000		1841	Audrey White	32,000
6		3992	33,500		3740	Elizabeth Kendrick	58,000
7							

Figure 7-23. *Exact match is specified and the VLOOKUP works*

Ranges Must Be in Ascending Order

As we already know, the ranges need to be in ascending order when performing range lookups (approximate match lookups). If a lookup table has been ordered differently for any reason, this will present a problem for VLOOKUP.

In Figure 7-24, the VLOOKUP formulas in range J3:J8 are having trouble returning the correct results. This is because the scores in range L3:L6 are not in ascending order.

✓	fx	=VLOOKUP(I3,$L$3:$M$6,2,TRUE)			

I	J	K	L	M
Score	Grade		Score	Grade
93	Very Good		60	Good
56	Poor		0	Poor
95	Very Good		90	Superb
46	Poor		75	Very Good
89	Poor			
74	Poor			

Figure 7-24. *Ranges not in order breaking VLOOKUP*

To fix this issue, the first column of the lookup table needs to be sorted into ascending order.

Figure 7-25 shows a functional VLOOKUP now that the scores are in the correct order.

```
=VLOOKUP(I3,$L$3:$M$6,2,TRUE)
```

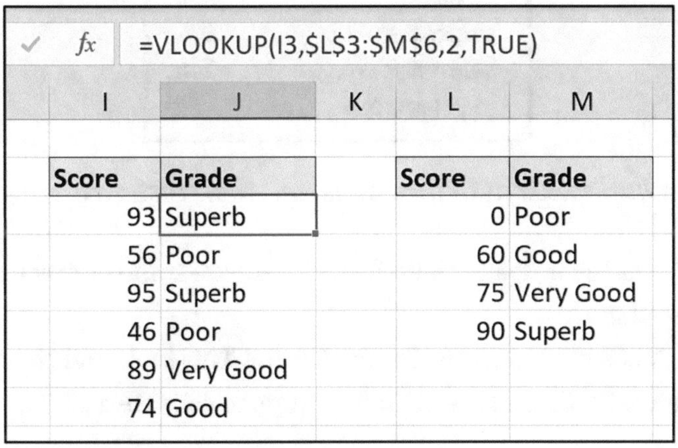

✓	fx	=VLOOKUP(I3,$L$3:$M$6,2,TRUE)			
	I	J	K	L	M
	Score	Grade		Score	Grade
	93	Superb		0	Poor
	56	Poor		60	Good
	95	Superb		75	Very Good
	46	Poor		90	Superb
	89	Very Good			
	74	Good			

Figure 7-25. *VLOOKUP working now that the ranges are in ascending order*

Handling Fake Errors with VLOOKUP

Now, not all errors that VLOOKUP returns are real errors. VLOOKUP is very eager to return #N/A if it cannot complete its job. And sometimes there are logical and valid reasons why it cannot complete its job.

In these circumstances, an alternative action is desired over the error returned by VLOOKUP.

In this example, we have a simple claim form for mileage expenses in Excel. When a user specifies the site that they traveled to, we want a VLOOKUP to return the distance in miles of that site.

Figure 7-26 shows a lookup range with the locations that someone may travel to and the distance in miles.

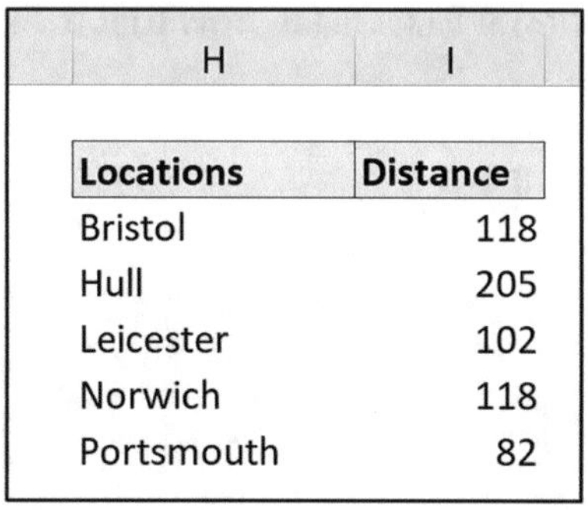

H	I
Locations	**Distance**
Bristol	118
Hull	205
Leicester	102
Norwich	118
Portsmouth	82

Figure 7-26. *Lookup range with locations and their distance*

Figure 7-27 shows the mileage claim form. There are some empty rows where there are no expenses to claim.

The following VLOOKUP returns the #N/A error. This looks ugly and is also breaking the formulas in range E3:E7 and the SUM functions in cells D9 and E9.

```
=VLOOKUP(C3,$H$3:$I$7,2,FALSE)
```

We would like to replace the #N/A errors with the value of 0. This is a more appropriate response, looks neater, and, most importantly, ensures the formulas will return the correct results.

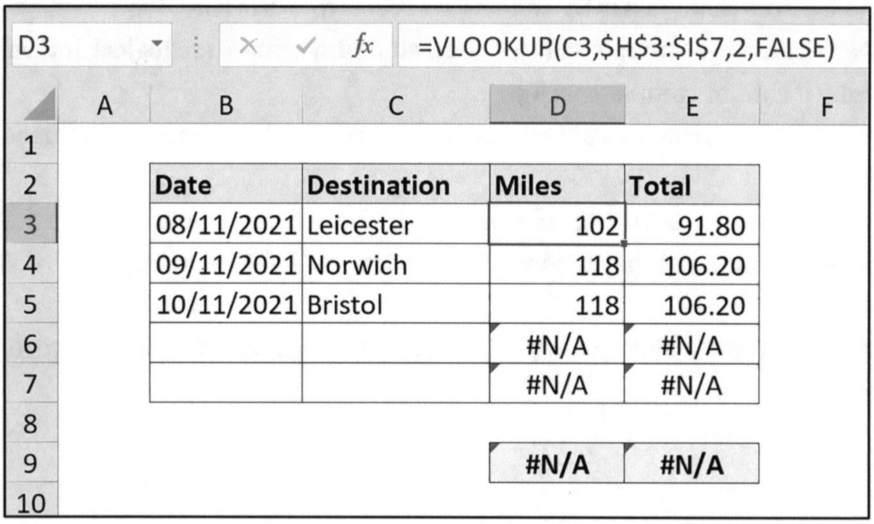

D3		✕	✓	*fx*	=VLOOKUP(C3,$H$3:$I$7,2,FALSE)	

	A	B	C	D	E	F
1						
2		**Date**	**Destination**	**Miles**	**Total**	
3		08/11/2021	Leicester	102	91.80	
4		09/11/2021	Norwich	118	106.20	
5		10/11/2021	Bristol	118	106.20	
6				#N/A	#N/A	
7				#N/A	#N/A	
8						
9				#N/A	#N/A	
10						

Figure 7-27. *VLOOKUP returning errors for the empty destination cells*

There are two main functions for this task – IFERROR and IFNA. These functions use the same syntax and were covered in detail in Chapter 2, so we will dive straight in and use these now.

In Figure 7-28, the following formula uses IFERROR to handle the errors returned by VLOOKUP. If the VLOOKUP returns an error, a 0 is shown as the alternate action.

```
=IFERROR(VLOOKUP(C3,$H$3:$I$7,2,FALSE),0)
```

Note   The IFERROR function will return an alternate action if any error is returned by VLOOKUP; IFNA focuses on the #N/A error only.

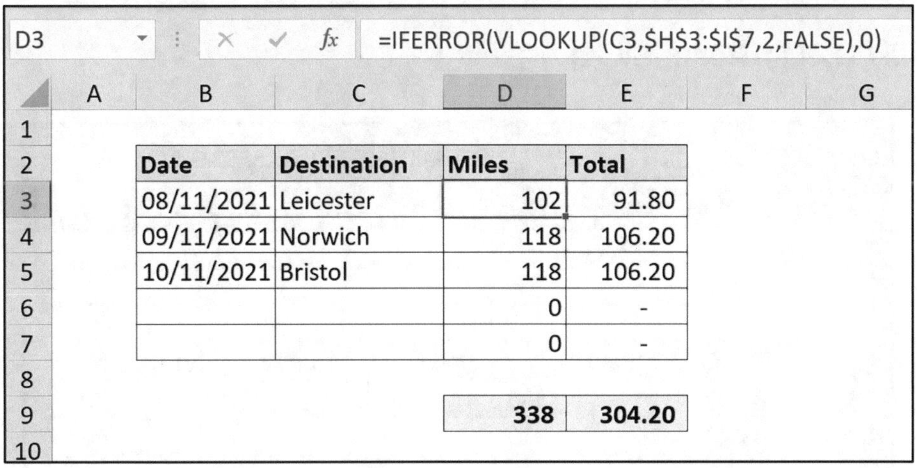

Figure 7-28. *IFERROR function added to replace errors with 0*

Although entering the value 0 is used in this example, we could have displayed any value or run an alternate formula.

The HLOOKUP Function

Availability: All versions

VLOOKUP has a lesser-known sibling – HLOOKUP. As you may have guessed, this stands for horizontal lookup.

The HLOOKUP function has the same syntax as VLOOKUP, though the third argument asks for a row index number instead of a column index number:

```
=HLOOKUP(lookup_value, table_array, row_index_number, [range_lookup])
```

Due to its less common usage compared to VLOOKUP, we will see only one example of HLOOKUP. However, every example demonstrated with VLOOKUP in this chapter can be performed with HLOOKUP, if required.

Figure 7-29 shows a lookup table/range with weekly performance values relating to some individuals. The headers are in the first column of the range (column B) with each field's data stored in rows.

In Figure 7-29, the following HLOOKUP function is entered in cell C2 and is returning the value for week 4 from the fifth row of the lookup range C4:F8 for Cyndy:

```
=HLOOKUP(B2,$C$4:$F$8,5,FALSE)
```

C2			×	✓	fx	=HLOOKUP(B2,$C$4:$F$8,5,FALSE)		
	A	B	C		D	E	F	
1			Wk 4					
2		Cyndy	234					
3								
4		Name	Paul		Cyndy	Audrey	Elizabeth	
5		Wk 1	563		892	1,179	397	
6		Wk 2	815		747	415	560	
7		Wk 3	610		675	369	414	
8		Wk 4	538		234	1,055	1,052	
9								

Figure 7-29. *HLOOKUP returning the value from the fifth row of the lookup range*

Get VLOOKUP to Look to the Left

One of the limitations of VLOOKUP is that it can only return a value from a column to the right of the one containing the lookup value (the first column).

Now this is not often a problem, as the first column of a table is typically a unique identifier. However, there is a trick to get VLOOKUP to look to its left.

Take the example shown in Figure 7-30. We need a VLOOKUP to return the grade for the score earned by each person.

The following VLOOKUP formula is returning errors in column D. This is due to VLOOKUP looking for the score in the [Grade] column, as that is the first column of the lookup range.

```
=VLOOKUP(C3,$F$3:$G$6,2,TRUE)
```

Now, we could reorder the data in columns F and G, and VLOOKUP would work fine. But let's look at a trick to get VLOOKUP looking to its left, and we do not need to reorder any columns.

D3	▾	⋮	×	✓	_fx_	=VLOOKUP(C3,$F$3:$G$6,2,TRUE)		
	A	B	C	D	E	F	G
1							
2		Name	Score	Grade		Grade	Score
3		Gill	93	#N/A		Poor	0
4		Bryan	56	#N/A		Good	60
5		Kevin	95	#N/A		Very Good	75
6		Barbara	46	#N/A		Superb	90
7		Rachel	89	#N/A			
8		Sue	74	#N/A			

Figure 7-30. *VLOOKUP returning errors as the score is not the leftmost column*

This trick requires the use of the CHOOSE function in Excel. The CHOOSE function will change the order of the columns for VLOOKUP to work from.

The CHOOSE function returns a value, or performs an action, from a list of given values and actions. The value or action it chooses from the list is based on an index number.

It requires only the index number and the list of possible values and actions:

```
=CHOOSE(index_num, value1, [value2],...)
```

In Figure 7-31, the following formula is used to change the order of the columns within VLOOKUP. It, therefore, returns the correct grade without physically changing the column order of the lookup range.

```
=VLOOKUP(C3,
CHOOSE({1,2},$G$3:$G$6,$F$3:$F$6),
2,TRUE)
```

The CHOOSE function is used in the *table array* argument of VLOOKUP. It is given the array of constants {1,2} for its index number. It is then told to return range $G$3:$G$6 first and $F$3:$F$6 second, therefore reversing the column order.

This is an array formula, so press **Ctrl + Shift + Enter** to run it if you are not using Excel for Microsoft 365, Excel for the Web, or Excel 2021.

Note   The CHOOSE function is covered in more detail in Chapter 11, when we explore more lookup functions.

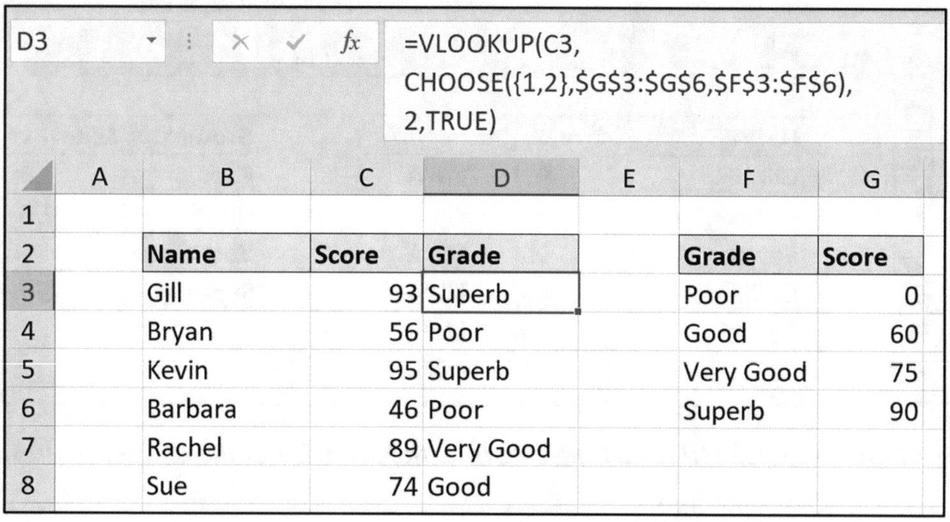

| D3 | | | ✕ | ✓ | *fx* | =VLOOKUP(C3, CHOOSE({1,2},$G$3:$G$6,$F$3:$F$6), 2,TRUE) |

	A	B	C	D	E	F	G
1							
2		Name	Score	Grade		Grade	Score
3		Gill	93	Superb		Poor	0
4		Bryan	56	Poor		Good	60
5		Kevin	95	Superb		Very Good	75
6		Barbara	46	Poor		Superb	90
7		Rachel	89	Very Good			
8		Sue	74	Good			

Figure 7-31.   CHOOSE function included to change the column order

---

Note   This technique is fun and good to be aware of. However, for a more flexible lookup formula, the INDEX and MATCH combination or XLOOKUP functions in Excel are encouraged.

Partial Match Lookup

A partial match is when only part of the lookup value text needs to match. Sometimes, you may be looking to perform a partial match instead of an exact text match.

For example, Figure 7-32 shows a table named [tblTargets]. It contains the performance targets for different offices that are in different cities. The [City] column contains the country name in addition to the city.

We need to match a city to one in the [City] column of [tblTargets]. However, we cannot get an exact match because the country name is also in those cell values. We need to perform a partial match.

G	H
City	**Target**
Copenhagen, Denmark	240
London, UK	710
Berlin, Germany	890
Lisbon, Portugal	610
Newcastle, UK	860

Figure 7-32. *Table of offices and their respective targets*

The VLOOKUP function allows the use of wildcard characters directly in the function. This makes it easy to create partial matches with VLOOKUP.

There are three wildcard characters that can be used in your VLOOKUP formulas:

- *** (Asterisk):** Represents any number of characters. For example, New* would match with Newport, Newcastle, New York, and New Zealand.

- **? (Question mark):** Represents a single character. For example, L????n would match with both London and Lisbon.

- **~ (Tilde):** Used to treat a wildcard character as a text character. For example, *don would match any text that ends in the characters don, but ~*don will look for an exact match of *don, treating the asterisk as its character and not a wildcard.

In Figure 7-33, the following formula uses the asterisk wildcard to perform a partial match on the city in the [tblTargets]:

```
=VLOOKUP(C3&"*",tblTargets,2,0)
```

The asterisk is joined after the city name in cell C3. Perfect for this scenario. We do not know how many characters will follow the city name, but we know there will be some.

Notice that the asterisk is enclosed in double quotations and joined using the ampersand.

| E3 | ▾ | ⋮ | ✕ | ✓ | *fx* | =VLOOKUP(C3&"*",tblTargets,2,0) |

	A	B	C	D	E	F
1						
2		Name	City	Value	Target	
3		Pedro Afonso	London	470	710	
4		Elizabeth Brown	Copenhagen	391	240	
5		Sven Ottlieb	Lisbon	417	610	
6		Janine Labrune	Berlin	282	890	
7		Ann Devon	Newcastle	1197	860	
8		Roland Mendel	Lisbon	771	610	
9		Aria Cruz	Copenhagen	1112	240	

Figure 7-33. *VLOOKUP with a wildcard character for a partial match*

If we want to create a partial match where the city is mentioned anywhere within the cell value, then an asterisk would also be added before the value in cell C3:

```
=VLOOKUP("*"&C3&"*",tblTargets,2,0)
```

Case-Sensitive VLOOKUP

Excel formulas rarely consider the case of characters when matching values. There are exceptions to this, for example, the FIND function is case-sensitive.

Figure 7-34 shows a VLOOKUP formula returning incorrect results for the lookup values written in lowercase – *a* and *b*.

Let's look at how we can fix this by creating a case-sensitive VLOOKUP.

| E3 | ▼ | ⋮ | × | ✓ | *fx* | =VLOOKUP(C3,$G$3:$H$8,2,FALSE) |

◢	A	B	C	D	E	F	G	H
1								
2		**Name**	**Level**	**Value**	**Discount**		**Level**	**Discount**
3		Pedro Afonso	A	1,199	15.0%		A	15.0%
4		Elizabeth Brown	b	936	12.0%		B	12.0%
5		Sven Ottlieb	b	1,360	12.0%		C	10.0%
6		Janine Labrune	a	1,098	15.0%		a	7.5%
7		Ann Devon	B	1,401	12.0%		b	5.0%
8		Roland Mendel	A	1,419	15.0%		c	2.5%
9		Aria Cruz	C	858	10.0%			

Figure 7-34. *VLOOKUP returning incorrect results due to case discrepancy*

To create a case-sensitive VLOOKUP, the CHOOSE and EXACT functions will be used together. This is an advanced example that creates a two-dimensional array for VLOOKUP to use.

We saw an example of EXACT being used to match case in Chapter 2 of this book. Back then, we were working with the IF function. Let's quickly remind ourselves on the EXACT function.

The EXACT function compares two text strings to see if they are exactly the same, including their case. It returns True if they are the same; otherwise, False is returned.

It requires two arguments – the two text strings to compare.

```
=EXACT(text1, text2)
```

We saw the CHOOSE function two examples ago, when we made VLOOKUP look to its left.

In Figure 7-35, the following formula has been used for a case-sensitive VLOOKUP formula. The correct results are now being returned for levels *a* and *b*.

```
=VLOOKUP(TRUE,
CHOOSE({1,2},EXACT(C3,$G$3:$G$8),$H$3:$H$8),
2,FALSE)
```

This is an array formula. If you are using a version of Excel with the array engine, the formula will work as normal. Otherwise, you will need to press **Ctrl + Shift + Enter** to run the formula.

E3	▼	⋮	✕	✓	*fx*	=VLOOKUP(TRUE,
						CHOOSE({1,2},EXACT(C3,$G$3:$G$8),$H$3:$H$8),
						2,FALSE)

◢	A	B	C	D	E	F	G	H
1								
2		Name	Level	Value	Discount		Level	Discount
3		Pedro Afonso	A	1,199	15.0%		A	15.0%
4		Elizabeth Brown	b	936	5.0%		B	12.0%
5		Sven Ottlieb	b	1,360	5.0%		C	10.0%
6		Janine Labrune	a	1,098	7.5%		a	7.5%
7		Ann Devon	B	1,401	12.0%		b	5.0%
8		Roland Mendel	A	1,419	15.0%		c	2.5%
9		Aria Cruz	C	858	10.0%			

Figure 7-35. *Case-sensitive VLOOKUP formula*

So, how does this work?

Firstly, the EXACT function compares the strings from the lookup value in C3 and the values in the lookup range of G3:G8. The following array of logical values is returned:

{TRUE;FALSE;FALSE;FALSE;FALSE;FALSE}

The array of constants {1,2} has been provided as the index number for CHOOSE. So, the CHOOSE function then combines the results of the EXACT function and the values in range H3:H8 into a two-dimensional array.

{TRUE,0.15;FALSE,0.12;FALSE,0.1;FALSE,0.075;FALSE,0.05;FALSE,0.025}

The VLOOKUP function has been given the lookup value of TRUE, so it now looks for TRUE down the first column of the two-dimensional array it has been given and returns the value from the second column.

Multiple Column VLOOKUP

It may be that you have two or more columns that need to be used in a lookup. VLOOKUP was not made with this scenario in mind, and it is much easier to perform with a function such as XLOOKUP or with a Merge Query in Power Query.

However, of course, it can be done. In Figure 7-36, we have a table (columns G:I) named [tblLastMonth] that contains a [Regional Code] column and a [Client ID] column along with last month's [Total] value.

In column E, we need a VLOOKUP to return the [Total] value for the matching combination of regional code and client ID.

B	C	D	E	F	G	H	I
Regional Code	**Client ID**	**Total**	**Previous**		**Regional C**	**Client ID**	**Total**
HUM	009	651			HUM	009	437
CHE	180	1,127			CRA	213	1,023
CRA	213	473			HUM	415	703
HUM	415	1,391			IPS	772	999
IPS	438	1,227			CHE	180	824
IPS	772	1,050			IPS	438	1,243
					HUM	911	819
					CRA	034	690
					SWA	552	497

Figure 7-36. Sample data with two columns to match with our lookup

We will do this by first creating a new column in [tblLastMonth] with the combined [Regional Code] and [Client ID]. This column will be the one used for the lookup, so it needs to be the first column of the table.

To insert a new column in a table (not the worksheet)

1. Right-click any cell in the [Regional Code] column of the table.

2. Point to **Insert** and click **Table Columns to the Left** (Figure 7-37).

3. Type the header "Reference" for the new column.

Note You can also insert a table column by clicking **Home ➤ Insert ➤ Insert Table Columns to the Left**.

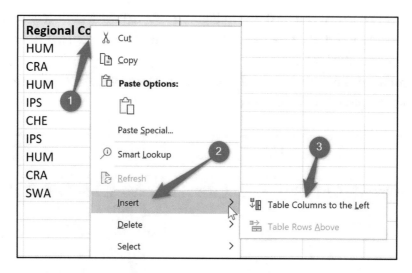

Figure 7-37. *Insert a table column to the left of the first column*

The following formula has been entered in the new [Reference] column to concatenate the [Regional Code] and [Client ID] column values (Figure 7-38):

```
=[@[Regional Code]]&[@[Client ID]]
```

f_x	=[@[Regional Code]]&[@[Client ID]]			
Reference	**Regional Code**	**Client ID**	**Total**	
HUM009	HUM	009	437	
CRA213	CRA	213	1,023	
HUM415	HUM	415	703	
IPS772	IPS	772	999	
CHE180	CHE	180	824	
IPS438	IPS	438	1,243	
HUM911	HUM	911	819	
CRA034	CRA	034	690	
SWA552	SWA	552	497	

Figure 7-38. *Reference column from combined regional code and client ID*

In Figure 7-39, the following VLOOKUP formula is then used to return the previous month's value:

```
=VLOOKUP(B3&C3,tblLastMonth,4,0)
```

The two *lookup value* columns have been combined to search in the first column of [tblLastMonth] and return the value from column 4.

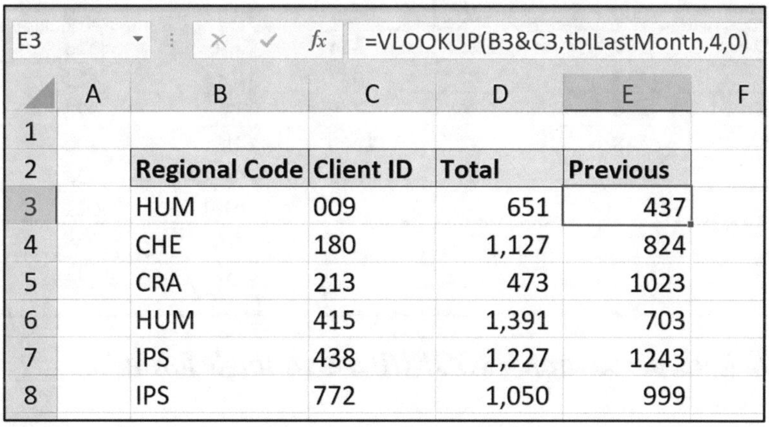

	A	B	C	D	E	F
1						
2		Regional Code	Client ID	Total	Previous	
3		HUM	009	651	437	
4		CHE	180	1,127	824	
5		CRA	213	473	1023	
6		HUM	415	1,391	703	
7		IPS	438	1,227	1243	
8		IPS	772	1,050	999	

E3 ▾ : × ✓ fx =VLOOKUP(B3&C3,tblLastMonth,4,0)

Figure 7-39. Multicolumn VLOOKUP formula

This technique can easily be extended to work for more than two columns, if required.

Taking this a step further, you can create a multicolumn VLOOKUP using a single formula. So, we can achieve this without inserting a new table column and creating the merged [Regional Code] and [Client ID] column.

In Figure 7-40, the following formula is entered in cell E3. It uses the CHOOSE function to create an array (a virtual table you could say) consisting of two columns. The first column is a merged [Regional Code] and [Client ID] column and the second column is the [Total] column. The VLOOKUP then searches for the multicolumn lookup value in this array and returns the matching value from the second column.

```
=VLOOKUP(B3&C3,
CHOOSE({1,2},
tblLastMonth[Regional Code]&tblLastMonth[Client ID],
tblLastMonth[Total]),
2,0)
```

	E3	✓	⋮	× ✓	*fx*	=VLOOKUP(B3&C3, CHOOSE({1,2}, tblLastMonth[Regional Code]&tblLastMonth[Client ID], tblLastMonth[Total]), 2,0)				

	A	B	C	D	E	F	G	H	I
1									
2		Regional Code	Client ID	Total	Previous		Regional Code	Client ID	Total
3		HUM	009	651	437		HUM	009	437
4		CHE	180	1,127	824		CRA	213	1,023
5		CRA	213	473	1023		HUM	415	703
6		HUM	415	1,391	703		IPS	772	999
7		IPS	438	1,227	1243		CHE	180	824
8		IPS	772	1,050	999		IPS	438	1,243
9							HUM	911	819
10							CRA	034	690
11							SWA	552	497
12									

Figure 7-40. Multiple column VLOOKUP with a single formula

We saw the CHOOSE function recently when getting VLOOKUP to look to its left. This brilliant function is covered in more detail in Chapter 11.

Return the Nth Match

The VLOOKUP function always returns a value for the first occurrence of the lookup value that it matches, searching from top to bottom.

Now, if you want to return multiple results, this is not something that VLOOKUP can do. You want to use the FILTER function, covered in Chapter 13.

We can however use VLOOKUP to return a specific instance of the lookup value, such as the second, third, fourth, or nth instance.

In Figure 7-41, we have a lookup range that contains multiple instances of participant names and their scores in a contest. Each participant has three attempts, so they occur three times.

We will use a VLOOKUP to return all three scores to range C5:C7 for the name stated in cell C2.

B	C	D	E	F	G
Name	Kelly		Date	Name	Score
			16/03/2021	David	60
Instance	Score		23/03/2021	Kelly	61
1			30/03/2021	Sue	93
2			20/04/2021	Sue	66
3			28/04/2021	David	84
			30/04/2021	Kelly	96
			30/05/2021	David	59
			15/06/2021	Sue	87
			14/07/2021	Kelly	71

Figure 7-41. *Multiple occurrences of participant scores*

Like the previous example, our first task is to create a lookup column in the first column position of the lookup table that we can use to uniquely identify each instance.

In Figure 7-42, the following formula is used to combine the value in the [Name] column and the instance number it occurs:

```
=G3&COUNTIFS($G$3:G3,G3)
```

The COUNTIFS function (covered in Chapter 8) is used to count the occurrences of each name.

The interesting part of this formula is the criteria range given to COUNTIFS. It has an absolute cell reference at the start of the range and a relative cell at the end of the range. This ensures that the criteria range expands as the formula is filled down the cells of column E.

So, in range $G$3:G3, David occurs only once. But when the formula gets to the second occurrence of David, the criteria range is $G$3:G7 and includes the second occurrence.

fx	=G3&COUNTIFS($G$3:G3,G3)			
D	**E**	**F**	**G**	**H**
	Lookup	**Date**	**Name**	**Score**
	David1	16/03/2021	David	60
	Kelly1	23/03/2021	Kelly	61
	Sue1	30/03/2021	Sue	93
	Sue2	20/04/2021	Sue	66
	David2	28/04/2021	David	84
	Kelly2	30/04/2021	Kelly	96
	David3	30/05/2021	David	59
	Sue3	15/06/2021	Sue	87
	Kelly3	14/07/2021	Kelly	71

Figure 7-42. *Lookup column with name and instance number combined*

In Figure 7-43, the following VLOOKUP formula is used to return the first, second, and third scores for the name entered in cell C2:

=VLOOKUP($C$2&B5,$E$3:$H$11,4,FALSE)

The lookup value is a combined value of the name in cell C2 and the instance number from range B5:B7. When the name in cell C2 is changed, the scores for that participant are returned.

		fx	=VLOOKUP($C$2&B5,$E$3:$H$11,4,FALSE)				
B	**C**	**D**	**E**	**F**	**G**	**H**	
Name	Kelly		**Lookup**	**Date**	**Name**	**Score**	
			David1	16/03/2021	David	60	
Instance	**Score**		Kelly1	23/03/2021	Kelly	61	
1	61		Sue1	30/03/2021	Sue	93	
2	96		Sue2	20/04/2021	Sue	66	
3	71		David2	28/04/2021	David	84	
			Kelly2	30/04/2021	Kelly	96	
			David3	30/05/2021	David	59	
			Sue3	15/06/2021	Sue	87	
			Kelly3	14/07/2021	Kelly	71	

Figure 7-43. *VLOOKUP returning the first, second, and third instances of a value*

It is possible to achieve the same result using a VLOOKUP formula without the helper column identifying each unique instance. It is a more advanced formula.

In Figure 7-44, the following array formula is entered in cell C5. As it is an array formula, if you are using a non-dynamic array version of Excel, you need to press **Ctrl + Shift + Enter** to run the formula.

```
=VLOOKUP(
SMALL(IF($F$3:$F$11=$C$2,ROW($F$3:$F$11)),B5),
CHOOSE({1,2},ROW($F$3:$F$11),$G$3:$G$11),
2,0)
```

So, how does this formula work?

In the *lookup value* argument of VLOOKUP, the IF function tests the names in range $F$3:$F$11 against the name in cell $C$2. It then uses the ROW function to return an array consisting of the row number of the matching name or FALSE if the name does not match. The following array is returned by IF when "Kelly" is entered in cell $C$2:

```
{FALSE;4;FALSE;FALSE;FALSE;8;FALSE;FALSE;11}
```

The ROW function returns the row number of the worksheet, not the row number with range $F$3:$F$11. "Kelly" is matched to rows 4, 8, and 11.

C5		✓ : ✕ ✓ *fx*	=VLOOKUP(SMALL(IF($F$3:$F$11=$C$2,ROW($F$3:$F$11)),B5), CHOOSE({1,2},ROW($F$3:$F$11),$G$3:$G$11), 2,0)					
	A	B	C	D	E	F	G	
1								
2		Name	Kelly		Date	Name	Score	
3					16/03/2021	David	60	
4		Instance	Score		23/03/2021	Kelly	61	
5		1	61		30/03/2021	Sue	93	
6		2	96		20/04/2021	Sue	66	
7		3	71		28/04/2021	David	84	
8					30/04/2021	Kelly	96	
9					30/05/2021	David	59	
10					15/06/2021	Sue	87	
11					14/07/2021	Kelly	71	

Figure 7-44. *Returning the Nth match with a single VLOOKUP formula*

The SMALL function then returns the Nth smallest number in this array. This number is specified by the values in range B5:B7. For the formula in cell C5, the SMALL function returns 4 as that is the first smallest number.

The CHOOSE function is used in the *table array* argument of VLOOKUP (Again! What a useful function!). It creates an array consisting of two columns.

In column 1, the ROW function returns a list of the sheet row numbers for range $F$3:$F$11. The result is {3;4;5;6;7;8;9;10;11}. Column 2 is simply the values from range $G$3:$G$11.

The VLOOKUP function searches for the row number returned by the SMALL and IF combo, in the column of row number provided by ROW, and returns the score value from column 2 of the array created by CHOOSE. Awesome!

VLOOKUP with Other Excel Features

As always, we will conclude the chapter with some examples of how VLOOKUP can be used with other Excel features. Let's see two examples, one with Conditional Formatting and another with a chart.

Conditional Formatting and VLOOKUP

For a Conditional Formatting example, we want to format the values that exceeded a target score. The target score resides in a different table to the one with the formatted values, so we will use VLOOKUP to retrieve it for testing.

Figure 7-45 shows a list of staff, their locale, and their performance value. A second table lists the different targets by locale.

We want to format only the values in range D3:D9 that are greater than or equal to the respective target for that staff member's locale.

B	C	D	E	F	G
Name	**Locale**	**Value**		**Locale**	**Target**
Pedro Afonso	GB	1,753		AU	1500
Elizabeth Brown	NZ	903		BE	600
Sven Ottlieb	NZ	581		DE	900
Janine Labrune	AU	1,666		GB	1800
Ann Devon	DE	751		NZ	850
Roland Mendel	GB	1,884			
Aria Cruz	BE	242			

Figure 7-45. *Performance values and a separate target by locale table*

1. Select range D3:D9.

2. Click **Home ➤ Conditional Formatting ➤ New Rule ➤ Use a formula to determine which cells to format**.

3. Enter the following formula into the *Format values where this formula is true:* box (Figure 7-46):

   `=D3>=VLOOKUP(C3,$F$3:$G$9,2,FALSE)`

Note   It is often easier to type a formula into a cell first and then copy and paste it into the Conditional Formatting rule. The formula box is quite small and offers little help, and you need to be careful to be in the correct cell mode when moving through the formula.

---

4. Click **Format** and specify the formatting you want to use.

5. Click **OK** to apply and close each window.

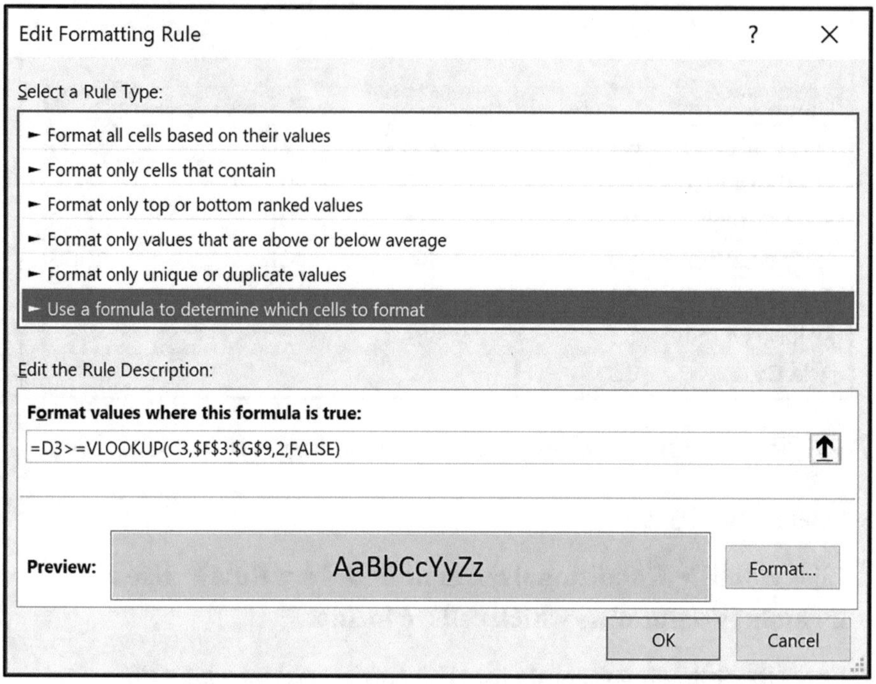

Figure 7-46. *VLOOKUP in a Conditional Formatting rule*

Figure 7-47 shows the formatting rule successfully applied to range D3:D9.

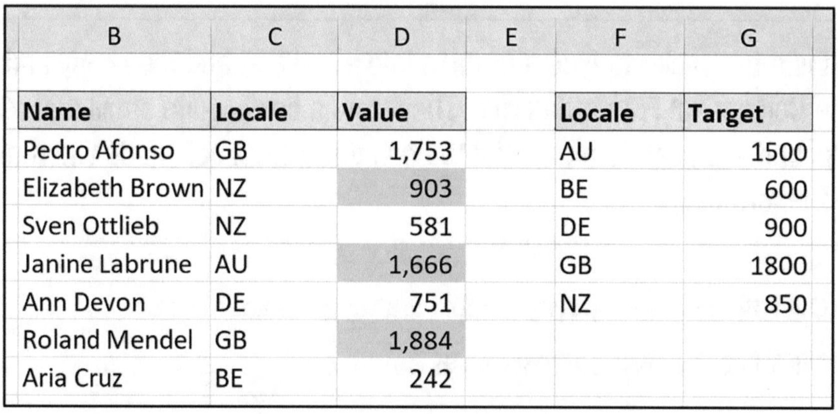

	B	C	D	E	F	G
	Name	Locale	Value		Locale	Target
	Pedro Afonso	GB	1,753		AU	1500
	Elizabeth Brown	NZ	903		BE	600
	Sven Ottlieb	NZ	581		DE	900
	Janine Labrune	AU	1,666		GB	1800
	Ann Devon	DE	751		NZ	850
	Roland Mendel	GB	1,884			
	Aria Cruz	BE	242			

Figure 7-47. *Formatting rule to format only values that are >= the target value*

Dynamic Chart Range

In this chart example, we will create a dynamic chart range that changes on the selection of a value from a drop-down list.

In Figure 7-48, there is a table named [tblWeekly] with six weeks' performance data by different staff members. Below the table are headers in preparation for our range that will feed the chart, and in cell J3 is a drop-down list of the different staff members' names.

When someone selects a name from the drop-down list, we want the values for that selected staff member to show in the range below the table. The chart will be based on that range, so will change when the drop-down list value changes.

B	C	D	E	F	G	H	I	J
Name	Wk 1	Wk 2	Wk 3	Wk 4	Wk 5	Wk 6		Name
Ann Devon	446	1,880	1,548	2,281	1,944	647		Janine Labrune
Aria Cruz	1,109	1,488	1,160	1,457	1,690	522		
Elizabeth Brown	2,366	1,860	1,523	1,474	1,407	2,380		
Janine Labrune	1,785	1,428	1,464	2,216	1,881	2,150		
Pedro Afonso	1,621	1,920	1,729	2,260	1,267	1,842		
Roland Mendel	1,541	2,047	1,210	1,462	1,937	925		
Sven Ottlieb	2,251	1,264	772	1,269	2,230	502		
Name	Wk 1	Wk 2	Wk 3	Wk 4	Wk 5	Wk 6		

Figure 7-48. *Table of data with a chart range below and a list in cell J3*

Note   Typically, the table of data, chart range, and chart with drop-down list would all be on different worksheets – a data sheet, calculation sheet, and a report/presentation sheet. It is displayed all-in-one here only to show the mechanics of the technique easier.

First, we want the selected name to appear in cell B12. This is achieved with a simple link to the value in cell J3. This cell value will be used as the chart title.

```
=J3
```

In range C12:H12, the following VLOOKUP formula is used to return the weekly values for the selected name (Figure 7-49):

```
=VLOOKUP($J$3,tblWeekly,COLUMN(C11)-1,FALSE)
```

The COLUMN function is used to return the column index number so that we do not need to enter it ourselves in six different VLOOKUP formulas, when we fill the formula.

It references the cell directly above the formula (C11 in the formula shown), and one is subtracted from the COLUMN function result because [tblWeekly] begins in column B. So, [Wk1] is the second column of the table, but the third column of the sheet.

	A	B	C	D	E	F	G	H	I	J
				fx	=VLOOKUP($J$3,tblWeekly,COLUMN(C11)-1,FALSE)					
1										
2		Name	Wk 1	Wk 2	Wk 3	Wk 4	Wk 5	Wk 6		Name
3		Ann Devon	446	1,880	1,548	2,281	1,944	647		Janine Labrune
4		Aria Cruz	1,109	1,488	1,160	1,457	1,690	522		
5		Elizabeth Brown	2,366	1,860	1,523	1,474	1,407	2,380		
6		Janine Labrune	1,785	1,428	1,464	2,216	1,881	2,150		
7		Pedro Afonso	1,621	1,920	1,729	2,260	1,267	1,842		
8		Roland Mendel	1,541	2,047	1,210	1,462	1,937	925		
9		Sven Ottlieb	2,251	1,264	772	1,269	2,230	502		
10										
11		Name	Wk 1	Wk 2	Wk 3	Wk 4	Wk 5	Wk 6		
12		Janine Labrune	1,785	1,428	1,464	2,216	1,881	2,150		
13										

Figure 7-49. VLOOKUP formula for a dynamic chart range

With the chart range created, the chart can now be created. For this example, let's create a simple line chart:

1. Select range B11:H12.

2. Click **Insert ➤ Insert Line or Area Chart ➤ Line**.

3. Make the necessary improvements to the chart to make it look awesome.

Figure 7-50 shows a basic line chart with no modifications positioned underneath the drop-down list.

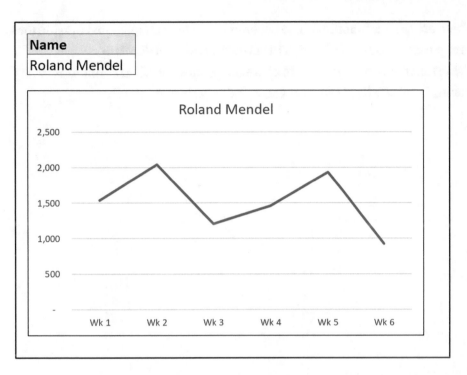

Figure 7-50. *Dynamic chart based on the value from the drop-down list above it*

Note   Creating the chart is explained very briefly here as working with charts is not the purpose of this book. It is the formulas and the creation of the dynamic chart range that is our focus.

Summary

In this chapter, we learned the VLOOKUP function in Excel along with some tricks to creating a more robust and effective VLOOKUP formula and an understanding of common mistakes that users make. We then progressed to some advanced examples that included multi-criteria and case-sensitive lookups.

In the next chapter, we will look at formulas that perform aggregations such as sum, count, and average dependent on conditions that are met. There is a group of functions in Excel built for these purposes. This group includes SUMIFS, COUNTIFS, and AVERAGEIFS.

There are similar functions, also covered in the next chapter, just outside the scope of this group that includes MEDIAN, TRIMMEAN, and MODE.MULT.

Using functions such as these to aggregate values based on conditions is very popular in Excel. We have lots to cover, so let's get started.

CHAPTER 8

The Awesome SUMIFS, COUNTIFS, and Friends

There is a group of functions in Excel that perform conditional aggregations. The two most well-known functions of this group are the SUMIFS and COUNTIFS functions. However, this also includes the AVERAGEIFS, MAXIFS, and MINIFS functions.

These functions are quick to learn, as they look very similar to each other. So, once you know one, you kind of know them all. They are an incredibly useful group of functions, especially COUNTIFS.

In this chapter, we will begin with the SUMIFS function. We will understand its syntax and how to write the different logical tests and see multiple examples of its use. This will also build an understanding for the other functions in the group as we progress through the chapter.

We will then explore the brilliant COUNTIFS function and the other functions in the group. The chapter also covers formulas to achieve similar tasks that are just outside the scope of this group of functions.

The SUMIFS Function

Availability: All versions

File   sumifs.xlsx

The SUMIFS function sums the values in a column, for the rows that meet one or more criteria. For example, sum the sales values for sales of a specific product, or sum the attendance values for a specific training course in a specific region.

© Alan Murray 2022
A. Murray, *Advanced Excel Formulas*, https://doi.org/10.1007/978-1-4842-7125-4_8

This is a wonderful and well-rounded function. It is simple to use and works very well with table data and with arrays (we will see array examples in Chapter 10).

The following is the syntax of the SUMIFS function:

```
=SUMIFS(sum_range, criteria_range1, criteria1, [criteria_range2],
    [criteria2], ...)
```

- **Sum range:** The values to be summed. This can be a range, table column, or an array.

- **Criteria range1:** The range or array of values to be tested using *criteria1*. If the criterion is met, the corresponding value from the *sum range* is summed.

- **Criteria1:** The criterion to be evaluated in *criteria range1*. This can be entered as a string, a number, or an expression. The following are all valid ways to enter the criterion: "London", B4, "<"&B4.

- **[Criteria range2], [Criteria2], …:** Additional criteria ranges and associated criterion when testing more than one condition.

Note   The size of the criteria ranges and the sum range must be the same.

The following examples (except the using wildcards with SUMIFS example) will be using the data in the table named [tblSales] on the [Data] worksheet. The first few rows of this table are shown in Figure 8-1.

	A	B	C	D	E	F
1	ID	Date	Product Name	Store	Units Sold	Total
2	19775	11/01/2021	Coffee	North	39	59.06
3	19776	12/01/2021	Hot Chocolate	West	16	424.80
4	19777	24/01/2021	Wine	North	25	207.30
5	19778	25/01/2021	Water	West	35	436.53
6	19779	30/01/2021	Coffee	South	38	424.30
7	19780	01/02/2021	Tea	North	10	174.45
8	19781	03/02/2021	Tea	North	30	456.55
9	19782	08/02/2021	Hot Chocolate	West	20	424.50

Figure 8-1. tblSales data to be used for the SUMIFS examples

SUMIF or SUMIFS

This chapter is primarily focused on the group of functions that names end in IFS. However, when typing SUMIFS, you will notice a SUMIF function in the intellisense list (Figure 8-2).

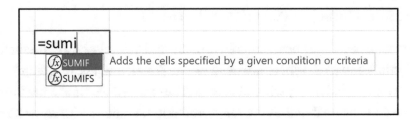

Figure 8-2. *SUMIF and SUMIFS functions in intellisense list*

The SUMIF function was essentially made redundant when Microsoft released the SUMIFS function with Excel 2007. The SUMIF function can only test one condition, while the SUMIFS can do one or more conditions.

Now, the SUMIF function is heavily used to this day and, therefore, is important to understand, despite its redundant nature.

The syntax of the SUMIF function is as follows:

```
=SUMIF(criteria_range, criteria, [sum_range])
```

Notice the key difference is that the SUMIF function begins with the *criteria range* argument, while SUMIFS begins with the *sum range* argument due to its handling of multiple conditions.

From this point, the book moves on only with the SUMIFS function, but be mindful that SUMIF can achieve the same examples, but for a single condition only.

Note   There are also COUNTIF and AVERAGEIF functions to accompany the COUNTIFS and AVERAGEIFS functions we see later. However, there is no singular version for MAXIFS and MINIFS.

Using Text Criteria

For our first example, we will use the SUMIFS function to test a single condition. We will sum the values in the [Total] column for the sales from the East store only.

In Figure 8-3, the following formula is entered into cell B6:

```
=SUMIFS(tblSales[Total],tblSales[Store],"East")
```

The text value "East" has been entered directly into the *Criteria* argument of the SUMIFS function. Table references are used for the [Total] and [Store] columns.

SUMIFS works wonderfully with table data. These references make the formula easier to read and ensure that the sum range and criteria range are of equal size.

Note   The SUMIFS function is not case-sensitive. Entering "East" or "east" for the criteria is both accepted.

B6	∨ ⋮ ✕ ✓ *fx*	=SUMIFS(tblSales[Total],tblSales[Store],"East")		
	A	B	C	D	E
1					
2		Product Name	Store		
3					
4					
5		Total			
6		3,023.55			
7					

Figure 8-3. *SUMIFS function with criteria entered directly*

To be clear, the use of tables is not necessary. The formula could have been written as follows:

```
=SUMIFS(Data!F:F,Data!D:D,"East")
```

or even as follows:

```
=SUMIFS(Data!$F$2:$F$50,Data!$D$2:$D$50,"East")
```

However, you probably agree that this is less efficient. It is harder to understand, is not dynamic, and is more prone to user error. The many advantages of using tables were outlined in detail in Chapter 4.

By entering the criteria directly into the *Criteria* argument, it is a constant. This could be an advantage of its use. But, if we want the user of the spreadsheet to be able to easily change the store being summed, then the formula can reference a cell value, instead of having the criteria "hardcoded" into it.

In Figure 8-4, the following formula sums the values for the store entered in cell C3:

```
=SUMIFS(tblSales[Total],tblSales[Store],C3)
```

Cell C3 contains a drop-down list of the different stores, making it easy for a user to interact with it.

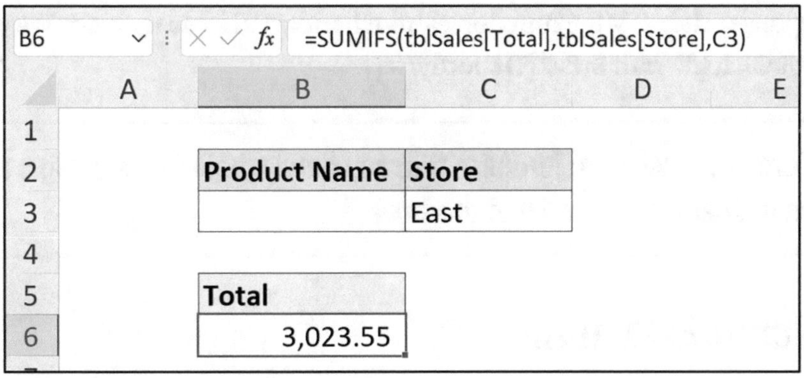

Figure 8-4. *SUMIFS function using a cell value for the criteria*

Working with Multiple Criteria

Continuing with the previous example, we will use the SUMIFS function with two conditions. We will sum the values in the [Total] column for a specific product and store. The product and store will both be specified by cell values.

The following formula is shown in Figure 8-5. Cell B3 contains the product name criteria and cell C3 contains the store criteria.

```
=SUMIFS(tblSales[Total],
    tblSales[Product Name],B3,tblSales[Store],C3)
```

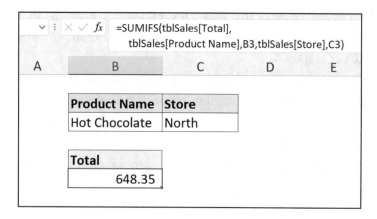

Figure 8-5. SUMIFS function with two conditions

In this example, AND logic is used between the two conditions, and this is the desired response. The SUMIFS function cannot handle OR logic natively. We will see a little trick for OR logic with SUMIFS shortly.

Note   More advanced sum formulas that can handle both types of logic and more are shown in Chapters 9 and 10 of this book.

Using Numeric Criteria

Testing numeric criteria with SUMIFS is quite different to how numbers are tested in functions such as IF.

Remember that with SUMIFS, the criteria must be entered as text, a number, or an expression. So, you can enter a number into the criteria, but if you want to test if the number is ">=", "<", or some other logical test, then this must be entered as text or written as an expression.

In the following formula, the numeric criterion is entered as text directly into the formula (Figure 8-6). It sums the [Total] column values only where 30 or more units were sold:

```
=SUMIFS(tblSales[Total],tblSales[Units Sold],">=30")
```

Entering this as text within the double quotation characters ("") is unexpected as we do not do this when entering similar criteria in IF. But this is a different function, and they all have their little quirks, just like us.

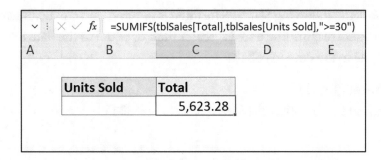

Figure 8-6. *SUMIFS function with a numeric condition entered directly*

If you want to use a cell value for the number criteria, then the logical characters can be combined with the cell value using an ampersand (&).

In Figure 8-7, cell B3 contains the number of units sold to be tested. In the following formula, the ">=" characters are combined with cell B3 in the formula:

```
=SUMIFS(tblSales[Total],tblSales[Units Sold],">="&B3)
```

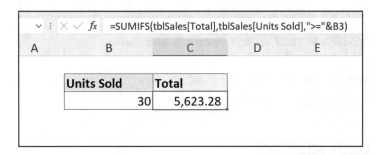

Figure 8-7. *SUMIFS function with text and cell values combined for criteria*

Sum Values Between Two Dates

The SUMIFS function is perfect for the task of summing values with date conditions.

In this example, we will sum values between two dates. However, the scenario could be to sum values with a single date condition, for instance, the values since a specified date or until a specified date.

Remember, dates in Excel are numbers. So, the technique used is a repetition of the previous example when we tested numeric criteria.

In Figure 8-8, the following SUMIFS formula is entered into cell B6. It sums the values where the corresponding date is greater than or equal to the date in cell B3 and less than or equal to the date in cell D3:

```
=SUMIFS(tblSales[Total],
    tblSales[Date],">="&B3,tblSales[Date],"<="&D3)
```

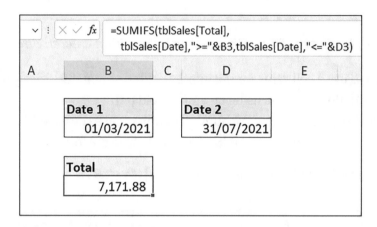

Figure 8-8. *SUMIFS to sum values between two dates*

Additional criteria could be added to test for a specific product or store. The SUMIFS function can handle up to 127 conditions.

OR Logic with SUMIFS

The SUMIFS function performs AND logic between its corresponding criteria ranges and criterion. SUMIFS does not support the use of OR logic in its truest form. So, many users would produce a separate SUMIFS for each condition that forms part of the OR expression and add the result of each SUMIFS together.

For example, the following formula in Figure 8-9 would return the sum of the [Total] column for the stores of the regions in the "East" or "West":

```
=SUMIFS(tblSales[Total],tblSales[Store],"East")
    +SUMIFS(tblSales[Total],tblSales[Store],"West")
```

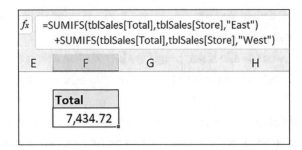

Figure 8-9. *Adding separate SUMIFS functions to create an OR logic result*

This works fine. However, there is a trick to perform OR logic with multiple conditions. Let's see some examples of how to do this.

Continuing to use the data in the [tblSales] table, we will sum only the values in the [Total] column that match multiple specified regions.

In this first example, the store regions are entered directly into the formula as an array of constants (Figure 8-10).

In the following formula, the regions of "East" and "West" are used. They are entered as an array, so are enclosed in the curly braces, and separated by a comma. The SUMIFS function returns two totals – one for "East" and another for "West." The SUM function then sums the two totals to produce a single result:

```
=SUM(
SUMIFS(tblSales[Total],tblSales[Store],{"East","West"})
)
```

Of course, more than two criteria can be added to the array. You need to separate each criterion with a comma, or a semicolon (;), and enclose them all in the curly braces of the array.

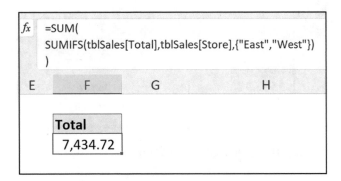

Figure 8-10. *Array of constants in SUMIFS for OR logic with multiple conditions*

This is great, but I am sure you are thinking – can we refer to cell values instead of typing the text directly into the array?

Well, yes you can. And to take it further, if we format the range of cells as a table, it will create a dynamic criteria range that we can easily add and remove criterion to and from.

In Figure 8-11, the following formula uses the values in a table named [tblStores]. The table is in cells I1:I3. We have the same result as before, but this time the criteria range is dynamic, and the formula is more concise:

```
=SUM(
SUMIFS(tblSales[Total],tblSales[Store],tblStores)
)
```

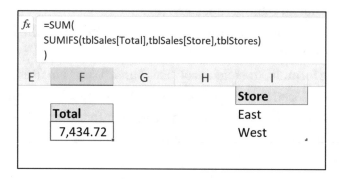

Figure 8-11. *Using a table as the source for OR logic values*

In Figure 8-12, another store region is added to [tblStores]. The table automatically expands, and the SUMIFS function updates the result.

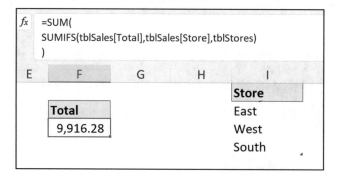

Figure 8-12. *SUMIFS criteria range expanded*

Note   In non-dynamic array–enabled versions of Excel, you need to press **Ctrl + Shift + Enter** for the formulas that reference a range for OR logic.

When using a range or an array of constants for OR logic, you can still take advantage of the up to 127 criteria offered by the SUMIFS function (and its friends).

The following formula has the added criteria that the product must be "Wine" (Figure 8-13):

```
=SUM(SUMIFS(tblSales[Total],
    tblSales[Product Name],"Wine",tblSales[Store],tblStores))
```

Note   The SUMPRODUCT and SUM (in Excel for Microsoft 365 and 2021 versions) functions offer great alternatives to SUMIFS when the logic gets more complex.

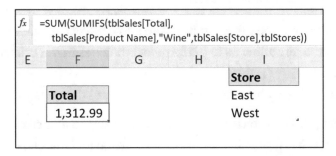

Figure 8-13. *SUMIFS function with both AND and OR logic included*

The examples so far have focused on text criteria only. And this is much more likely to be required. However, the same technique can be used with numeric criteria too.

In Figure 8-14, the following SUMIFS formula sums the values from the [Total] column that correspond to the dates that lie within two different date ranges: 1st March 2021–31st March 2021 and 1st September 2021–30th September 2021.

```
=SUM(SUMIFS(tblSales[Total],
    tblSales[Date],">="&tblDates1,tblSales[Date],"<="&tblDates2))
```

Both date ranges are formatted as tables ([tblDates1] and [tblDates2]), so that they can be easily referenced and expanded or reduced, if required.

Testing numeric values is not as common a requirement as testing multiple text values with OR logic. But cool to know that it is possible.

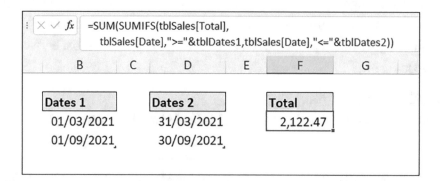

Figure 8-14. *SUMIFS summing values between two date ranges*

Using Wildcards with SUMIFS

The SUMIFS function and the others in its group allow the use of wildcard characters. These wildcard characters allow us to perform text matches in our criteria that are similar but not exact.

There are two wildcard characters, the asterisk (*) and the question mark (?):

- **Asterisk (*):** The asterisk is used in place of any sequence of characters. It is fantastic for performing partial text matches and is the more commonly used wildcard character. For example, the criterion "*America" can be used to match both "South America" and "North America."

- **Question mark (?):** The question mark is used in place of a single character. This is useful when the matching text needs to be a specific number of characters. For example, the criterion "SR???" will match any five-character text string that begins with "SR". It would match "SR371," but not "SR9271," "SR4," or "DF736."

Note   If you need to use an actual asterisk or question mark within the criteria, precede the asterisk or question mark with the tilde (~) character. The tilde forces the function to use the actual character and not treat it as a wildcard.

Let's look at two examples of using the SUMIFS function with wildcard characters. These examples use the [tblOrders] table on the [Wildcard Characters] worksheet.

In Figure 8-15, the SUMIFS function is used to sum the [Total] column for only the order numbers that begin with the characters entered in cell B3 ("VO" in this example):

```
=SUMIFS(tblOrders[Total],tblOrders[Order No],B3&"*")
```

The asterisk has been entered as text (enclosed in double quotations) and concatenated to the value in cell B3.

Notice that all three orders that begin with the characters "VO" are summed (313 = 166 + 107 + 40). This is because the asterisk wildcard replaces any number of characters.

	A	B	C	D	E	F	G	H
C3				f_x =SUMIFS(tblOrders[Total],tblOrders[Order No],B3&"*")				
1					Order No	Product	Total	
2		Code	Total		HJ57462	THL	89	
3		VO	313		KR209	BBN	46	
4					VO2019	QSD	166	
5					KR2811	AMD	67	
6					KR0087	THL	73	
7					VO4271	QSD	107	
8					HJ2251	AMD	113	
9					KR94624	AMD	12	
10					VO33005	BBN	40	
11								

Figure 8-15. *SUMIFS function with the asterisk wildcard character*

In Figure 8-16, the criteria of the following SUMIFS function have a string of four question marks "????" concatenated to the value in cell B3:

```
=SUMIFS(tblOrders[Total],tblOrders[Order No],B3&"????")
```

This time, only two of the three order numbers that begin with the characters "VO" are summed (273 = 166 + 107). The question marks replace a single character, so in this example, the order number must have exactly four characters following the characters "VO".

C3		✓ : ✕ ✓ *fx*	=SUMIFS(tblOrders[Total],tblOrders[Order No],B3&"????")					
	A	B	C	D	E	F	G	H
1					Order No	Product	Total	
2		Code	Total		HJ57462	THL	89	
3		VO	273		KR209	BBN	46	
4					VO2019	QSD	166	
5					KR2811	AMD	67	
6					KR0087	THL	73	
7					VO4271	QSD	107	
8					HJ2251	AMD	113	
9					KR94624	AMD	12	
10					VO33005	BBN	40	
11								

Figure 8-16. *SUMIFS function with the question mark wildcard character*

The Versatile COUNTIFS Function

Availability: All versions

File   countifs.xlsx

The COUNTIFS function counts the number of times its given criteria are met. It can handle up to 127 corresponding criteria ranges and criteria.

The syntax of the COUNTIFS function is similar to the SUMIFS function but has one fewer argument. The COUNTIFS function does not require a column to aggregate (SUMIFS required a sum range).

```
=COUNTIFS(criteria_range1, criteria1, [criteria_range2], [criteria2], ...)
```

This makes the COUNTIFS function an exception in this group, as all the other functions require a column to aggregate – sum, average, maximum, and minimum.

The COUNTIFS function works in the same manner as the SUMIFS function before, except it counts instead of sums. All the examples demonstrated with SUMIFS, including testing numeric criteria, the use of wildcard characters, and handling OR logic, also apply to COUNTIFS.

Note These techniques also apply to the AVERAGEIFS, MAXIFS, and MINIFS functions. They all have the same fundamental way of working.

As the COUNTIFS function works in the same way as SUMIFS, we will not repeat the same examples. However, let's look at a couple of simple COUNTIFS formulas to get a feel for this function.

The following two examples use the same [tblSales] table that was used for the majority of the SUMIFS examples before.

In Figure 8-17, the following COUNTIFS function returns the number of orders for the product entered in cell B3:

```
=COUNTIFS(tblSales[Product Name],B3)
```

There is a COUNTIF function in Excel that we could have used to achieve this same result. Be aware of its existence, but COUNTIFS is its successor and therefore a superior function.

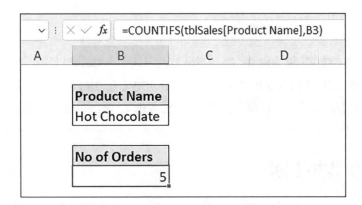

Figure 8-17. *COUNTIFS function with a single condition*

Let's add another condition. In Figure 8-18, the following COUNTIFS function returns the number of orders for the product entered in cell B3 and since the date entered in cell C3:

```
=COUNTIFS(tblSales[Product Name],B3,tblSales[Date],">="&C3)
```

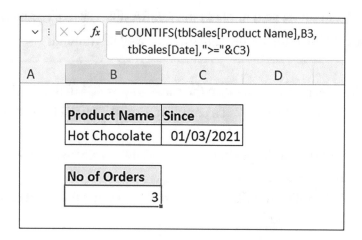

Figure 8-18. *COUNTIFS with more than one condition*

The COUNTIFS function is one of my favorite functions. It is very versatile and has been a savior many times over the years for me.

So, let's see a few examples that are a little outside the traditional scope of how it is used.

Note   You can expect to see more of the COUNTIFS function later in this book. It is an incredibly useful function, and there are future examples of it being used with functions such as FILTER, SUMPRODUCT, and MIN to achieve specific objectives.

Comparing Two Lists

The COUNTIFS function is fantastic for the task of comparing two lists. If you are trying to find the items that appear in one list but not another, or maybe you want to know the items that do appear in both, COUNTIFS is ideal for these tasks.

Figure 8-19 shows two tables – [tblFirst] and [tblSecond]. We want to identify the names in the first table [tblFirst] that do not appear in the second table [tblSecond].

Date	Name
07/03/2021	Martin
27/03/2021	Victoria
01/05/2021	Katherine
16/05/2021	Deborah
25/05/2021	David
07/06/2021	Jason
11/07/2021	Beth
07/08/2021	Carly
09/08/2021	Joe
15/08/2021	Lyndsey
01/09/2021	Rachel
05/09/2021	Claire
10/09/2021	Jeff
02/10/2021	Heather

Date	Name
05/04/2021	Martin
12/06/2021	Victoria
26/06/2021	Deborah
26/07/2021	David
30/07/2021	Jason
14/08/2021	Carly
19/08/2021	Lyndsey
16/08/2021	Rachel
20/09/2021	Claire
07/10/2021	Heather

Figure 8-19. *Two lists to compare and identify the missing values*

We will use the COUNTIFS function to count the occurrences of the names in the first table in the second table. This will flag to us if the names are present in the second table or not.

The following function is entered in a new column named [Flag] in the [tblFirst] table (Figure 8-20):

```
=COUNTIFS(tblSecond[Name],[@Name])
```

The [Name] column of [tblSecond] is given as the *criteria range,* and the name in the current row (the @ symbol indicates this row of a table) is given as the *criteria.*

All results are returned as a 1 or a 0 as there are no duplicated names in this example.

			fx	=COUNTIFS(tblSecond[Name],[@Name])		

A	B	C	D	E	F	G
	Date	**Name**	**Flag**		**Date**	**Name**
	07/03/2021	Martin	1		05/04/2021	Martin
	27/03/2021	Victoria	1		12/06/2021	Victoria
	01/05/2021	Katherine	0		26/06/2021	Deborah
	16/05/2021	Deborah	1		26/07/2021	David
	25/05/2021	David	1		30/07/2021	Jason
	07/06/2021	Jason	1		14/08/2021	Carly
	11/07/2021	Beth	0		19/08/2021	Lyndsey
	07/08/2021	Carly	1		16/08/2021	Rachel
	09/08/2021	Joe	0		20/09/2021	Claire
	15/08/2021	Lyndsey	1		07/10/2021	Heather
	01/09/2021	Rachel	1			
	05/09/2021	Claire	1			
	10/09/2021	Jeff	0			
	02/10/2021	Heather	1			

Figure 8-20. *COUNTIFS function returning the number of times the names appear*

Now, this is serving a purpose, but it would be nice to have a more meaningful output than a bunch of 1s and 0s. So, let's wrap an IF function around our COUNTIFS to request a different response to be returned.

In Figure 8-21, the following formula uses an IF function to return an empty string (the cell appears empty) if the name is present in [tblSecond] and the string "Missing" if the name is not present:

```
=IF(COUNTIFS(tblSecond[Name],[@Name]),"","Missing")
```

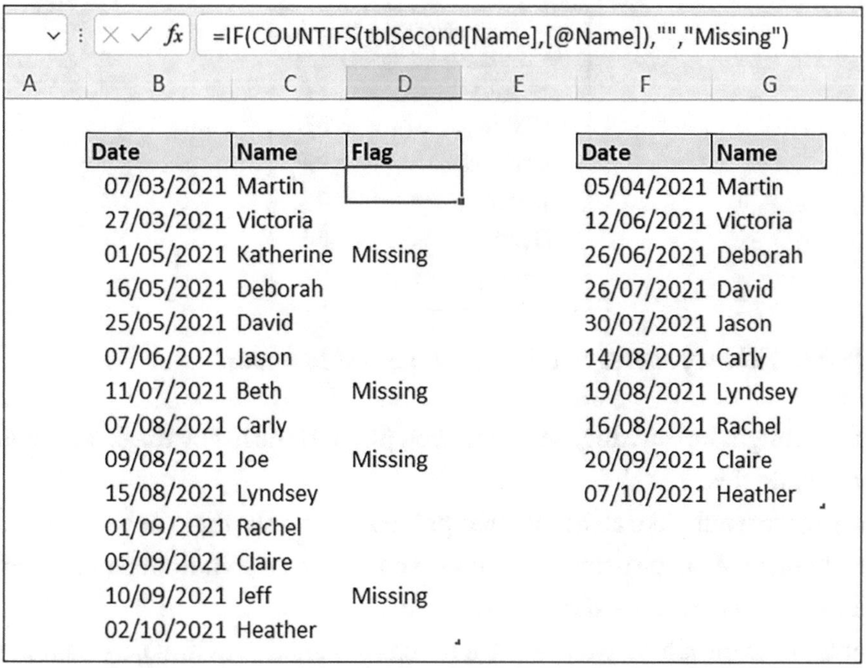

Figure 8-21. *IF function added to return a more meaningful result*

Note   We will see the COUNTIFS function comparing lists again in Chapter 13 of this book. It will be used with the FILTER function to return only the matching or missing rows.

Generating Unique Rankings

There are functions in Excel that will rank values in a range in either an ascending or descending order. However, independently they do not create a unique ranking if any of the values are tied.

In Figure 8-22, we have a range of names and their associated score that they achieved. We want to calculate a ranking of each of the scores and then order them by that rank.

Name	Score
Joseph	84
Susan	65
Michael	99
Javier	72
Garth	84
Mandy	87

Figure 8-22. *Table of scores to be ranked highest to lowest*

Now, you might be thinking, why don't you just sort the list by the score values? Well, sure we could do this.

However, we would like an automated process that ranks them as the scores are added or changed. Also, by using formulas we could create something more complex and rank by other conditions, if required.

To rank the score values, we will use a function named RANK.EQ, a function that ranks a number relative to the other numbers in a list.

The following is the syntax of the RANK.EQ function:

```
=RANK.EQ(number, ref, [order])
```

- **Number:** The number whose rank you want to return.

- **Ref:** The range of numbers to rank the number within.

- **Order:** The order to rank the numbers. Enter 0 or omit the argument to rank in descending order. Enter 1 to rank in ascending order.

Note   The RANK.EQ function was released in Excel 2010 as the successor to the RANK function. The RANK function still exists for compatibility reasons. There is also a less common RANK.AVG function that is not covered in this book.

In Figure 8-23, the following formula was used to generate a rank for each score. The *order* argument was omitted as we want to rank the values in descending order:

```
=RANK.EQ(C3,$C$3:$C$8)
```

You can see that the scores for Joseph and Garth are tied. Because of this, the RANK. EQ function has duplicated the rank and skipped the following rank (there is no rank of 4).

D3		✕ ✓ fx	=RANK.EQ(C3,$C$3:$C$8)	
	A	B	C	D
1				
2		**Name**	**Score**	**Unique Rank**
3		Joseph	84	3
4		Susan	65	6
5		Michael	99	1
6		Javier	72	5
7		Garth	84	3
8		Mandy	87	2

Figure 8-23. *Ranking values in a range using RANK.EQ*

We need to return a unique rank for each score. This is so that we can use a lookup formula to generate a table with the names and scores ordered by their rank.

The COUNTIFS function will help us here. The following formula is shown in Figure 8-24:

```
=RANK.EQ(C3,$C$3:$C$8)+COUNTIFS($C$3:$C3,C3)-1
```

The COUNTIFS function is used to count the instances of a score up to the current row. Subtract 1 from this result and add it to the rank to make it a unique value.

D3		✕ ✓ fx	=RANK.EQ(C3,$C$3:$C$8) +COUNTIFS($C$3:$C3,C3)-1	
	A	B	C	D
1				
2		**Name**	**Score**	**Unique Rank**
3		Joseph	84	3
4		Susan	65	6
5		Michael	99	1
6		Javier	72	5
7		Garth	84	4
8		Mandy	87	2
9				

Figure 8-24. *Unique ranking calculated with COUNTIFS and RANK.EQ*

Let's break that down a little more.

The *criteria range* used in the COUNTIFS function has a fixed start but a relative end. So, for each row, the range expands:

$C$3:$C3

Joseph's score is the first occurrence of the score 84 in the range $C$3:$C3. So, COUNTIFS returns 1. A 1 is subtracted from this result and then added to the rank. This means that the rank does not change.

Garth's score is the second occurrence of the score 84 in the range $C$3:$C7. So, COUNTIFS returns 2. A 1 is subtracted, leaving 1. And this 1 is added to the rank to become a rank of 4.

The COUNTIFS function has helped us create a unique ranking which the rank functions of Excel could not do alone. Amazing!

To complete this task, we will now order them by their rankings. And for this, we will use the VLOOKUP function that was covered in Chapter 7.

Remember, the VLOOKUP function looks down the first column of a range and returns from a column to its right. Currently, the unique rankings are in the last column. So, we need to change this before we start writing a VLOOKUP.

There are a few different techniques to quickly move a range of cells in Excel. To move the unique rankings, we will use the "insert cut cells" technique:

1. Select range D2:D8 and cut the cells.

2. Right-click cell B2 and click **Insert Cut Cells** from the context menu (Figure 8-25).

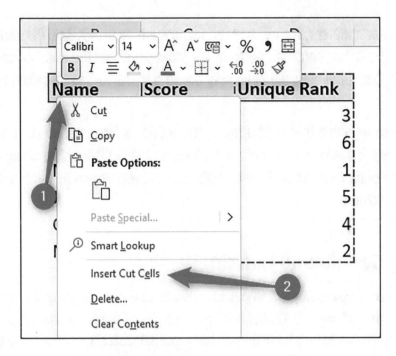

Figure 8-25. *Insert cut cells to quickly move a range of cells*

We can now create a rankings table and use the VLOOKUP function to return the names and scores in order by looking up their rank.

In Figure 8-26, rankings have been typed in column F and then VLOOKUP functions written into columns G and H to return the required information.

The following VLOOKUP function was used in cell G3:

=VLOOKUP(F3,$B$3:$D$8,2,0)

					fx =VLOOKUP(F3,$B$3:$D$8,2,0)		
B	C	D	E	F	G	H	

Unique Rank	Name	Score		Rank	Name	Score
3	Joseph	84		1	Michael	99
6	Susan	65		2	Mandy	87
1	Michael	99		3	Joseph	84
5	Javier	72		4	Garth	84
4	Garth	84		5	Javier	72
2	Mandy	87		6	Susan	65

Figure 8-26. *VLOOKUP function to return the scores in the order by rank*

395

Note   In later chapters, we will see functions such as INDEX-MATCH and XLOOKUP. These functions can perform the lookup without the need to have moved the column first. Until now, we have only covered VLOOKUP, so therefore took that approach.

It should also be noted that in Chapter 7, we did see a formula that used VLOOKUP with CHOOSE to overcome the built-in limitation of VLOOKUP only looking down the first column of its *table array*. That technique could have been applied instead of moving the column.

Creating Conditional Rankings

Let's take the rankings example a step further, and instead of using the RANK.EQ function, we can do it all with COUNTIFS. Not only that, but let's add another condition.

In Figure 8-27, we have a table named [tblRegionalScores] with names and scores that are divided into three different regions.

We want to rank the score values again in a largest first manner, but this time we need three groups of rankings. We want to rank the scores in each region separately.

	A	B	C	D
1	Region	Name	Score	Rank
2	East	Michelle	89	
3	East	Victoria	95	
4	East	Jason	61	
5	East	Darryl	89	
6	East	Heather	56	
7	South	Rachel	78	
8	South	David	59	
9	South	Kevin	66	
10	South	Hannah	91	
11	West	Carl	69	
12	West	Natalie	77	
13	West	Deborah	96	

Figure 8-27. *Table with scores from different regions*

In Figure 8-28, the following formula creates separate rankings for each region:

```
=COUNTIFS([Region],[@Region],
   [Score],">"&[@Score])+1
```

The COUNTIFS function tests the region and then returns how many scores are larger than the score in that row. 1 is then added to this result.

The 1 is added because if there are 0 scores larger than the current one, then that score is rank 1. If there is 1 score larger than the current one, then that score is rank 2, and so on.

So, the COUNTIFS function can create rankings on its own and can include any extra conditions that may be required.

However, we do have an issue with a duplicate rank again. In Figure 8-28, in the East, Michelle and Darryl both have a rank of 2.

	A	B	C	D	E
				D2	fx =COUNTIFS([Region],[@Region], [Score],">"&[@Score])+1
1	Region	Name	Score	Rank	
2	East	Michelle	89	2	
3	East	Victoria	95	1	
4	East	Jason	61	4	
5	East	Darryl	89	2	
6	East	Heather	56	5	
7	South	Rachel	78	2	
8	South	David	59	4	
9	South	Kevin	66	3	
10	South	Hannah	91	1	
11	West	Carl	69	3	
12	West	Natalie	77	2	
13	West	Deborah	96	1	
14					

Figure 8-28. Conditional ranking formula that creates rankings for each region

We can use the same technique as we did previously and add a COUNTIFS function to this result to generate a unique ranking.

In the following formula (Figure 8-29), the second COUNTIFS function is added to the first COUNTIFS instead of the 1:

```
=COUNTIFS([Region],[@Region],[Score],">"&[@Score])
   +COUNTIFS($C$2:$C2,[@Score])
```

This is similar to how we added COUNTIFS to the RANK.EQ function before. However, this time we do not need to subtract 1 like earlier, because we replaced the plus 1 from the first COUNTIFS.

You will also notice that a range has been used in the *criteria range* of the second COUNTIFS. This is to create that ever-expanding range. This is awkward to achieve using a table's structured reference, so we referenced the grid instead.

	A	B	C	D	E	F
D2	✓ : × ✓ *fx*	=COUNTIFS([Region],[@Region], [Score],">"&[@Score]) +COUNTIFS($C$2:$C2,[@Score])				
1	Region	Name	Score	Rank		
2	East	Michelle	89	2		
3	East	Victoria	95	1		
4	East	Jason	61	4		
5	East	Darryl	89	3		
6	East	Heather	56	5		
7	South	Rachel	78	2		
8	South	David	59	4		
9	South	Kevin	66	3		
10	South	Hannah	91	1		
11	West	Carl	69	3		
12	West	Natalie	77	2		
13	West	Deborah	96	1		

Figure 8-29. *Second COUNTIFS to make the ranking unique*

From here, we could create separate ranking tables for each region or whatever our end goal may be.

But the focus of this chapter is COUNTIFS, so with this result, we will move on.

Creating a Frequency Distribution

For the final COUNTIFS example, let's create a frequency distribution table. Excel has a function named FREQUENCY for this purpose, but it is limited when compared to COUNTIFS.

In Figure 8-30, there is a table of scores named [tblScores] and a frequency distribution range with bins defined. The bin ranges can be set up in different ways. In this spreadsheet, the bins are defined with the lowest value, a hyphen or dash, and then the upper bound value of that bin range.

Name	Score		Bin	Count
Joseph	97		50-64	
Susan	81		65-79	
Michael	69		80-89	
Javier	85		90-100	
Garth	95			
Mandy	92			
Hannah	66			
Ben	92			
Tim	76			
Francesca	62			

Figure 8-30. Table of scores and a bin range

We want to return a count of the scores in each bin. To do this, we will include the LEFT and RIGHT functions that were covered in Chapter 5 to extract the lowest and highest values in each bin range for testing.

In Figure 8-31, the following COUNTIFS function is used in range F4:F6 to create the frequency distribution for the first three bin ranges:

```
=COUNTIFS(tblScores[Score],">="&LEFT(E4,2),
    tblScores[Score],"<="&RIGHT(E4,2))
```

The LEFT and RIGHT functions are used to extract the first two and last two characters from the ranges in column E for testing.

The following formula is entered in cell F7. For the last bin, we only need to test the lowest bound of the bin range.

`=COUNTIFS(tblScores[Score],">="&LEFT(E7,2))`

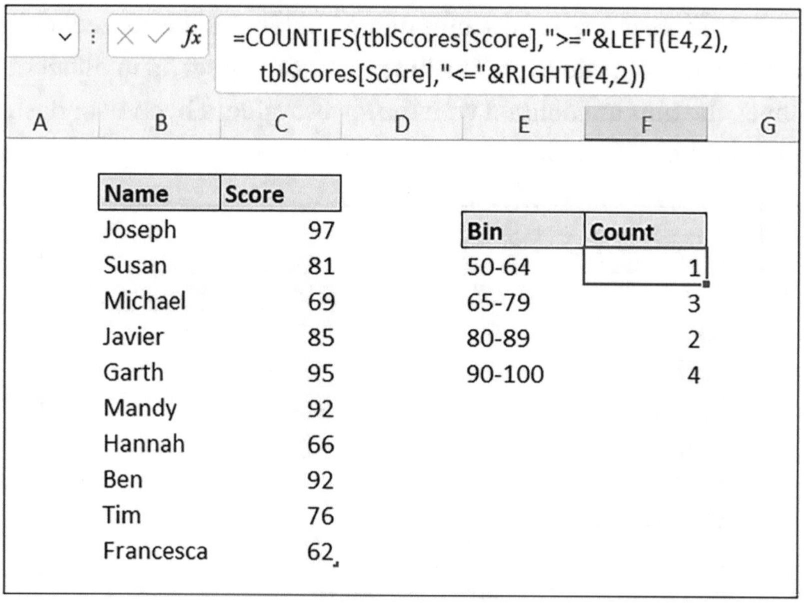

Figure 8-31. *Frequency distribution created with COUNTIFS*

This frequency distribution table could be the result, or it could be used as the source for a histogram for a graphical representation.

The AVERAGEIFS Function

Availability: All versions

File   averageifs.xlsx

The next function in our journey through the IFS family of functions is AVERAGEIFS. It returns the mean average for the values that meet the given criteria.

The following is the syntax of the AVERAGEIFS function:

```
=AVERAGEIFS(average_range, criteria_range1, criteria1, criteria_range2,
    criteria2,...)
```

The AVERAGEIFS function requires the range of values to perform the average calculation on and the up to 127 *criteria range* and *criteria* pairs.

Let's continue with the [tblSales] table that many of our examples in this chapter have used. A snapshot of the first few rows of the table is shown in Figure 8-32.

	A	B	C	D	E	F
1	ID	Date	Product Name	Store	Units So	Total
2	19775	11/01/2021	Coffee	North	39	59.06
3	19776	12/01/2021	Hot Chocolate	West	16	424.80
4	19777	24/01/2021	Wine	North	25	207.30
5	19778	25/01/2021	Water	West	35	436.53
6	19779	30/01/2021	Coffee	South	38	424.30
7	19780	01/02/2021	Tea	North	10	174.45
8	19781	03/02/2021	Tea	North	30	456.55
9	19782	08/02/2021	Hot Chocolate	West	20	424.50
10	19783	08/02/2021	Water	East	12	90.88
11	19784	24/02/2021	Wine	West	50	216.34
12	19785	13/03/2021	Tea	North	14	230.87

Figure 8-32. *The tblSales table showing product sales*

We want to return the average of the values in the [Total] column for a specified product and region.

In Figure 8-33, the following formula is entered in cell B6:

```
=AVERAGEIFS(tblSales[Total],
    tblSales[Store],B3,tblSales[Product Name],C3)
```

The AVERAGEIFS function is like the SUMIFS function earlier in the chapter, so there is no need to go into much detail on how this works.

One of the many great things about this group of functions is how similar they are. Once you are familiar with one, you know them all.

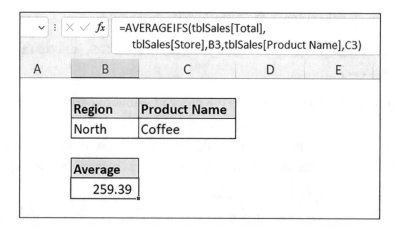

Figure 8-33. *AVERAGEIFS function to return the average sales value*

A common use of the AVERAGEIFS function is to use it to ignore zero values in an average range.

In Figure 8-34, we have a table named [tblRegionalScores], and there are a couple of zero values in the [Score] column.

When performing an average calculation, these zero values are included by the function, and this may not be the behavior that we want. The result of an AVERAGE function is shown in cell E3.

The following formula is entered in cell E6 and uses the AVERAGEIFS function that includes criteria to exclude any zero or negative values:

```
=AVERAGEIFS(tblRegionalScores[Score],tblRegionalScores[Score],">0")
```

| E6 | ⌄ | : | ✕ ✓ fx | =AVERAGEIFS(tblRegionalScores[Score], tblRegionalScores[Score],">0") |

	A	B	C	D	E	F
1	**Region**	**Name**	**Score**			
2	East	Michelle	89		**Average**	
3	East	Victoria	95		67.0	
4	East	Jason	61			
5	East	Darryl	89		**Average Exc 0**	
6	East	Heather	0		80.4	
7	South	Rachel	78			
8	South	David	59			
9	South	Kevin	0			
10	South	Hannah	91			
11	West	Carl	69			
12	West	Natalie	77			
13	West	Deborah	96			

Figure 8-34. *Table of scores that include zero values*

This is a cool use of the AVERAGEIFS function. Of course, with its ability to handle multiple criteria, we could return the average for a specified region in addition to excluding the zero values.

In Figure 8-35, the following formula is entered in cell E9 to return the average for the region entered in cell E8 and exclude zero values:

```
=AVERAGEIFS(tblRegionalScores[Score],
    tblRegionalScores[Score],">0",tblRegionalScores[Region],E8)
```

| E9 | | | | | =AVERAGEIFS(tblRegionalScores[Score], tblRegionalScores[Score],">0",tblRegionalScores[Region],E8) |

	A	B	C	D	E	F	G
1	Region	Name	Score				
2	East	Michelle	89		**Average**		
3	East	Victoria	95		67.0		
4	East	Jason	61				
5	East	Darryl	89		**Average Exc 0**		
6	East	Heather	0		80.4		
7	South	Rachel	78				
8	South	David	59		**East**		
9	South	Kevin	0		83.5		
10	South	Hannah	91				
11	West	Carl	69				
12	West	Natalie	77				
13	West	Deborah	96				

Figure 8-35. *Average score for a specified region and excluding zero values*

TRIMMEAN Function

Availability: All versions

File   trimmean.xlsx

The TRIMMEAN function returns the mean average for an array of values excluding a specified percentage of outlying values. It calculates the mean of the interior values of the array. The specified percentage of data is trimmed from the top and bottom ends of the array of values.

The anatomy of the TRIMMEAN function is

```
=TRIMMEAN(array, percent)
```

- **Array:** The values to trim and average. This can be provided as a range, table column, or an array.

- **Percent:** The percentage of values to exclude from the array. It can be entered into the function as a percentage or as a decimal value.

  This percentage is taken in equal portion from the top and bottom ends of the array. So, for example, if there were 10 values and the percent was 20%, then 20% of 10 equals 2. So, one value would be excluded from the bottom and one value excluded from the top end of the array.

Figure 8-36 shows a table named [tblSales] with a column of totals. The following AVERAGE function is entered into cell D3 to return the mean average of all values in the [Total] column:

=AVERAGE(tblSales[Total]

You may notice that there are two outliers in the [Total] column that are affecting the average result. These are the 27 in row 4 and the 11 in row 8.

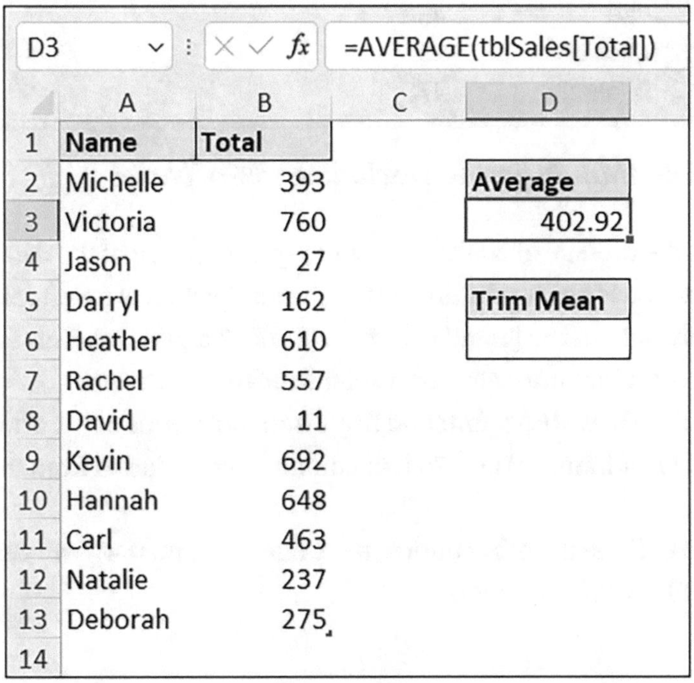

D3		✕ ✓ fx	=AVERAGE(tblSales[Total])	
	A	B	C	D
1	Name	Total		
2	Michelle	393		Average
3	Victoria	760		402.92
4	Jason	27		
5	Darryl	162		Trim Mean
6	Heather	610		
7	Rachel	557		
8	David	11		
9	Kevin	692		
10	Hannah	648		
11	Carl	463		
12	Natalie	237		
13	Deborah	275		
14				

Figure 8-36. *Average of all values in the [Total] column*

Let's trim this average with the TRIMMEAN function to exclude the outliers and return an average that is a better semblance of the data.

In Figure 8-37, the following TRIMMEAN function excludes 20% of the values in the [Total] column:

```
=TRIMMEAN(tblSales[Total],0.2)
```

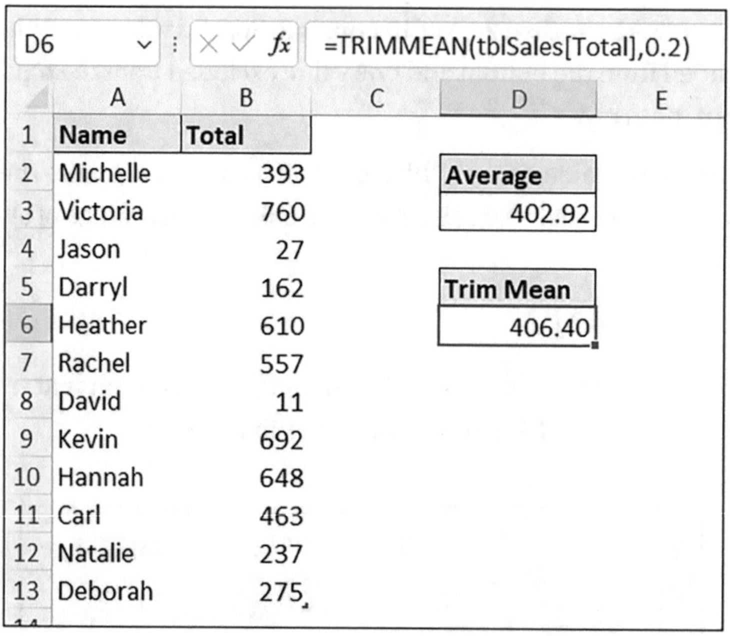

Figure 8-37. TRIMMEAN function excluding 20% of values

This returns the average of 406.40 – a better representation of the data. However, this TRIMMEAN function is only excluding one of the outlier values noted earlier.

There are 12 values in the [Total] column. 20% of 12 equals 2.4. This result is truncated to 2, so 2 values are excluded from the mean calculation.

Remember, the TRIMMEAN function trims from both ends of the array of values. So, the values of 11 (minimum) and 760 (maximum) are excluded from the mean calculation.

If we want to exclude the other outlier, the value of 27, then we will enter a larger percent in the TRIMMEAN function.

In Figure 8-38, the following TRIMMEAN function excludes 35% of the values in the [Total] column returning the result of 418.13, a better average of the [Total] column values:

```
=TRIMMEAN(tblSales[Total],0.35)
```

D6		✕ ✓ fx	=TRIMMEAN(tblSales[Total],0.35)		
	A	B	C	D	E
1	Name	Total			
2	Michelle	393		Average	
3	Victoria	760		402.92	
4	Jason	27			
5	Darryl	162		Trim Mean	
6	Heather	610		418.13	
7	Rachel	557			
8	David	11			
9	Kevin	692			
10	Hannah	648			
11	Carl	463			
12	Natalie	237			
13	Deborah	275			
14					

Figure 8-38. *TRIMMEAN function excluding 35% of the values*

This formula excluded both small outlier values and the two largest values in the column too.

We know this because 35% of 12 equals 4.2. This result is truncated to 4. So, TRIMMEAN trims the bottom 2 and top 2 values from the array. In this example, they are values 11, 27, 692, and 760.

Finally, a cell could be used as the input for the percent as an alternative to typing it directly into the formula. This would make it more dynamic and easily visible to those using the spreadsheet what percentage was used.

In Figure 8-39, the following formula references cell D6 for the percentage input:

```
=TRIMMEAN(tblSales[Total],D6)
```

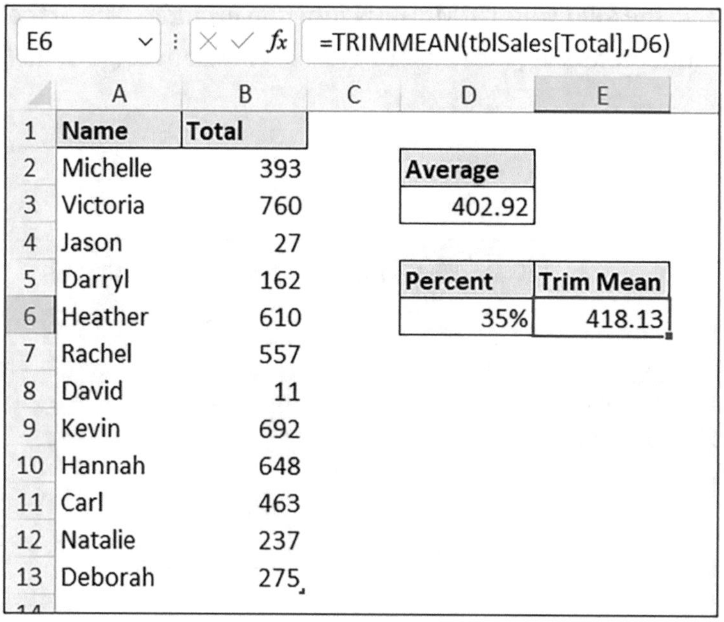

| E6 | ⌄ | ⋮ | ✕ ✓ fx | =TRIMMEAN(tblSales[Total],D6) |

	A	B	C	D	E
1	Name	Total			
2	Michelle	393		**Average**	
3	Victoria	760		402.92	
4	Jason	27			
5	Darryl	162		**Percent**	**Trim Mean**
6	Heather	610		35%	418.13
7	Rachel	557			
8	David	11			
9	Kevin	692			
10	Hannah	648			
11	Carl	463			
12	Natalie	237			
13	Deborah	275			

Figure 8-39. *Using a cell as input for the percentage to trim*

Note   This is a small set of data (only 12 values) used for demonstration and to explain how TRIMMEAN works. In a larger array of values, 35% is a lot of values to exclude.

Conditional MEDIAN and MODE Functions

Availability: All versions

File   conditional-mode-and-median.xlsx

The average calculations so far have all been focusing on the mean average. Excel also contains functions to calculate the median and mode averages – fittingly named MEDIAN and MODE.

However, Excel does not have a conditional version of these functions like we have in AVERAGEIFS. So, we will create a formula by combining the MEDIAN or MODE function with the IF function.

Calculating the Median

Let's start with the median average. Figure 8-40 shows a table named [tblScores]. It contains a [Score] column with a couple of outliers (rows 6 and 14).

	A	B	C	D
1	**Region**	**Name**	**Score**	
2	North	Michelle	89	
3	South	Victoria	95	
4	North	Jason	61	
5	North	Darryl	89	
6	North	Heather	14	
7	South	Rachel	78	
8	South	David	84	
9	North	Kevin	66	
10	South	Hannah	91	
11	South	Carl	69	
12	South	Natalie	77	
13	North	Deborah	96	
14	South	Ben	19	
15	South	Francesca	88	
16	North	Stephen	71	
17				

Figure 8-40. *Table of scores for median calculation*

So, calculating the median may be a better average than the mean in this scenario.

The median is the middle number in a set of numbers. If there is an even set of numbers, MEDIAN will calculate the average of the middle two numbers.

The MEDIAN function requires only the range of numbers from which to return the median. It can handle multiple number ranges:

```
=MEDIAN(number1, [number2], ...)
```

In Figure 8-41, the following MEDIAN function is entered in cell E4 and returns 78:

```
=MEDIAN(tblScores[Score])
```

But we want to create a conditional median formula. We want to know the median value for a specific region.

The following formula is entered in cell F7 in Figure 8-41. It returns the median value for the "South" region. This is specified in cell E7.

```
=MEDIAN(IF(tblScores[Region]=E7,tblScores[Score]))
```

In this formula, the IF function tests the values in the [Region] column against the value in cell E7 and returns an array of all the corresponding values in the [Score] column where the test evaluated to True. This array was used by the MEDIAN function.

If you are using a version of Excel outside of Excel for Microsoft 365 or Excel 2021, you will need to press **Ctrl + Shift + Enter** to run the formula. In modern versions of Excel, you can just press **Enter** (dynamic array formulas are discussed in detail in Chapter 10).

F7	⌄ ┊ ✕ ✓ *fx*	=MEDIAN(IF(tblScores[Region]=E7,tblScores[Score]))						
	A	B	C	D	E	F	G	
1	**Region**	**Name**	Score					
2	North	Michelle	89					
3	South	Victoria	95		**Median**			
4	North	Jason	61		78			
5	North	Darryl	89					
6	North	Heather	14		**Region**	**Median**		
7	South	Rachel	78		South	81		
8	South	David	84					
9	North	Kevin	66					

Figure 8-41. *Combined with IF for a conditional MEDIAN formula*

Note   Other functions such as IFS, SWITCH, or CHOOSE could be used with the MEDIAN and MODE functions, instead of IF, to create the conditional element, especially if you have a more complex multiple condition scenario.

Calculating the Mode

The mode is the most common number in a set of numbers. In Excel, there are three mode functions – MODE, MODE.SNGL, and MODE.MULT.

The most used is the MODE function, but this was succeeded back in Excel 2007 by the MODE.SNGL function. MODE is only kept around for compatibility reasons; however, it is still the one most people use to this day.

All three mode functions require only the ranges of numbers from which to return the most frequently occurring number(s). The following syntax is for the MODE.SNGL function, but it applies to all three functions:

```
=MODE.SNGL(number1, [number2], ...)
```

Note   The MODE functions only work with numeric values. In Chapter 11, when we discuss the INDEX and MATCH functions in Excel, we will see a technique to return the most frequent and least frequent text value.

Let's focus on the two modern mode functions – MODE.SNGL and MODE.MULT. As you may have suspected, the SNGL stands for single and MULT stands for multiple.

In Figure 8-42, the MODE.SNGL function is used to return the single most common number in the [Attendance] column of the [tblAttendances] table. The image is only a snapshot of the table. The table has 30 rows.

```
=MODE.SNGL(tblAttendances[Attendance])
```

There are three numbers in the [Attendance] column that are equal in being the most frequently occurring. These are 6, 3, and 4. The MODE.SNGL function returns a single value. The 6 is returned as it is the first of the three numbers to occur in the column.

E4		✕ ✓ *fx*	=MODE.SNGL(tblAttendances[Attendance])		
	A	B	C	D	E
1	Date	Region	Attendance		
2	02/09/2021	South	2		
3	03/09/2021	South	6		MODE.SNGL
4	08/09/2021	North	6		6
5	11/09/2021	North	3		
6	13/09/2021	South	4		

Figure 8-42. *MODE.SNGL function used to return the most common number*

In Figure 8-43, the MODE.MULT function returns all three numbers in the order that they appear in the [Attendance] column.

```
=MODE.MULT(tblAttendances[Attendance])
```

E7		⋮	× ✓ ƒx	=MODE.MULT(tblAttendances[Attendance])			
	A		B	C	D	E	F
1	Date		Region	Attendance			
2	02/09/2021	South		2			
3	03/09/2021	South		6		MODE.SNGL	
4	08/09/2021	North		6		6	
5	11/09/2021	North		3			
6	13/09/2021	South		4		MODE.MULT	
7	15/09/2021	North		6		6	
8	16/09/2021	South		8		3	
9	21/09/2021	South		5		4	
10	01/10/2021	North		4			

Figure 8-43. *MODE.MULT returning the three most common numbers*

If you are using a version of Excel that can natively handle arrays (Excel for Microsoft 365, Excel 2021, or Excel for the Web), then the three results are returned in a spilled array (covered in Chapter 10).

If you are using an older version of Excel, then you would need to select the three cells to store each of the returned numbers before writing the MODE.MULT function. Of course, this would mean that you would have to know that three answers would be returned. This makes the MODE.MULT function almost pointless to be used in this manner in older Excel versions.

Regardless of the version we are using, we may not want to return all three values. The MIN or MAX functions could be wrapped around MODE.MULT to return only the smallest or largest of the returned values.

This is a different behavior to MODE.SNGL, as that function returned the first of the three numbers to appear in the column.

In Figure 8-44, the following formula uses the MIN function to return the smallest of the most frequent numbers:

```
=MIN(MODE.MULT(tblAttendances[Attendance]))
```

| E7 | | ⌄ | : | ✕ ✓ fx | =MIN(MODE.MULT(tblAttendances[Attendance])) | | |

	A	B	C	D	E	F
1	Date	Region	Attendance			
2	02/09/2021	South	2			
3	03/09/2021	South	6		MODE.SNGL	
4	08/09/2021	North	6			6
5	11/09/2021	North	3			
6	13/09/2021	South	4		MODE.MULT	
7	15/09/2021	North	6			3
8	16/09/2021	South	8			
9	21/09/2021	South	5			

Figure 8-44. *Wrapping the MIN function around MODE.MULT*

Now, let's look at applying a condition to a mode function by including the brilliant IF function.

In Figure 8-45, the following formula shows the IF function working with MODE. SNGL to return the most common number for the region of the "North" in a table named [tblAttendances2]:

```
=MODE.SNGL(IF(tblAttendances2[Region]="North",tblAttendances2[Attendance]))
```

This combination works in the same way as was discussed with the MEDIAN function.

E4		⌄	:	✕ ✓ fx	=MODE.SNGL(
					IF(tblAttendances2[Region]="North",
					tblAttendances2[Attendance]))

	A	B	C	D	E
1	Date	Region	Attendance		
2	02/09/2021	South	2		
3	03/09/2021	South	6		MODE IF
4	08/09/2021	North	6		6
5	11/09/2021	North	3		
6	13/09/2021	South	4		

Figure 8-45. *MODE.SNGL function with IF for a conditional mode formula*

MAXIFS and MINIFS Functions

Availability: Excel 2019, Excel 2021, Excel for Microsoft 365, Excel for the Web, Excel 2019 for Mac, Excel 2021 for Mac, Excel for Microsoft 365 for Mac

---

File   maxifs-and-minifs.xlsx

Completing the IFS family of functions are the MAXIFS and MINIFS functions. They will return the largest and smallest numeric values in a list that meet one or more criteria.

Their syntax and behavior are the same as the SUMIFS and AVERAGEIFS functions discussed before. The following is the syntax of the MAXIFS function:

```
=MAXIFS(max_range, criteria_range1, criteria1, [criteria_range2,
    [criteria2], ...)
```

They require the range of values to perform the maximum or minimum calculation on and the up to 127 *criteria range* and *criteria* pairs.

For the first example of these functions, we will use the [tblScores] table shown in Figure 8-46. It contains score values for two different regions – North and South.

	A	B	C
1	**Region**	**Name**	**Score**
2	North	Michelle	89
3	South	Victoria	95
4	North	Jason	61
5	North	Darryl	89
6	North	Heather	67
7	South	Rachel	78
8	South	David	84
9	North	Kevin	66
10	South	Hannah	91
11	South	Carl	69
12	South	Natalie	77
13	North	Deborah	96
14	South	Ben	83
15	South	Francesca	88
16	North	Stephen	71

Figure 8-46. *Table of scores from two different regions*

In Figure 8-47, the following MAXIFS function is entered in cell E6. It returns the maximum value in the [Score] column for the region entered in cell E3:

=MAXIFS(tblScores[Score],tblScores[Region],E3)

The following MINIFS function is used in cell F7:

=MINIFS(tblScores[Score],tblScores[Region],E3)

E6		⌄	⋮ × ✓ fx	=MAXIFS(tblScores[Score],tblScores[Region],E3)			

	A	B	C	D	E	F	G
1	**Region**	**Name**	Score				
2	North	Michelle	89		**Region**		
3	South	Victoria	95		North		
4	North	Jason	61				
5	North	Darryl	89		**Max**	**Min**	
6	North	Heather	67		96	61	
7	South	Rachel	78				
8	South	David	84				
9	North	Kevin	66				

Figure 8-47. *MAXIFS and MINIFS functions returning results for the North*

The MAXIFS and MINIFS functions can also be useful for analysis of dates. For example, the MAXIFS function will return the latest date in a range that meets specific criteria.

In Figure 8-48, we have a table named [tblWorkshops] that lists workshops and the date that they were held. We want to return the last date that each workshop was run. The MAXIFS function is perfect for this task.

The following formula was used in cell E3 and filled down range E4:E6. The formula returns the latest date for each workshop in range D3:D6:

```
=MAXIFS(tblWorkshops[Date],tblWorkshops[Workshop],D3)
```

Of course, additional conditions could be added to these functions, if needed. And all the techniques demonstrated with SUMIFS at the beginning of this chapter, such as using OR logic and wildcard characters, also apply to MAXIFS and MINIFS.

| E3 | | ⌄ | ⋮ | ✕ ✓ | *fx* | =MAXIFS(tblWorkshops[Date],tblWorkshops[Workshop],D3) |

	A	B	C	D	E	F
1	**Workshop**	**Date**				
2	Workshop C	12/06/2021		**Workshop**	**Date**	
3	Workshop D	21/06/2021		Workshop A	27/11/2021	
4	Workshop D	23/06/2021		Workshop B	26/09/2021	
5	Workshop B	09/07/2021		Workshop C	01/11/2021	
6	Workshop B	11/07/2021		Workshop D	03/10/2021	
7	Workshop D	16/07/2021				
13	Workshop B	19/09/2021				
14	Workshop B	22/09/2021				
15	Workshop B	26/09/2021				
16	Workshop D	03/10/2021				
17	Workshop C	21/10/2021				
18	Workshop C	22/10/2021				
19	Workshop C	01/11/2021				
20	Workshop A	27/11/2021				
21						

Figure 8-48. *MAXIFS function returning the latest date for each workshop*

Using the Functions with Other Excel Features

File   ifs-other-features.xlsx

As always, we will conclude the chapter with some examples of how some of the functions in this chapter can be used with other Excel features. Let's see examples with COUNTIFS and a use of the MEDIAN function.

Identifying Duplicates with Conditional Formatting

Working with duplicates is a common task for Excel users. So, it's a good thing that Excel has many methods for tackling duplicates. These range from the Remove Duplicates and Advanced Filter features to using Power Query.

Instead of removing the duplicates though, we want to format them to make them easy to see when conducting further tasks.

Excel already has a built-in Conditional Formatting rule to highlight duplicate or unique values in a range. However, it is not as flexible as a custom rule that we can create ourselves with the COUNTIFS function.

Figure 8-49 shows a table named [tblAppointments] that contains some duplicate names. We want to identify the names that occur more than once in the table by formatting both cells of that row in a different color.

Date	Name
07/03/2021	Martin
27/03/2021	Victoria
01/05/2021	Katherine
16/05/2021	Deborah
25/05/2021	Martin
07/06/2021	Jason
11/07/2021	Beth
07/08/2021	Carly
09/08/2021	Deborah
15/08/2021	Lyndsey
01/09/2021	Rachel
05/09/2021	Jason
10/09/2021	Martin
02/10/2021	Heather

Figure 8-49. *Table of appointments that contains duplicate entries*

1. Select the cells in the data of the table, range B3:C16.

2. Click **Home ➤ Conditional Formatting ➤ New Rule ➤ Use a formula to determine which cells to format**.

3. Enter the following COUNTIFS formula into the *Format values where this formula is true* field (Figure 8-50):

   =COUNTIFS($C$3:$C$16,$C3)>1

4. Click **Format** and choose the desired formatting to apply. Click **OK**.

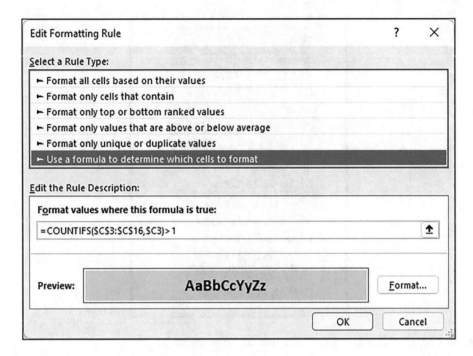

Figure 8-50. *Conditional Formatting rule to format duplicate entries*

The formula counts the occurrences of each name in the range C3:C16 and returns True if the name occurs more than once. Conditional Formatting then applies the chosen format.

Note   Range references are used in the COUNTIFS formula because Conditional Formatting does not accept a table's structured references directly within a rule. However, if more names are added to the table, the COUNTIFS formula will automatically expand with the table.

Figure 8-51 shows the finished article with both columns of the duplicated names formatted.

Figure 8-51. *Duplicate entries in a table formatted*

Now, by writing our own formulas, we have greater control than the standard built-in rules that come with Excel. So, let's say that we want to format the names that occur more than twice in the table. This is a more niche scenario of duplicate testing that goes beyond the built-in rules that Excel provides. This rule will be in addition to the previous rule.

Follow the same steps as before to create a new Conditional Formatting rule, use the following formula, and specify a different color for the format:

```
=COUNTIFS($C$3:$C$16,$C3)>2
```

Figure 8-52 shows the results with both Conditional Formatting rules applied to the table. There is one name (Martin) that occurs more than twice.

Date	Name
07/03/2021 Martin	
27/03/2021 Victoria	
01/05/2021 Katherine	
16/05/2021 Deborah	
25/05/2021 Martin	
07/06/2021 Jason	
11/07/2021 Beth	
07/08/2021 Carly	
09/08/2021 Deborah	
15/08/2021 Lyndsey	
01/09/2021 Rachel	
05/09/2021 Jason	
10/09/2021 Martin	
02/10/2021 Heather	

Figure 8-52. *Additional rule to identify names occurring more than twice*

Incidentally, if you only wanted to format the second or third occurrence of the name, and not every instance of the name, edit the second half of the *criteria range* to have a relative row reference and begin from the first cell of the range. This creates a range that expands each row at a time.

The following formula shows an example of this. It uses the test for names that occur more than twice. It will only format the third instance of a name and onward.

```
=COUNTIFS($C$3:$C3,$C3)>2
```

Identifying Unmatched Values Between Two Lists

Earlier in the chapter, we saw the COUNTIFS function being used to compare two lists and flag the names that appeared in the first list but were missing from the second list.

Figure 8-53 shows the two tables that we used for this example. Let's revisit this task, but this time apply a Conditional Formatting rule to highlight the names in the first list that do not appear in the second list.

Date	Name		Date	Name
07/03/2021	Martin		05/04/2021	Martin
27/03/2021	Victoria		12/06/2021	Victoria
01/05/2021	Katherine		26/06/2021	Deborah
16/05/2021	Deborah		26/07/2021	David
25/05/2021	David		30/07/2021	Jason
07/06/2021	Jason		14/08/2021	Carly
11/07/2021	Beth		19/08/2021	Lyndsey
07/08/2021	Carly		16/08/2021	Rachel
09/08/2021	Joe		20/09/2021	Claire
15/08/2021	Lyndsey		07/10/2021	Heather
01/09/2021	Rachel			
05/09/2021	Claire			
10/09/2021	Jeff			
02/10/2021	Heather			

Figure 8-53. *Two lists to compare and highlight missing names*

1. Select the cells in the data of the first table, range B3:C16.

2. Click **Home ➤ Conditional Formatting ➤ New Rule ➤ Use a formula to determine which cells to format**.

3. Enter the following COUNTIFS formula into the *Format values where this formula is true* field (Figure 8-54):

   `=NOT(COUNTIFS($F$3:$F$12,$C3))`

This formula counts the number of times the names in the first table occur in the second table. If they do not occur in the second table, then 0 is returned. 0 evaluates to False in the result in a logical expression, and all values except 0 evaluate to True. The NOT function then reverses this result. So, the names that are not found return True.

4. Click **Format** and choose the desired formatting to apply.

5. Click **OK**.

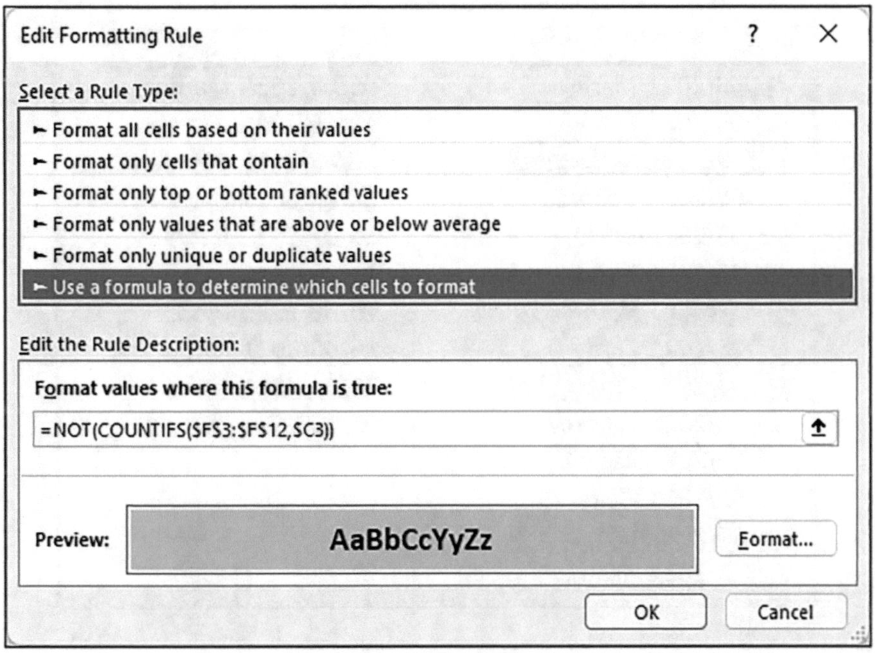

Figure 8-54. COUNTIFS formula with NOT for unmatched values

Of course, there are a few alternatives to this formula that would also work. For example, instead of the NOT function, the following formula tests if the result is less than 1:

```
=COUNTIFS($F$3:$F$12,$C3)<1
```

Figure 8-55 shows the names that are missing from the second list highlighted by the Conditional Formatting rule.

Date	Name		Date	Name
07/03/2021	Martin		05/04/2021	Martin
27/03/2021	Victoria		12/06/2021	Victoria
01/05/2021	**Katherine**		26/06/2021	Deborah
16/05/2021	Deborah		26/07/2021	David
25/05/2021	David		30/07/2021	Jason
07/06/2021	Jason		14/08/2021	Carly
11/07/2021	**Beth**		19/08/2021	Lyndsey
07/08/2021	Carly		16/08/2021	Rachel
09/08/2021	**Joe**		20/09/2021	Claire
15/08/2021	Lyndsey		07/10/2021	Heather
01/09/2021	Rachel			
05/09/2021	Claire			
10/09/2021	**Jeff**			
02/10/2021	Heather			

Figure 8-55. *Missing names identified in the first list*

Highlight Values Larger Than the Median

The Conditional Formatting feature in Excel has built-in rules to highlight values that are above or below the average in the selected range (Figure 8-56).

These rules use the favored mean average just like the AVERAGE function of Excel. However, you may require the use of a different average calculation such as MEDIAN, TRIMMEAN, or MODE.

In this example, we will create a rule to highlight the values that are larger than the median of a specified range.

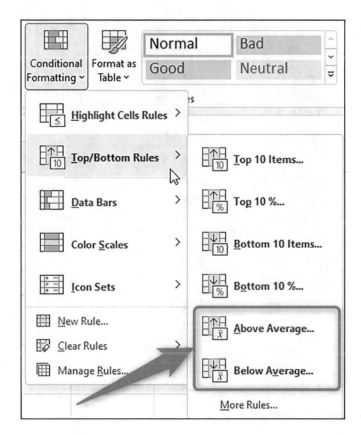

Figure 8-56. *The standard above and below average Conditional Formatting rules*

For this example, we will use the same table of scores that we used earlier in the chapter when we discussed the MEDIAN and conditional median formulas (Figure 8-57).

	A	B	C
1	**Region**	**Name**	**Score**
2	North	Michelle	89
3	South	Victoria	95
4	North	Jason	61
5	North	Darryl	89
6	North	Heather	14
7	South	Rachel	78
8	South	David	84
9	North	Kevin	66
10	South	Hannah	91
11	South	Carl	69
12	South	Natalie	77
13	North	Deborah	96
14	South	Ben	19
15	South	Francesca	88
16	North	Stephen	71

Figure 8-57. *Table of scores*

1. Select the range of scores in the table, range C2:C16.

2. Click **Home ➤ Conditional Formatting ➤ Highlight Cells Rules ➤ Greater Than**.

3. Enter the following formula into the *Format cells that are GREATER THAN* box provided (Figure 8-58):

   =MEDIAN($C$2:$C$16)

4. Specify the format you want to apply from the drop-down list.

5. Click **OK**.

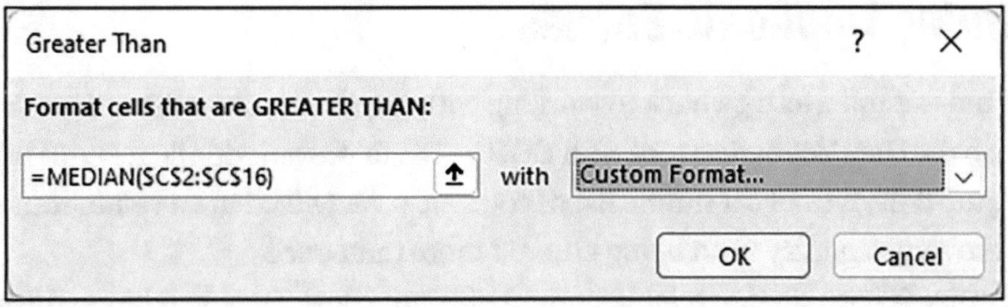

Figure 8-58. *Format cells greater than the median value*

All values in the [Scores] column that are greater than the median value are highlighted (Figure 8-59).

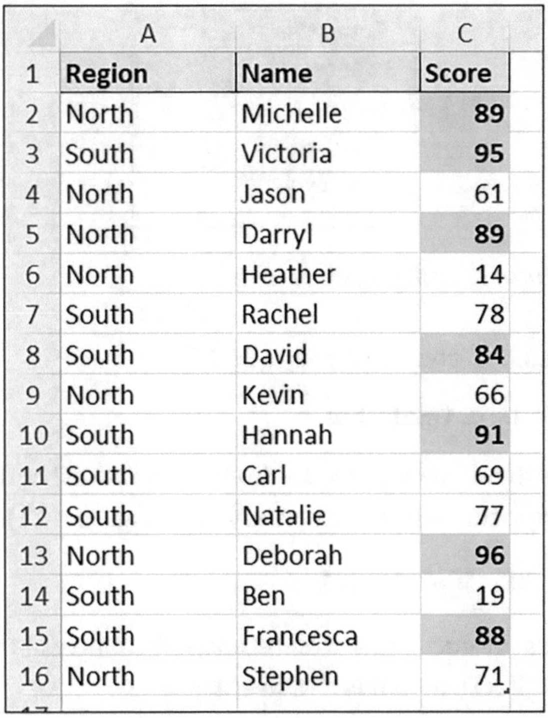

	A	B	C
1	**Region**	**Name**	**Score**
2	North	Michelle	**89**
3	South	Victoria	**95**
4	North	Jason	61
5	North	Darryl	**89**
6	North	Heather	14
7	South	Rachel	78
8	South	David	**84**
9	North	Kevin	66
10	South	Hannah	**91**
11	South	Carl	69
12	South	Natalie	77
13	North	Deborah	**96**
14	South	Ben	19
15	South	Francesca	**88**
16	North	Stephen	71

Figure 8-59. *All scores greater than the median are highlighted*

Preventing Duplicate Entries

For the final example, let's go back to working with duplicate values. This time though, we will use the Data Validation tool with COUNTIFS to prevent duplicate entries in a list.

In Figure 8-60, we have a simple list of countries. We will create a validation rule to prevent the same country from being entered more than once.

This range is formatted as a table named [tblCountries]. Data Validation does not allow the use of a table's structured references within the validation rules directly. So, we will use range references in our formula, but the rule will still update and automatically expand with the table.

Figure 8-60. *Table with country names*

1. Select the range of countries, range B3:B6.

2. Click **Data ➤ Data Validation**.

3. On the *Settings* tab, select **Custom** from the *Allow* list and enter the following formula into the *Formula* box (Figure 8-61):

    `=COUNTIFS($B$3:$B$6,$B3)<1`

The formula counts the occurrences of the entered country in the table and tests if the result is less than 1. If it is, then it is a valid entry.

Data Validation	?	×

Settings   Input Message   Error Alert

Validation criteria

Allow:

Custom ∨	☑ Ignore blank

Data:

between ∨

Formula:

=COUNTIFS($B$3:$B$6,$B3)<1	⬆

☐ Apply these changes to all other cells with the same settings

Clear All		OK	Cancel

Figure 8-61. *COUNTIFS formula in a Data Validation rule*

4. Click the **Error Alert** tab and enter a meaningful error for an invalid entry.

5. Click **OK**.

In Figure 8-62, the custom error alert is shown when a duplicate country is added to the table.

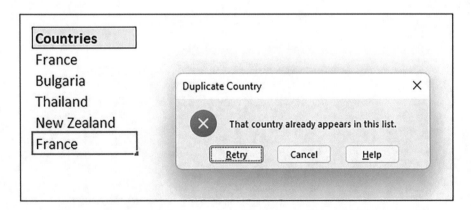

Figure 8-62. *Duplicate country detected and error alert shown*

Summary

In this chapter, we learned functions that perform aggregations dependent upon conditions that are met. These included SUMIFS, COUNTIFS, and combining functions such as MEDIAN with IF.

We learned some cool tricks to apply with these functions, for example, using OR logic with SUMIFS and creating conditional rankings with COUNTIFS.

In the next chapter, we will look at two functions that take it to the next level in aggregating data – SUMPRODUCT and AGGREGATE. These functions are incredible, and each one has a special set of abilities that makes it so useful. Let's dig in.

CHAPTER 9

Next-Level Aggregation Functions

In the previous chapter, we saw functions such as SUMIFS and COUNTIFS performing aggregations dependent upon criteria. They are incredible functions, but as with everything in life, they have their limitations. You may need to perform aggregations outside of the scope of those functions' capabilities.

This chapter covers two next-level aggregation functions – SUMPRODUCT and AGGREGATE. These functions are amazing, and each one has specific abilities that make them extremely useful.

We will begin with the SUMPRODUCT function. This function has achieved infamy with many advanced Excel users who label it as their favorite function. It's ability to handle arrays is possibly its greatest strength, and this makes it very valuable to users of Excel versions prior to Excel 365.

We then move on to the AGGREGATE function. This function is a powerful toolset of 19 different aggregations including sum, large, median, and mode. But it does not stop there. It has additional abilities such as to ignore errors and hidden values in a range when aggregating.

SUMPRODUCT Function

Availability: All versions

File	sumproduct.xlsx

The SUMPRODUCT function returns the sum of the products from one or more arrays. Its syntax is straightforward, as it is simply a list of the arrays you want it to use.

`=SUMPRODUCT(array1, [array2], [array3], ...)`

Each array can be a range of values or an array returned by a function or a logical expression. Each array must be of the same height or width.

The SUMPRODUCT function multiplies the values of the corresponding arrays and then sums the results.

Let's start with a simple example of SUMPRODUCT being used in its conventional way. And then explore more powerful examples including handling multiple conditions and working with arrays.

Classic SUMPRODUCT

The conventional use of the SUMPRODUCT function can remove the need for performing intermediary row calculations, therefore reducing calculation time and improving spreadsheet performance.

In Figure 9-1, there is some transactional data, and formulas have been entered in column D to multiply the price by the number sold. These row totals are then summed in cell D8 with a simple SUM function.

`=SUM(D2:D6)`

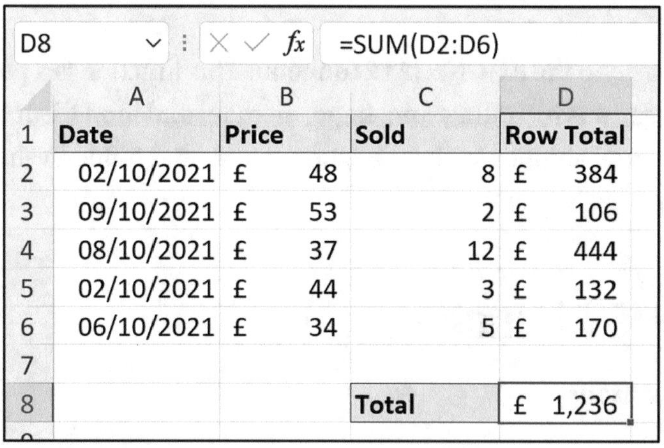

D8		✕ ✓ ƒx	=SUM(D2:D6)	
	A	B	C	D
1	Date	Price	Sold	Row Total
2	02/10/2021	£ 48	8	£ 384
3	09/10/2021	£ 53	2	£ 106
4	08/10/2021	£ 37	12	£ 444
5	02/10/2021	£ 44	3	£ 132
6	06/10/2021	£ 34	5	£ 170
7				
8			Total	£ 1,236

Figure 9-1. *Summing the row totals*

This is fine, and the row totals may be useful. However, if there were thousands of rows in this dataset, this may be an unnecessary volume of calculations and strain on the spreadsheet.

The total could be calculated with one SUMPRODUCT formula. In Figure 9-2, the following formula is used:

=SUMPRODUCT(B2:B6,C2:C6)

SUMPRODUCT multiplies the values in the corresponding arrays of B2:B6 and C2:C6, for example, 48*8, 53*2, 37*12. These intermediary totals are then summed to produce the result 1236.

C8		✕ ✓ ƒx	=SUMPRODUCT(B2:B6,C2:C6)	
	A	B	C	D
1	Date	Price	Sold	
2	02/10/2021	£ 48	8	
3	09/10/2021	£ 53	2	
4	08/10/2021	£ 37	12	
5	02/10/2021	£ 44	3	
6	06/10/2021	£ 34	5	
7				
8		Total	£ 1,236	
9				

Figure 9-2. *One formula solution with SUMPRODUCT*

Only two arrays were used in this example, and SUMPRODUCT can handle up to 255 arrays. Let's move on and see further examples of the extreme power and versatility of this function.

Sum Values That Meet Multiple Criteria

The SUMPRODUCT function is fantastic for summing and counting values that meet multiple criteria. It can handle both AND and OR logic, so the criteria can be complex.

It is much more efficient at handling different logical tests than the IFS family of functions (SUMIFS, COUNTIFS, etc.). We saw a technique to use OR logic with the SUMIFS function in the previous chapter, as natively it cannot apply OR logic.

Let's start by using the SUMPRODUCT function to sum values that meet a single condition. We will then increase the complexity of the criteria by adding more conditions and explain how it all works.

For these examples, we will use the data in the table named [tblSales] on the [Data] worksheet. The first few rows of this table are shown in Figure 9-3.

	A	B	C	D	E	F
1	ID	Date	Product Name	Store	Units Sold	Total
2	19775	11/01/2021	Coffee	North	39	59.06
3	19776	12/01/2021	Hot Chocolate	West	16	424.80
4	19777	24/01/2021	Wine	North	25	207.30
5	19778	25/01/2021	Water	West	35	436.53
6	19779	30/01/2021	Coffee	South	38	424.30
7	19780	01/02/2021	Tea	North	10	174.45
8	19781	03/02/2021	Tea	North	30	456.55
9	19782	08/02/2021	Hot Chocolate	West	20	424.50

Figure 9-3. *Sales table to be used for SUMPRODUCT examples*

In Figure 9-4, the following formula sums the [Total] values for all sales of the product entered in cell B3:

```
=SUMPRODUCT((tblSales[Product Name]=B3)*tblSales[Total])
```

Figure 9-4. *SUMPRODUCT function summing values that meet one condition*

This formula is quite different to others that we have seen so far in this book. Two things that stand out are that the condition is enclosed within its own set of brackets and that the results of that condition are multiplied by the values in the [Total] column.

Let's break down how this all works.

Looking at just the first five rows in Figure 9-3, the logical tests return the following array of values. The first and fifth rows contain the [Product Name] of "Coffee." So TRUE is returned, while the other rows return FALSE.

```
{TRUE; FALSE; FALSE; FALSE; TRUE}
```

434

Note   A semicolon (;) is used for a break in row, while a comma (,) is used for a break in column.

This array of values is multiplied by the corresponding value from the [Total] column. On performing a mathematical calculation, the TRUE and FALSE values are converted to 1s and 0s. Then the following calculations are performed:

```
{1; 0; 0; 0; 1}
*
{59.06; 424.80; 207.30; 436.53; 424.30}
```

These calculations result in the following array. And this array of values is summed by SUMPRODUCT.

```
{59.06; 0; 0; 0; 424.30}
```

Now that we understand how this is working, let's add a second condition to our SUMPRODUCT formula.

In Figure 9-5, the following formula sums the [Total] values for all sales of the product entered in cell B3 and the store entered in cell C3:

```
=SUMPRODUCT(
(tblSales[Product Name]=B3)*(tblSales[Store]=C3),
tblSales[Total]
)
```

In this formula, each condition is enclosed within its own brackets. Each condition will return an array of TRUE and FALSE values dependent on the result of that logical test. The asterisk (*) is used to multiply the corresponding values of the two arrays. This applies AND logic between the two conditions.

Looking at the first five rows of the sales table, the following two arrays represent the results of the two conditions:

```
{TRUE; FALSE; FALSE; FALSE; TRUE}
*
{TRUE; FALSE; TRUE; FALSE; FALSE}
```

After the values of the two arrays are multiplied together, the following array is returned:

{1; 0; 0; 0; 0}

The asterisk, or multiply symbol, is used for AND logic because you only get a non-zero value if all logical tests return TRUE. For example, 1*1=1 but 1*0=0 and 0*1=0.

Note   All numbers except zero evaluate to TRUE including both negative and positive values, while zero evaluates to FALSE.

The resulting array from the conditions is then multiplied by the corresponding values in the [Total] column. And the resulting values from that are then summed by SUMPRODUCT.

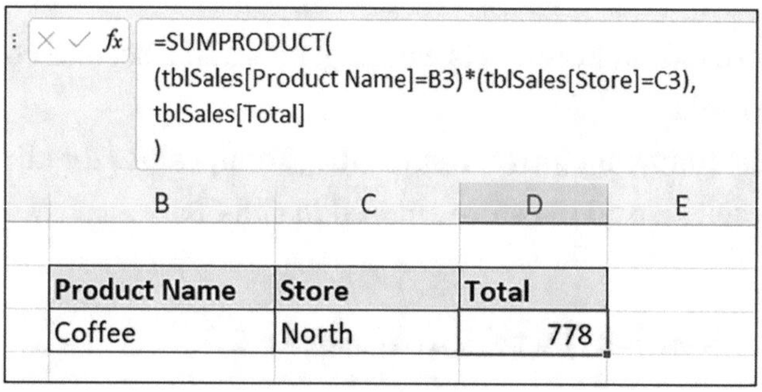

Figure 9-5. *Summing values that meet two conditions with AND logic*

To perform OR logic between conditions with SUMPRODUCT, the plus symbol (+) is used. Let's see an example.

In Figure 9-6, the following formula is used to sum the [Total] values for both the products in cells B3 and C3:

```
=SUMPRODUCT(
(tblSales[Product Name]=B3)+(tblSales[Product Name]=C3),
tblSales[Total]
)
```

Why is the plus symbol used for OR logic? Let's dive into the detail.

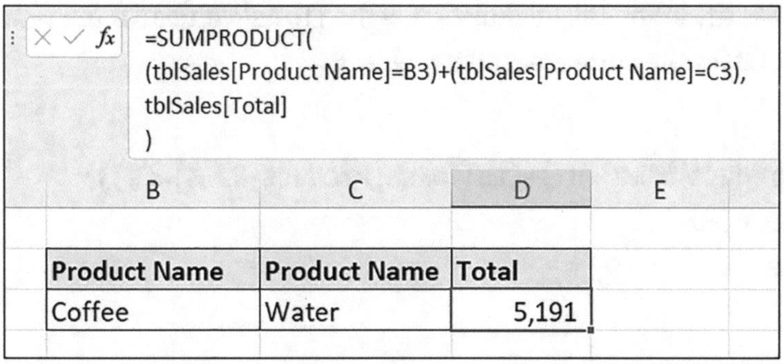

```
× ✓ fx    =SUMPRODUCT(
          (tblSales[Product Name]=B3)+(tblSales[Product Name]=C3),
          tblSales[Total]
          )
```

B	C	D	E
Product Name	**Product Name**	**Total**	
Coffee	Water	5,191	

Figure 9-6. Applying OR logic between conditions with SUMPRODUCT

As always, each condition is enclosed in its own set of brackets. When looking at the first five rows only, the following arrays are returned as the results of the two conditions in this formula:

{TRUE; FALSE; FALSE; FALSE; TRUE}
+
{FALSE; FALSE; FALSE; TRUE; FALSE}

The corresponding values from these arrays are added together. This results in the following array being returned:

{1; 0; 0; 1; 1}

These values are then multiplied by the corresponding value from the [Total] column and summed by SUMPRODUCT.

By adding the corresponding values returned by all conditions, as long as one of the logical tests returns TRUE, then the overall result is TRUE. This is perfect OR logic.

If we tested multiple columns, and more than one column returned TRUE, this is fine. Any non-zero value evaluates to TRUE. So, (TRUE + TRUE) = TRUE.

Let's see one final example, where we will use a combination of both AND and OR logic in a SUMPRODUCT function. These conditional tests can, of course, get more complex than we will take them in this chapter.

In Figure 9-7, the following formula sums the [Total] values for the products entered in cells B3 and C3 for the store entered in cell D3:

```
=SUMPRODUCT(
((tblSales[Product Name]=B3)+(tblSales[Product Name]=C3))*
(tblSales[Store]=D3),
tblSales[Total]
)
```

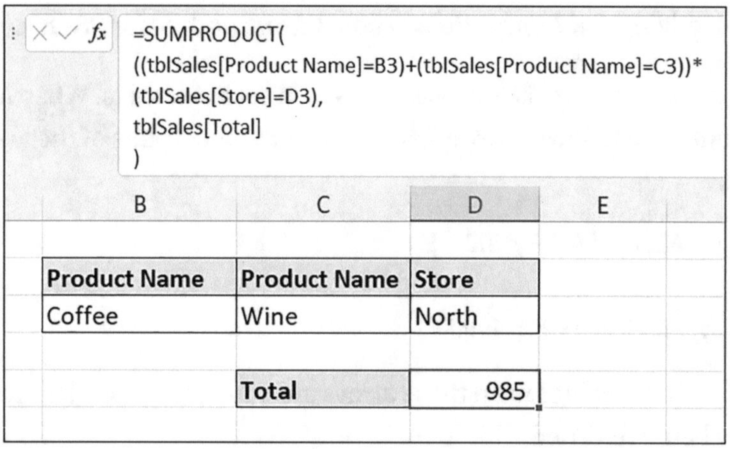

Figure 9-7. *Using both AND and OR logic in SUMPRODUCT*

In this formula, the OR segment is enclosed in its own set of brackets. This is to follow the mathematical order of precedence and ensure that the OR segment evaluates before applying the AND logical expression to the selected store.

Let's break this down.

Looking at the first five rows only, the following arrays are returned by the conditions:

```
{TRUE; FALSE; FALSE; FALSE; TRUE}
+
{FALSE; FALSE; TRUE; FALSE; FALSE}
*
{TRUE; FALSE; TRUE; FALSE; FALSE}
```

The OR segment then evaluates to return the following arrays:

```
{1; 0; 1; 0; 1}
*
{TRUE; FALSE; TRUE; FALSE; FALSE}
```

The values of the corresponding arrays are then multiplied (AND segment):

```
{1; 0; 1; 0; 0}
```

The values in this array are then multiplied by the corresponding values in the [Total] column and summed by SUMPRODUCT. So, for the first five rows (Figure 9-3), the following values are summed:

```
{59.06; 0; 207.30; 0; 0}
```

Note   Conditions are entered in the same manner in the FILTER function, discussed in Chapter 13. So, what we are learning here is directly transferable to criteria in the FILTER function.

Count Values That Meet Multiple Criteria

To count values instead of summing them, we simply need to remove the array from the formula that contains the values to be summed.

The following formula is the same formula from the previous example, but without the [Total] column. This is shown in Figure 9-8.

```
=SUMPRODUCT(
((tblSales[Product Name]=B3)+(tblSales[Product Name]=C3))*
(tblSales[Store]=D3)
)
```

Because the [Total] column is omitted from the formula, SUMPRODUCT is summing the values returned from the conditions only. So, for the first five rows, it is summing the following values:

```
{1; 0; 1; 0; 0}
```

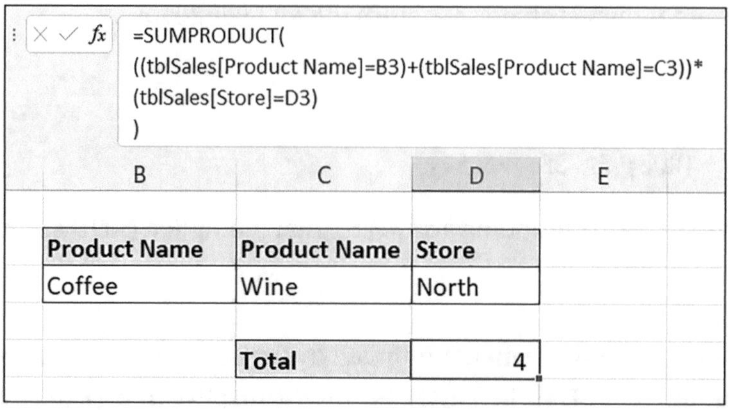

Figure 9-8. *Counting values that meet multiple conditions with SUMPRODUCT*

All the conditions used in the examples so far have tested text values. So, let's finish with an example that tests a numeric value.

In Figure 9-9, the following formula counts the number of sales for the store entered in cell B3 where the number of units sold was greater than or equal to the number entered in cell C3:

```
=SUMPRODUCT(
(tblSales[Store]=B3)*(tblSales[Units Sold]>=C3)
)
```

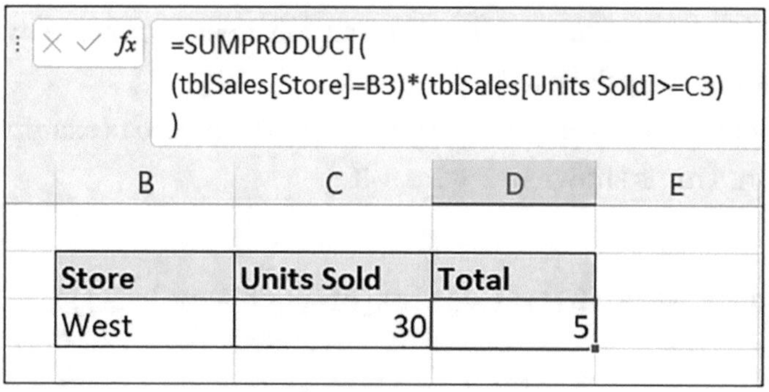

Figure 9-9. *SUMPRODUCT including a test of a numeric value*

Aggregating Multiple Columns

An area that showcases the flexibility of the SUMPRODUCT function well is its ability to handle criteria ranges of different dimensions.

Figure 9-10 shows a matrix of student names and their results to five different questions. "C" stands for correct and "I" for incorrect. A blank cell represents no answer to the question.

We want to return the number of correct questions answered for the student specified in cell B2. Cell B2 has been named [rngStudent].

The following COUNTIFS function fails to produce a result because the IFS functions (SUMIFS, COUNTIFS, etc.) require the criteria ranges to be of the same dimensions. And in this example, the student names' range is one column wide, while the questions' range is five columns wide.

```
=COUNTIFS(A5:A8,rngStudent,B5:F8,"C")
```

C2		⌄ : ✕ ✓ fx	=COUNTIFS(A5:A8,rngStudent,B5:F8,"C")			
	A	B	C	D	E	F
1		Student	# Correct			
2		Jason	#VALUE!			
3						
4	Students	Q1	Q2	Q3	Q4	Q5
5	Victoria	C	C	C	I	C
6	Kate	C	C	C	C	C
7	Claire	I	I		C	C
8	Jason	C	I	C	C	C
9						

Figure 9-10. *COUNTIFS function failing to produce a result*

This task is no problem for SUMPRODUCT. It can easily handle criteria ranges of irregular dimensions.

In Figure 9-11, the following SUMPRODUCT formula is used to return the number of correct answers for the student "Jason":

```
=SUMPRODUCT((A5:A8=rngStudent)*(B5:F8="C"))
```

C2	⌄ : ✕ ✓ fx	=SUMPRODUCT((A5:A8=rngStudent)*(B5:F8="C"))				

	A	B	C	D	E	F	G
1		**Student**	**# Correct**				
2		Jason	4				
3							
4	**Students**	**Q1**	**Q2**	**Q3**	**Q4**	**Q5**	
5	Victoria	C	C	C	I	C	
6	Kate	C	C	C	C	C	
7	Claire	I	I		C	C	
8	Jason	C	I	C	C	C	
9							

Figure 9-11. *SUMPRODUCT function handling irregular criteria ranges*

Distinct Count Formula

A function that is unfortunately missing from the library of functions in Excel is one that counts only the distinct items in a range.

Figure 9-12 shows a list of webinars that have been delivered. We would like to return the distinct number of different webinars delivered.

Date	Webinar
04/10/2021	PivotTables
06/10/2021	Excel Formulas Advanced
07/10/2021	PivotTables
08/10/2021	Pro Formatting in Excel
09/10/2021	Excel Formulas Advanced
10/10/2021	Power BI for Beginners
11/10/2021	PivotTables
11/10/2021	Excel Formulas Basics
15/10/2021	Excel Formulas Basics

Figure 9-12. *Table of a schedule of webinars that were delivered*

This list is formatted as a table named [tblWebinars]. We will achieve the distinct count with a formula that combines the SUMPRODUCT and COUNTIFS functions together.

In Figure 9-13, the following formula is entered in cell D6 to return the distinct count of values in the [Webinar] column:

```
=SUMPRODUCT(1/COUNTIFS(tblWebinars[Webinar],tblWebinars[Webinar]))
```

D6	⌄ : ✕ ✓ ƒx	=SUMPRODUCT(1/ COUNTIFS(tblWebinars[Webinar],tblWebinars[Webinar]))		
	A	B	C	D
1	Date	Webinar		
2	04/10/2021	PivotTables		Count
3	06/10/2021	Excel Formulas Advanced		9
4	07/10/2021	PivotTables		
5	08/10/2021	Pro Formatting in Excel		Count Distinct
6	09/10/2021	Excel Formulas Advanced		5
7	10/10/2021	Power BI for Beginners		
8	11/10/2021	PivotTables		
9	11/10/2021	Excel Formulas Basics		
10	15/10/2021	Excel Formulas Basics		
11				

Figure 9-13. *Distinct count formula with SUMPRODUCT*

Let's break down how this formula works.

The COUNTIFS function counts the number of occurrences of each value in the [Webinar] column and returns the results in an array.

{3; 2; 3; 1; 2; 1; 3; 2; 2}

One is then divided by each of the values in the array returned by COUNTIFS. This returns the following array of results:

{0.33;0.5;0.33;1;0.5;1;0.33;0.5;0.5}

SUMPRODUCT then sums the values in this array.

This is a nice technique to produce a distinct count. It takes advantage of SUMPRODUCT's ability to work with arrays and the fabulously useful COUNTIFS function.

Note   A distinct count formula is even easier to create with the new UNIQUE function in Excel. We will cover this technique in Chapter 10.

Weighted Average

Excel also does not have a built-in function to calculate a weighted average. Fortunately, SUMPRODUCT with its ability to handle arrays natively makes this task simple.

In Figure 9-14, we have a table named [tblAssessments]. The arithmetic mean has been calculated using the AVERAGE function on the [Score] column and returns 78.2.

However, this is wrong because the assessments are not weighted equally. Some assessments make a greater contribution to the final average than others. This is acknowledged by the [Weight] column. For example, the final exam carries the most weight toward the final average.

Average	78.2
Weighted Average	

Assessment	Score	Weight
Assignment 1	91	10%
Assignment 2	66	15%
Exam 1	79	20%
Assignment 3	84	20%
Final exam	71	35%

Figure 9-14. *Arithmetic mean on the assessment scores*

The following formula is shown in Figure 9-15. The values in the [Score] column are multiplied by the values in the [Weight] column. This produces an array of values for SUMPRODUCT to sum.

```
=SUMPRODUCT(tblAssessments[Score]*tblAssessments[Weight])
```

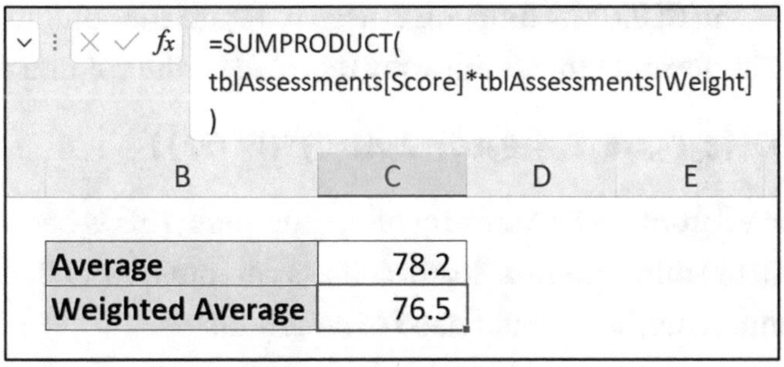

	B	C	D	E
Average		78.2		
Weighted Average		76.5		

Figure 9-15. *Weighted average with SUMPRODUCT*

Sum Every Nth Cell

You may come across a scenario where the values you want to sum are not in consecutive cells. Figure 9-16 shows a range that includes quarterly totals in every fourth column (every quarter).

We want to sum only the quarter values as they are subtotals of the months in that quarter. Of course, Figure 9-16 shows only two quarters, but imagine this is a larger range. In a different dataset, there may be many columns occurring every Nth column that you want to sum.

Name	Total	Jan	Feb	Mar	Qtr 1	Apr	May	Jun	Qtr 2
David		425	1,240	651	2,316	930	1,210	1,130	3,270
Claire		1,275	1,072	1,044	3,391	153	417	540	1,110
Victoria		266	354	268	888	161	693	1,219	2,073
Sarah		858	946	198	2,002	849	1,270	593	2,712
Fred		1,201	1,165	194	2,560	381	1,029	728	2,138
Michelle		873	240	311	1,424	485	806	375	1,666

Figure 9-16. *Range with quarterly values in every fourth column*

In Figure 9-17, the following formula has been entered in cell B2 and filled down range B3:B7:

```
=SUMPRODUCT((MOD(COLUMN(C2:J2)-2,4)=0)*(C2:J2))
```

In this formula, the COLUMN function is used to return the column number of each cell in the range. This formula shows the array returned by the column function:

=SUMPRODUCT((MOD({3,4,5,6,7,8,9,10}-2,4)=0)*(C2:J2))

Two is subtracted from each of these column numbers. This is because the range starts in column C, the third column. So, this offsets columns A and B. If the range used started from column A, nothing would need to be subtracted.

The MOD function divides each number in the array by 4 and returns the remainder. The following formula shows what we have at this point:

=SUMPRODUCT((({1,2,3,0,1,2,3,0}=0)*(C2:J2))

Each value in the array is then tested to see if it evaluated to 0. After dividing by 4, if the MOD function returned the remainder of 0, that would indicate that the value is in the fourth column of the range. The following TRUE and FALSE values are returned:

=SUMPRODUCT({FALSE,FALSE,FALSE,TRUE,FALSE,FALSE,FALSE,TRUE}*(C2:J2))

From here, the TRUE and FALSE (1 and 0) values are multiplied by the values in range C2:J2, and the resulting values are summed by SUMPRODUCT.

B2			$\times$ $\checkmark$ f_x	=SUMPRODUCT((MOD(COLUMN(C2:J2)-2,4)=0)*(C2:J2))					
	A	B	C	D	E	F	G	H
1	Name	Total	Jan	Feb	Mar	Qtr 1	Apr	May
2	David	5,586	425	1,240	651	2,316	930	1,
3	Claire	4,501	1,275	1,072	1,044	3,391	153	
4	Victoria	2,961	266	354	268	888	161	
5	Sarah	4,714	858	946	198	2,002	849	1,
6	Fred	4,698	1,201	1,165	194	2,560	381	1,
7	Michelle	3,090	873	240	311	1,424	485	
8								

Figure 9-17. SUMPRODUCT summing the values in every fourth column

This formula could easily be adapted to sum every Nth row. The main change would be to swap the COLUMN function for the ROW function.

Sum Values for a Specific Weekday

The SUMPRODUCT function is a built-in array formula. Its ability to work with arrays is one of its great strengths. This makes the function incredibly valuable to users of older versions of Excel that cannot natively handle arrays (discussed in Chapter 10).

We have seen examples of SUMPRODUCT working with arrays already in the last two examples. However, this example is here to demonstrate a common scenario that avoids the need for creating helper columns.

In Figure 9-18, we have a table named [tblDailySales] with sales transactions on different dates. We want to sum only the values that occurred at a weekend (Saturday or Sunday).

Date	Total
Fri 01/10/2021	489
Sat 02/10/2021	181
Sat 02/10/2021	445
Mon 04/10/2021	164
Thu 07/10/2021	361
Sun 10/10/2021	462
Sun 10/10/2021	101
Mon 11/10/2021	315
Fri 15/10/2021	369

Figure 9-18. *Table with daily transactions*

A common solution is to insert a column and use the WEEKDAY function to return the weekday numbers in all cells of that column. Then use a separate function such as SUMIFS to sum the [Total] values using the weekday number column for the criteria range. Functions like SUMIFS cannot handle the WEEKDAY function directly within its criteria.

With SUMPRODUCT, it can store the weekday numbers returned by WEEKDAY in an array. No need to create an additional physical column. This array of weekday numbers is then tested and calculated all in one formula.

In Figure 9-19, the following formula uses the WEEKDAY function to return the weekday numbers for each date. The 2 within the WEEKDAY function specifies that the weekday numbers should begin with Monday as 1 and end with Sunday as 7.

SUMPRODUCT tests if the number is greater than 5 (after Friday), and then the results are multiplied by the [Total] values and summed.

```
=SUMPRODUCT(
(WEEKDAY(tblDailySales[Date],2)>5)*
tblDailySales[Total]
)
```

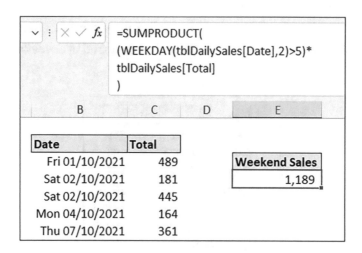

Figure 9-19. *SUMPRODUCT summing only values that occurred at a weekend*

Without the use of an array function, you would not be able to provide an entire column of values to a function such as WEEKDAY. This also applies to functions such as LEFT, RIGHT, MONTH, etc. By using SUMPRODUCT, we do not have to force an array formula by pressing **Ctrl + Shift + Enter**.

Note In Chapter 10, we will discuss dynamic arrays in Excel for Microsoft 365, Excel for the web, and Excel 2021. With this modern development, even the standard SUM function could handle this array task.

Sum the Top Five Values Only

For the final SUMPRODUCT examples, let's see it being used to sum the top five values in a range only. Once again, this is a showcase of SUMPRODUCT handling arrays.

Figure 9-20 shows the first eight rows of the [tblSales] table that we worked with earlier in this chapter when summing and counting values that met multiple criteria. We will use this table again now and look to sum the top five values only.

	A	B	C	D	E	F
1	ID	Date	Product Name	Store	Units Sold	Total
2	19775	11/01/2021	Coffee	North	39	59.06
3	19776	12/01/2021	Hot Chocolate	West	16	424.80
4	19777	24/01/2021	Wine	North	25	207.30
5	19778	25/01/2021	Water	West	35	436.53
6	19779	30/01/2021	Coffee	South	38	424.30
7	19780	01/02/2021	Tea	North	10	174.45
8	19781	03/02/2021	Tea	North	30	456.55
9	19782	08/02/2021	Hot Chocolate	West	20	424.50

Figure 9-20. *Table of sales data*

To do this, we will combine SUMPRODUCT with the LARGE function. The LARGE function returns the kth largest value in a range, for example, the second, third, or fifth largest value.

This is the syntax of the LARGE function:

```
=LARGE(array, k)
```

- **Array:** The range, table column, or array from which to return the kth largest value

- **K:** The position of the value in the array (from the largest) that you want to return

---

Note   There is also a SMALL function in Excel to return the kth smallest value in a range.

We want to return the top five values for SUMPRODUCT to sum, not just a single value. So, for the *k* argument, we will feed the LARGE function an array of constants containing all the values that we want.

The following is the array that we will use. This requests the first, second, third, fourth, and fifth largest values to be returned. As you can imagine, you can enter whatever values you want in this array, for example, top three, top eight, or top ten.

```
{1, 2, 3, 4, 5}
```

In Figure 9-21, the following formula sums the top five values only:

```
=SUMPRODUCT(
LARGE(tblSales[Total],{1,2,3,4,5})
)
```

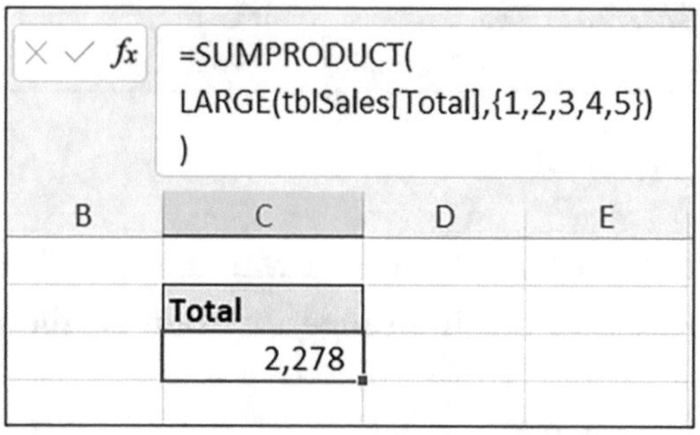

Figure 9-21. *Summing the top five values with SUMPRODUCT and LARGE*

The LARGE function could be replaced by the SMALL function to return the smallest values to be summed.

Let's now take this a step further and add criteria to the example. Say, we want to sum the top five values for a specific store only.

In Figure 9-22, the following SUMPRODUCT formula sums the top five values for the store entered in cell B3. Notice that the criterion has been entered within the *array* argument of the LARGE function.

```
=SUMPRODUCT(
LARGE((tblSales[Store]=B3)*tblSales[Total],
{1,2,3,4,5})
)
```

This ensures that the array the LARGE function returns values from only includes values where that criterion was met. Additional criteria could be added just as was discussed earlier in this chapter with SUMPRODUCT.

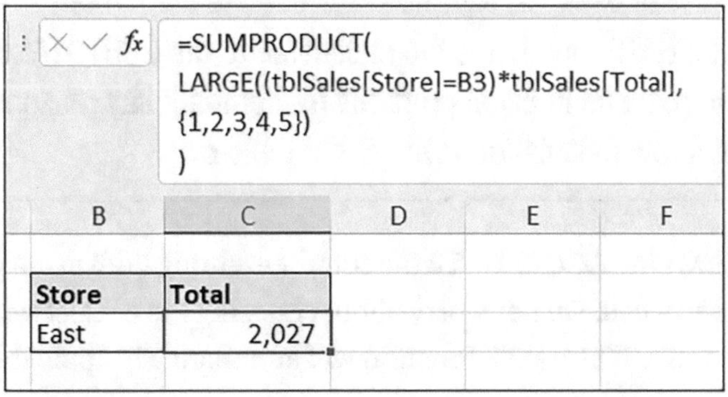

Figure 9-22. *Summing the top five values with additional criteria*

The importance of SUMPRODUCT in older versions of Excel is indisputable, from their general purpose of calculating the products of arrays followed by a sum to complex criteria sums and counts and finally its ability to natively handle arrays.

AGGREGATE Function

Availability: Excel 2010, Excel 2013, Excel 2016, Excel 2019, Excel 2021, Excel for Microsoft 365, Excel for the Web, Excel 2011 for Mac, Excel 2016 for Mac, Excel 2019 for Mac, Excel 2021 for Mac, Excel for Microsoft 365 for Mac

---

File   aggregate.xlsx

The AGGREGATE function was introduced in Excel 2010. This terrific function can apply a plethora of different aggregate functions (19 in fact) to a dataset with the option to ignore hidden rows, error values, and/or subtotals.

It has two different syntaxes. There is the array form:

```
=AGGREGATE(function_num, options, array, [k])
```

And there is the reference form:

```
=AGGREGATE(function_num, options, ref1, ref2, ...
```

Note   The AGGREGATE function is the successor to the SUBTOTAL function in Excel. SUBTOTAL remains in Excel primarily for compatibility reasons. SUBTOTAL is also used for total row calculations with Excel Tables.

Figure 9-23 shows the AGGREGATE function presenting both syntaxes as the function is written in a cell. Do not worry about choosing the correct syntax at this point however, because the AGGREGATE function will automatically apply the correct syntax based on the information that you provide.

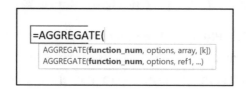

Figure 9-23. *AGGREGATE has two syntax options*

Let's have a look at the different arguments of the AGGREGATE function:

- **Function num:** A number from 1 to 19 that specifies which aggregate function to use. The following list details all 19 functions:

    - 1 – AVERAGE

    - 2 – COUNT

    - 3 – COUNTA

    - 4 – MAX

    - 5 – MIN

    - 6 – PRODUCT

    - 7 – STDEV.S

    - 8 – STDEV.P

    - 9 – SUM

    - 10 – VAR.S

    - 11 – VAR.P

- 12 – MEDIAN

- 13 – MODE.SNGL

- 14 – LARGE

- 15 – SMALL

- 16 – PERCENTILE.INC

- 17 – QUARTILE.INC

- 18 – PERCENTILE.EXC

- 19 – QUARTILE.EXC

Fortunately, you do not need to remember these index numbers because AGGREGATE provides you with a list to select the function from (Figure 9-24).

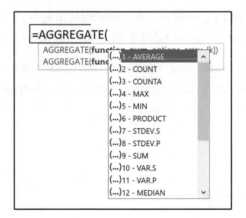

Figure 9-24. *List of the different functions in AGGREGATE*

- **Options:** A number between 0 and 7 that specifies which values to ignore, if any, when performing the aggregation function.

Once again, the AGGREGATE function provides a list making it easy to select the option that you need (Figure 9-25).

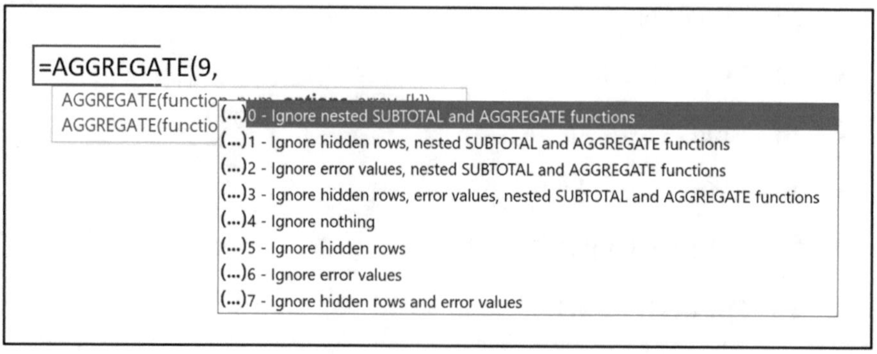

Figure 9-25. *List of the options to be ignored when performing the aggregate*

- **Array, ref1:** The array formula, array of values, or range of cells for the function to be applied.

- **Ref2:** Additional ranges of values for which to apply the aggregation function. Up to 253 can be added. This is an optional argument.

- **K:** The position in the array to return. It is used by the functions in the following list only – kth largest, kth smallest, kth percentile, kth quartile:

  - LARGE

  - SMALL

  - PERCENTILE.INC

  - QUARTILE.INC

  - PERCENTILE.EXC

  - QUARTILE.EXC

Advantages of using the AGGREGATE function include

- The vast array of aggregate functions it offers

- Its ability to handle arrays (great for non-dynamic array–enabled versions of Excel)

- Its special skill at ignoring hidden rows, errors, and other subtotals

It is not all rosy though. There are some disadvantages:

- It is not easy to understand. As the function and options arguments return the selection as an index number, it is confusing to the user reading the formula.

- It was designed to aggregate vertical ranges of data. If it is used to aggregate data in rows, aggregate cannot ignore hidden columns. The aggregate result will include the hidden values.

- Criteria can be added to the AGGREGATE function just like with SUMPRODUCT (an example is shown); however, when adding criteria, the options such as ignoring hidden rows are not applied. This is because once criteria are applied, the range is converted to an array, and arrays cannot have hidden values.

Let's see some examples of the AGGREGATE function. The following examples will use the table of data named [tblSales].

ID	Product Name	Region	Units Sold	Total
19775	Coffee	North	39	59.06
19776	Hot Chocolate	West	16	424.80
19777	Wine	North	25	207.30
19778	Water	West	35	436.53
19779	Coffee	South	38	424.30
19780	Tea	North	10	174.45
19781	Tea	North	30	456.55
19782	Hot Chocolate	West	20	424.50
19783	Water	East	12	90.88

Figure 9-26. *Table of sales data*

Ignoring Hidden Rows

When using functions such as SUM and AVERAGE on a range that contains hidden rows, the hidden values are still included by the function.

The AGGREGATE function can be requested to perform calculations on the visible cells only, ignoring any hidden rows, which are probably the result of filtering a list.

In Figure 9-27, the following formula is entered in cell F2 to sum the [Total] values and ignore the hidden rows. The values for the "West" have been hidden by a filter applied to the [Region] column.

```
=AGGREGATE(9,5,tblSales[Total])
```

In the formula, the number 9 is the index number for the SUM function, and number 5 specifies the option to ignore hidden rows.

fx	=AGGREGATE(9,5,tblSales[Total])				
B		C	D	E	F
				Sum	1,412.54
ID	Product Name	Region	Units Sold	Total	
19775	Coffee	North	39	59.06	
19777	Wine	North	25	207.30	
19779	Coffee	South	38	424.30	
19780	Tea	North	10	174.45	
19781	Tea	North	30	456.55	
19783	Water	East	12	90.88	

Figure 9-27. AGGREGATE function summing visible values only

Let's now look at an example where we want to return the second largest value in the [tblSales] table while ignoring hidden rows. When using the LARGE function, we will be required to use the *K* argument.

In Figure 9-28, the following formula specifies function number 14 – the LARGE function. Position 2 is specified for the *K* argument.

```
=AGGREGATE(14,5,tblSales[Total],2)
```

The "West" values are filtered out of the list. In Figure 9-26, you can see that there is a total value of 436.53 for the "West." This is the second largest value in the complete list.

As the AGGREGATE formula in Figure 9-28 is requested to ignore hidden rows, it returns the correct result of 424.30.

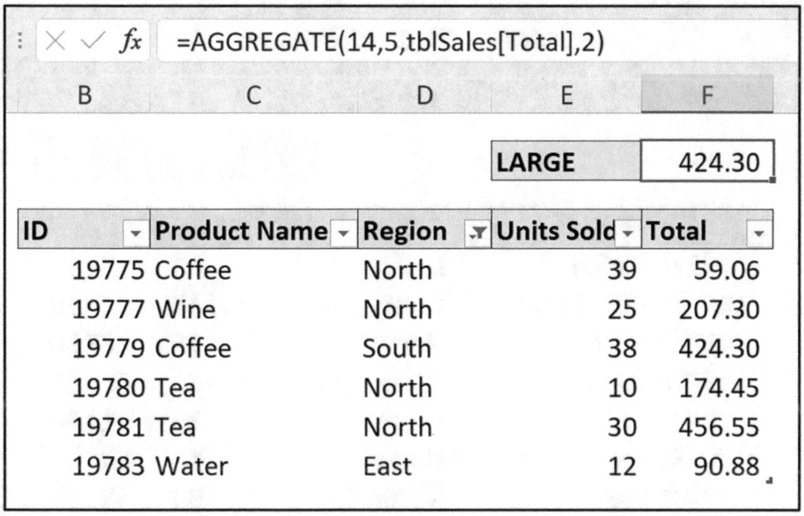

⋮ ✕ ✓ *fx*	=AGGREGATE(14,5,tblSales[Total],2)			
B	C	D	E	F

			LARGE	424.30

ID ▾	Product Name ▾	Region ⊤	Units Sold ▾	Total ▾
19775	Coffee	North	39	59.06
19777	Wine	North	25	207.30
19779	Coffee	South	38	424.30
19780	Tea	North	10	174.45
19781	Tea	North	30	456.55
19783	Water	East	12	90.88

Figure 9-28. Returning the second largest value while ignoring hidden rows

Ignoring Errors in a Range

Functions such as SUM, LARGE, and MEDIAN will not work if a table column or range contains error values. However, the AGGREGATE function has a nifty option to ignore error values.

In Figure 9-29, the following AGGREGATE formula applies the SUM function (number 9) to the [Total] column. Option 6 is specified to ignore error values in the range.

```
=AGGREGATE(9,6,tblSales[Total])
```

Note   These examples aggregate a single column of values; however, the AGGREGATE function can handle multiple value ranges and ranges that are multiple columns wide.

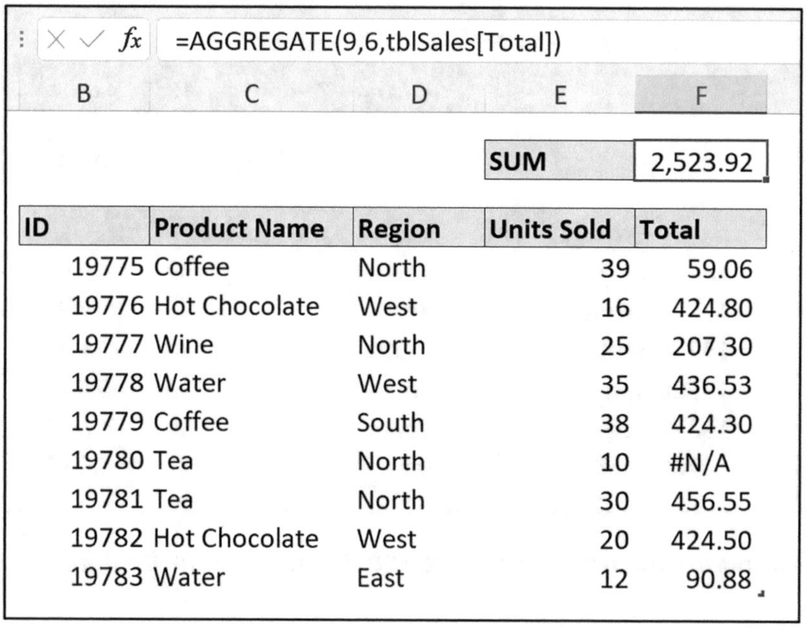

| : | × | ✓ | *fx* | =AGGREGATE(9,6,tblSales[Total]) |

B	C	D	E	F
			SUM	2,523.92

ID	Product Name	Region	Units Sold	Total
19775	Coffee	North	39	59.06
19776	Hot Chocolate	West	16	424.80
19777	Wine	North	25	207.30
19778	Water	West	35	436.53
19779	Coffee	South	38	424.30
19780	Tea	North	10	#N/A
19781	Tea	North	30	456.55
19782	Hot Chocolate	West	20	424.50
19783	Water	East	12	90.88

Figure 9-29. *Sum values ignoring errors with AGGREGATE*

The AGGREGATE function provides seven different options. These include the individual options to ignore hidden rows, ignore error values, and ignore other totals. But there are also combined options.

In Figure 9-30, the AVERAGE function (number 1) is applied to the [Total] column. Option 7 has been specified. This option requests the AGGREGATE function to ignore hidden rows and error values.

=AGGREGATE(1,7,tblSales[Total])

A filter is applied to the table to hide the sales of "Hot Chocolate" and "Wine" in the [Product Name] column.

⋮ ✕ ✓ fx	=AGGREGATE(1,7,tblSales[Total])

B	C	D	E	F
			AVERAGE	293.46

ID ▾	Product Name ⊤	Region ▾	Units Sold ▾	Total ▾
19775	Coffee	North	39	59.06
19778	Water	West	35	436.53
19779	Coffee	South	38	424.30
19780	Tea	North	10	#N/A
19781	Tea	North	30	456.55
19783	Water	East	12	90.88

Figure 9-30. *Average ignoring errors and hidden rows*

Adding Criteria to AGGREGATE

The AGGREGATE function, like SUMPRODUCT, can process arrays. This makes it a very useful function for those on older versions of Excel, as it negates the requirement to press **Ctrl + Shift + Enter** when entering an array formula.

Note   In Excel for Microsoft 365, Excel 2021, and Excel for the Web, all formulas can handle arrays (covered in Chapter 10), so this benefit of the AGGREGATE function is not as important.

This is a fantastic functionality; however, options such as ignore hidden rows cannot be used when adding criteria to the AGGREGATE function.

This is a shame as it removes one of the key strengths of AGGREGATE, but it can still be a very useful technique.

In Figure 9-31, the following formula has been used to return the second largest value in the [Total] column for the "North" region only:

```
=AGGREGATE(14,4,tblSales[Total]*(tblSales[Region]="North"),2)
```

A criterion has been added within a set of brackets and multiplied by the [Total] column values, just like we did in SUMPRODUCT.

Function number 14 is used to specify the LARGE function, and option 4 is used to ignore nothing. Remember, when adding criteria in an array, options such as hidden rows will not be applied anyhow.

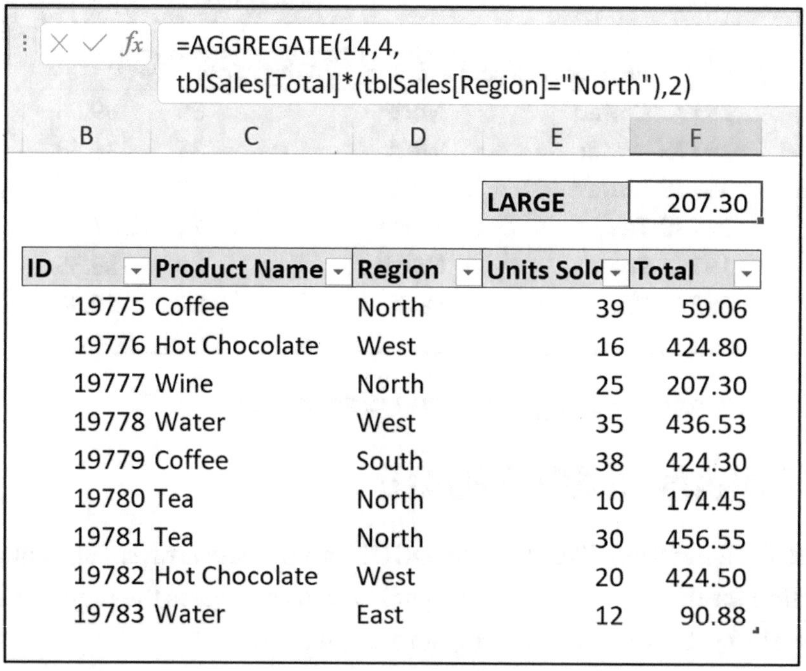

⋮ ✕ ✓ *fx*	=AGGREGATE(14,4, tblSales[Total]*(tblSales[Region]="North"),2)				
	B	C	D	E	F
				LARGE	207.30
ID ▾	Product Name ▾	Region ▾	Units Sold ▾	Total ▾	
19775	Coffee	North	39	59.06	
19776	Hot Chocolate	West	16	424.80	
19777	Wine	North	25	207.30	
19778	Water	West	35	436.53	
19779	Coffee	South	38	424.30	
19780	Tea	North	10	174.45	
19781	Tea	North	30	456.55	
19782	Hot Chocolate	West	20	424.50	
19783	Water	East	12	90.88	

Figure 9-31. *Second largest value for the North region only*

Criteria can only be added like this, for the six functions that can handle arrays, as stated earlier in the chapter.

Function Specified by a Cell Value

For the final examples, let's use a drop-down list to make it easy for the user to select the function they would like to apply. The user can simply select the aggregate function from a list, instead of typing those awkward index numbers in.

Figure 9-32 shows a table named [tblFunctions]. The [Function] column contains five functions that are being used as the source for a drop-down list. The [Index] column contains the index number associated with each of these functions.

Function	Index
AVERAGE	1
COUNT	2
MEDIAN	12
MODE	13
SUM	9

Figure 9-32. *Lookup table with function names and their index number*

Figure 9-33 shows the drop-down list of functions in cell E2 above [tblSales].

We will use the VLOOKUP function (other lookup functions are covered in Chapter 11) to look up the selected function in cell E3 within [tblFunctions] and return the index number for the AGGREGATE function to use.

Figure 9-33. *Drop-down list of functions above the sales table*

In Figure 9-34, the following formula is entered in cell F2. The AVERAGE function has been selected from the drop-down list in cell E2.

```
=AGGREGATE(
VLOOKUP(E2,tblFunctions,2,0),
7,tblSales2[Total])
```

The VLOOKUP function is nested within the *function num* argument of AGGREGATE. It returns the function number from [tblFunctions] for the selected function in E2.

Option 7 is specified to ignore hidden rows and error values. A filter has been applied to the [Product Name] column to exclude "Wine" and also to the [Region] column to exclude "South."

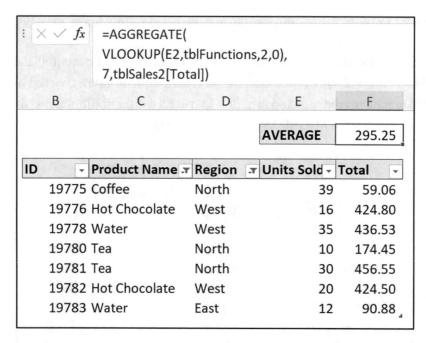

⋮ ✕ ✓ *fx*   =AGGREGATE(
VLOOKUP(E2,tblFunctions,2,0),
7,tblSales2[Total])

	B	C	D	E	F
				AVERAGE	295.25
ID	Product Name	Region	Units Sold	Total	
	19775 Coffee	North	39	59.06	
	19776 Hot Chocolate	West	16	424.80	
	19778 Water	West	35	436.53	
	19780 Tea	North	10	174.45	
	19781 Tea	North	30	456.55	
	19782 Hot Chocolate	West	20	424.50	
	19783 Water	East	12	90.88	

Figure 9-34.   VLOOKUP with AGGREGATE for function based on cell value

With the 19 different functions on offer by AGGREGATE, it makes it simple to create this interactivity and enable a user to choose the function from a nice drop-down list.

Summary

In this chapter, we learned the SUMPRODUCT and AGGREGATE functions in Excel – two powerful functions that offer various benefits over other aggregation functions such as SUMIFS and AVERAGE.

Different examples were shown to demonstrate the full capability of these functions and detail of their limitations.

In the next chapter, we will dive into dynamic array formulas in Excel. One of the greatest updates in Excel history, the ability to handle arrays natively, and have them dynamically update in size, has changed how we write formulas.

We will explain what dynamic arrays are and how to use them effectively with Excel functions and features such as charts. We will also detail, with practical examples, a bunch of dynamic array functions including SORTBY, SEQUENCE, and SUM (OK, that one isn't very new, but this is SUM 2.0, the dynamic array version).

CHAPTER 10

Dynamic Array Formulas

The introduction of dynamic array formulas in Excel is one of the greatest updates in Excel history. It completely changes the way that we think and write our formulas in Excel.

This fundamental change in how formulas calculate in Excel affects all formulas. So, this change can affect how you, or somebody else, write a classic Excel function such as SUM, IF, or VLOOKUP.

In addition to the introduction of the dynamic array formula engine, Microsoft released six new functions. These functions are commonly referred to as the dynamic array functions, though that is not an official function category.

Dynamic array formulas are only available in the Excel for Microsoft 365, Excel 2021, and Excel for the Web versions. When collaborating with Excel users from external organizations, you should exercise some caution, as they may have a different version of Excel to you.

In this chapter, we will begin by getting to know dynamic arrays. How do you use them, how would you recognize them on a spreadsheet, and what are their limitations?

We then go into detail on five of the six new dynamic array functions – UNIQUE, SORT, SORTBY, SEQUENCE, and RANDARRAY. The sixth function, FILTER, is covered on its own in Chapter 13.

Finally, we explore some examples of how the introduction of dynamic arrays has improved how we use existing Excel formulas. We focus on the FREQUENCY, TRANSPOSE, and SUM functions in this chapter, but the improvements go way beyond just those functions.

Getting to Know Dynamic Array Formulas

Availability: Excel for Microsoft 365, Excel for the Web, Excel 2021, Excel for Microsoft 365 for Mac, Excel 2021 for Mac

---

File   dynamic-arrays.xlsx

465

© Alan Murray 2022
A. Murray, *Advanced Excel Formulas*, https://doi.org/10.1007/978-1-4842-7125-4_10

The formulas that we know and love in Excel have always been one cell, one formula. A formula would be filled, probably by clicking and dragging the fill handle, to any other cells in the range requiring that formula.

Dynamic arrays change all that. With the dynamic array formula engine, a formula can return multiple results. If a formula returns more than one value, the additional values are spilled to the adjacent cells. The range of cells that contain the formula is known as the spill range.

In Figure 10-1, the following formula has been entered in cell D2. It returns all the values for the range A1:B6.

```
=A1:B6
```

Notice the blue border surrounding the spill range. This appears when you click any cell within the spill range, making dynamic array formulas easy to identify on a spreadsheet.

Now, this is a simple example that is not very practical. However, it demonstrates the concept of dynamic arrays nicely. It also shows that a dynamic array formula can spill across rows and columns.

D2	∨ ⋮ ✕ ✓ *fx*	=A1:B6		
	A	**B**	**C**	**D**	**E**
1	**Name**	**Score**			
2	Michelle	89		Name	Score
3	Victoria	95		Michelle	89
4	Jason	61		Victoria	95
5	Darryl	89		Jason	61
6	Heather	73		Darryl	89
7				Heather	73
8					

Figure 10-1. *Dynamic array returning multiple values*

To achieve this in an Excel version that doesn't support dynamic arrays, you would need to

1. Select the output range D2:E7.

2. Write the formula: =A1:B6.

3. Press **Ctrl + Shift + Enter**.

The formula would be entered into all the cells in range D2:E7 and would be enclosed in curly braces, as shown in the following. You would never type these curly braces; they were automatically input by Excel on pressing **Ctrl + Shift + Enter**.

`{=A1:B6}`

Figure 10-2 shows an array formula as it would appear when entered in an Excel version that does not support dynamic arrays. Cell E4 is active, and the formula is shown in the Formula Bar. All 12 cells contain the same formula.

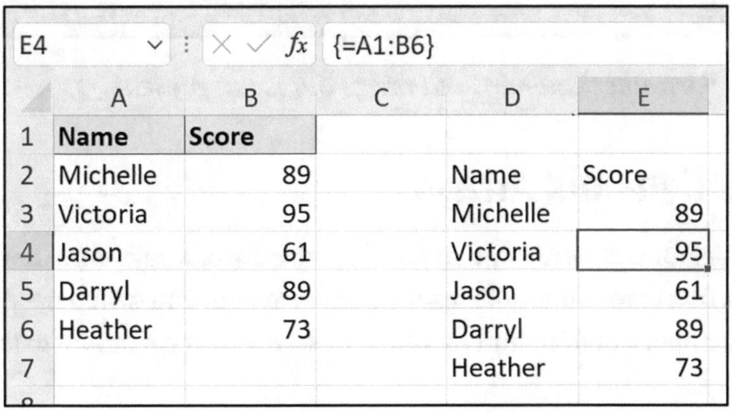

E4				fx	{=A1:B6}		
	A	B		C	D	E	
1	Name	Score					
2	Michelle	89			Name	Score	
3	Victoria	95			Michelle	89	
4	Jason	61			Victoria	95	
5	Darryl	89			Jason	61	
6	Heather	73			Darryl	89	
7					Heather	73	

Figure 10-2. Array formula in an Excel version without dynamic arrays

---

Note   Array formulas were often referred to as CSE formulas due to the requirement to press **Ctrl + Shift + Enter** on running them.

The dynamic array formula back in Figure 10-1 only exists in the origin cell and spills the results (not the formula) to the other cells in the spill range.

In Figure 10-3, cell D3 is active. In the Formula Bar, the formula is shown in a light gray font. This is a visual so that we can understand how the result was achieved; the formula is not actually existing in the cell. If you were to click in the Formula Bar, nothing is shown.

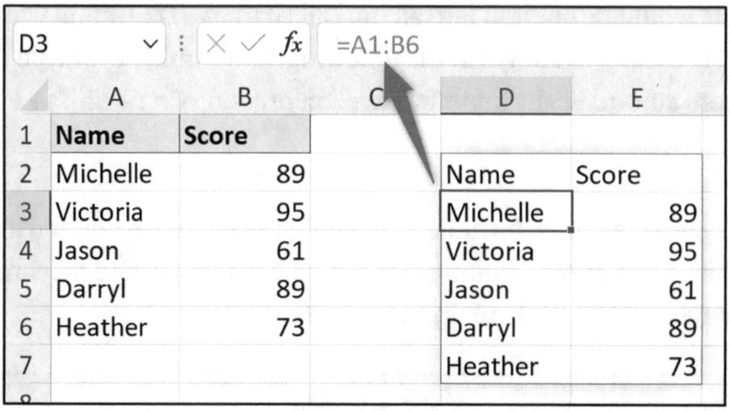

Figure 10-3. *Formula shown in spill range but is not present*

Arrays vs. Dynamic Arrays

This example demonstrates nicely that although the use of arrays is not new in Excel, array formulas that output multiple results were awkward. You would need to know the cells that the formula would output to, which was a massive constraint to their use. They were static arrays.

So, dynamic arrays really are a combination of two key developments – dynamic + arrays.

These formulas are entered in the same way as any other formula and will handle arrays without the need to press **Ctrl + Shift + Enter**. And they are dynamic. You do not need to know the range of cells to output to. The spill range will dynamically grow and shrink depending on the number of values being returned by the formula.

Now, not all array formulas return multiple values, so single cell array formulas were easier to apply in the Excel of the past. You just needed to recall pressing **Ctrl + Shift + Enter**, and not just **Enter**.

However, did your colleagues know to press **Ctrl + Shift + Enter**, and what were the curly braces around the formula? Did you need to type them?

These limitations meant that, in the past, writing array formulas ended up being for advanced uses only, and the SUMPRODUCT function gained a lot of love as it could handle the arrays natively.

With dynamic array formulas, this is all a thing of the past.

Dynamic Arrays with Tables

In Figure 10-4, the following formula returns all the values from the table in range A1:B6 named [tblData]. If the [#All] was omitted, the formula would only return the table data excluding the headers.

```
=tblData[#All]
```

D2		⌄	⋮	×	✓	*fx*	=tblData[#All]		
	A	B		C		D	E		
1	**Name**	**Score**							
2	Michelle	89				Name	Score		
3	Victoria	95				Michelle	89		
4	Jason	61				Victoria	95		
5	Darryl	89				Jason	61		
6	Heather	73				Darryl	89		
7						Heather	73		
8									

Figure 10-4. *Dynamic array formula referencing all values in a table*

Using dynamic array formulas with table data is a dream combination. The first example that referenced range A1:B6 works great. However, it is not a fully dynamic solution as using the range as the source is not dynamic. So, you are losing 50% of the brilliant dynamic + array capabilities.

Tables are dynamic and grow and shrink with data automatically. So, using table data as the source for a dynamic array formula ensures a completely dynamic solution.

Figure 10-5 shows a new row added to the table. The table expands, and the dynamic array formula expands in sync.

D2	⌄ ⋮ × ✓ fx	=tblData[#All]		
	A	B	C	D	E

	A	B	C	D	E
1	**Name**	**Score**			
2	Michelle	89		Name	Score
3	Victoria	95		Michelle	89
4	Jason	61		Victoria	95
5	Darryl	89		Jason	61
6	Heather	73		Darryl	89
7	Carly	84		Heather	73
8				Carly	84
9					

Figure 10-5. *Dynamic array formula and table provide a fully dynamic solution*

Dynamic Array Formula Example

Let's look at a more practical case for a dynamic array formula. Figure 10-6 shows a table named [tblScores]. We will use an AVERAGEIFS function to calculate the mean average score for each region.

Region	Name	Score
East	Michelle	89
East	Victoria	95
East	Jason	61
East	Darryl	89
East	Heather	73
South	Rachel	78
South	David	59
South	Kevin	85
South	Hannah	91
West	Carl	69
West	Natalie	77
West	Deborah	96

Figure 10-6. *Table of scores*

The common method to achieve this would be to write an AVERAGEIFS function like the following and fill it down to cell F5, as shown in Figure 10-7:

```
=AVERAGEIFS(tblScores[Score],tblScores[Region],E3)
```

The formula references the scalar value in cell E3 for the criteria. The formula is then filled down to cells F4 and F5, which reference the values in cells E4 and E5 consecutively. This is classic Excel.

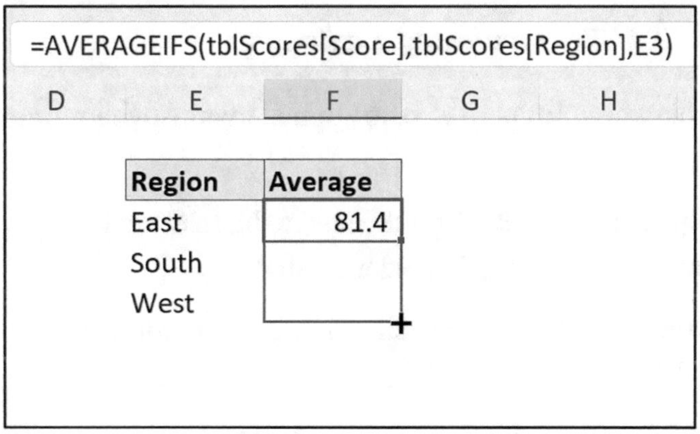

Figure 10-7. *Classic AVERAGEIFS being filled across other cells*

With dynamic array formulas, we could reference the range of criteria values, instead of a single criteria value at a time.

Figure 10-8 shows the following formula as an alternative to the previous approach. Notice the blue border around the results identifying the perimeter of the spill range.

```
=AVERAGEIFS(tblScores[Score],tblScores[Region],E3:E5)
```

Instead of producing three formulas – one formula per cell – the dynamic array formula is one formula that returns three results.

Once again, this example is not dynamically complete as the criteria is not based on table data or a DA spill range. It, therefore, is not maximizing the full potential of dynamic arrays. We will soon be constructing our dynamic array formulas on table data and spill ranges only.

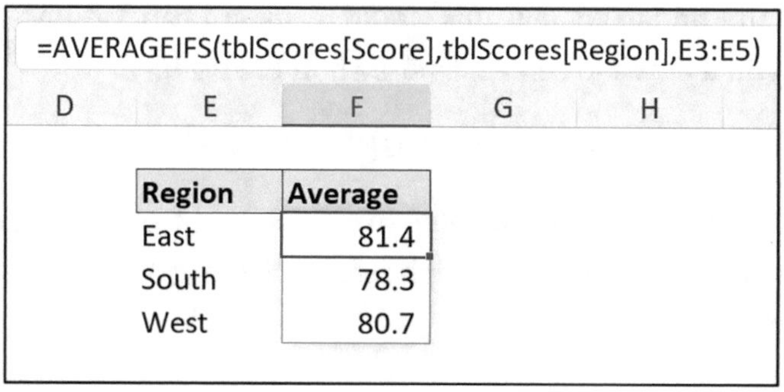

Figure 10-8. *AVERAGEIFS returning a spill range*

The last formula example could also be applied in non-dynamic array–enabled versions of Excel. However

- The output range of F3:F5 would need to be selected before writing the formula. No "spilling" in older versions.

- The formula would exist in each cell, while dynamic arrays are one cell, multiple results.

- The formula range would need to be in line with the range being referenced as implicit intersection would be applied. In this example, F3:F5 is in line with E3:E5 so it would work. The formula can be run as an array formula by pressing **Ctrl + Shift + Enter** to override the implicit intersection.

With dynamic arrays, none of this needs to be considered. The formula is written just like any other formula and wherever you want.

Note   Implicit intersection is denoted by the @ symbol. In modern Excel, this is mainly seen in formulas in a table that reference other cells in the same row of a table, for example, =[@Country].

Welcome the # Operator

You may be wondering how one would reference the spill range of a dynamic array formula. You may want to use the results of a dynamic array formula in another formula or maybe in a chart.

If the spill range is dynamic, you wouldn't necessarily know the final cell of the range.

Well, the answer, as I'm sure you have concluded from the title of this section, is the # symbol (typically referred to as the hash or pound sign).

To refer to all the cells in the spill range, you reference the origin cell that contains the dynamic array formula followed by the # symbol, for example, A2#.

In Figure 10-9, the following COUNT function is being entered and refers to the spill range that exists in cell F3. Notice the range F3:F5 changes color as it is recognized as the spill range on entering the # symbol.

=COUNT(F3#)

Note   The # symbol references the entire spill range including a spill range that contains multiple columns and rows. In Chapter 11, we will cover how the INDEX function can be used to reference specific columns or rows of a spill range only.

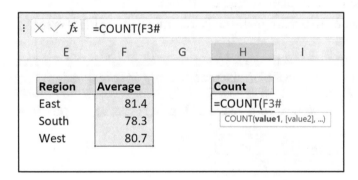

Figure 10-9. *Spill operator accesses all values in a spill range*

The #SPILL! Error

The #SPILL! error is created when the results of a dynamic array formula cannot be returned to the grid. This is typically caused by other content blocking the spill range.

In Figure 10-10, some text is causing the #SPILL! error to be returned. The DA formula needs blank cells in the spill range to return the results to. To remove the error, this text needs to be moved or deleted.

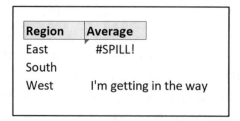

Figure 10-10. *#SPILL! error caused by content blocking the spill range*

Note   This is a similar behavior to what you may have encountered with PivotTables. They return an error when they are refreshed and need to expand in size but do not have the space to expand into.

The #SPILL! error is also returned if there are merged cells in the range that the formula needs to spill to or if a dynamic array formula is used within a table.

Figure 10-11 shows the #SPILL! error caused by merged cells in the spill range. The cells in range F5:G5 have been merged in this example.

You would need to unmerge the cells to remove the #SPILL! error.

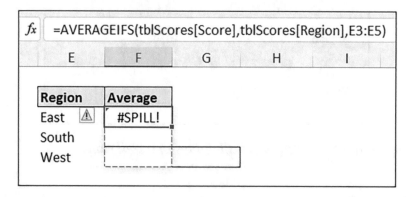

Figure 10-11. *Merged cells causing a #SPILL! error*

Merged cells should only be applied in very specific cases in Excel. Very few actions can attract the ire of an Excel user more than the sight of merged cells.

DA Formulas Cannot Be Used Within Tables

The #SPILL! error is also caused by a dynamic array formula being used within a table. An example of this is shown in Figure 10-12. Note the blue corner in the bottom right indicating that the range is formatted as a table.

Using tables as the source data for dynamic arrays is an ideal relationship as it provides a fully dynamic solution. However, dynamic arrays are their own range and cannot be used within tables.

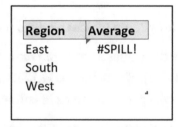

Figure 10-12. *#SPILL! error caused by using a DA within a table*

Let's now look at the dynamic array functions that were released to take advantage of this new formula behavior.

UNIQUE Function

Availability: Excel for Microsoft 365, Excel for the Web, Excel 2021, Excel for Microsoft 365 for Mac, Excel 2021 for Mac

---

File   unique.xlsx

The UNIQUE function is a tremendous addition to Excel. It is incredibly helpful, and I find myself using it in most spreadsheets that I create.

Creating a distinct list of values is a very common Excel task. The Remove Duplicates button, the Advanced Filter, and PivotTables are popular tools to generate a distinct list of values in Excel. This distinct list may be used as the source for a Data Validation list or to create labels for a report.

This function is often used as a formula alternative for creating a distinct list of values. Being a dynamic array function, this approach would ensure a dynamic list that updates when values are added, removed, or changed in the source data.

In addition to returning a distinct list of values, this function can also return a unique list of values (as its name implies). We will cover the distinction (pun fully intended) between the often misunderstood terms of distinct and unique shortly.

The syntax for the UNIQUE function is as follows:

=UNIQUE(array, [by_col], [exactly_once])

- **Array:** The range or array from which to return the values.

- **[By col]:** To compare the values in rows or columns. Entered as a logical value (True/False). The default is FALSE to compare values in rows. Enter TRUE to compare the values in columns.

- **[Exactly once]:** A logical value. The default is FALSE to return a distinct list of values. Enter TRUE to return a list of the unique values (those that only occur once).

Returning Distinct and Unique Values

The UNIQUE function, despite its name, actually returns the distinct values by default. A list of the distinct values is a list with the duplicate values removed. This is the most common use of this function.

A list of the unique values is a list of values that occur only once in the list. This is specified by entering TRUE for the final argument of the UNIQUE function.

There is a lot of confusion over the terms distinct and unique. Users often refer to a list of distinct values as a list of unique values. So be prepared for that when conversing with other Excel users.

It does not help that Microsoft named the function UNIQUE, yet it returns a distinct list by default. I believe it was named UNIQUE as that is the more common term, and Excel users would be more familiar with it. The final argument does however coincide with the function name. Enter TRUE for a unique list, or enter FALSE or omit the response for a distinct list.

In Figure 10-13, the following formula returns the distinct values from the [Customer] column. Five names are returned as there are three duplicates in the column.

```
=UNIQUE(tblAttendances[Customer])
```

Note   Remember that these dynamic array functions automatically update as the source data changes. This formula has a table source for a dynamically complete formula.

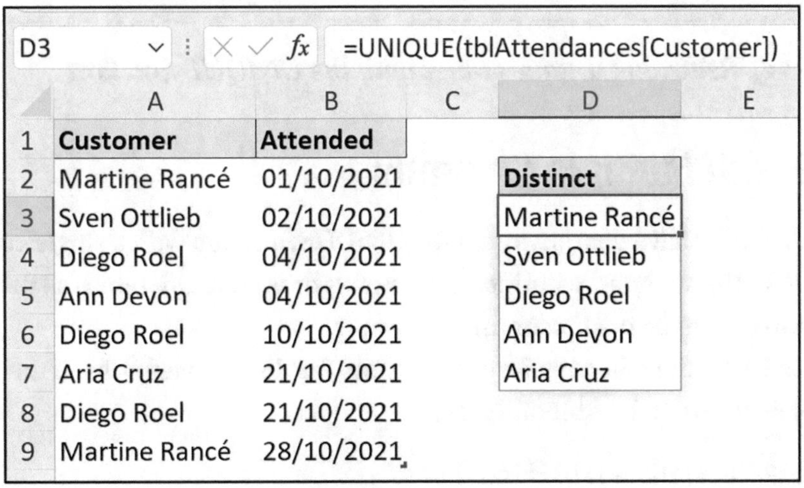

Figure 10-13. *Distinct list of values returned by UNIQUE*

In Figure 10-14, the following formula returns the unique names from the [Customer] column. The second argument is ignored, and TRUE is entered for the *exactly once* argument. There are three names that occur exactly once.

```
=UNIQUE(tblAttendances[Customer],,TRUE)
```

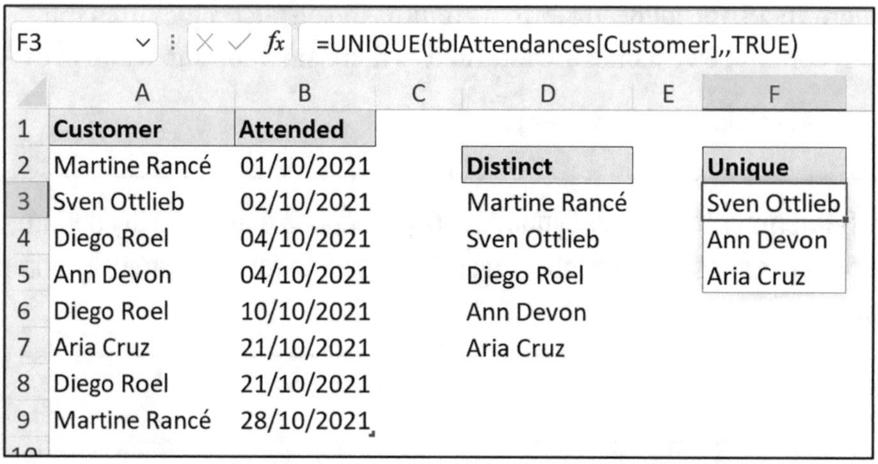

Figure 10-14. *Returning unique values with the UNIQUE function*

UNIQUE with Multiple Columns

The examples so far have demonstrated the UNIQUE function with a single column. However, UNIQUE can handle multicolumn arrays or even entire tables as the array from which to return the distinct or unique results.

In Figure 10-15, the following formula returns the distinct values from the [Name] and [Office] columns of the [tblPoints] table:

```
=UNIQUE(tblPoints[[Name]:[Office]])
```

The results show that an "Elizabeth Brown" has been returned twice. This is because the offices are different (London and York), so they must be two distinct Elizabeth Browns. However, there is a duplicate of "Maria Larsson" in [tblPoints], so only the first of those records was returned.

E2	⌄	:	×	✓	*fx*	=UNIQUE(tblPoints[[Name]:[Office]])

	A	B	C	D	E	F
1	**Name**	**Office**	**Points**		**Distinct Names**	**Office**
2	Elizabeth Brown	London	89		Elizabeth Brown	London
3	Sven Ottlieb	Belfast	63		Sven Ottlieb	Belfast
4	Maria Larsson	London	64		Maria Larsson	London
5	Ann Devon	London	82		Ann Devon	London
6	Roland Mendel	Belfast	95		Roland Mendel	Belfast
7	Aria Cruz	London	71		Aria Cruz	London
8	Diego Roel	York	72		Diego Roel	York
9	Elizabeth Brown	York	95		Elizabeth Brown	York
10	Maria Larsson	London	97			
11						

Figure 10-15. *UNIQUE function using a multiple column array*

In this multiple column array example, the columns were adjacent. In fact, the formula used the range `tblPoints[[Name]:[Office]]`.

Let's see how the UNIQUE function can be used with a multiple column array where the columns are non-adjacent.

In Figure 10-16, the following formula returns the distinct values from the [Name] and [Office] columns again, but in the [tblPoints2] table, they are separated by the [Points] column. The CHOOSE function (covered in Chapter 11) is used to supply UNIQUE with the [Name] and [Office] columns only.

```
=UNIQUE(
CHOOSE({1,2},tblPoints2[Name],tblPoints2[Office])
)
```

This is a technique that can be used to choose which columns you want to extract from any table or array. The CHOOSE function is given the array of constants {1,2}. It is then told to return the [Name] column as column 1 and the [Office] column as column 2. This is passed to UNIQUE to work with.

E2	⌄	⋮ ✕ ✓ *fx*	=UNIQUE(
			CHOOSE({1,2},tblPoints2[Name],tblPoints2[Office])
			)

	A	B	C	D	E	F	G
1	**Name**	**Points**	**Office**		**Distinct Names**	**Office**	
2	Elizabeth Brown	89	London		Elizabeth Brown	London	
3	Sven Ottlieb	63	Belfast		Sven Ottlieb	Belfast	
4	Maria Larsson	64	London		Maria Larsson	London	
5	Ann Devon	82	London		Ann Devon	London	
6	Roland Mendel	95	Belfast		Roland Mendel	Belfast	
7	Aria Cruz	71	London		Aria Cruz	London	
8	Diego Roel	72	York		Diego Roel	York	
9	Elizabeth Brown	95	York		Elizabeth Brown	York	
10	Maria Larsson	97	London				
11							

Figure 10-16. *Returning non-adjacent columns with UNIQUE*

You can also specify the order that the columns should be returned. We could have returned the [Office] column to the left of the [Name] column by using the following formula:

```
=UNIQUE(
CHOOSE({1,2},tblPoints2[Office],tblPoints2[Name])
)
```

UNIQUE to Compare Columns

The UNIQUE function compares the values in rows by default. This is the more common practice as we handle columnar data usually.

It is no problem for UNIQUE to work with data stored in rows though, if required. The second argument of the UNIQUE function allows us to switch to comparing values in columns. This is done by entering TRUE for the second argument named *By col.*

In Figure 10-17, the following formula returns the distinct values from range B4:G4:

```
=UNIQUE(B4:G4,TRUE)
```

B2		⌄	:	✕ ✓	*fx*	=UNIQUE(B4:G4,TRUE)		

	A	B	C	D	E	F	G
1							
2		Bristol	Cambridge	Preston			
3							
4		Bristol	Bristol	Cambridge	Cambridge	Preston	Preston
5		Sales	Upsells	Sales	Upsells	Sales	Upsells
6	Fortune	814	71	860	180	581	53
7	Wings	486	178	621	240	619	82
8	Nirvana	676	193	302	231	556	120
9	Mano	422	219	867	173	512	83
10	Halo	442	129	454	145	754	192

Figure 10-17. *UNIQUE function comparing columns*

The results are returned along a row. The TRANSPOSE function could be used to convert the results into a column. This example is shown when we cover TRANSPOSE later in the chapter.

Distinct Labels for SUMIFS

We covered an example earlier in the chapter that used the AVERAGEIFS function on a range of criteria values. This generated a spill range with the results for each criterion in that range (Figure 10-8).

That example was a static report as the criteria values were simply typed into the cells. Let's explore a dynamic solution where the UNIQUE function will return the distinct values from a table. A SUMIFS function will then use the spill range generated by UNIQUE for its criteria values.

Figure 10-18 shows the first few rows of a table named [tblSales] that we will use for this example. Our goal is to create a small report showing the sum of the [Total] column for each product in the [Product Name] column.

A	B	C	D	E	F
ID	Date	Product Name	Store	Units Sold	Total
19775	11/01/2021	Coffee	North	39	59.06
19776	12/01/2021	Hot Chocolate	West	16	424.80
19777	24/01/2021	Wine	North	25	207.30
19778	25/01/2021	Water	West	35	436.53
19779	30/01/2021	Coffee	South	38	424.30
19780	01/02/2021	Tea	North	10	174.45
19781	03/02/2021	Tea	North	30	456.55

Figure 10-18. *Table of sales data*

In Figure 10-19, the summary report is created. The following UNIQUE formula has been used in cell B3 to generate the distinct values from the [Product Name] column of [tblSales]:

```
=UNIQUE(tblSales[Product Name])
```

The following SUMIFS function is entered in cell C3 to sum the [Total] column for each of the product names in the spill range of cell B3:

```
=SUMIFS(tblSales[Total],tblSales[Product Name],B3#)
```

This report is completely dynamic. If new rows are added to the [tblSales] table, the report will update. And if new product names are added, the report will automatically expand with the new product and its total.

✓ ⋮ ✕ ✓ *fx*	=UNIQUE(tblSales[Product Name])			
B		C	D	E
Product Name		**Total**		
Coffee		3,534.98		
Hot Chocolate		1,497.65		
Wine		1,934.52		
Water		1,656.23		
Tea		2,469.09		
Beer		1,778.81		
Orange Juice		1,098.91		

Figure 10-19. *Table showing sales by product using UNIQUE and SUMIFS*

Distinct Count Formula

The examples so far have all returned values to the grid. The UNIQUE function can, of course, also be nested within other functions. A natural example of this would be to count the number of distinct values returned.

In Chapter 9, we created a distinct count formula using SUMPRODUCT and COUNTIFS. With dynamic arrays and the UNIQUE function, this is much simpler.

In Figure 10-20, the following formula is entered in cell D7. It uses the UNIQUE function with COUNTA to count the distinct values only. In this example, that returns the number of different webinars that occurred.

```
=COUNTA(UNIQUE(tblWebinars[Webinar]))
```

The following formula is entered in cell E7 to return the number of webinars that only occurred once in the table. The result is two, the "Pro Formatting in Excel" and the "Power BI for Beginners" webinars.

```
=COUNTA(UNIQUE(tblWebinars[Webinar],,TRUE))
```

D7	∨ : × ✓ fx	=COUNTA(UNIQUE(tblWebinars[Webinar]))		
	A	B	C	D	E
1	Date	Webinar			
2	04/10/2021	PivotTables		Count	
3	06/10/2021	Excel Formulas Advanced		9	
4	07/10/2021	PivotTables			
5	08/10/2021	Pro Formatting in Excel		Count	Count
6	09/10/2021	Excel Formulas Advanced		Distinct	Unique
7	10/10/2021	Power BI for Beginners		5	2
8	11/10/2021	PivotTables			
9	11/10/2021	Excel Formulas Basics			
10	15/10/2021	Excel Formulas Basics			
11					

Figure 10-20. *Count distinct and count unique formulas*

SORT Function

Availability: Excel for Microsoft 365, Excel for the Web, Excel 2021, Excel for Microsoft 365 for Mac, Excel 2021 for Mac

---

File   sort.xlsx

Sorting the data in a table is one of the most common everyday tasks that an Excel user performs. The introduction of the SORT function to automate the sorting of the data is a revelation for how we create in Excel.

In the past, PivotTables, VBA, or an overly complex formula would be used to automate the sorting of data in Excel reports and models. With the SORT function, this is now very easy to do.

This is the syntax of the SORT function:

```
=SORT(array, [sort_index], [sort_order], [by_col])
```

- **Array:** The range or array of data that you want to sort and return.

- **[Sort index]:** An index number that represents the column or row of the array to sort by. If omitted, the first column or row of the array is used.

- **[Sort order]:** The order that the column or row should be sorted. Enter 1 to sort in ascending order and –1 to sort in descending order. If omitted, it will sort in ascending order.

- **[By col]:** A logical value that specifies whether to sort by row or by column. The default value is FALSE, which sorts by row (vertical sort). Enter TRUE to sort by column (horizontal sort).

Simple SORT Example

Let's start with a simple example of the SORT function being used to sort a single column of data.

In Figure 10-21, the following formula sorts the list of country names in ascending order.

As the table is a single column of data, there is no need to specify a column to sort by (*sort index*). The SORT function also defaults to sorting in an ascending order, which is what we want. So, no other arguments outside of the array to sort are given in this example. Very simple!

```
=SORT(tblCountries[Name])
```

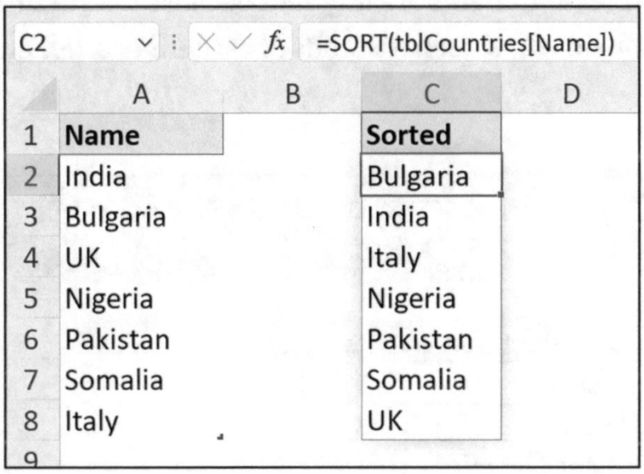

Figure 10-21. Simple example of the SORT function

Sort the Distinct Values

When discussing the UNIQUE function previously, we created a small report showing the total sales by product from data in [tblSales] (Figure 10-18). This report is shown in Figure 10-22.

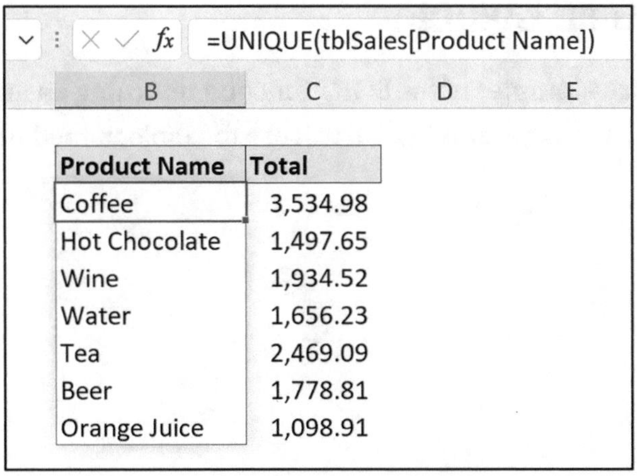

Figure 10-22. Total sales by product in no particular order

The results in this report are in no particular order. They actually appear in the order that UNIQUE finds them in [tblSales]. This is not useful. Let's use the SORT function to sort the distinct list of product names in ascending order.

In Figure 10-23, the SORT function is added to sort the values returned by UNIQUE.

```
=SORT(UNIQUE(tblSales[Product Name]))
```

Once again, no other arguments are required because we are sorting a single column, and we require the argument defaults of ascending order and sort by row (vertical sort).

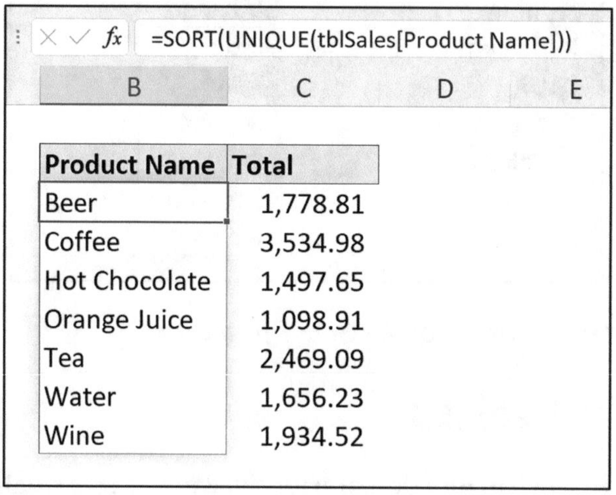

Product Name	Total
Beer	1,778.81
Coffee	3,534.98
Hot Chocolate	1,497.65
Orange Juice	1,098.91
Tea	2,469.09
Water	1,656.23
Wine	1,934.52

fx =SORT(UNIQUE(tblSales[Product Name]))

Figure 10-23. *Sorting the values returned by UNIQUE*

Sort by Specified Column

Let's move on and see examples of the SORT function returning an array with multiple columns. For these examples, we will use the table named [tblProductSales] (Figure 10-24).

	A	B	C	D
1	**Product Name**	**Category**	**Units**	**Total**
2	Orange Juice	Beverages	80	87.95
3	Coffee	Beverages	47	51.75
4	Beer	Beverages	41	43.61
5	Wine	Beverages	77	82.31
6	Sandwich	Food	60	116.51
7	Samosa	Food	81	192.86
8	Baguette	Food	35	162.59
9	Soup	Food	80	222.12
10	Blueberry Muffin	Cakes	14	54.90
11	Flapjack	Cakes	42	72.26
12	Shortbread	Cakes	48	32.12
13				

Figure 10-24. *Table of product sales*

For our first example in Figure 10-25, the following formula is using the entire [tblProductSales] table for its array. None of the optional arguments are specified, so the SORT function has applied an ascending sort to the first column in the array.

=SORT(tblProductSales)

So, in this example, the results are in ascending order by the product name.

⌄ ⋮ ✕ ✓ *fx*	=SORT(tblProductSales)				
B		C	D	E	F
Product Name		**Category**	**Units**	**Total**	
Baguette		Food	35	162.59	
Beer		Beverages	41	43.61	
Blueberry Muffin		Cakes	14	54.90	
Coffee		Beverages	47	51.75	
Flapjack		Cakes	42	72.26	
Orange Juice		Beverages	80	87.95	
Samosa		Food	81	192.86	
Sandwich		Food	60	116.51	
Shortbread		Cakes	48	32.12	
Soup		Food	80	222.12	
Wine		Beverages	77	82.31	

Figure 10-25. *SORT function returning a multiple column array*

Let's specify a different column for the results to be sorted by. We want the results to be in a descending order by the [Total] column.

We need to provide the SORT function with the *sort index*. So, for the [Total] column, this will be column 4.

In Figure 10-26, the following SORT formula has been used. –1 has been entered for the *sort order* to sort the values in a descending order.

```
=SORT(tblProductSales,4,-1)
```

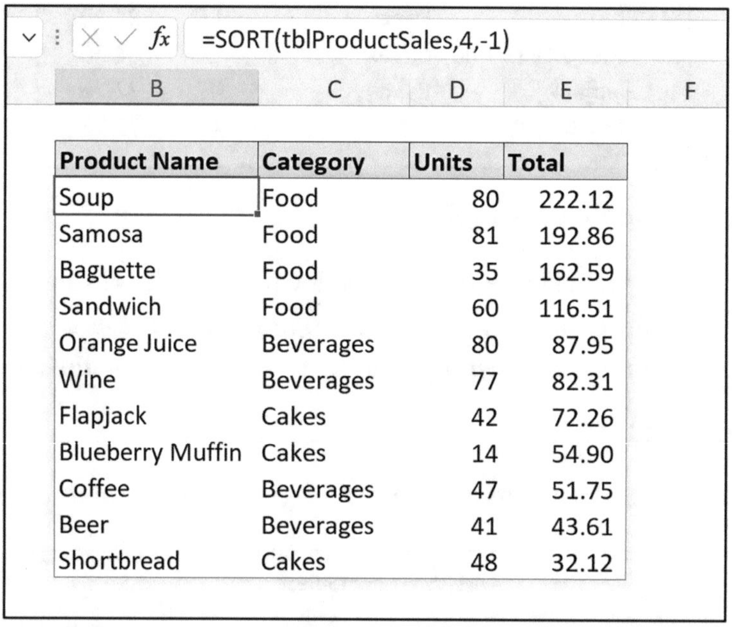

Product Name	Category	Units	Total
Soup	Food	80	222.12
Samosa	Food	81	192.86
Baguette	Food	35	162.59
Sandwich	Food	60	116.51
Orange Juice	Beverages	80	87.95
Wine	Beverages	77	82.31
Flapjack	Cakes	42	72.26
Blueberry Muffin	Cakes	14	54.90
Coffee	Beverages	47	51.75
Beer	Beverages	41	43.61
Shortbread	Cakes	48	32.12

fx =SORT(tblProductSales,4,-1)

Figure 10-26. *SORT results by column 4 in descending order*

Sort by Multiple Columns

It is possible to request the SORT function to sort using multiple columns. To do this, we will enter the multiple sort indexes and sort orders within arrays.

For this example, we will sort the [tblProductSales] data by two levels: first by the [Category] column in ascending order and then by the [Total] column in descending order.

In Figure 10-27, the following SORT formula is entered in cell B3:

```
=SORT(tblProductSales,{2,4},{1,-1})
```

The array {2,4} is used in the *sort index* argument to specify that the data should be sorted by column 2 and then by column 4.

The array {1,-1} is used in the *sort order* argument to state that column 2 should be sorted in an ascending order and column 4 should be sorted in a descending order.

This formula could be extended to sort by more columns if required.

	=SORT(tblProductSales,{2,4},{1,-1})				
A	B	C	D	E	F
	Product Name	**Category**	**Units**	**Total**	
	Orange Juice	Beverages	80	87.95	
	Wine	Beverages	77	82.31	
	Coffee	Beverages	47	51.75	
	Beer	Beverages	41	43.61	
	Flapjack	Cakes	42	72.26	
	Blueberry Muffin	Cakes	14	54.90	
	Shortbread	Cakes	48	32.12	
	Soup	Food	80	222.12	
	Samosa	Food	81	192.86	
	Baguette	Food	35	162.59	
	Sandwich	Food	60	116.51	

Figure 10-27. *Sorting an array by multiple columns with SORT*

SORT Function Returning Specific Columns from a Table

For the final SORT function example, we will return specific columns from [tblProductSales].

Dynamic array functions in isolation can only return columns that are adjacent to each other. In this example, we will return the [Product Name], [Units], and [Total] columns only.

These columns are split by the [Category] column in the table, so SORT will need some assistance to work with these columns as they are non-adjacent.

To do this, we will nest the CHOOSE function within the SORT function to specify the columns to work with. We saw the CHOOSE function assuming this role previously in this chapter within the UNIQUE function.

Note   In Chapter 11, we will see the INDEX and MATCH functions together
to create a more dynamic method for returning non-adjacent columns in
dynamic arrays.

In Figure 10-28, the following SORT formula returns the three required columns and
sorts the data in descending order by the [Total] column. Column 3 is specified as the
sort index as the [Total] column is the third column of the array returned by CHOOSE.

```
=SORT(
CHOOSE({1,2,3},
tblProductSales[Product Name],tblProductSales[Units],tblProductSale
s[Total]),
3,-1)
```

B	C	D	E	F	G
Product Name	**Units**	**Total**			
Soup	80	222.12			
Samosa	81	192.86			
Baguette	35	162.59			
Sandwich	60	116.51			
Orange Juice	80	87.95			
Wine	77	82.31			
Flapjack	42	72.26			
Blueberry Muffin	14	54.9			
Coffee	47	51.75			
Beer	41	43.61			
Shortbread	48	32.12			

Figure 10-28. *SORT function returning specific columns from a table*

When returning only three columns, this works quite well and is simple to deploy. In more complex examples, this CHOOSE technique can be bulky, and a more advanced technique would involve the INDEX function. We will see examples of this technique in Chapters 11 and 13 of the book.

Note   No examples are shown in this chapter of sorting data by column (sorting horizontally) due to the rarity of this behavior. Excel data is better in a columnar layout. However, TRUE can be entered for the *By col* argument to sort horizontally. An example of the *By col* argument was shown with the UNIQUE function previously.

SORTBY Function

Availability: Excel for Microsoft 365, Excel for the Web, Excel 2021, Excel for Microsoft 365 for Mac, Excel 2021 for Mac

---

File   sortby.xlsx

If the SORT function is not enough for you, Microsoft also gave us SORTBY. There are benefits for using each of these two sort functions.

The SORT function is perfect for very simple single column sorting. It is also better for sorting based on dynamic columns, as the columns are specified using index numbers.

The SORTBY function has two key advantages over SORT:

- The column to sort by is specified using the range or array. This absolute reference to the column to sort by makes it fantastic for use with table data.

- With the SORTBY function, you can sort an array by a column that is outside of the array being returned.

This is the syntax for the SORTBY function:

```
=SORTBY(array, by_array1, [sort_order1], [by_array2], [sort_order2])
```

- **Array:** The range or array of data that you want to sort and return.

- **By array1:** The range or array to sort by. The array must be one column wide or one row high.

- **[Sort order1]:** The order that the column or row should be sorted. Enter 1 to sort in ascending order and –1 to sort in descending order. If omitted, it will sort in ascending order.

- **[By array2], [sort order2]:** The corresponding arrays to sort by and sort orders for any additional sort levels you require.

Note   The SORTBY function can sort data that is arranged in rows or columns. It does not have a special argument for this functionality like UNIQUE and SORT do. SORTBY will automatically understand the direction of the sort and spill range.

The following examples of the SORTBY function will use the table shown in Figure 10-29 named [tblProductSales].

	A	B	C	D
1	**Product Name**	**Category**	**Units**	**Total**
2	Orange Juice	Beverages	80	87.95
3	Coffee	Beverages	47	51.75
4	Beer	Beverages	41	43.61
5	Wine	Beverages	77	82.31
6	Sandwich	Food	60	116.51
7	Samosa	Food	81	192.86
8	Baguette	Food	35	162.59
9	Soup	Food	80	222.12
10	Blueberry Muffin	Cakes	14	54.90
11	Flapjack	Cakes	42	72.26
12	Shortbread	Cakes	48	32.12
13				

Figure 10-29. *Table of product sales*

Simple SORTBY Example

Let's begin with a simple example that returns all columns from the [tblProductSales] table sorted in descending order by the [Total] column.

In Figure 10-30, the following formula is entered in cell B3. This SORTBY formula is more meaningful than its SORT equivalent (Figure 10-26) as it uses the structured reference of tblProductSales[Total] instead of the *sort index* of 4. The –1 specifies the descending order.

```
=SORTBY(tblProductSales,tblProductSales[Total],-1)
```

Product Name	Category	Units	Total
Soup	Food	80	222.12
Samosa	Food	81	192.86
Baguette	Food	35	162.59
Sandwich	Food	60	116.51
Orange Juice	Beverages	80	87.95
Wine	Beverages	77	82.31
Flapjack	Cakes	42	72.26
Blueberry Muffin	Cakes	14	54.90
Coffee	Beverages	47	51.75
Beer	Beverages	41	43.61
Shortbread	Cakes	48	32.12

Figure 10-30.   Simple SORTBY example sorting the array by the [Total] column

Sort by Multiple Columns with SORTBY

The SORTBY function can sort an array by multiple columns, and, once again, it is an easier task than the equivalent formula with the SORT function (Figure 10-27).

SORTBY has arguments for us to keep specifying the additional columns and sort orders that we want to apply.

In Figure 10-31, the following formula sorts the data from the [tblProductSales] table by [Category] in ascending order and then by [Total] in descending order:

```
=SORTBY(tblProductSales,
tblProductSales[Category],1,tblProductSales[Total],-1)
```

A 1 is entered in the *sort order 1* argument to specify ascending order for the [Category] column. This could have been omitted, and the formula would have worked fine, as ascending order is the default. However, it is a more meaningful formula, I believe, when this sort order is stated.

⋮ ✕ ✓ *fx*	=SORTBY(tblProductSales,			
	tblProductSales[Category],1,tblProductSales[Total],-1)			

	B	C	D	E	F
	Product Name	**Category**	**Units**	**Total**	
	Orange Juice	Beverages	80	87.95	
	Wine	Beverages	77	82.31	
	Coffee	Beverages	47	51.75	
	Beer	Beverages	41	43.61	
	Flapjack	Cakes	42	72.26	
	Blueberry Muffin	Cakes	14	54.90	
	Shortbread	Cakes	48	32.12	
	Soup	Food	80	222.12	
	Samosa	Food	81	192.86	
	Baguette	Food	35	162.59	
	Sandwich	Food	60	116.51	

Figure 10-31. Sort by multiple columns with SORTBY

Sort by Column Outside of the Returned Array

A great advantage that the SORTBY function has over SORT is the ability to sort an array using a column, or row, that is not included in the returned array.

In Figure 10-32, the [Product Name] and [Total] columns are returned with some help from the CHOOSE function. This array has been sorted in a descending order by the [Units] column, which is not included in the returned array. Pretty cool!

```
=SORTBY(
CHOOSE({1,2},tblProductSales[Product Name],tblProductSales[Total]),
tblProductSales[Units],-1)
```

_fx_ =SORTBY(
CHOOSE({1,2},tblProductSales[Product Name],tblProductSales[Total]),
tblProductSales[Units],-1)

Product Name	Total
Samosa	192.86
Orange Juice	87.95
Soup	222.12
Wine	82.31
Sandwich	116.51
Shortbread	32.12
Coffee	51.75
Flapjack	72.26
Beer	43.61
Baguette	162.59
Blueberry Muffin	54.9

Figure 10-32. *SORTBY sorting by a column not included in the returned array*

This can be a very useful technique. Let's see another example.

Sort Product Name by Sales Totals

Let's return to the sales by product report that we have used in a few examples of this chapter so far. Figure 10-33 shows this report with the total sales by product and the results in an ascending order by the product name.

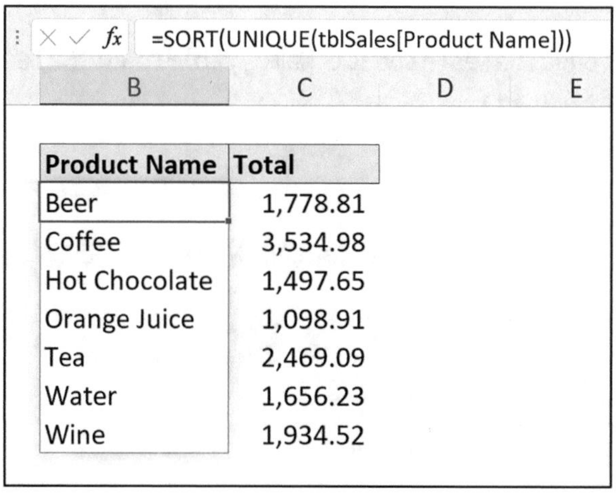

Product Name	Total
Beer	1,778.81
Coffee	3,534.98
Hot Chocolate	1,497.65
Orange Juice	1,098.91
Tea	2,469.09
Water	1,656.23
Wine	1,934.52

Formula bar: `=SORT(UNIQUE(tblSales[Product Name]))`

Figure 10-33. *Sales by product sorted by the product name*

We will change this to sort the results by the total sales in a descending order. It will be more practical to order the products by the sales total rather than their name. And it's a great example of how useful SORTBY is.

We will start by using the SORTBY function to sort the product names by the sales totals. The SUMIFS function will be used to sum the [Total] column for each product. With the product names ordered correctly, the SUMIFS function will then be used again to create the column of total sales values.

In Figure 10-34, the following formula sorts the distinct list of product names returned by UNIQUE in a descending order by the totals returned by SUMIFS:

```
=SORTBY(UNIQUE(tblSales[Product Name]),
SUMIFS(tblSales[Total],tblSales[Product Name],UNIQUE(tblSales[Product
Name])),
-1)
```

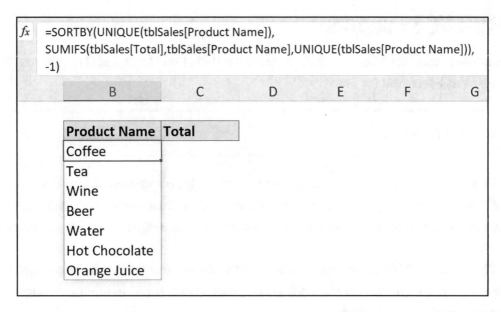

Figure 10-34. *Sort product names by sales totals in descending order*

This is another nice example of using SORTBY to sort by an array outside of the one being ordered. We now need to return the totals.

In Figure 10-35, the following formula uses the SUMIFS function to sum the values in the [Total] column for each product in the spill range B3#:

```
=SUMIFS(tblSales[Total],tblSales[Product Name],B3#)
```

We will use these spill ranges in a bar chart later in this chapter. This dynamic sorting by sales totals will ensure that our bar chart orders the bars from largest to smallest.

Product Name	Total
Coffee	3,534.98
Tea	2,469.09
Wine	1,934.52
Beer	1,778.81
Water	1,656.23
Hot Chocolate	1,497.65
Orange Juice	1,098.91

fx =SUMIFS(tblSales[Total],tblSales[Product Name],B3#)

Figure 10-35. *SUMIFS to sum the totals for each product*

SEQUENCE Function

Availability: Excel for Microsoft 365, Excel for the Web, Excel 2021, Excel for Microsoft 365 for Mac, Excel 2021 for Mac

---

File   sequence.xlsx

The first time that you see it, it may not immediately be apparent how brilliant the SEQUENCE function is. Certainly not in the way that functions such as SORT and UNIQUE will instantly earn your affection. But believe me, SEQUENCE is an awesome function.

The SEQUENCE function returns a series of numbers. It is the formula equivalent of the Fill Series feature in Excel. As a function, we can nest it within other functions to create some real formula magic.

It accepts four arguments, but only the first argument (rows) is required:

```
=SEQUENCE(rows, [columns], [start], [step])
```

- **Rows:** The number of rows to return.

- **[Columns]:** The number of columns to return.

- **[Start]:** The first number in the sequence. If omitted, the sequence begins from one.

- **[step]:** The amount to increment each subsequent value in the sequence. If omitted, it will step one at a time.

Stepping into the SEQUENCE Function

Let's start with some basic examples to get a feel for how to operate the SEQUENCE function. This will prepare us for the more practical examples to come in this chapter and the next.

In Figure 10-36, a simple SEQUENCE function is entered in cell B2 to generate a series of numbers from one to eight. Only the *rows* argument is entered. A *start* and *step* value of one is used as these arguments were omitted.

```
=SEQUENCE(8)
```

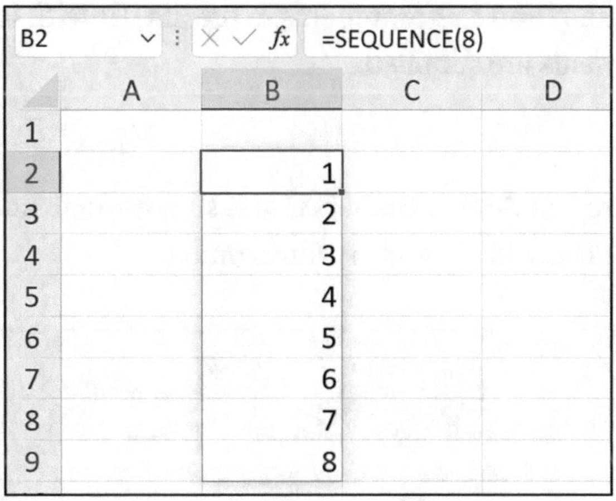

Figure 10-36. *Number series across rows with SEQUENCE*

In Figure 10-37, the columns argument is included in the SEQUENCE function. The formula generates a series of numbers starting from one that is eight rows high and three columns wide.

=SEQUENCE(8,3)

The order of the number sequence goes row by row. Shortly, we will see how this order can be changed to column by column.

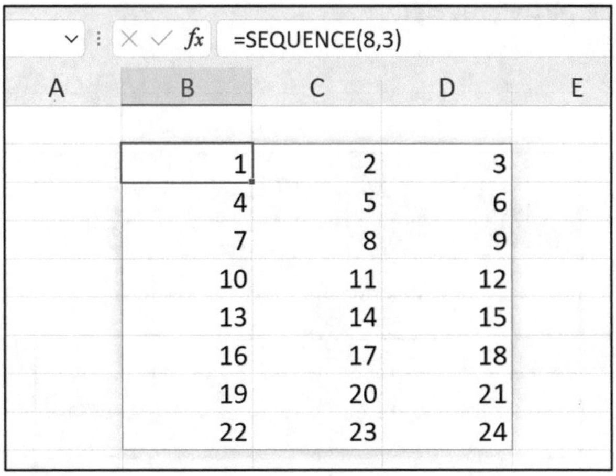

Figure 10-37. *Using the rows and columns arguments of SEQUENCE*

Let's now add the *start* and *step* arguments to the SEQUENCE function. In Figure 10-38, all arguments are supplied.

=SEQUENCE(6,4,5,5)

The formula returns a series of numbers that is six rows high and four columns wide. It begins from number five and steps every fifth number.

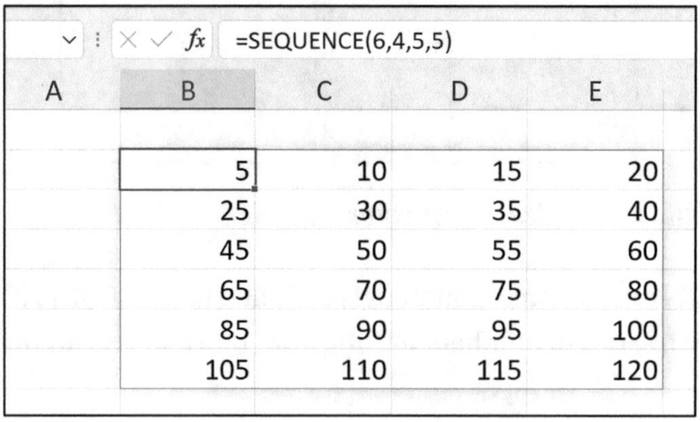

	fx	=SEQUENCE(6,4,5,5)		
A	B	C	D	E
	5	10	15	20
	25	30	35	40
	45	50	55	60
	65	70	75	80
	85	90	95	100
	105	110	115	120

Figure 10-38. *SEQUENCE function with all arguments specified*

A negative step can be used to reverse the sequence of values returned. In Figure 10-39, the following SEQUENCE function returns a series that is five rows high, starts from five, and steps negatively:

=SEQUENCE(5,,5,-1)

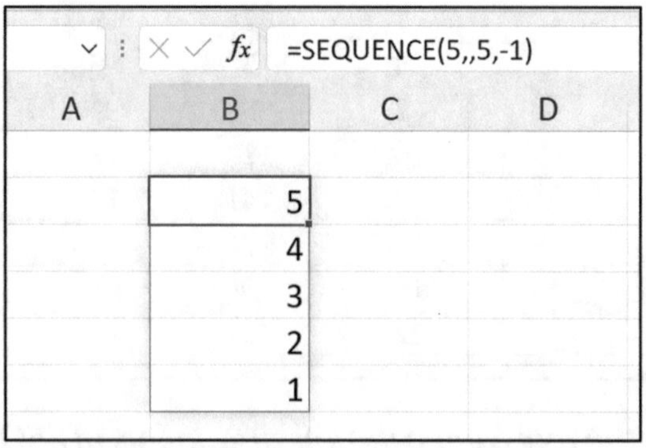

	fx	=SEQUENCE(5,,5,-1)	
A	B	C	D
	5		
	4		
	3		
	2		
	1		

Figure 10-39. *Reversing a sequence with a negative step*

In this example, the *columns* argument is skipped. The default one column wide is used.

Changing the Row/Column Order

When returning a two-dimensional array, we saw that the numbering of the series goes across columns, before going to the next row (Figure 10-38).

To switch the ordering of the numbers in the series, the TRANSPOSE function could be wrapped around SEQUENCE.

In Figure 10-40, the following formula switches the direction of the series of the formula shown in Figure 10-38 to down across rows before moving to the next column:

=TRANSPOSE(SEQUENCE(4,6,5,5)

The TRANSPOSE function has been added, and the number of *rows* and *columns* has been reversed. SEQUENCE returns an array of four rows and six columns, and this is transposed. Awesome!

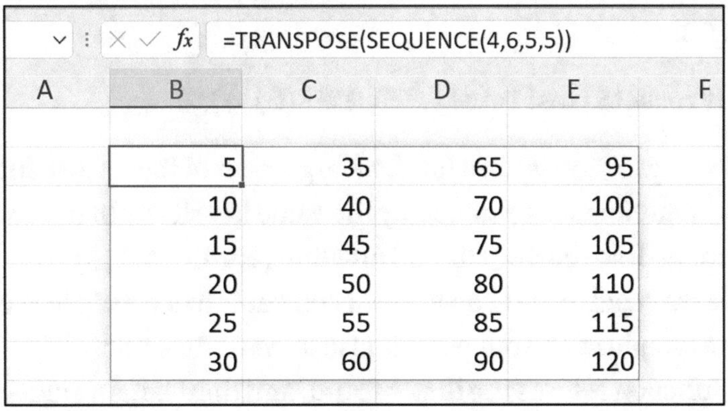

	✓ ⋮ ✕ ✓ *fx* =TRANSPOSE(SEQUENCE(4,6,5,5))				
A	B	C	D	E	F
	5	35	65	95	
	10	40	70	100	
	15	45	75	105	
	20	50	80	110	
	25	55	85	115	
	30	60	90	120	

Figure 10-40. *Changing the row/column order with TRANSPOSE*

Let's see some examples now that really showcase the flexibility and potential of the SEQUENCE function.

Sum the Top N Values

Performing a calculation on the top N values is a common task for reporting in Excel. For this example, we will sum the top N values, but a calculation such as average could also be applied.

We saw a method to sum the top five values in Chapter 9 with the SUMPRODUCT function. This was great as it works for all versions of Excel.

If you have a dynamic array–enabled version of Excel though, there is a better way. It is simpler and more dynamic. And of course, SEQUENCE plays an important role.

The LARGE function will also be used in our formula. This function has been covered already in this book, but let's briefly remind ourselves of the purpose and syntax of the LARGE function.

The LARGE function returns the kth largest value in a range, for example, the second, third, or fifth largest value. Here is its syntax:

`=LARGE(array, k)`

- **Array:** The range, table column, or array from which to return the kth largest value

- **K:** The position of the value in the array (from the largest) that you want to return

In Figure 10-41, the following formula sums the top N values where N is specified by the value in cell D3:

`=SUM(LARGE(tblProductSales[Total],SEQUENCE(D3)))`

The SEQUENCE function is used for the *K* argument of the LARGE function. It returns an array of numbers determined by the value in cell D3. In this example, cell D3 contains the number 3, so the SEQUENCE function returns {1,2,3}.

This replaces the need to enter an array of constants like we did in the SUMPRODUCT example in Chapter 9. This also keeps it dynamic.

The LARGE function returns the first, second, and third largest values from the [Total] column, and these are summed by SUM.

	A	B	C	D	E	F
	E3	⌄ : ✕ ✓ *fx*	=SUM(LARGE(tblProductSales[Total],SEQUENCE(D3)))			
1	**Product Name**	**Total**				
2	Orange Juice	87.95		**Top**	**Total**	
3	Coffee	148.59		3	563.57	
4	Beer	43.61				
5	Wine	82.31				
6	Sandwich	116.51				
7	Samosa	192.86				
8	Baguette	72.26				
9	Soup	222.12				
10	Shortbread	32.12				
11						

Figure 10-41. Summing the top N values

Sum the Last N Days

The SEQUENCE function is great for creating a series of dates that occur at specific intervals. The activity on these dates can then be analyzed with other formulas or charted.

For this example, we will use the SEQUENCE function to return the last N days. We will find the last date in a range and then return each date for the last N days. The number of days will be specified by a cell value.

Figure 10-42 shows the first few rows of a table named [tblSales]. This table will be used as the data source for the next two examples. It contains sales data with daily transactions. The table has been sorted by [Sales Rep] to show the different dates in the [Date] column.

	A	B	C	D	E	
1	**Date** ⌄	**Sales Rep** ⌄↑	**Region** ⌄	**Category** ⌄	**Sales**	⌄
2	18/03/2021	Benjamen Strathe	Australia	Fruit	£ 19.01	
3	19/03/2021	Benjamen Strathe	Australia	Sweets and chocolate	£ 152.97	
4	23/03/2021	Benjamen Strathe	Australia	Fruit juice	£ 172.70	
5	26/03/2021	Benjamen Strathe	Australia	Fruit	£ 111.85	
6	27/03/2021	Benjamen Strathe	Australia	Meat and proteins	£ 32.73	
7	29/03/2021	Benjamen Strathe	Australia	Preserves	£ 61.09	
8	29/03/2021	Benjamen Strathe	Australia	Beverages and drinks	£ 10.36	

Figure 10-42. tblSales data with daily transactions

503

In Figure 10-43, the following formula uses SEQUENCE to return the dates for the number of rows entered in cell C2. The MAX function has been used to return the latest date in the [Date] column. A negative one has been used for the *step* argument to reverse the series of dates and return the last seven dates from the latest date.

```
=SEQUENCE(C2,,MAX(tblSales[Date]),-1)
```

The following SUMIFS function returns the total for each date in the spill range returned by SEQUENCE. You can see the B5# reference for the criteria argument.

```
=SUMIFS(tblSales[Sales],tblSales[Date],B5#)
```

This is a fully dynamic solution.

If new dates are added to [tblSales], the MAX function will pick it up, and SEQUENCE will adjust to the new data. And if a different value is entered into cell C2, the SEQUENCE function will return that number of rows. The SUMIFS function references the spill range, so this will also update.

	fx	=SEQUENCE(C2,,MAX(tblSales[Date]),-1)		
A	B	C	D	E
	No of Days	7		
	Dates	**Total**		
	04/11/2021	958.60		
	03/11/2021	1,484.84		
	02/11/2021	1,724.37		
	01/11/2021	1,383.90		
	31/10/2021	1,414.44		
	30/10/2021	916.55		
	29/10/2021	2,112.52		

Figure 10-43. *SEQUENCE returning a series of dates for analysis*

Sum the Last N Months

Let's expand on this example and get the SEQUENCE function to return the last N months from the last month in the [tblSales] table.

In Figure 10-44, the following formula returns the last seven months from the latest date in the [Date] column. The number of months is specified by the value in cell F2.

```
=DATE(2021,
SEQUENCE(F2,,MONTH(MAX(tblSales[Date]))),-1),
1)
```

The DATE function is used to construct a date value for the results. These values could be formatted to show month names using the custom number formatting feature of Excel. I have not bothered with this in the example, as I'm happy to show the first date of each month.

The MAX function is used again to return the latest date in the [Date] column of [tblSales]. The MONTH function extracts the month number of the latest date.

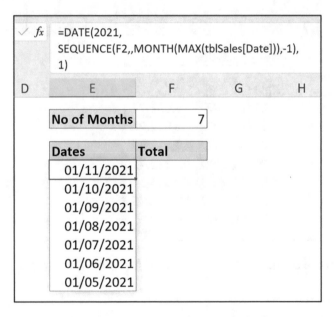

Figure 10-44. *DATE and SEQUENCE functions to return last N months*

In Figure 10-45, the following SUMIFS function totals the values from the [Sales] column that occurred between the first and last day of the month in context:

```
=SUMIFS(tblSales[Sales],
tblSales[Date],">="&E5#,
tblSales[Date],"<="&EOMONTH(+E5#,0)
)
```

The spill range is accessed using E5# for the first date of the month.

The EOMONTH function is used to return the last date of a month a specified number of months in the future or past. A zero is entered for the *months* argument to return the last date of the current month.

You may notice the + sign before the spill reference in the EOMONTH function. The EOMONTH function is one of a few functions in Excel that does not spill. An error is returned if the spill reference E5# is used. A trick to work around this issue is simply to add the + before the spill reference.

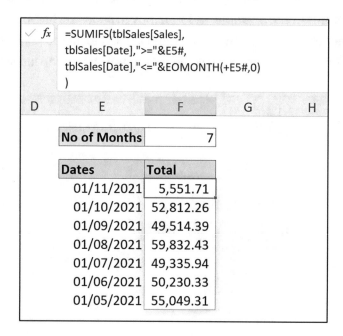

Figure 10-45. *Total values between first and last day of a month*

Note   The DATE and EOMONTH functions were covered in detail in Chapter 6.

Last N Months by Country – Pivot Style Report

The last two examples have used the SEQUENCE function to spill the date values across rows. But, of course, SEQUENCE can spill across columns also. This feature can be used to create awesome pivot style reports with time-based analysis.

In Figure 10-46, the following formula is used in cell C4 to spill the last N months across columns. The number of months spilled is based on the value in cell D2.

```
=DATE(2021,
SEQUENCE(,D2,MONTH(MAX(tblSales[Date]))-D2+1,1),
1)
```

There are some differences in this formula compared to the previous one that spilled across rows.

Notably, the *rows* argument is omitted. The other key difference is that the dates are ordered smallest to largest. In the previous example, they were largest to smallest. To do this, the value in cell D2 was subtracted from the month of the maximum date. This takes us a month too far, so one is added. The SEQUENCE function steps one month at a time from that date.

✓ ✕ ✓ *fx*	=DATE(2021, SEQUENCE(,D2,MONTH(MAX(tblSales[Date]))-D2+1,1), 1)							
B	C	D	E	F	G	H	I
	Months		6					
		01/06/2021	01/07/2021	01/08/2021	01/09/2021	01/10/2021	01/11/2021	
Australia	5,733	5,210	6,832	4,540	7,903	725
Belgium	7,408	3,977	6,335	6,742	6,006	1,003
Canada	5,433	7,717	5,908	5,235	6,048	332
France	4,442	3,618	7,563	6,480	5,021	653
India	5,542	5,714	5,957	4,830	4,963	696
Italy	6,373	5,604	7,134	4,892	5,515	507
Netherlands	4,252	5,694	7,797	6,285	5,983	887
UK	6,080	4,884	6,564	5,563	4,913	374
USA	4,967	6,916	5,743	4,947	6,461	375

Figure 10-46. SEQUENCE for last N months spilled across columns

The following SORT and UNIQUE function combination is used to generate the list of countries:

```
=SORT(UNIQUE(tblSales[Region]))
```

507

The following SUMIFS formula is used to sum the values in the [Sales] column for the country entered in the B5# spill range and month in the C4# spill range. The + is entered before the spill range for the EOMONTH function again to get this function to work with the dynamic array.

```
=SUMIFS(tblSales[Sales],
tblSales[Region],B5#,
tblSales[Date],">="&C4#,
tblSales[Date],"<="&EOMONTH(+C4#,0)
)
```

Sum Values from Alternate Rows/Columns

There are many scenarios in Excel where we can take advantage of the SEQUENCE function and its ability to return a sequence of values. Another of these scenarios is to perform a calculation on the values in every Nth cell. In the first of these examples, we will sum the values in alternate rows.

Figure 10-47 shows the following formula being used to sum the "Income" values only:

```
=SUM(
INDEX(tblAccounts[Amount],
SEQUENCE(ROUNDUP(ROWS(tblAccounts[Amount])/2,0),,,2))
)
```

E3	⌄ ⋮ ✕ ✓ *fx*	=SUM(

```
=SUM(
INDEX(tblAccounts[Amount],
SEQUENCE(ROUNDUP(ROWS(tblAccounts[Amount])/2,0),,,2))
)
```

	A	B	C	D	E	F	G	H
1	**Location**	**Type**	**Amount**					
2	Bristol	Income	4,726		**Total Income**			
3	Bristol	Expenses	1,875		17,734			
4	Derby	Income	4,227					
5	Derby	Expenses	1,924					
6	Liverpool	Income	4,835					
7	Liverpool	Expenses	2,499					
8	Swansea	Income	3,946					
9	Swansea	Expenses	1,539					
10								

Figure 10-47.   Sum alternate rows with SEQUENCE

The SEQUENCE function returns the following array of numbers. These numbers are the row numbers of the table for which we want to sum the values.

{1;3;5;7}

Four numbers are returned, as the ROWS function returns the total number of rows in the table (eight), and this is divided by two as we want every other row, that is, half the rows.

The ROUNDUP function is included in the scenario that we have an odd number of rows. In this example, it is not relevant, as we are dealing with income and expenses, so the total rows will be an even number. However, it has been added for completeness. If there were 9 rows in total, half would produce 4.5 and ROUNDUP would make this 5. The rows {1;3;5;7;9} would be returned in that scenario.

The *columns* and *start* arguments are omitted, and the SEQUENCE function is asked to *step* by two.

The INDEX function is used to return the values from the [Amount] column for each of the rows. It returns the following array for the SUM function:

{4726;4227;4835;3946}

With the SEQUENCE function, the values that we step through can represent rows or columns, and we can specify any Nth value. For a second example, we will return to a task that we completed with the SUMPRODUCT function along with others in Chapter 9.

In Figure 10-48, the following formula is entered in column B and sums the values in every fourth column (the two quarter totals):

```
=SUM(
INDEX(C2:J2,,
SEQUENCE(,COLUMNS(C2:J2)/4,4,4))
)
```

	A	B	C	D	E	F	G	H	I	J
		Total	Jan	Feb	Mar	Qtr 1	Apr	May	Jun	Qtr 2
1	Name	Total	Jan	Feb	Mar	Qtr 1	Apr	May	Jun	Qtr 2
2	David	5,586	425	1,240	651	2,316	930	1,210	1,130	3,270
3	Claire	4,501	1,275	1,072	1,044	3,391	153	417	540	1,110
4	Victoria	2,961	266	354	268	888	161	693	1,219	2,073
5	Sarah	4,714	858	946	198	2,002	849	1,270	593	2,712
6	Fred	4,698	1,201	1,165	194	2,560	381	1,029	728	2,138
7	Michelle	3,090	873	240	311	1,424	485	806	375	1,666

Cell reference B2 with formula bar showing:
```
=SUM(
INDEX(C2:J2,,
SEQUENCE(,COLUMNS(C2:J2)/4,4,4))
)
```

Figure 10-48. Summing the value in every Nth column

This time, the *rows* argument is omitted, and the COLUMNS function is used to return the total columns in the range C2:J2 (eight columns). This value is then divided by four (the number of columns we want to step) to return the result of two columns.

SEQUENCE is then told to *start* from four and *step* every four. The following array is returned:

{4,8}

The INDEX function then returns the values from columns 4 and 8 in the range C2:J2 to be summed. Notice that the *rows* argument of INDEX is omitted.

Note   We will see more of the INDEX and SEQUENCE functions working together when we discuss the INDEX function in detail in Chapter 11.

RANDARRAY Function

Availability: Excel for Microsoft 365, Excel for the Web, Excel 2021, Excel for Microsoft 365 for Mac, Excel 2021 for Mac

---

File   randarray.xlsx

For years, Excel has had two functions that are used to return random values – RAND and RANDBETWEEN. There is now a third musketeer – the RANDARRAY function. This function merges the characteristics of the two existing functions along with further advantages.

RAND and RANDBETWEEN

Availability: All versions

Let's begin with a quick look at the RAND and RANDBETWEEN functions. They are still great to use, and understanding them will help us appreciate the role that RANDARRAY plays.

The RAND function returns a random number between 0 and 1. For example, RAND will generate a number like 0.657233. Its syntax is very simple as it has no arguments:

=RAND()

Figure 10-49 shows the RAND function entered in cell B2 and filled down to cell B6 to return five random numbers between 0 and 1. Five formulas are used here as we are using a non-DA formula. RANDARRAY will be able to achieve this in one formula.

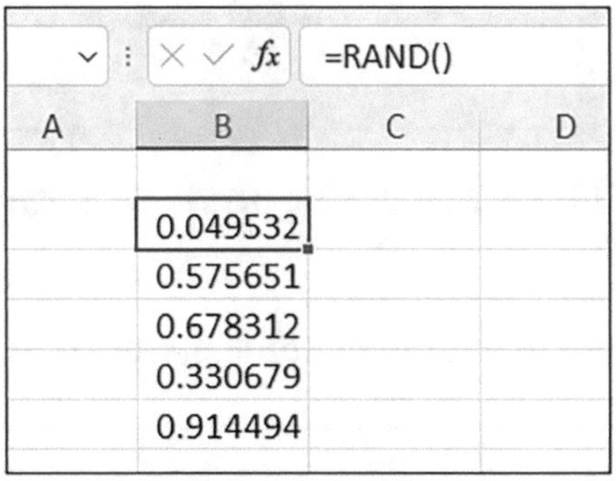

Figure 10-49. *RAND function generating random numbers between 0 and 1*

The RANDBETWEEN function returns a random integer number from within a given range. The bottom and top values of this range are specified by us. The RANDBETWEEN function requires only two arguments:

=RANDBETWEEN(bottom, top)

- **Bottom:** The smallest integer number that RANDBETWEEN can return

- **Top:** The largest integer number that RANDBETWEEN can return

Figure 10-50 shows the RANDBETWEEN function returning random integer numbers between 50 and 250.

=RANDBETWEEN(50,250)

It has been entered in cell B2 and filled down five rows and across three columns to cell D6. There are 15 formulas entered to produce these random values. It is probably no surprise that RANDARRAY can handle this task also with just one formula that spills.

So, the two key differences between RAND and RANDBETWEEN are that RAND returns decimal values while RANDBETWEEN returns integers and that RANDBETWEEN allows us to specify the range of values from which to return.

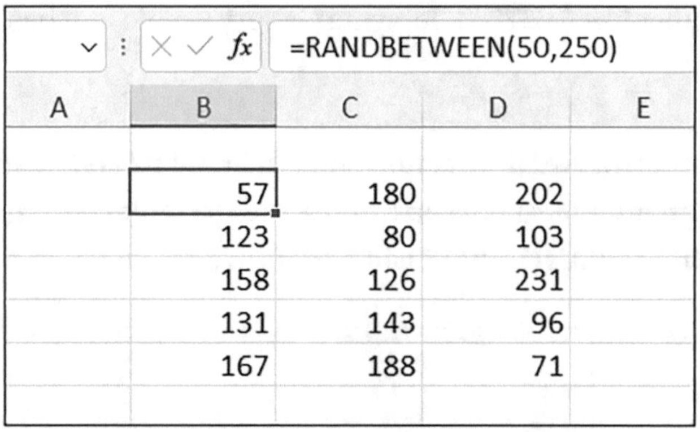

	A	B	C	D	E
			fx =RANDBETWEEN(50,250)		
		57	180	202	
		123	80	103	
		158	126	231	
		131	143	96	
		167	188	71	

Figure 10-50. RANDBETWEEN returning random integer numbers between 50 and 250

Both functions generate a new random number every time the worksheet calculates.

Note   Functions that behave in this manner are known as volatile functions.

Introduction to RANDARRAY

The RANDARRAY function returns an array of random numbers. All the finest qualities of RAND and RANDBETWEEN are included, with the added ability to return a dynamic array that spills.

You can specify the number of rows and columns to spill, whether you want decimal values or integers, and you can specify the bottom and top values from which to return the random number(s).

The syntax of the RANDARRAY function is as follows. Interestingly, all the arguments are optional:

=RANDARRAY([rows], [columns], [min], [max], [integer])

- **[Rows]:** The number of rows to return.

- **[Columns]:** The number of columns to return.

- **[Min]:** The smallest number that the RANDARRAY function can return.

- **[Max]:** The largest number that the RANDARRAY function can return.

- **[Integer]:** Would you like an integer value returned? Type TRUE to return an integer value or FALSE for a decimal value. If omitted, FALSE is applied and decimal values are returned.

Let's look at a few examples that show different applications of these arguments. Then we will see two practical examples of RANDARRAY.

Figure 10-51 shows the RANDARRAY function being used with no arguments. It behaves like the RAND function and returns a random number between 0 and 1 to a single cell. Remember, the default of RANDARRAY is to return a decimal value.

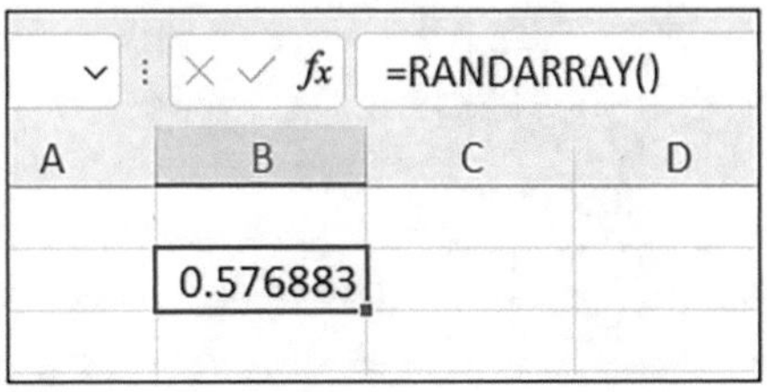

Figure 10-51. *RANDARRAY with no arguments entered*

And in Figure 10-52, the RANDARRAY function returns a random integer number between 5 and 250. It is behaving like RANDBETWEEN in this example.

The *rows* and *columns* arguments have been omitted, and TRUE is specified to return an integer.

```
=RANDARRAY(,,5,250,TRUE)
```

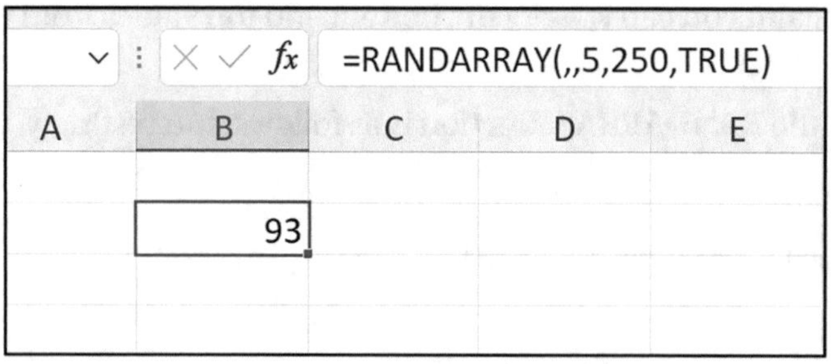

Figure 10-52. *RANDARRAY being applied like RANDBETWEEN*

Now, these examples show us nothing that we could not have achieved with the existing RAND and RANDBETWEEN functions. They are only shown to provide an extensive understanding of using RANDARRAY and to show that the characteristics of both existing random number–generating functions exist within RANDARRAY.

A key advantage of RANDARRAY is clearly its ability to return an array and therefore be used within our dynamic array formulas.

In Figure 10-53, the formula returns five rows of values that are between 1 and 10. The *columns* argument is omitted, so a single column of values is returned. The *integer* argument is also omitted, so RANDARRAY returns decimal values.

```
=RANDARRAY(5,,1,10)
```

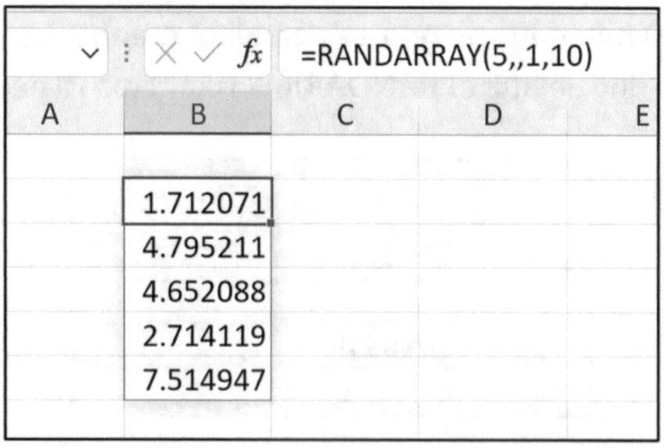

Figure 10-53. *RANDARRAY returning five rows of decimal values between 1 and 10*

This example not only demonstrates an array being returned but also RANDARRAY returning decimal values larger than 1. This is something that the RAND and RANDBETWEEN functions alone do not offer. RANDBETWEEN returns integers only, and RAND returns decimal values, but only between 0 and 1.

Finally, in Figure 10-54, all arguments of RANDARRAY are completed. An array of five rows and five columns is returned with integer numbers between 1 and 500.

```
=RANDARRAY(5,5,1,500,TRUE)
```

A	B	C	D	E	F
	367	86	50	62	113
	351	256	244	238	227
	406	128	373	298	474
	372	392	165	405	61
	321	74	28	197	223

fx =RANDARRAY(5,5,1,500,TRUE)

Figure 10-54. *RANDARRAY with all arguments completed*

Pick a Name from a List at Random

A practical example of using the RANDARRAY function is to return a value at random from a list. In this example, we want to return a name at random from a table named [tblNames].

In Figure 10-55, the following formula is entered in cell D3. A single value is being returned, so the *rows* and *columns* arguments are omitted. The ROWS function is used to return the total count of names in the table. This is used as the maximum number to be returned. Integer values are specified.

```
=INDEX(tblNames,
RANDARRAY(,,1,ROWS(tblNames),TRUE)
)
```

The random value returned by RANDARRAY is used as the row number to return the name from. This is the row of the table, not the row of the spreadsheet. The INDEX function is used to return the name from that row of the [tblNames] table.

In this example, as a single value is being returned, the RANDBETWEEN function works just as well. The following formula shows the RANDBETWEEN function being used instead of RANDARRAY:

```
=INDEX(tblNames,
RANDBETWEEN(1,ROWS(tblNames))
)
```

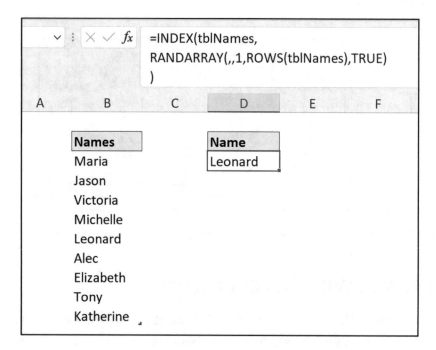

Figure 10-55. *Returning a name at random from a list*

A different name is returned every time the worksheet calculates. The F9 key is pressed to run calculations on the worksheet.

Shuffle a List of Names

In this example, we will shuffle a list of names, changing the order every time the sheet is calculated. This is a solid example of dynamic arrays in action, as we are now returning an array that is dynamic.

In Figure 10-56, the following formula is entered in cell F3 to return a randomized list of the names in the [tblNamesList] table in columns B and C:

```
=SORTBY(tblNamesList[Names],
RANDARRAY(ROWS(tblNamesList))
)
```

The RANDARRAY function has been inserted into the *by array* argument of the SORTBY function. So, the names are sorted by randomly generated numbers.

The number of rows to return has been calculated by using the ROWS function on [tblNamesList]. No other arguments in RANDARRAY are used, so the function is returning decimal values between 0 and 1.

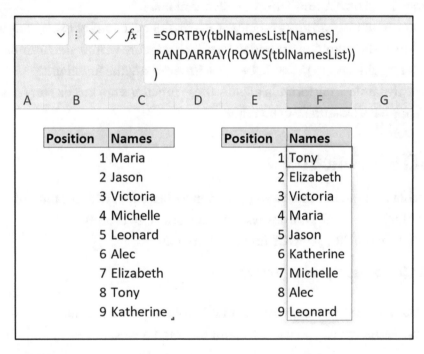

Figure 10-56. *Using RANDARRAY and SORTBY to shuffle a list*

Dynamic arrays make tasks such as this easy. The following SEQUENCE formula is used in cell E3 to generate the position numbers. So, this solution is fully dynamic.

```
=SEQUENCE(ROWS(tblNamesList))
```

Note   An example of the RANDARRAY function is shown with the CHOOSE function in the next chapter to randomly generate some sample data. This is useful for testing and practice.

FREQUENCY and TRANSPOSE Functions

Availability: All versions

File   frequency-and-transpose.xlsx

Dynamic array formulas are not all about the fabulous new functions. Existing Excel functions also benefit from the array engine. Two functions that really saw a new lease of life were the FREQUENCY and TRANSPOSE functions.

These two functions are array functions. So, in older versions of Excel, they were very awkward to use. The output range had to be selected before writing the formula, and then the user would have to press **Ctrl + Alt + Enter** to run the function.

With the dynamic array formula engine, these functions are just like any other Excel function. They have essentially been reborn.

FREQUENCY Function

The FREQUENCY function calculates how often values occur within a range of values (known as bins). The results are always returned as a vertical array.

The syntax of the FREQUENCY function is as follows:

```
=FREQUENCY(data_array, bins_array)
```

- **Data array:** The range, array, or table column that contains the values for which you want to count the frequencies.

- **Bins array:** The range or array that contains the intervals for which to group the values.

In Figure 10-57, the following FREQUENCY function returns the frequencies that the values in the [Score] column occur within the intervals specified in range E4:E7:

```
=FREQUENCY(tblScores[Score],E4:E7)
```

The score must be greater than the interval value to be grouped in that range. So, the *bins array* can be read as 1–50, 51–65, 66–80, 81–90, and >90.

The FREQUENCY function always returns one extra value to the number of intervals in the *bins array*. This extra value is the count of values greater than the largest interval.

To cater for this behavior, the formula was entered into cell F3, one cell before the range specified for the *bins array*.

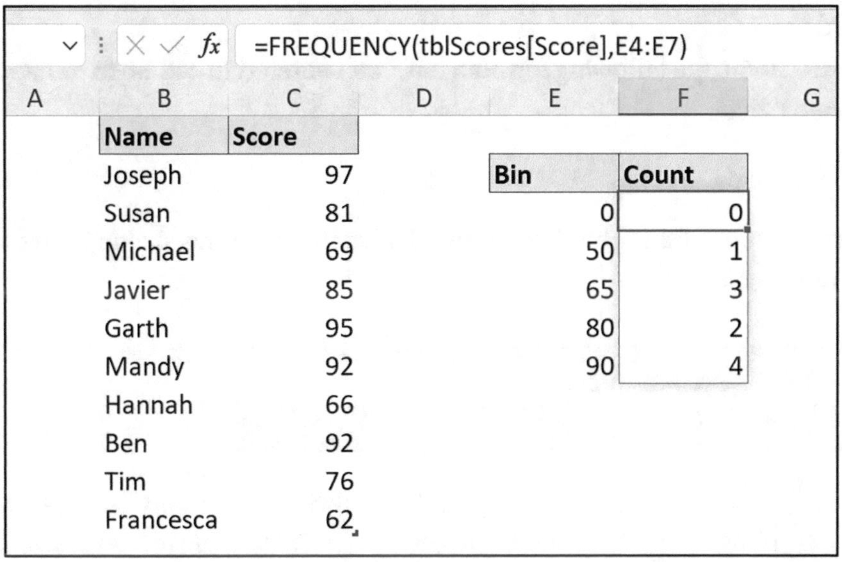

Figure 10-57. FREQUENCY function returning the frequencies of scores

---

Note   In Chapter 8, we saw the COUNTIFS function used to create a frequency distribution table. This is my preferred approach due to the extra flexibility it provides. However, FREQUENCY is great and was built for this purpose.

TRANSPOSE Function

Not many functions benefitted from the introduction of the dynamic array engine more than TRANSPOSE. The TRANSPOSE function was a sleeping giant shackled by Excel's inability to natively handle arrays in older versions.

The shackles have now been broken for this function to show its value. Welcome to TRANSPOSE 2.0.

The TRANSPOSE function rotates data that is arranged horizontally to being arranged vertically and vice versa. It requires only the array to be transposed.

=TRANSPOSE(array)

Many people are familiar with the transpose functionality that is available when you copy and paste data. This is very useful. With the TRANSPOSE function, you can automatically transpose the results of a formula or feed a formula with a transposed array.

In Figure 10-58, the following formula has been entered in cell B6 to transpose the data in range B2:H4:

```
=TRANSPOSE(B2:H4)
```

The data in range B2:H4 has been rotated from being arranged along rows to being arranged down columns.

	B	C	D	E	F	G	H
fx	=TRANSPOSE(B2:H4)						
Name	Maria	Bob	Victoria	Jen	Paula	Henry	
Location	London	Manchester	London	London	Manchester	London	
Score		93	66	85	80	67	75
Name	Location	Score					
Maria	London	93					
Bob	Manchester	66					
Victoria	London	85					
Jen	London	80					
Paula	Manchester	67					
Henry	London	75					

Figure 10-58. Switching horizontal data to vertical with TRANSPOSE

In versions of Excel that do not have dynamic arrays, the TRANSPOSE function is a horrible experience.

To achieve the same result for this example, you would need to select the output cells for the TRANSPOSE function. The range to be transposed is seven columns wide and three rows high. So, you would need to select an output range that is three columns wide and seven rows high and then type the TRANSPOSE function followed by pressing **Ctrl + Shift + Enter**.

This is not a feasible way to work. It is awkward, not dynamic, and required **Ctrl + Shift + Enter** to operate.

520

Thankfully, it now works like any formula – one cell, one formula that spills.

Let's see a quick second example.

Earlier in this chapter, we used the UNIQUE function as shown in Figure 10-59. It is entered in cell B2 to compare columns in the range B4:G4 and return the distinct values.

B2	⌄ ⋮ ✕ ✓ *fx*	=UNIQUE(B4:G4,TRUE)				
	A	B	C	D	E	F	G
1							
2		Bristol	Cambridge	Preston			
3							
4		Bristol	Bristol	Cambridge	Cambridge	Preston	Preston
5		Sales	Upsells	Sales	Upsells	Sales	Upsells
6	Fortune	814	71	860	180	581	53
7	Wings	486	178	621	240	619	82
8	Nirvana	676	193	302	231	556	120
9	Mano	422	219	867	173	512	83
10	Halo	442	129	454	145	754	192

Figure 10-59. *Data containing duplicate values in range B4:G4*

We may need this array to be rotated into a vertical array. This could be to feed a Data Validation list or maybe to feed an Excel function that only works with vertical arrays (there are a few).

In Figure 10-60, the following formula is entered into cell I2:

```
=TRANSPOSE(UNIQUE(B4:G4,TRUE))
```

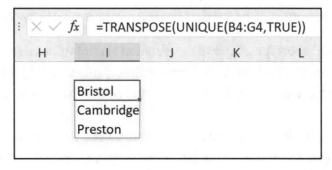

Figure 10-60. *Transposing a horizontal array returned by UNIQUE*

Note   The TRANSPOSE function was shown with the SEQUENCE function earlier in this chapter to change the column-row order that SEQUENCE uses when producing two-dimensional arrays.

PivotTable Style Report Using Formulas

A fantastic use of the TRANSPOSE function is how it can be used to produce labels for a PivotTable style report.

We saw an example earlier in the chapter of the SEQUENCE function generating time-series data across columns for a PivotTable style report. This is simple with SEQUENCE as it has a *columns* argument, and this is great for numeric values. But to get text values dynamically displayed across columns, TRANSPOSE is superb.

Figure 10-61 shows a table named [tblSales]. This will be used as the source data for our pivot style report.

	A	B	C	D	E	F
1	ID	Date	Product Name	Store	Units Sold	Total
2	19775	11/01/2021	Coffee	Chicago	39	59.06
3	19776	12/01/2021	Hot Chocolate	Brussels	16	424.80
4	19777	24/01/2021	Wine	Chicago	25	207.30
5	19778	25/01/2021	Water	Brussels	35	436.53
6	19779	30/01/2021	Coffee	London	38	424.30
7	19780	01/02/2021	Tea	Chicago	10	174.45
8	19781	03/02/2021	Tea	Chicago	30	456.55

Figure 10-61. *Sales data to be used as the source for a pivot style report*

We will create a report that displays the [Product Name] values as row labels and the [Store] values as column labels. To show the [Store] values across columns, they will need to be transposed. The values in the [Total] column will be summed for each product and store.

In Figure 10-62, the following formula is used in cell C2 to create the column labels of the report. The distinct values from the [Store] column are sorted and then transposed.

```
=TRANSPOSE(SORT(UNIQUE(tblSales[Store])))
```

✓ : × ✓ fx	=TRANSPOSE(SORT(UNIQUE(tblSales[Store])))				
B	C	D	E	F	G

	Brussels	Chicago	London	Toronto
Beer	1,544.28	1,070.23	190.88	1,032.69
Coffee	662.34	778.17	1,103.83	1,341.33
Hot Chocolate	849.30	893.43	-	382.19
Orange Juice	814.19	182.93	134.91	389.44
Tea	568.83	1,392.93	329.73	506.56
Water	792.29	465.08	319.37	94.66
Wine	2,593.89	2,047.59	414.23	2,896.91

Figure 10-62. *TRANSPOSE for column labels in a pivot style report*

This is the reverse of the previous two examples where the TRANSPOSE function was used to switch data that was arranged horizontally to vertically.

The following formula is entered in cell B3 to generate the row labels:

=SORT(UNIQUE(tblSales[Product Name]))

And finally, the following SUMIFS formula is entered in cell C3 to produce the totals for each product and store. The two spill ranges are used for the criteria.

=SUMIFS(tblSales[Total],tblSales[Product Name],B3#,tblSales[Store],C2#)

By using dynamic array formulas based on a table, we have a completely dynamic solution here that updates automatically, unlike PivotTables. It also provides greater flexibility than a built-in tool like PivotTables would allow.

SUM v2.0 – The DA Version

Availability: Excel for Microsoft 365, Excel for the Web, Excel 2021, Excel for Microsoft 365 for Mac, Excel 2021 for Mac

---

File   sum.xlsx

Excel's number one function, the SUM function, has also had a new lease of life thanks to the array engine available in Excel 365, Online, and 2021.

In modern versions of Excel, a simple SUM can perform the tasks that we would previously rely on SUMPRODUCT for. It can handle complex arrays, multiple conditional sums, and multiple columns of values (unlike SUMIFS).

Let's welcome SUM 2.0.

Sum Based on Complex Criteria

Let's dive straight in and see the SUM function performing a sum that is based on complex criteria. We need to perform both AND and OR logic in the criteria of this formula.

Figure 10-63 shows the first few rows of a table named [tblSales]. This is the source data that our formula will be using.

	A	B	C	D	E	F
1	ID	Date	Product Name	Store	Units Sold	Total
2	19775	11/01/2021	Coffee	North	39	59.06
3	19776	12/01/2021	Hot Chocolate	West	16	424.80
4	19777	24/01/2021	Wine	North	25	207.30
5	19778	25/01/2021	Water	West	35	436.53
6	19779	30/01/2021	Coffee	South	38	424.30
7	19780	01/02/2021	Tea	North	10	174.45
8	19781	03/02/2021	Tea	North	30	456.55
9	19782	08/02/2021	Hot Chocolate	West	20	424.50

Figure 10-63. Table of sales data

In Figure 10-64, the following formula sums the values in the [Total] column for sales where the [Product Name] was equal to the value in cell B3 or C3 and the [Store] was equal to the value in cell D3:

```
=SUM(
((tblSales[Product Name]=B3)+(tblSales[Product Name]=C3))*
(tblSales[Store]=D3)*
tblSales[Total]
)
```

The following formula returns the count of orders for the same criteria:

```
=SUM(
((tblSales[Product Name]=B3)+(tblSales[Product Name]=C3))*
(tblSales[Store]=D3)
)
```

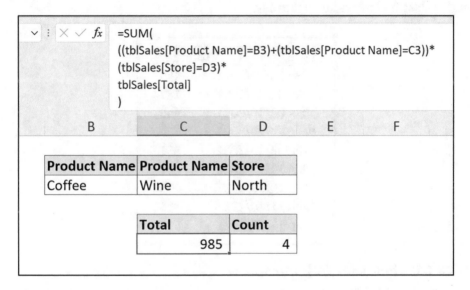

Figure 10-64. *SUM based on complex criteria including AND and OR logic*

When performing formulas such as this, the "+" operator is used to stipulate OR logic between conditions, and the "*" specifies AND logic. An extra set of brackets surround the OR logic part of the formula to force that operation to calculate before the AND operation.

We saw this example in Chapter 9 when we covered the SUMPRODUCT function in detail. In modern Excel, SUMPRODUCT is no longer required for this work. For a detailed breakdown of how this formula works, visit the "SUMPRODUCT Function" section of Chapter 9.

Note   In Chapter 8, we saw a neat trick to combine the SUM function with the SUMIFS and COUNTIFS functions for a more dynamic version of a formula like this.

Sum with Arrays

As formulas in Excel can now handle arrays, this reduces the requirement for using intermediary formulas that store their results in columns.

In Figure 10-65, we have daily sales transactions in a table named [tblDailySales]. We would like to sum the values that occurred at a weekend only. In this example, the weekend is classified as Friday to Sunday.

Date	Total
Fri 01/10/2021	489
Sat 02/10/2021	181
Sat 02/10/2021	445
Mon 04/10/2021	164
Thu 07/10/2021	361
Sun 10/10/2021	462
Sun 10/10/2021	101
Mon 11/10/2021	315
Fri 15/10/2021	369

Figure 10-65. *Table with daily transaction*

In non-dynamic array–enabled versions of Excel, the typical approach would be to use the WEEKDAY function in a column to return the number that identifies the day of the week. A function such as SUMIFS can then be used that tests the values from the weekday column to sum the required values.

In Figure 10-66, the following formula is entered in cell E4 and sums the values that occurred on a Friday-Sunday all in one formula:

```
=SUM(
(WEEKDAY(tblDailySales[Date],2)>4)*
tblDailySales[Total]
)
```

The WEEKDAY function returns a number that identifies the day of the week. The week starts from a Monday as 1 and ends with Sunday as 7. The formula tests if the value returned by the WEEKDAY function is greater than 4.

The results of this logical expression are multiplied by the values in the [Total] column and then summed by the SUM function.

This formula can be achieved in non-DA versions of Excel also, but it requires the user to press **Ctrl + Shift + Enter** on completion to specify an array formula.

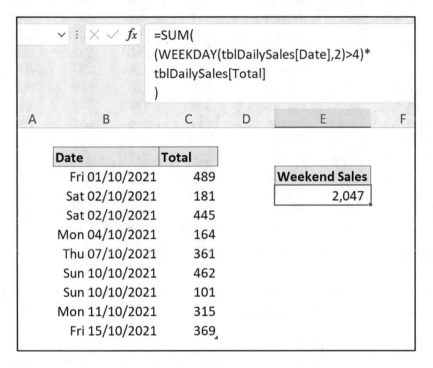

Figure 10-66. *Summing the sales from Friday to Sunday*

Sum Based on Multiple Columns

The SUM function is extremely versatile and can sum values of any array dimensions and include any criteria.

Figure 10-67 shows a matrix of sales data in range D1:I16. It contains product names in range D2:D16 and location names in range F1:I1.

	D	E	F	G	H	I
1	Product	Month	Dublin	Frankfurt	Sofia	Milan
2	Cake	January	592	392	537	306
3	Coffee	January	111	329	536	412
4	Fruit	January	342	413	453	398
5	Juice	January	457	264	402	138
6	Tea	January	393	106	110	289
7	Cake	February	340	701	592	560
8	Coffee	February	556	238	287	624
9	Fruit	February	244	448	580	432
10	Juice	February	164	527	642	353
11	Tea	February	707	444	362	511
12	Cake	March	373	484	636	450
13	Coffee	March	555	721	570	344
14	Fruit	March	416	660	562	167
15	Juice	March	275	796	451	197
16	Tea	March	503	647	590	584

Figure 10-67. *Sales matrix by product and location*

In Figure 10-68, the following SUM function sums the values from range F2:I16, but only for sales of the product stated in cell A2:

=SUM((D2:D16=A2)*(F2:I16))

You would not be able to sum values from multiple columns (F to I) like this with the SUMIFS function. So, this demonstrates the versatility of SUM nicely.

B2	⌄ : ✕ ✓ *fx*	=SUM((D2:D16=A2)*(F2:I16))			
	A	B	C	D	E
1	Product			Product	Month
2	Coffee	5,283		Cake	January
3				Coffee	January

Figure 10-68. *Summing values from multiple columns*

Taking it a step further, we can set both row and column criteria, creating a two-way SUM.

In Figure 10-69, the following SUM function is summing the values at the intersection of the rows for the product stated in cell A2 and the column for the location stated in cell B1. How cool is that?

```
=SUM((D2:D16=A2)*(F1:I1=B1)*(F2:I16))
```

B2		⌄	⋮	╳ ✓ *fx*	=SUM((D2:D16=A2)*(F1:I1=B1)*(F2:I16))		
	A	B	C	D	E	F
1	Product	Sofia		Product	Month	Dublin
2	Juice	1,495		Cake	January	592
3				Coffee	January	111

Figure 10-69. *Two-way SUM with row and column criteria*

Note   Although this section of the chapter is dedicated to SUM, it is worth noting that all aggregation functions benefit from the array engine. We have seen other examples in this book that showcase this, for example, the conditional median function using MEDIAN and IF shown in Chapter 8.

Dynamic Array Formulas with Other Excel Features

Dynamic array formulas have a mixed relationship with other Excel features. Some features work well with DA formulas, although we may need to reference them indirectly, while others do not recognize DA formulas at all.

Let's look at how DA formulas can be used in combination with Conditional Formatting rules, Data Validation rules, and charts in Excel.

DA Formulas with Conditional Formatting

Unfortunately, Conditional Formatting does not recognize a spill range. You cannot reference a spill range directly in a Conditional Formatting rule. And if you select a spill range and apply a Conditional Formatting rule to it, it will not update dynamically with the spill range.

Figure 10-70 shows a dynamic report with two spill ranges – one in range B3 and another in range C3. The spill range in cell C3 returns the total sales for each product.

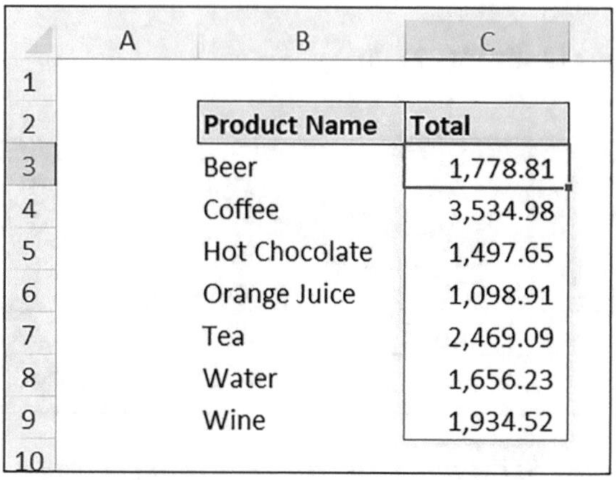

	A	B	C
1			
2		Product Name	Total
3		Beer	1,778.81
4		Coffee	3,534.98
5		Hot Chocolate	1,497.65
6		Orange Juice	1,098.91
7		Tea	2,469.09
8		Water	1,656.23
9		Wine	1,934.52
10			

Figure 10-70. Spilled range in range C3

We will apply a Conditional Formatting rule to change the cell color for all values that are greater than or equal to 1700.

Because the Conditional Formatting feature will not accept a reference to a spill range, you cannot enter the following formula into the formatting rule:

```
=C3#>=1700
```

The approach we will take to make the best of an unfortunate situation is to select more cells than is required. The dynamic array formula may expand the spill range in the future, and we want the rule to apply to the additional cells.

As mentioned, Conditional Formatting cannot work directly with a spill range, so we must resort to selecting cells on the grid and plan a little for future changes.

In Figure 10-71, two additional cells are selected beyond the spill range to cater for the spill range expanding. The Conditional Formatting rule is then created as usual.

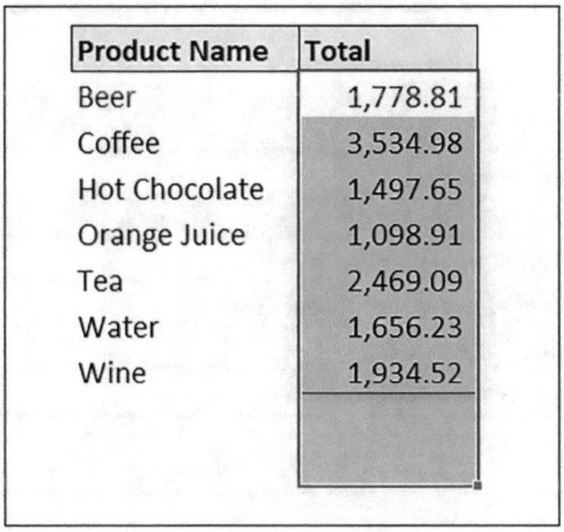

Product Name	Total
Beer	1,778.81
Coffee	3,534.98
Hot Chocolate	1,497.65
Orange Juice	1,098.91
Tea	2,469.09
Water	1,656.23
Wine	1,934.52

Figure 10-71. *Selecting additional cells beyond the spill range*

1. Click **Home ➤ Conditional Formatting ➤ New Rule**.

2. Click **Format only cells that contain**.

3. Select **greater than or equal to** from the list of logical operations and type "1700" into the box provided (Figure 10-72).

4. Click **Format** and specify the formatting you want to apply.

5. Click **OK**.

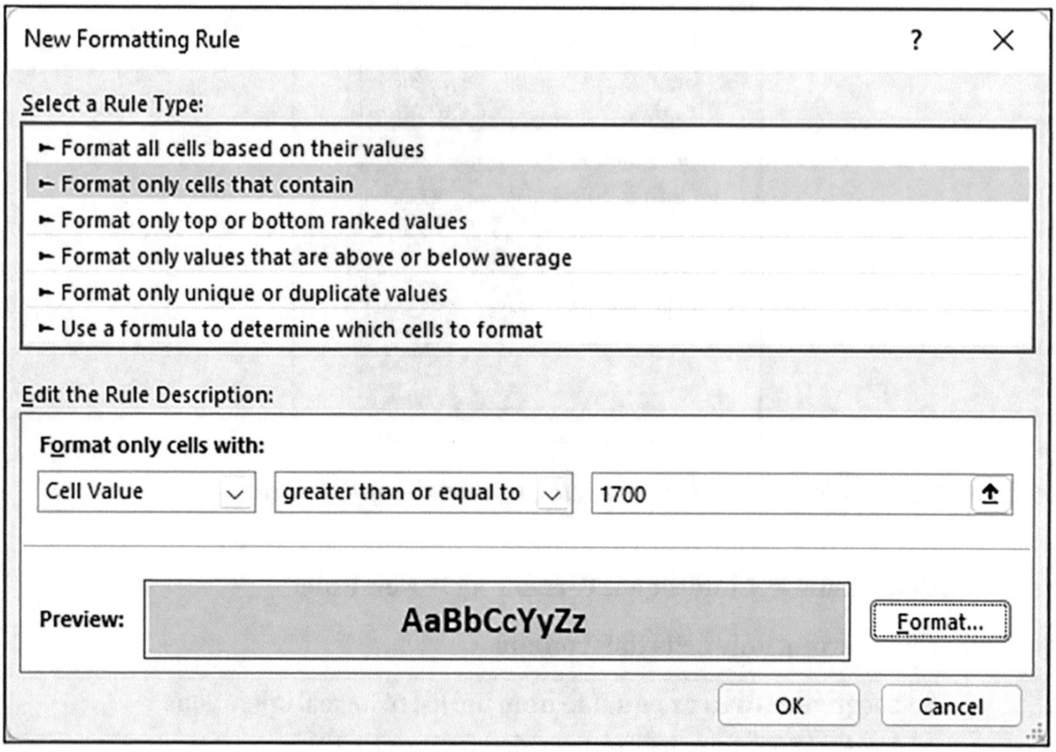

Figure 10-72. *Format cells greater than or equal to 1700*

The Conditional Formatting rule is applied to the selected range as shown in Figure 10-73. If the spill range expanded within the additional two selected cells (we could have selected more), the formatting rule would automatically be applied.

Product Name	Total
Beer	1,778.81
Coffee	3,534.98
Hot Chocolate	1,497.65
Orange Juice	1,098.91
Tea	2,469.09
Water	1,656.23
Wine	1,934.52

Figure 10-73. *Conditional Formatting rule applied*

DA Formulas with Data Validation

The good news is that Data Validation works with dynamic array formulas. You cannot enter DA formulas directly in the Data Validation window, but you can reference spill ranges on the grid. When the spill range updates, the Data Validation rule will update with it.

For this example, we will use the UNIQUE and SORT functions together to create a source for a Data Validation list. Figure 10-74 shows a table named [tblSubscribers].

	A	B	C
1	ID	Name	Country
2	95	Victoria Ashworth	France
3	87	Sven Ottlieb	Canada
4	96	Pedro Alfonso	UK
5	61	Ann Devon	France
6	51	Francisco Chang	Mexico
7	28	Aria Cruz	Belgium
8	36	Diego Roel	UK
9	94	Elizabeth Lincoln	USA
10			

Figure 10-74. *Table with subscriber data*

We will create a dynamic Data Validation list from the countries in the [Country] column. If subscribers are added from new countries, the Data Validation list will automatically update to include them.

In cell B3, the following formula is used to create a distinct list of the countries and is sorted in ascending order (Figure 10-75):

```
=SORT(UNIQUE(tblSubscribers[Country]))
```

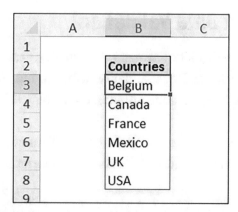

Figure 10-75. *Spill range to be used as the source for a DV list*

To create the Data Validation list

1. Click the cell(s) you want the Data Validation list in.

2. Click **Data ➤ Data Validation**.

3. From the **Settings** tab, click the *Allow* list and click **List**.

4. Click in the *Source* box, click the cell that contains the spill range, and type the # operator after the reference (Figure 10-76). The following reference is used in this example. Click **OK**.

    =$B$3#

Note   A defined name could be created for this reference, such as *lstCountries*, and then the defined name used for the source of the Data Validation rule. This is not required but is a nice technique for a more meaningful reference than *$B$3#*, especially if the spill range was on another sheet.

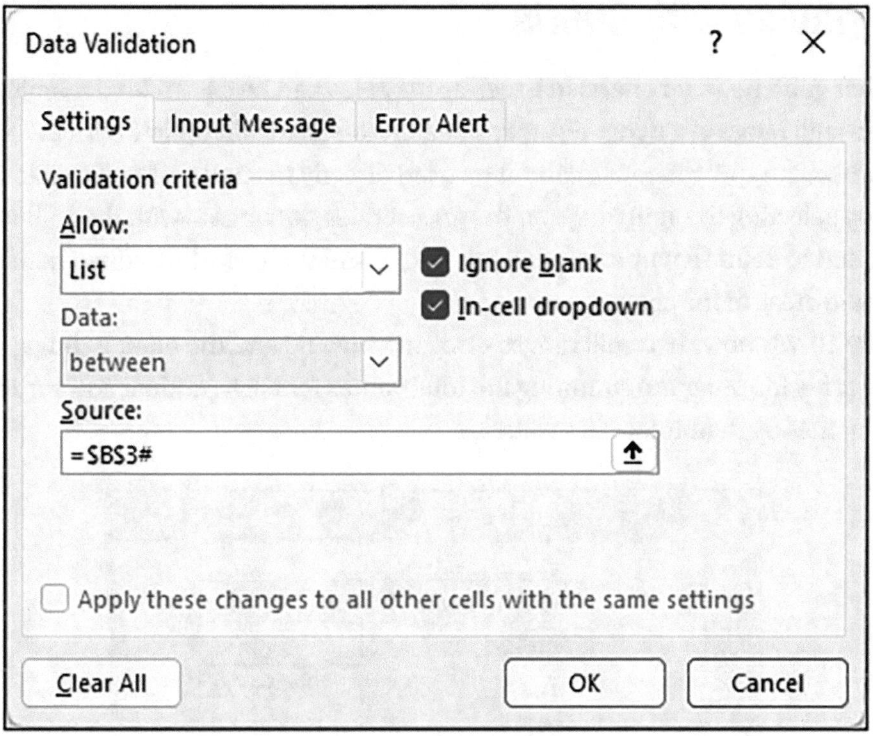

Figure 10-76. *Data Validation list referencing a spill range*

Figure 10-77 shows the Data Validation list. The spill range in cell B3 will update with the data in the [tblSubscribers] table, and the Data Validation list will automatically update as it references the spill range.

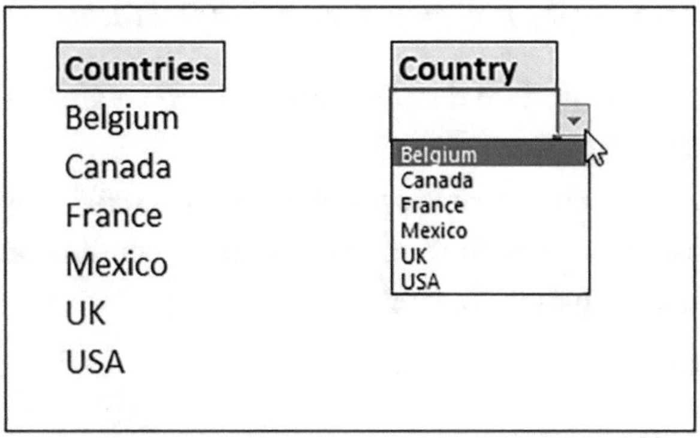

Figure 10-77. *A dynamic Data Validation list of countries*

DA Formulas with Charts

It is further good news for charts in Excel, as they also can be used with dynamic arrays. When the spill range of a dynamic array updates, the chart will update with it.

However, the spill reference cannot be used directly in charts. Also, if a chart is created by selecting the spill range on the grid, it does not update with the spill range.

We need to define a name for each spill range and then use the defined name in the appropriate areas of the chart.

Figure 10-78 shows two spill ranges – one in range B3 and the other in range C3. The dynamic array formulas are summing the total values for each product and sorting the product names by their total sales values.

	A	B	C	D
1				
2		Product Name	Total	
3		Coffee	3,534.98	
4		Tea	2,469.09	
5		Wine	1,934.52	
6		Beer	1,778.81	
7		Water	1,656.23	
8		Hot Chocolate	1,497.65	
9		Orange Juice	1,098.91	
10				

Figure 10-78. Spill ranges for products sorted by sales totals

This is a cool technique, and we demonstrated how to create this report earlier in the chapter with the SORTBY function.

We will insert a column chart that is connected to these spill ranges, so that the chart always sorts the product names by their sales totals in descending order.

First, we need to define names for each spill range:

1. Click cell B3.

2. Click **Formulas ➤ Define Name**.

3. Type a *Name* for the defined name. In Figure 10-79, "rngProducts" is used.

4. The reference to cell B3 should automatically appear in the *Refers to* box, as we clicked the cell before defining the name. Add the # operator to the end of the reference. Click **OK**.

=Charts!$B$3#

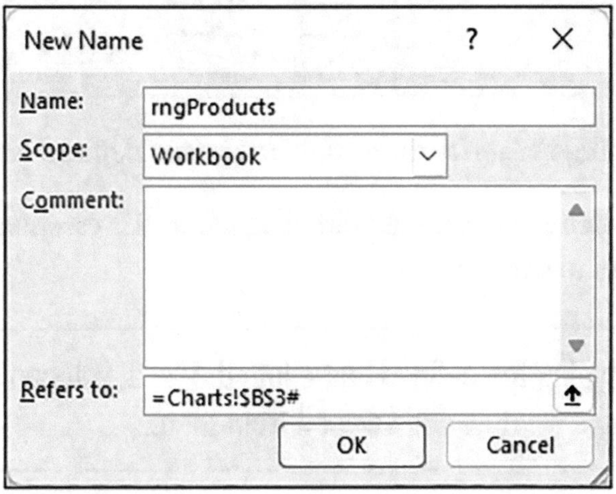

Figure 10-79. *Define a name for the product name's spill range*

This defined name will be used for the axis labels. We need to define another name for the sales total spill range in range C3#.

5. Click cell C3 and repeat the previous steps using the following reference. In this example, the name "rngSalesTotals" is used for the defined name.

=Charts!$C$3#

The next step is to insert the chart and then connect it to our defined names.

6. Click **Insert ➤ Insert Column or Bar Chart ➤ Clustered Column**.

7. With the chart selected, click **Chart Design ➤ Select Data**.

8. Click the **Add** button in the *Legend Entries (Series)* area on the left.

9. Type "Product Sales" for the *Series name* and type the following reference in the *Series values* box (Figure 10-80). Click **OK**.

=Charts!rngSalesTotals

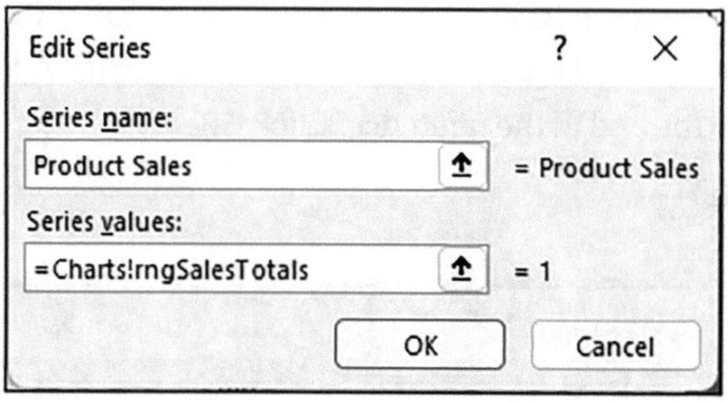

Figure 10-80. *Editing the series for a chart to use the defined name*

Even though the defined name has workbook scope, it is essential that the references in charts include the sheet name.

Note   Instead of typing the defined name into the field, you can also press **F3** to open the *Paste Name* window and select it from there.

---

10. Click the **Edit** button in the *Horizontal (Category) Axis Labels* area on the right.

11. Type the following reference into the *Axis label range* box and click **OK** (Figure 10-81).

    =Charts!rngProducts

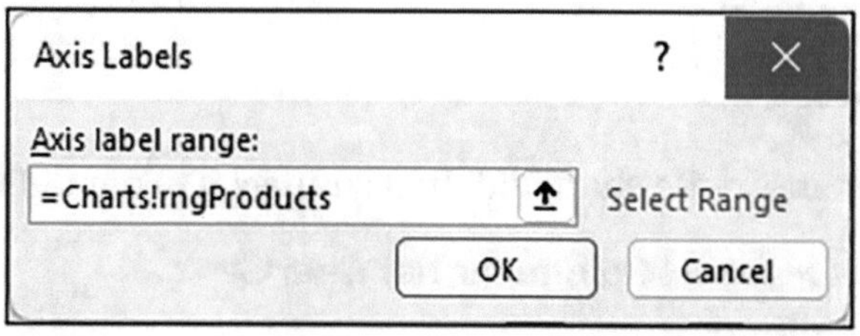

Figure 10-81. *Editing the axis labels to use the defined name*

12. Click **OK** to close the *Select Data Source* window.

Figure 10-82 shows the completed column chart based indirectly on the spill ranges. This chart will automatically update to reflect any changes in the spill ranges.

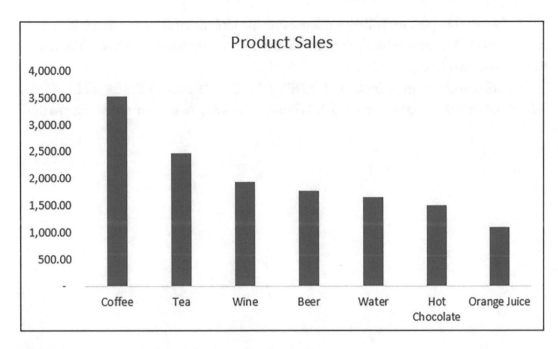

Figure 10-82. *Completed chart using dynamic array sources*

Summary

In this chapter, we learned all about dynamic arrays in modern Excel. The key takeaways from this chapter were

- Understanding what exactly a dynamic array is and how to use them effectively in Excel.

- Learning a few of the dynamic array functions in Excel including SORTBY, UNIQUE, and SEQUENCE. Others such as TEXTSPLIT, FILTER, and STOCKHISTORY are covered in other chapters of the book.

- How existing functions in Excel such as SUM, TRANSPOSE, EOMONTH, and SUMIFS work with arrays. Functions such as SUM are better than ever, while EOMONTH requires some tricks to work effectively.

- How dynamic array are used with existing features of Excel such as charts and Data Validation.

In the next chapter, we will dive deeper into the lookup functions of Excel. We have covered VLOOKUP in this book already, but there are many more (and better) lookup functions in Excel than VLOOKUP.

We will cover functions including INDEX, CHOOSE, OFFSET, VSTACK, and INDIRECT. It is the largest chapter of this book, containing many examples and pro tips.

CHAPTER 11

Advanced Lookup Functions

One of the most important skills to learn in Excel is understanding how to reference values and arrays. Whatever you use Excel for, you need to know how to specify the location of a value or array. One could argue that it is the most important skill.

This does not just apply to formulas, but charts, PivotTables, formatting, validation rules, etc. It all boils down to being able to tell Excel the locations of the values or array that you need.

Data could be stored on the grid, in a table, a defined name, a spill range, an array returned by a formula, or stored as a date type (covered in Chapter 14). There are so many options, and this is partly what makes Excel so exciting.

There are many lookup and reference functions in Excel, and these functions provide us with the means to access the values and arrays in the manner we require.

We covered the VLOOKUP function in Chapter 7. It has its own chapter in this book due to its overwhelming popularity as a function. But Excel has so many more functions that extend beyond the capabilities of VLOOKUP. Therefore, the chapter has been coined "Advanced Lookup Functions."

We will cover many of the most useful lookup and reference functions in this chapter. There will be dedicated chapters for the new XLOOKUP and FILTER functions to follow this one. These are two of the finest lookup and reference functions in Excel.

In this chapter, we will cover the CHOOSE, INDIRECT, OFFSET, VSTACK, and XMATCH functions, to name just a few. The INDEX function is also covered and deserves a special mention independently from the others as it is possibly the best function in Excel.

© Alan Murray 2022
A. Murray, *Advanced Excel Formulas*, https://doi.org/10.1007/978-1-4842-7125-4_11

MATCH Function

Availability: All versions

File   match.xlsx

The MATCH function is one that we will see a lot of in this chapter. It is a real workhorse that performs a lot of the legwork for other lookup functions to perform dynamic relative references.

The MATCH function returns the relative position of a value within a range or array. This is the syntax for the MATCH function:

```
=MATCH(lookup_value, lookup_array, [match_type])
```

- **Lookup value:** The value you want to look for and return its relative position.

- **Lookup array:** The range or array to search in for the *lookup value*. This can be a vertical or horizontal array.

- **[Match type]:** The number 1, 0, or –1 that defines the match type.

  - 0 is entered to specify an exact match. This is the most used match type.

  - 1 is entered to perform a range lookup that returns the position of the largest value less than the *lookup value*, if the *lookup value* is not found. The *lookup array* must be sorted in ascending order when using this match type. This is also the default match type.

  - –1 is entered to perform a range lookup that returns the position of the smallest value greater than the *lookup value*, if the *lookup value* is not found. The *lookup array* must be sorted in descending order when using this match type.

Note   The MATCH function is case-insensitive. It does not distinguish between lowercase, proper case, and uppercase when matching text values.

Figure 11-1 shows a MATCH function being used to return the position of the name entered in cell F2 within the range B3:B7. An exact match has been specified as the match type.

=MATCH(F2,B3:B7,0)

Notice that the relative position of 4 is returned. The MATCH function returns the position of a value within the lookup range or array, and not its position on the worksheet, that is, row 6.

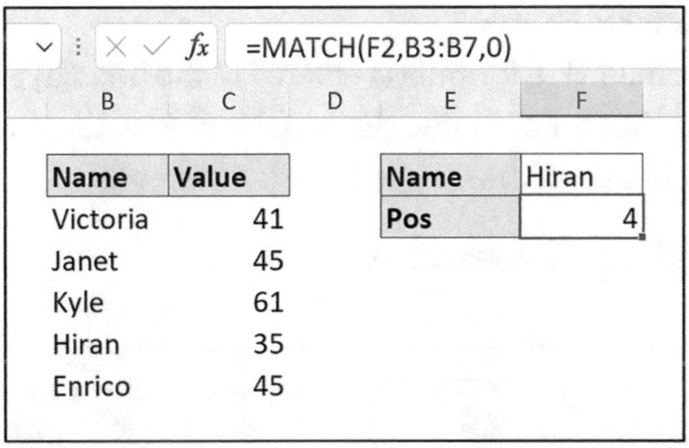

Figure 11-1. *Simple MATCH example returning the relative position of a name*

If the *lookup array* contains duplicate values, the MATCH function will return the position of the first occurrence of the value that it finds.

If a matching value is not found, the #N/A error is returned (Figure 11-2).

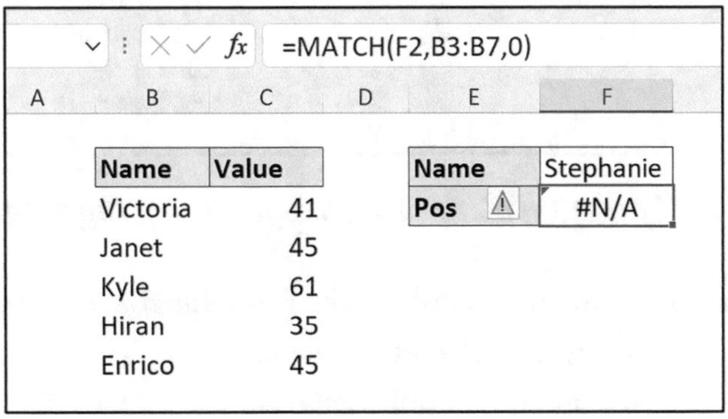

Figure 11-2. *#N/A error returned when a value is not matched*

Let's look at some more practical examples of the MATCH function in action. There are further examples of MATCH throughout this chapter, especially when combined with the INDEX function, its most familiar partner.

Compare Two Lists

The MATCH function provides a neat way to compare two lists and identify the differences.

When comparing two lists, if a value is matched, its relative position is returned; otherwise, the #N/A error is returned.

In Figure 11-3, the following formula is entered in the [Match] column of the first table. It checks for matches for the values in the [Number] column of the first table within the [Number] column of the second table [tblSecond]:

```
=MATCH([@Number],tblSecond[Number],0)
```

Number	Name	Match		Number	Name
20034	Oz	4		412	Pamela
21099	Kenneth	#N/A		23384	Kirsty
3415	Martin	7		24461	Patrick
20075	Jane	6		20034	Oz
412	Pamela	1		91158	Jon
9081	Laurence	#N/A		20075	Jane
23384	Kirsty	2		3415	Martin
1273	Ian	#N/A		412	Pamela
				5173	Harry
				47661	Mike

Figure 11-3. *MATCH function comparing lists for matching values*

You can see that there are three names in the first table that are not matched in the second table. This is shown by the #N/A error message.

Although this works, it is not a very polished result.

The MATCH function can be nested within other functions to display an alternative value or to perform an action based on the result. It could also be inserted into a Conditional Formatting rule to visualize the differences between the two lists better.

In Figure 11-4, the IF function along with the ISNUMBER function has been used to tidy up the results. A "Yes" is displayed for the matched values and "No" for the unmatched values.

```
=IF(
ISNUMBER(MATCH([@Number],tblSecond[Number],0)),
"Yes","No")
```

The ISNUMBER function returns TRUE if MATCH returns a number relating to the value's position and FALSE if the #N/A error is returned. IF uses these results to then display the "Yes" and "No" values.

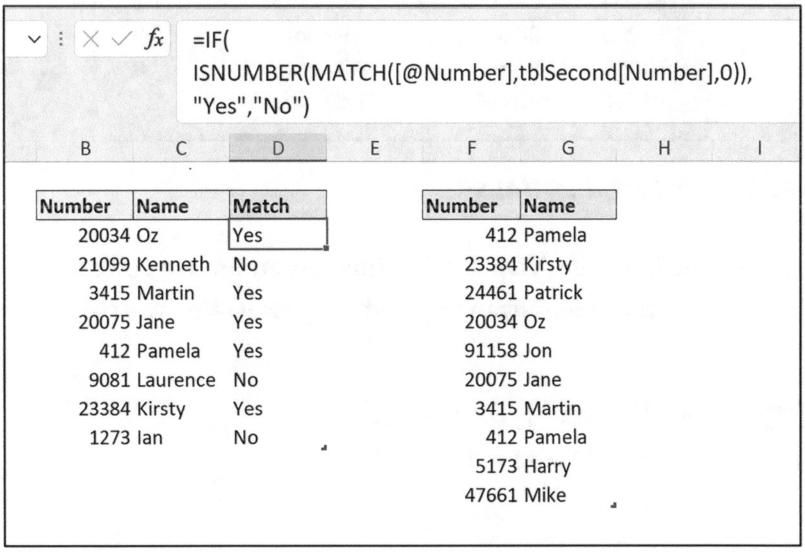

Figure 11-4. Tidying up the results to display "Yes" and "No" values

Dynamic Column Index Number in VLOOKUP

We covered the VLOOKUP function in Chapter 7 in great detail, including tricks for returning the column index number as an alternative to typing in the column number directly.

The MATCH function is a terrific method for fetching the column index number for VLOOKUP. It provides an approach that is robust, durable, and dynamic.

We will use the MATCH function to search for the header text of the column we want, along the header row of the lookup table, and return the relative position of that column to VLOOKUP.

Figure 11-5 shows the lookup table named [tblProducts]. It contains information about products being sold including the [P Code] column. These values are used to uniquely identify a product.

	A	B	C	D
1	P Code	Product Name	Category	Price
2	P1001	Orange Juice	Cold Drink	1.2
3	P1002	Coffee	Hot Drink	2.4
4	P1003	Tea	Hot Drink	1.5
5	P1004	Hot Chocolate	Hot Drink	1.6
6	P1005	Beer	Alcohol	3.9
7	P1006	Wine	Alcohol	8
8	P1007	Water	Cold Drink	1.1
9				

Figure 11-5. *Table of product data*

In Figure 11-6, the following VLOOKUP formula is entered in cell D2 of the table to return the [Product Name] values from [tblProducts] associated with the [P Code] value in that row:

```
=VLOOKUP([@[P Code]:[P Code]],tblProducts,
MATCH(D$1,tblProducts[#Headers],0),
FALSE)
```

The MATCH function searches the header row of [tblProducts] to return the column number of the header stated in cell D1. The header text of the value in cell D1 and that in the *lookup array* must match exactly.

Notice the absolute reference to the P Code *lookup value*. This technique was covered in Chapter 4, when we covered tables in detail. Also, the row has been made absolute in the reference to the header text in cell D1.

These references have been applied so that the VLOOKUP formula can be filled across the [Category] and [Price] columns too.

No need to manually edit the column number returned, as the MATCH function returns the required column number automatically. It is also durable and will not break if someone changed the order of the columns in [tblProducts] or inserted a new column before the column being returned.

		fx	=VLOOKUP(tblSalesData[@[P Code]:[P Code]],tblProducts,
			MATCH(D$1,tblProducts[#Headers],0),
			FALSE)

	B	C	D	E	F	G	H
	Order Date	P Code	Product Name	Category	Price	Units Sold	
75	02-Jan-19	P1001	Orange Juice	Cold Drink	1.2	12	
84	03-Jan-19	P1005	Beer	Alcohol	3.9	40	
85	03-Jan-19	P1003	Tea	Hot Drink	1.5	80	
86	03-Jan-19	P1007	Water	Cold Drink	1.1	70	
87	03-Jan-19	P1005	Beer	Alcohol	3.9	55	
88	03-Jan-19	P1004	Hot Chocolate	Hot Drink	1.6	18	
89	04-Jan-19	P1004	Hot Chocolate	Hot Drink	1.6	8	
90	04-Jan-19	P1003	Tea	Hot Drink	1.5	40	
91	04-Jan-19	P1005	Beer	Alcohol	3.9	8	
92	04-Jan-19	P1002	Coffee	Hot Drink	2.4	14	
93	04-Jan-19	P1007	Water	Cold Drink	1.1	5	

Figure 11-6. Returning product details with VLOOKUP and MATCH

Sort a Range by Drop-Down List Value

Using the MATCH function combined with the SORT function, we can create a nice effect for our Excel reports and models, where a user can sort a range by selecting the column to sort by from a drop-down list.

This is a great technique, as it makes our reports interactive from functionality on the grid, instead of a user having to know how to use built-in Excel features. It also gives us more control to setting up how a feature of a report should be used.

The SORT function requires that the column to sort by is entered as an index number. This is a perfect scenario for the MATCH function to assist.

Figure 11-7 shows a table named [tblCoffee] that contains aggregated sales data for six different products.

On a different sheet, we would like to use the SORT function to sort this data dependent upon the value in a cell.

Product Name	Rating	Quantity	Total
Americano	4.10	558	2,167
Super M Blend	4.89	621	1,556
Choccocino	4.08	648	2,689
Espresso X	4.37	622	1,589
Iced Tea	4.01	473	2,406
Caramel Latte	3.69	539	2,623

Figure 11-7. *Table with data about coffee sales*

In Figure 11-8, the following formula is entered in cell B5 to return all columns from [tblCoffee] sorted by the column specified in cell B2. Cell B2 contains a drop-down list so that the user can easily and accurately select the column to sort by.

```
=SORT(tblCoffee,
MATCH(B2,tblCoffee[#Headers],0),
IF(MATCH(B2,tblCoffee[#Headers],0)=1,1,-1)
)
```

The same MATCH function is used twice in the formula. The first MATCH is used to return the *sort index*. It matches the text in cell B2 to the headers in [tblCoffee] and returns the column number.

The second time the MATCH function is used is within an IF function. The IF function is used here to ensure that the correct *sort order* is applied.

It checks if the column stated in cell B2 is column 1, the [Product Name] column. If it is, the SORT function is instructed to order the list in ascending order. If the selected column is not column 1, then a descending sort order is applied.

| B5 | | ⌄ | ⋮ | ✕ | ✓ | *fx* | =SORT(tblCoffee,
MATCH(B2,tblCoffee[#Headers],0),
IF(MATCH(B2,tblCoffee[#Headers],0)=1,1,-1)
) |

	A	B	C	D	E	F
1						
2		Rating				
3						
4		Product Name	Rating	Quantity	Total	
5		Super M Blend	4.89	621	1,555.87	
6		Espresso X	4.37	622	1,589.10	
7		Americano	4.10	558	2,166.63	
8		Choccocino	4.08	648	2,688.75	
9		Iced Tea	4.01	473	2,406.02	
10		Caramel Latte	3.69	539	2,623.29	
11						

Figure 11-8. *Sorting table data based on drop-down list selection*

To avoid the repetition of the same MATCH function in one formula, we could define a name for the MATCH function and use that name in the formula instead. This would help us to create a more meaningful and concise formula.

We covered this technique in Chapter 3, and this is a great opportunity to resurface this technique in a practical application:

1. Click **Formulas ➤ Define Name**.

2. Type "SelectedColumn" for the *Name* (Figure 11-9).

3. Enter, or copy, the MATCH formula into the *Refers to* box. Click **OK**.

```
=MATCH($B$2,tblCoffee[#Headers],0)
```

The reference to B2 has been made an absolute reference for the defined name. In Figure 11-9, you can see the sheet name precedes the $B$2 reference. This was automatically entered by Excel, as it is required for a defined name with workbook scope.

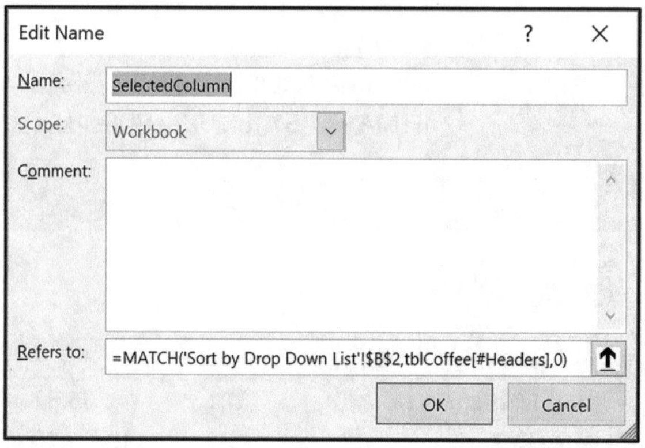

Figure 11-9. *Named formula for the MATCH function*

The formula in cell B5 can now be edited to use the defined name instead of the MATCH formula. The following formula shows the edited version:

```
=SORT(tblCoffee,
SelectedColumn,
IF(SelectedColumn=1,1,-1)
)
```

This formula is much more concise and meaningful.

Note   In Chapter 15, we cover the LET function in Excel. With LET, we can save variables with meaningful names and repurpose them within a formula. Using LET prevents us from having to define named formulas like we did here for this example.

XMATCH Function

Availability: Excel 2021, Excel for Microsoft 365, Excel for the Web, Excel 2021 for Mac, Excel for Microsoft 365 for Mac

---

File   xmatch.xlsx

The XMATCH function is the successor to the MATCH function and offers a few refinements and added functionality over its predecessor. It is only available in the 365, Online, and 2021 versions of Excel though, so MATCH is still very important to know.

The key changes with XMATCH are that it defaults to an exact match type and that it has the ability to search an array from first to last or from last to first.

This is the syntax of the XMATCH function. It is similar to the MATCH function, but there are differences with the *match mode* argument, and it has the additional *search mode* argument:

```
=XMATCH(lookup_value, lookup_array, [match_mode], [search_mode])
```

- **Lookup value:** The value you want to look for and return its relative position.

- **Lookup array:** The range or array to search in for the *lookup value*. This can be a vertical or horizontal array.

- **[Match mode]:** The number –1, 0, 1, or 2 that defines the match type.

  - 0 is entered to specify an exact match. This is the most used match type and the default option.

  - –1 is entered to return the position of the exact match or the next smaller value to the *lookup value*, if the *lookup value* is not found.

  - 1 is entered to return the position of the exact match or the next larger value to the *lookup value*, if the *lookup value* is not found.

  - 2 is entered to specify a wildcard character match. The asterisk (*), question mark (?), and tilde (~) wildcard characters can be used for partial matches.

- **[Search mode]:** The number 1, –1, 2, or –2 that defines the type of search to perform.

  - 1 is entered to specify a search from first to last. This is the default search mode.

  - –1 is entered to reverse the search and search from last to first.

- 2 is entered to specify a binary search from first to last. Performing this type of search requires the *lookup array* to be sorted in ascending order.

- –2 is entered to specify a binary search from last to first. The *lookup array* needs to be sorted in descending order for this type of search.

Note   The numbers used to specify the "next item smaller than" and "next item larger than" match modes are the reverse of the numbers used by MATCH. Be careful with this change when you start using XMATCH.

Because we have covered the MATCH function already, the following examples will focus on highlighting the differences between XMATCH and MATCH.

XMATCH Defaults to an Exact Match

The most used match type is the exact match, and this is the default match type of XMATCH, unlike the MATCH function. So, when performing an exact match, we do not need to answer the third argument.

In Figure 11-10, the following formula is entered in cell F3 to return the relative position of the name stated in cell F2. Only the first two arguments have been specified.

=XMATCH(F2,B3:B7)

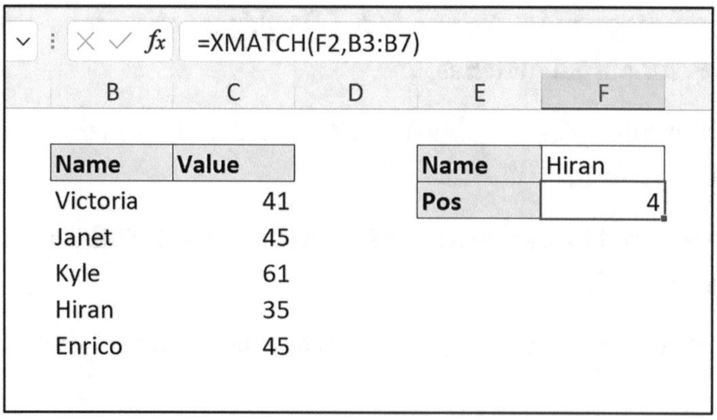

	fx	=XMATCH(F2,B3:B7)			
B	C	D	E	F	
Name	Value		Name	Hiran	
Victoria	41		Pos	4	
Janet	45				
Kyle	61				
Hiran	35				
Enrico	45				

Figure 11-10.   XMATCH function defaults to exact match

Returning the Position of the Last Match

The *search mode* argument of the XMATCH function provides the ability to search an array from last to first. This is useful for returning the position of the last match in an array.

Figure 11-11 shows team names in range B3:B8 and 12 rounds of results: W = Win, D = Draw, and L = Loss. This data is on a worksheet named [Horizontal].

	A	B	C	D	E	F	G	H	I	J	K	L	M	N
1														
2		Team	R1	R2	R3	R4	R5	R6	R7	R8	R9	R10	R11	R12
3		Albatross	L	L	D	L	W	D	L	D	L	D	W	L
4		Tigers	D	D	D	W	D	D	W	L	L	W	L	L
5		The Eagles	D	L	D	L	D	D	W	D	D	D	L	W
6		Leopards	D	D	D	W	W	W	D	L	L	W	L	D
7		The Chargers	L	W	D	D	D	L	L	W	W	L	W	D
8		Beetles	L	D	D	D	W	W	D	W	D	L	D	L
9														

Figure 11-11. *Rounds of results for different teams*

In Figure 11-12, the XMATCH function has been used to return the round that a team recorded their first win and the number of rounds it has been since their last win.

The following formula is entered in cell C3 to return the relative position of the first match of a "W":

```
=XMATCH("W",Horizontal!C3:N3)
```

To return the number of rounds since a team won their last match, we need to return the relative position of the last match of a "W."

The following formula searches the range Horizontal!C3:N3 from last to first. The *match mode* argument is ignored, and –1 is entered for the *search mode* argument:

```
=XMATCH("W",Horizontal!C3:N3,,-1)
```

The following formula is entered in cell D3 in Figure 11-12. The value returned by the XMATCH function is subtracted from the results of a COUNTA function that returns the number of rounds played:

```
=COUNTA(Horizontal!C3:N3)-
XMATCH("W",Horizontal!C3:N3,,-1)
```

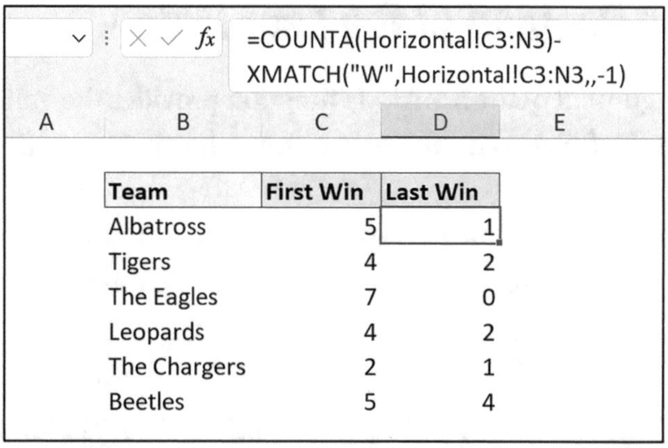

| | fx | =COUNTA(Horizontal!C3:N3)-XMATCH("W",Horizontal!C3:N3,,-1) |

A	B	C	D	E
	Team	First Win	Last Win	
	Albatross	5	1	
	Tigers	4	2	
	The Eagles	7	0	
	Leopards	4	2	
	The Chargers	2	1	
	Beetles	5	4	

Figure 11-12. *Returning the number of rounds since the last win*

Note   We will see further examples of the XMATCH function and showcase other uses of its arguments when we discuss the INDEX function later in this chapter.

CHOOSE Function

Availability: All versions

File   choose.xlsx

The CHOOSE function is a simple yet very effective function in Excel. It chooses a value, range, or an action from a list based on an index number.

We have seen a few examples of the CHOOSE function in this book so far. It has been demonstrated in Chapters 6, 7, and 10. It was used to return fiscal quarters from dates in Chapter 6. And in Chapters 7 and 10, it was used to reorder or extract specific columns for the VLOOKUP and SORT functions.

It is a very useful function in Excel, so in this chapter we will see some further examples of its use.

This is the syntax of the CHOOSE function:

```
=CHOOSE(index_num, value, [value2])
```

- **Index num:** The index number of the value, range, or action in the list that you want to use

- **Value, [value 2]:** The list of values, ranges, and actions that you want to return from

In Figure 11-13, a simple CHOOSE function is shown returning a value based on the index number of 3.

```
=CHOOSE(3,"Banana","Melon","Cherry","Mango")
```

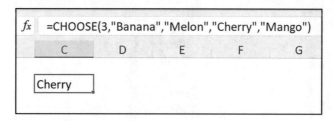

Figure 11-13. *Simple CHOOSE function*

The true power of the CHOOSE function is revealed when the index number is provided by the result of a formula or via a form control. So, let's take the CHOOSE function further.

Generating Random Sample Data

CHOOSE is great for generating random sample data that can be used for testing formulas and models that you create. In fact, much of the sample data provided in this book was generated using these methods.

In Figure 11-14, the following formula returns the name of a region based on a random index number generated by the RANDARRAY function:

```
=CHOOSE(
RANDARRAY(10,,1,3,TRUE),
"West","North","East")
```

The RANDARRAY function returns an array containing ten rows of integer values between 1 and 3. The CHOOSE function returns the region from its list based on the index number provided by RANDARRAY and spills the results to the grid.

Note   The RANDBETWEEN function can be used instead of RANDARRAY in Excel versions that do not support the RANDARRAY function.

| C2 | | ✓ | ∶ | ✕ | ✓ | *fx* | =CHOOSE(
RANDARRAY(10,,1,3,TRUE),
"West","North","East") |

	A	B	C	D	E
1	ID	Date	Region	Product	Total
2			North		
3			East		
4			West		
5			North		
6			North		
7			East		
8			North		
9			East		
10			North		
11			North		
12					

Figure 11-14. *Generating text values at random*

To quickly generate some product names in the [Product] column, the following formula could be used. This formula uses RANDARRAY to return a random value between 1 and 4 as there are four values in its list:

```
=CHOOSE(
RANDARRAY(10,,1,4,TRUE),
"Melon","Apple","Kiwi","Mango")
```

Remember, when using the random number–generating functions – RAND, RANDBETWEEN, and RANDARRAY – they return new results every time the worksheet calculates.

So, after producing the random values, you want to replace the formulas with the values only. There are many techniques to accomplish this, but my favorite is the following:

1. Select the range you want to convert to values.

2. Position the cursor on the border of the selection until you see the "move" cursor (four arrows facing away from the center).

3. Right-click and drag away and then back to the range and release the mouse.

4. Click **Copy Here as Values Only** (Figure 11-15).

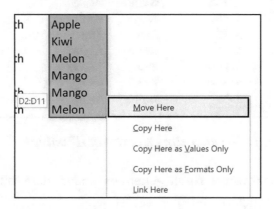

Figure 11-15. *Converting formulas to values only*

To complete the sample data, we will generate random values for the [ID], [Date], and [Total] columns. We will not be using the CHOOSE function for this task, despite it being the focus of this part of the chapter, but it is important to finish the job.

To generate the ID values, we could use RANDBETWEEN or RANDARRAY, but I like to use SEQUENCE for this task as it returns a series of values in order (Figure 11-16).

=SEQUENCE(10,,1422)

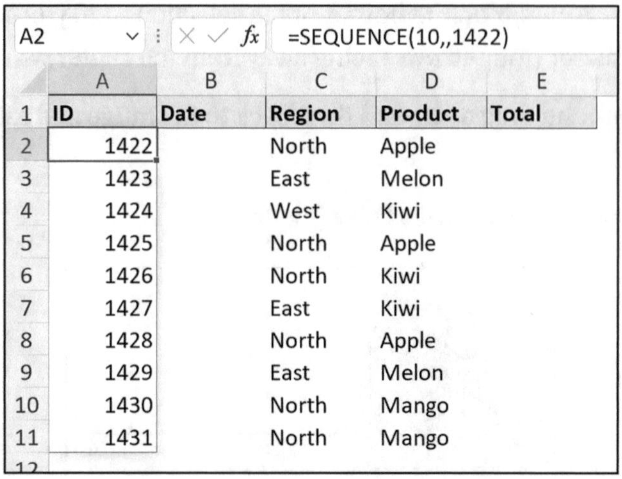

A2	⌄ : ✕ ✓ *fx*	=SEQUENCE(10,,1422)		
	A	B	C	D	E
1	ID	Date	Region	Product	Total
2	1422		North	Apple	
3	1423		East	Melon	
4	1424		West	Kiwi	
5	1425		North	Apple	
6	1426		North	Kiwi	
7	1427		East	Kiwi	
8	1428		North	Apple	
9	1429		East	Melon	
10	1430		North	Mango	
11	1431		North	Mango	
12					

Figure 11-16. *SEQUENCE generating a series of ID values*

For the dates, the following formula generates random date values between 1st July 2021 and 31st July 2021 (Figure 11-17):

```
=SORT(RANDARRAY(10,,DATE(2021,7,1),DATE(2021,7,31),TRUE))
```

The DATE function is used in the *min* and *max* arguments of RANDARRAY to specify the start and end dates of the date range. The SORT function is added to order the dates returned in an ascending order.

Note   Instead of adding the SORT function, we could have generated the dates before generating the ID values and sorted the dates manually using the commands in Excel.

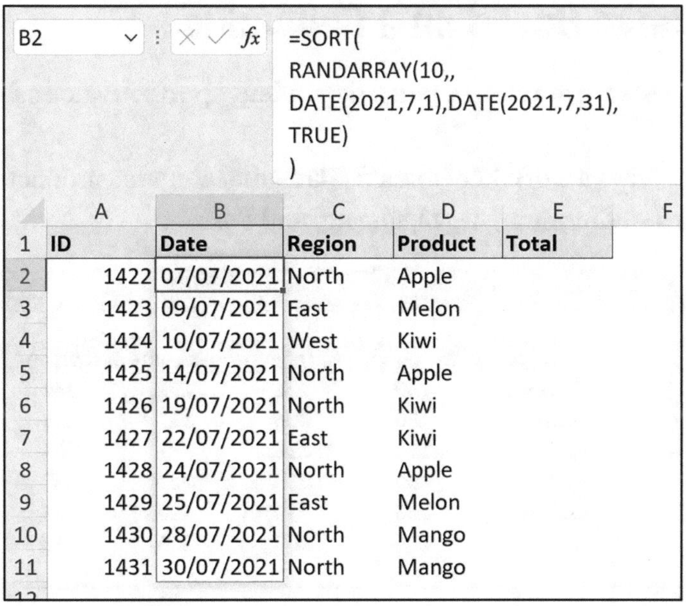

B2 =SORT(
RANDARRAY(10,,
DATE(2021,7,1),DATE(2021,7,31),
TRUE)
)

	A	B	C	D	E
1	ID	Date	Region	Product	Total
2	1422	07/07/2021	North	Apple	
3	1423	09/07/2021	East	Melon	
4	1424	10/07/2021	West	Kiwi	
5	1425	14/07/2021	North	Apple	
6	1426	19/07/2021	North	Kiwi	
7	1427	22/07/2021	East	Kiwi	
8	1428	24/07/2021	North	Apple	
9	1429	25/07/2021	East	Melon	
10	1430	28/07/2021	North	Mango	
11	1431	30/07/2021	North	Mango	

Figure 11-17. *Random date values in July 2021 in ascending order*

Finally, the following formula is used to produce the values for the [Total] column (Figure 11-18). The RANDARRAY function returns decimal values between 10 and 300. These values are then rounded to two decimal places.

```
=ROUND(RANDARRAY(10,,10,300),2)
```

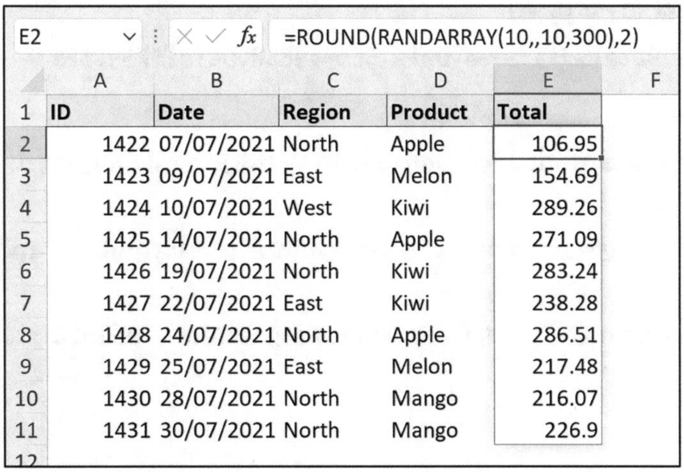

E2 =ROUND(RANDARRAY(10,,10,300),2)

	A	B	C	D	E
1	ID	Date	Region	Product	Total
2	1422	07/07/2021	North	Apple	106.95
3	1423	09/07/2021	East	Melon	154.69
4	1424	10/07/2021	West	Kiwi	289.26
5	1425	14/07/2021	North	Apple	271.09
6	1426	19/07/2021	North	Kiwi	283.24
7	1427	22/07/2021	East	Kiwi	238.28
8	1428	24/07/2021	North	Apple	286.51
9	1429	25/07/2021	East	Melon	217.48
10	1430	28/07/2021	North	Mango	216.07
11	1431	30/07/2021	North	Mango	226.9

Figure 11-18. *Generating random decimal values*

Return a Range Based on a Cell Value

In this example, we want to return a range dependent upon the value selected from a drop-down list.

Figure 11-19 shows a worksheet named [Data] that contains product sales for four different locations – Edmonton, Argyll, Regent, and Euston.

	A	B	C	D	E	F
1						
2		Product	Edmonton	Argyll	Regent	Euston
3		Coffee	230	141	191	147
4		Toast	156	406	157	106
5		Eggs	174	356	377	304
6		Muffins	405	336	220	238
7		Waffles	160	258	469	328
8		Bacon	334	405	296	358
9						

Figure 11-19. *Data for range selection by CHOOSE*

In Figure 11-20, the following formula returns the range that matches the location specified in cell C4. The MATCH function returns the index number of the range to be used. It looks for the value in cell C4 along the headers of the data in range C2:F2 and returns the index number of the matching location.

```
=CHOOSE(
MATCH(C4,Data!$C$2:$F$2,0),
Data!$C$3:$C$8,Data!$D$3:$D$8,Data!$E$3:$E$8,Data!$F$3:$F$8
)
```

When a different location is chosen in cell C4, the formula returns the required results.

In a dynamic array version of Excel, the results of this formula are spilled to the cells below.

In a non-DA version of Excel, use the following formula and fill the formula down to cell C10:

```
=CHOOSE(
MATCH($C$4,Data!$C$2:$F$2,0),
Data!C3,Data!D3,Data!E3,Data!F3
)
```

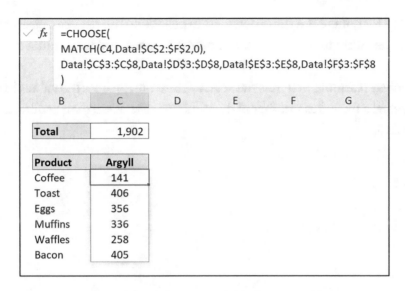

Figure 11-20. *Returning a range based on the value in cell C4*

The following formula is entered in cell C2 to sum the values in the range returned by the CHOOSE function:

```
=SUM(
CHOOSE(MATCH(C4,Data!$C$2:$F$2,0),
Data!$C$3:$C$8,Data!$D$3:$D$8,Data!$E$3:$E$8,Data!$F$3:$F$8)
)
```

Sure! In this example, the total could have been produced by referencing the range in C5:C10. In a dynamic array version of Excel, the spill range could be used, =SUM(C5#), but in other versions the fixed range could be used, =SUM(C5:C10).

However, we wanted to demonstrate the use of the CHOOSE function returning a range based on a cell value and passing this directly to the SUM function. This formula would sum the values for the chosen location without the need to return the values to the worksheet.

Choosing a Function from a List

The technique of selecting a different function from a list is one of my favorite uses of the CHOOSE function. The list can contain any functions you want. In this example, the SUM, AVERAGE, and MAX functions are made available for a user to choose from.

In Figure 11-21, there is a drop-down list in cell B2, so the user can easily select the function they want to use. The table of product names and total values is named [tblSales].

The following formula matches the selected function against the values in range E1:E3 and returns the index number of that function. CHOOSE then actions the specified function in its list.

```
=CHOOSE(
MATCH(B2,E1:E3,0),
SUM(tblSales[Total]),
AVERAGE(tblSales[Total]),
MAX(tblSales[Total])
)
```

The function list in range E1:E3 is shown on the same sheet to simplify the demonstration of the technique. This would typically be on a hidden sheet.

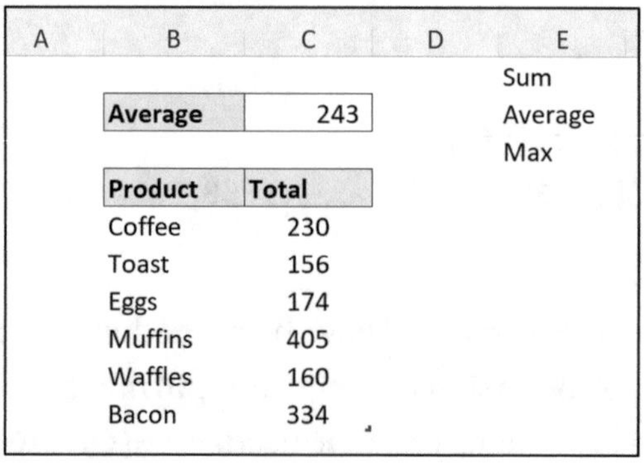

Figure 11-21. *Choosing a function from a drop-down list*

Simple and very effective. We have seen in the examples so far how easily the CHOOSE function can be used to insert some interactivity into an Excel report or model, and how a user could change the calculation being applied or the range that is being used.

Using CHOOSE with Form Controls

A few of the form controls in Excel, such as the list box, combo box, and option buttons, return an index number to represent the selection made in the control. This makes them ideal to be used with the CHOOSE function, as CHOOSE also uses an index number to identify the selection made.

Continuing with the previous example, let's provide a form control for the user to make the function selection instead of the drop-down list. We will use the option button control for the example.

Figure 11-22 shows three option buttons, one for each of the three functions to choose from – SUM, AVERAGE, and MAX. The table of product names and totals is named [tblProductSales].

Cells C2 and D2 are currently empty. We will use the CHOOSE function in cell C2 to return the chosen function name, and in cell D2, the CHOOSE function will run the chosen function and return its result.

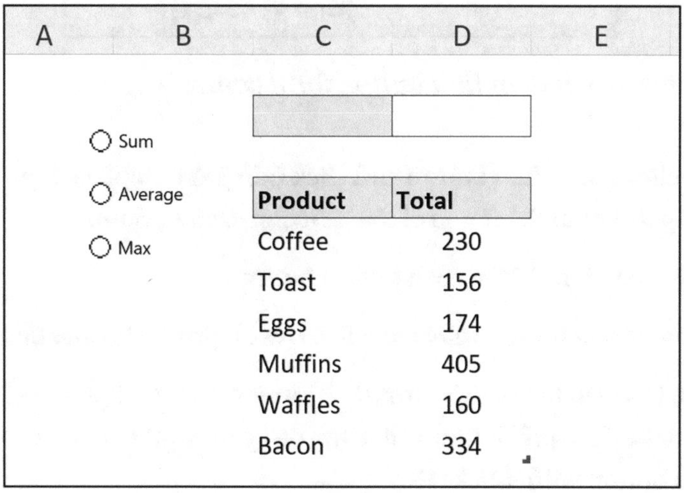

A	B	C	D	E
	◯ Sum			
	◯ Average	**Product**	**Total**	
	◯ Max	Coffee	230	
		Toast	156	
		Eggs	174	
		Muffins	405	
		Waffles	160	
		Bacon	334	

Figure 11-22. *Option buttons to enable the user selection of a function*

Let's first take a quick look at how to insert the option button controls:

1. Click **Developer ➤ Insert ➤ Option Button (Form Control)** (Figure 11-23).

Note   No Developer tab on the Ribbon? Right-click the Ribbon, click **Customize the Ribbon** and check the **Developer** box in the list on the right. Click **OK**. On a Mac, click **Excel ➤ Preferences ➤ Ribbon & Toolbar ➤ Customize the Ribbon** and check **Developer**.

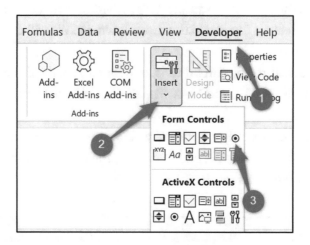

Figure 11-23. *Inserting an option button form control*

2. Right-click the option button and click **Edit Text**. Replace the existing text with the name of the function, that is, Sum.

3. Repeat steps 1 and 2 for each option button.

4. With an option button selected, click **Developer ➤ Properties**.

5. On the **Control** tab of the *Format Control* window (Figure 11-24), click in the *Cell link* box and click the cell you want to connect the option button with. Click **OK**.

   Cell F1 has been used in this example. This means that the index number of the selected option button will appear in this cell.

Figure 11-24. *Formatting the option button controls*

Now that we have our option button controls inserted, let's get back to the CHOOSE function.

In Figure 11-25, the following CHOOSE function is entered in cell C2 to return the name of the chosen function. It uses the index number from cell F1, the cell linked to the option buttons.

```
=CHOOSE(F1,"Sum","Average","Max")
```

And the following formula is entered in cell D2 to return the result of the chosen function:

```
=CHOOSE(F1,
SUM(tblProductSales[Total]),
AVERAGE(tblProductSales[Total]),
MAX(tblProductSales[Total])
)
```

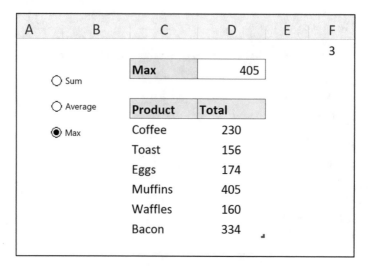

Figure 11-25. *Choosing a function via option buttons*

INDIRECT Function

Availability: All versions

File   indirect.xlsx

The INDIRECT function converts a text string into a reference to a cell, table, named range, or some other reference.

It is used to create dynamic references within formulas. Instead of directly typing a reference into a formula, a cell value can be used as the input of the reference text. The reference within the formula is then updated when the cell value is changed.

The INDIRECT function has two arguments, though only the first is generally used:

=INDIRECT(ref_text, [a1])

- **Ref text:** The reference to a cell, range name, or table entered as text.

- **[a1]:** A logical value that specifies the type of reference to be used – A1 or R1C1. Enter TRUE or omit the argument to specify the A1 reference style. Enter FALSE for the R1C1 reference style.

When using INDIRECT, the A1 style is generally used; therefore, the second argument is normally omitted. The A1 style is the style that Excel users are more familiar with. For example, B3 and D10 are both A1 style references.

An R1C1 reference style is when numbers are used to reference the row and column of a cell. It is always entered with the row first and the column second. For example, R4C5 is a reference to cell E4. Cell E4 is in the fourth row and the fifth column.

INDIRECT is one of the eight volatile functions in Excel. These functions recalculate, along with all dependents, every time Excel recalculates. Heavy reliance on these functions can slow calculation time, so should be used sparingly. Worth knowing, however it does not detract from INDIRECT being very useful.

To demonstrate a simple example of how INDIRECT works, in Figure 11-26, cell D2 indirectly references cell B2.

Cell B4 is used as an input cell and provides a text reference to cell B2 for the INDIRECT function. The value in cell B2 is returned. Only the *ref text* argument is provided, so an A1 style reference is applied.

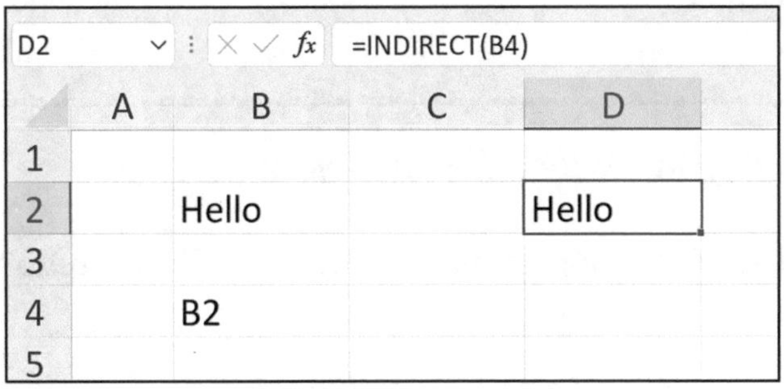

***Figure 11-26.** Basic example of INDIRECT*

Let's see some more practical examples of the application of the INDIRECT function. We will see examples that demonstrate the dynamic referencing of ranges on other worksheets, named ranges, and data stored in tables.

Indirect Table Reference in VLOOKUP

In this first example, we will use the INDIRECT function to indirectly reference a table.

We want to use the VLOOKUP function to return the grade associated with the score a student achieved in a subject. Each subject has its own grading system, so they have their own separate lookup tables. VLOOKUP will know which lookup table to refer to because it is specified in a cell. INDIRECT will perform the task of converting this cell value into a reference for VLOOKUP.

Figure 11-27 shows the three lookup tables – [French], [Maths], and [Art].

B	C	D	E	F	G	H	I
French			Maths			Art	
Score	Grade		Score	Grade		Score	Grade
0	Poor		0	Poor		0	Poor
50	Average		60	Good		60	Basic
65	Good		75	Very Good		75	Good
75	Very Good		90	Superb		85	Very Good
90	Excellent					95	Master

Figure 11-27. *Lookup tables for different subjects*

In Figure 11-28, the following formula is entered in cell E2 to return the grade for each row of the table:

```
=VLOOKUP([@Score],INDIRECT([@Subject]),2,TRUE)
```

The INDIRECT function is nested in the *table array* argument of VLOOKUP. It takes the value from the [Subject] column for the current row and converts it to a reference. The values in the [Subject] column match the names of the three lookup tables, so this is a simple reference to make.

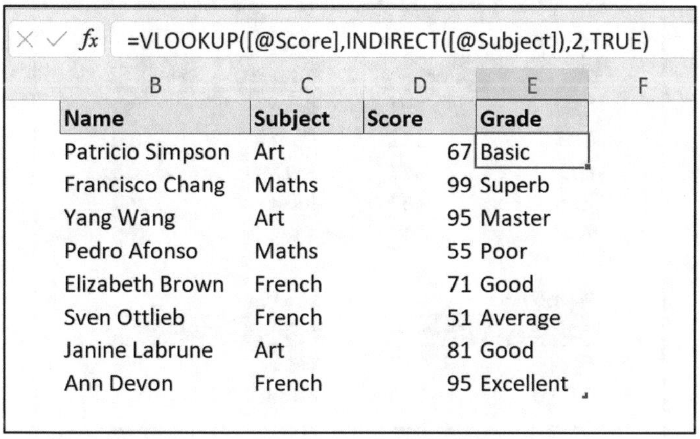

	B	C	D	E	F

× ✓ *fx*   =VLOOKUP([@Score],INDIRECT([@Subject]),2,TRUE)

Name	Subject	Score	Grade	
Patricio Simpson	Art	67	Basic	
Francisco Chang	Maths	99	Superb	
Yang Wang	Art	95	Master	
Pedro Afonso	Maths	55	Poor	
Elizabeth Brown	French	71	Good	
Sven Ottlieb	French	51	Average	
Janine Labrune	Art	81	Good	
Ann Devon	French	95	Excellent	

Figure 11-28. *VLOOKUP indirectly referencing a table*

Referencing Table Columns with INDIRECT

In this example, instead of referencing an entire table we will reference a specific column within a table.

We have four tables, each containing sales data for a different city – [tblManchester], [tblLeeds], [tblPlymouth], and [tblLincoln]. We want to use the SUM function to sum values from the table specified by a cell value.

Figure 11-29 shows the four different tables. We want to sum the values in the [Total] column for the specified table. To do this, we need to build a reference from some text strings and a cell value in INDIRECT.

The reference is made up of three separate sections, the "tbl" prefix, the table name, and then the column reference as text "[Sales]."

Manchester		Leeds	
Product	Sales	Product	Sales
Cake	592	Cake	392
Coffee	111	Coffee	329
Fruit	342	Fruit	413
Juice	457	Juice	264
Tea	393	Tea	106

Plymouth		Lincoln	
Product	Sales	Product	Sales
Cake	537	Cake	306
Coffee	536	Coffee	412
Fruit	453	Fruit	398
Juice	402	Juice	138
Tea	110	Tea	289

Figure 11-29. *Separate tables for different cities*

In Figure 11-30, the following formula sums the [Sales] values from the table stated in cell B3:

```
=SUM(INDIRECT("tbl"&B3&"[Sales]"))
```

		=SUM(INDIRECT("tbl"&B3&"[Sales]"))			
B	C	D	E	F

City	Total
Lincoln	1,543

Figure 11-30. *INDIRECT to reference a table column*

Referencing Other Worksheets

The INDIRECT function can be used to dynamically reference other worksheets using the value in a cell.

In Figure 11-31, we have sales values like the previous example, but this time they are ranges on separate worksheets instead of separate tables. There are four worksheets – [Milton Keynes], [Derby], [Hartlepool], and [Gloucester]. The sales values in each worksheet are in range C3:C7.

	A	B	C	D	E	F
1						
2		**Product**	**Sales**			
3		Cake	592			
4		Coffee	111			
5		Fruit	342			
6		Juice	457			
7		Tea	393			
8						
9						
10						
23						
24						

◀ ▶ ... | INDIRECT other Sheets | **Milton Keynes** | Derby | Hartlepool | Gloucester

Figure 11-31. *Sales data on separate worksheets*

In Figure 11-32, the following formula sums the values from range C3:C7 on the worksheet specified by the value in cell B3:

```
=SUM(INDIRECT("'"&B3&"'!C3:C7"))
```

Within the INDIRECT function, the reference to the sum range is made up of three parts. There is a single quotation ('), followed by the value in cell B3, and then the final string. The final text string contains the closing single quotation, an exclamation mark, and then range C3:C7.

The three parts combined form the following reference. The single quotations are required because one of the sheet names (Milton Keynes) contains spaces.

```
'Hartlepool'!C3:C7
```

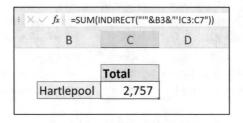

Figure 11-32. *INDIRECT to reference a sheet using a cell value*

When the sheet name in cell B3 is changed, the formula updates to sum the correct values.

In Chapter 1, we covered the topic of sheet references. If any aspect of the references is unclear, I encourage reading through that chapter and the dedicated chapters for defined names and working with tables. A strong understanding of how to reference cells is imperative for advanced formula skills.

Pivot Style Report with Dynamic Row Labels

We have created a couple of pivot style reports in this book using dynamic array formulas. In this example, we take it further by using the INDIRECT function to create dynamic row labels. The example uses dynamic arrays and so requires an Excel for the Web, Excel for Microsoft 365, or Excel 2021 version of Excel.

The report will be created using the table shown in Figure 11-33. This table is named [tblSales]. The image shows a snapshot of the first nine rows of the table.

For the pivot style report, we will display the last N months along the column labels using the SEQUENCE formula on the [Date] column that we detailed in Chapter 10.

For the row labels, we will provide a drop-down list for the user to pick between the [Sales Rep] column and the [Region] column. The INDIRECT function will be used to create the functionality for a user to switch between columns via a drop-down list.

A SUMIFS function will then be used to total the values in the [Sales] column for the month specified in that column and the sales rep or region value stated in that row.

	A	B	C	D	E
1	Date	Sales Rep	Region	Category	Sales
2	17/03/2021	Marga Muck	France	Alcoholic drinks	£ 8.98
3	17/03/2021	Olivier Beggi	Italy	Alcoholic drinks	£ 11.37
4	19/03/2021	Olivier Beggi	Australia	Alcoholic drinks	£ 174.83
5	22/03/2021	Cecilius Rockall	Canada	Alcoholic drinks	£ 154.80
6	22/03/2021	Tam Matthessen	Italy	Alcoholic drinks	£ 170.51
7	23/03/2021	Jean Giampietro	USA	Alcoholic drinks	£ 34.15
8	25/03/2021	Cecilius Rockall	USA	Alcoholic drinks	£ 109.43
9	26/03/2021	Jean Giampietro	Italy	Alcoholic drinks	£ 63.68
10	27/03/2021	Rock Bemwell	USA	Alcoholic drinks	£ 97.92

Figure 11-33. *Sales data for the pivot style report*

Figure 11-34 shows the setup of the pivot style report before we introduce the dynamic row labels and sales totals.

The following SEQUENCE formula is entered in cell D4 to produce the first date of the month for the last N months. The N value is specified by the value in cell D2.

```
=DATE(2021,
SEQUENCE(,D2,MONTH(MAX(tblSales[Date]))-D2+1,1),
1)
```

A Data Validation list is added to cell C4 to make it easy for a user to pick the column they want to use for the row labels.

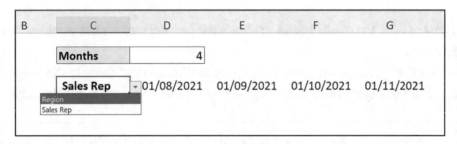

Figure 11-34. *Drop-down list to pick the column to use for row labels*

To create the dynamic row labels, we will create a distinct list for each of the [Sales Rep] and [Region] column values using dynamic array formulas. We will then define names for these spill ranges and use the INDIRECT function to dynamically refer to these names.

In Figure 11-35, the following formula is entered in cells A1 and C1 of a sheet named [Lists] to create the distinct and ordered lists:

```
=SORT(UNIQUE(tblSales[Sales Rep]))
```

	A	B	C	D
1	Benjamen Strathe		Australia	
2	Cecilius Rockall		Belgium	
3	Jean Giampietro		Canada	
4	Marga Muck		France	
5	Olivier Beggi		India	
6	Phillip Godbehere		Italy	
7	Rock Bemwell		Netherlands	
8	Tam Matthessen		UK	
9			USA	
10				

Figure 11-35. *Lists for the sales reps and region labels*

In Figure 11-36, the *Name Manager* shows the two defined names established for each spill range.

The [Sales_Rep] name has been defined for the "Sales Rep" value in the drop-down list. You cannot use spaces in a name, so the underscore was used as the delimiter.

Note   Unsure how to define a named range? Please refer to Chapter 3, where we learn all about defined names in Excel.

Name Manager

New...	Edit...	Delete

Name	Value	Refers To	Scope	Co
Art	{"0","Poor";"60","Basic";...	='VLOOKUP Tables'!$H...	Workbook	
French	{"0","Poor";"50","Avera...	='VLOOKUP Tables'!$B...	Workbook	
Maths	{"0","Poor";"60","Good"...	'VLOOKUP Tables'!$E...	Workbook	
Region	{...}	=Lists!$C$1#	Workbook	
Sales_Rep	{...}	=Lists!$A$1#	Workbook	
tblLeeds	{"Cake","392";"Coffee",...	='SUM & INDIRECT'!$...	Workbook	
tblLincoln	{"Cake","306";"Coffee",...	='SUM & INDIRECT'!$...	Workbook	
tblManchester	{"Cake","592";"Coffee",...	='SUM & INDIRECT'!$...	Workbook	
tblPlymouth	{"Cake","537";"Coffee",...	='SUM & INDIRECT'!$...	Workbook	
tblSales	{"17/03/2021","Marga ...	=Data!$A$2:$E$3896	Workbook	
tblSubjectGrades	{"Patricio Simpson","Ar...	=VLOOKUP!$B$2:$E$9	Workbook	

Figure 11-36. *Defined names for the two list spill ranges*

In Figure 11-37, the following formula is entered in cell C5 to return the dynamic row labels. The SUBSTITUTE function is applied within INDIRECT to replace spaces with an underscore so that the "Sales Rep" drop-down value and the [Sales_Rep] named range match.

```
=INDIRECT(SUBSTITUTE(C4," ","_"))
```

As an alternative approach to the dynamic array formulas and defined names, the following formula could be used in cell C5 to generate the dynamic row labels:

```
=SORT(UNIQUE(INDIRECT("tblSales["&C4&"]")))
```

This formula refers to the table column using a reference that is a combination of text strings and the value in cell C4, like we covered a couple of examples previously.

The decision to use defined names instead of a table column reference in the main example was because in a "real-world" scenario, we may require those distinct lists for other formulas or tasks, such as the labels of a category axis in a column chart. The defined names can be reused as many times as required.

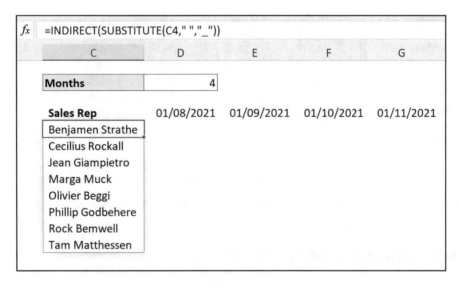

Figure 11-37. Dynamic row labels with INDIRECT

To complete the pivot style report, the following formula is entered in cell D5 (Figure 11-38):

```
=SUMIFS(tblSales[Sales],
INDIRECT("tblSales["&C4&"]"),C5#,
tblSales[Date],">="&D4#,
tblSales[Date],"<="&EOMONTH(+D4#,0)
)
```

In the *criteria range 1* argument of SUMIFS, the INDIRECT function is used to refer to the correct table column as stated in cell C4.

The spill ranges for the row labels and column labels are both referenced. The "+" operator is entered before the D4# reference in the EOMONTH function to enable the spill range reference. EOMONTH does not natively work with spill ranges.

C	D	E	F	G	H
Months	5				
Region	01/07/2021	01/08/2021	01/09/2021	01/10/2021	01/11/2021
Australia	5,210	6,832	4,540	7,903	725
Belgium	3,977	6,335	6,742	6,006	1,003
Canada	7,717	5,908	5,235	6,048	332
France	3,618	7,563	6,480	5,021	653
India	5,714	5,957	4,830	4,963	696
Italy	5,604	7,134	4,892	5,515	507
Netherlands	5,694	7,797	6,285	5,983	887
UK	4,884	6,564	5,563	4,913	374
USA	6,916	5,743	4,947	6,461	375

Figure 11-38. Dynamic SUMIFS added to complete the pivot style report

R1C1 Reference with INDIRECT

In addition to the A1 style of reference generally used with INDIRECT, the R1C1 reference style can also be applied. With the R1C1 style, row and column numbers are used to specify the cell reference. This is especially useful for columns as the A1 style does not enable us to refer to a column using a number.

In Figure 11-39, the following formula is entered in cell C2 to return the value associated with the name stated in cell B2 and for the last column:

```
=INDIRECT(
"R"&MATCH(B2,tblMonthly[Name],0)+4&
"C"&COLUMNS(tblMonthly)+1,
FALSE)
```

A MATCH function is used to return the row number of the name specified in cell B2. The R1C1 reference of INDIRECT refers to the row and column numbers of the sheet, so four is added to this value to offset the four rows above the names in the table (B1:B4).

The COLUMNS function is used to return the number of columns in the [tblMonthly] table. One is added to account for column A to the left of the table.

This is all then joined together to form the R1C1 reference. The completed R1C1 reference used in Figure 11-39 would read R9C7. FALSE is entered for the *a1* argument to specify that an R1C1 reference style has been used.

	A	B	C	D	E	F	G
1			Last Month	Total			
2		Enrico	102	399			
3							
4		Name	Jan	Feb	Mar	Apr	May
5		Victoria	120	26	57	112	107
6		Janet	95	135	38	89	81
7		Kyle	111	49	90	79	50
8		Hiran	83	108	81	118	131
9		Enrico	81	97	63	56	102
10		Amber	122	123	93	94	121
11		Stephanie	31	120	124	85	39
12							

Figure 11-39. *R1C1 reference style used with INDIRECT*

The INDIRECT function can also be used to return a range.

The following formula is entered in cell D2 to sum all values for the name stated in cell B2:

```
=SUM(
INDIRECT("R"&MATCH(B2,tblMonthly[Name],0)+4&"C3",FALSE):
```

```
INDIRECT("R"&MATCH(B2,tblMonthly[Name],0)+4&"C"&COLUMNS(tblMonthly)
+1,FALSE)
)
```

In this formula, two INDIRECT functions using R1C1 reference styles are used to form a range by entering a colon (:) between them. This is given to a SUM function to sum the values.

The first INDIRECT is fixed to start from column 3, while the second INDIRECT returns the final column in the table using the COLUMNS function with one added to it. MATCH is again used to return the row number for the name entered in cell B2.

Note   The INDEX function is a better function for referring to cells using numbers. This example of an R1C1 reference style is only shown for the purposes of a deeper understanding of the INDIRECT function.

OFFSET Function

Availability: All versions

File   offset.xlsx

The OFFSET function returns a reference to a range that is a given number of rows and/or columns from a start range. This reference can be a single cell or multiple cells that are a specified number of rows high and columns wide.

This function is fantastic for dynamic references that may change in size over time or are specified by the value in a cell.

The syntax for the OFFSET function is as follows:

```
=OFFSET(reference, rows, cols, [height], [width])
```

- **Reference:** The start reference from which to offset.

- **Rows:** The number of rows above or below the start reference you want to offset. Enter a positive number to reference the range the given number of rows below, or a negative number to reference the range the given number of rows above.

- **Cols:** The number of columns to the right or left of the start reference you want to offset. Enter a positive number to reference the range the given number of columns to the right, or a negative number to reference the range the given number of columns to the left.

- **[Height]:** The number of rows in height of the returned range. This is an optional argument, and if omitted, the range returned is the same height as the start reference.

- **[Width]:** The number of columns in width of the returned range. This is an optional argument, and if omitted, the range returned is the same width as the start reference.

Note   The OFFSET function gets a somewhat unfair reputation of being bad due to it being a volatile function. This means it recalculates every time Excel recalculates, regardless of which cell values were changed. It is, however, a very useful function that should not be disregarded so easily.

Simple Examples

Let's begin by looking at some simple examples of OFFSET to get a strong understanding of how it operates before we progress to more practical examples.

In Figure 11-40, the following OFFSET function returns the value that is four rows below and one column to the right of the start reference A1. This is cell B5. The number of rows to offset is specified by the value in cell D3.

```
=OFFSET(A1,H2,1)
```

The *height* and *width* arguments are omitted, so a single cell reference is used, as this matches the height and width of the start reference.

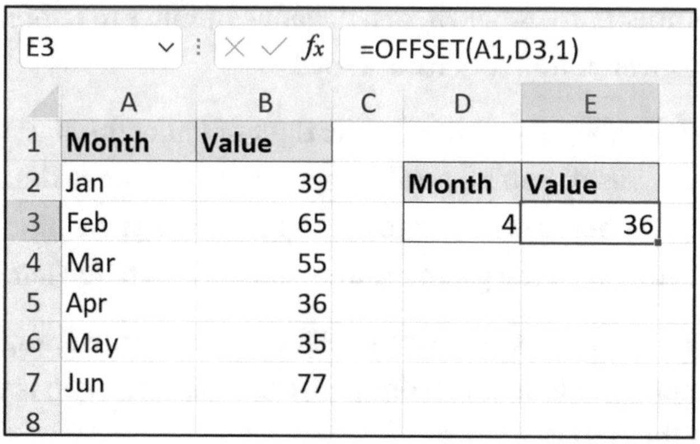

E3 =OFFSET(A1,D3,1)

	A	B	C	D	E
1	**Month**	**Value**			
2	Jan	39		**Month**	**Value**
3	Feb	65		4	36
4	Mar	55			
5	Apr	36			
6	May	35			
7	Jun	77			
8					

Figure 11-40. *Simple OFFSET example*

Functions such as COUNT, MATCH, and COLUMNS are often used to calculate the number of rows or columns to offset. So, let's see an example.

In Figure 11-41, the following formula returns the value for the name specified in cell G2 and the month specified in cell H2:

```
=OFFSET(G4,MATCH(G2,G5:G9,0),H2)
```

The start reference is G4. This is the top-left corner of the range that we are returning the value. This start reference can be any reference. However, it is often the top-left corner cell of the range or table from which you are returning the reference.

The MATCH function is used to find the number of rows to offset, and an input cell (H2) is used for the number of columns to offset.

Both these examples return a single cell reference, but we will start to look at returning multiple cell ranges next.

fx	=OFFSET(G4,MATCH(G2,G5:G9,0),H2)			
G	H	I	J	K
Name	**Month**	**Value**		
Janet	4	53		
Name	**Jan**	**Feb**	**Mar**	**Apr**
Victoria	41	42	61	27
Janet	45	26	34	53
Kyle	61	41	68	61
Hiran	35	50	23	66
Enrico	45	60	53	32

Figure 11-41. OFFSET example using cell values for row and column offsets

Sum the Values in the Nth Column

The OFFSET function can return a range of cells, and this range can be given to another function for use. This delivers the ability to provide dynamic ranges to functions.

In Figure 11-42, the following formula sums all values for a specified column in the [tblNCol] table:

```
=SUM(OFFSET(B5,1,B3,ROWS(tblNCol),1))
```

The start reference is cell B5, so the range to return is offset by one row. If the OFFSET function was given a start reference of B6 (same row that the numbers start), we would not need to offset a row. However, it is important to be consistent in the way you work, and I like to use the top-left corner cell. The number of columns to offset is specified by the value in cell B3.

The ROWS function is used to ascertain the height of the range to return. The ROWS function returns the number of rows in the table, excluding the headers.

The width of the range is a fixed value of 1. This did not need to be stated, as if omitted, the same width as the start reference is used. However, it is included for a fully documented function.

| ✓ | : | X ✓ | *fx* | =SUM(OFFSET(B5,1,B3,ROWS(tblNCol),1)) |

B	C	D	E	F	G
Month	**Month**	**Value**			
	2	219			
Name	**Jan**	**Feb**	**Mar**	**Apr**	**May**
Victoria	41	42	61	27	65
Janet	45	26	34	53	47
Kyle	61	41	68	61	58
Hiran	35	50	23	66	66
Enrico	45	60	53	32	26

Figure 11-42. *Summing all values for a specified column*

The cell input being provided may be the month name instead of the month number. This is no problem, as a function such as MATCH can be used.

In Figure 11-43, the same formula is used as before, except the introduction of the MATCH function to return the number of columns to offset from cell B5:

```
=SUM(OFFSET(B5,1,
MATCH(C3,tblNCol[#Headers],0)-1,
ROWS(tblNCol),1))
```

One is subtracted from the result returned by MATCH. This is because the MATCH function is searching for the matching month name in all headers of the table. And because the start reference is in the first column of the table, MATCH returns a column number one more than is required.

This is a key point to understand when familiarizing yourself with OFFSET. It is not using the column or row number of the table or range like the INDEX function does, it is using the number of columns or rows away from the start reference.

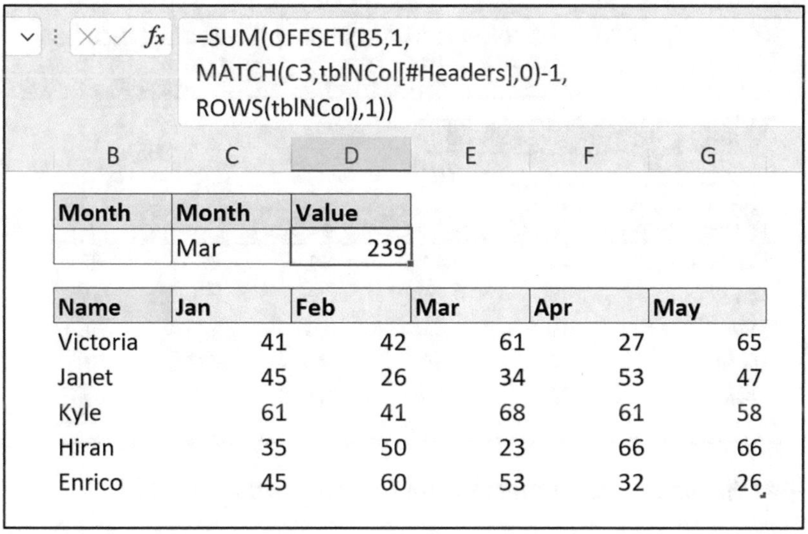

| ✓ | : | ✕ ✓ | fx | =SUM(OFFSET(B5,1, |

=SUM(OFFSET(B5,1,
MATCH(C3,tblNCol[#Headers],0)-1,
ROWS(tblNCol),1))

B	C	D	E	F	G
Month	Month	Value			
	Mar	239			
Name	Jan	Feb	Mar	Apr	May
Victoria	41	42	61	27	65
Janet	45	26	34	53	47
Kyle	61	41	68	61	58
Hiran	35	50	23	66	66
Enrico	45	60	53	32	26

Figure 11-43. *Summing the values of a specified column with MATCH*

Finally, let's sum the values for the last column in the table (Figure 11-44). The following formula uses the COLUMNS function to return the number of columns to offset. Again, one is subtracted to cater for the start reference being in the first column of the table.

```
=SUM(OFFSET(B5,1,COLUMNS(tblNCol)-1,ROWS(tblNCol),1))
```

Of course, instead of subtracting one, we could have specified a start reference as the first column to the left of the table. You may prefer this adaptation to get OFFSET to return the correct range. However, as mentioned before, I like to keep consistency to my approach, so I know what to expect.

	fx	=SUM(OFFSET(B5,1,COLUMNS(tblNCol)-1,ROWS(tblNCol),1))

	B	C	D	E	F	G	H
	Month	Month	Last Month				
			262				
	Name	Jan	Feb	Mar	Apr	May	
	Victoria	41	42	61	27	65	
	Janet	45	26	34	53	47	
	Kyle	61	41	68	61	58	
	Hiran	35	50	23	66	66	
	Enrico	45	60	53	32	26	

Figure 11-44. *Summing all values in the last column of a table*

Return the Last X Columns

Instead of returning a range to another function, it could be returned to the worksheet.

Figure 11-45 shows a table named [tblResults] containing 12 rounds of competition results for six different teams. There are three types of result: "W" = win, "D" = draw, and "L" = loss.

	A	B	C	D	E	F	G	H	I	J	K	L	M	N
1														
2		Team	R1	R2	R3	R4	R5	R6	R7	R8	R9	R10	R11	R12
3		Albatross	L	L	D	L	W	D	L	D	L	D	W	L
4		Tigers	D	D	D	W	D	D	W	L	L	W	L	L
5		The Eagles	D	L	D	L	D	D	W	D	D	D	L	W
6		Leopards	D	D	D	W	W	W	D	L	L	W	L	D
7		The Chargers	L	W	D	D	D	L	L	W	W	L	W	D
8		Beetles	L	D	D	D	W	W	D	W	D	L	D	L
9														

Figure 11-45. *Table of team results*

From another sheet, we want to return the last six results for a specified team. It is common in sports dashboards to see recent results for teams like this.

In Figure 11-46, the following formula is entered in cell C2 to return the name of the last six rounds:

```
=OFFSET(Results!B2,,COLUMNS(tblResults)-6,1,6)
```

And the following formula returns the last six results of the team stated in cell B3 to cell C3:

```
=OFFSET(Results!B2,
MATCH(B3,tblResults[Team],0),
COLUMNS(tblResults)-6,1,6)
```

The COLUMNS function is used to find the starting column. COLUMNS returns the number of columns in the table, and six is then subtracted from this result to return the correct number of columns to offset.

The returned array is specified as one row high and six columns wide. Although these values are entered into the formula, they could be provided by a cell value, so a user can specify the number of results to return.

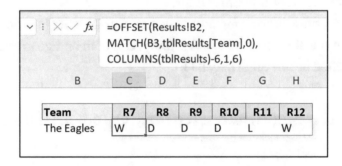

Figure 11-46. *Returning the last six results for a specified team*

Note   These formulas are being demonstrated in a dynamic array–enabled version of Excel. In non-dynamic array–enabled versions of Excel, the range of cells to return the reference will need to be selected before typing the formula. Also, **Ctrl + Shift + Enter** needs to be pressed to run an array formula.

The start reference used in both formulas is a reference to cell B2 of the [Results] worksheet. This is the cell in the top-left corner of the table. This works great, but an alternative approach could be to refer to the table itself.

When a start reference containing multiple cells is used, the cell in the top-left corner of that range is the start reference. The following formula shows the previous formula that returns the last six results, but with the start reference specified as tblResults[#All]:

```
=OFFSET(tblResults[#All],
MATCH(B3,tblResults[Team],0),
COLUMNS(tblResults)-6,1,6)
```

The OFFSET function returns a reference with the same dimensions as the start reference if the *height* and *width* arguments are not stated. This is important to remember if you are going to use multiple cell start references.

OFFSET with COUNTIFS

The OFFSET function can be used to provide a range to any function that requests one. We have seen an example of this already with the SUM function. Let's use the formula from this example with the COUNTIFS function to return the number of wins for a specific team in the last X number of rounds.

In Figure 11-47, the following formula uses a similar OFFSET function to before, except in this formula, the columns to offset and width of the range to return (number of rounds) are specified by the value in cell J3:

```
=COUNTIFS(
OFFSET(Results!B2,MATCH(K3,tblResults[Team],0),COLUMNS(tblResults)-
J3,1,J3),
"W")
```

The COUNTIFS function uses the range returned by OFFSET for its *criteria range* and counts the occurrences of "W."

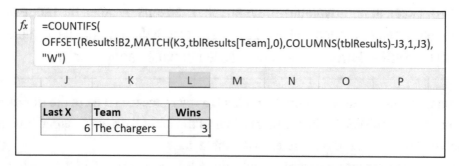

Figure 11-47. *OFFSET with COUNTIFS to count number of wins*

Note   This same technique can be applied to return the last X rows in a range by applying the ROWS function instead of COLUMNS, for example, to sum the last X rows.

INDEX Function

Availability: All versions

File   index.xlsx

The INDEX function is an absolutely incredible function in Excel. It does not sound very sexy, but it is stunningly useful. This section of the book will run through numerous examples that demonstrate the amazing power and versatility of this function.

The INDEX function is often teamed up with the MATCH or XMATCH function to create a flexible lookup formula. You may have heard of or used an INDEX-MATCH combination before.

The usefulness of the INDEX function stretches far beyond its role in the INDEX-MATCH combo. And in modern versions of Excel, with the dynamic array formulas, applications of INDEX have broadened even further. It is better and more important to know than ever before.

Introduction to the INDEX Function

The power of the INDEX function is really down to its simplicity and flexibility. The role of the INDEX function is to return the value or reference of a cell from a specified row and column number, in a given range.

A key part of that INDEX function description was its ability to return a value or a reference. It is incredibly helpful in accessing values in ranges, arrays, and spill ranges, but also creating dynamic references for other formulas or Excel features such as charts.

The description also stated that we need to provide the row and column number from which it returns the value or reference. This indexing approach is its superpower. We can state the row and column number in an absolute manner or find them using another function such as MATCH, COLUMN, COUNTA, and so on.

The sky is the limit for the INDEX function.

Let's take a look at its syntaxes. Yes, it has two different syntaxes (Figure 11-48).

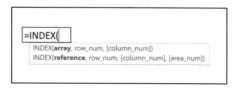

Figure 11-48. *The two syntaxes of the INDEX function*

The following is the first syntax of the INDEX function:

`=INDEX(array, row_num, [column_num])`

- **Array:** The range or array from which to return the value or reference.

- **Row num:** The row number in the array from which to return the value or reference. This argument is optional. If omitted, a column number should be provided.

- **[Column Num]:** The column number in the array from which to return the value or reference. If omitted, a row number should be provided.

When using the INDEX function, you will nearly always be using the first syntax. It is only the final INDEX function example in this book that demonstrates a use of the second syntax.

This is the second syntax of the INDEX function. This syntax is used to return a reference from a list. The chosen reference is specified by an index number:

`=INDEX(reference, row_num, [column_num], [area_num])`

- **Reference:** This is a list of one or more references enclosed within brackets.

- **Row Num:** The row number in the chosen reference from which to return the value or reference. This is an optional argument.

- **[Column num]:** The column number in the chosen reference from which to return the value or reference. This is an optional argument.

- **[Area num]:** The index number of the reference you want to return from the list of references.

Basics of the INDEX Function

To get a solid understanding of how the INDEX function operates, we will start with some basic examples and progress to the more exciting stuff.

In Figure 11-49, the following formula is used to return the value from the fourth row and second column of the range B3:C8:

```
=INDEX(B3:C8,4,2)
```

The purpose of this example is to show that the INDEX function returns from the row and column numbers of the array provided in the first argument, and not the row and column numbers of the sheet. This is a common mistake when beginning with INDEX.

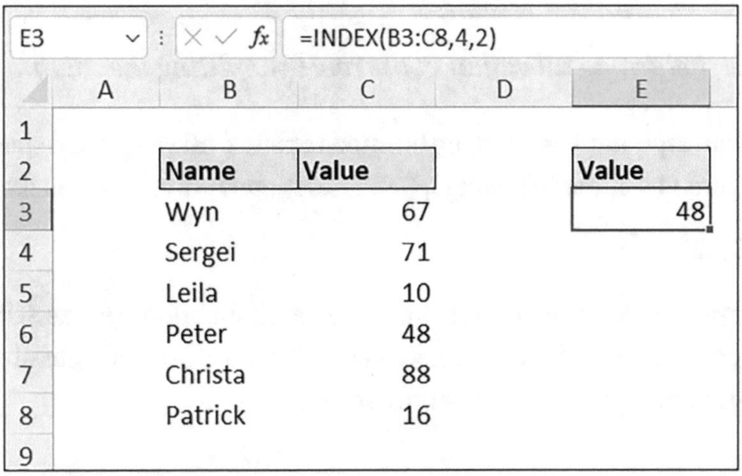

	A	B	C	D	E
1					
2		Name	Value		Value
3		Wyn	67		48
4		Sergei	71		
5		Leila	10		
6		Peter	48		
7		Christa	88		
8		Patrick	16		
9					

E3   =INDEX(B3:C8,4,2)

Figure 11-49. *Simple INDEX example*

An interesting aspect of the INDEX function is that it returns the values or reference of all cells in a row or column, if a row or column number is omitted.

This is very useful for users with a dynamic array–enabled version of Excel. It is a powerful method to access elements of an array. And we will see this technique later in this "INDEX Function" section and again later in the book.

Let's see exactly what I mean by this using the same range of B3:C8.

In Figure 11-50, the following INDEX function is entered in cell F3 and returns a spilled array of all values from the fifth row of the range B3:C8. Notice the comma after the *row num* argument. This is required.

```
=INDEX(B3:C8,5,)
```

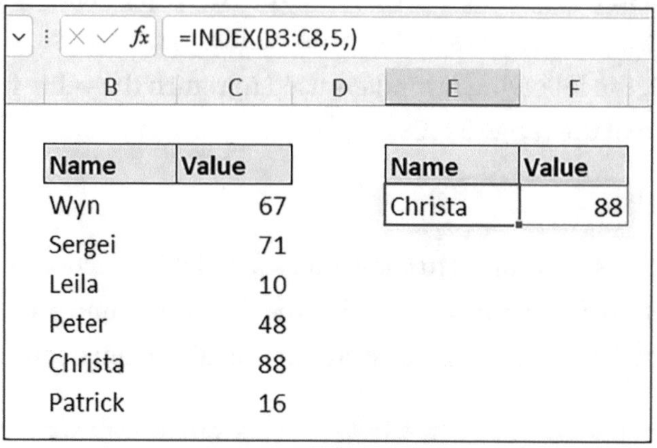

B	C	D	E	F
Name	**Value**		**Name**	**Value**
Wyn	67		Christa	88
Sergei	71			
Leila	10			
Peter	48			
Christa	88			
Patrick	16			

Formula bar: =INDEX(B3:C8,5,)

Figure 11-50. *Returning all values in the row by omitting the column number*

The *row num* argument can also be omitted to return all values in a specified column. In Figure 11-51, the following INDEX function is entered in cell E3:

```
=INDEX(B3:C8,,2)
```

These returned arrays can be fed to an aggregation function such as SUM or AVERAGE or given to a chart via a defined name. There are fantastic possibilities for such a simple little function that does something so awesome.

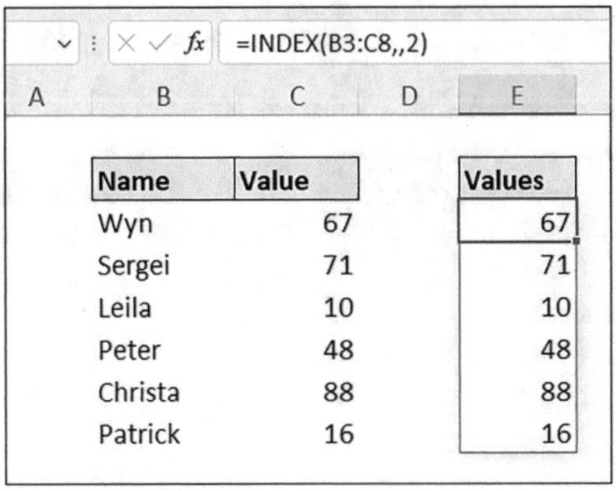

Figure 11-51. *Returning all values in a column by omitting the row number*

In all the examples so far, the column and row numbers have been entered directly into the formula. These numbers are normally returned by a function such as MATCH, COLUMNS, ROWS, or COUNTA for a dynamic and more robust method. Form controls such as the list box and option buttons are also great for serving index numbers to the INDEX function.

The most popular function to be affiliated with INDEX is the MATCH function. And in modern versions of Excel, it is the XMATCH function. With these functions, we can return the row or column number that matches a value we are looking for.

In Figure 11-52, the following formula is entered in cell F3 to return the value from range B3:C8 that is in column 2 and in the row where there is a match for the name entered in cell E3:

```
=INDEX(B3:C8,MATCH(E3,B3:B8,0),2)
```

The MATCH function is used to return the row number from range B3:B8 where there is a match for the name. In this example, the name "Sergei" is used. The MATCH function returns the row number 2. INDEX then returns the value in row 2 and column 2 from range B3:C8.

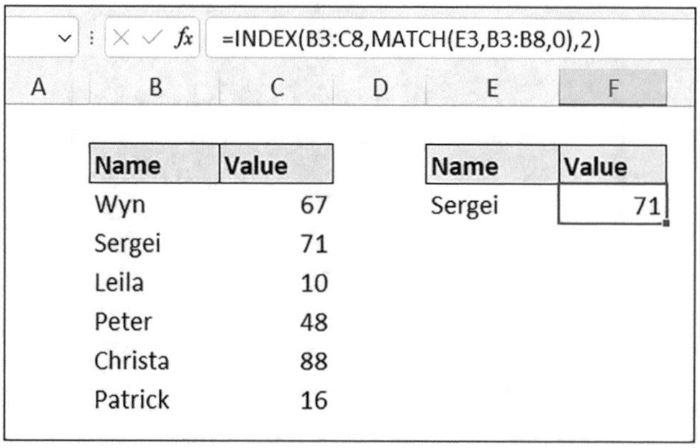

Figure 11-52. *INDEX and MATCH functions to look up a specific value*

This example uses a sheet range for the *array* that INDEX returns from and for the *lookup array* that MATCH searches in. This is adequate, but using data formatted as a table is more commonplace and provides additional advantages. Therefore, many, though not all, forthcoming examples will be working with data formatted as a table or an array returned by another function.

INDEX and MATCH/XMATCH for Versatile Lookups

Let's continue with further examples of the fantastic combination of INDEX and MATCH or INDEX and XMATCH functions. Together they provide an extremely versatile lookup formula that is available to all versions of Excel.

We saw a workaround in Chapter 7 that used the CHOOSE function to enable VLOOKUP to return a value from a column to the left of the lookup column. Now, the better alternative to that approach is the INDEX and MATCH combination. And these functions are available in all versions of Excel, unlike the newer XLOOKUP and FILTER options.

With INDEX and MATCH, you can look for a value down any column of a range or table (VLOOKUP only looks down the first column) and return from any column of the range or table.

Note   INDEX and MATCH will also look along and return from data arranged in rows, and we will see examples of this shortly.

In Figure 11-53, we have two tables. The table on the right is named [tblGrades]. It contains four different grades, each one associated with achieving a particular score. This is the lookup table, and notice that the [Grade] column is to the left of the [Score] column.

The table on the left is named [tblScores] and contains the scores achieved by different people.

The following formula is entered in cell D3 to return the grade attained by each person in [tblScores]. It looks for the score down the [Score] column of [tblGrades] and returns the corresponding grade from the [Grade] column.

```
=INDEX(tblGrades[Grade],MATCH([@Score],tblGrades[Score],1))
```

This formula demonstrates the versatility of INDEX and MATCH. It makes it simple to look for and return a value from any column of a table. It also highlights that INDEX-MATCH works brilliantly with data formatted as a table.

And finally, this formula shows the use of a range lookup. The 1 in the *match type* argument of MATCH specifies to return the exact match or next item smaller than the *lookup value*.

fx	=INDEX(tblGrades[Grade],MATCH([@Score],tblGrades[Score],1))						
B	C	D	E	F	G	H	
Name	**Score**	**Grade**		**Grade**	**Score**		
Gill	93	Superb		Poor	0		
Bryan	56	Poor		Good	60		
Kevin	95	Superb		Very Good	75		
Barbara	46	Poor		Superb	90		
Rachel	89	Very Good					
Sue	74	Good					

Figure 11-53. *Versatile INDEX and MATCH returning from a column to the left*

In Figure 11-54, the following formula achieves the same task using the INDEX and XMATCH combination. A different number (–1) is used to specify an exact match or next smaller item with XMATCH.

```
=INDEX(tblGrades[Grade],XMATCH([@Score],tblGrades[Score],-1))
```

In this example, the rows in the lookup table [tblGrades] are jumbled. This is a little unrealistic but demonstrates the robustness of the XMATCH function. It continues to function correctly. When using MATCH to look in ranges, the values in the *lookup array* must be in ascending order.

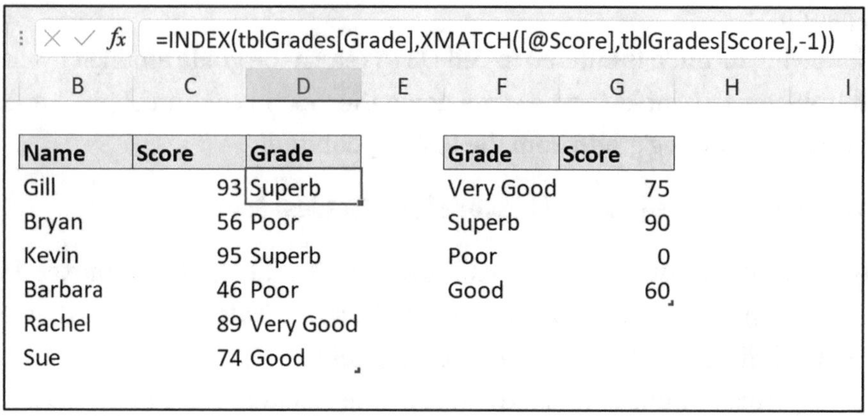

	fx	=INDEX(tblGrades[Grade],XMATCH([@Score],tblGrades[Score],-1))					
B	C	D	E	F	G	H	I

Name	Score	Grade		Grade	Score
Gill	93	Superb		Very Good	75
Bryan	56	Poor		Superb	90
Kevin	95	Superb		Poor	0
Barbara	46	Poor		Good	60
Rachel	89	Very Good			
Sue	74	Good			

Figure 11-54. INDEX and XMATCH performing a versatile range lookup

Two-Way Lookup with INDEX and MATCH/XMATCH

A two-way lookup can be created by using two MATCH or XMATCH functions with INDEX – one to search for a value down a column and another to search along a row.

Figure 11-55 shows a matrix of data. It contains prices for different holiday accommodations. The price is dependent upon the type of accommodation and the location. The type of accommodation is labeled in range B3:B7, and the different locations are labeled along range C2:F2.

We need a lookup formula to return the price for a given accommodation type and location. We will write this formula on another sheet. The sheet containing the price matrix is named [Prices].

	A	B	C	D	E	F
1						
2		Accommodation	Norfolk	Cumbria	Suffolk	Derbyshire
3		Woodland	133	137	130	129
4		Waterside	111	127	136	158
5		Treehouse	139	119	122	162
6		Spa Suite	155	169	174	177
7		Exclusive	241	293	297	295
8						

Figure 11-55. *Data matrix of accommodation prices by location*

In Figure 11-56, the following formula uses INDEX and MATCH to return the prices for the values stated in the [Accommodation] and [Location] columns of the table:

```
=INDEX(Prices!$C$3:$F$7,
MATCH([@Accommodation],Prices!$B$3:$B$7,0),
MATCH([@Location],Prices!$C$2:$F$2,0)
)
```

| E3 | | ∨ | ⋮ | ✕ ✓ | *fx* | =INDEX(Prices!$C$3:$F$7, MATCH([@Accommodation],Prices!$B$3:$B$7,0), MATCH([@Location],Prices!$C$2:$F$2,0)) |

	A	B	C	D	E	F
1						
2		ID	Accommodation	Location	Price	
3		1121	Woodland	Derbyshire	129	
4		1209	Spa Suite	Cumbria	169	
5		1333	Treehouse	Norfolk	139	
6		1344	Spa Suite	Suffolk	174	
7		1422	Exclusive	Derbyshire	295	
8		1441	Waterside	Norfolk	111	
9		1451	Treehouse	Derbyshire	162	
10						

Figure 11-56. *Two-way lookup with INDEX and MATCH*

It is important in this formula that the *array* given to INDEX is the same height as the vertical *lookup array* and the same width as the horizontal *lookup array* given to the MATCH functions.

Using Wildcards with INDEX and MATCH/XMATCH

The MATCH function will handle wildcard characters natively. This makes it simple to perform partial text matches with the INDEX and MATCH combination. With the XMATCH function however, a wildcard character match needs to be specified.

Figure 11-57 shows a lookup table named [tblTargets]. It contains target values for different cities. The cities are not alone in the cell though. The cells contain a string of city followed by country.

City	Target
Copenhagen, Denmark	240
London, UK	710
Berlin, Germany	890
Lisbon, Portugal	610
Newcastle, UK	860

Figure 11-57. *Table of target values by city*

We need to perform a lookup using the city name only, so will perform a partial match for any value that begins with the city we are looking for.

There are three wildcard characters that can be used in your MATCH and XMATCH functions:

- *** (Asterisk):** Represents any number of characters. For example, New* would match with Newport, Newcastle, New York, and New Zealand.

- **? (Question mark):** Represents a single character. For example, L????n would match with both London and Lisbon.

- **~ (Tilde):** Used to treat a wildcard character as a text character. For example, *don would match any text that ends in the characters don, but ~*don will look for an exact match of *don, treating the asterisk as its character and not a wildcard.

In Figure 11-58, the following formula uses the asterisk wildcard character in the MATCH function. A string is created by joining the value in cell C3 with the asterisk character. The wildcard character match does not need to be specified with MATCH.

```
=INDEX(tblTargets[Target],
MATCH(C3&"*",tblTargets[City],0)
)
```

Name	City	Value	Target
Pedro Afonso	London	470	710
Elizabeth Brown	Copenhagen	391	240
Sven Ottlieb	Lisbon	417	610
Janine Labrune	Berlin	282	890
Ann Devon	Newcastle	1197	860
Roland Mendel	Lisbon	771	610
Aria Cruz	Copenhagen	1112	240

Figure 11-58. *Using wildcard characters with INDEX and MATCH*

The following is the alternative formula using XMATCH with INDEX. The wildcard character match is specified by entering option 2 for the *match mode* argument.

```
=INDEX(tblTargets[Target],
XMATCH(C3&"*",tblTargets[City],2)
)
```

Last Occurrence of a Value with XMATCH

One of the advantages that XMATCH has over MATCH is the ability to search an array from last to first. By searching from last to first, XMATCH can be used to return a value relating to the last match in a row or column.

This option is specified in the *search mode* argument of XMATCH (Figure 11-59).

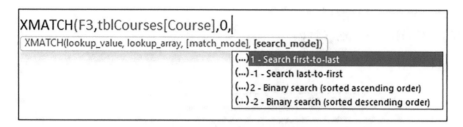

Figure 11-59. Search mode option in the XMATCH function

In Figure 11-60, the INDEX and XMATCH combination is used in cells G3 and H3 to return the date and number of attendees for the last occurrence of the training course entered in cell F3.

The following formula is entered in cell G3 to return the date. INDEX is provided with the single column array of [Date], and XMATCH returns the row from which INDEX will return. The last-to-first search mode is specified by entering –1 in the final argument.

```
=INDEX(tblCourses[Date],XMATCH(F3,tblCourses[Course],0,-1))
```

The following formula is entered in cell H3 to return the number of attendees:

```
=INDEX(tblCourses[Attendees],XMATCH(F3,tblCourses[Course],0,-1))
```

Date	Course	Attendees		Course	Date	Attendees
22/09/2021	Excel Adv	5		Excel Adv	04/09/2021	5
13/09/2021	Excel Adv	4				
23/09/2021	PivotTables	4				
10/09/2021	PivotTables	8				
30/09/2021	Excel Adv	6				
20/09/2021	Excel Basic	5				
09/09/2021	Excel Adv	10				
04/09/2021	Excel Adv	5				
26/09/2021	PivotTables	3				

Formula bar: `=INDEX(tblCourses[Date],XMATCH(F3,tblCourses[Course],0,-1))`

Figure 11-60. INDEX and XMATCH for the last match in column

Let's see another example. This time, we will use INDEX and XMATCH to search both down a column and along a row.

Figure 11-61 shows the results of 12 rounds of games for six different teams. The teams are listed down column B and the results arranged along rows. "W" represents a win, "D" is a draw, and an "L" is a loss.

This data matrix is stored on a sheet named [Results]. On another sheet, we will use a formula to return the round from range C2:N2 for the last win for each team, that is, the last win for "Tigers" was in round "R10."

	A	B	C	D	E	F	G	H	I	J	K	L	M	N
1														
2		Team	R1	R2	R3	R4	R5	R6	R7	R8	R9	R10	R11	R12
3		Albatross	L	L	D	L	W	D	L	D	L	D	W	L
4		Tigers	D	D	D	W	D	D	W	L	L	W	L	L
5		The Eagles	D	L	D	L	D	D	W	D	D	D	L	W
6		Leopards	D	D	D	W	W	W	D	L	L	W	L	D
7		The Chargers	L	W	D	D	D	L	L	W	W	L	W	D
8		Beetles	L	D	D	D	W	W	D	W	D	L	D	L
9														

Figure 11-61. *Team results over 12 rounds of games*

In Figure 11-62, the following formula is entered in range C3:C8. Indentation is applied to make the formula easier to digest.

```
=INDEX(Results!C$2:N$2,,
    XMATCH("W",
        INDEX(Results!$C$3:$N$8,
            XMATCH(B3,Results!$B$3:$B$8,0),
        ),
    0,-1)
)
```

There is a nested INDEX and XMATCH in this formula to return all results for the team name entered in the corresponding row of range B3:B8. This is important as the team names listed on this sheet are in a different order to those on the [Results] sheet.

Notice the comma entered after the XMATCH function. Remember, by omitting the *column num* argument, an array containing the values for all columns of the given range is returned.

The outer INDEX and XMATCH combination then searches last to first in this array for the "W" and returns the column number for the final occurrence of the "W." INDEX then returns the round number from range C2:N2 for that column.

	A	B	C	D
1				
2		Team	Last Win	
3		Albatross	R11	
4		Beetles	R8	
5		Leopards	R10	
6		The Chargers	R11	
7		The Eagles	R12	
8		Tigers	R10	

Figure 11-62. Returning the round of a team's last win with INDEX and XMATCH

Note   This formula demonstrates a few INDEX techniques that have been discussed. In this instance, a better alternative would be to use the XLOOKUP function. This function is covered in Chapter 12.

Last Value in a Row/Column

The INDEX function makes it simple to return the last value in a row or column. The versatility of this function is its superpower, and by combining it with the necessary functions, we can return whatever value or reference we require.

In Figure 11-63, the following formula is entered in cell E2. It uses the ROWS function to return the number of rows in the table named [tblMonthlyTotals]. INDEX then returns the value from the [Total] column of that row in the table.

```
=INDEX(tblMonthlyTotals[Total],ROWS(tblMonthlyTotals))
```

This example is taken further by entering the following formula in cell F2 to return the penultimate row in the table. One is subtracted from the number of rows returned by ROWS.

```
=INDEX(tblMonthlyTotals[Total],ROWS(tblMonthlyTotals)-1)
```

And then a formula is entered in cell E5 to calculate the percentage change in the two values.

```
=(E2-F2)/F2
```

	fx	=INDEX(tblMonthlyTotals[Total],ROWS(tblMonthlyTotals))				
B	**C**	**D**	**E**	**F**	**G**
Month-Year	Total		Last Month	Prev Month	
Jan-2022	320		279	307	
Feb-2022	201				
Mar-2022	692		% Variance		
Apr-2022	651		-9.1%		
May-2022	408				
Jun-2022	698				
Jul-2022	307				
Aug-2022	279				

Figure 11-63. *Returning the last value in a column with INDEX*

I like the use of the ROWS function (or COLUMNS for last value in a row), especially when working with data formatted as a table. Alternative methods to return the last row/column in a range/table include the use of the COUNT or COUNTA functions.

The following formula uses COUNTA instead of ROWS. COUNTA returns the number of non-blank cells in the [Month-Year] column of [tblMonthlyTotals].

```
=INDEX(tblMonthlyTotals[Total],COUNTA(tblMonthlyTotals[Month-Year]))
```

Sum Values in the Last Row/Column

The INDEX function makes it very simple to return all values in a row or column. Armed with this, let's return all values in the last column of a table and aggregate them with the SUM function.

In Figure 11-64, the following formula is entered in cell D2. It uses the COLUMNS function to return the last column in the [tblMonthly] table. The *row num* argument of INDEX is ignored to return all values in the column. SUM then totals all the values in the returned array.

```
=SUM(INDEX(tblMonthly,,COLUMNS(tblMonthly)))
```

X ✓ fx	=SUM(INDEX(tblMonthly,,COLUMNS(tblMonthly)))					

B	C	D	E	F	G	H
	Last Month	Total				
Stephanie		631				
Name	Jan	Feb	Mar	Apr	May	
Amber	122	123	93	94	121	
Enrico	81	97	63	56	102	
Hiran	83	108	81	118	131	
Janet	95	135	38	89	81	
Kyle	111	49	90	79	50	
Stephanie	31	120	124	85	39	
Victoria	120	26	57	112	107	

Figure 11-64. *Sum all values in the last column of a table*

Last Value in a Row/Column for a Specific Match

Taking it further, we now want to return the last value in a row for a specific match. The following formula is entered in cell C2 to return the last value in the row that matches the name entered in cell B2 (Figure 11-65). The MATCH function is used to return the row number.

```
=INDEX(tblMonthly,MATCH(B2,tblMonthly[Name],0),COLUMNS(tblMonthly))
```

X ✓ fx	=INDEX(tblMonthly,MATCH(B2,tblMonthly[Name],0),COLUMNS(tblMonthly))						

B	C	D	E	F	G	H	I
	Last Month	Total					
Stephanie	39	631					
Name	Jan	Feb	Mar	Apr	May		
Amber	122	123	93	94	121		
Enrico	81	97	63	56	102		
Hiran	83	108	81	118	131		
Janet	95	135	38	89	81		
Kyle	111	49	90	79	50		
Stephanie	31	120	124	85	39		
Victoria	120	26	57	112	107		

Figure 11-65. *Last value in a row for a specific match*

Most and Least Frequently Occurring Values

In Chapter 8, we discussed different functions in Excel for calculating averages, and there were three different MODE functions. The MODE functions return the most frequently occurring value in an array, but they only work with numeric values.

In this example, we have a table of ice cream flavors purchased from two different regions, north and south. We want to return the most popular and least popular ice cream flavors.

In Figure 11-66, the following formula is entered in cell D7 to return the most frequently occurring ice cream flavor from the [Flavour] column:

```
=INDEX(tblIceCreams[Flavour],
MATCH(
MAX(COUNTIFS(tblIceCreams[Flavour],tblIceCreams[Flavour])),
COUNTIFS(tblIceCreams[Flavour],tblIceCreams[Flavour]),
0))
```

The same COUNTIFS function is used twice in the formula. They return the number of occurrences for each ice cream flavor. This is returned as an array of values, for example, {7;7;7;9;8;8...}.

The MAX function is used in the *lookup value* argument of MATCH. It returns the maximum value from the first COUNTIFS array. This is number 9 in this example and relates to the "Cookies & Cream" flavor.

The MATCH function searches for number 9 in the second COUNTIFS array and returns the position of the first instance of this number. INDEX then returns the value (flavor) in that position.

	A	B	C	D	E
1	**Region**	**Flavour**			
2	North	Peanut Butter			
3	North	Peanut Butter		**Region**	
4	North	Peanut Butter			
5	South	Cookies & Cream			
6	South	Strawberry		**Most Popular**	
7	South	Strawberry		Cookies & Cream	
8	North	Strawberry			
9	North	Strawberry		**Least Popular**	
10	North	Peanut Butter		Peanut Butter	
11	North	Peanut Butter			
12	South	Cookies & Cream			
23	South	Strawberry			
24	North	Cookies & Cream			
25	South	Strawberry			

Figure 11-66. Most and least frequently purchased ice cream flavors

The following formula is entered in cell D10 to return the least frequent ice cream flavor. The MIN function is used instead of MAX.

```
=INDEX(tblIceCreams[Flavour],
MATCH(
MIN(COUNTIFS(tblIceCreams[Flavour],tblIceCreams[Flavour])),
COUNTIFS(tblIceCreams[Flavour],tblIceCreams[Flavour]),
0))
```

With the COUNTIFS function providing a key role in this formula by returning the number of occurrences of each flavor, we can easily incorporate extra conditions, by adding them to the COUNTIFS.

In Figure 11-67, the following formula is entered in cell D7 to return the most frequently occurring ice cream flavor for the region stated in cell D4. The extra condition is added to both COUNTIFS functions.

```
=INDEX(tblIceCreams[Flavour],
MATCH(
MAX(COUNTIFS(tblIceCreams[Flavour],tblIceCreams[Flavour],tblIceCreams[Region],D4)),
```

```
COUNTIFS(tblIceCreams[Flavour],tblIceCreams[Flavour],tblIceCreams
[Region],D4),
0))
```

The following formula is entered in cell D10 to return the least frequent ice cream flavor for the region stated in cell D4:

```
=INDEX(tblIceCreams[Flavour],
MATCH(
MIN(COUNTIFS(tblIceCreams[Flavour],tblIceCreams[Flavour],tblIceCreams
[Region],D4)),
COUNTIFS(tblIceCreams[Flavour],tblIceCreams[Flavour],tblIceCreams
[Region],D4),
0))
```

	A	B	C	D	E
1	**Region**	**Flavour**			
2	North	Peanut Butter			
3	North	Peanut Butter		**Region**	
4	North	Peanut Butter		North	
5	South	Cookies & Cream			
6	South	Strawberry		**Most Popular**	
7	South	Strawberry		Peanut Butter	
8	North	Strawberry			
9	North	Strawberry		**Least Popular**	
10	North	Peanut Butter		Strawberry	
11	North	Peanut Butter			
23	South	Strawberry			
24	North	Cookies & Cream			
25	South	Strawberry			
26					

Figure 11-67. *Most and least frequent values with criteria*

For the "South" region, there are two flavors that are tied as the most frequent. The INDEX and MATCH combination will only return the first instance of these two flavors. So, the one that occurs first in the [Flavour] column is returned.

To return all flavors when there is a tie, the formula can be adapted to use the FILTER function. The FILTER function is covered in detail in Chapter 13 and is only available to users of Excel 365, Excel 2021, and Excel Online.

In Figure 11-68, the following formula is entered in cell D7 to return all flavors when there are multiple flavors that occur the most. Both the "Cookies & Cream" and "Strawberry" flavors are returned.

```
=SORT(UNIQUE(FILTER(tblIceCreams[Flavour],
COUNTIFS(tblIceCreams[Flavour],tblIceCreams[Flavour],tblIceCreams
[Region],D4)=
MAX(COUNTIFS(tblIceCreams[Flavour],tblIceCreams[Flavour],tblIceCreams
[Region],D4))
)))
```

The MATCH function is adapted into a logical test between the two COUNTIFS functions. This returns an array of TRUE and FALSE values.

The INDEX function is swapped for FILTER to return the flavors where the logical test evaluates to TRUE. SORT and UNIQUE are added to order the flavors and prevent duplicates.

	A	B	C	D	E
1	**Region**	**Flavour**			
2	North	Peanut Butter			
3	North	Peanut Butter		**Region**	
4	North	Peanut Butter		South	
5	South	Cookies & Cream			
6	South	Strawberry		**Most Popular**	
7	South	Strawberry		Cookies & Cream	
8	North	Strawberry		Strawberry	
9	North	Strawberry			
10	North	Peanut Butter		**Least Popular**	
11	North	Peanut Butter		Peanut Butter	
12	South	Cookies & Cream			
23	South	Strawberry			
24	North	Cookies & Cream			
25	South	Strawberry			

Figure 11-68. Returning all values that occur the most

Returning a Range with INDEX

A special feature of INDEX is that it is a function that can return a reference. There are only a few functions in Excel that can do this. Others include, but are not limited to, OFFSET, XLOOKUP, and IF.

As INDEX is an incredibly versatile function that accepts numeric inputs for the rows and columns of a reference, it makes it a very effective way to create rolling ranges.

Figure 11-69 shows a table named [tblResults]. It contains 12 rounds of results for six different teams. You may recognize this data from an earlier example; however, it was not formatted as a table previously.

We want to use a formula to return the last five rounds of results from the table for each team. When additional columns are added to the table (new rounds of games), the formula continues to return the last five.

Team	R1	R2	R3	R4	R5	R6	R7	R8	R9	R10	R11	R12
Albatross	L	L	D	L	W	D	L	D	L	D	W	L
Tigers	D	D	D	W	D	D	W	L	L	W	L	L
The Eagles	D	L	D	L	D	D	W	D	D	D	L	W
Leopards	D	D	D	W	W	W	D	L	L	W	L	D
The Chargers	L	W	D	D	D	L	L	W	W	L	W	D
Beetles	L	D	D	D	W	W	D	W	D	L	D	L

Figure 11-69. *Table of results*

In Figure 11-70, the following formula is entered in cell C3. A key aspect of this is the use of the range operator, the colon (:), to create a range with the two references returned by INDEX.

The MATCH function is used to find the position of the team in the table. COLUMNS is used to find the last column in the table. And for the first INDEX, four is subtracted to return the reference four columns to the left of the last column.

```
=INDEX(tblResults,MATCH(B3,tblResults[Team],0),COLUMNS(tblResults)-4):
INDEX(tblResults,MATCH(B3,tblResults[Team],0),COLUMNS(tblResults))
```

The following formula is entered in cell C2 to return the names of the last five rounds. It returns the values from the header row of [tblResults]. The header row is one row high, so the *row num* argument is omitted.

```
=INDEX(tblResults[#Headers],,COLUMNS(tblResults)-4):
INDEX(tblResults[#Headers],,COLUMNS(tblResults))
```

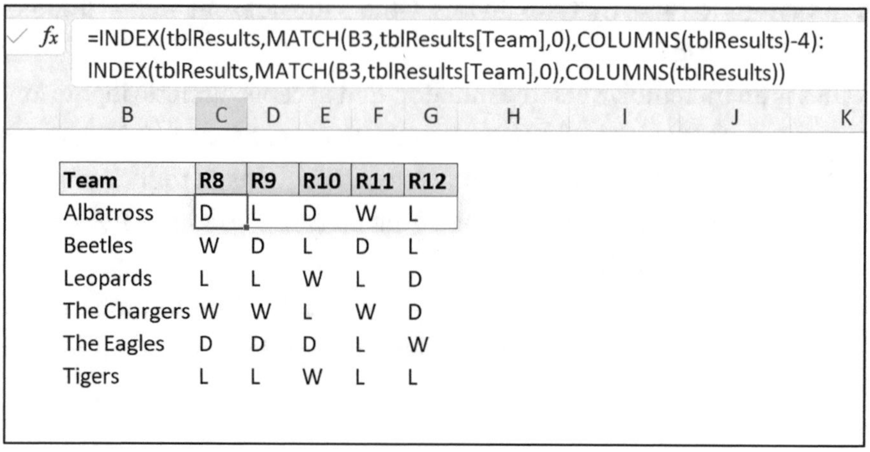

Figure 11-70. *Returning the range to the grid with INDEX*

Instead of returning the range to the grid to be spilled across five different columns, the TEXTJOIN function can be added to combine the returned values in one cell (Figure 11-71). In the following formula, the hyphen "-" is used as the delimiter between the five results:

```
=TEXTJOIN("-",,
INDEX(tblResults,MATCH(I3,tblResults[Team],0),COLUMNS(tblResults)-4):
INDEX(tblResults,MATCH(I3,tblResults[Team],0),COLUMNS(tblResults))
)
```

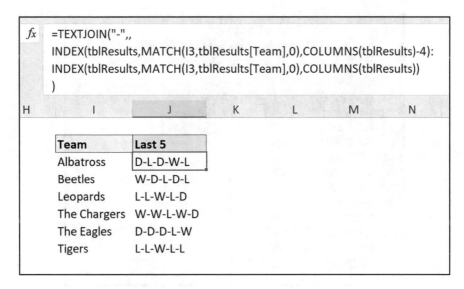

Figure 11-71. *Combining the range values with TEXTJOIN*

Moving Average Formula

This technique to return a range can be used to create calculations on dynamic ranges. A common example of this is the moving average calculation.

In this example, we have a table of values named [tblDaily], and we will use a moving average formula to return the average for the last seven days only.

In Figure 11-72, the following formula is entered in cell D2. The INDEX function is used with the ROWS function to build a range for the last seven values in the [Value] column of [tblDaily]. The average is then performed with these values.

```
=AVERAGE(
INDEX(tblDaily[Value],ROWS(tblDaily)-6):
INDEX(tblDaily[Value],ROWS(tblDaily))
)
```

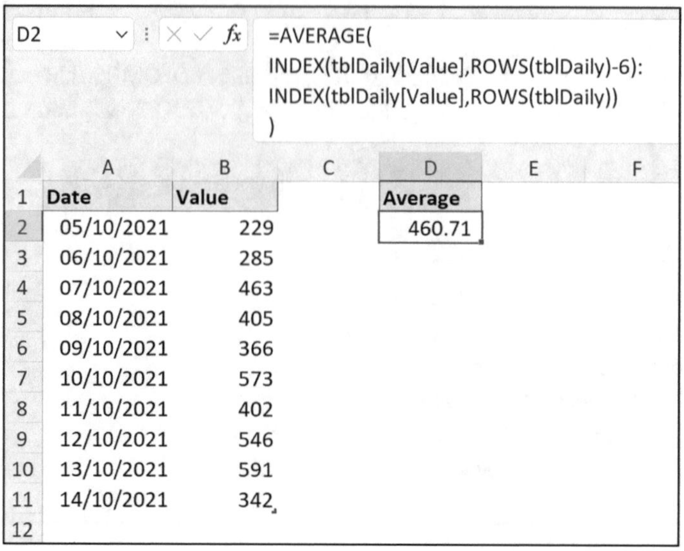

Figure 11-72. *Moving average formula using INDEX*

Note   The OFFSET function can also be used to create dynamic ranges. In fact, it is often a simpler approach. However, I prefer the INDEX function.

Working with Arrays and Spilled Ranges

The INDEX function is fantastic for working with arrays. It enables us to extract specific rows, columns, or cells from arrays and from the spilled ranges of other formulas. Let's see some examples.

Creating a Top N List

A great example of the INDEX function extracting specific rows from an array is when used with SORT to create a top N report.

Figure 11-73 shows a table named [tblProductSales]. It is a small table for the purposes of this demonstration.

We want to return the top selling products, and this will be determined by sorting the data in descending order by the [Total] column using SORT. The number of rows (products) to return will be specified by a cell value. This makes it dynamic, and a user can easily change the number of products returned.

	A	B	C	D
1	**Product Name**	**Category**	**Units**	**Total**
2	Orange Juice	Beverages	80	87.95
3	Coffee	Beverages	47	51.75
4	Beer	Beverages	41	43.61
5	Wine	Beverages	77	82.31
6	Blueberry Muffin	Cakes	14	54.90
7	Flapjack	Cakes	42	72.26
8	Shortbread	Cakes	48	32.12
9	Sandwich	Food	60	116.51
10	Samosa	Food	81	192.86
11	Baguette	Food	35	162.59
12	Soup	Food	80	222.12
13				

Figure 11-73. *Table of product sales*

In Figure 11-74, the following formula is entered in cell B5. The SORT function is used to return an array of sorted product names for INDEX. The products table is sorted in descending order by column 4, the [Total] column.

```
=INDEX(
SORT(tblProductSales,4,-1),
SEQUENCE(C2),
SEQUENCE(,COLUMNS(tblProductSales))
)
```

Two SEQUENCE functions are then used – one to return the rows and another for the columns.

The first SEQUENCE function uses the value stated in cell C2 for the number of rows to return. If the value is 5, the SEQUENCE function returns an array of {1, 2, 3, 4, 5}. So, the first five rows are returned. The number of rows is dependent on the value in cell C2.

The second SEQUENCE function returns all columns of the table. The COLUMNS function is used to return how many columns there are. This is passed to SEQUENCE to generate, well, the sequence of column numbers. Notice that the *rows* argument is omitted in the second SEQUENCE.

B5	⌄ ⋮ ✕ ✓ *fx*	=INDEX(				
		SORT(tblProductSales,4,-1),				
		SEQUENCE(C2),				
		SEQUENCE(,COLUMNS(tblProductSales))				
		)				

	A	B	C	D	E	F
1						
2		No of Products	5			
3						
4	Rank	Product Name	Category	Units	Total	
5		1 Soup	Food	80	222	
6		2 Samosa	Food	81	193	
7		3 Baguette	Food	35	163	
8		4 Sandwich	Food	60	117	
9		5 Orange Juice	Beverages	80	88	
10						

Figure 11-74. Top N report with INDEX, SORT, and SEQUENCE

Prefer the SORTBY function? No problem. This could be used instead of SORT. The following formula shows the SORTBY alternative for creating a top N report. This enables us to specify the [Total] column absolutely instead of referencing it as column 4.

```
=INDEX(
SORTBY(tblProductSales,tblProductSales[Total],-1),
SEQUENCE(C2),
SEQUENCE(,COLUMNS(tblProductSales))
)
```

Extracting Headers from a Table/Range

Functions such as SORT, FILTER, and many others do not return headers with a returned array, especially when based on a data formatted as a table. This is a good thing, because headers are not data and therefore should be kept distinct.

This means that the headers are typed or pasted into cells when creating a report in Excel. This is not much of an issue and indeed has its benefits (we will create dynamic headers shortly). However, if you want to return the headers using a formula, then this is simple. And when we require specific headers, then INDEX is up to the task.

Figure 11-75 shows the following simple formula entered in cell B4 to return the header names. If a header is changed in the table, it will automatically update on the report.

```
=tblProductSales[#Headers]
```

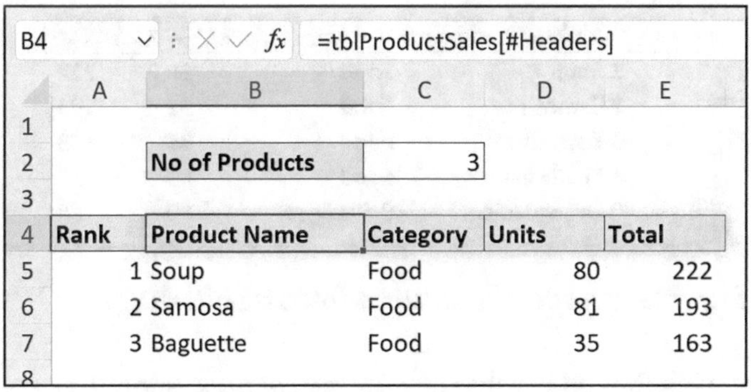

Figure 11-75. *Returning the header names with a simple formula*

The rank column is not part of the original table data, so this header needs to be entered manually.

If headers for specific columns were required, then INDEX could be used to specify the column index numbers. The following formula would return the column headers for columns 1 and 4 only.

```
=INDEX(tblProductSales[#Headers],,{1,4})
```

Returning Rows/Columns from a Spill Range

Extracting specific rows and/or columns from a spill range is no different to extracting them from a table or array.

For this example, let's imagine we want to sum the total values from the spill range of the previous formula. This formula returned a spill range that is four columns wide. The [Total] column is the fourth column of the spill range. So, we need to specify that the SUM function uses column 4 only.

In Figure 11-76, the following formula uses INDEX to extract all values from the fourth column of the spill range B5#. The *row num* argument is omitted to return all rows, and the column is explicitly entered as 4.

```
=SUM(INDEX(B5#,,4))
```

E2		⌄ ⋮ ✕ ✓ fx	=SUM(INDEX(B5#,,4))		
	A	B	C	D	E
1					
2		No of Products	5	Total	782
3					
4	Rank	Product Name	Category	Units	Total
5	1	Soup	Food	80	222
6	2	Samosa	Food	81	193
7	3	Baguette	Food	35	163
8	4	Sandwich	Food	60	117
9	5	Orange Juice	Beverages	80	88

Figure 11-76. Summing a specific column from a spill range

Instead of entering the index value of 4 for the *col num*, sometimes using a function may be a better option, as it is dynamic. We will see examples of dynamically returning columns in the next example.

For now, in addition to being column 4, the [Total] column is also the last column in the spill range, so an alternative approach could include the COLUMNS function.

```
=SUM(INDEX(B5#,,COLUMNS(B5#)))
```

Returning Non-adjacent Columns from a Table with INDEX-MATCH

Functions such as FILTER, SORT, and SORTBY do not natively allow the selection of specific columns from a table or array. They will only allow the return of a group of adjacent columns. Fortunately, we know INDEX, and INDEX does not understand the words "it can't be done."

The INDEX and MATCH/XMATCH combination provides an effective way to dynamically return specific columns from a table or array using cell values.

In Figure 11-77, the following formula returns the top N values using the SORTBY function with SEQUENCE and INDEX. The MATCH function is entered in the *column num* argument of INDEX. It returns the array of column numbers for the column names entered in range B4:C4.

```
=INDEX(
SORTBY(tblProductSales,tblProductSales[Total],-1),
SEQUENCE(C2),
MATCH(B4:C4,tblProductSales[#Headers],0)
)
```

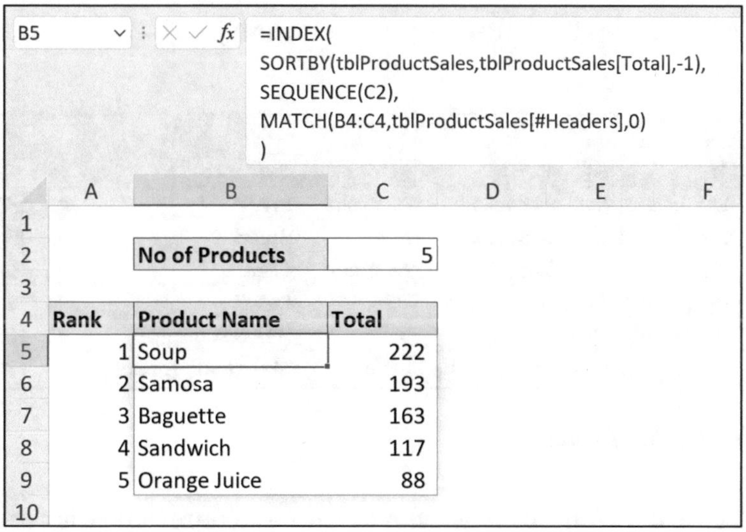

Figure 11-77. *Returning specific columns from an array with INDEX-MATCH*

Note   The CHOOSECOLS function is covered shortly and is a great alternative method for returning specific columns from an array. CHOOSE has also been discussed in this book. It is fantastic to have so many different options for this task.

In this example, INDEX was already being used to return the top N values, so was the obvious choice in preference of the aforementioned functions.

Returning a Reference from a List

In this final example of the INDEX function, we will be using its second syntax. By using INDEX in this way, we can internally list a collection of references, and then return the reference we want dynamically using an index number.

For this example, we will be using the table of sales data shown in Figure 11-78. This shows only the first few rows of the table named [tblData].

We want to create a report that includes a drop-down list to dynamically choose the column from which to summarize the total sales values. We will have three columns in the drop-down list – [Sales Rep], [Region], and [Category].

	A	B	C	D	E
1	Date	Sales Rep	Region	Category	Sales
2	15/03/2021	Cecilius Rockall	Australia	Bread	£ 142.72
3	15/03/2021	Cecilius Rockall	India	Bread	£ 194.59
4	15/03/2021	Jean Giampietro	Australia	Cakes	£ 98.48
5	15/03/2021	Tam Matthessen	USA	Cakes	£ 88.60
6	15/03/2021	Olivier Beggi	India	Herbs and spices	£ 108.62
7	15/03/2021	Benjamen Strathe	India	Meat and proteins	£ 136.78

Figure 11-78. *Table of sales data*

In Figure 11-79, the drop-down list with the three column names is in cell C2, with "Region" currently specified.

The following formula is entered in cell C3. It spills the sorted and distinct values from the column specified in cell C2.

```
=SORT(UNIQUE(INDEX(
(tblData[Category],tblData[Region],tblData[Sales Rep]),,,
MATCH(C2,A1:A3,0)
)))
```

The first argument within INDEX is the collection of references. The three columns [Category], [Region], and [Sales Rep] are entered here within brackets. The order is important, as they are indexed as references 1, 2, and 3.

The *row num* and *column num* arguments are ignored as we want to return all values for the stated column.

The MATCH function is entered in the *area num* argument. It searches for the value stated in cell C2 within the range A1:A3 and returns the index number of the found value. It is essential that the order of the references in range A1:A3 match the order of the references in the first argument of INDEX.

The following formula is entered in cell D3 and uses the SUMIFS function to sum the values in the [Total] column for each value of the spill range in cell C3:

```
=SUMIFS(tblData[Sales],
INDEX((tblData[Category],tblData[Region],tblData[Sales Rep]),,,
MATCH(C2,A1:A3,0)),
C3#)
```

The INDEX function is used again in this formula to return the stated reference for the *criteria range* argument of SUMIFS.

C3		⌄	⋮	× ✓	*fx*	=SORT(UNIQUE(INDEX((tblData[Category],tblData[Region],tblData[Sales Rep]),,, MATCH(C2,A1:A3,0))))

	A	B	C	D	E	F	G
1	Category						
2	Region		**Region**	**Total**			
3	Sales Rep		Australia	45,747			
4			Belgium	44,977			
5			Canada	45,313			
6			France	41,272			
7			India	42,996			
8			Italy	45,608			
9			Netherlands	43,348			
10			UK	45,982			
11			USA	44,225			
12							

Figure 11-79. Using INDEX to dynamically return row labels

This is a pretty cool technique that further demonstrates the sheer number of tasks that INDEX can help us to achieve. However, this type of task is easier to accomplish with the CHOOSE or INDIRECT functions or by using a newer function such as SWITCH or XLOOKUP.

CHOOSECOLS and CHOOSEROWS Functions

Availability: Excel for Microsoft 365, Excel for the Web, Excel for Microsoft 365 for Mac

---

File   choosecols-and-chooserows.xlsx

The CHOOSECOLS and CHOOSEROWS functions are very new functions that have been released to Excel 365 and Excel Online only, during the writing of this chapter.

They have been introduced to simplify the extraction and ordering of specific columns or rows from a table or array.

There have been examples in this book that use functions such as CHOOSE and INDEX to perform these tasks. And they are great, especially CHOOSE as it offers a specific advantage over these new functions. That advantage is that you can specify columns absolutely. This is very helpful, especially when data is formatted as a table.

However, these are the new kids in town, and they are fantastic. The columns or rows you require are specified by providing the column or row index numbers. The true power of these functions is realized when functions such as SEQUENCE, COUNTA, and MATCH are used to return the column or row numbers.

The following are the syntaxes for the two functions:

```
=CHOOSECOLS(array, col_num1, [col_num2] ...)
```

and

```
=CHOOSEROWS(array, row_num1, [row_num2], ...)
```

- **Array:** The table, range, or array that you want to return specific columns of rows from.

- **Col num or Row num:** The index numbers for the columns or rows that you want to return from the array. The column and row numbers can be entered as separate arguments or provided as an array of index numbers.

CHOOSECOLS to Return Specific Columns

The CHOOSECOLS function, as its name beautifully describes, enables us to choose specific columns from an array. This function has been eagerly awaited by Excel users as soon as we realized that dynamic array functions such as SORT and FILTER would not allow the selection of non-adjacent columns.

Now, we know that there are already preexisting methods of overcoming this issue such as the INDEX function. But the CHOOSECOLS function is built for this purpose and is therefore simpler and more discoverable by Excel users needing this functionality.

Figure 11-80 shows a table of product sales data named [tblProductSales]. For this example, we will use the SORT function in Excel to sort the data by the fourth column [Total]. We only want to return the [Product Name] and [Total] columns in the resulting array. This is where CHOOSECOLS will assist us.

	A	B	C	D
1	Product Name	Category	Units	Total
2	Orange Juice	Beverages	80	87.95
3	Coffee	Beverages	47	51.75
4	Beer	Beverages	41	43.61
5	Wine	Beverages	77	82.31
6	Blueberry Muffin	Cakes	14	54.90
7	Flapjack	Cakes	42	72.26
8	Shortbread	Cakes	48	32.12
9	Sandwich	Food	60	116.51
10	Samosa	Food	81	192.86
11	Baguette	Food	35	162.59
12	Soup	Food	80	222.12
13				

Figure 11-80. *Table of product sales data*

In Figure 11-81, the following formula is entered in cell B3. The SORT function returns an array with all columns of the table [tblProductSales] sorted by column 4 in descending order. CHOOSECOLS then returns only columns 1 and 4 from that array.

```
=CHOOSECOLS(
SORT(tblProductSales,4,-1),
1,4)
```

B3	⌄	⋮	× ✓ *fx*	=CHOOSECOLS(SORT(tblProductSales,4,-1), 1,4)

	A	B	C	D	E
1					
2		**Product Name**	**Total**		
3		Soup	222.12		
4		Samosa	192.86		
5		Baguette	162.59		
6		Sandwich	116.51		
7		Orange Juice	87.95		
8		Wine	82.31		
9		Flapjack	72.26		
10		Blueberry Muffir	54.90		
11		Coffee	51.75		
12		Beer	43.61		
13		Shortbread	32.12		
14					

Figure 11-81. CHOOSECOLS returning the first and fourth columns only

CHOOSECOLS with MATCH

Typing the column index numbers to be returned is not ideal, especially with tables that have many columns. The MATCH function can be used to return the column numbers based on cell values.

The CHOOSECOLS function accepts an array of column numbers as an alternative to entering them as separate arguments. The following formula is a repeat of the previous example, but with columns 1 and 4 entered as an array:

```
=CHOOSECOLS(
SORT(tblProductSales,4,-1),
{1,4})
```

Because of this functionality, other functions can be used to return the array of column numbers to CHOOSECOLS.

In Figure 11-82, the following formula uses the MATCH function to return the column numbers from the header row of [tblProductSales] where there is a match for the values entered in range B2:C2:

```
=CHOOSECOLS(
```

```
SORT(tblProductSales,4,-1),
MATCH(B2:C2,tblProductSales[#Headers],0)
)
```

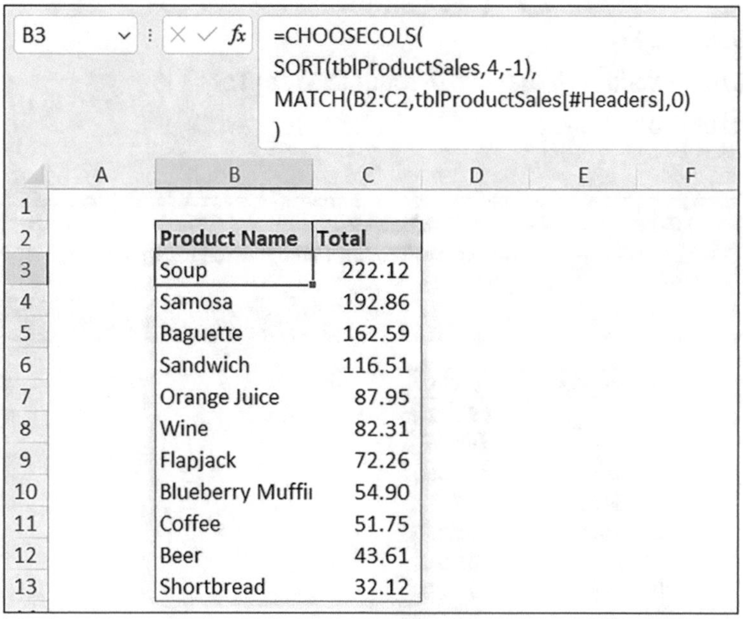

Figure 11-82. *CHOOSECOLS with MATCH for dynamic column numbers*

This technique does require that the values in range B2:C2 match the header name exactly. However, it also means that you can change the value in cell B2 or C2 to return a different column, for example, "Product Name" to "Category." This could be a cool feature in a reporting scenario.

CHOOSE for Absolute Column Selection

I know, I know, the CHOOSE function has been covered in this chapter and in other parts of this book already. But it feels appropriate to demonstrate it here along with CHOOSECOLS as an alternative approach.

CHOOSECOLS is great for dynamic reports and models. It can be combined with other formulas or controls to return the column numbers such as MATCH and SEQUENCE. But you may want to just specify the columns to return by their name. And in that scenario, one could argue that CHOOSE is better.

In Figure 11-83, the following formula uses the CHOOSE function to provide the SORTBY function with an array containing the [Product Name] and [Total] columns only. As this example uses absolute table column references, it made sense to use SORTBY instead of SORT to avoid entering column numbers when sorting also.

```
=SORTBY(CHOOSE({1,2},
tblProductSales[Product Name],tblProductSales[Total]),
tblProductSales[Total],-1)
```

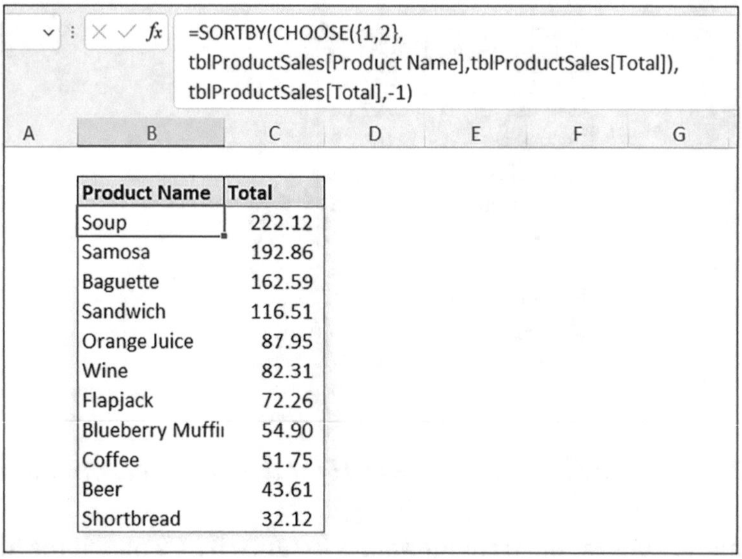

Figure 11-83. *CHOOSE and SORTBY alternative formula*

The structure of this formula is different to before in respect that CHOOSE is serving an array to SORTBY, while previously SORT was serving CHOOSECOLS with the array. So, the sequence is reversed.

In simple examples, you can choose the method that you prefer. CHOOSECOLS offers more potential when it comes to dynamic, robust, and interactive spreadsheets.

Finally, with the CHOOSE example, if there were many columns to return, the SEQUENCE function could be added to avoid entering the sequence of column numbers manually.

The following formula shows the SEQUENCE function used to return the array {1,2} instead of us entering it manually. The *rows* argument of SEQUENCE is omitted, and 2 is entered for *columns*.

```
=SORTBY(
CHOOSE(SEQUENCE(,2),
tblProductSales[Product Name],tblProductSales[Total]),
tblProductSales[Total],-1
)
```

Reordering Columns with CHOOSECOLS

In addition to returning specific columns from an array, CHOOSECOLS enables us to position the columns in any order that we require.

Following on from the previous examples, let's return the [Category], [Product Name], and [Total] columns from the SORT function and position them in the order just stated.

In Figure 11-84, you can see in the snapshot of the [tblProductSales] table that the [Category] column is column 2 and the [Product Name] column is column 1. However, in our results we want the [Category] column to precede the [Product Name] column.

	A	B	C	D
1	Product Name	Category	Units	Total
2	Orange Juice	Beverages	80	87.95
3	Coffee	Beverages	47	51.75
4	Beer	Beverages	41	43.61
5	Wine	Beverages	77	82.31
6	Blueberry Muffin	Cakes	14	54.90

Figure 11-84. *Order of columns in the product sales table*

In Figure 11-85, the following formula is entered in cell B3. With CHOOSECOLS, you simply enter the column numbers in the order that you want them to appear.

```
=CHOOSECOLS(
SORT(tblProductSales,4,-1),
2,1,4)
```

B3		∨ : × ✓ fx	=CHOOSECOLS(SORT(tblProductSales,4,-1), 2,1,4)		

▲	A	B	C	D	E
1					
2		Category	Product Name	Total	
3		Food	Soup	222.12	
4		Food	Samosa	192.86	
5		Food	Baguette	162.59	
6		Food	Sandwich	116.51	
7		Beverages	Orange Juice	87.95	
8		Beverages	Wine	82.31	
9		Cakes	Flapjack	72.26	
10		Cakes	Blueberry Muffin	54.9	
11		Beverages	Coffee	51.75	
12		Beverages	Beer	43.61	
13		Cakes	Shortbread	32.12	

Figure 11-85. *CHOOSECOLS changing an array's column order*

In this example, the MATCH function could have been used to return the column numbers from range B2:D2 instead of the entry of the 2, 1, 4 numbers, if preferred.

Returning Every Nth Column

By combining the CHOOSECOLS function with SEQUENCE, you can return all columns that occur at specific intervals.

Figure 11-86 shows a table named [tblQuartely]. It contains a [Name] column and then quarterly totals for an entire calendar year. We want to return the [Name] column followed by the quarterly totals only. All month columns should be neglected.

▲	A	B	C	D	E	F	O	P	Q
1	Name	Jan	Feb	Mar	Qtr 1	Apr	Nov	Dec	Qtr 4
2	David	425	1,240	651	2,316	930	644	381	1,638
3	Claire	1,275	1,072	1,044	3,391	153	526	1,188	2,477
4	Victoria	266	354	268	888	161	241	1,673	2,809
5	Sarah	858	946	198	2,002	849	1,125	227	2,676
6	Fred	1,201	1,165	194	2,560	381	551	331	1,131
7	Michelle	873	240	311	1,424	485	249	456	2,287
8									

Figure 11-86. *Table of quarterly data*

In this example, the columns that we require occur in every fourth column. We want to return columns 1, 5, 9, 13, and 17.

In Figure 11-87, the following formula is entered in cell A2. CHOOSECOLS is extracting columns from the [tblQuartely] table, and the columns to extract are determined by the SEQUENCE function.

```
=CHOOSECOLS(tblQuartely,
SEQUENCE(,ROUNDUP(COLUMNS(tblQuartely)/4,0),,4)
)
```

In the SEQUENCE function, the number of columns to return is calculated by dividing the total number of table columns by 4 and rounding the result up. In this example, this results in 17 divided by 4 equals 4.25. This is then rounded up to 5. So, 5 columns are returned. The *step* argument of SEQUENCE is entered as 4.

This approach can be used for any number of columns and any divisor that you require.

The following formula is entered in cell A1 to return the headers of the required columns:

```
=CHOOSECOLS(tblQuartely[#Headers],
SEQUENCE(,ROUNDUP(COLUMNS(tblQuartely)/4,0),,4)
)
```

A2		f_x	=CHOOSECOLS(tblQuartely,				
			SEQUENCE(,ROUNDUP(COLUMNS(tblQuartely)/4,0),,4)				
			)				

	A	B	C	D	E	F	G
1	Name	Qtr 1	Qtr 2	Qtr 3	Qtr 4		
2	David	2,316	3,270	1796	1638		
3	Claire	3,391	1,110	3557	2477		
4	Victoria	888	2,073	4254	2809		
5	Sarah	2,002	2,712	3102	2676		
6	Fred	2,560	2,138	3563	1131		
7	Michelle	1,424	1,666	2704	2287		
8							

Figure 11-87. *Returning every Nth column with CHOOSECOLS and SEQUENCE*

CHOOSEROWS to Return Every Nth Row

The CHOOSEROWS function is used to return specific rows from an array. This function is generally not as commonly used as CHOOSECOLS, because there are many other Excel functions to return rows, and values from rows, including FILTER and VLOOKUP.

The FILTER function enables us to return rows from a table that meets specific criteria. So, the specific advantage of CHOOSEROWS is that we can specify the exact rows we need or the rows that follow a specific pattern.

In Figure 11-88, we have a table containing payments that have been received from different sources. The table is named [tblPayments], and it contains subtotal rows.

We will use the CHOOSEROWS function to return only the total rows from the table. The totals occur in every third row, so we will use the SEQUENCE function to return the array of row numbers for CHOOSEROWS.

	A	B	C
1	Source	Total	
2	Single Payment	1,448	
3	Europe	697	
4	RoW	751	
5	Recurring Payments	613	
6	Europe	451	
7	RoW	162	
8	Subscriptions	1,703	
9	Europe	662	
10	RoW	1,041	
11			

Figure 11-88. *Table of payment data that includes subtotals*

In Figure 11-89, the following formula returns the total rows only. The number of rows to return is calculated by dividing the total rows by three. SEQUENCE is told to step every third row.

```
=CHOOSEROWS(tblPayments,
SEQUENCE(ROWS(tblPayments)/3,,,3)
)
```

A2	⌄	:	× ✓ *fx*	=CHOOSEROWS(tblPayments, SEQUENCE(ROWS(tblPayments))/3,,,3))

	A	B	C	D	E
1	**Source**	Total			
2	Single Payment	1,448			
3	Recurring Payments	613			
4	Subscriptions	1,703			
5					

Figure 11-89. *CHOOSEROWS function returning every third row*

Returning the Top and Bottom N Values

Another example where the CHOOSEROWS function can be useful is to return the top and bottom N values from an array.

In previous examples, we returned an array of products and their totals, sorted in descending order by the total value (Figure 11-81). CHOOSECOLS was used to return specific columns in this array. The following formula was used for this task:

```
=CHOOSECOLS(SORT(tblProductSales,4,-1),1,4)
```

In Figure 11-90, the following formula is entered in cell A5 to return the top number of rows specified in cell B1. The SEQUENCE function is used to provide the array of row numbers for CHOOSEROWS. As 3 is entered in cell B1, SEQUENCE returns {1,2,3}.

```
=CHOOSEROWS(
CHOOSECOLS(SORT(tblProductSales,4,-1),1,4),
SEQUENCE(B1))
```

The following formula is entered in cell D5 to return the bottom number of rows specified in cell B1. SEQUENCE is used again, and in the *start* argument of SEQUENCE, ROWS is used to find the first row of the array to return. In this example, the array {9,10,11} is returned.

```
=CHOOSEROWS(
CHOOSECOLS(SORT(tblProductSales,4,-1),1,4),
SEQUENCE(B1,,ROWS(tblProductSales)-B1+1))
```

A5		$\vee$: $\times$ $\checkmark$ fx	=CHOOSEROWS(CHOOSECOLS(SORT(tblProductSales,4,-1),1,4), SEQUENCE(B1))			

	A	B	C	D	E	F
1	**No of Rows**	3				
2						
3	**Top**			**Bottom**		
4	**Product Name**	**Total**		**Product Name**	**Total**	
5	Soup	222.12		Coffee	51.75	
6	Samosa	192.86		Beer	43.61	
7	Baguette	162.59		Shortbread	32.12	
8						

Figure 11-90. *CHOOSEROWS returning top and bottom N rows*

TAKE and DROP Functions

Availability: Excel for Microsoft 365, Excel for the Web, Excel for Microsoft 365 for Mac

---

File   take-and-drop.xlsx

The TAKE and DROP functions enable us to resize arrays within a formula. The definitions for the two functions are as follows:

- **TAKE:** The TAKE function is used to return a specific number of consecutive rows or columns from the start or end of an array.

- **DROP:** The DROP function removes a specific number of consecutive rows or columns from the start or end of an array.

The following are the syntaxes for the two functions:

```
=DROP(array, rows, [columns])
```

and

```
=TAKE(array, rows, [columns])
```

- **Array:** The array from which to take or drop rows or columns.

- **Rows:** The number of consecutive rows to take or drop. A positive value will take or drop rows from the start of an array, and a negative value will take or drop rows from the end of an array.

- **[Columns]:** The number of consecutive columns to take or drop. A positive value will take or drop columns from the start of an array, and a negative value will take or drop columns from the end of an array.

The following examples will be based on the product data shown in Figure 11-91. For some examples, the data is formatted as a table named [tblProducts], and in others it is a range on the [Data] sheet.

Note The TAKE and DROP functions do not accept arrays of row or column numbers like CHOOSEROWS and CHOOSECOLS can.

	A	B	C	D
1	**Product Name**	**Category**	**Units**	**Total**
2	Orange Juice	Beverages	80	87.95
3	Coffee	Beverages	47	51.75
4	Beer	Beverages	41	43.61
5	Wine	Beverages	77	82.31
6	Blueberry Muffin	Cakes	14	54.90
7	Flapjack	Cakes	42	72.26
8	Shortbread	Cakes	48	32.12
9				

Figure 11-91. *Product data for take and drop examples*

In this first example, the DROP function is used to remove the first row, and last two columns, from the range A1:D8 on the [Data] sheet (Figure 11-92).

```
=DROP(Data!A1:D8,1,-2)
```

In the formula, 1 is entered for the *rows* argument and –2 for *columns* to remove the two columns from the end of the array.

When working with data in a range, the header row is often returned by other functions. DROP offers a simple way to remove this header row, as it is not data that we want included in calculations or in spill ranges for charts to use.

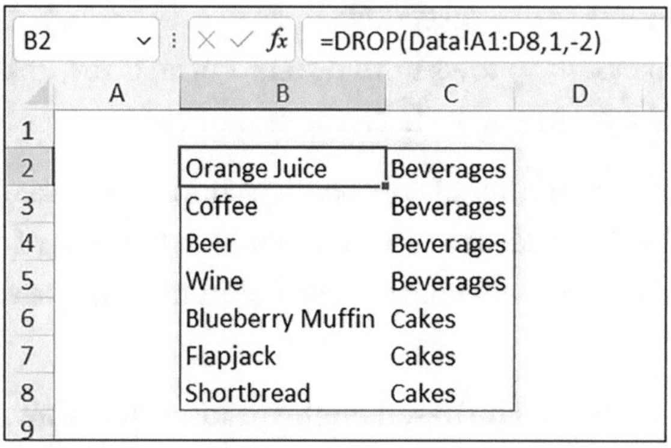

Figure 11-92. *Dropping rows and columns from a range*

With the TAKE and DROP functions, both the *rows* and *columns* arguments are optional. However, you must provide at least one of these arguments.

In Figure 11-93, the following formula uses the TAKE function to return the first two columns from the table named [tblProducts]. The *rows* argument has been omitted. The SORT function orders the array in ascending order by the first column.

```
=SORT(TAKE(tblProducts,,2))
```

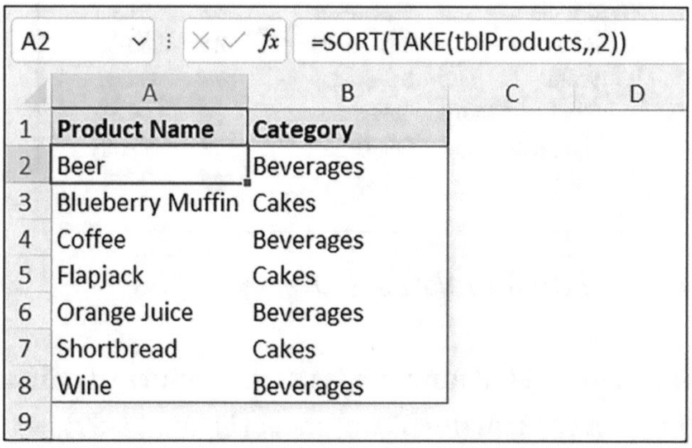

Figure 11-93. *TAKE function returning the first two columns from a table*

The TAKE function makes it easy to provide a function such as SUM with the last column of a table or array. In Figure 11-94, the following formula sums the last column in [tblProducts]:

```
=SUM(TAKE(tblProducts,,-1))
```

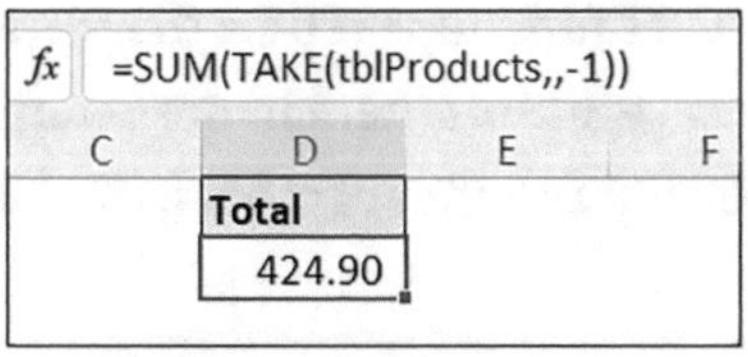

f_x =SUM(TAKE(tblProducts,,-1))

C	D	E	F
	Total		
	424.90		

Figure 11-94. *TAKE returning the last column only*

Of course, we could have achieved this with the DROP function instead using the following formula. This is interesting to know; however, the TAKE example is more effective.

```
=SUM(DROP(tblProducts,,3))
```

If we want to sum the [Units] column, we could use the DROP and TAKE functions together (Figure 11-95). The [Units] column is the penultimate column of the table. In this formula, TAKE returns the last two columns, and then DROP dumps the last column, leaving the second from the last column to be served to SUM.

```
=SUM(DROP(TAKE(tblProducts,,-2),,-1))
```

f_x =SUM(DROP(TAKE(tblProducts,,-2),,-1))

C	D	E	F
	Total		
	349		

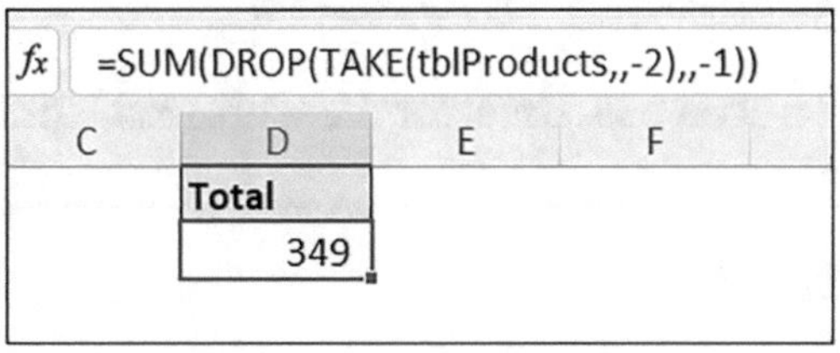

Figure 11-95. *The TAKE and DROP functions together in a formula*

Finally, the TAKE and DROP functions can accept arrays from other functions and the number of rows or columns from a cell value.

In Figure 11-96, the following formula is entered in cell A4. It returns the top selling products. The number of products is specified by the value in cell B1.

```
=TAKE(
CHOOSECOLS(SORT(tblProducts,4,-1),1,4),
B1)
```

The CHOOSECOLS and SORT functions return the [Product Name] and [Total] columns only from [tblProducts] and sort them in descending order by the [Total] column. TAKE then returns the top number of rows specified by cell B1.

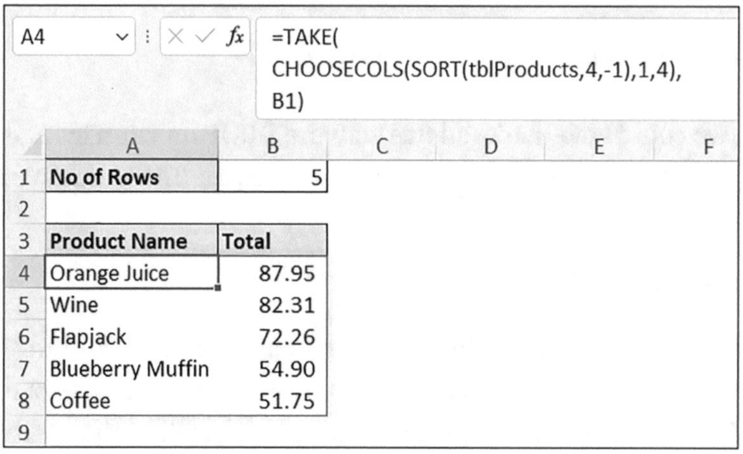

| A4 | ⌄ : ✕ ✓ fx | =TAKE(
CHOOSECOLS(SORT(tblProducts,4,-1),1,4),
B1) |

	A	B	C	D	E	F
1	No of Rows	5				
2						
3	Product Name	Total				
4	Orange Juice	87.95				
5	Wine	82.31				
6	Flapjack	72.26				
7	Blueberry Muffin	54.90				
8	Coffee	51.75				
9						

Figure 11-96. Using a cell value to specify the number of rows

VSTACK and HSTACK Functions

Availability: Excel for Microsoft 365, Excel for the Web, Excel for Microsoft 365 for Mac

---

File   vstack-and-hstack.xlsx

The VSTACK and HSTACK functions are used to combine, or stack, multiple arrays vertically or horizontally into a single array.

These functions have been eagerly anticipated by Excel users. They make particular tasks that were once awkward now very easy.

The syntaxes of the two functions are as follows:

=VSTACK(array1, [array2], ...)

and

=HSTACK(array1, [array2], ...)

- **Array1, [array2]:** The arrays that you want to stack vertically or horizontally

Stacking Multiple Tables with VSTACK

Combining multiple tables is a task that previously required endless copy and paste operations, a Power Query, or a macro to perform. Now, with VSTACK, it is incredibly simple and will automatically update when data in the tables update.

In Figure 11-97, we have two tables named [tblNorth] and [tblSouth]. We want to combine the data from both tables into a single table. This is a simplified example, and the VSTACK function can handle as many tables as you need.

	A	B	C	D	E
1	Name	Value		Name	Value
2	Celia	45		Sergei	86
3	Faraz	103		Tania	69
4	John	114		Sue	24
5	Malina	46		Jan	122
6				Michael	96
7					

Figure 11-97. *Multiple tables to be stacked*

In Figure 11-98, the following formula is used to stack both tables – [tblNorth] first, followed by [tblSouth]:

```
=VSTACK(tblNorth,tblSouth)
```

We could sort the data after stacking to change the order if required:

```
=SORT(VSTACK(tblNorth,tblSouth))
```

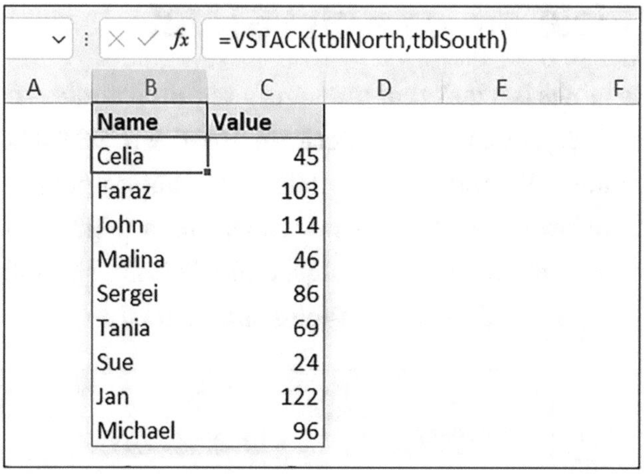

Figure 11-98. Stacking tables together into a single table

Adding Calculated Columns to an Array with HSTACK

The HSTACK function is used to stack arrays horizontally. This function can be great for adding calculated columns to an array. With the VSTACK and HSTACK functions, we can create reports with a single formula.

For an example of this, we will create a report that we have covered previously in this book, but this time, with a single formula.

Note   The HSTACK function is used again in Chapter 15 to create our own function that generates a report.

In Figure 11-99, we have a table of sales data named [tblSales]. We will create a report that lists the distinct product names in one column and the sum of the [Total] column for each product in another column. The report will be sorted in descending order by the total.

	A	B	C	D	E	F
1	ID	Date	Product Name	Store	Units Sold	Total
2	19775	11/01/2021	Coffee	North	39	59.06
3	19776	12/01/2021	Hot Chocolate	West	16	424.80
4	19777	24/01/2021	Wine	North	25	207.30
5	19778	25/01/2021	Water	West	35	436.53
6	19779	30/01/2021	Coffee	South	38	424.30
7	19780	01/02/2021	Tea	North	10	174.45

Figure 11-99. *Table of sales data*

In Figure 11-100, the following formula is entered in cell B3:

```
=SORT(HSTACK(
UNIQUE(tblSales[Product Name]),
SUMIFS(tblSales[Total],tblSales[Product Name],UNIQUE(tblSales[Product Name]))
),2,-1)
```

The HSTACK function combines two arrays together. The first array is the distinct list of product names. And the second is the SUMIFS function to return the total for each product name.

The SORT function then sorts the returned array by the second column in descending order.

The HSTACK function can handle more than two arrays, so more calculated columns can be added if required.

In Chapter 15, the LET function is covered. This function allows us to perform intermediate calculations, leading to faster operation and cleaner formulas. This function is a great help when creating more complex examples of the VSTACK and HSTACK functions.

fx	=SORT(HSTACK(
	UNIQUE(tblSales[Product Name]),
	SUMIFS(tblSales[Total],tblSales[Product Name],UNIQUE(tblSales[Product Name]))
	),2,-1)

	B	C	D	E	F	G	H

Product Name	Total
Coffee	3,535
Tea	2,469
Wine	1,935
Beer	1,779
Water	1,656
Hot Chocolate	1,498
Orange Juice	1,099

Figure 11-100. *Creating a report with one formula*

Lookup Functions with Other Excel Features

Lookup functions are some of the best functions to use with other Excel features. With functions such as INDEX, INDIRECT, and CHOOSEROWS, you can create some cool dynamic functionality to charts, Data Validation rules, and formatting in Excel.

Dynamic Data Validation List with INDEX or OFFSET

One of the most common requirements for the INDEX and OFFSET functions is to create a dynamic range. And a reason for this can be to feed a Data Validation list. When items are added or removed from the range used as the source for the list, the list automatically updates to include or exclude the items.

My personal preference for this task is to use the INDEX function, but it is useful to be familiar with both.

Figure 11-101 shows four separate ranges of city names by country. For each range, additional cities may be added, or some removed over time. We want to make these ranges dynamic to accommodate such changes automatically.

For this example, we will create a dynamic range of the cities in Germany only. The technique can then be replicated for the other lists.

	A	B	C	D	E	F	G
1	**Germany**		**Spain**		**USA**		**UK**
2	Berlin		Bilbao		Atlanta		Birmingham
3	Bremen		Seville		Boston		Brighton
4	Dortmund		Valencia		Dallas		Cambridge
5	Dresden				Philadelphia		Hull
6	Stuttgart				Sacramento		London
7							Manchester
8							

Figure 11-101. *Different lists of cities by country*

The following formula uses the INDEX function to create a dynamic range. A fixed start reference of A2 is entered, followed by the range operator, and then an INDEX function that uses COUNTA to find the last used cell in the range A2:A15 (a range expected to be sufficient in size to handle additional city names).

`=$A$2:INDEX($A$2:$A$15,COUNTA($A$2:$A$15))`

This formula cannot be entered directly into a Data Validation rule due to the use of the range operator (:). Figure 11-102 shows the type of error you can expect to receive if you try.

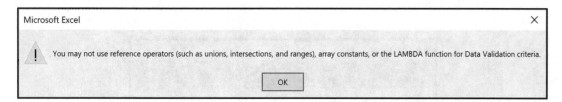

Figure 11-102. *Error due to use of the range operator in a Data Validation rule*

A name will need to be defined for the formula, and that name is then used in the Data Validation rule. Even if we were able to enter it directly, I would be inclined to define a name anyway for better management of the workbook.

Figure 11-103 shows the formula entered as the source for a name defined as "lstGermany."

As the name has workbook scope, Excel will automatically add the sheet name before each range of the formula. We can let Excel handle this and save ourselves a job.

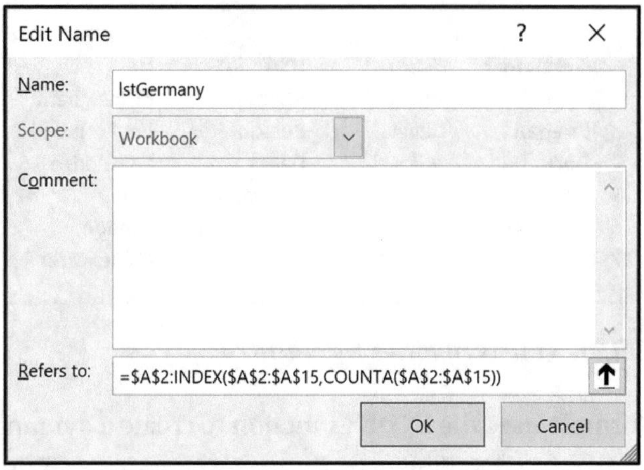

Figure 11-103. *Define a name for the dynamic range*

This name can now be used as the source for a Data Validation rule:

1. Click **Data ➤ Data Validation**.

2. On the **Settings** tab, select **List** for the *Allow* list and enter the
   following reference in the *Source* box (Figure 11-104). Click **OK**.

   =lstGermany

Figure 11-104. *Data Validation list using lstGermany as its source*

To achieve the same with OFFSET, the following formula can be used. Cell A2 is set as the start cell, and the COUNTA function is entered for the *height* argument. This determines the height of the range returned. All other arguments were omitted.

```
=OFFSET($A$2,,,COUNTA($A$2:$A$15))
```

This formula can be entered directly into the Data Validation rule as it does not include a range operator or other illegal characters. This, I suppose, is an advantage over INDEX, though I do like the concept of defining names for ranges such as this still.

You may be thinking "if a Data Validation list is based on a range formatted as a table, would the list auto-expand and contract in size with the table?". Well, at the time of writing this book, a Data Validation list only effectively updates with a table when they are on the same sheet.

Now, we do not need this formula approach, because if we simply define a name for a range formatted as a table, the name and table work together to create the dynamic range.

However, due to this confusion, until Microsoft has a Data Validation rule and table data working together efficiently, using INDEX or OFFSET for a dynamic range is still very beneficial. It should also be noted that understanding this technique assists us in scenarios outside of Data Validation list too.

Dependent Data Validation List with INDIRECT

Creating dependent drop-down lists with Data Validation is a common question asked in training courses and across Excel forums. Often, a list of items is too large, and it is useful to have a first list that reduces the items shown in a second list.

In modern Excel versions, the searchable list functionality recently introduced has lessened the requirement for creating dependent drop-down lists. But this is only available for those using Excel 365 or Excel Online. This technique is still important for previous Excel versions.

In Figure 11-105, we have four lists of cities by country. Each range has been named using the country name as shown in row 1 prefixed with the text "lst" – for example, lstGermany, lstSpain, etc.

	A	B	C	D	E	F	G
1	**Germany**		**Spain**		**USA**		**UK**
2	Berlin		Bilbao		Atlanta		Birmingham
3	Bremen		Seville		Boston		Brighton
4	Dortmund		Valencia		Dallas		Cambridge
5	Dresden				Philadelphia		Hull
6	Stuttgart				Sacramento		London
7							Manchester
8							

Figure 11-105. *Ranges of city names by country*

Figure 11-106 shows the setup for a dependent list scenario. Cell B3 contains a list with the four country names and "Germany" currently selected. The dependent drop-down list of cities will be in cell D3.

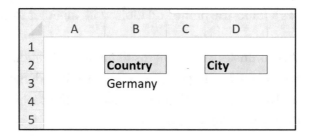

Figure 11-106. *Setup for dependent list*

1. Click cell D3.

2. Click **Data ➤ Data Validation**.

3. On the **Settings** tab, select **List** for the *Allow* list and enter the following INDIRECT formula in the *Source* box (Figure 11-107). Click **OK**.

   ```
   =INDIRECT("lst"&$B$3)
   ```

This formula creates a reference by combining the text string "lst" with the value in cell B3. This allows us to indirectly reference the named range of cities for the country stated in cell B3.

Note   This technique works for named ranges only, and not for named formulas.

Figure 11-107. *INDIRECT for a dependent drop-down list*

Figure 11-108 shows the completed dependent drop-down list showing cities from the USA as that is the country specified in the first list.

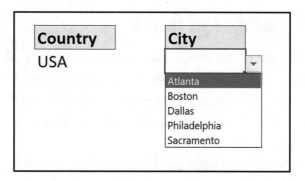

Figure 11-108. *List of cities dependent upon country selection*

Note   Although this example shows the dependent drop-down list in a single cell, it can be applied to multiple cells. The reference type in the INDIRECT function would need modifying to fit the sheet layout, that is, $B3 for multiple rows.

In this example, all country names are single words – Germany, Spain, UK, and USA. If there was a country with more than one word in its name such as South Korea or New Zealand, then the formula would be a little different.

Why? Well, you cannot use spaces in the name of a range, yet the name of the range and the name of the country selected in cell B3 must match exactly.

A common solution for this is to use an underscore in the named range of that country's cities, that is, lstnew_zealand. The name of the country in the first drop-down would be "New Zealand," as one would expect.

For the named range and cell value to then match, the SUBSTITUTE function can be used with INDIRECT to replace the space with an underscore. The following formula would be used for the Data Validation criteria:

```
=INDIRECT("lst"&SUBSTITUTE($B$3," ","_"))
```

Note   Modern techniques to create dependent drop-down lists using XLOOKUP and FILTER are shown in Chapters 12 and 13, respectively.

Format Last X Number of Rows

In the INDEX function part of this chapter, we saw INDEX used to calculate the moving average for a specified number of days. Now, this could be any calculation; the key is that the range being calculated is moving as new rows are added to a table.

For a nice visual touch, it has been decided to format the rows being used in the calculation.

We will use the OFFSET in a Conditional Formatting rule for this task. INDEX would be an obvious choice for this task, but mixing up the techniques used is good for learning.

In Figure 11-109, the last x number of days is formatted. The number of days is specified by the value in cell D2. The following formula is entered in cell E2 to return the moving average for the number of days stated in cell D2:

```
=AVERAGE(OFFSET($B$2,ROWS(tblDaily)-D2,,D2))
```

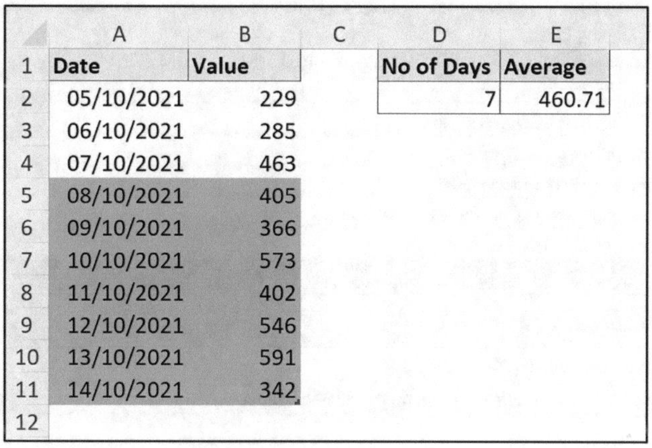

	A	B	C	D	E
1	Date	Value		No of Days	Average
2	05/10/2021	229		7	460.71
3	06/10/2021	285			
4	07/10/2021	463			
5	08/10/2021	405			
6	09/10/2021	366			
7	10/10/2021	573			
8	11/10/2021	402			
9	12/10/2021	546			
10	13/10/2021	591			
11	14/10/2021	342			
12					

Figure 11-109. *Format the last x number of rows*

To create the Conditional Formatting rule

1. Select the table.

2. Click **Home ➤ Conditional Formatting ➤ New Rule**.

3. Click **Use a formula to determine which cells to format**.

4. Enter the following formula into the *Format values where this formula is true* box (Figure 11-110):

    `=ROW(B2)>=ROW(OFFSET($B$2,COUNTA($B$2:$B$500)-$D$2,))`

    The formula tests if the current row number is greater than or equal to the row number the stated number of rows ago specified by cell D2. The OFFSET function is used to offset the stated number of rows back from the last row. This is done with the `COUNTA($B$2:$B$500)-$D$2` part used for the *rows* argument of OFFSET.

5. Click **Format** and specify the format to apply. Click **OK**.

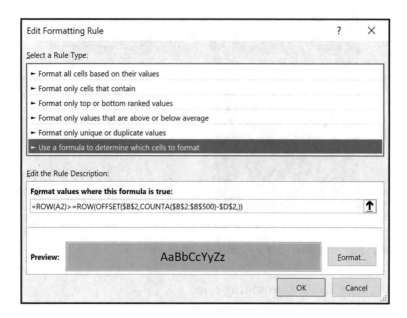

Figure 11-110. *Conditional Formatting rule to format the last x number of rows*

Interactive Chart with INDIRECT

The INDIRECT function offers a simple method to return data from a table dependent upon user selection. In this example, we have four tables containing sales data (Figure 11-111). Each table shares its name with the name of the city written above the table prefixed by the characters "tbl".

Each table has the same number of rows and columns, so we will not concern ourselves with a dynamic approach (like the following two examples). We simply want to return the data for the specified table to a range on the sheet, to then create a chart from.

Manchester			Leeds		
Product	Total		Product	Total	
Cake	592		Cake	392	
Coffee	111		Coffee	329	
Fruit	342		Fruit	413	
Juice	457		Juice	264	
Tea	393		Tea	106	
Plymouth			Lincoln		
Product	Total		Product	Total	
Cake	537		Cake	306	
Coffee	536		Coffee	412	
Fruit	453		Fruit	398	
Juice	402		Juice	138	
Tea	110		Tea	289	

Figure 11-111. *Four sales tables to be used for the chart source*

In Figure 11-112, the following INDIRECT formula is entered in cell B5 to return the sales data from the [tblLincoln] table. Cell B2 contains a drop-down list of the four cities' names. The formula references this cell to know which table to return data from. The characters "tbl" are concatenated to the beginning of the reference.

```
=INDIRECT("tbl"&B2)
```

This formula returns an array of values that are spilled to the adjacent cells. Although we do not require a dynamic approach for this example, this is great because we only have one formula returning the values.

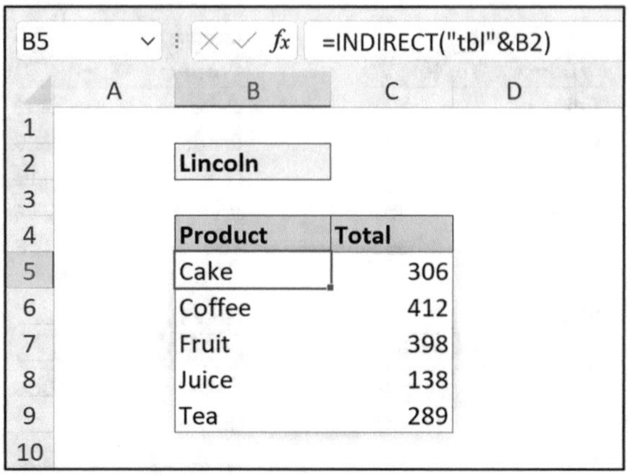

Figure 11-112. *INDIRECT function returning data dependent upon cell value*

If you are using a version of Excel that cannot handle dynamic arrays, the following adapted formula can be used (Figure 11-113):

```
=INDEX(INDIRECT("tbl"&$B$2),
ROW(A1),COLUMN(A1)
)
```

The INDEX function is wrapped around the INDIRECT function to return the value from the row and column numbers of cell A1. So, the formula in cell B5 returns the value from row 1 and column 1 of the [tblLincoln] table.

When this formula is filled to the four rows below cell B5 and then the column to the right, the INDEX function returns the row and column numbers from the relative cell. For example, the formula in cell B6 returns the value from row 2 and column 1 of the table. And the formula in cell C5 returns the value from row 1 and column 2 of the table.

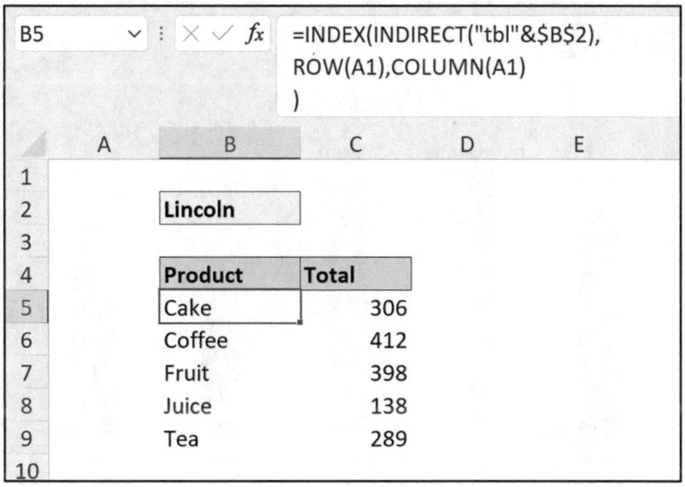

B5	⌄ ⋮ ✕ ✓ ƒx	=INDEX(INDIRECT("tbl"&$B$2), ROW(A1),COLUMN(A1))

	A	B	C	D	E
1					
2		Lincoln			
3					
4		**Product**	**Total**		
5		Cake	306		
6		Coffee	412		
7		Fruit	398		
8		Juice	138		
9		Tea	289		
10					

Figure 11-113. *INDIRECT with INDEX for a non-dynamic array method*

The chart can then be created from the data returned by the formula(s). In this example, a column chart will be used:

1. Select range B4:C9.

2. Click **Insert ➤ Insert Column or Bar Chart ➤ Clustered Column**.

Figure 11-114 shows the finished column chart. A few modifications have been made (never stick with the standard chart Excel inserts), and it has been positioned over the data that the chart is using as its source.

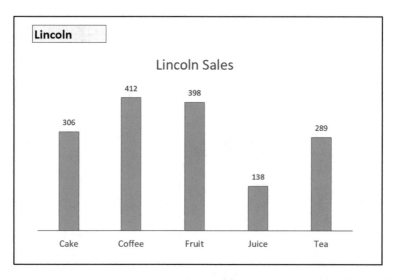

Figure 11-114. *Column chart presenting data from the tblLincoln table*

Interactive Chart with CHOOSEROWS

For this example, we will be using the table of monthly data shown in Figure 11-115. The table is named [tblMonthly].

Name	Jan	Feb	Mar	Apr	May
Amber	122	123	93	94	121
Enrico	81	97	63	56	102
Hiran	83	108	81	118	131
Janet	95	135	38	89	81
Kyle	111	49	90	79	50
Stephanie	31	120	124	85	39
Victoria	120	26	57	112	107

Figure 11-115. *Table of monthly data*

We want to chart all monthly values for the name selected from the drop-down list in cell C2 (Figure 11-116). This cell has been named [rngName].

The row of values that we require is specified by a cell value, so a combination of CHOOSEROWS and MATCH would be a nice choice of functions for this task.

We want a dynamic method, so that when new months (columns) are added to the [tblMonthly] table, the chart automatically picks them up.

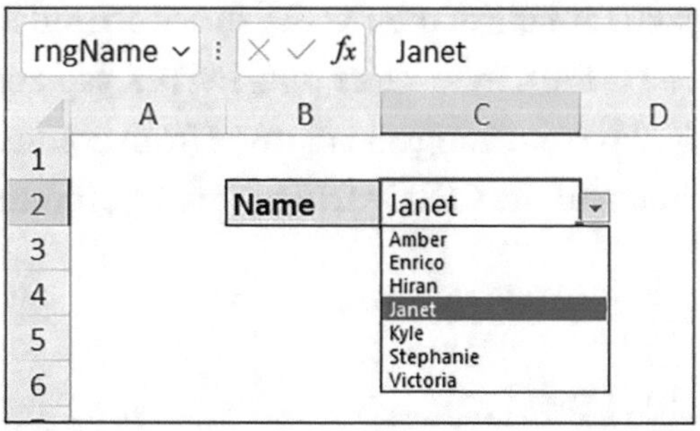

Figure 11-116. *Drop-down list of names for interactive chart*

In Figure 11-117, the following formula is entered in cell A2 of the sheet named [CHOOSEROWS Data]. It uses the MATCH function to return the row number for the name stated in the [rngName] cell. CHOOSEROWS returns an array with all values for this chosen row. The DROP function then removes the first column from the array, as the [Name] column from [tblMonthly] is not needed.

```
=DROP(CHOOSEROWS(tblMonthly,
MATCH(rngName,tblMonthly[Name],0)
),,1)
```

The following formula is entered in cell A1 to return the headers. The first column has been dropped again as we do not need the [Name] header.

```
=DROP(tblMonthly[#Headers],,1)
```

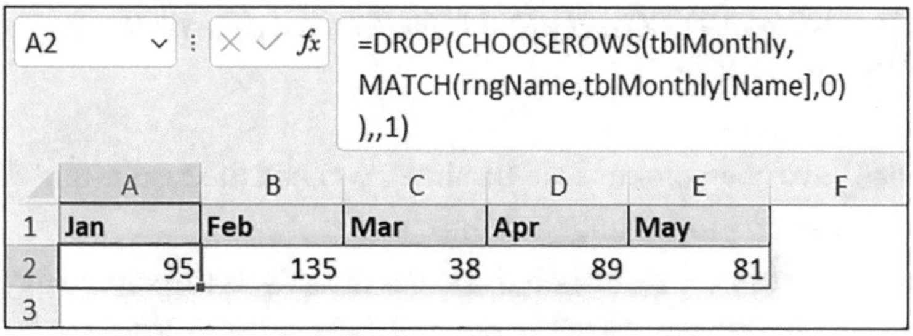

Figure 11-117. *CHOOSEROWS formula entered on the sheet*

An alternative approach for fans of the INDEX function and SEQUENCE could be the following formula (Figure 11-118). In this formula, INDEX replaces CHOOSEROWS, and SEQUENCE replaces DROP by returning all columns from column 2 to the last column. 2 is entered as the *start* value, and the COLUMNS minus 1 part returns how many column numbers to return.

```
=INDEX(tblMonthly,
MATCH(rngName,tblMonthly[Name],0),
SEQUENCE(,COLUMNS(tblMonthly)-1,2,1)
)
```

The following formula returns the headers:

```
=INDEX(tblMonthly[#Headers],
,SEQUENCE(,COLUMNS(tblMonthly)-1,2,1)
)
```

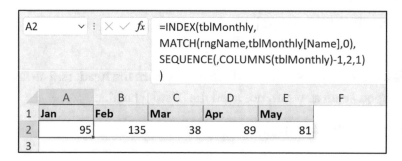

Figure 11-118. *Using INDEX and SEQUENCE as an alternative to CHOOSEROWS and DROP*

The formulas have been entered on the sheet to check the results and that they function correctly before proceeding with the chart.

We do not want to use the results on the sheet directly as the source for the chart because we cannot take advantage of the dynamic arrays there. We want the chart to automatically update when new months are added to the [tblMonthly] table. So, we will define names for the two spill ranges and use the names for the chart data:

1. Click **Formulas ➤ Define Name**.

2.   In the *New Name* window, type a *Name* for the chart values.
Then click in the *Refers to* box, and click cell A2 that contains the
formula on the sheet [CHOOSEROWS Data]. Add the "#" on the
end to reference the dynamic spill range. In Figure 11-119, the
reference has been named "chooserowsValues". Click **OK**.

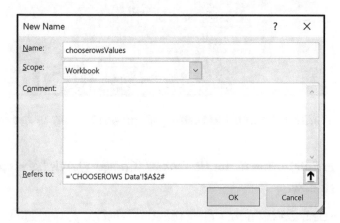

Figure 11-119. *Defining a name for the CHOOSEROWS formula*

3.   Repeat these steps for the formula that returns the chart labels. In
this example, this formula has been named "chooserowsLabels".

We will now create the chart and use the defined names for the chart source data. In
this example, we will create a line chart.

4.   Click **Insert ➤ Insert Line or Area Chart ➤ Line**.

5.   Click **Chart Design ➤ Select Data**.

6.   In the *Select Data Source* window, click the **Add** button in the
Legend Entries (Series) area of the window.

7.   In the *Edit Series* window (Figure 11-120), click in the *Series values*
box, remove any text, click a cell on the sheet to enter a sheet
name, remove the cell reference, and type "chooserowsValues".
Click **OK**.

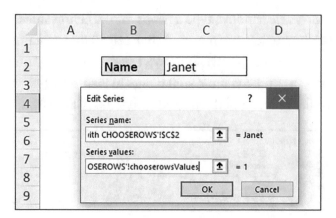

Figure 11-120. *Adding the defined name for the series data of the line chart*

8. Click the **Edit** button in the *Horizontal (Category) Axis Labels* part of the window.

9. In the *Axis Labels* window, click the *Axis label range* box, click a cell on the sheet, remove the cell reference, and type the name used for the labels "chooserowsLabels". Click **OK**.

10. Click **OK** to close the *Select Data Source* window.

Figure 11-121 shows the inserted line chart with some further modifications applied.

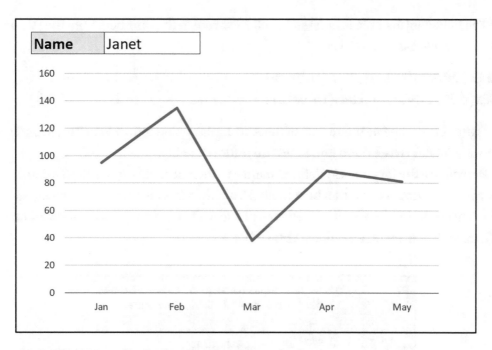

Figure 11-121. *Line chart plotting the values for Janet*

Rolling Chart with INDEX

For the final example, we will create a rolling chart using INDEX to chart the last seven days of values. With INDEX, we can create a dynamic range easily. This makes it perfect for the task of creating a chart that presents the last x number of values only, that is, the last 13 months, the last 6 weeks, etc.

This technique was demonstrated earlier in the chapter to create a moving average formula with INDEX. This time, we will chart the values instead of aggregating them. When new rows are added, the chart automatically adjusts.

In Figure 11-122, we have a table named [tblData] containing values at a daily level. The following formula is entered in cell D2 to return the dates for the last seven days. Two INDEX functions have been used on either side of the colon (:) to return a range.

```
=INDEX(tblData[Date],ROWS(tblData)-6):
INDEX(tblData[Date],ROWS(tblData))
```

The following formula is entered in cell E2 to return the numbers from the [Values] column for the last seven days:

```
=INDEX(tblData[Value],ROWS(tblData)-6):
INDEX(tblData[Value],ROWS(tblData))
```

Figure 11-122 shows the results of these formulas being returned to the sheet. This is only done to help write them and to test their functionality.

We will use the formulas in defined names to then be used for the chart's data sources. The formulas will then be removed from the sheet as they are not required there. This technique works in all versions of Excel. Do not worry about the sight of the spill ranges if you are on an older version of Excel.

D2				fx	=INDEX(tblData[Date],ROWS(tblData)-6):INDEX(tblData[Date],ROWS(tblData))

	A	B	C	D	E	F
1	Date	Value				
2	05/10/2021	229		08/10/2021	405	
3	06/10/2021	285		09/10/2021	366	
4	07/10/2021	463		10/10/2021	573	
5	08/10/2021	405		11/10/2021	402	
6	09/10/2021	366		12/10/2021	546	
7	10/10/2021	573		13/10/2021	591	
8	11/10/2021	402		14/10/2021	342	
9	12/10/2021	546				
10	13/10/2021	591				
11	14/10/2021	342				
12						

Figure 11-122. *Rolling data ranges using INDEX*

1. Copy the formula that returns the dates in cell D2. This name will form the axis labels of a line chart.

2. Click **Formulas ➤ Define Name**.

3. In the *New Name* window, type a *Name* for the date labels. Click the *Refers to* box and paste in the formula. In Figure 11-123, the formula has been named "dateLabels". Click **OK**.

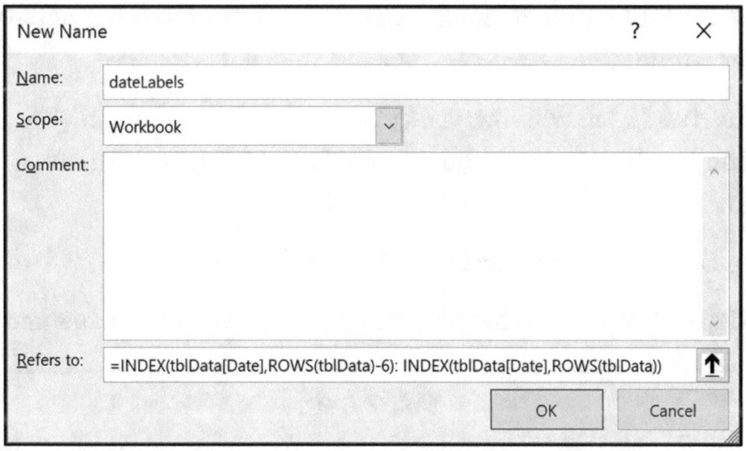

New Name

Name: dateLabels

Scope: Workbook

Comment:

Refers to: =INDEX(tblData[Date],ROWS(tblData)-6): INDEX(tblData[Date],ROWS(tblData))

OK   Cancel

Figure 11-123. *Defined name for the date labels*

4. Repeat these steps for the formula that returns the chart values. In this example, this formula has been named "chartValues".

We will now create the chart and use the defined names for the chart source data. In this example, we will create a line chart.

5. Click **Insert ➤ Insert Line or Area Chart ➤ Line**.

6. Click **Chart Design ➤ Select Data**.

7. In the *Select Data Source* window, click the **Add** button in the *Legend Entries (Series)* area of the window.

8. In the *Edit Series* window (Figure 11-124), click the *Series values* box, remove any text, click a cell on the sheet to enter a sheet name, remove the cell reference, and type "chartValues". Click **OK**.

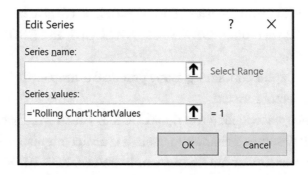

Edit Series

Series name:

▮ Select Range

Series values:

='Rolling Chart'!chartValues ▮ = 1

OK   Cancel

Figure 11-124. *Adding the chartValues name for the chart data series*

9. Click the **Edit** button in the *Horizontal (Category) Axis Labels* part of the window.

10. In the *Axis Labels* window, click the *Axis label range* box, click a cell on the sheet, remove the cell reference, and type the name used for the labels "dateLabels". Click **OK**.

11. Click **OK** to close the *Select Data Source* window.

Figure 11-125 shows the line chart showing the last seven days' dates and values only.

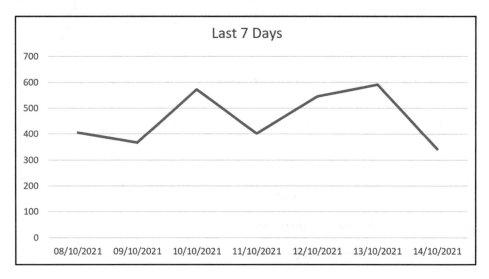

Figure 11-125. *Line chart showing the last seven days' values only*

Summary

In this chapter, we learned many of the best lookup functions in Excel, including INDEX, OFFSET, MATCH, and INDIRECT, to name a few. We also covered functions newly released to 2022, including VSTACK, CHOOSECOLS, and DROP. Excel is forever expanding and evolving.

This was a large chapter containing many practical examples to demonstrate the application of the different functions.

In the next chapter, we will focus on the XLOOKUP function in Excel, another lookup function. XLOOKUP deserves a chapter to itself. It is an accomplished function with many key strengths over similar functions including VLOOKUP, HLOOKUP, and the INDEX-MATCH combination.

CHAPTER 12

XLOOKUP: The New Kid on the Block

The XLOOKUP function was released in 2020 to provide a superior lookup function to others that have existed in Excel for years.

This function is the new kid on the block of lookup functions. It gains more fans every week as Excel users discover XLOOKUP and the simplicity it provides in looking up and returning values.

This function is only available for users of Excel 2021 (Windows and Mac), Excel for Microsoft 365 (Windows and Mac), and Excel for the Web. It is a fine representation of how we work in modern Excel.

In this chapter, we will begin with the basics of XLOOKUP and use the function to accomplish some typical lookup tasks. We then progress through numerous examples that demonstrate the power of this function.

File   xlookup.xlsx

Introduction to XLOOKUP

Availability: Excel 2021, Excel for Microsoft 365, Excel for the Web, Excel 2021 for Mac, Excel for Microsoft 365 for Mac

The XLOOKUP function combines a blend of the key attributes of the INDEX and MATCH functions into one function. It is a brilliant function with some special abilities.

Its modest definition is that it looks for a value, within a range or array, and returns the corresponding item from a second range or array. However, you soon realize it goes a little beyond this scope.

© Alan Murray 2022

A. Murray, *Advanced Excel Formulas*, https://doi.org/10.1007/978-1-4842-7125-4_12

There are several key developments that were included within XLOOKUP:

- It defaults to an exact match. This is the most common match type yet is not the default with the older VLOOKUP and MATCH functions.

- It contains a built-in *if not found* argument. No requirement for a function such as IFERROR or IFNA to handle unmatched values.

- It can return ranges as well as values. VLOOKUP cannot do this. This complements the dynamic array engine wonderfully.

- It is a robust lookup function. It can look vertically or horizontally, left or right, and does not require the values of its *lookup array* to be in any specific order.

- It can look for a value from first to last or last to first.

The XLOOKUP function is especially well equipped at performing lookups on data in tables, returning ranges and working with dynamic arrays. These are key qualities of XLOOKUP.

Lookup functions such as INDEX, VLOOKUP, HLOOKUP, and OFFSET request index numbers for their row and column arguments. This makes them great for relative references and more flexible. XLOOKUP works with explicit references to the range or table element to be used for its lookup and return arrays. XLOOKUP is a perfect match for use with structured data in tables. They go together like mint and chocolate. A dream team.

The syntax of the XLOOKUP function may seem daunting at first as it contains six arguments. This is testimony to its extra functionality mentioned before. However, only the first three arguments are required:

```
=XLOOKUP(lookup_value, lookup_array, return_array, [if_not_found],
[match_mode], [search_mode])
```

- **Lookup value:** The value you are looking for

- **Lookup array:** The range or array to look within

- **Return array:** The range or array to return from

- **[If not found]:** The value to return if a match is not found

- **[Match mode]:** The number –1, 0, 1, or 2 that defines the match type

- • 0 is entered to specify an exact match. This is the most used match type and the default option.

- • –1 is entered to return the position of the exact match or the next smaller value to the *lookup value*, if the *lookup value* is not found.

- • 1 is entered to return the position of the exact match or the next larger value to the *lookup value*, if the *lookup value* is not found.

- • 2 is entered to specify a wildcard character match. The asterisk (*), question mark (?), and tilde (~) wildcard characters can be used for partial matches.

- **[Search mode]:** The number 1, –1, 2, or –2 that defines the type of search to perform

  - • 1 is entered to specify a search from first to last (top to bottom). This is the default search mode.

  - • –1 is entered to reverse the search and search from last to first (bottom to top).

  - • 2 is entered to specify a binary search from first to last. Performing this type of search requires the *lookup array* to be sorted in ascending order.

  - • –2 is entered to specify a binary search from last to first. The *lookup array* needs to be sorted in descending order for this type of search.

XLOOKUP for an Exact Match

XLOOKUP makes exact match lookups very simple and very durable, especially when used with data formatted as a table.

Figure 12-1 shows a table of product data named [tblProductData]. This table can be found on the [Exact Match Data] sheet. It contains a unique ID for each product and a couple of attribute columns – [Category] and [Product Name].

	A	B	C
1	Category	ID	Product Name
2	Beverages	738	Orange Juice
3	Beverages	184	Coffee
4	Beverages	222	Beer
5	Beverages	250	Wine
6	Food	320	Sandwich
7	Food	197	Samosa
8	Food	179	Baguette
9	Food	349	Soup
10	Cakes	151	Blueberry Muffin
11	Cakes	289	Flapjack
12	Cakes	205	Shortbread

Figure 12-1. *Table of product data*

Note   All data sheets in the example [xlookup.xlsx] file have been hidden.

In Figure 12-2, the following formula is entered in column D to return the product name for each product ID in a dataset. The default *match mode* in XLOOKUP is the exact match, so this argument does not need to be specified.

=XLOOKUP(C2,tblProductData[ID],tblProductData[Product Name])

The [ID] column of the lookup table [tblProductData] has been specified as the *lookup array*, and the *return array* is stated as the [Product Name] column.

fx	=XLOOKUP(C2,tblProductData[ID],tblProductData[Product Name])				
	C	D	E	F	G
	Product ID	Product Name	Category	Units	Total
2021	205	Shortbread		80	87.95
2021	289	Flapjack		47	51.75
2021	151	Blueberry Muffin		41	43.61
2021	738	Orange Juice		77	82.31
2021	222	Beer		60	116.51

Figure 12-2. *XLOOKUP returning the product name for each ID value*

This is very simple. There is no requirement to enter a *column index number* as requested by VLOOKUP or to nest a MATCH function as commonly used with INDEX.

Specifying table columns instead of ranges that lack meaning, such as column 5 or range E2:E14, makes it even better. It is faster to enter the formula too – less clicking with a mouse to select ranges, typing in meaningful references instead.

The XLOOKUP function has a built-in argument to specify an *if not found* value to return instead of the #N/A error. This is optional and is often not required.

In Figure 12-3, the text "Incorrect ID" is returned instead of the #N/A error. The value in cell C4 has been changed from 151 to 152, so now contains an invalid product ID. This ID is not matched with a [Product ID] in the *lookup array*, and the *if not found* value is returned.

```
=XLOOKUP(C2,tblProductData[ID],tblProductData[Product Name],"Incorrect ID")
```

In this example, the #N/A error makes it easier to spot the issue with the lookup value, but sometimes you want an alternative response. There can be valid reasons why a lookup value is not matched.

fx	=XLOOKUP(C2,tblProductData[ID],tblProductData[Product Name],"Incorrect ID")					
	C	D	E	F	G	H
	Product ID	**Product Name**	**Category**	**Units**	**Total**	
2021	205	Shortbread		80	87.95	
2021	289	Flapjack		47	51.75	
2021	152	Incorrect ID		41	43.61	
2021	738	Orange Juice		77	82.31	
2021	222	Beer		60	116.51	

Figure 12-3. *If not found argument returning a value instead of #N/A*

Because the XLOOKUP function uses distinct lookup and return arrays (VLOOKUP looks in and returns from the same *table array*), the *lookup array* and *return array* can be in any order within the lookup table.

In Figure 12-4, the following formula returns the [Category] for each product ID. You can see back in Figure 12-1 that the [Category] column sits to the left of the [ID] column in [tblProductData]. This is no problem for XLOOKUP.

```
=XLOOKUP(C2,tblProductData[ID],tblProductData[Category])
```

fx	=XLOOKUP(C2,tblProductData[ID],tblProductData[Category])				
	C	D	E	F	G
	Product ID	**Product Name**	**Category**	**Units**	**Total**
/2021	205	Shortbread	Cakes	80	87.95
/2021	289	Flapjack	Cakes	47	51.75
/2021	151	Blueberry Muffin	Cakes	41	43.61
/2021	738	Orange Juice	Beverages	77	82.31
/2021	222	Beer	Beverages	60	116.51

Figure 12-4. *Returning the category name for each product ID*

Note   The value in cell C4 has been changed back from 152 to 151 to return a matching value.

XLOOKUP to Look Up a Value in Ranges

The different *match modes* of XLOOKUP can be split into three different types of lookups – exact matches, range lookups, and wildcard lookups.

There are two types of range lookup – *exact match or next smaller item* and *exact match or next larger item* (Figure 12-5). Returning the next smaller item when a match is not found (–1) is the more commonplace of the two.

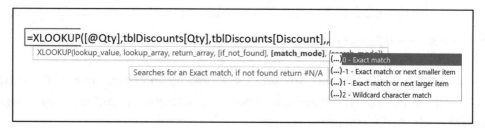

Figure 12-5. *The different match modes of XLOOKUP*

Figure 12-6 shows a table named [tblDiscounts] on a sheet named [Range Lookup Data]. It contains ranges of quantity values in a column named [Qty] and a [Discount] value associated with that range.

	A	B
1	**Qty**	**Discount**
2	0	0.0%
3	15	3.0%
4	50	5.0%
5	65	7.5%
6	90	10.0%
7	100	11.5%
8		

Figure 12-6. *Table of quantity ranges and discounts*

In Figure 12-7, the following XLOOKUP formula is entered in column D to return the applicable discount from [tblDiscounts] dependent upon the quantity ordered:

```
=XLOOKUP([@Qty],tblDiscounts[Qty],tblDiscounts[Discount],0,-1)
```

A 0 is entered for the *if not found* argument, and –1 is specified for the *match mode*.

fx	=XLOOKUP([@Qty],tblDiscounts[Qty],tblDiscounts[Discount],0,-1)						
B	C	D	E	F	G	H	
Qty	**Total**	**Discount**	**Minus Disc**				
63	504	5.0%	479				
70	490	7.5%	453				
20	100	3.0%	97				
77	539	7.5%	499				
31	124	3.0%	120				
5	25	0.0%	25				
64	384	5.0%	365				
101	505	11.5%	447				
45	180	3.0%	175				

Figure 12-7. *Looking up a value in ranges with XLOOKUP*

Although the ranges of [Qty] values in [tblDiscounts] are in ascending order, and it is great that they are, the XLOOKUP function returns the correct discount regardless of the order of the ranges.

This provides a more robust range lookup formula than offered by the older VLOOKUP and MATCH functions. They required the range values to be in order.

XLOOKUP with Wildcards

The XLOOKUP function can handle the use of wildcard characters such as the asterisk (*) and question mark (?) in the *lookup value*, but this needs to be specified as the *match mode*.

Figure 12-8 shows a table named [tblTargets] on a sheet named [Target Data]. It contains names of cities and a target value associated with the city. The [City] column includes the country that the city resides in.

City	Target
Copenhagen, Denmark	240
London, UK	710
Berlin, Germany	890
Lisbon, Portugal	610
Newcastle, UK	860

Figure 12-8. *Table containing cities and targets*

From another range, we have a column that contains city names only, for example, "Lisbon," and we need to look up the city in the [tblTargets] table and return the [Target] value.

We need to perform a partial match on the city name, as there is not an exact match between the two column values. For this, we can perform a wildcard search.

There are three wildcard characters that can be used in your XLOOKUP formulas:

- *** (Asterisk):** Represents any number of characters. For example, New* would match with Newport, Newcastle, New York, and New Zealand.

- **? (Question mark):** Represents a single character. For example, L????n would match with both London and Lisbon.

- **~ (Tilde):** Used to treat a wildcard character as a text character. For example, *don would match any text that ends in the characters don, but ~*don will look for an exact match of *don, treating the asterisk as its character and not a wildcard.

In Figure 12-9, the following formula is entered in column E:

```
=XLOOKUP(C3&"*",tblTargets[City],tblTargets[Target],,2)
```

For the *lookup value,* the city name in column C is combined with the asterisk wildcard character. This creates a *lookup value* that begins with the value in column C but can have any text after that.

The *if not found* argument is skipped, and 2 (wildcard character match) is entered for the *match mode* argument.

Name	City	Value	Target
Pedro Afonso	London	470	710
Elizabeth Brown	Copenhagen	391	240
Sven Ottlieb	Lisbon	417	610
Janine Labrune	Berlin	282	890
Ann Devon	Newcastle	1197	860
Roland Mendel	Lisbon	771	610
Aria Cruz	Copenhagen	1112	240

Figure 12-9. *XLOOKUP function using wildcard characters in the lookup value*

If we wanted to perform a wildcard character match where the city name can occur anywhere within the cells of the *lookup array,* an additional asterisk can be joined before the city name in cell C3:

```
=XLOOKUP("*"&C3&"*",tblTargets[City],tblTargets[Target],,2)
```

XLOOKUP for the Last Match

One of the key developments with the XLOOKUP function compared to some other lookup functions is its ability to search its lookup array from last to first in addition to the standard first to last.

Figure 12-10 shows a table named [tblCourses] that contains a list of training courses that were conducted recently. The courses are ordered by the date that they were delivered.

665

We want to specify a training course from a drop-down list and return the date and number of attendees for the last instance of that training course.

	A	B	C
1	Date	Course	Attendees
2	04/09/2021	Excel Adv	5
3	09/09/2021	Excel Adv	10
4	10/09/2021	PivotTables	8
5	13/09/2021	Excel Adv	4
6	20/09/2021	Excel Basic	5
7	22/09/2021	Excel Adv	5
8	23/09/2021	PivotTables	4
9	26/09/2021	PivotTables	3
10	30/09/2021	Excel Adv	6
11			

Figure 12-10. *Table of recently delivered training courses*

In Figure 12-11, the following formula is entered in cell F3. It searches for the course name in cell E3 in the [Course] column of the table from last to first (from bottom to top). It returns the date of the first matching value.

```
=XLOOKUP(E3,tblCourses[Course],tblCourses[Date],"No courses booked",0,-1)
```

If no matching courses are found, the text "No courses booked" is returned. A 0 is entered to request an exact match, and –1 is entered to specify a last-to-first *search mode.*

F3		✕ ✓ *fx*	=XLOOKUP(E3,tblCourses[Course],tblCourses[Date],"No courses booked",0,-1)						
	A	B	C	D	E	F	G	H
1	Date	Course	Attendees					
2	04/09/2021	Excel Adv	5		Course	Date	Attendees	
3	09/09/2021	Excel Adv	10		PivotTables	26/09/2021	3	
4	10/09/2021	PivotTables	8					
5	13/09/2021	Excel Adv	4					
6	20/09/2021	Excel Basic	5					
7	22/09/2021	Excel Adv	5					
8	23/09/2021	PivotTables	4					
9	26/09/2021	PivotTables	3					
10	30/09/2021	Excel Adv	6					

Figure 12-11. *Returning the last matching value in a list*

The following XLOOKUP formula is entered in cell G3 to return the number of attendees for the matching course:

```
=XLOOKUP(E3,tblCourses[Course],tblCourses[Attendees],"",0,-1)
```

An empty string "" is specified for the *if not found* argument. The XLOOKUP formula in cell F3 returns "No courses booked" if there is no matching value, so it is not necessary to provide a meaningful *if not found* response again. We just want to hide the #N/A error, and an empty string is ideal for that task.

Multiple Column XLOOKUP

With XLOOKUP, it is simple to create lookup formulas that return values or ranges where the values in multiple columns must match. These formulas are sometimes referred to as multi-criteria lookup formulas.

Figure 12-12 shows a table named [tblPrices], found on the [Multi-Column Data] sheet. It contains membership prices that are dependent upon the membership type and the location of the membership.

	A	B	C	
1	Membership	Location	Price	
2	Executive	Dublin	90	
3	Gold	Dublin	75	
4	Silver	Dublin	65	
5	Bronze	Dublin	40	
6	Executive	Edinburgh	105	
7	Gold	Edinburgh	90	
8	Silver	Edinburgh	75	
9	Bronze	Edinburgh	55	
10				

Figure 12-12. Table containing prices by membership type and location

In Figure 12-13, the following formula returns the price for each member based on their membership type and location:

```
=XLOOKUP(B2&C2,
tblPrices[Membership]&tblPrices[Location],
tblPrices[Price])
```

The values in cells B2 (membership) and C2 (location) are combined into one value using the ampersand (&). The same technique is applied to the columns required for the *lookup array* – [Membership] and [Location].

This simple technique is used to combine any number of criteria needed for the *lookup value* and *lookup array*.

D2		× ✓ fx	=XLOOKUP(B2&C2, tblPrices[Membership]&tblPrices[Location], tblPrices[Price])		

	A	B	C	D	E
1	Name	Membership	Location	Price	
2	Patricio Simpson	Silver	Edinburgh	75	
3	Francisco Chang	Bronze	Dublin	40	
4	Yang Wang	Gold	Edinburgh	90	
5	Pedro Afonso	Gold	Edinburgh	90	
6	Elizabeth Brown	Bronze	Edinburgh	55	
7	Sven Ottlieb	Silver	Dublin	65	
8	Janine Labrune	Executive	Dublin	90	
9					

Figure 12-13. *Multiple column XLOOKUP formula*

Two-Way Lookup with XLOOKUP

What is better than XLOOKUP? Two XLOOKUPs. And with two XLOOKUP functions, we can create a two-way lookup.

This two-way lookup formula uses an XLOOKUP to return the matching value from an array returned by an accompanying XLOOKUP function.

Figure 12-14 shows the prices for holiday accommodation based on the type of accommodation and the location. The accommodation types are stored in range B3:B7, and the locations are stored in range C2:F2, on the worksheet [Prices].

	A	B	C	D	E	F
1						
2		Accommodation	Norfolk	Cumbria	Suffolk	Derbyshire
3		Woodland	133	137	130	129
4		Waterside	111	127	136	158
5		Treehouse	139	119	122	162
6		Spa Suite	155	169	174	177
7		Exclusive	241	293	297	295
8						
9						

Figure 12-14. *Accommodation prices for the two-way lookup*

In Figure 12-15, the following formula returns the prices for the given accommodation and location to the [Price] column in the table:

```
=XLOOKUP([@Accommodation],Prices!$B$3:$B$7,
XLOOKUP([@Location],Prices!$C$2:$F$2,Prices!$C$3:$F$7)
)
```

⋮ ✕ ✓ *fx*	=XLOOKUP([@Accommodation],Prices!$B$3:$B$7, XLOOKUP([@Location],Prices!$C$2:$F$2,Prices!$C$3:$F$7))

	B	C	D	E	F
	ID	Accommodation	Location	Price	
	1121	Woodland	Derbyshire	129	
	1209	Spa Suite	Cumbria	169	
	1333	Treehouse	Norfolk	139	
	1344	Spa Suite	Suffolk	174	
	1422	Exclusive	Derbyshire	295	
	1441	Waterside	Norfolk	111	
	1451	Treehouse	Derbyshire	162	

Figure 12-15. *Two-way XLOOKUP formula*

The second XLOOKUP is finding the matching column, while the first finds the matching row.

The second XLOOKUP function is used as the *return array* for the first XLOOKUP. The second XLOOKUP returns the array of values corresponding to the value stated in the [Location] column.

The following formula shows the results after the first XLOOKUP is calculated. The following results show the array of values returned for "Derbyshire":

```
=XLOOKUP([@Accommodation],Prices!$B$3:$B$7,
{129;158;162;177;295}
)
```

The first XLOOKUP then returns the corresponding value in this array for the value stated in the [Accommodation] column.

It does not matter which order the two XLOOKUP functions are used; however, I have written them in order of row and then column to match R1C1 notation.

Three-Way Lookup

We can combine the techniques of the last two examples to create what some refer to as a three-way lookup.

In Figure 12-16, the following formula is entered in cell D2 to return the room rate dependent upon the room type, board, and the day of the week:

```
=XLOOKUP(A2&B2,A5:A10&B5:B10,
XLOOKUP(C2,C4:I4,C5:I10)
)
```

The second XLOOKUP function is returning the array of values for the matching column like we saw in the two-way lookup example. It is matching the day of week value in cell C2 against the range of values in C4:I4.

The first XLOOKUP then returns the corresponding value in that array for the matching row. The room type and board conditions are met by combining the values from A2 and B2 and A5:A10 and B5:B10. This creates a merged *lookup value* and *lookup array*.

All three matches, or conditions, are easily met with these two XLOOKUP functions in a relatively concise formula.

D2	: × ✓ fx	=XLOOKUP(A2&B2,A5:A10&B5:B10,XLOOKUP(C2,C4:I4,C5:I10))							

	A	B	C	D	E	F	G	H	I
1	Room Type	Board	Day	Rate					
2	Executive	Half	Friday	733					
3									
4	Room Type	Board	Monday	Tuesday	Wednesday	Thursday	Friday	Saturday	Sunday
5	Executive	Full	871	906	899	888	923	842	806
6	Executive	Half	667	747	612	729	733	648	723
7	Gold	Full	723	726	747	751	724	800	765
8	Gold	Half	521	641	522	668	539	599	679
9	Silver	Full	518	536	480	498	515	542	496
10	Silver	Half	415	359	361	402	378	413	384
11									

Figure 12-16. *Three-way lookup with XLOOKUP*

Three-Way Lookup with Mixed Match Modes

Taking the previous example further, the XLOOKUP functions can use different match modes. In Figure 12-17, we have a range containing different room rates that are dependent upon the room type, board, and the time of the year. This range is on a sheet named [Room Rates].

In range C1:F1 are ranges of dates beginning from 10th March 2021. The price of a room changes at different times of the year.

We want to use a three-way lookup to return the room rate for a specified room type, board, and date that the room is booked.

	A	B	C	D	E	F
1	Room Type	Board	10/03/2021	22/07/2021	01/10/2021	10/12/2021
2	Executive	Full	871	906	899	888
3	Executive	Half	667	747	612	729
4	Gold	Full	723	726	747	751
5	Gold	Half	521	641	522	668
6	Silver	Full	518	536	480	498
7	Silver	Half	415	359	361	402
8						

Figure 12-17. *Room rates over different date periods*

In Figure 12-18, the following formula returns the room rates to range D2:D7. This formula is like the previous example, except in the second XLOOKUP, –1 is specified for the *match mode* to apply the *exact match or next smaller item* mode for the date range.

```
=XLOOKUP(A2&B2,
'Room Rates'!$A$2:$A$7&'Room Rates'!$B$2:$B$7,
XLOOKUP(C2,'Room Rates'!$C$1:$F$1,'Room Rates'!$C$2:$F$7,,-1))
```

	A	B	C	D
1	Room Type	Board	Date	Rate
2	Gold	Full	23/07/2021	726
3	Silver	Full	12/03/2021	518
4	Gold	Half	16/07/2021	521
5	Executive	Full	30/12/2021	888
6	Executive	Half	08/06/2021	667
7	Silver	Full	09/11/2021	480
8				

Figure 12-18. *Three-way lookup including date ranges*

Returning Multiple Values with XLOOKUP

In the last few examples demonstrating two- and three-way lookups, we have seen that an XLOOKUP function can return an array of values for a matching value in a row or column. In each of those examples, the array was passed to another XLOOKUP to return a single matching value.

This array returned by XLOOKUP can, of course, be passed to other Excel functions for use or to the grid itself.

In Figure 12-19, the following formula searches for the product stated in cell B2 in range B5:B10 and returns the values for all months:

```
=XLOOKUP(B2,B5:B10,C5:G10)
```

In this example, the values are returned to the grid to be displayed. A defined name could be made for this spill range of values and then used as the data source for a chart like the example at the end of Chapter 10.

Such a simple formula to create a powerful lookup that returns multiple values. The range used for the *lookup array* and *return array* could be formatted as a table to fully take advantage of this dynamic array behavior.

C2	⌄	:	✕ ✓ *fx*	=XLOOKUP(B2,B5:B10,C5:G10)			

	A	B	C	D	E	F	G
1		Product	Jan	Feb	Mar	Apr	May
2		Eggs	1,178	418	894	1291	628
3							
4		Product	Jan	Feb	Mar	Apr	May
5		Coffee	1,322	1,051	381	1,012	238
6		Toast	518	1,185	620	458	953
7		Eggs	1,178	418	894	1,291	628
8		Muffins	875	639	1,110	1,194	330
9		Waffles	508	1,000	815	1,189	267
10		Bacon	1,276	678	494	330	1,212
11							

Figure 12-19. *Returning multiple values with XLOOKUP*

In this example, the values are returned in the same order as displayed in the *lookup array*. This works in this scenario, and because the labels in range C1:G1 are month names, the order is unlikely to change.

However, in a situation where you want the returned array of values in a different order to the lookup array, the following formula could be used:

=XLOOKUP(C1:G1,C4:G4,XLOOKUP(B2,B5:B10,C5:G10))

Another XLOOKUP is added to the formula to match the values in range C1:G1 to the header labels in range C4:G4. This returns an array with the values in the order that they are matched, as opposed to inferring that the order of the two ranges is the same.

In Figure 12-20, the formula is entered in cell C2. The order of the headers in range C1:G1 has been changed to demonstrate the matching of the header values.

C2		∨ : ✕ ✓ *fx*	=XLOOKUP(C1:G1,C4:G4,XLOOKUP(B2,B5:B10,C5:G10))					
	A	B	C	D	E	F	G	H
1		Product	May	Apr	Mar	Feb	Jan	
2		Eggs	628	1,291	894	418	1,178	
3								
4		Product	Jan	Feb	Mar	Apr	May	
5		Coffee	1,322	1,051	381	1,012	238	
6		Toast	518	1,185	620	458	953	
7		Eggs	1,178	418	894	1,291	628	
8		Muffins	875	639	1,110	1,194	330	
9		Waffles	508	1,000	815	1,189	267	
10		Bacon	1,276	678	494	330	1,212	
11								

Figure 12-20. *Returning multiple values in a different order with XLOOKUP*

This also provides a more robust formula – one that is unaffected by users changing the order of the values in the *lookup array* or the lookup values in range C1:G1.

The formula returns a spill range of the resulting values. This is efficient, as it is only one formula returning multiple results.

Instead of returning the values to the grid, they can be returned to another function for use, such as an aggregation function like SUM.

In Figure 12-21, the following formula sums the returned values:

=SUM(XLOOKUP(B2,B5:B10,C5:G10))

C2		∨ : ✕ ✓ *fx*	=SUM(XLOOKUP(B2,B5:B10,C5:G10))				
	A	B	C	D	E	F	G
1		Product	Total				
2		Eggs	4,409				
3							
4		Product	Jan	Feb	Mar	Apr	May
5		Coffee	1,322	1,051	381	1,012	238
6		Toast	518	1,185	620	458	953
7		Eggs	1,178	418	894	1,291	628
8		Muffins	875	639	1,110	1,194	330
9		Waffles	508	1,000	815	1,189	267
10		Bacon	1,276	678	494	330	1,212
11							

Figure 12-21. *Summing the array of values returned by XLOOKUP*

XLOOKUP with SUMIFS for a Dynamic Sum Range

The XLOOKUP function can be used with SUMIFS to provide a dynamic column for the *sum range*. The sum range column can be specified by a cell value. This technique works equally well with AVERAGEIFS, COUNTIFS, etc.

In Figure 12-22, the following formula is entered in cell B4. The XLOOKUP function returns the array of values for the location specified in cell B2. SUMIFS then sums the values in this array for the rows where the values in the [Expense] column match the criteria entered in cell A2.

```
=SUMIFS(
XLOOKUP(B2,tblExpenses[#Headers],tblExpenses),
tblExpenses[Expense],A2)
```

B4		⌄	:	× ✓ ƒx	=SUMIFS(XLOOKUP(B2,tblExpenses[#Headers],tblExpenses), tblExpenses[Expense],A2)				
	A	B	C	D	E	F	G	H
1	Expense	Location		Expense	Qtr	Swindon	Exeter	Oxford
2	Advertising	Oxford		Advertising	Q1	1,072	749	1,091
3				Equipment	Q1	988	798	724
4	Total	2,659		Maintenance	Q1	667	889	353
5				Advertising	Q2	408	321	1,070
6				Equipment	Q2	296	803	216
7				Maintenance	Q2	379	671	816
8				Advertising	Q3	356	256	235
9				Equipment	Q3	1,018	827	444
10				Maintenance	Q3	816	637	679
11				Advertising	Q4	1,031	681	263
12				Equipment	Q4	783	204	272
13				Maintenance	Q4	746	933	890
14								

Figure 12-22. *XLOOKUP with the SUMIFS function*

To keep the formula as meaningful as possible, XLOOKUP is told to check the entire header row of the [tblExpenses] table, even though only the location columns need checking.

If only the location columns were selected, the following reference would be used. This was avoided, as it is a little convoluted.

```
tblExpenses[[#Headers],[Swindon]:[Oxford]]
```

Plus, by referencing the entire header row, if a new location/column is added, the formula continues to work.

XLOOKUP with Other Excel Features

We will conclude the chapter by going beyond the grid and use XLOOKUP with other Excel features. We start with an example of using XLOOKUP to create dependent drop-down lists. This example demonstrates a special technique of using the spill reference appended to the end of a function.

Dependent Drop-Down List with XLOOKUP

A dependent drop-down list is when the items in a list are dependent upon the item selected from a previous list. XLOOKUP provides a neat way for us to set up these dependent drop-down lists in Excel.

Figure 12-23 shows a range that has been prepared for use as the source for the drop-down lists. Dynamic array formulas are used to return the city names for four different countries from a table named [tblCities]. This range is on a sheet named [Lists].

D2		✓ : ✕ ✓ fx	=FILTER(tblCities[City],tblCities[Country]=D1)			
	A	B	C	D	E	F	G
1	Country	City		USA	Germany	Spain	UK
2	USA	Atlanta		Atlanta	Berlin	Bilbao	Birmingham
3	Germany	Berlin		Boston	Bremen	Seville	Brighton
4	Spain	Bilbao		Dallas	Dortmund	Valencia	Cambridge
5	UK	Birmingham		Philadelphia	Dresden		Hull
6	USA	Boston		Sacramento	Stuttgart		London
7	Germany	Bremen					Manchester
8	UK	Brighton					
18	Spain	Seville					
19	Germany	Stuttgart					
20	Spain	Valencia					
21							

Figure 12-23. Spill ranges to be used for dependent drop-down list

The following formula is entered in cell D1 to return a distinct list of the country names and transpose them to be used as headers:

```
=TRANSPOSE(UNIQUE(tblCities[Country]))
```

The following FILTER function is entered in each cell in range D2:G2 to return the cities for the country stated in range D1:G1:

```
=FILTER(tblCities[City],tblCities[Country]=D1)
```

Note   The FILTER function is covered in detail in Chapter 13. This is a brilliant function.

We will create a dependent drop-down list so that when a user picks a country from the list, the second list only displays the cities for that selected country.

We want to use the XLOOKUP function to work with the spill ranges returned by the FILTER function. There may be additional cities added or cities removed in the future. By accessing the spill ranges, the drop-down lists would automatically update.

Also, by working directly with the spill ranges, we can avoid the additional blank cells that would appear if we selected the ranges manually. In this example, there are fewer cities in "Spain" in our data than for other countries.

In Figure 12-24, the first drop-down list has been set up in range B2:B4. The following formula is entered for the Data Validation rule. This is a simple reference to the spill range of country names in cell D1 of the [Lists] sheet.

```
=Lists!$D$1#
```

	A	B	C
1	ID	Country	City
2		426 USA	
3		184 Spain	
4		790	
5			USA
6			Germany
			Spain
7			UK

Figure 12-24. *Drop-down list of country names*

We can now create the dependent lists in range C2:C4:

1. Select range C2:C4.

2. Click **Data ➤ Data Validation**.

3. Click the *Allow* list and click **List**. Enter the following formula into the *Source* box (Figure 12-25). Click **OK**.

```
=XLOOKUP(B2,Lists!$D$1:$G$1,Lists!$D$2:$G$2)#
```

The formula searches for the country specified in the first drop-down along range Lists!$D$1:$G$1. An absolute reference is used as the Data Validation rule is applied to multiple cells in this example.

For the *return array*, only the first row is referenced: Lists!$D$2:$G$2. These cells contain the spill ranges of the cities. The # sign is appended to the end of the XLOOKUP formula to access the spill ranges.

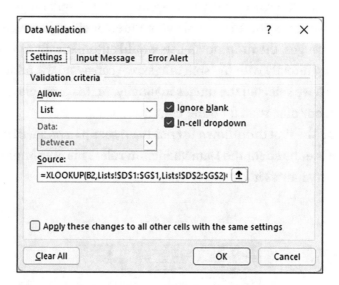

Figure 12-25. *XLOOKUP formula in a Data Validation rule*

Note   A name could have been defined for the XLOOKUP formula and then referenced in the Data Validation rule. We have covered this technique previously in this book. It is useful to aid the management of formulas.

Figure 12-26 shows the completed dependent lists. Only the cities for the UK are shown, as that country is specified in cell B4.

	A	B	C	D
1	**ID**	**Country**	**City**	
2	426	USA	Dallas	
3	184	Spain	Valencia	
4	790	UK		
5			Birmingham	
6			Brighton Cambridge	
7			Hull London Manchester	
8				

Figure 12-26. *Dependent drop-down list of cities*

This Data Validation rule can be applied to as many cells in columns B and C as required. To simplify the example, the rule is applied to rows 2:4 only. However, we could easily have selected a larger range to apply the Data Validation rules to.

Return a Range for a Chart

The XLOOKUP function can be used to return a range like we saw with the INDEX function in Chapter 11. While INDEX is excellent at relative references and working with index values such as column numbers, XLOOKUP is better for explicit column references and is more succinct for ranges between text values.

Figure 12-27 shows a range of sales values for different products and all 12 months of the year. Range B2:D2 contains input cells to specify a product and the first and last month of a date range.

B	C	D
Product	**Range**	
Waffles	Mar	Oct

Product	**Jan**	**Feb**	**Mar**	**Apr**	**May**	**Jun**	**Jul**	**Aug**	**Sep**	**Oct**	**Nov**	**Dec**
Coffee	1,175	312	984	967	514	832	391	747	253	456	849	544
Toast	1,078	606	511	402	779	499	997	827	957	508	283	829
Eggs	884	918	1,115	275	571	298	828	462	1,137	960	407	647
Muffins	767	375	704	825	892	546	941	901	708	598	1,106	643
Waffles	881	952	709	389	794	962	1,023	861	390	310	798	900
Bacon	986	300	717	1,150	1,068	1,107	1,142	804	991	329	724	985

Figure 12-27. *Sales for all months with input cells to specify a range*

We want to create a line chart showing the sales for the product specified in cell B2 and for the date range specified by the months in cells C2 and D2.

To do this, we will create two different XLOOKUP formulas: one for the month names to be used in the chart's X axis and another for the sales values to be used for the chart data series.

Names will be defined for each of the two XLOOKUP formulas and then used for the two elements of the line chart.

Let's enter the two formulas on the worksheet first. This is not necessary; however, it is good practice, as it provides an opportunity to check that the formulas work correctly, before proceeding to define the names and the subsequent chart steps.

Enter the following formula somewhere on the sheet to return the month names for the specified range in cells C2 and B2:

```
=XLOOKUP($C$2,$C$4:$N$4,$C$4:$N$4):
XLOOKUP($D$2,$C$4:$N$4,$C$4:$N$4)
```

Now, enter the following formula to return the sales values for the given product and the specified range in cells C2 and B2 (Figure 12-28):

```
=XLOOKUP($B$2,$B$5:$B$10,XLOOKUP($C$2,$C$4:$N$4,$C$5:$N$10)):
XLOOKUP($B$2,$B$5:$B$10,XLOOKUP($D$2,$C$4:$N$4,$C$5:$N$10))
```

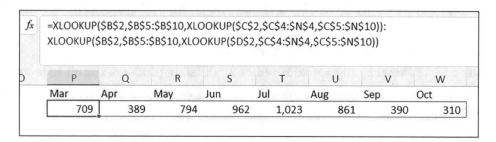

Figure 12-28. XLOOKUP formulas entered on the worksheet

With confirmation that the formulas are working accurately, we can proceed to define the names:

1. Copy the text for the formula returning the month names.

2. Click **Formulas ➤ Define Name**.

3. Type "MonthLabels" for the *Name* of the formula.

4. Paste the formula into the *Refers to* box (Figure 12-29). Click **OK**.

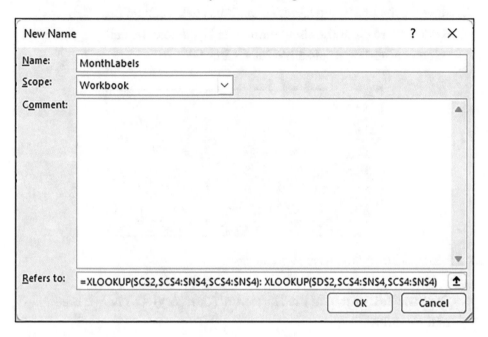

Figure 12-29. *Defining a name for the chart labels*

5. Repeat these steps to define a name for the formula that returns the sales values. Name it "MonthValues."

Note   The sheet name is added automatically by Excel to each of the references in the named formulas.

Now, we can insert the line chart and assign the defined names to the axis and data series:

1. Click **Insert ➤ Insert Line or Area Chart ➤ Line** to insert a blank line chart.

2. With the chart selected, click **Chart Design ➤ Select Data**. This opens the *Select Data Source* window (Figure 12-32).

3. Click the **Add** button in the *Legend Entries (Series)* area of the window.

4. Click in the *Series name* box and click cell B2 containing the name of the selected product (Figure 12-30).

5. Remove the text in the *Series values* box, click a cell on the worksheet to enter the sheet name quickly, delete the cell reference, and type "MonthValues". Click **OK**.

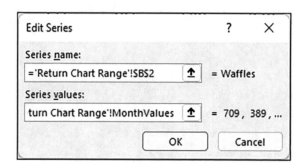

Figure 12-30. *Editing the chart data series*

6. Click the **Edit** button in the *Horizontal (Category) Axis Labels* area of the window.

7. Remove the text in the *Axis label range* box, click a cell on the worksheet to enter the sheet name quickly, delete the cell reference, and type "MonthLabels" (Figure 12-31). Click **OK**.

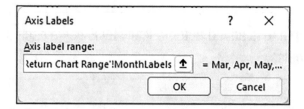

Figure 12-31. *Editing the chart labels*

Note   Instead of typing the name, you can also press **F3** to open the *Paste Name* window, select the name, and click **OK**.

The completed *Select Data Source* window is shown in Figure 12-32. You can see the "Waffles" data series and month range correctly picked up.

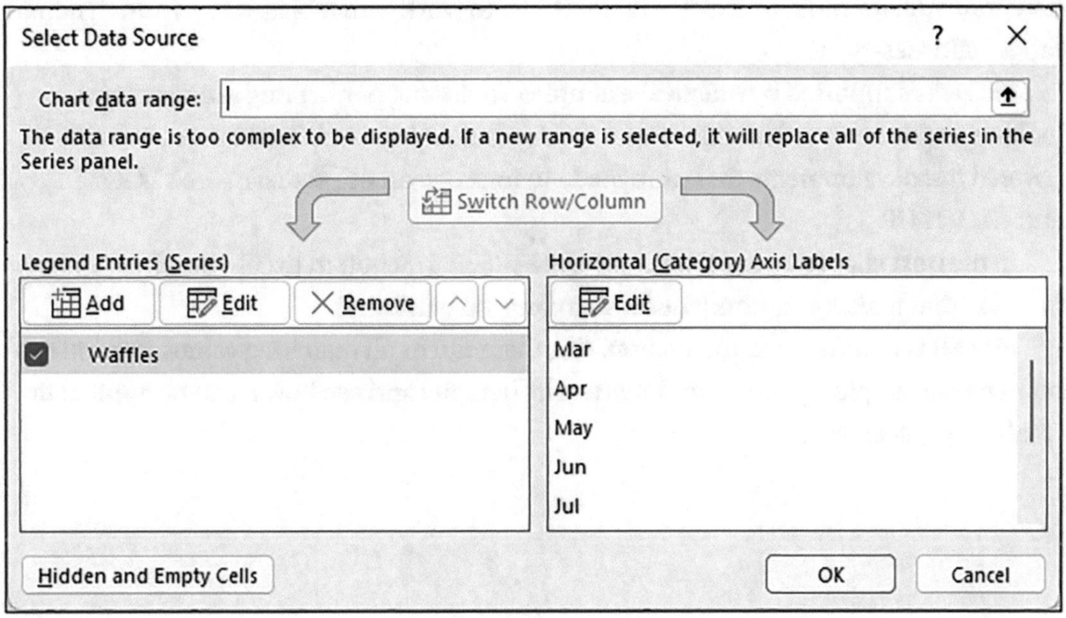

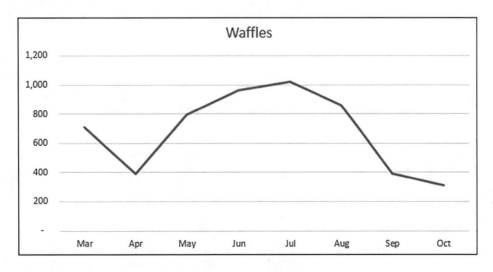

Figure 12-32. *Completed data source for the chart*

Figure 12-33 shows the completed line chart. Further formatting can be applied to enhance the chart.

Figure 12-33. *Completed chart from a specified range*

Summary

In this chapter, we learned the new XLOOKUP function – a powerful and robust function, built for modern Excel, with its ability to work with tables, arrays, and dynamic ranges effortlessly.

This was supported by practical examples, including performing multi-criteria lookups and returning dynamic ranges for dependent lists and chart ranges. We also covered the developments that were made to improve on its predecessors VLOOKUP and HLOOKUP.

In the next chapter, we will dive into the FILTER function in Excel – another fantastic function that makes you wonder how we managed without it.

FILTER is another lookup function, one that returns all matching values. We will see numerous examples of its use to showcase its benefits and see how it can be applied in "real-world" scenarios.

CHAPTER 13

FILTER Function: The Game Changer

When the dynamic array formulas were covered in Chapter 10, the FILTER function was omitted. FILTER was introduced in Excel at the same time as the other dynamic array formulas – SORT, UNIQUE, SEQUENCE, etc. This function will make you wonder, how did I work before the FILTER function? And for this reason, it has its own chapter.

A common question I receive in my training sessions and comments on my YouTube channel is how to write a lookup formula to return all matching results. Functions such as VLOOKUP, the INDEX-MATCH combo, and XLOOKUP cannot do this. This is where the FILTER function steps up.

Now we did see the INDEX and XLOOKUP functions returning ranges, and therefore multiple values, earlier in this book. However, that is not truly returning all results for the value you are looking up. The FILTER function will return the values for each matching item found and not only the first or last matching value.

The FILTER function is quite simply a formula alternative to the popular filter tool in Excel. The filter tool is amazing but is limited in that it requires a user to reapply the filter every time they want to update the results.

FILTER will automate this task of filtering a table of data. It also gives us the capability of combining it with other formulas and Excel features for an even richer Excel experience. FILTER is *insert your chosen superlative here*!

In this chapter, we will begin with the basics of FILTER and learn how to structure the logical tests that determine the results to return. We will then start using FILTER with other functions such as SORT, TEXTJOIN, and NETWORKDAYS.INTL to become familiar with how FILTER can be applied in different scenarios.

© Alan Murray 2022
A. Murray, *Advanced Excel Formulas*, https://doi.org/10.1007/978-1-4842-7125-4_13

The chapter is concluded with examples of using FILTER with other Excel features such as Data Validation and charts.

File   filter.xlsx

Introduction to the FILTER Function

Availability: Excel 2021, Excel for Microsoft 365, Excel for the Web, Excel 2021 for Mac, Excel for Microsoft 365 for Mac

The FILTER function filters a range or array based on specified criteria. It returns a spill range with the results of the filter.

This function is terrific for creating dynamic reports and models where the values to return are dependent upon the value of an input cell.

The syntax for FILTER is short and simple:

```
=FILTER(array, include, [if_empty])
```

- **Array:** The range or array that you want to filter and return

- **Include:** The filter criterion that determines the rows or columns to return

- **[If empty]:** The action to take, or value to return, if no results are returned by FILTER

Simple FILTER Example

Let's jump straight into a simple example of the FILTER function in action.

For the next few examples, the FILTER function will be used to assist the tracking of due dates for a review process. Figure 13-1 shows the first few rows of a table named [tblReviewDates]. It contains only three columns – an individual's name, their region, and the date that their review is due.

	A	B	C
1	Name	Region	Review By
2	Maria Anders	West	19/04/2022
3	Ana Trujillo	North	26/05/2022
4	Antonio Moreno	East	05/05/2022
5	Thomas Hardy	East	15/06/2022
6	Christina Berglund	South	16/06/2022
7	Hanna Moos	West	02/05/2022

Figure 13-1. *First few rows of the table with review due dates*

Note   The [Review By] column contains a formula to ensure that the sample file, and therefore FILTER results, behaves the same for you as it does for me in these examples.

In our first FILTER example, we will return a range containing all three columns from [tblReviewDates] for the rows where the review due date has passed.

In Figure 13-2, the following formula is entered in cell B3:

```
=FILTER(tblReviewDates,
tblReviewDates[Review By]<TODAY(),
"No review dates have passed"
)
```

The criterion tblReviewDates[Review By]<TODAY() is entered as the *include* argument to ensure only rows with a past date in the [Review By] column are returned. The text "No review dates have passed" would be returned if the returned array contained no results.

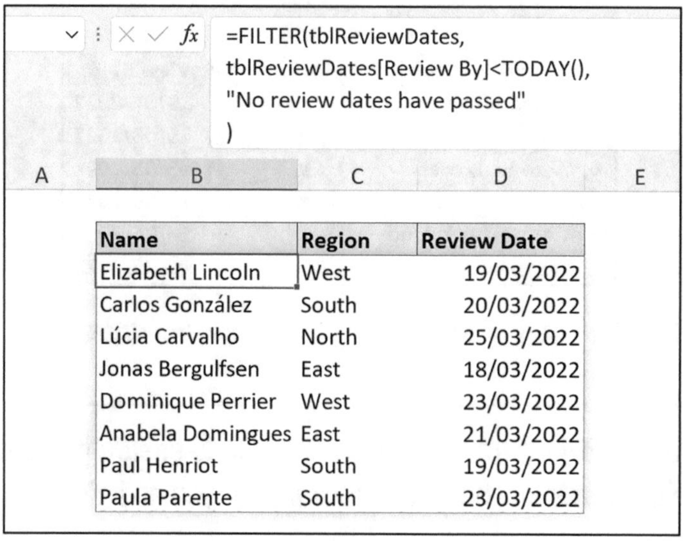

Name	Region	Review Date
Elizabeth Lincoln	West	19/03/2022
Carlos González	South	20/03/2022
Lúcia Carvalho	North	25/03/2022
Jonas Bergulfsen	East	18/03/2022
Dominique Perrier	West	23/03/2022
Anabela Domingues	East	21/03/2022
Paul Henriot	South	19/03/2022
Paula Parente	South	23/03/2022

Figure 13-2. *FILTER returning overdue review dates*

FILTER with Multiple Conditions

Often, there may be more than one condition that determines the results to return. Let's progress from our first example and see examples that include multiple conditions and handle both AND and OR logic.

In the first of these examples, we will create a report that returns those who have a review due in the next x number of days. The number of days will be determined by a cell value.

In Figure 13-3, the following formula is entered in cell B5:

```
=FILTER(tblReviewDates,
(tblReviewDates[Review By]>=TODAY())*
(tblReviewDates[Review By]<TODAY()+B2),
"No review dates are due"
)
```

| B5 | | : × ✓ fx | =FILTER(tblReviewDates,
(tblReviewDates[Review By]>=TODAY())*
(tblReviewDates[Review By]<TODAY()+B2),
"No review dates are due"
) |

	A	B	C	D	E
1		**No of Days**	**Region 1**	**Region 2**	
2		14			
3					
4		**Name**	**Region**	**Review Date**	
5		Victoria Ashworth	South	05/04/2022	
6		Elizabeth Brown	East	28/03/2022	
7		Diego Roel	West	08/04/2022	
8		Eduardo Saavedra	North	28/03/2022	
9		Howard Snyder	West	31/03/2022	
10		Liu Wong	West	29/03/2022	
11		Pirkko Koskitalo	East	07/04/2022	
12		Karl Jablonski	North	31/03/2022	

Figure 13-3. *FILTER function with multiple conditions and AND logic*

The *include* argument of FILTER in this example contains two conditions. When writing multiple conditions in the FILTER function, each condition must be enclosed in its own set of brackets.

In this example, we need to apply AND logic between the two conditions. They are that the [Review By] date must be between today's date and the date in the number of days specified by the value in cell B2.

To apply AND logic, the asterisk (*) operator is used between the two conditions. If OR logic was required, the plus (+) operator would be used (we will see an example of this shortly).

How the FILTER Function Logic Works

Let's briefly recap on why the * and + operators are used to apply AND and OR logic, respectively.

Let's imagine we have six rows of data in a table, and the two conditions returned the following two arrays:

{TRUE; FALSE; FALSE; TRUE; TRUE; FALSE}

and

{TRUE; TRUE; FALSE; FALSE; TRUE; FALSE}

Note   A semicolon separates rows in an array, and a comma separates columns in an array.

The asterisk is the multiplication operator and ensures that the corresponding values in each array are multiplied. This converts the TRUE and FALSE values to 1 and 0, respectively, and performs the operation between each corresponding value.

The following array is returned. 1*1=1, 0*1=0, 0*0=0, and so on.

{1; 0; 0; 0; 1; 0}

The rows of the array that are equal to 1 are then returned. So, rows 1 and 5 are returned in this example.

If OR logic is applied between the two arrays, the following array is returned. 1+1=2, 0+1=1, 0+0=0, and so on. Any value except 0 is equal to TRUE in a logical expression. So, rows 1, 2, 4, and 5 are returned in this OR logic example.

{2; 1; 0; 1; 2; 0}

Note   This same application of logical expressions with arrays was seen with the SUMPRODUCT and SUM functions earlier in this book.

Further Examples

Now that we understand why the * and + operators are used to perform the different logical operations, let's proceed and see further examples with the FILTER function.

In Figure 13-4, the following formula returns the rows where the [Review By] date is in the next x number of days for a specified region only. The region is stated by the value in cell C2.

```
=FILTER(tblReviewDates,
(tblReviewDates[Review By]>=TODAY())*(tblReviewDates[Review
By]<TODAY()+B2)*
(tblReviewDates[Region]=C2),
"No review dates are due"
)
```

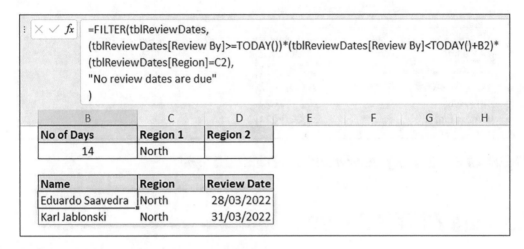

Figure 13-4. *FILTER function with multiple conditions*

Two AND logical tests are applied between the three conditions. Each condition is enclosed in its own set of brackets. Let's now add some OR logic into the formula.

In Figure 13-5, the following formula includes a second specified region. In this example, the number of days is stated in cell B2, and the regions are in cells C2 and D2. The OR logical tests are enclosed in its own set of brackets to ensure that it calculates independently (multiplication has precedence over addition in the order of calculation).

```
=FILTER(tblReviewDates,
(tblReviewDates[Review By]>=TODAY())*(tblReviewDates[Review
By]<TODAY()+B2)*
((tblReviewDates[Region]=C2)+(tblReviewDates[Region]=D2)),
"No review dates are due"
)
```

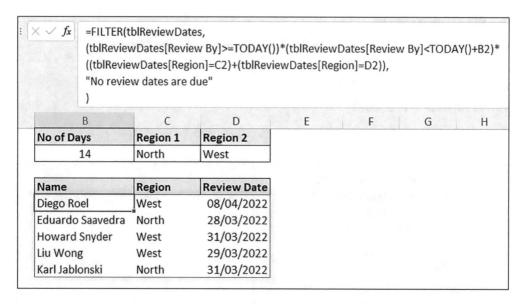

Figure 13-5. FILTER function with AND and OR logic

Sort the FILTER Results

The results of the FILTER function will appear in the same order that they appear in the source data. In this example, that is the [tblReviewDates] table. This may not be the order that you require. Also, if someone sorts the data in [tblReviewDates], this change will propagate through to the FILTER results.

To specify the order for our FILTER results, we can add the SORT function.

In Figure 13-6, the following formula uses the SORT function to order the returned array by the third column, the [Review By] column of the table, in ascending order. This ensures that the more urgent review dates will appear first in the results.

```
=SORT(FILTER(tblReviewDates,
(tblReviewDates[Review By]>=TODAY())*(tblReviewDates[Review
By]<TODAY()+B2)*
((tblReviewDates[Region]=C2)+(tblReviewDates[Region]=D2)),
"No review dates are due"
),3,1)
```

Number 1 is entered for the *sort order* argument of the SORT function to specify the ascending order. This was not necessary as ascending is the default order, but I like to be explicit in a formula and specify the order.

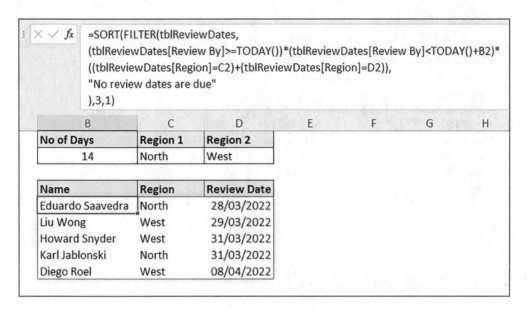

Figure 13-6. *Sorting the filter results by review date in ascending order*

The SORT function supports the ability to sort an array by multiple columns. In Figure 13-7, the following formula is used to sort the FILTER results by region (column 2) in ascending order followed by the review date (column 3) in ascending order:

```
=SORT(FILTER(tblReviewDates,
(tblReviewDates[Review By]>=TODAY())*(tblReviewDates[Review
By]<TODAY()+B2)*
((tblReviewDates[Region]=C2)+(tblReviewDates[Region]=D2)),
"No review dates are due"
),{2,3},{1,1})
```

An array of constants has been used in the *sort index* and *sort order* arguments of the SORT function to specify this multilevel sort.

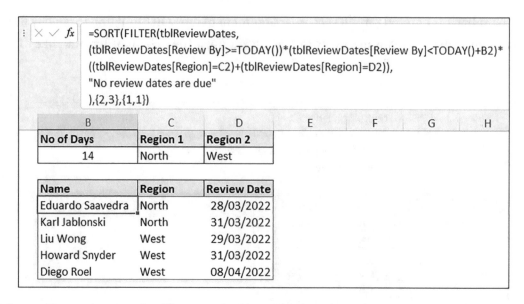

Figure 13-7. Sorting the filter results by multiple columns

#CALC! Error with FILTER

The #CALC! error is returned by the FILTER function when there are no results for the FILTER function to return.

In the previous examples, the text "No review dates are due" was entered in the *if empty* argument of FILTER. This text would be returned instead of the #CALC! error if there were no results to return.

In Figure 13-8, the following formula is used. The *if empty* argument is omitted, and the returned array is empty as there are no review dates in the next seven days for the south region. The #CALC! error is returned.

```
=FILTER(tblReviewDates,
(tblReviewDates[Review By]>=TODAY())*(tblReviewDates[Review
By]<TODAY()+B2)*
(tblReviewDates[Region]=C2)
)
```

The solution to this would be to use the *if empty* argument to return a logical response such as the text "No review dates are due."

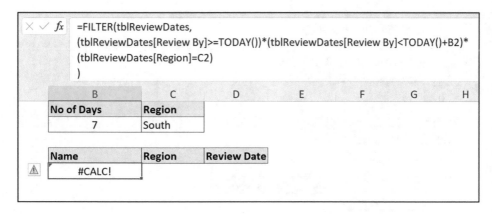

Figure 13-8. *CALC error due to the returned array being empty*

However, another common cause for the #CALC! error is when an input value is omitted. In Figure 13-9, the region in cell C2 has not been specified. The #CALC! error is returned.

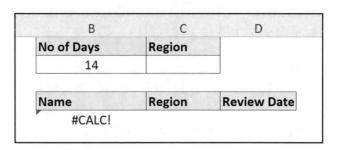

Figure 13-9. *CALC error caused by an empty input cell*

In this scenario, it would be good to return an alternative response. The cause of the #CALC! error is different, and the response shown in Figure 13-10 is not relevant. There are definitely review dates due within the next 14 days; the cause is the empty region cell.

We will adapt the formula to show all review dates due within the specified timeframe regardless of the region if the cell C2 is left empty.

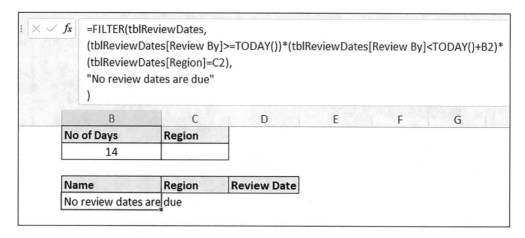

Figure 13-10. *If empty argument returning a message*

In Figure 13-11, the following formula is entered in cell B5. It uses an IF function to test if cell C2 is blank. If it is, the value TRUE is returned so that the FILTER function can use all regions in its returned array. If cell C2 is not blank, then the region in that cell is used in the logical expression as before.

```
=FILTER(tblReviewDates,
(tblReviewDates[Review By]>=TODAY())*(tblReviewDates[Review
By]<TODAY()+B2)*
(IF(ISBLANK(C2),TRUE,tblReviewDates[Region]=C2))
)
```

This formula can be enhanced further to handle cell B2 being left empty and other considerations. However, you cannot plan for every eventuality, and the #CALC! error is good for telling the user that they have done something wrong, such as omitting required information. Not all errors are bad.

This was a demonstration of how we could refine the formula beyond the built-in *if empty* argument.

```
⋮  ✕  ✓  fx    =FILTER(tblReviewDates,
                (tblReviewDates[Review By]>=TODAY())*(tblReviewDates[Review By]<TODAY()+B2)*
                (IF(ISBLANK(C2),TRUE,tblReviewDates[Region]=C2))
                )
```

	B	C	D	E	F	G
	No of Days	Region				
	14					
	Name	Region	Review Date			
	Victoria Ashworth	South	05/04/2022			
	Elizabeth Brown	East	28/03/2022			
	Diego Roel	West	08/04/2022			
	Eduardo Saavedra	North	28/03/2022			
	Howard Snyder	West	31/03/2022			
	Liu Wong	West	29/03/2022			
	Pirkko Koskitalo	East	07/04/2022			
	Karl Jablonski	North	31/03/2022			

Figure 13-11. *Results returned even when criteria are omitted*

Adding a Calculated Column to the Returned Array

You may need to add calculated columns to your report that use the results returned by the FILTER function. This will require being able to access specific columns, and maybe rows, of the returned array.

In this example, we will add a calculated column to return the number of days remaining until the review date. This provides a puzzle to us, because the FILTER function in this example returns an array that is three columns wide. Yet, we want to use only the third column [Review Date] in our calculation.

In Chapter 11, we covered the INDEX function and saw how it is the ultimate function for working with arrays. Let's use it here to isolate the third column of this multicolumn array for our calculated column.

In Figure 13-12, the following formula is entered in cell E5 to calculate the number of days until the review date. The INDEX function is used to access the spill range of FILTER and return all values from the third column only. Today's date is subtracted from these to return the number of days remaining.

```
=INDEX(B5#,,3)-TODAY()
```

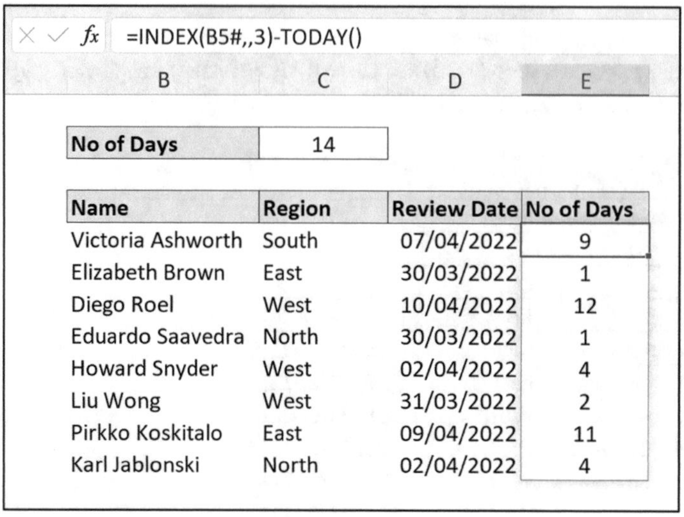

	B	C	D	E
	× ✓ fx	=INDEX(B5#,,3)-TODAY()		

No of Days	14

Name	Region	Review Date	No of Days
Victoria Ashworth	South	07/04/2022	9
Elizabeth Brown	East	30/03/2022	1
Diego Roel	West	10/04/2022	12
Eduardo Saavedra	North	30/03/2022	1
Howard Snyder	West	02/04/2022	4
Liu Wong	West	31/03/2022	2
Pirkko Koskitalo	East	09/04/2022	11
Karl Jablonski	North	02/04/2022	4

Figure 13-12. *Calculated column on a multicolumn array*

Note   By using the TODAY() function in this formula, the result in cell E5 is returned in a date format. It will need reformatting to be presented correctly.

The CHOOSECOLS function provides a neat alternative to INDEX for this task. This is exactly the type of task that the CHOOSECOLS function was developed for.

In Figure 13-13, the following formula is entered in cell E5. The CHOOSECOLS function takes the place of INDEX to return the values in the third column of the spill range for the calculated column.

```
=CHOOSECOLS(B5#,3)-TODAY()
```

| | | fx | =CHOOSECOLS(B5#,3)-TODAY() |

	B	C	D	E	F
No of Days		14			

Name	Region	Review Date	No of Days
Victoria Ashworth	South	07/04/2022	9
Elizabeth Brown	East	30/03/2022	1
Diego Roel	West	10/04/2022	12
Eduardo Saavedra	North	30/03/2022	1
Howard Snyder	West	02/04/2022	4
Liu Wong	West	31/03/2022	2
Pirkko Koskitalo	East	09/04/2022	11
Karl Jablonski	North	02/04/2022	4

Figure 13-13. *CHOOSECOLS to extract the values for the calculated column*

Having the calculated column separate from the FILTER function results will have its advantages. It will be easier to use in other formulas if required or for values in a chart.

But maybe we want to include this column in a combined array with the FILTER results. For this, we can use the HSTACK function.

In Figure 13-14, the following formula returns the results as a single array:

```
=LET(
reviews,
FILTER(tblReviewDates,
(tblReviewDates[Review By]>=TODAY())*(tblReviewDates[Review
By]<TODAY()+C2),
"No review dates have passed"),
days,CHOOSECOLS(reviews,3)-TODAY(),
HSTACK(reviews,days)
)
```

This formula uses the LET function which is covered in Chapter 15 of this book. Using LET ensures that the FILTER function is only calculated once. The FILTER function is assigned to the name *reviews*. CHOOSECOLS then references *reviews* for its array. Skip to Chapter 15 to read more detail on how to use LET and why the LET function is important.

Both formulas are calculated and defined as a name or variable (reviews and *days*). These names are then used in the HSTACK function to form the single array to return.

B	C	D	E	F
No of Days	14			
Name	Region	Review Date	No of Days	
Victoria Ashworth	South	07/04/2022	9	
Elizabeth Brown	East	30/03/2022	1	
Diego Roel	West	10/04/2022	12	
Eduardo Saavedra	North	30/03/2022	1	
Howard Snyder	West	02/04/2022	4	
Liu Wong	West	31/03/2022	2	
Pirkko Koskitalo	East	09/04/2022	11	
Karl Jablonski	North	02/04/2022	4	

Figure 13-14. *Results returned as a single array*

Note   The CHOOSECOLS and HSTACK functions are available in the Excel for Microsoft 365 version for Windows and Mac and Excel for the Web version only.

FILTER and Return Non-adjacent Columns

The FILTER function cannot independently return specific columns from a table or array. It requires the columns to be together or adjacent as Excel will typically describe it.

For these examples, we will return the [Name] and [Review By] columns from the [tblReviewDates] table only. These are columns 1 and 3.

Fortunately, there are numerous ways to accomplish this, and they are nice and simple. Let's start with the CHOOSECOLS function.

In Figure 13-15, the CHOOSECOLS function is used in the *array* argument of FILTER to provide it with the columns to return. Columns 1 and 3 from [tblReviewDates] are specified.

```
=SORT(FILTER(CHOOSECOLS(tblReviewDates,1,3),
(tblReviewDates[Review By]>=TODAY())*
(tblReviewDates[Review By]<TODAY()+C2),
"No review dates are due"
),2,1)
```

The SORT function is added to order the results in ascending order by the [Review By] column. This is stated as column 2 in the SORT function as it is the second column in the returned array.

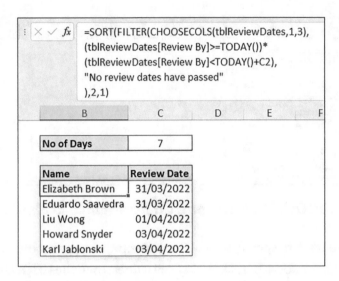

Figure 13-15. *CHOOSECOLS for non-adjacent columns with FILTER*

Entering the column numbers to return is not tough when there are only two out of three to return. However, you may be looking for a more dynamic approach.

The CHOOSECOLS function will accept an array of constants to specify the columns to return, for example, =CHOOSECOLS(tblReviewDates,{1,3}). Because of this, the MATCH function could be used to return the columns stated in range B4:C4 on the worksheet. This will prevent the need to type in the column numbers manually, as the columns will be dynamically returned based on the cell values.

In Figure 13-16, the following formula uses the MATCH function to return the array of column numbers for CHOOSECOLS to use. It matches the values in range B4:C4 against the values in the header row of [tblReviewDates]. The value in cell C4 has been changed from "Review Date" to "Review By" to match the column header in [tblReviewDates].

```
=SORT(FILTER(
CHOOSECOLS(tblReviewDates,MATCH(B4:C4,tblReviewDates[#Headers],0)),
(tblReviewDates[Review By]>=TODAY())*(tblReviewDates[Review
By]<TODAY()+C2),
"No review dates are due"
),2,1)
```

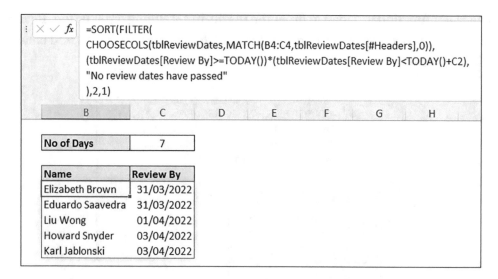

Figure 13-16. *CHOOSECOLS with MATCH for dynamic columns to return*

If your preference is to specify the columns to return in an absolute manner, instead of entering column numbers or referencing cell values, then the CHOOSE function is a great alternative.

In Figure 13-17, the following formula uses the CHOOSE function to specify that we want the [Name] and [Review By] columns returned only. This approach is ideal when working with data formatted as a table.

Numbers 1 and 2 are entered in an array for CHOOSE. It is then provided with the columns to return for each of those index numbers. The columns could have been specified in any order.

```
=SORT(FILTER(
CHOOSE({1,2},tblReviewDates[Name],tblReviewDates[Review By]),
(tblReviewDates[Review By]>=TODAY())*(tblReviewDates[Review
By]<TODAY()+C2),
"No review dates are due"
),2,1)
```

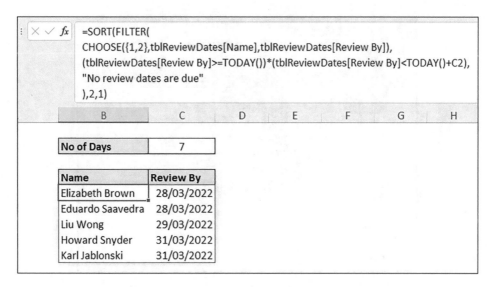

Figure 13-17. *CHOOSE function for absolute column references*

UNIQUE Ignoring Blanks

The FILTER function is great for removing blanks from a range. A typical scenario for this technique would be to prepare a range of values for use in a drop-down list or labels of a report.

In Figure 13-18, the following formula is entered in cell D2 to remove the blank cells from the country names in [tblCountries]. The SORT and UNIQUE functions are also applied to order them and remove any duplicate values that may occur.

```
=SORT(UNIQUE(
FILTER(tblCountries[Location],tblCountries[Location]<>"")
))
```

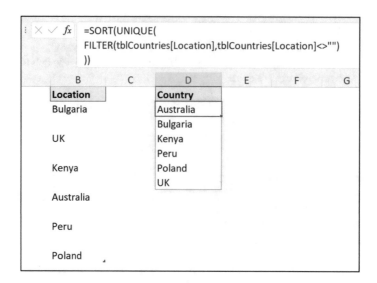

Figure 13-18. *Removing blanks from an array of values*

FILTER with NETWORKDAYS.INTL

The FILTER function can be used to provide other functions with a filtered array to be used. This provides a lot of potential and fun when you think of the different ways that this can be utilized.

In this example, we will use the FILTER function with NETWORKDAYS.INTL to return a range of *holidays* dates that are dependent on criteria.

Note   This example could be applied to the NETWORKDAYS function just as well. However, the NETWORKDAYS.INTL function (covered in Chapter 6) is a superior function.

Figure 13-19 shows a table named [tblClosures]. It contains the dates for three different sites/locations for when they are closed, and tasks of a project therefore cannot be worked.

H	I	J
Site 1	Site 2	Site 3
16/02/2022	09/02/2022	18/02/2022
17/02/2022	11/02/2022	08/03/2022
18/02/2022		09/03/2022
11/03/2022		

Figure 13-19. *Site closure dates in a table*

In Figure 13-20, the following formula is entered in cell E2 to calculate the number of working days for the different tasks of a project.

The FILTER function returns the dates from the [tblClosures] table where there is a match for the site name in the header row of [tblClosures].

```
=NETWORKDAYS.INTL(B2,C2,,
FILTER(tblClosures,tblClosures[#Headers]=D2,0)
)
```

Something interesting about this example when compared to the previous examples is that this formula is filtering by column instead of by row. You typically see the FILTER function returning matching rows from a table; however, as demonstrated with this example, the FILTER function can filter by column also.

E2		⌄	:	×	✓	fx	=NETWORKDAYS.INTL(B2,C2,,
							FILTER(tblClosures,tblClosures[#Headers]=D2,0)
							)

	A	B	C	D	E	F
1	Task Name	From	To	Site	No of Workdays	No FILTER
2	Task 1	07/02/2022	10/02/2022	Site 2	3	4
3	Task 2	11/02/2022	22/02/2022	Site 1	5	8
4	Task 3	16/02/2022	01/03/2022	Site 3	9	10
5	Task 4	02/03/2022	04/03/2022	Site 2	3	3
6	Task 5	02/03/2022	11/03/2022	Site 3	6	8
7	Task 6	10/03/2022	23/03/2022	Site 1	9	10

Figure 13-20. *NETWORKDAYS.INTL and FILTER for dependent non-working days*

The formula =NETWORKDAYS.INTL(B2,C2) is entered in column F to help demonstrate that the FILTER function successfully returns the correct dates.

705

FILTER and Combine Results in One Cell

The FILTER results can be combined in a single cell using the TEXTJOIN function. This can offer a neat alternative to spilling the results into the adjacent cells on the sheet.

Figure 13-21 shows a table of product data named [tblProducts]. It contains a [Product] column for the product name and a [Category] that it is assigned to.

	A	B	C	D
1	Product	Product	Category	Price
2	R1001	Orange Juice	Beverages	1.20
3	R1002	Coffee	Beverages	2.40
4	R1003	Tea	Beverages	1.50
5	R1004	Hot Chocolate	Beverages	1.80
6	R1005	Beer	Beverages	3.90
7	R1006	Wine	Beverages	6.60
8	R1007	Water	Beverages	1.00
9	R1008	Sandwich	Food	3.30
10	R1009	Samosa	Food	2.50
11	R1010	Baguette	Food	2.80
12	R1011	Soup	Food	2.00
13	R1012	Jacket Potato	Food	3.20
14	R1013	Cornish Pasty	Food	3.40
15	R1014	Sausage Roll	Food	2.50
16	R1015	Blueberry Muffin	Cakes	1.40
17	R1016	Chocolate Chip Muffin	Cakes	1.40
18	R1017	Croissant	Cakes	1.70
19	R1018	Flapjack	Cakes	1.50
20	R1019	Caramel Shortbread	Cakes	2.20
21	R1020	Crisps	Cakes	0.90

Figure 13-21. *Table of product data*

Let's imagine that we want to list the different product categories in a column and, in the adjacent column, list all products assigned to that category combined into a single cell.

In Figure 13-22, the following formula is entered in cell B3. It lists the distinct product categories in ascending order:

```
=SORT(UNIQUE(tblProducts[Category]))
```

The following formula is then entered in cell C3 and filled down to C5:

```
=TEXTJOIN(", ",,
SORT(FILTER(tblProducts[Product],tblProducts[Category]=B3))
)
```

The FILTER function returns the array of products that match the category entered in the corresponding cell of column B. The values in this array are sorted in ascending order by SORT.

TEXTJOIN then has the simple task of joining each value together in a single cell separated by a comma and space ", ". The *ignore empty* argument of TEXTJOIN is ignored.

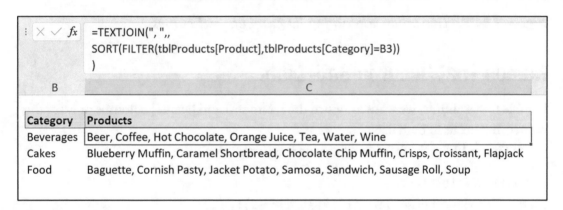

Figure 13-22. *Filter results combined in one cell*

Compare Lists with FILTER

The FILTER function combined with COUNTIFS enables us to easily compare two lists and return the results we require.

This could be that we want all values that occur in both lists, those that occur in one list and not the other, or even the values that occur in either list but not both.

Let's look at answering all these queries using the tables shown in Figure 13-23. The first table is named [tblFirst], and the second is named [tblSecond].

Number	Name		Number	Name
20034	Oz		412	Pamela
21099	Kenneth		23384	Kirsty
3415	Martin		24461	Patrick
20075	Jane		20034	Oz
412	Pamela		91158	Jon
9081	Laurence		20075	Jane
23384	Kirsty		3415	Martin
1273	Ian		5173	Harry
			47661	Mike

Figure 13-23. *Two tables containing ID numbers and names*

Names That Occur in Both Lists

For this first example, we want to return the [Number] and [Name] columns only for the names that occur in both lists.

In Figure 13-24, the following formula is entered in cell H3:

```
=SORT(FILTER(tblFirst,
COUNTIFS(tblSecond[Number],tblFirst[Number]),
"No names appear in both lists"
))
```

It uses the COUNTIFS function to count the occurrences of the ID numbers from [tblFirst] within [tblSecond]. The resulting array is passed to the FILTER function. Remember, any non-zero value evaluates to TRUE. So, if the ID number is found, then FILTER will return the record. The returned results are sorted by the [Number] column in ascending order.

When returning the names that appear in both lists, it does not matter which list we return from, the results will be the same. The following formula returns the names from [tblSecond] that also appear in [tblFirst]:

```
=SORT(FILTER(tblSecond,
COUNTIFS(tblFirst[Number],tblSecond[Number]),
"No names appear in both lists"
))
```

708

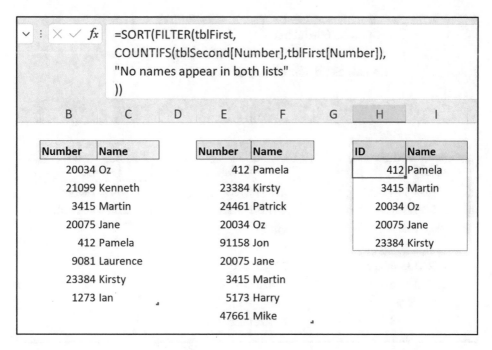

Figure 13-24. *Formula to return all names that appear in both tables*

Names That Occur in One List Only

Let's now return the names that occur in either the first or second table only.

In Figure 13-25, the following formula returns the names that occur in [tblFirst] only:

```
=SORT(FILTER(tblFirst,
NOT(COUNTIFS(tblSecond[Number],tblFirst[Number])),
"No names appear in only table 1"
))
```

The only adaptation that has been made from the previous formula is the addition of the NOT function to reverse the results of the COUNTIFS. It now returns the names in [tblFirst] that do not appear in [tblSecond].

The text "No names appear in only table 1" is entered for the *if empty* argument to provide a logical response if an empty array is returned.

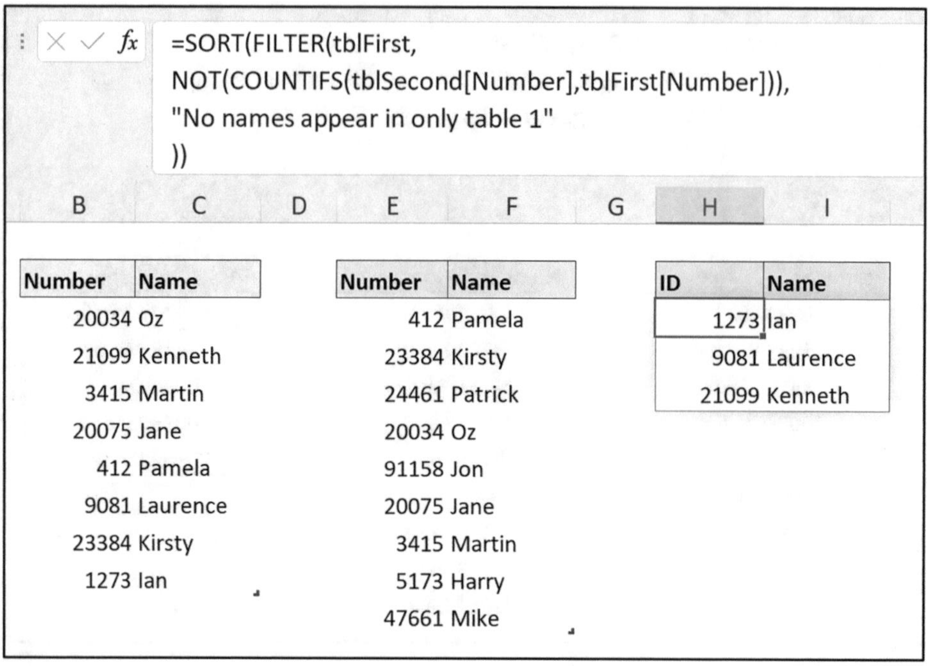

Figure 13-25. *Returning the names that occur in the first table only*

As before, this formula can easily be switched to return the names in [tblSecond] that do not appear in [tblFirst]. This is shown in the following formula, and we will see this formula successfully returning the names that occur in the second table only, in the next example:

```
=SORT(FILTER(tblSecond,
NOT(COUNTIFS(tblFirst[Number],tblSecond[Number])),
"No names appear in only table 2"
))
```

Names That Occur in Either List but Not Both

We now want to return the names that occur in either [tblFirst] or [tblSecond] only. This is really a table with the appended results of the two formulas from the previous example.

In Figure 13-26, the following formula uses the VSTACK function to append the results of the two formulas. This combined table is then sorted by the first column [Number].

```
=SORT(VSTACK(FILTER(tblFirst,
NOT(COUNTIFS(tblSecond[Number],tblFirst[Number])))),
FILTER(tblSecond,
NOT(COUNTIFS(tblFirst[Number],tblSecond[Number])))
))
```

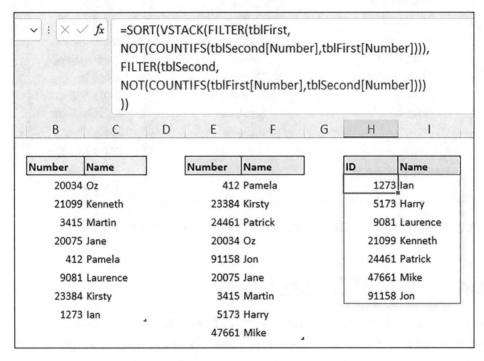

Figure 13-26. *Formula returning the names that appear in either of the tables*

Return All Names from Both Lists

Finally, let's use an Excel formula to return a distinct list of all names that appear in both tables.

This example does not require the FILTER function; however, it has been included for a thorough coverage of comparing two lists.

In Figure 13-27, the following formula uses the VSTACK function to stack both tables vertically. Any duplicate values are then removed and sorted in ascending order by the [Number] column (the first column of the returned array).

```
=SORT(UNIQUE(VSTACK(tblFirst,tblSecond)))
```

			fx	=SORT(UNIQUE(VSTACK(tblFirst,tblSecond)))

B	C	D	E	F	G	H	I

Number	Name		Number	Name		ID	Name
20034	Oz		412	Pamela		412	Pamela
21099	Kenneth		23384	Kirsty		1273	Ian
3415	Martin		24461	Patrick		3415	Martin
20075	Jane		20034	Oz		5173	Harry
412	Pamela		91158	Jon		9081	Laurence
9081	Laurence		20075	Jane		20034	Oz
23384	Kirsty		3415	Martin		20075	Jane
1273	Ian		5173	Harry		21099	Kenneth
			47661	Mike		23384	Kirsty
						24461	Patrick
						47661	Mike
						91158	Jon

Figure 13-27. *Distinct list of all names that occur in both tables*

Aggregate FILTER Results

We have seen a few aggregation functions in this book. These include SUMIFS, SUMPRODUCT, and AGGREGATE, to name a few. These amazing functions all have small disadvantages which help you decide which one is best for your chosen task.

Well, let's add another to the list in terms of the FILTER function. It is an extremely well-rounded function that does not suffer from some of the ailments that the other aggregation functions do.

The FILTER function can be used to perform the logical expressions required and return an array of values for an aggregation function to work on. As we know from this chapter, FILTER can handle AND and OR logic, multiple column and row arrays, and arrays provided by other functions. This makes it a fantastic provider for an aggregation function.

Let's see a few examples. We will use the table of student scores shown in Figure 13-28 for all examples. This table is named [tblScores].

	A	B	C
1	Region	Name	Score
2	East	Michelle	89
3	East	Victoria	95
4	East	Jason	61
5	East	Darryl	89
6	East	Heather	56
7	South	Rachel	78
8	South	David	59
9	South	Kevin	66
10	South	Hannah	91
11	West	Carl	69
12	West	Natalie	77
13	West	Deborah	96
14			

Figure 13-28. *Table of student scores*

In Figure 13-29, the following formula is used in cell E3 to return the average for the top five student scores. The LARGE function is used to return the fifth largest score for FILTER to test. The scores that meet this criterion are then returned to AVERAGE to calculate.

```
=AVERAGE(
FILTER(tblScores[Score],tblScores[Score]>=LARGE(tblScores[Score],5))
)
```

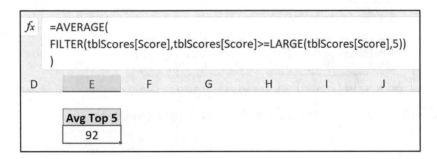

Figure 13-29. *Average the top five values*

Figure 13-30 shows the results of two more examples. The following formula is entered in cell H6 to return the maximum score for a student based in the regions entered in E6 (East) or F6 (West):

```
=MAX(
FILTER(tblScores[Score],(tblScores[Region]=E6)+(tblScores[Region]=F6))
)
```

And this formula is entered in cell G6 to count the number of students from the regions specified in cells E6 and F6. This is easily done with the ROWS function working of the returned array by FILTER.

```
=ROWS(
FILTER(tblScores[Score],(tblScores[Region]=E6)+(tblScores[Region]=F6))
)
```

The FILTER function makes applying logical expressions using OR logic simple. And along with its other strengths, it can be used as the engine for a versatile aggregator.

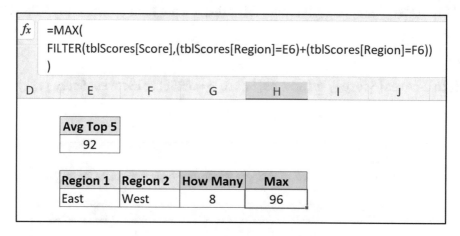

Figure 13-30. *Maximum score from two specified regions*

FILTER with Other Excel Features

There are some fantastic ways that the FILTER function can be used with other Excel features. Let's see some examples of FILTER being used to provide a filtered array for Data Validation and for charts.

Shrinking Drop-Down List

In this first example, we will create a shrinking drop-down list. This is a list that decreases in size each time an item in the list is used. Once an item is used, it is removed from the list to prevent it from being used again.

For this example, we will use the data shown in Figure 13-31. The table on the left is named [tblNames]. It contains names of individuals that we want to assign to the tasks in the table on the right, named [tblTasks].

	A	B	C	D
1	**Names**		**Task**	**Assigned**
2	Debra		Task A	
3	Oz		Task B	
4	Celia		Task C	
5	Mynda		Task D	
6	Bill		Task E	
7	Cristiano			
8	Heather			
9	Anders			
10				

Figure 13-31. *Names to be assigned to tasks*

To create the shrinking drop-down list, we will perform a three-step process:

1. Write the required formula and check that it works.
2. Define a name for the spill range generated by FILTER.
3. Reference the defined name as the source of the Data Validation list.

In Figure 13-32, the following formula is entered in cell F2. It returns the names that are not yet assigned to any task:

```
=FILTER(tblNames[Names],
NOT(COUNTIFS(tblTasks[Assigned],tblNames[Names]))
)
```

The COUNTIFS function checks if the names occur in [tblTasks]. The NOT function then reverses the logic to show TRUE if the names do not occur and FALSE if they do. FILTER then returns the unused names.

This formula is only displayed beside the tables for testing purposes. Now we are confident that it works, it is moved to another sheet named [List Data]. We will define a name for the spill range and then hide the sheet.

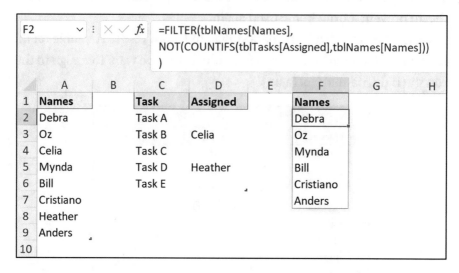

Figure 13-32. *Formula to return the remaining names unassigned to any tasks*

Figure 13-33 shows the name "lstNames" being defined by referring to the spill range of unassigned names in cell A2 of the [List Data] sheet.

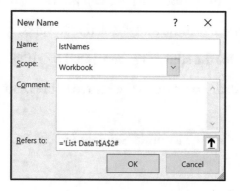

Figure 13-33. *Defining a name for the unassigned names' list*

Note   Please refer to Chapter 3 on defined names or Chapter 10 on dynamic arrays if you are unsure on how to define a name for a range.

This name can now be used as the source for the Data Validation list:

1. Select the [Assigned] column of [tblTasks].

2. Click **Data ➤ Data Validation**.

3. On the **Settings** tab, select **List** in the *Allow* field and then enter "=lstNames" in the *Source* field (Figure 13-34).

4. Click **OK**.

Figure 13-34. *Creating the shrinking Data Validation list*

Figure 13-35 shows the shrinking drop-down list being used to assign names to tasks. Only the remaining unassigned names are shown in the list.

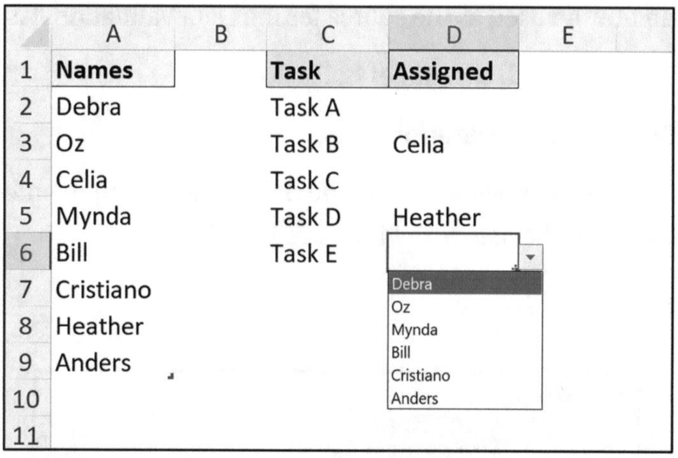

	A	B	C	D	E
1	**Names**		**Task**	**Assigned**	
2	Debra		Task A		
3	Oz		Task B	Celia	
4	Celia		Task C		
5	Mynda		Task D	Heather	
6	Bill		Task E		
7	Cristiano			Debra	
8	Heather			Oz	
9	Anders			Mynda	
10				Bill	
11				Cristiano	
				Anders	

Figure 13-35. *Shrinking drop-down list showing unassigned names only*

Dependent Drop-Down List

For a second Data Validation example, we will see how the FILTER function offers a neat method of creating dependent drop-down lists.

A dependent drop-down list is when the items shown in a drop-down list are dependent on the item specified in a previous drop-down list.

Figure 13-36 shows a table named [tblProducts]. It contains information about products that we sell. For this example, we are interested in just the [Product] and [Category] columns of this table.

We want to create a drop-down list for the three different categories of product. And then create a second drop-down list for the product names. The second list of product names will be dependent on the selection made in the first list. Only products relating to the specified category will be shown.

The table shown in Figure 13-36 is stored on a worksheet named [Product Data & Lists]. We will use this worksheet to store the spill ranges of both formulas that are used to serve the drop-down lists. To make referencing the spill ranges easier, names will be defined for them and used in the Data Validation rules.

	A	B	C	D
1	Product ↓↑	Product ▾	Category ▾	Price ▾
2	R1001	Orange Juice	Beverages	1.20
3	R1002	Coffee	Beverages	2.40
4	R1003	Tea	Beverages	1.50
5	R1004	Hot Chocolate	Beverages	1.80
6	R1005	Beer	Beverages	3.90
7	R1006	Wine	Beverages	6.60
8	R1007	Water	Beverages	1.00
9	R1008	Sandwich	Food	3.30
10	R1009	Samosa	Food	2.50
11	R1010	Baguette	Food	2.80
12	R1011	Soup	Food	2.00
13	R1012	Jacket Potato	Food	3.20
14	R1013	Cornish Pasty	Food	3.40
15	R1014	Sausage Roll	Food	2.50
16	R1015	Blueberry Muffin	Cakes	1.40
17	R1016	Chocolate Chip Muffin	Cakes	1.40
18	R1017	Croissant	Cakes	1.70
19	R1018	Flapjack	Cakes	1.50
20	R1019	Caramel Shortbread	Cakes	2.20
21	R1020	Crisps	Cakes	0.90
22				

Figure 13-36. *Table of product data*

In Figure 13-37, the first drop-down list of categories is created in cell B3. The following formula is used to return a distinct list of the categories and fed to the Data Validation list via a defined name:

```
=SORT(UNIQUE(tblProducts[Category]))
```

Cell B3 has been named [rngCategory] and will be referenced in the formula for the dependent list.

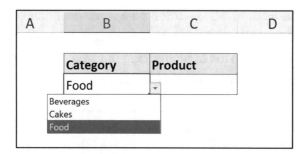

Figure 13-37. *First drop-down list showing the product categories*

Now let's create the dependent list. In Figure 13-38, the following formula returns the product names for the category specified in the first list (Food). That cell is defined as [rngCategory] for the purposes of this tutorial.

```
=SORT(FILTER(tblProducts[Product],
tblProducts[Category]=rngCategory,
"No category selected"))
```

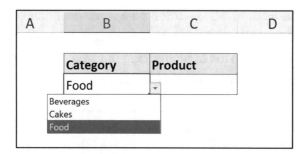

Figure 13-38. *Formula to return values for the dependent list*

The spill range is defined as the name "lstProduct" and then used as the source for the list in the Data Validation rule.

```
=lstProduct
```

Figure 13-39 shows the dependent list showing food products only, as that has been stated via the first list.

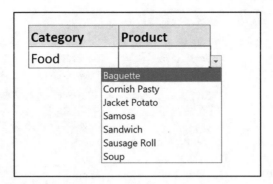

Figure 13-39. *Dependent drop-down list showing food products only*

If no selection is made in the previous list, then the text "No category selected" is returned (Figure 13-40). This text was entered for the *if empty* argument of the FILTER function.

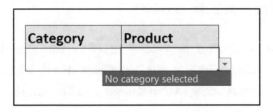

Figure 13-40. *Text returned when no selection is made in the previous list*

Interactive Chart

The FILTER function can be used to easily add an interactive element to a chart in Excel. In this example, we will use a drop-down list for a user to make a selection, and that selection determines the data to be charted.

For this example, we have a table of product sales data, named [tblProductSales] (Figure 13-41).

	A	B	C	D
1	Product ↓↑	Product ▾	Category ▾	Total ▾
2	R1001	Orange Juice	Beverages	6,580
3	R1002	Coffee	Beverages	6,075
4	R1003	Tea	Beverages	6,956
5	R1004	Hot Chocolate	Beverages	2,545
6	R1005	Beer	Beverages	6,429
13	R1012	Jacket Potato	Food	3,527
14	R1013	Cornish Pasty	Food	4,954
15	R1014	Sausage Roll	Food	1,834
16	R1015	Blueberry Muffin	Cakes	5,356
17	R1016	Chocolate Chip Muffin	Cakes	4,705
18	R1017	Croissant	Cakes	2,090
19	R1018	Flapjack	Cakes	4,344
20	R1019	Caramel Shortbread	Cakes	3,481
21	R1020	Crisps	Cakes	6,542

Figure 13-41. *Table of product sales data*

On a separate sheet, we have a drop-down list of the three product categories. The cell containing the drop-down list is named [rngChosenCat]. When a user selects a category, only the products relating to that category will be charted and will be sorted in descending order by their sales total.

Figure 13-42 shows two different formulas producing spill ranges in cells B2 and C2.

The following formula is entered in cell C2 to return the sales total for all products of the chosen category, sorted in descending order:

```
=SORT(FILTER(
tblProductSales[Total],
tblProductSales[Category]=rngChosenCat),
,-1)
```

And the following formula is entered in cell B2 to return the product names for the chosen category. The SORTBY function is applied to order the product names by the sales total array in descending order.

```
=SORTBY(
FILTER(tblProductSales[Product],tblProductSales[Category]=rngChosenCat),
FILTER(tblProductSales[Total],tblProductSales[Category]=rngChosenCat),
-1)
```

			fx	=SORTBY(

```
=SORTBY(
FILTER(tblProductSales[Product],
tblProductSales[Category]=rngChosenCat),
FILTER(tblProductSales[Total],
tblProductSales[Category]=rngChosenCat),
-1)
```

	B	C	D	E
	Products	**Total**		
	Crisps	6542		
	Blueberry Muffin	5356		
	Chocolate Chip Muffin	4705		
	Flapjack	4344		
	Caramel Shortbread	3481		
	Croissant	2090		

Figure 13-42. *Formula to return the arrays to be used for the chart data source*

These formulas are entered on a sheet named [Chart Data]. A name has been defined for each spill range so they can be referenced in the chart.

The product name range is defined as "rngProductNames" and the sales total range defined as "rngSalesTotals." Figure 13-43 shows the product name range being defined.

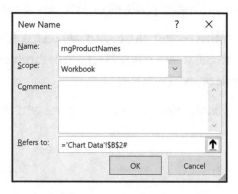

Figure 13-43. *Defining a name for the product name spill range*

Now, we will insert the chart and use the defined names for the source of the axis labels and the data to be charted. For this example, a column chart will be used:

1. On the [Dynamic Chart] sheet, click **Insert ➤ Insert Column or Bar Chart ➤ Clustered Column**.

2. With the chart selected, click **Chart Design ➤ Select Data**.

3. In the *Legend Entries (Series)* area, click **Add**.

4. Type "Sales Totals" for the *Series name* (this will become the chart title and can be changed later for something more meaningful).

5. Click in the *Series values* field, remove the content, click a cell on the [Chart Data] sheet, remove the cell reference, and type "rngSalesTotals" after the sheet name (Figure 13-44). Charts require an explicit reference that includes the sheet name. Click **OK**.

Figure 13-44. *Adding the sales totals for the data series*

6. Click **Edit** in the *Horizontal (Category) Axis Labels* area.

7. Click in the *Axis label range* field, click a cell on the [Chart Data] sheet, remove the cell reference, and type "rngProductNames" after the sheet reference. Click **OK**.

Figure 13-45 shows the completed *Select Data Source* window.

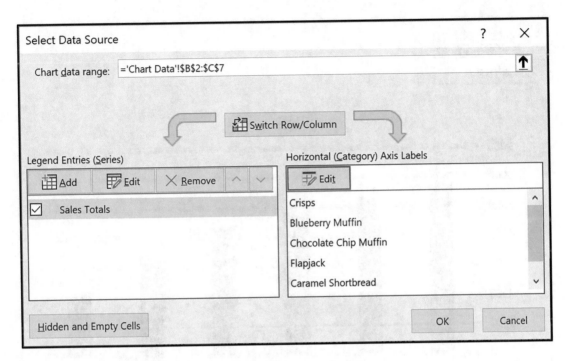

Figure 13-45. *Completed Select Data Source window*

Note   Excel will actually edit the data series and axis label references in the chart to the workbook name followed by the defined name. But we can let Excel handle that.

Figure 13-46 shows the finished chart. Improvements can and should be made to the chart to take it further.

When the value in the drop-down list is changed, the chart reacts and plots the correct values.

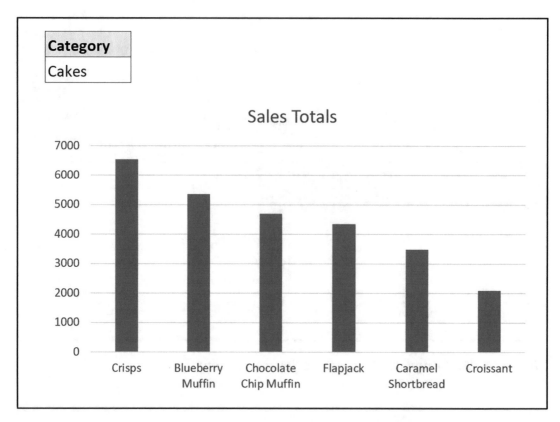

Figure 13-46. Completed chart dependent on drop-down list selection

Summary

In this chapter, we learned the excellent FILTER function of Excel – a very powerful and flexible function. We saw many examples that supported this and complemented the strengths of FILTER compared to other lookup functions. It has changed the game in how we perform certain tasks in modern Excel.

In the next chapter, we will look at using formulas with data types in Excel. Data types are a recent development that is still evolving and finding its place in the Excel jigsaw. They are a rich data type that enables us to store many columns of values in a single cell.

In the chapter, we will discuss in detail the different data types available and how to access their data with some of the most popular functions in Excel, plus a couple of new functions – FIELDVALUE and STOCKHISTORY.

CHAPTER 14

Formulas with Data Types in Excel

In modern Excel, a single cell can contain multiple fields of data. This is possible thanks to data types in Excel. These data types are often referred to as rich data types to distinguish them from existing data types such as number, string, and Boolean.

We will begin this chapter with a short explanation of the different data types available in Excel. We then get down to the purpose of this book and learn how we can use formulas to access and perform calculations on data type fields.

This chapter is not intended to provide a complete understanding on using data types in Excel, but how we can access data within the data types using formulas.

These formulas will include popular requirements for Excel users such as returning live exchange rate data and performing currency conversions and retrieving historical stock market data. We will also see how we can use some of our favorite Excel functions such as SUM, FILTER, and XLOOKUP with data types.

File   data-types.xlsx

Introduction to Data Types in Excel

Availability: Excel for Microsoft 365, Excel for the Web, and Excel for Microsoft 365 for Mac

Data types are a real game changer in how we think about Excel. Being able to store many fields of data in a single cell is quite radical. These additional hidden fields of data can still be accessed using formulas in Excel while remaining hidden on the sheet.

© Alan Murray 2022
A. Murray, *Advanced Excel Formulas*, https://doi.org/10.1007/978-1-4842-7125-4_14

There are a few different data types in Excel. These include data types that are connected to an online data source to pull in live data, such as currency exchange rates, and the ability to create your own custom data types using Power Query or Power BI.

The data types available to you are dependent upon a few factors including your version of Excel, what has been enabled by your IT administrators, and the language that you use for Excel.

This is a very new feature to Excel that is expanding fast with new data types and further language support becoming available.

The following is a list of the different data types available in Excel:

- **Stocks:** Return data related to types such as stock, equity, mutual fund, ETF, currency pairs, and commodity. For example, Microsoft Corp or Barclays PLC.

- **Currencies:** Return live exchange rates. Enter the two currencies separated by a forward slash (/) or a colon (:). For example, USD/EUR or GBP:EUR.

- **Geography:** Return data related to countries, cities, states, provinces, counties, and districts. For example, Canada or Ottawa.

- **Wolfram:** Data powered by Wolfram to provide additional data about food, movies, yoga, terrain, chemistry, animals, and more. These data types are only available in Excel for Microsoft 365 Home/Student edition, so will not be covered in any examples.

- **Organization:** A custom data type that is created in Power BI and published to the Power BI Service. These data types are then pulled into Excel using your organization account. For example, data related to an organization such as sales or inventory could be made a data type and then accessed in Excel as an organization data type.

- **Power Query:** A custom data type that is created in Power Query in Excel. You can convert any data in Power Query into a data type and then load it to an Excel table.

Figure 14-1 shows the Data Types gallery on the **Data** tab in Excel.

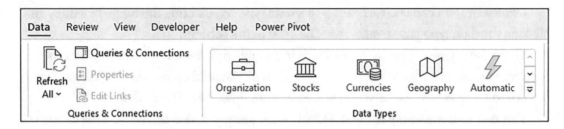

Figure 14-1. *Data Types on the Excel Ribbon*

Note   Data Types information is updated by clicking **Data ➤ Refresh All**. Some data types such as Stocks allow you to specify the refresh interval such as every five minutes, while others can only be manually refreshed. The default refresh interval is set by the data provider for the data type.

Accessing the Data Type Fields with Formulas

Let's get into the exciting stuff and write some formulas. We will see examples that extract and analyze data using the Geography, Currencies, Stock, and Power Query data types in this chapter. We will start with the Geography data type, but the examples shown apply to all data types.

When converting text values into a linked data type, this will often happen automatically as you type data onto a worksheet. In Figure 14-2, I am asked if I would like to convert the country names written in range B2:B4 to the Geography data type.

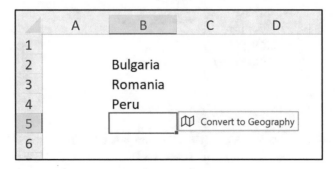

Figure 14-2. *Automatic recognition of Geography data type*

Otherwise, you can convert values to a data type by selecting the range of values and clicking the data type you need on the **Data** tab of the Ribbon.

These data types can store many fields in a single cell. We can access the fields of a data type using formulas, without having to display the field on the sheet. However, let's start by looking at how we can insert some chosen fields onto the grid of Excel.

This can be done easily using the UI of Excel. Simply click a cell containing a data type and use the **Insert Data** button that appears in the top-right corner of that cell (Figure 14-3).

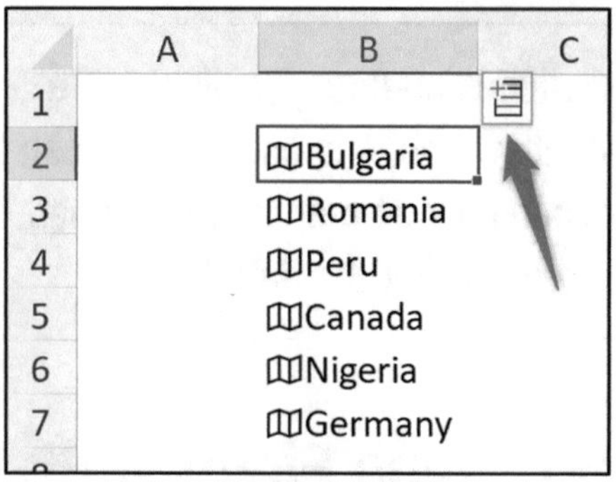

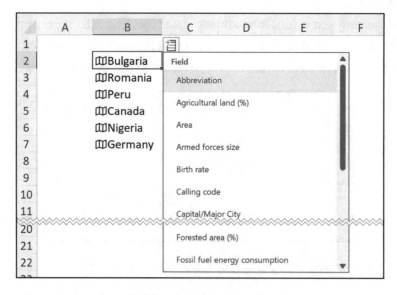

Figure 14-3. *Inserting data type field using the UI*

A list of the available fields is displayed (Figure 14-4). Simply click the field that you want to add. Excel writes the formula for you when you use the **Insert Data** button.

Figure 14-4. *Inserting a data field using the UI*

The same list of fields can be accessed using formulas. In Figure 14-5, the formula to access the list of fields for a data type is shown. Typing a period (.) after the reference to a cell containing a data type shows the list of available fields.

Note   You may be wondering where Excel is getting the data from. If you click the data type icon to the left of its name, a card is displayed. Scroll to the bottom of the card to see a list of sources that Excel uses to retrieve the data.

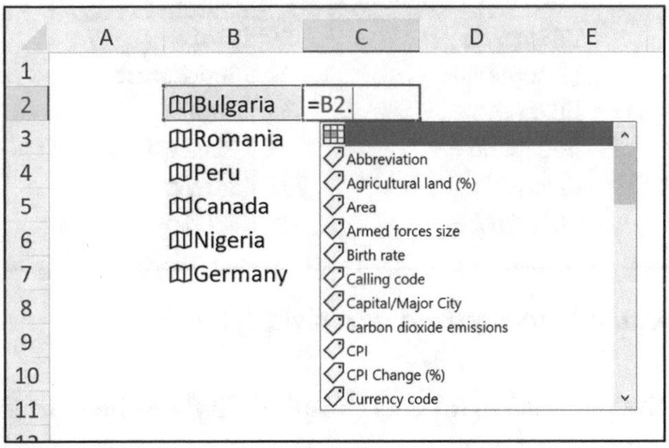

Figure 14-5. *Inserting data fields using a formula*

Click the field you want to use to insert the data. In Figure 14-6, the [Calling Code] field has been added using a formula. Because the name of the field contains a space, the square brackets [ ] are used to enclose the field name.

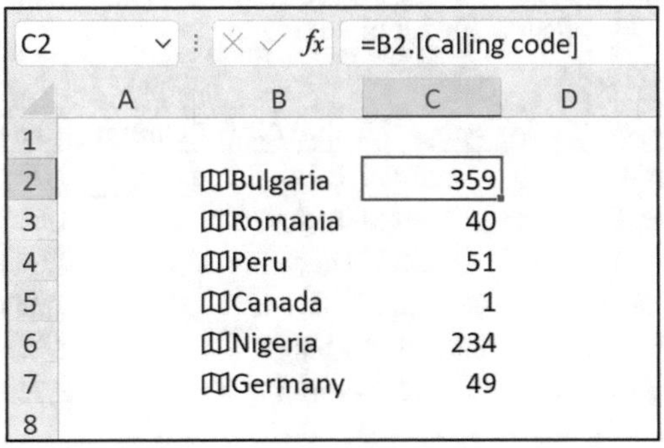

Figure 14-6. *Formula input by the Insert Data feature*

Further fields that you insert can themselves be a data type. In Figure 14-7, the [Capital/Major City] field has been added for each country. These cities are automatically recognized as Geography data types by Excel.

The range has also been formatted as a table. The data does not need to be in a table to utilize data types. However, there are many advantages to managing and working with data formatted as a table.

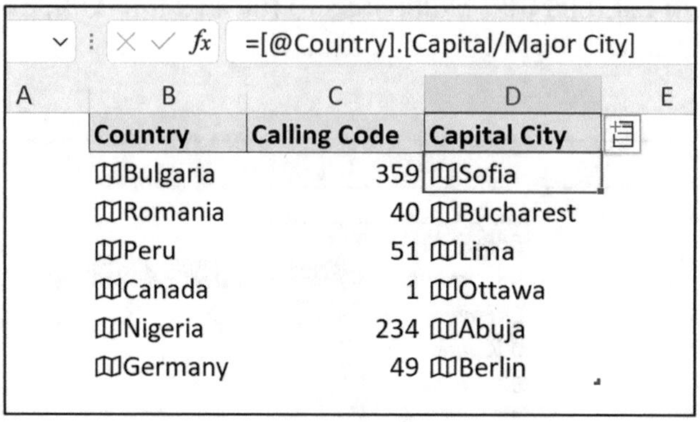

***Figure 14-7.** Capital city recognized as a data type*

In Figure 14-8, the population for each [Capital City] has been returned with a simple formula. When referring to a data type, you refer to the cell in the same manner as we would if it contained a standard text or numeric value.

In this example, notice that the reference to the [Population] field in the formula does not contain square brackets []. This is because the field name does not contain a space or other illegal character such as the forward slash "/" used in the [Capital/Major City] field.

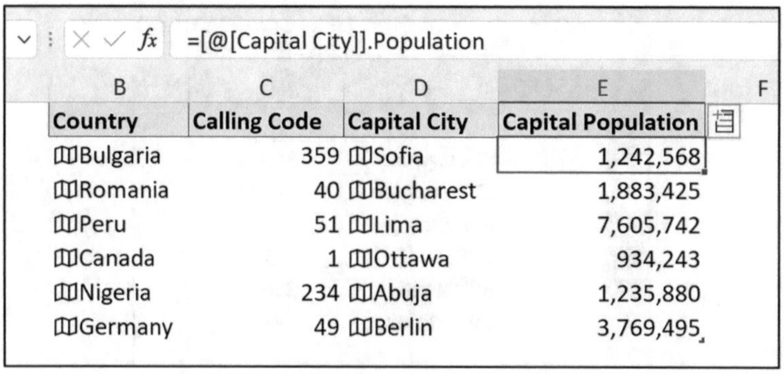

***Figure 14-8.** Population field without square brackets*

Aggregating the Values in a Data Type Field

Let's move on to using functions with data type fields and begin with an aggregation function.

Now, a data type field does not need to be visible on the sheet to be used. In Figure 14-9, the following formula uses the AVERAGE function on the [Population] field of the data type in the [capital city] column of the table:

```
=AVERAGE(tblCountries[Capital City].Population)
```

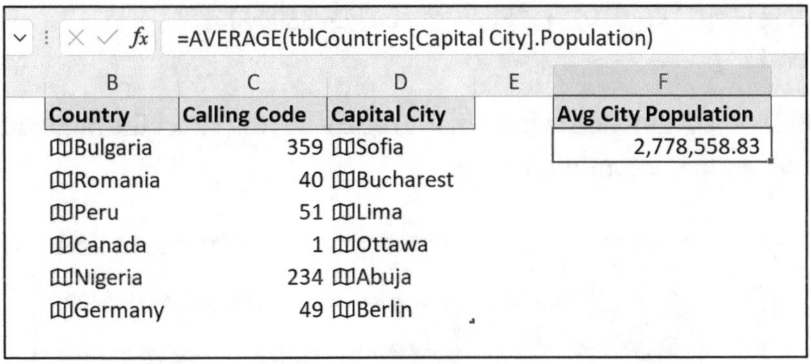

Figure 14-9. *Average city population using geography data types*

FIELDVALUE Function

Availability: Excel for Microsoft 365, Excel for the Web, and Excel for Microsoft 365 for Mac

The FIELDVALUE function is used to extract a value from a specified field of a data type. We have just seen examples of how to achieve this using the "." operator following a cell that contains a data type, for example, B2.[Calling Code] or [@Country]. Population. So, you might be thinking why we would use the FIELDVALUE function.

The simple formula to extract a field from a data type does not work in all scenarios. The most common of these scenarios is when performing conditional calculations.

We will see an example using the FIELDVALUE within an IF function now and within a SUM function to perform a conditional sum later in this chapter.

This is the syntax of the FIELDVALUE function:

```
=FIELDVALUE(value, field_name)
```

- **Value:** A reference to the data type. It returns all fields from the referenced data type.

- **[field name]:** Name or names of the fields from which to extract the value. The field name must be entered within double quotes (" ").

In Figure 14-10, the following formula uses a simple IF function to display the text "Large" if the population of the capital city is greater than or equal to 3.5 million. Otherwise, the text "Small" is shown.

```
=IF(
FIELDVALUE([@[Capital City]],"Population")>=3500000,
"Large","Small")
```

The FIELDVALUE function is used in the *logical test* to extract the population of the capital city for use in the conditional test.

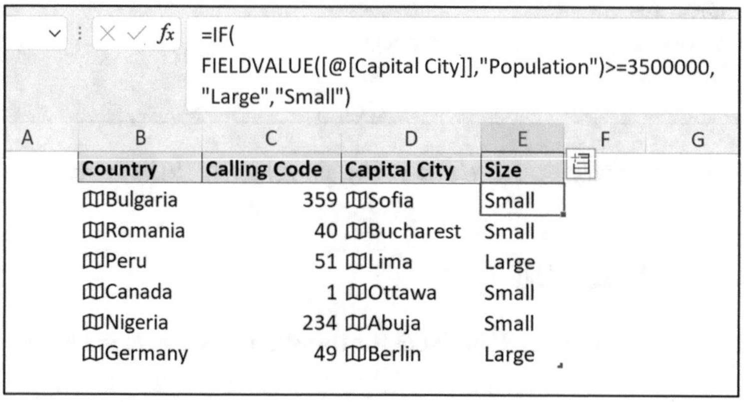

Figure 14-10. FIELDVALUE in an IF function

Using Functions with Data Type Data

Let's now explore how some of our favorite Excel functions, such as XLOOKUP, SUM, and FILTER, can be used to extract and calculate data from these rich data types.

The technique for using formula and functions with data types applies for all kinds of data type. For the next few examples, we will demonstrate the functions with Power Query data types.

Although this book is about formulas, I feel it would be remiss of me to fully disregard a demonstration of how to create a Power Query data type. However, this will be brief, as it is not the focus of the chapter.

Creating a Custom Data Type with Power Query

Figure 14-11 shows a table of data about company stores named [tblStores]. This includes information such as the store name, region, last year's revenue, and the name of the top performing sales representative.

	A	B	C	D	E	F
1	Store Code	Store Name	Region	No of Staff	Last Year Revenue	Top Sale Rep
2	1	Southgate Gardens	East	16	20,072	Elizabeth Brown
3	2	Hopkins Circle	East	17	39,601	Sven Ottlieb
4	3	Bartholomew Drive	South	14	26,580	Janine Labrune
5	4	Evans Street	West	20	32,059	Ann Devon
6	5	Heather Gardens	East	14	31,513	Roland Mendel
7	6	Allum Avenue	South	8	53,849	Aria Cruz
8	7	Shaverin House	West	11	56,966	Diego Roel
9	8	Buckley Drive	West	19	50,661	Martine Rancé
10	9	Wright Lane	East	19	35,762	Maria Larsson
11	10	The Bailie	South	15	34,384	Peter Franken
12						

Figure 14-11. *Table of company store data*

This table can be found in the [data-types.xlsx] workbook, but one of the great strengths of Power Query is to pull data from external sources. This is not a Power Query guide, so we will briefly cover how to convert the data into a custom data type and then use the functions to work with that data type. We will not go into detail on any Power Query topic.

1. Click the [tblStores] table and click **Data ➤ From Table/Range** to load it into Power Query.

2. Select the columns to be used in the data type.

3. Click **Transform ➤ Create Data Type** (Figure 14-12).

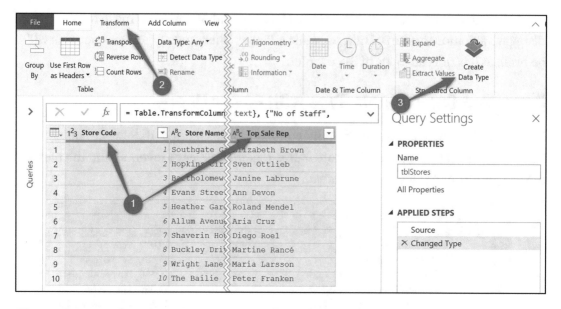

Figure 14-12. Creating a Power Query data type

4. In the *Create Data Type* window, type a name for the data type in
    the *Data type name* box and specify the *Display column* from the
    list (Figure 14-13). Click **OK**.

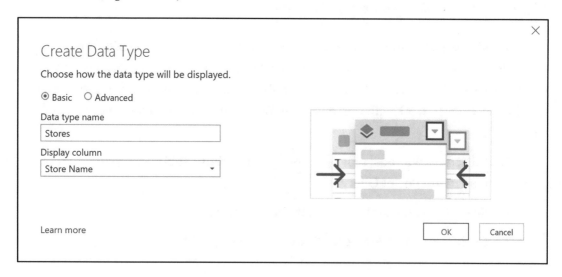

Figure 14-13. Specifying the details of the new data type

5. **Close & Load** to a table in Excel.

Figure 14-14 shows the table loaded to cell A1 of a sheet named [Stores]. The table is named [StoresData], and the [Store Name] field is displayed on the cell as that was specified as the *Display column* in the *Create Data Type* window (Figure 14-13). The data type icon is shown to the left of the store name.

In cell C2, the beginning of a formula is shown to demonstrate that all fields of the custom data type can be accessed in the same manner as shown with the Geography linked data type.

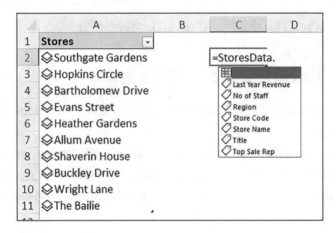

Figure 14-14. *Power Query data type loaded as a table named StoresData*

XLOOKUP with Data Types

For the first function example, let's see the XLOOKUP being used to search for and return a value from the data type based on a cell value.

In Figure 14-15, the following formula is entered in cell B2 to return the region for the store code stated in cell A2 and copied down:

```
=XLOOKUP(A2,StoresData[Stores].[Store Code],StoresData[Stores].Region)
```

And the following formula is entered in cell C2 to return the store name. Using XLOOKUP with data in a data type is simple:

```
=XLOOKUP(A2,StoresData[Stores].[Store Code],StoresData[Stores].
[Store Name])
```

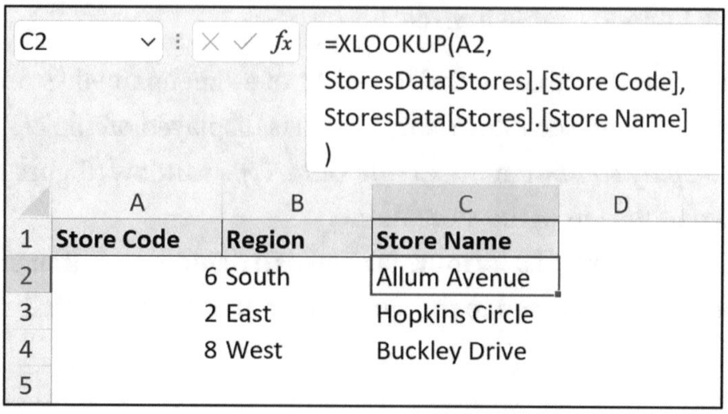

C2	⌄ ⋮ ╳ ✓ *fx*	=XLOOKUP(A2, StoresData[Stores].[Store Code], StoresData[Stores].[Store Name])		
	A	B	C	D
1	Store Code	Region	Store Name	
2		6 South	Allum Avenue	
3		2 East	Hopkins Circle	
4		8 West	Buckley Drive	
5				

Figure 14-15. Using XLOOKUP with a custom data type

Conditional SUM Function with Data Types

Now, let's use the incredible SUM function to count and sum values of the data type based on conditions.

In Figure 14-16, two SUM function examples are demonstrated. In cell C3, the following formula is used to count the number of stores where last year's revenue was greater than or equal to 35,000. The last year's revenue threshold to test against is stated in cell B3.

```
=SUM(--(FIELDVALUE(StoresData,"Last Year Revenue")>=B3))
```

The FIELDVALUE function is used to return the last year's revenue value for testing. An array for TRUE and FALSE values is returned as results for the conditional test. To sum these values, the double unary (--) is used to convert the TRUE and FALSE values to 1 and 0.

The following formula is entered in cell C6 to sum the [No of Staff] values for stores in the region stated in cell B6 only. In Figure 14-16, the results for the region of the West are shown.

```
=SUM(
(FIELDVALUE(StoresData,"Region")=B6)*(FIELDVALUE(StoresData,"No of Staff"))
)
```

fx	=SUM(

```
=SUM(
(FIELDVALUE(StoresData,"Region")=B6)*(FIELDVALUE(StoresData,"No of Staff"))
)
```

	B	C	D	E	F	G	H

Last Year revenue >=

35,000	5

Total Staff in

West	50

Figure 14-16. Conditional SUM formula to return the total staff in the West

---

Note Using the SUM function with arrays as demonstrated in these examples was explained in Chapter 10. Visit that chapter if you are interested in understanding how these formulas work in more detail.

FILTER Function with Data Types

For the final example of using some of our favorite functions with data types, we will see the FILTER function.

In Figure 14-17, the following formula is used to return results for the region stated in cell B3 only:

```
=SORT(
FILTER(CHOOSE({1,2,3},
StoresData.[Store Name],StoresData.[Last Year Revenue],StoresData.[Top
Sale Rep]),
StoresData[Stores].Region=B3,""),
2,-1)
```

The CHOOSE function is used to specify the return of the [Store Name], [Last Year Revenue], and [Top Sale Rep] fields only. FILTER returns the rows for the South region only. And SORT then orders the results in descending order by column 2, the [Last Year Revenue] column.

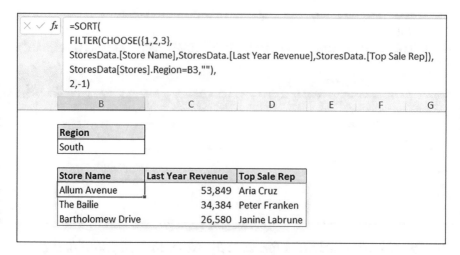

Figure 14-17. FILTER function working with data from a data type

Currency Conversion Using Data Types

With the Currencies data type in Excel, you can return live currency data such as exchange rates. If you do not see a Currencies data type in your version of Excel, the Stocks data type can be used instead. Both data types pull their information from the Stocks source.

Figure 14-18 shows the exchange rate being returned for two currency pairs – US Dollars to Euros and Danish Krone to Euros.

The [Price] field is used to return the exchange rate. The [Last Trade Time] field can be used to display the date that the [Price] was last updated.

To create the Currencies or Stocks data type, simply enter the two ISO currency codes separated by a forward slash (EUR/GBP), a colon (EUR:GBP), or by nothing at all (EURGBP). Select the cells containing the currency pairs and click **Data ➤ Currencies** or **Data ➤ Stocks**.

Note   You can return the ISO currency code for a country using the [Currency Code] field of the Geography data type.

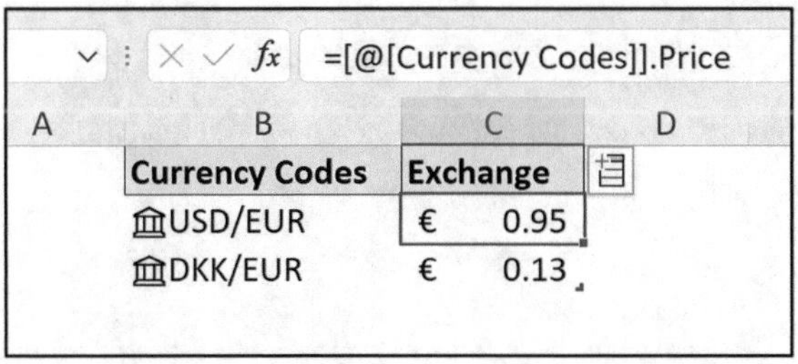
=[@[Currency Codes]].Price

Currency Codes	Exchange
USD/EUR	€ 0.95
DKK/EUR	€ 0.13

Figure 14-18. *Returning the price after converting a currency to euros*

The values returned from the Currencies data type can be used within a formula to convert currencies. In Figure 14-19, the following formula is used to convert different currencies to the British Pound (GBP):

```
=[@Codes].Price*[@Total]
```

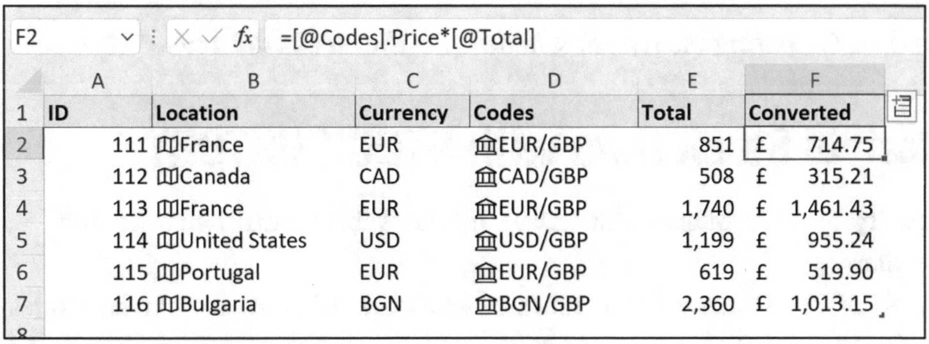
F2 =[@Codes].Price*[@Total]

ID	Location	Currency	Codes	Total	Converted
111	France	EUR	EUR/GBP	851	£ 714.75
112	Canada	CAD	CAD/GBP	508	£ 315.21
113	France	EUR	EUR/GBP	1,740	£ 1,461.43
114	United States	USD	USD/GBP	1,199	£ 955.24
115	Portugal	EUR	EUR/GBP	619	£ 519.90
116	Bulgaria	BGN	BGN/GBP	2,360	£ 1,013.15

Figure 14-19. *Converting values to GBP*

The exchange rate data being pulled into Excel can be updated by clicking **Data ➤ Refresh All**. The refresh schedule for Stocks data can be changed, if required, to set an automatic refresh schedule or to update when the workbook is opened:

1. Right-click a cell containing the data type.
2. Click **Data Type ➤ Refresh Settings**.
3. Click the **Stocks** data type in the *Data Types Refresh Settings* pane to expand the refresh settings (Figure 14-20).
4. Click the refresh option you want to use from *Automatically every 5 minutes*, *On file open*, or *Manually*.

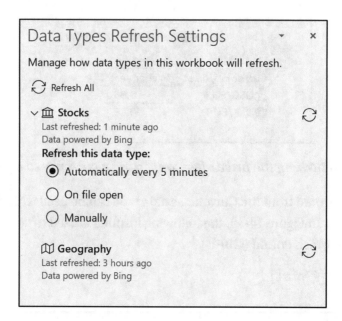

Figure 14-20. *Setting the refresh schedule for the Stocks data type*

Historical Stock Data with STOCKHISTORY

Availability: Excel for Microsoft 365, Excel for the Web, and Excel for Microsoft 365 for Mac

The STOCKHISTORY function returns historical stock price and currency rates based on a given symbol and date range. It can return a dynamic array of results from a single formula.

The syntax for the STOCKHISTORY function is as follows:

```
=STOCKHISTORY(stock, start_date, [end_date], [interval], [headers],
[properties1], ...)
```

- **Stock:** Reference to a cell containing the Stocks data type or the ticker symbol entered within double quotes (e.g., "MSFT"). Data is pulled from the default exchange; however, you can specify the exchange by entering the four-character ISO market identifier followed by a colon (:) before the ticker symbol (e.g., XNAS:MSFT).

- **Start date:** The earliest date for the data to be returned. The date can be entered as a fixed date enclosed in double quotes (e.g., "01/04/2022"), a formula (e.g., TODAY()-10), or a reference to a cell containing a date value.

- **[End date]:** The latest date for which to retrieve stock data. This argument is optional, and when omitted the *start date* is used.

- **[Interval]:** Specify the interval that each value represents. Type 0 for daily, 1 for weekly, or 2 for monthly. If omitted, a daily interval is used.

- **[Headers]:** Specify whether headers should be displayed. Enter 0 for no headers, 1 for with headers, or 2 for headers prefixed with the instrument identifier. The default is to display the headers.

- **[Properties]:** The columns to be returned for each stock. The properties are specified by the following index numbers: 0 = Date, 1 = Close, 2 = Open, 3 = High, 4 = Low, 5 = Volume. The columns/properties are returned in the order provided, for example, 0, 2, 1. The default is Date and Close (i.e., 0, 1).

The following is a definition for the different properties:

- **Date:** The first valid trading day in the period

- **Close:** The closing price on the last trading day in the period

- **Open:** The opening price on the last trading day in the period

- **High:** Highest price of the highest day's high in the period

- **Low:** Lowest price of the lowest day's low in the period

- **Volume:** The volume traded during the period

Note   When using an *interval* other than daily, the *start date* will revert to the first date of the specified period, so may be earlier than the stated *start date*.

Simple STOCKHISTORY Example

Let's start with a simple STOCKHISTORY example that pulls stock prices for a specified stock in the London Stock Exchange.

In Figure 14-21, cell B2 contains a drop-down list of four different stocks. The following formula is entered in cell B4 to return the daily close price for the last 15 days including today's date. Trading does not occur at weekends and some holidays, so the number of dates listed by the formula will vary.

```
=SORT(STOCKHISTORY(B2,TODAY()-14,TODAY()),,-1)
```

The default values are used for the *interval, headers,* and *properties* arguments. So, the *interval* is set as daily, *headers* are inserted as part of the array, and the default *properties* of *Date* and *Close* are used.

The SORT function is added to order the array by the [Date] column in descending order.

B4	∨	⋮	× ✓	*fx*	=SORT(STOCKHISTORY(B2,TODAY()-14,TODAY()),,-1)			
	A	B	C	D	E	F	G	

1		
2	🏛 TESLA, INC. (XLON:0R0X)	
3		
4	**Date**	**Close**
5	29/04/2022	$ 906.35
6	28/04/2022	$ 839.50
7	27/04/2022	$ 904.70
8	26/04/2022	$ 932.90
9	25/04/2022	$ 998.40
10	22/04/2022	$1,026.90
11	21/04/2022	$1,045.00
12	20/04/2022	$ 994.50
13	19/04/2022	$1,027.60

Figure 14-21. *Simple STOCKHISTORY example*

Adding Properties to STOCKHISTORY

STOCKHISTORY provides six properties that can be returned by the function. These properties are entered in the order that you would like them to be returned.

In Figure 14-22, the following formula is entered in cell B7. It returns the stock data for the stock and exchange stated in cell B2. The date range for the information returned is specified in cells B5 and C5.

```
=SORT(STOCKHISTORY(B2,B5,C5,2,,0,5,2,1),,-1)
```

In this formula, the *interval* is set as monthly, and four properties are returned: *Date, Volume, Open,* and *Close.*

∨ ⋮ ✕ ✓ *fx*	=SORT(STOCKHISTORY(B2,B5,C5,2,,0,5,2,1),,-1)				
A	B	C	D	E	F

🏛 MICROSOFT CORPORATION (XLON:0QYP)

Start Date	End Date		
01/01/2022	30/04/2022		

Date	Volume	Open	Close
01/04/2022	2,422,433	$ 309.80	$ 284.48
01/03/2022	8,273,834	$ 297.19	$ 312.20
01/02/2022	7,245,164	$ 310.48	$ 297.88
01/01/2022	4,421,801	$ 335.57	$ 307.48

Figure 14-22. Setting the properties to return with STOCKHISTORY

Inserting a Stock Chart Using STOCKHISTORY Data

The data returned by STOCKHISTORY can be presented in a chart for a greater visual of the stock trend over time.

When using STOCKHISTORY in its default manner, which returns the *Date* and *Close* price data only, a line chart would be great. But to play around more with STOCKHISTORY, let's insert one of the stock charts available in Excel.

Excel provides four different stock charts natively (there are chart techniques to create your own variations). We will insert the Open-High-Low-Close stock chart.

When looking at the different stock charts in the *Insert Chart* window, the description of the Open-High-Low-Close stock chart states clearly that the columns need to be in that order (Figure 14-23). It also states that a label column is required such as dates or stock names. We will use the date column for the category labels in our chart.

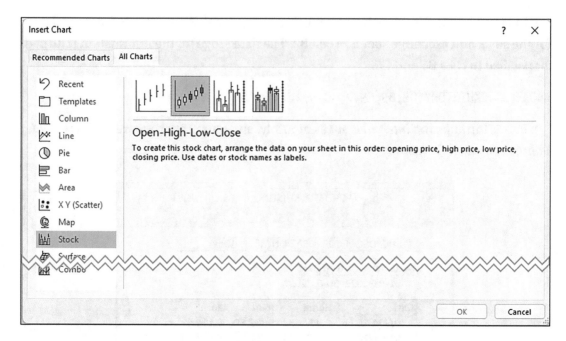

Figure 14-23. *Inserting an Open-High-Low-Close stock chart in Excel*

In Figure 14-24, the following formula is entered in cell B4 to return the required information:

```
=STOCKHISTORY(B2,TODAY()-14,TODAY(),,,0,2,3,4,1)
```

It returns the properties of *Date, Open, High, Low, Close* (0,2,3,4,1) in that order, as requested by the stock chart description.

Data for the stock stated in cell B2 is returned and within the range of the last 15 days. The headers are also returned with the data.

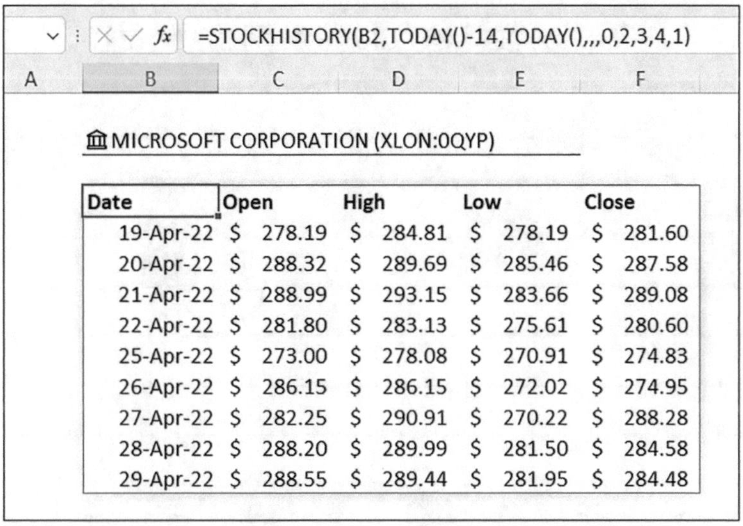

		f_x	=STOCKHISTORY(B2,TODAY()-14,TODAY(),,,0,2,3,4,1)

A	B	C	D	E	F

🏛 MICROSOFT CORPORATION (XLON:0QYP)

Date	Open	High	Low	Close
19-Apr-22	$ 278.19	$ 284.81	$ 278.19	$ 281.60
20-Apr-22	$ 288.32	$ 289.69	$ 285.46	$ 287.58
21-Apr-22	$ 288.99	$ 293.15	$ 283.66	$ 289.08
22-Apr-22	$ 281.80	$ 283.13	$ 275.61	$ 280.60
25-Apr-22	$ 273.00	$ 278.08	$ 270.91	$ 274.83
26-Apr-22	$ 286.15	$ 286.15	$ 272.02	$ 274.95
27-Apr-22	$ 282.25	$ 290.91	$ 270.22	$ 288.28
28-Apr-22	$ 288.20	$ 289.99	$ 281.50	$ 284.58
29-Apr-22	$ 288.55	$ 289.44	$ 281.95	$ 284.48

Figure 14-24. *STOCKHISTORY data for the stock chart*

To insert the stock chart

1. Select range to be used for the chart data.

2. Click **Insert ➤ Insert Waterfall, Funnel, Stock, Surface, or Radar Chart** button ➤ **Open-High-Low-Close**.

The chart is inserted and can be refined further as desired. Figure 14-25 shows the Open-High-Low-Close stock chart inserted in this example. The chart title has been linked to the value in cell B2.

In this stock chart, the vertical line represents the range between the *High* and *Low* values. The floating bar represents the range between the *Open* and *Close* values. If the close price is higher than the open price, the floating bar is filled with a color (white by default), and if it is lower, a different fill color is used (black by default). These colors can be changed.

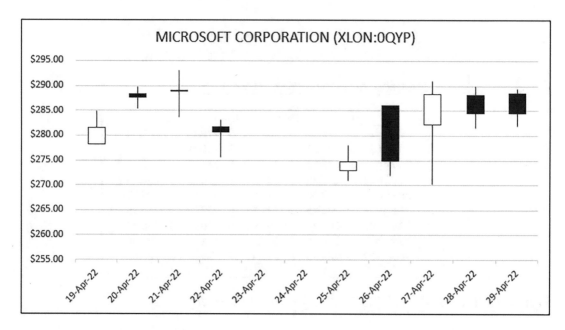

Figure 14-25. *Open-High-Low-Close stock chart*

Returning Historical Exchange Rates with STOCKHISTORY

As we saw earlier in this chapter, exchange rate data comes from the Stocks data type, even though a Currencies type is provided for simplicity. The STOCKHISTORY function can return historical exchange rate data just as it does for stocks.

For a demonstration of this, we will return historical exchange rate data for multiple currency pairs and for a specified five-day period.

In Figure 14-26, the following SEQUENCE formula is entered in cell D3 to return the sequence of five dates from the date stated in cell C1:

```
=SEQUENCE(,5,C1)
```

The following formula is then entered in cell D4 to return the exchange rate data. The range of currency pairs listed in range B4:B10 is used for the *stock* argument, and the reference to the spill range in D3 is used for the *start date*. No end date is provided.

```
=STOCKHISTORY(B4:B10,D3#,,,0,1)
```

In this example, the headers are disabled, as they are not required. And a single property of the *close* price is requested.

Line Sparklines are inserted in range C4:C10 for a quick visual of the exchange rate trend.

748

	fx	=STOCKHISTORY(B4:B10,D3#,,,0,1)

B	C	D	E	F	G	H
Date	25/04/2022					
Currency Pairs	Trend	25/04/2022	26/04/2022	27/04/2022	28/04/2022	29/04/2022
🏛 USD/GBP		£ 0.78	£ 0.80	£ 0.80	£ 0.80	£ 0.80
🏛 EUR/GBP		£ 0.84	£ 0.85	£ 0.84	£ 0.84	£ 0.84
🏛 CHF/GBP		£ 0.82	£ 0.83	£ 0.82	£ 0.83	£ 0.82
🏛 SAR/GBP		£ 0.21	£ 0.21	£ 0.21	£ 0.21	£ 0.21
🏛 AUD/GBP		£ 0.56	£ 0.57	£ 0.57	£ 0.57	£ 0.56
🏛 CAD/GBP		£ 0.62	£ 0.62	£ 0.62	£ 0.63	£ 0.62
🏛 NZD/GBP		£ 0.52	£ 0.52	£ 0.52	£ 0.52	£ 0.51

Figure 14-26. *Historical exchange rates with STOCKHISTORY*

Summary

In this chapter, we learned how to use formulas to access and analyze data stored in rich data types.

The chapter began with an introduction to what data types are and the different data types available in Excel. We then saw how to use some popular functions such as SUM, FILTER, and IF to work with data types. We also covered a couple of new functions – FIELDVALUE and STOCKHISTORY.

Data types are a new feature of Excel, only a few years old, and it is exciting to see how they grow and mature as a tool.

In the next chapter, we will learn lots of new Excel functions – LET, LAMBDA, and the seven LAMBDA helper functions.

The LET function is a fantastic addition that makes complex formulas more efficient. It improves their calculation speed and readability.

With LAMBDA, we can create our own custom functions. This is so much fun. We now have the tools to create the functions that we want from within the Excel experience. These functions can then be distributed to others.

CHAPTER 15

LET, LAMBDA, and the Helper Functions

Formulas in Excel have seen numerous fantastic advances in recent years including the introduction of dynamic array formulas and many brilliant new functions such as TEXTJOIN, XLOOKUP, and STOCKHISTORY. The development of LAMBDA functions in Excel was another tremendous leap in the advancement of formulas in Excel.

With LAMBDA, you can create your own functions in Excel. So, if Excel does not have it, you can create it. This is very special. What an awesome functionality to be introduced. It is also a lot of fun. Seeing your own Excel functions in the lights of the Excel grid as you type is a wonderful sight.

This chapter is not just about the LAMBDA function, although it is a focal point. We also see the wonderful LET function and the helper functions that can be used with LAMBDA.

In this chapter, we will start with the LET function. You will learn the benefits of using this function in your Excel formulas and see a few examples of its application.

It is then the turn of the LAMBDA function. We will see how to create a LAMBDA function and assign it to a name. Learn some best practices when creating LAMBDAs and see it used with the LET function.

We then move on to the LAMBDA helper functions. These are an array of functions that have been created to be used with your LAMBDA functions.

Finally, we introduce the Advanced Formula Environment, also known simply as AFE – an improved environment for creating complex formulas and ideal for LAMBDA creation. We will see how this environment improves our ability to write formulas and how it can be used to share our LAMBDAs with others and import the LAMBDAs of others into our own environment.

© Alan Murray 2022
A. Murray, *Advanced Excel Formulas*, https://doi.org/10.1007/978-1-4842-7125-4_15

LET Function: Speed Up and Simplify Your Formulas

Availability: Excel for Microsoft 365, Excel for the Web, and Excel 2021

File   let.xlsx

With the LET function, you can define names for calculations, ranges, and values in your formulas. These names, or variables, can then be called within the formula.

This is great! If you are using the same calculation multiple times in a formula, you can calculate it once and assign a name to it and then reuse it as many times as required in the formula.

The names only have scope within the formula of which they are created, so this is no replacement for the technique of defining names in the Name Manager of Excel, as they can have worksheet or workbook scope. However, LET offers a neat method, directly in the formula, to define names and create meaningful formulas.

There are two key benefits to using the LET function in your formulas:

- **Speed:** By performing a calculation once instead of multiple times, there is an improved performance in the speed Excel calculates your formulas.

- **Simplicity:** By assigning meaningful names to calculations and values, the formula is easier to understand and use by others and yourself. Your formulas are also more concise, as it nullifies the requirement to repeat the same calculation or range within the formula.

The following is the syntax of the LET function. You can assign up to 126 *name* and *name value* pairs:

```
=LET(name1, name_value1, calculation or name2, [name_value2], [calculation
or name3], ...)
```

- **Name1, name2, ...:** The name of the variable. These names adhere to the same rules as when defining names in the Name Manager. So, they must begin with a letter, not contain spaces and other specific characters.

- **Name value1, name value2, …:** The calculation, range, or value to assign to the corresponding *name*.

- **Calculation:** A calculation that uses all names defined with the LET function. The *calculation* argument must be the final argument of LET.

OK, let's see some examples of the LET function in formulas.

Using LET in Your Formulas

We will revisit one of our examples from earlier in this book and improve it with LET.

In Figure 15-1, the following formula is used to extract the characters between two delimiters. In this example, the delimiters are the open bracket "(" and the close bracket ")".

```
=MID(A2,
SEARCH("(",A2)+1,
SEARCH(")",A2)-SEARCH("(",A2)-1)
```

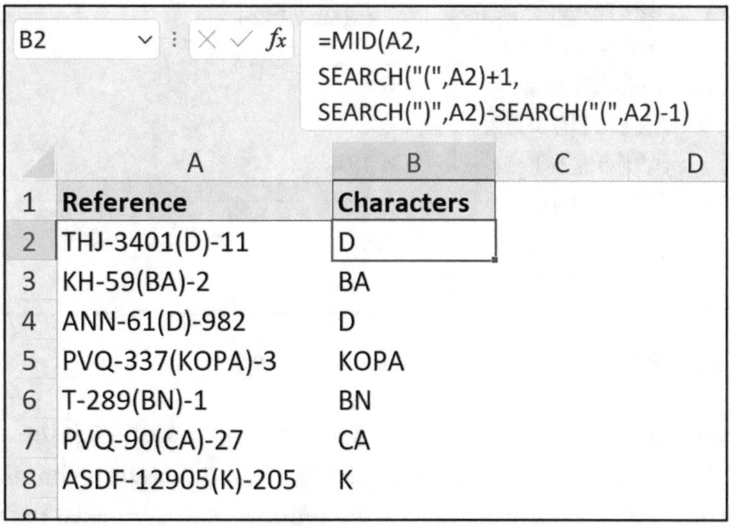

Figure 15-1. *Formula to extract characters between two delimiters*

There are three SEARCH functions in this formula, and the one that returns the position of the open bracket "(" is used twice.

In Figure 15-2, the following formula uses the LET function to define a name for each of the SEARCH functions. The names are then used in the final calculation.

```
=LET(
Char1,SEARCH("(",A2),
Char2,SEARCH(")",A2),
MID(A2,Char1+1,Char2-Char1-1)
)
```

The *Char1* name stores the result of the SEARCH function that returns the position of the open bracket. And the *Char2* name stores the result of the SEARCH function that returns the position of the close bracket.

B2	⌄ ⋮ ✕ ✓ *fx*	=LET(
		Char1,SEARCH("(",A2),
		Char2,SEARCH(")",A2),
		MID(A2,Char1+1,Char2-Char1-1)
		)

	A	B	C	D
1	Reference	Characters		
2	THJ-3401(D)-11	D		
3	KH-59(BA)-2	BA		
4	ANN-61(D)-982	D		
5	PVQ-337(KOPA)-3	KOPA		
6	T-289(BN)-1	BN		
7	PVQ-90(CA)-27	CA		
8	ASDF-12905(K)-205	K		

Figure 15-2. *LET function for an improved formula*

This is a meaningful formula that is easier to read and maintain. If the delimiter changed in the future, or the calculation required to find the second character did, then someone need only edit the formula beside the name and not concern themselves with the final calculation.

Even in a simple formula such as this, you can see the benefits that LET offers us. Imagine the benefits of LET in more complex examples.

To add some final comments on this example, we could have taken it further and defined a name for the cell reference also (Figure 15-3).

```
=LET(
Text,A2,
Char1,SEARCH("(",Text),
Char2,SEARCH(")",Text),
MID(Text,Char1+1,Char2-Char1-1)
)
```

In this example, you can see that the name *Text* has been used to store the reference A2. This name has been referred to in the calculations of the other two names and the final calculation.

B2		✕ ✓ *fx*	=LET(

```
Text,A2,
Char1,SEARCH("(",Text),
Char2,SEARCH(")",Text),
MID(Text,Char1+1,Char2-Char1-1)
)
```

	A	B	C	D
1	**Reference**	**Characters**		
2	THJ-3401(D)-11	D		
3	KH-59(BA)-2	BA		
4	ANN-61(D)-982	D		
5	PVQ-337(KOPA)-3	KOPA		
6	T-289(BN)-1	BN		
7	PVQ-90(CA)-27	CA		
8	ASDF-12905(K)-205	K		
9				

Figure 15-3. *Range assigned to a name within LET*

In a simple example such as this, one may question how necessary this is, especially if we had used data formatted as a table instead of a range. Tables provide meaningful references for us.

However, this does demonstrate that the names within LET are not only for calculations but can be used to store ranges also. And this can be very helpful in our quest for fast, concise, and meaningful formulas.

LAMBDA: Create Your Own Functions

Availability: Excel for Microsoft 365 and Excel for the Web

File   lambda.xlsx

With LAMBDA functions, you can create your own Excel functions. These functions can then be used in a workbook like any other Excel function and shared with others. That is truly amazing.

There are many functions that do not exist in Excel. There may be calculations you perform in your specific line of work for which there is no existing function or formulas you write that may be complex, and you want to simplify for use by yourself and others in the future.

This is the syntax of the LAMBDA function:

```
=LAMBDA(parameter_or_calculation, [parameter_or_calculation])
```

- **Parameter or calculation:** Each argument in the LAMBDA function is either a parameter or a calculation. The final argument supplied to the LAMBDA must be a calculation.

  - **Parameter:** A value to be passed to the function. This can be a cell reference, text string, number, or an array. Up to 253 parameters can be entered.

  - **Calculation:** The formula you want to execute. This argument is required.

A LAMBDA function is typically created in four distinct phases:

1. Write the formula you want to create a LAMBDA for.

2. Create the LAMBDA function for the formula.

3. Test that the LAMBDA works.

4. Define a name and description for the LAMBDA function.

Writing the LAMBDA Function

For this example, we will refer to a formula we created earlier in this book to count the number of words in a cell.

The following formula is shown in Figure 15-4. We will create a LAMBDA function for this formula. This will make it much easier for everyone to use.

```
=LEN(TRIM(A2))-
LEN(SUBSTITUTE(TRIM(A2)," ",""))
+1
```

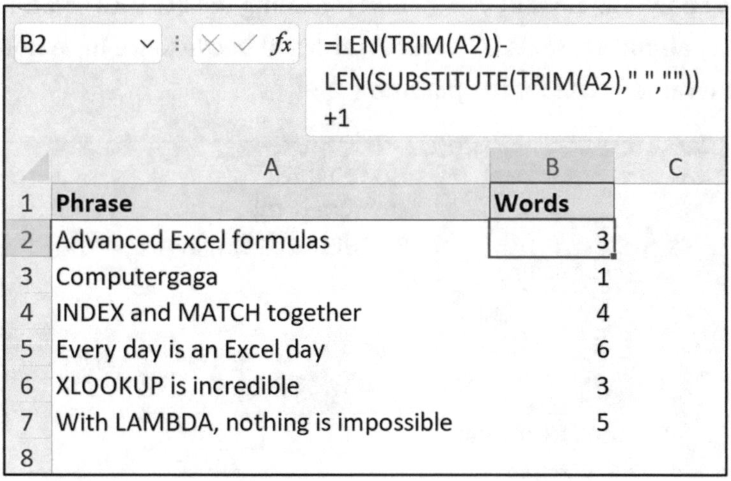

Figure 15-4. *Excel formula to count the number of words in a cell*

A brief explanation on how this works.

The formula uses two LEN functions – one to return the number of characters in a cell and the other to return the number of characters once spaces are removed. The difference between the two results is returned.

So, really this is returning the number of spaces in the cell. One is added to the result, as there will be one more word than there are spaces.

TRIM is used to ensure that there are no erroneous spaces before or after the cell content.

So, we have our formula. And we can see that it works. That is step 1 done. Let's now create the LAMBDA.

The following formula shows the LAMBDA function. It contains a single *parameter*, which is "text." This is the cell or text string that the user needs to provide for the function to operate. The *calculation* is then the formula we created to count words, but with the parameter used in place of the cell reference.

```
=LAMBDA(text,
LEN(TRIM(text))-
LEN(SUBSTITUTE(TRIM(text)," ",""))
+1
)
```

Figure 15-5 shows the LAMBDA function returning the #CALC! error. This is nothing to worry about. The #CALC! error is returned because we have not provided the LAMBDA with a value to use for the parameter yet.

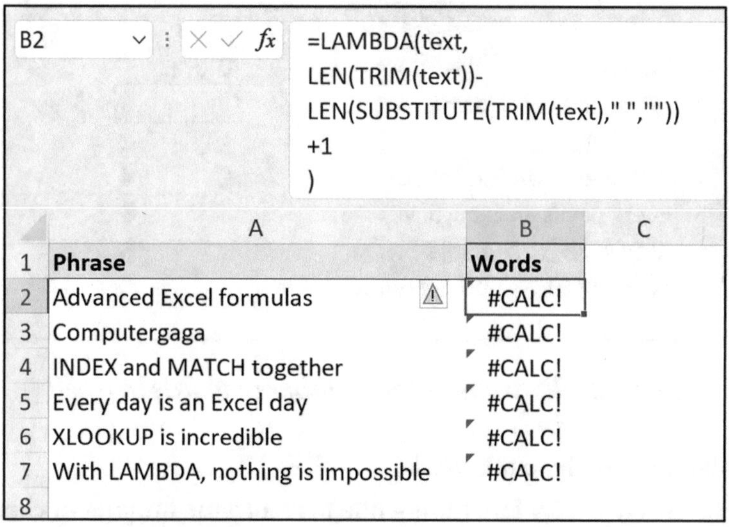

Figure 15-5. *LAMBDA function returning the #CALC! error*

Testing Your LAMBDA Function

It is good practice to test your LAMBDA functions before you start defining a name and description for them. To test a LAMBDA, you need to provide it with any necessary parameters. In this example, we have the single parameter of *text*.

To use the LAMBDA in a testing scenario, provide the results to any parameters by entering them in brackets after the function. In the following formula, cell A2 is provided to use for the *text* parameter (Figure 15-6):

```
=LAMBDA(text,
LEN(TRIM(text))-
LEN(SUBSTITUTE(TRIM(text)," ",""))
+1
)(A2)
```

This confirms for us that the LAMBDA is working great, and we can proceed with defining the name and description for it.

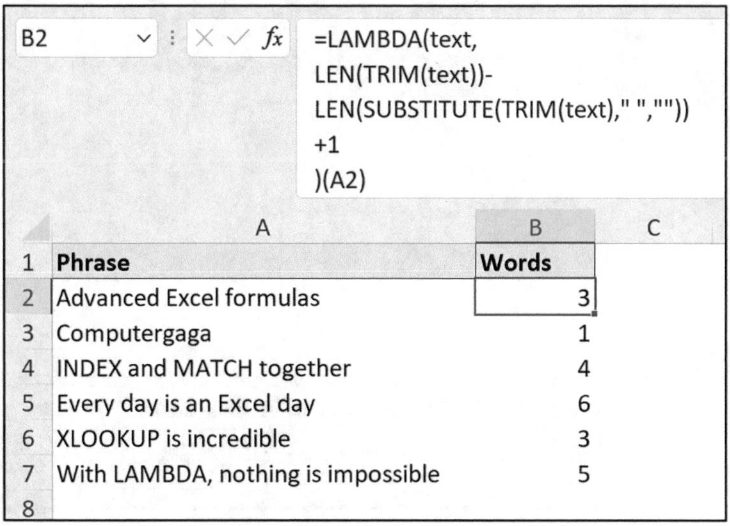

Figure 15-6. *Testing your LAMBDA function*

Defining a Name for Your LAMBDA

We will now define the name for the LAMBDA using the Name Manager. This is an exciting step, as this is where the LAMBDA is born for natural use in Excel.

1. Copy all the LAMBDA function text, except the test value we entered in brackets at the end.

2. Click **Formulas ➤ Define Name**.

3. Type "COUNTWORDS" in the *Name* field as the name for this new Excel function (Figure 15-7).

4. Type a description for the function into the *Comment* field. This description will appear when users enter the function into a cell, so keep it simple and clear for others.

5. Paste the LAMBDA function into the *Refers to* field.

6. Click **OK**.

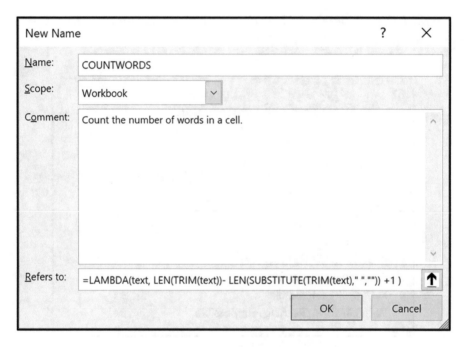

Figure 15-7. *Defining a name for a LAMBDA function*

Done! We have created our very own function in Excel.

Click a cell on the worksheet, type "=", and then start typing COUNTWORDS. The function will appear as you type. Figure 15-8 shows the function appearing as you type with the description that we defined.

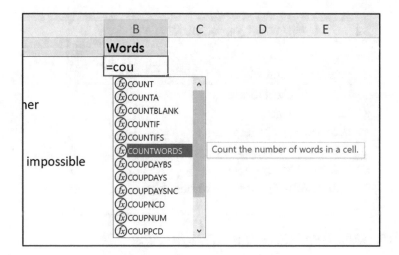

Figure 15-8. *The COUNTWORDS function in Excel*

On starting the COUNTWORDS function, the *text* argument is shown to us (Figure 15-9).

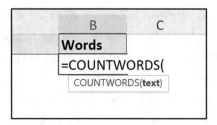

Figure 15-9. *Arguments of the new function are shown*

Figure 15-10 shows the COUNTWORDS function used to count the number of words in each cell of range A2:A7.

```
=COUNTWORDS(A2)
```

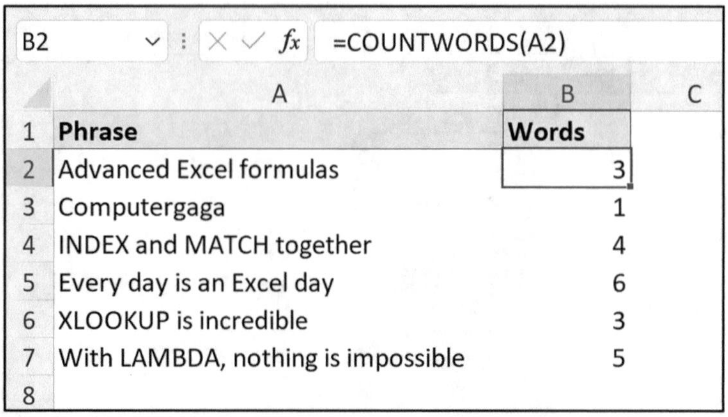

Figure 15-10. *Completed COUNTWORDS function*

That is certainly a lot easier than entering the original formula to count the number of words in a cell.

This function is available in this workbook only. Anyone who has access to this workbook would also have access to the function. And the function can be copied to another workbook by simply copying a cell containing the written function.

By copying the cell, or the worksheet, containing the function, the defined name would be copied with it. This provides a simple method for making the function available in other workbooks.

Later in this chapter, we will cover the Advanced Formula Environment and GitHub. These provide a more official approach to sharing your LAMBDAs with others.

Second LAMBDA Example

Let's create a second LAMBDA function that requires multiple parameters. For this example, we will create a function to extract the characters between two delimiters in a cell. This will be like the formula we used in the LET function example, but slightly improved.

The first step to creating a LAMBDA is to write the formula. Figure 15-11 shows the following formula extracting the characters between the open and close brackets:

```
=MID(A2,
SEARCH("(",A2)+1,
SEARCH(")",A2,SEARCH("(",A2)+1)-SEARCH("(",A2)-1)
```

	A	B
1	Reference	Character
2	THJ-3401(D)-11	D
3	KH-59(BA)-2	BA
4	ANN-61(D)-982	D
5	PVQ-337(KOPA)-3	KOPA
6	T-289(BN)-1	BN
7	PVQ-90(CA)-27	CA
8	ASDF-12905(K)-205	K
9		

Figure 15-11. *Formula to extract characters between two delimiters*

Now, this formula is a little different to the one used earlier in this chapter with LET. The earlier formula worked only if the two delimiters were different, but we would like the LAMBDA function to also work if the delimiters are the same.

So, using this formula, we will convert it into a LAMBDA with three parameters – the text to extract from, the first delimiter character, and the second delimiter character.

The following LAMBDA function is created and tested using the values A2, "(", and ")" for the three parameters (Figure 15-12). The three parameters are named *text*, *char1*, and *char2* and have been used in the LAMBDA in place of the entered values.

```
=LAMBDA(text,char1,char2,
MID(text,
SEARCH(char1,text)+1,
SEARCH(char2,text,SEARCH(char1,text)+1)-SEARCH(char1,text)-1)
)(A2,"(",")")
```

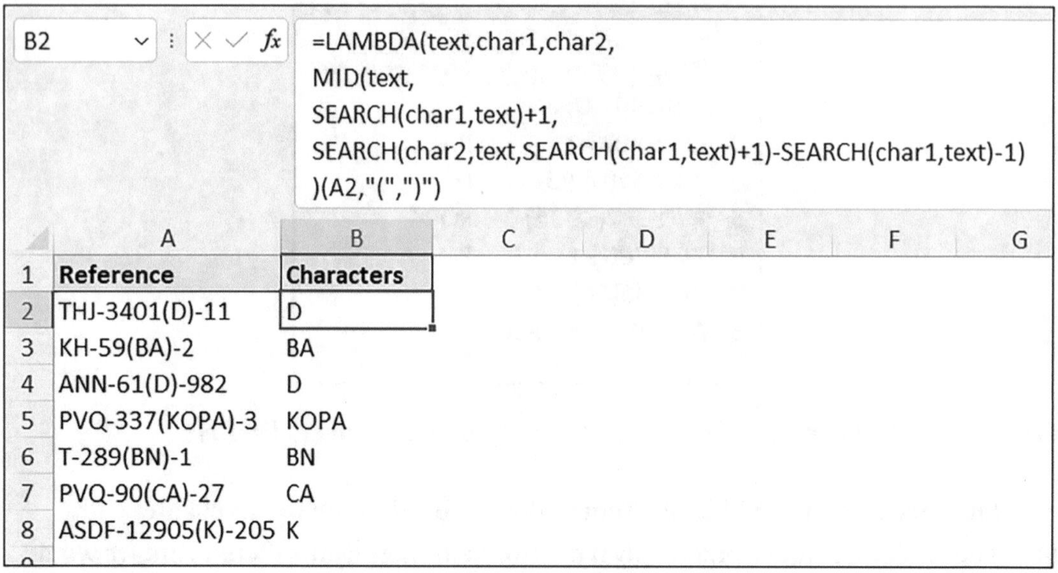

B2	⌄ ⋮ ✕ ✓ *fx*	=LAMBDA(text,char1,char2,
		MID(text,
		SEARCH(char1,text)+1,
		SEARCH(char2,text,SEARCH(char1,text)+1)-SEARCH(char1,text)-1)
		)(A2,"(",")")

	A	B	C	D	E	F	G
1	Reference	Characters					
2	THJ-3401(D)-11	D					
3	KH-59(BA)-2	BA					
4	ANN-61(D)-982	D					
5	PVQ-337(KOPA)-3	KOPA					
6	T-289(BN)-1	BN					
7	PVQ-90(CA)-27	CA					
8	ASDF-12905(K)-205	K					

Figure 15-12. *Testing the second LAMBDA function*

Note   This LAMBDA extracts text between the first instance of the two delimiters. If the delimiter occurs more than once in the string, there is no option to handle this. This presents a nice challenge. The instance number could be a LAMBDA argument. Hint: SUBSTITUTE.

We can now define a name and description for our second LAMBDA function.

In Figure 15-13, the function has been named TEXTBETWEEN, and a description is entered. The LAMBDA function minus the bracketed test values is pasted into the *Refers to* box.

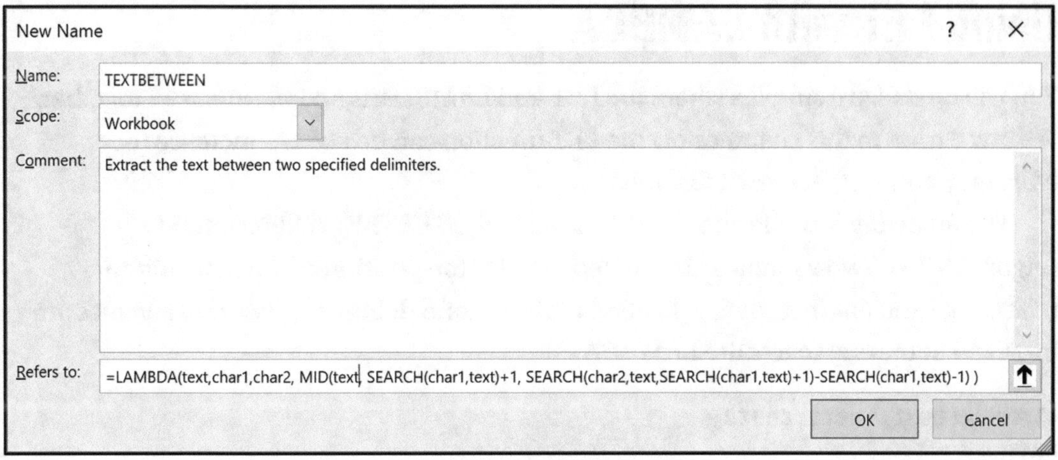

New Name		?	×
Name:	TEXTBETWEEN		
Scope:	Workbook ∨		
Comment:	Extract the text between two specified delimiters.		
Refers to:	=LAMBDA(text,char1,char2, MID(text, SEARCH(char1,text)+1, SEARCH(char2,text,SEARCH(char1,text)+1)-SEARCH(char1,text)-1))	↑	
		OK	Cancel

Figure 15-13. *Defining a name and description for the second LAMBDA*

The TEXTBETWEEN function is now ready to be used wherever needed in Excel. In Figure 15-14, the function has been used to extract the text between the two hyphens "-" in range A2:A7. The LAMBDA function is so much fun!

```
=TEXTBETWEEN(A2,"-","-")
```

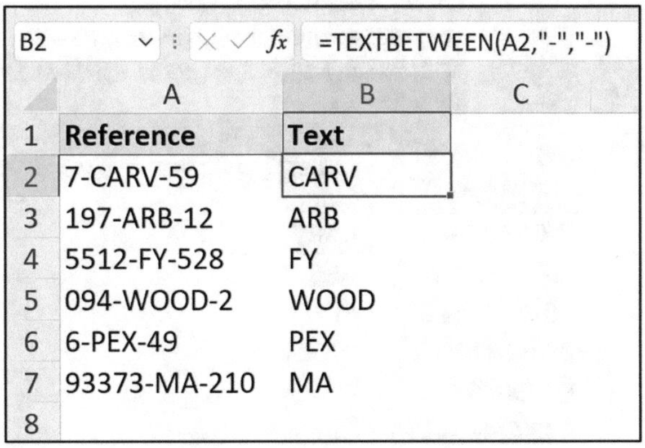

B2	∨ : × ✓ *fx*	=TEXTBETWEEN(A2,"-","-")	
	A	B	C
1	**Reference**	**Text**	
2	7-CARV-59	CARV	
3	197-ARB-12	ARB	
4	5512-FY-528	FY	
5	094-WOOD-2	WOOD	
6	6-PEX-49	PEX	
7	93373-MA-210	MA	
8			

Figure 15-14. *Using the TEXTBETWEEN function*

Using LET with LAMBDA

You will often see examples where the LET and LAMBDA functions are used together. We saw earlier in this chapter how the LET function can be used to increase the efficiency and simplicity of a formula.

The following formula shows LET added to the TEXTBETWEEN function (Figure 15-15). Two variables are created, one for the position of the first delimiter (*char1Pos*) and another for the position of the second delimiter (*char2Pos*). Values are provided at the end to test the LAMBDA.

```
=LAMBDA(text,char1,char2,
LET(
char1Pos,SEARCH(char1,text),
char2Pos,SEARCH(char2,text,char1Pos+1),
MID(text,char1Pos+1,char2Pos-char1Pos-1)
))(B2,"-","-")
```

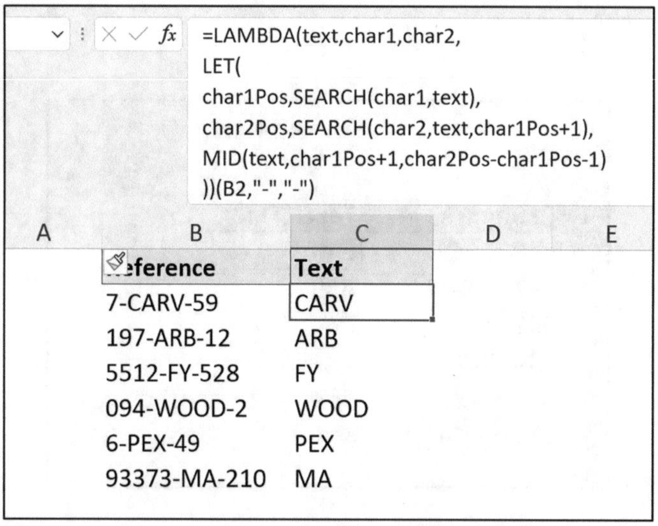

Figure 15-15.   *LAMBDA and LET functions together*

This has reduced the complexity of the formula and ensured that the delimiter 1 calculation only occurs once.

The LAMBDA Helper Functions

Availability: Excel for Microsoft 365 and Excel for the Web

File   lambda-helpers.xlsx

In addition to the LAMBDA function itself, there are seven further LAMBDA functions, commonly referred to as the LAMBDA helper functions. They are ISOMITTED, BYROW, BYCOL, MAP, REDUCE, SCAN, and MAKEARRAY.

They can be used to support the creation of our own custom functions with LAMBDA or entered as stand-alone functions themselves.

ISOMITTED: Optional Arguments in LAMBDA Functions

The ISOMITTED function is used within a custom function created with LAMBDA to handle the use of optional arguments. It tests a given LAMBDA parameter, or argument, to see if the value has been omitted and returns TRUE if it has and FALSE if not.

The syntax of ISOMITTED is simple:

```
=ISOMITTED(argument)
```

- **Argument:** The LAMBDA parameter that you want to test.

For this example, we will make the *char2* parameter of our TEXTBETWEEN function optional. If a user omits to provide a *char2* value, the same value specified for the *char1* delimiter will be assumed.

To enter an optional parameter in a LAMBDA function, you simply enter it within square brackets []. This illustrates to the user that the argument is optional. You then use the ISOMITTED function to ensure that the LAMBDA handles the argument correctly.

The following LAMBDA function is an adapted version of the previous TEXTBETWEEN function with the optional *char2* argument:

```
=LAMBDA(text,char1,[char2],
LET(
char1Pos,SEARCH(char1,text),
char2Pos,SEARCH(IF(ISOMITTED(char2),char1,char2),text,char1Pos+1),
MID(text,char1Pos+1,char2Pos-char1Pos-1)
))
```

For the *char2Pos* variable of the LET function, the ISOMITTED function is included within an IF to test the *char2* parameter. If omitted, the *char1* value is supplied to the SEARCH function. Otherwise, the provided value for the *char2* parameter is used.

In Figure 15-16, the TEXTBETWEEN function is used to extract the characters between the two hyphens "-". The *char2* argument has been omitted, so the *char1* value is repeated and the formula works correctly.

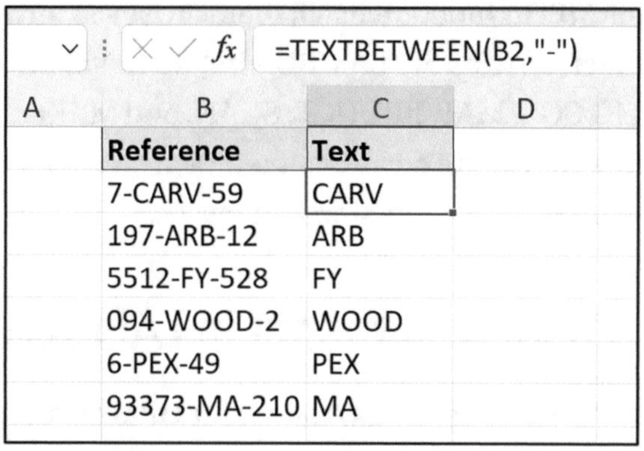

Figure 15-16. *TEXTBETWEEN function with optional argument omitted*

When entering the TEXTBETWEEN function (Figure 15-17), the *char2* argument is displayed within the square brackets [ ], identifying itself as an optional argument to users.

Figure 15-17. *Optional argument displayed in square brackets*

In Figure 15-18, all three arguments are specified as the delimiters are different for the *char1* and *char2* arguments. This example is provided to show that the TEXTBETWEEN function works fine in both scenarios – when the *char2* argument is omitted and when not.

✓ fx	=TEXTBETWEEN(E2,"(",")")		
D	E	F	G
	Reference	**Text**	
	THJ-3401(D)-11	D	
	KH-59(BA)-2	BA	
	ANN-61(D)-982	D	
	PVQ-337(KOPA)-3	KOPA	
	T-289(BN)-1	BN	
	PVQ-90(CA)-27	CA	
	ASDF-12905(K)-205	K	

Figure 15-18. *All three arguments specified in TEXTBETWEEN*

BYROW

With the BYROW function, a LAMBDA function is applied to each row of a given array and returns an array of results.

This is the syntax for the BYROW function:

```
=BYROW(array, [function])
```

- **Array:** The multiple row array to process.

- **Function:** The LAMBDA function to perform on each row of the array. This LAMBDA takes a single parameter only. This parameter represents each row of the array.

Figure 15-19 shows a table named [tblAttendance]. It contains the average attendances for eight classes over different weeks.

The following simple BYROW formula is entered in cell A2. It returns a spill range with the average for each row of the [tblAttendance] table.

```
=BYROW(tblAttendance,LAMBDA(row,AVERAGE(row)))
```

The LAMBDA function accepts the array given by the BYROW function. It then performs the AVERAGE function for each row of the array and returns the results as a single column array.

The parameter in the LAMBDA is named *row*. Any legal name could have been used for this parameter. It did not have to be named *row*. This parameter always represents each row of the array for which the LAMBDA function is processed.

A2			f_x	=BYROW(tblAttendance,LAMBDA(row,AVERAGE(row)))				
	A	B	C	D	E	F	G	H
1	Average		Class	Week 1	Week 2	Week 3	Week 4	Week 5
2	22.2		1TC	25	19	24	20	23
3	20.8		1SM	18	23	21	23	19
4	22		2AM	25	21	24	22	18
5	21		2DB	22	18	22	23	20
6	21.6		3HB	23	19	21	20	25
7	22.4		3JE	23	19	23	22	25
8	22.2		4CT	22	23	23	19	24
9	22.2		4RS	25	18	25	19	24
10								

Figure 15-19. BYROW function returning the average for each row in a table

This is a simple example but demonstrates the behavior of BYROW nicely.

Ordinarily, a single AVERAGE function could not be applied to each row of the table. It is an aggregation function and would return the average from all values.

Sure, we could have written a separate AVERAGE function for each row. However, BYROW is more efficient for two reasons. It is one calculation as opposed to multiple AVERAGE calculations. And it is dynamic. The spill range will automatically adjust to reflect changes to the [tblAttendance] table.

The true advantages of using BYROW are realized by applying more complex calculations. So, let's take our formula a little further.

In Figure 15-20, the following formula is entered in cell J2 to return the class names where the average attendance is under 22 students. These are classes that we need to focus on and improve their attendance figures.

```
=FILTER(tblAttendance[Class],
BYROW(tblAttendance,LAMBDA(row,AVERAGE(row)))<22
)
```

The FILTER function is added to filter the [Class] column of [tblAttendance] where the values in the array returned by BYROW are less than 22.

770

⋮ ✕ ✓ *fx*   =FILTER(tblAttendance[Class],
              BYROW(tblAttendance,LAMBDA(row,AVERAGE(row)))<22
)

C	D	E	F	G	H	I	J
Class	Week 1	Week 2	Week 3	Week 4	Week 5		Classes
1TC	25	19	24	20	23		1SM
1SM	18	23	21	23	19		2DB
2AM	25	21	24	22	18		3HB
2DB	22	18	22	23	20		
3HB	23	19	21	20	25		
3JE	23	19	23	22	25		
4CT	22	23	23	19	24		
4RS	25	18	25	19	24		

Figure 15-20.   FILTER with the BYROW function

One of the cool aspects of these LAMBDA helper functions is that they can be applied as stand-alone functions on the sheet. We can, however, use them in our own custom functions by adding another LAMBDA.

The following formula creates a custom function with two arguments – *classes* and *table*. *Classes* is the list of class names to be filtered and returned, and *table* is the table that BYROW will apply its LAMBDA function to.

```
=LAMBDA(classes,table,
FILTER(classes,BYROW(table,LAMBDA(row,AVERAGE(row)))<22)
)
```

A defined name is created for this custom LAMBDA function and named ATTENDANCE.CHASE. This function can then be used to return the class names that have underperforming attendance figures, whenever and wherever it's required.

In Figure 15-21, the following formula is entered in cell J2:

```
=ATTENDANCE.CHASE(tblAttendance[Class],tblAttendance)
```

This is a simple function that can be provided in the workbook for others to use. It avoids the requirement of writing the more complex FILTER, BYROW, and LAMBDA combination when we need to produce these results.

Class	Week 1	Week 2	Week 3	Week 4	Week 5		Classes
1TC	25	19	24	20	23		1SM
1SM	18	23	21	23	19		2DB
2AM	25	21	24	22	18		3HB
2DB	22	18	22	23	20		
3HB	23	19	21	20	25		
3JE	23	19	23	22	25		
4CT	22	23	23	19	24		
4RS	25	18	25	19	24		

fx =ATTENDANCE.CHASE(tblAttendance[Class],tblAttendance)

Figure 15-21. ATTENDANCE.CHASE custom function to return class names

BYCOL

The BYCOL function works in the same manner as BYROW, but with columns. With BYCOL, a LAMBDA function is applied to each column of a given array and returns a single row array of results.

This is the syntax for the BYCOL function:

```
=BYCOL(array, [function])
```

- **Array:** The multiple column array to process.

- **Function:** The LAMBDA function to perform on each column of the array. This LAMBDA takes a single parameter only. This parameter represents each column of the array.

In Figure 15-22, the following formula is entered in cell A2. It uses the BYCOL function to process a LAMBDA over each column in the [tblExams] table. This LAMBDA uses the COUNTIFS function to count the number of student exam scores that are greater than or equal to 75.

```
=BYCOL(tblExams,LAMBDA(column,COUNTIFS(column,">=75")))
```

The LAMBDA parameter is named *column*. Any legal name can be used for this parameter name. This is the name for each column of the BYCOL array.

A single row array of results is returned to cell A2 and spilled for all columns of [tblExams]. 0 is returned for the [Student] column. This column could have been disregarded in the formula as it does not contain any student scores; however, the formula looks neater referring to the [tblExams] table, and including that column does not affect the next development of this formula.

A2		fx	=BYCOL(tblExams, LAMBDA(column,COUNTIFS(column,">=75")))				
	A	B	C	D	E	F	G
1							
2	0	7	6	5	6	4	6
3							
4	Student	Maths	French	Business	History	Art	Tech
5	Student A	93	90	79	68	75	77
6	Student B	96	87	79	83	67	59
7	Student C	80	83	85	97	85	94
8	Student D	87	61	62	85	70	95
9	Student E	93	97	91	92	90	84
10	Student F	98	95	91	81	88	72
11	Student G	62	64	58	94	74	87
12	Student H	91	82	55	66	71	92
13							

Figure 15-22. BYCOL returning results for each column of an array

Like the previous BYROW example, we will add the FILTER function. We will use FILTER to return only the subjects with greater than five student passes (student scoring 75 or more in the exam).

In Figure 15-23, the following formula is entered in cell I2:

```
=TRANSPOSE(FILTER(tblExams[#Headers],
BYCOL(tblExams,
LAMBDA(column,COUNTIFS(column,">=75"))
)>5
))
```

The FILTER function filters the header row of the table to return only the subjects that meet the criteria of five or more student passes. TRANSPOSE is added to switch the single row array into a single column array.

This formula can be converted into a LAMBDA custom function or left as a stand-alone function as demonstrated in Figure 15-23.

| I2 | | ✓ ⋮ ✕ ✓ *fx* | =TRANSPOSE(FILTER(tblExams[#Headers], BYCOL(tblExams, LAMBDA(column,COUNTIFS(column,">=75")))>5)) |

	A	B	C	D	E	F	G	H	I
1	Student	Maths	French	Business	History	Art	Tech		Subjects
2	Student A	93	90	79	68	75	77		Maths
3	Student B	96	87	79	83	67	59		French
4	Student C	80	83	85	97	85	94		History
5	Student D	87	61	62	85	70	95		Tech
6	Student E	93	97	91	92	90	84		
7	Student F	98	95	91	81	88	72		
8	Student G	62	64	58	94	74	87		
9	Student H	91	82	55	66	71	92		
10									

Figure 15-23. *Returning subjects where the number of student passes meets the target*

The following is a LAMBDA formula that returns the subjects with five or more passes. Test values are provided in the brackets at the end.

```
=LAMBDA(subjects,table,
TRANSPOSE(FILTER(subjects,
BYCOL(table,
LAMBDA(column,COUNTIFS(column,">=75"))
)>5
)))(tblExams[#Headers],tblExams)
```

This LAMBDA could be enhanced by making the criteria, currently set as ">=5", the result of a LAMBDA parameter too. The user can then specify this when writing the function.

Try this and play around with these LAMBDAs. They are great fun!

To easily create our own functions in Excel without the need for VBA is awesome. We can put our own personal touch on versions of Excel functions we have used for years, but maybe thought "Oh, I wish it did this." Well, now it can, because you can do it.

It is like the *Lego* movie, but with Excel functions. You are a "Master Builder."

Complex Example: One Formula Report

Let's progress to a slightly more complex example and generate a multicolumn report with one formula.

For this example, we will return all subjects and the average student score for each subject. This two-column array will be sorted in descending order by the average student score.

The following formula is wrapped in a LET function. Figure 15-24 shows the results of this formula when entered on a worksheet.

```
=LET(
AverageScores,BYCOL(tblExams,LAMBDA(column,AVERAGE(column))),
SortedScores,SORT(TRANSPOSE(AverageScores),,-1),
Scores,TRANSPOSE(SORT(AverageScores,,-1)),
SortedSubjects,SORTBY(TRANSPOSE(tblExams[#Headers]),Scores,-1),
DROP(HSTACK(SortedSubjects,SortedScores),1)
)
```

Four variables are defined in the LET:

- An array with the average score for each subject (BYCOL used here)

- An array with the average scores sorted in descending order

- Another array with the sorted scores to be used to sort the subject names

- An array of the subject names sorted by the average scores using SORTBY

The HSTACK function is used to combine the two arrays into a single array. The DROP function removes the first row (header row that includes an error) from the combined array.

Subject	Average
Maths	87.5
History	83.3
Tech	82.5
French	82.4
Art	77.5
Business	75.0

Figure 15-24. Single formula to generate an average score report

This formula is focused on performing a very specific task with a specific set of data. A LAMBDA custom function can be created from this formula to make the generation of this report as easy as 1, 2, 3.

This LAMBDA fits a very different role to our previous examples of COUNTWORDS and TEXTBETWEEN. Those functions could be generally used by anyone and with any data. This LAMBDA would be created to make it simple for someone with the specific requirement of creating this report.

The following LAMBDA function has been defined as AVERAGE.SCORE.REPORT and entered in cell D2 to create the report (Figure 15-25):

```
=LAMBDA(subjects,table,
LET(
AverageScores,BYCOL(table,LAMBDA(column,AVERAGE(column))),
SortedScores,SORT(TRANSPOSE(AverageScores),,-1),
Scores,TRANSPOSE(SORT(AverageScores,,-1)),
SortedSubjects,SORTBY(TRANSPOSE(subjects),Scores,-1),
DROP(HSTACK(SortedSubjects,SortedScores),1)
))
```

This function accepts two parameters, the range containing the subjects and the table of exam scores:

```
=AVERAGE.SCORE.REPORT(tblExams[#Headers],tblExams)
```

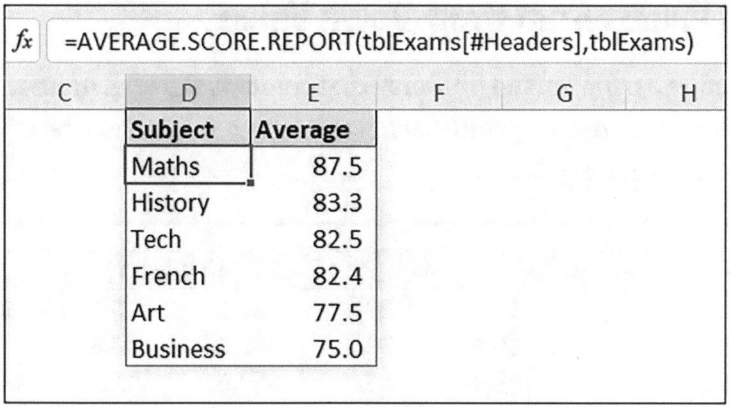

fx	=AVERAGE.SCORE.REPORT(tblExams[#Headers],tblExams)

C	D	E	F	G	H
	Subject	Average			
	Maths	87.5			
	History	83.3			
	Tech	82.5			
	French	82.4			
	Art	77.5			
	Business	75.0			

Figure 15-25. *Custom function for creating the average score report*

Note   There is a lot happening in this LAMBDA function. The Advanced Formula Environment, covered at the end of this chapter, would greatly simplify the creation and naming of a LAMBDA of this magnitude over the standard Excel Formula Bar and Name Manager dialogs.

MAP

The MAP function is used to apply a LAMBDA function to all values in an array or arrays. It has the following syntax:

```
=MAP(array, [lambda_or_array])
```

- **Array:** The array of values to transform with a LAMBDA. MAP can handle multiple arrays.

- **LAMBDA or array:** Another array to be mapped or the LAMBDA function to process on all values in the arrays. The final argument of the MAP function must be a LAMBDA.

Let's get straight into some examples of the MAP function.

Converting Values from Drop-Down Value

Figure 15-26 shows a table named [tblRuns] that contains the total miles ran each week by a few runners from a running club. Each week, a new column will be added to the table with the latest running data.

Name	Week 1	Week 2	Week 3	Week 4	Week 5
Stephanie	15.9	20.1	32.2	29.3	39.7
Peter	39.3	38.8	45.2	46.6	17.6
Cristiano	15.3	46.7	17.8	38.1	35.2
Debra	26.8	39.4	22.7	33.5	23.9
Julia	29.3	32.1	20	16.3	35.1

Figure 15-26. *Weekly run data in miles*

It is common in running to measure your distances in both miles and kilometers. Events often use a mixture of these measurements.

Because of this, the club would like the spreadsheet to have a drop-down list in a cell that allows easy switching between the two measurements. The total distances will be presented in the chosen measurement.

In Figure 15-27, the drop-down list is in cell C2 and currently contains "Km" for measurement in kilometers.

The following formula is entered in cell B4 to return the header row for our mapped data. As the formula references the headers of the table, it will automatically update when new weeks/columns are added to the [tblRuns] table.

```
=tblRuns[#Headers]
```

∨ ⋮ ✕ ✓ *fx*	=tblRuns[#Headers]				
B	C	D	E	F	G
Measurement Km					
Name	Week 1	Week 2	Week 3	Week 4	Week 5

Figure 15-27. *Dynamic header row from tblRuns*

The following formula is then entered in cell B5 to return the mapped values from [tblRuns] (Figure 15-28):

```
=MAP(tblRuns,LAMBDA(array,
IF(ISNUMBER(array),
IF(C2="Km",ROUND(CONVERT(array,"mi","m")/1000,1),array),
array)))
```

		fx	=MAP(tblRuns,LAMBDA(array, IF(ISNUMBER(array), IF(C2="Km",ROUND(CONVERT(array,"mi","m")/1000,1),array), array)))					
	B		C	D	E	F	G	H
Measurement		Km						
Name		Week 1	Week 2	Week 3	Week 4	Week 5		
Stephanie		25.6	32.3	51.8	47.2	63.9		
Peter		63.2	62.4	72.7	75.0	28.3		
Cristiano		24.6	75.2	28.6	61.3	56.6		
Debra		43.1	63.4	36.5	53.9	38.5		
Julia		47.2	51.7	32.2	26.2	56.5		

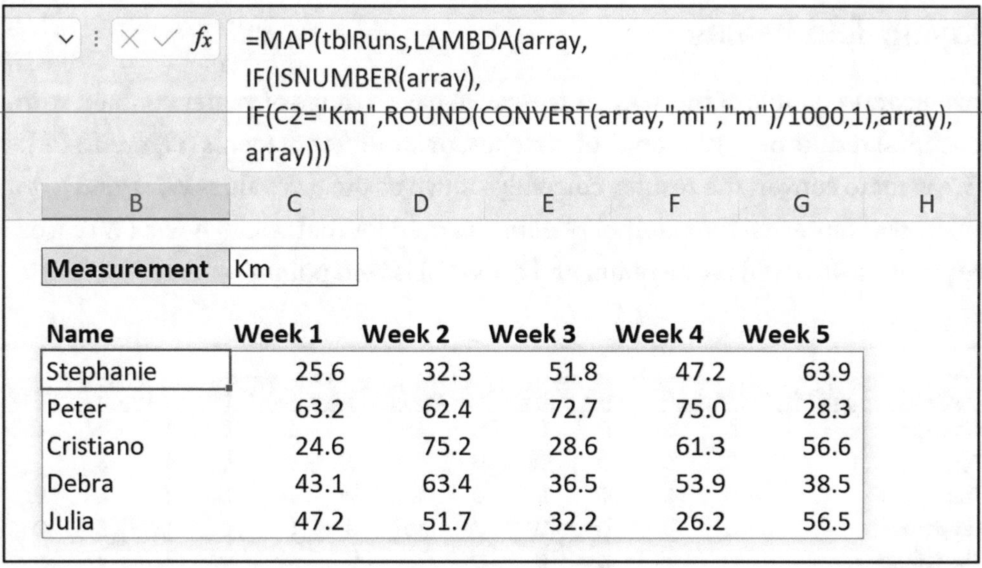

Figure 15-28. Formula to convert miles to kilometers based on cell value

The [tblRuns] table is entered as the array in the MAP function. The *array* parameter is then used in the LAMBDA.

Remember, this parameter can be named whatever you wish, as long as it is a legal name. Do not be deceived by the fact that the name of the LAMBDA parameter here matches the argument name in MAP, although that does make it a logical choice of name for the parameter. From this point on in the formula, *array* represents [tblRuns].

Two IF functions are used in the LAMBDA calculation. The first tests if the value in the array is a number. If it is, the formula to convert it to the requested measurement is performed, and if not, the current value in the array is returned unchanged.

The second IF function tests if cell C2 contains the text "Km". If it does, then the values in the array are converted from miles to kilometers. The CONVERT function is used for this. It converts the miles to meters, so this result is divided by 1000 and then rounded to one decimal place. If cell C2 does not contain "Km," then the value in the array is returned unchanged.

This is a completely dynamic solution based on the table and a drop-down value – a cool example of transforming values in an array with MAP.

Mapping Text Values

In this second example of the MAP function, we have a range of values containing the competition results over 12 rounds of matches for six different teams (Figure 15-29).

We want to convert the results, currently shown as the text values W, D, and L, to numbers that represent the number of points earned for that result. A win (W) earns three points, a draw (D) is one point, and a loss (L) is zero points.

Team	Points	R1	R2	R3	R4	R5	R6	R7	R8	R9	R10	R11	R12
Albatross		L	L	D	L	W	D	L	D	L	D	W	L
Tigers		D	D	D	W	D	D	W	L	L	W	L	L
The Eagles		D	L	D	L	D	D	W	D	D	D	L	W
Leopards		D	D	D	W	W	W	D	L	L	W	L	D
The Chargers		L	W	D	D	D	L	L	W	W	L	W	D
Beetles		L	D	D	D	W	W	D	W	D	L	D	L

Figure 15-29. *Sports teams results data*

In Figure 15-30, the following formula is entered in cell Q2. It maps the array of D3:O8 and uses an IFS function to test for the three possible results and returns the number for the matching value.

```
=MAP(D3:O8,
LAMBDA(results,IFS(results="W",3,results="D",1,results="L",0))
)
```

```
fx   =MAP(D3:O8,
       LAMBDA(results,IFS(results="W",3,results="D",1,results="L",0))
       )
```

Q	R	S	T	U	V	W	X	Y	Z	AA	AB
0	0	1	0	3	1	0	1	0	1	3	0
1	1	1	3	1	1	3	0	0	3	0	0
1	0	1	0	1	1	3	1	1	1	0	3
1	1	1	3	3	3	1	0	0	3	0	1
0	3	1	1	1	0	0	3	3	0	3	1
0	1	1	1	3	3	1	3	1	0	1	0

Figure 15-30. *Mapping text values to points*

Using BYROW with MAP

Let's take this example further by adding the BYROW function to sum the total points earned by each team.

In Figure 15-31, the following formula is entered in cell C3 to return the single column array with the total points for each team:

```
=BYROW(
MAP(D3:O8,LAMBDA(results,IFS(results="W",3,results="D",1,results="L",0))),
LAMBDA(points,SUM(points))
)
```

The BYROW function accepts the array returned by MAP as the array for it to apply its own LAMBDA function. It processes the SUM function for each row of the array, named *points*, to total the points.

This function could easily be turned into a LAMBDA to make it easier to return the total points in the future. All the function would need is the range to operate on.

```
=LAMBDA(range,
BYROW(
MAP(range,LAMBDA(results,IFS(results="W",3,results="D",1,results="L",0))),
LAMBDA(points,SUM(points))
))
```

It could be made more flexible by enabling the user to specify the possible results and number of points earned for each result.

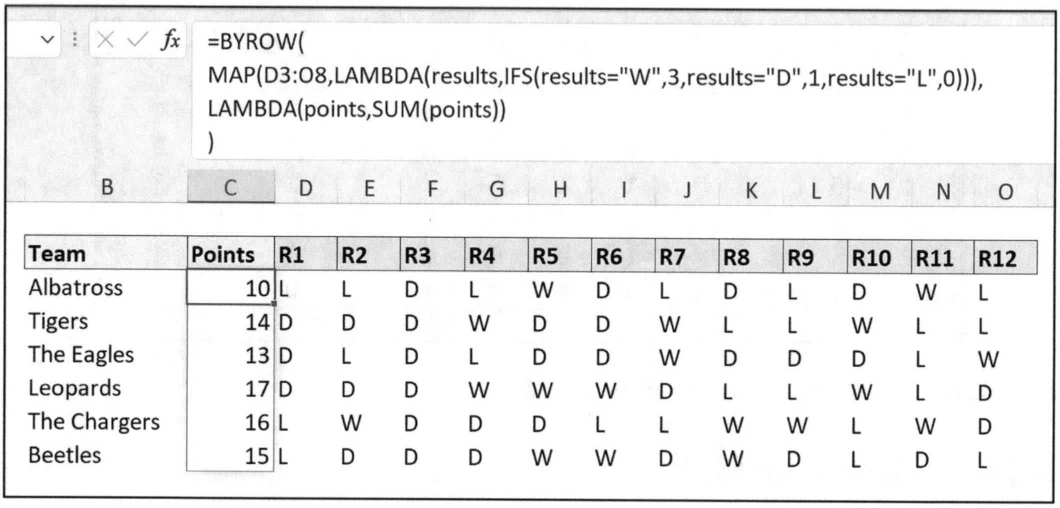

		=BYROW(
		MAP(D3:O8,LAMBDA(results,IFS(results="W",3,results="D",1,results="L",0))),
		LAMBDA(points,SUM(points))
		)

Team	Points	R1	R2	R3	R4	R5	R6	R7	R8	R9	R10	R11	R12
Albatross	10	L	L	D	L	W	D	L	D	L	D	W	L
Tigers	14	D	D	D	W	D	D	W	L	L	W	L	L
The Eagles	13	D	L	D	L	D	D	W	D	D	D	L	W
Leopards	17	D	D	D	W	W	W	D	L	L	W	L	D
The Chargers	16	L	W	D	D	D	L	L	W	W	L	W	D
Beetles	15	L	D	D	D	W	W	D	W	D	L	D	L

Figure 15-31. *Total points from results using BYROW and MAP*

Multiple Arrays with MAP

The MAP function can work with multiple arrays. This is demonstrated with the following formula entered in cell C3 to return the total points earned by each team (Figure 15-32):

```
=MAP(D3:D8,E3:E8,F3:F8,
LAMBDA(w,d,l,SUM(w*3,d*1,l*0))
)
```

This time, we have three separate ranges that contain the number of wins, draws, and losses each team has achieved.

Each range is given to MAP as a separate array. The LAMBDA then uses the named parameters of w, d, and l in a SUM function. Each parameter in the SUM is multiplied by the number of points applicable to each result.

In this example, because the values are aggregated with SUM, a single column array of values is returned.

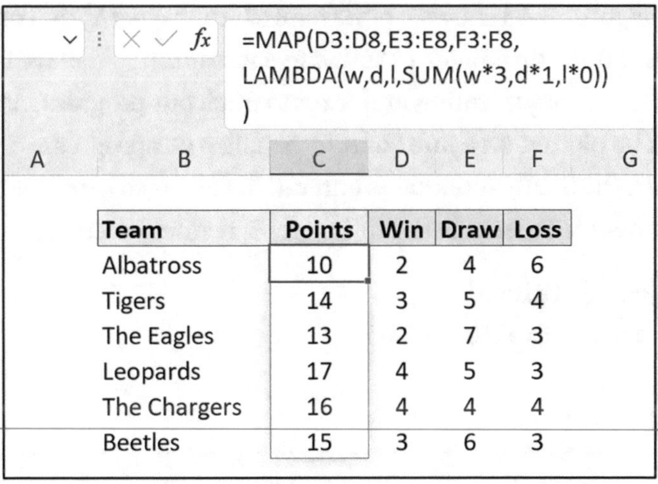

| | | fx | =MAP(D3:D8,E3:E8,F3:F8, LAMBDA(w,d,l,SUM(w*3,d*1,l*0))) |

A	B	C	D	E	F	G
	Team	Points	Win	Draw	Loss	
	Albatross	10	2	4	6	
	Tigers	14	3	5	4	
	The Eagles	13	2	7	3	
	Leopards	17	4	5	3	
	The Chargers	16	4	4	4	
	Beetles	15	3	6	3	

Figure 15-32. MAP with multiple arrays

SCAN

The SCAN function scans an array applying a LAMBDA function to every value in the array and returns an array with all intermediate values. This makes the scan function perfect for calculating running totals.

This is the syntax for the SCAN function:

```
=SCAN([initial_value], array, function)
```

- **[Initial value]:** The starting value for the accumulator. If omitted, the value is assumed to be blank and is treated as a 0 or an empty string ".

- **Array:** The array to be scanned.

- **Function:** The LAMBDA function to scan the array. It takes the following two arguments:

  - **Accumulator:** The accumulated value that is returned for each intermediate value and the end result

  - **Value:** The calculation to be applied to each value in the array

For example, Figure 15-33 shows a table named [tblProjectA] that contains the number of people trained on a piece of software each month. We have been set a target to train 3500 users in an organization and want to track our progress monthly. These values could then be plotted on a line chart to visualize our progress.

In Figure 15-33, the SCAN function is entered in cell D2 to produce the running total for the number of people trained in the tblProjectA[Trained] column.

```
=SCAN(0,tblProjectA[Trained],
LAMBDA(total,trained,total+trained)
)
```

	A	B	C	D	E	F
	D2 ⌄ ⋮ ✕ ✓ *fx* =SCAN(0,tblProjectA[Trained], LAMBDA(total,trained,total+trained))					
1	Month-Year	Trained		Running Total	%	
2	Jan-2020	149		149	96%	
3	Feb-2020	259		408	88%	
4	Mar-2020	250		658	81%	
5	Apr-2020	232		890	75%	
6	May-2020	180		1,070	69%	
7	Jun-2020	168		1,238	65%	
8	Jul-2020	103		1,341	62%	
9	Aug-2020	135		1,476	58%	
10	Sep-2020	225		1,701	51%	
11	Oct-2020	295		1,996	43%	
12	Nov-2020	261		2,257	36%	
13	Dec-2020	205		2,462	30%	
14	Jan-2021	105		2,567	27%	
15	Feb-2021	275		2,842	19%	
16	Mar-2021	148		2,990	15%	

Figure 15-33. *SCAN function for a simple running total*

The *initial value* is set as 0 (this could have been omitted) and the *array* to be scanned stated as the [Trained] column.

The LAMBDA uses two parameters, *total* for the accumulated value and *trained* for the next value to be added to the accumulated total. The LAMBDA calculation is simply to add the *trained* value to the existing accumulated *total*.

A spill range is returned for all intermediate values. The following formula is then entered in cell E2 to calculate the percent of users still to be trained:

```
=1-D2#/3500
```

The parameters could have been named anything you wanted, and the calculation could have been any operation, for example, a formula to multiply or concatenate the parameter values.

This example demonstrates how simple it is to create a running total from a single array formula with the SCAN function.

REDUCE

The REDUCE function applies a LAMBDA function to all values in an array and reduces the returned array to the total accumulated value. So, it behaves in the same way as SCAN but returns the final accumulated value only and not all intermediate values.

The following is the syntax for the REDUCE function. It matches the SCAN function syntax:

```
=REDUCE([initial_value], array, function)
```

- **[Initial value]:** The starting value for the accumulator. If omitted, the value is assumed to be 0.

- **Array:** The array to be reduced.

- **Function:** The LAMBDA function to reduce the array. It takes the following two arguments:

  - **Accumulator:** The accumulated value that is reduced and returned as the final total value

  - **Value:** The calculation to be applied to each value in the array

In Figure 15-34, the following formula is entered in cell D3 to return the reduced total for the [Trained] column in the [tblProjectB] table. This is the same data and the same LAMBDA function as used with SCAN previously. However, REDUCE returns the final total only.

```
=REDUCE(0,tblProjectB[Trained],
LAMBDA(total,trained,total+trained)
)
```

D3		⋮	✕ ✓ ƒx	=REDUCE(0,tblProjectB[Trained], LAMBDA(total,trained,total+trained))		

	A	B	C	D	E	F
1	Month-Year	Trained				
2	Jan-2020	149		Total	%	
3	Feb-2020	259		2,990	15%	
4	Mar-2020	250				
5	Apr-2020	232		Target		200
6	May-2020	180		Last Value		
7	Jun-2020	168		Date		
8	Jul-2020	103				
9	Aug-2020	135				
10	Sep-2020	225				
11	Oct-2020	295				
12	Nov-2020	261				
13	Dec-2020	205				
14	Jan-2021	105				
15	Feb-2021	275				
16	Mar-2021	148				

Figure 15-34. REDUCE function returning the total accumulated value

The formula in cell E3 is simply =1-D3/3500.

The LAMBDA functions for both the SCAN and REDUCE functions could be more involved than a simple accumulated value. An IF function could be used for conditional logic such as totaling only the positive values. Other operations such as multiplication could also have been used.

This example is shown as a demonstration of how the REDUCE function works, especially when compared to SCAN, and to provide ideas of how you could utilize it. However, this specific example is very simple and is achieving no more than a simple SUM could achieve.

Because of this, let's see another example of REDUCE.

Working with the same [tblProjectB] data, we want to return the last value from the [Trained] column that is greater than a specified target value.

In Figure 15-35, the following formula uses the REDUCE function to return the last value that was greater than the value entered in cell E5:

```
=REDUCE(,tblProjectB[Trained],
LAMBDA(FirstValue,CurrentValue,
IF(CurrentValue>E5,CurrentValue,FirstValue)
))
```

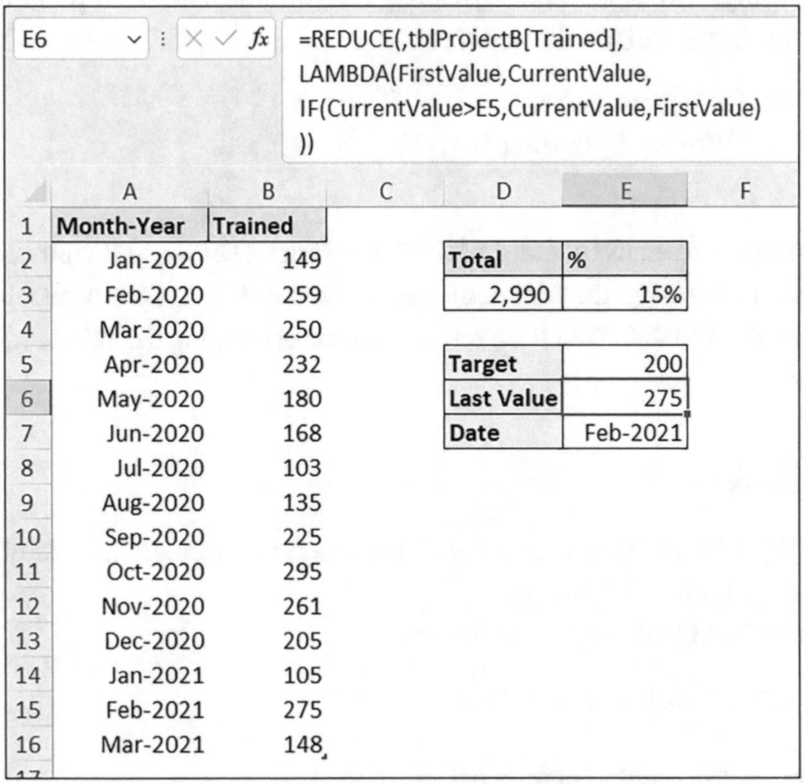

Figure 15-35. *REDUCE to return the last successful monthly total*

The *initial value* is omitted (so assumed to be 0), and the [Trained] column is provided for the *array* argument.

The LAMBDA function uses two parameters named *FirstValue* and *CurrentValue*. Remember, these parameters could be named anything you like, such as simply *a* and *b*; it still works the same. However, *FirstValue* and *CurrentValue* are meaningful in this context.

The REDUCE function uses the LAMBDA to iterate down the values in the [Trained] column. An IF function tests each value in the column against the target value in cell E5. If the current value being tested is greater than the target value, then the current value is displayed; otherwise, the first value in the column (149 in this example) is displayed.

The first value is displayed if no value achieves the target, because in this example, there is no calculation to accumulate the value (in the first example, the *total + trained* formula was used). So, it remains the first value in the array. Hopefully, this explains why the parameters were named *FirstValue* and *CurrentValue*.

The following formula is entered in cell E7 to return the date corresponding to the result returned by the REDUCE function:

```
=INDEX(tblProjectB[Month-Year],
XMATCH($E$6,tblProjectB[Trained],0,-1)
)
```

This formula uses an INDEX and XMATCH technique shown in Chapter 11. XMATCH is used to search the [Trained] column from last to first for the result of the REDUCE function in E6. INDEX then returns the corresponding [Month-Year] value for the matched row index.

MAKEARRAY

The MAKEARRAY function returns a calculated array of a specified number of rows and columns using a LAMBDA function.

The syntax for MAKEARRAY is as follows:

```
=MAKEARRAY(rows, columns, function)
```

- **Rows:** The number of rows in the array.

- **Columns:** The number of columns in the array.

- **Function:** The LAMBDA function to make the array. It takes the following two parameters:

  - **Row:** The row index of the array

  - **Col:** The column index of the array

The LAMBDA function is typically used within MAKEARRAY to perform a calculation using the *row* and *col* parameters. In Figure 15-36, the following formula is used to return a multiplication table. The size of the table is determined by the row and column values specified in cells C2 and E2.

```
=MAKEARRAY(C2,E2,LAMBDA(r,c,r*c))
```

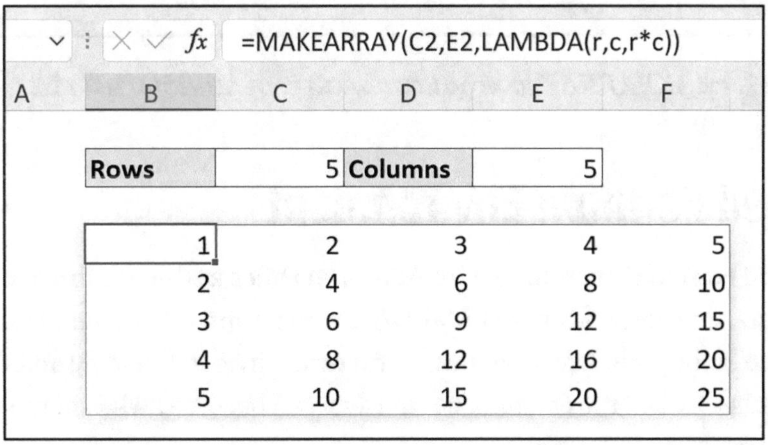

Figure 15-36. *Multiplication table with MAKEARRAY*

Interestingly, the *row* and *col* parameters do not need to be used by the LAMBDA. In Figure 15-37, the following MAKEARRAY function returns a matrix of randomized text values using CHOOSE and RANDBETWEEN. The *r* and *c* parameters are not referenced by the LAMBDA.

```
=MAKEARRAY(C2,E2,LAMBDA(r,c,
CHOOSE(RANDBETWEEN(1,4),"Red","Blue","Green","Black"))
)
```

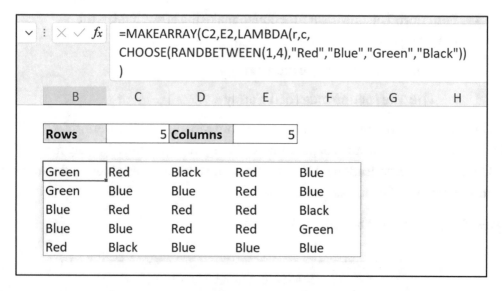

Figure 15-37. MAKEARRAY to produce a matrix of randomized text

Advanced Formula Environment

The Advanced Formula Environment, or AFE, is an Office add-in for Excel that makes it easier to create, manage, and share LAMBDA functions and other named formulas.

The Name Manager in Excel can be a torrid experience for creating and editing named formulas. In fact, the Formula Bar in Excel can become awkward too when working with complex formulas.

The Advanced Formula Environment provides many improvements to aid the formula creation and management experience. This includes the ability to add comments, indent your formula lines, receive immediate inline errors, and easy sharing via GitHub gists or simply copying between workbooks.

Let's look at how to find, install, and use the Advanced Formula Environment.

Getting the AFE Add-in

The Advanced Formula Environment can be quickly and easily installed from the Office store within Excel in just a few seconds. It will then appear on the far right of your **Home** tab in Excel.

To install the Advanced Formula Environment

1. Click **Insert ➤ Get Add-ins** (Figure 15-38).

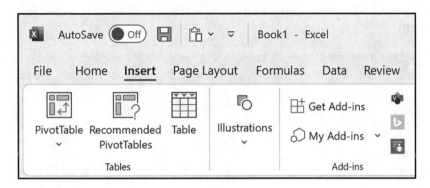

Figure 15-38. *Get Add-ins from the Insert tab*

2. Search for the add-in by typing "formula" into the search bar (Figure 15-39). Click ***Add*** beside the Advanced formula environment add-in.

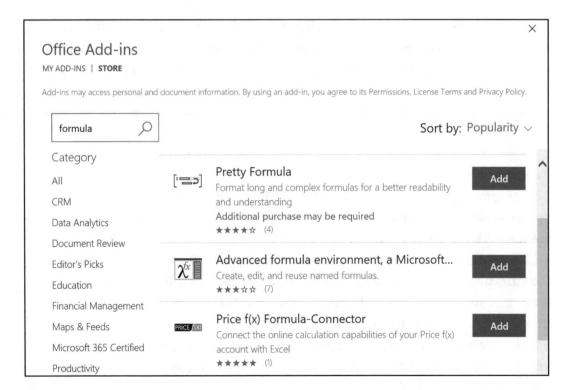

Figure 15-39. *Adding the Advanced Formula Environment add-in*

3.   If a window appears to accept the license terms and privacy
policy, click **Continue**.

The Advanced Formula Environment is added to the end of the **Home** tab in Excel
(Figure 15-40).

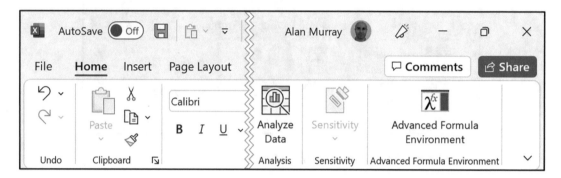

Figure 15-40. *Advanced Formula Environment on the Home tab*

Managing Your Named Formulas

The AFE makes it easy to manage your named formulas. All your named formulas (and
named ranges) will appear in the AFE pane in separate cards that distinguish them
clearly, show the formula in a neatly constructed manner, and provide buttons to edit,
delete, and share.

To open the Advanced Formula Environment, click **Home ➤ Advanced Formula
Environment**.

The Advanced Formula Environment pane appears on the right side of the
Excel window.

In Figure 15-41, you can see the "SUBJECTSLIST" LAMBDA function that was
created earlier in this chapter. This has been pulled into the AFE from the Name
Manager of Excel; it was not created in the AFE.

Notice the indentation on the different lines of the LAMBDA function. This was
automatically applied by the AFE. This indentation was not made when creating the
function in the Name Manager. Different colors are also applied to function names, text
strings, and number constants.

The Advanced Formula Environment pane can be resized and undocked from
the side of the screen. This is great as it can be moved to another connected screen,
providing more room to work.

If you have many functions and named ranges in the AFE, the *Filter names* field at the top can be used to search for the function name using keywords. It is very effective to jump quickly to the function you need.

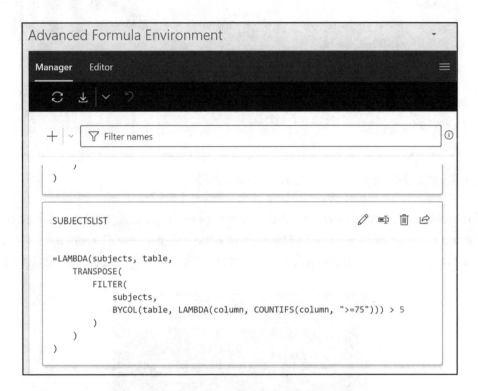

Figure 15-41. Named formulas in the Advanced Formula Environment

On each card, there are four buttons to manage your function (Figure 15-42):

1. **Edit** the formula using the AFE.

2. **Rename** the function.

3. **Delete** the function.

4. **Share** the function by copying it as a text snippet.

```
        /
      )                                              2

    SUBJECTSLIST                              ✏  ⏏  🗑  ↪
                                                    ↑
    =LAMBDA(subjects, table,                   ↗   |   ↑
        TRANSPOSE(                            1   3   4
            FILTER(
                subjects,
                BYCOL(table, LAMBDA(column, COUNTIFS(column, ">=75"))) > 5
            )
        )
    )
```

Figure 15-42. *Managing a LAMBDA in the AFE*

On making any changes to a named function or named range, click the **Sync** button to sync the changes with the Name Manager in Excel (Figure 15-43). Until the AFE and Name Manager are synced, you will not be able to utilize the updated name in Excel.

```
Advanced Formula Environment

 Manager    Editor
 ────────

    ⟳  ⭳  | ∨  ↺

    +  ∨   ▽ Filter names
```

Figure 15-43. *Sync names with the Name Manager in Excel*

Sharing Your LAMBDA Functions

Named formulas, such as your LAMBDAs, are only available in the workbook in which they are created.

There are two methods for making these formulas available in other workbooks:

- Using the share feature of the AFE to copy the formula text

- Creating a GitHub gist that contains the named formulas and using the URL for yourself and others to easily import the formulas into the AFE and Name Manager of Excel

To share a named formula in the AFE, click the **Share** button in the top-right corner of the formula card.

In the window that appears (Figure 15-44), click the **Copy text** button in the bottom right.

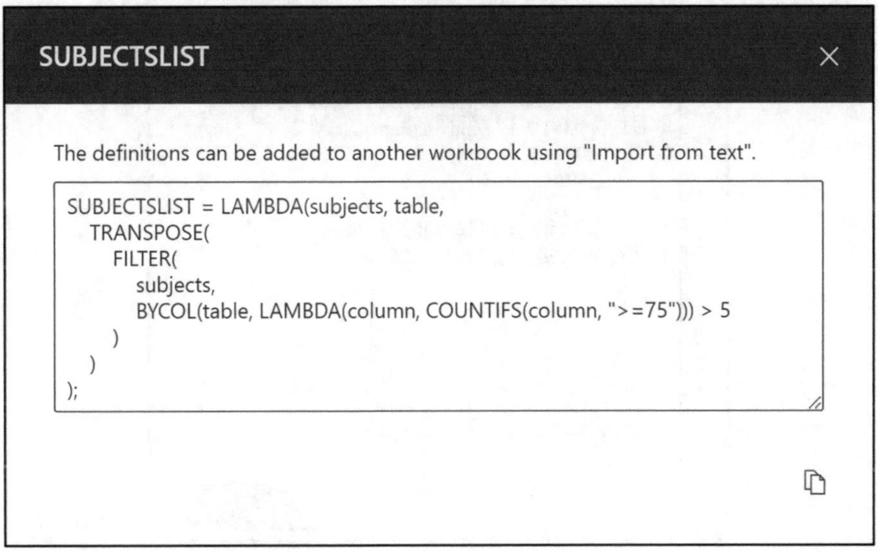

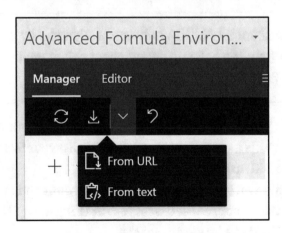

Figure 15-44. *Copying a LAMBDA to another workbook*

Switch to the workbook where you want the named formula, and in the AFE, click the arrow next to the **Import** button and click **From text** (Figure 15-45).

Figure 15-45. *Import from text*

Paste the formula text into the *Import text snippet* window and click **Import** (Figure 15-46).

```
Import text snippet                                    ✕

Import a series of names, such as those obtained  ⓘ
using the share functionality in this app.

SUBJECTSLIST = LAMBDA(subjects, table,
    TRANSPOSE(
        FILTER(
            subjects,
            BYCOL(table, LAMBDA(column,
    COUNTIFS(column, ">=75"))) > 5
        )
    )
);

                                              Import
```

Figure 15-46. *Importing a text snippet in the AFE*

The named formula is imported. Click the **Sync** button to push the changes through to the Name Manager in Excel.

Note   You can also share a LAMBDA between workbooks by simply copying and pasting the formula from the cell into a worksheet cell of another workbook. This automatically adds the function to the Name Manager.

You can also make your named formulas available to other workbooks by creating a gist at GitHub.com. A gist is a repository where you can list your formulas and then share them by providing the URL to others.

For more information on how to set up a GitHub account and create your own gist, visit https://docs.github.com/en/get-started/writing-on-github/editing-and-sharing-content-with-gists/creating-gists.

Importing LAMBDA Functions from a GitHub Gist

Importing formulas from a gist is very simple. Click the **Import** button in the Advanced Formula Environment (Figure 15-47).

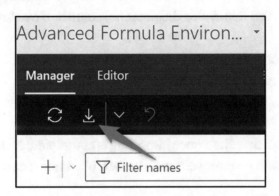

Figure 15-47. *Import button in the Advanced Formula Environment*

Copy and paste the gist URL into the *GitHub Gist URL* box provided (Figure 15-48). The following URL is used in this example. This URL is for my own gist and contains some of the LAMBDA functions created in this chapter.

This is the URL for my GitHub gist:

`https://gist.github.com/computergaga/f61f78ceaa89ed417e157e1e664a3f7a`

Figure 15-48. *Importing from a GitHub gist URL*

In this example, the *Add formulas to new namespace?* box is checked, and a *Namespace* of COMPUTERGAGA is entered. This is optional.

The advantage of creating a namespace is that it is easier to distinguish the imported formulas from the existing formulas as their names are preceded by the namespace name (Figure 15-49). And this avoids the potential conflict of two formulas having the same name.

This process imports all formulas from the gist. So, if there are 14 formulas, you will see 14 new formulas appear in the AFE.

When the AFE has finished importing the formulas from the gist, a message appears to say that importing was successful.

These formulas can be edited once importing is completed, including their names. So, the namespace could be removed from the formula name if desired.

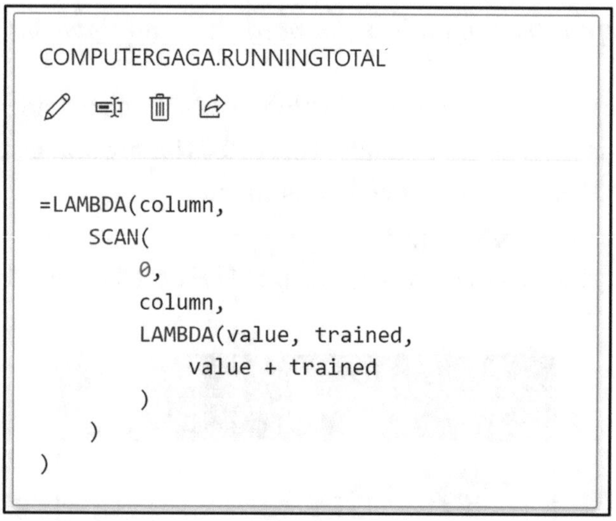

```
COMPUTERGAGA.RUNNINGTOTAL

   ✎  ⇥  🗑  ↪


=LAMBDA(column,
     SCAN(
          0,
          column,
          LAMBDA(value, trained,
               value + trained
          )
     )
)
```

Figure 15-49. *Imported LAMBDA in the AFE*

Click the **Sync** button to sync the changes with the Name Manager in Excel. Figure 15-50 shows the imported names with the COMPUTERGAGA namespace prefix in the *Name Manager*.

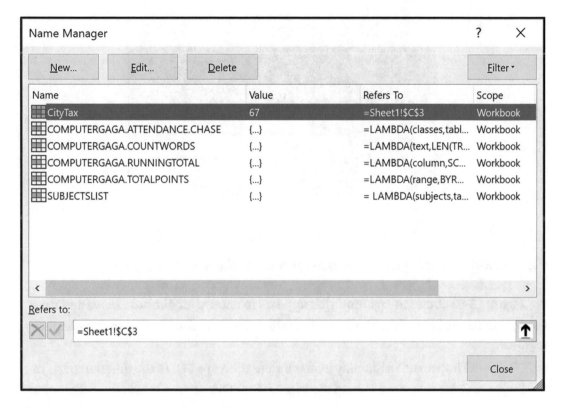

Figure 15-50. *Functions in the Name Manager after syncing*

Creating Named Formulas in the AFE

The Advanced Formula Editor provides an improved experience for creating your
LAMBDA functions and other named formulas. You can add comments, break up a
formula over multiple lines with indentation, and receive immediate inline errors.

Named formulas can be created in the AFE Manager or the Editor. The Editor offers
a stronger formula editing experience. However, the Manager offers a high-quality
experience itself that is far superior to the Name Manager of Excel.

To create a new named formula in the AFE Manager, click the **Add named formula**
button in the top-left corner of the *Manager* (Figure 15-51).

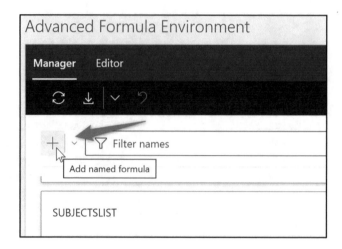

Figure 15-51. *Adding a new named formula in the AFE Manager*

Figure 15-52 shows the window that appears to enter your *Formula name* and then formula in the *Refers to* box. The TEXTBETWEEN function from earlier in this chapter is shown.

Notice the improved readability by the indentation applied to the different parts of the formula. Colors are used to help distinguish function names, brackets, and number constants.

This offers a similar experience, though vastly improved, to the Name Manager of Excel. This is great, as it makes it simple to get started.

Click **Add** when your formula is complete.

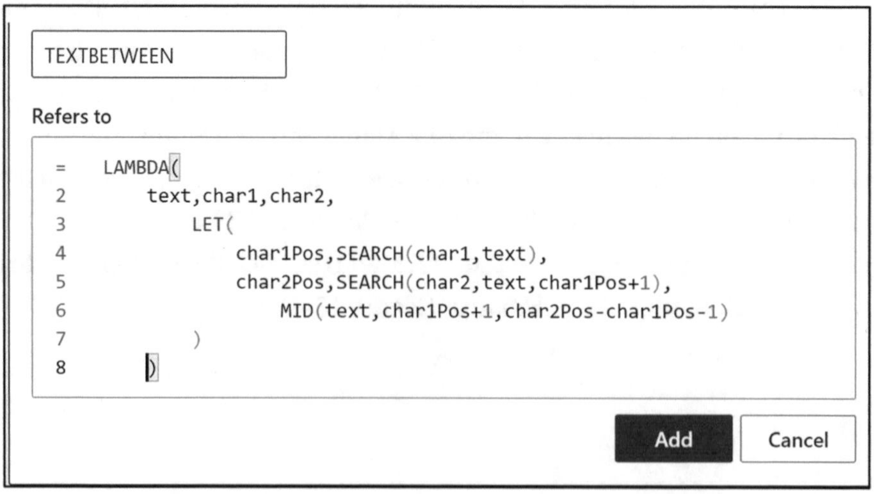

```
TEXTBETWEEN

Refers to

 =    LAMBDA(
 2          text,char1,char2,
 3              LET(
 4                  char1Pos,SEARCH(char1,text),
 5                  char2Pos,SEARCH(char2,text,char1Pos+1),
 6                      MID(text,char1Pos+1,char2Pos-char1Pos-1)
 7                  )
 8          )
```

Figure 15-52. *Creating a new LAMBDA in the AFE Manager*

To create named formulas in the AFE Editor, click the **Editor** tab at the top of the Advanced Formula Environment pane (Figure 15-53).

Different namespaces are listed along the top of the Editor. You always have a *Workbook* namespace. This is the default. Click **New** to add additional namespaces.

Note   An "AVERAGE" namespace is created for the AVERAGE.SCORE.REPORT function due to the period separator being used in the function name. This is not a problem. Using periods in a function name is not unusual, for example, NETWORKDAYS.INTL. If this is not desired however, the namespaces can be edited or a different function name used.

The Editor lists all the named formulas of the AFE for the selected namespace. A semicolon is used to signify the end of a named formula. When creating a new named formula in the Editor, be sure to finish it with a semicolon.

In Figure 15-53, you can see the SUBJECTSLIST and TEXTBETWEEN functions shown as examples of how a formula can be entered. The formula name is entered, followed by an "=" and then the formula.

Comments are entered before the TEXTBETWEEN function. You can enter single-line comments by preceding the text with a double slash "//". Multiline comments are started by entering "/*" and finished with "*/".

You will often see red squiggly lines to notify you of potential syntax errors as you type, like what you may encounter when using MS Word. This can be a little frustrating. At the time of writing this chapter, the Advanced Formula Environment is very new, and further developments and changes can be expected.

Manager   Editor   ≡

⟳ ↓ | ⌄

📗 Workbook   AVERAGE   + New

```
 1     SUBJECTSLIST = LAMBDA(subjects, table,
 2         TRANSPOSE(
 3             FILTER(
 4                 subjects,
 5                 BYCOL(table, LAMBDA(column, COUNTIFS(column, ">=75"))) > 5
 6             )
 7         )
 8     );
 9
10     //Start of text LAMBDA functions
11
12     /* Extract the characters between two delimiters in a cell
13     Each delimiter must be specified */
14     TEXTBETWEEN = LAMBDA(text,char1,char2,
15         LET(
16             char1Pos,SEARCH(char1,text),
17             char2Pos,SEARCH(char2,text,char1Pos+1),
18             MID(text,char1Pos+1,char2Pos-char1Pos-1)
19         )
20     );
21
```

Figure 15-53. *Creating LAMBDA functions in the Editor*

The AFE Editor is a rich formula development tool that Excel users with experience in writing VBA will appreciate. Another example of this richness, especially when compared to the Name Manager of Excel, is the tooltips you see when you hover over different elements of your formula.

Figure 15-54 shows the SEARCH function arguments in a tooltip on mouse hover of the SEARCH function in the formula.

```
/* Extract the characters between two delimiters in a cell
Each delimiter must be specified */
TEXTBETWEEN = LAMBDA(text char1 char2
    LET(              (function) SEARCH(find_text, within_text, [start_num])
        char1Pos,SEARCH(char1,text),
        char2Pos,SEARCH(char2,text,char1Pos+1),
        MID(text,char1Pos+1,char2Pos-char1Pos-1)
    )
);
```

Figure 15-54. Helpful tooltip on mouse hover

Do not forget to sync the Advanced Formula Environment with the Name Manager of Excel when you have finished creating and editing your formulas.

Summary

In this chapter, we learned the LET, LAMBDA, and the seven LAMBDA helper functions in Excel. These functions along with the Advanced Formula Environment are testimony to the growth in Excel formulas in recent years.

We saw how with the LET function, we can create faster, more efficient, and better documented formulas. That led us nicely to the LAMBDA function, where we learned how to create and share our own custom functions in Excel. Those functions are very special.

This is the final chapter of the book; however, your Excel formula journey does not end here. Far from it.

I hope that this book has provided some useful examples and insight into how the many functions of Excel can be utilized. I also hope that this book serves as a reference to be used time and time again to remind you on some of the intricacies of the different functions when applying them. You cannot remember every fact about every function.

Enjoy your Excel adventure and thank you for spending your time with me and my book.

Index

A

Absolute references, 13

Additional functionality, 139

Advanced Formula Environment (AFE)
    add-in, 801–803
    formula creation, 790
    Home tab, 792
    LAMBDA functions, 800–802
        creation, 802
        import from GitHub Gist, 797
    management experience, 790
    named formulas, 793, 800
    Name Manager in Excel, 794
    Sync names with Name Manager in
        Excel, 794

AGGREGATE function
    adding criteria, 459, 460
    advantages, 454, 455
    cell value, 460–462
    in Excel 2010, 451
    function_num, 452
    ignore error values in the range,
        457, 458
    ignore hidden rows, 455–457
    list options, 453, 454
    sales data, 455
    syntax options, 451, 452

Ampersand character, 217, 218

AND and OR functions, 67

AND function, 62, 64, 84

Australian financial year, 296

AVERAGEIFS function, 401–404, 470, 471

B

BYCOL function, 779–781

BYROW function, 770, 776–779, 787, 788

C

#CALC! error, 694–696

Case of text, 176–178

CEILING function, 299

CEILING.MATH function, 309, 310

CEILING rounds, 299

Cell F2, 98, 291, 336, 456, 505, 543, 600

Cell references
    absolute
        definition, 13
        making absolute, 15, 16
        mixed, 16, 18
        relative reference, 13–15
    sheet, 18–20
    workbook, 21–24

Chart data series, 655, 680, 682

Chart labels, 238, 240

Charts, 39, 158

CHOOSECOLS function, 698, 701
    absolute column selection, 621, 622
    MATCH, 620, 621
    Nth column, 624, 625
    reordering columns, 623, 624
    specific columns, 619, 620

CHOOSE function, 297, 298, 357, 366, 554
    cell value, 560, 561
    controls, 563, 565

Printed in the United States
by Baker & Taylor Publisher Services